THE
ITALIAN
RENAISSANCE
INTERIOR

1400–1600

THE
ITALIAN RENAISSANCE INTERIOR
1400–1600

PETER THORNTON

Harry N. Abrams, Inc., Publishers

NEW YORK

IMPARTIALL READER SEEST THOW THIS WORKE?
Beleeve me it cost me much Labour swett & tiresomenesse,
Through my toilsome travailes, viewing of places and turning
over of bookes. Sitt thou still if thow please & enjoy it.

Farewell

From the title-page of an unpublished translation of about 1630 of Scamozzi's
treatise on architecture of 1615, in Sir John Soane's Museum.

FRONTISPIECE:
Girolamo da Santa Croce, *Birth of the Virgin*, Scuola del Carmine, Padua
(photograph: Scala). Plate 142.

Library of Conress Cataloging-in-Publication Data

Thorton, Peter, 1926–
    The Italian Renaissance interior, 1400–1600 / by Peter Thornton.
        p.   cm.
    Includes index.
    ISBN 0-8109-3459-0
    1. Decorative arts, Renaissance—Italy.   2. Decorative arts–
– Italy.   I. Title.
    NK959.T47   1991
    747.25´09´024—dc20   91-1274

Published in 1991 by Harry N. Abrams, Incorporated, New York
A Times Mirror Company

Designed by Andrew Shoolbred
House Editor: Suzannah Gough

Printed and bound in Italy

CONTENTS

PREFACE AND
ACKNOWLEGEMENTS

This is a book about details – and mostly about details of a material kind. I happen to find this kind of thing interesting; that is why I write about them.[1] The list of contents at the beginning gives quite a good idea of what the book is about, and it should be evident that a reader seeking in these pages information about moral, spiritual or philosophical questions is unlikely to discover much that will hold his attention for long. Yet it was against the physical background described here that Italian Renaissance culture evolved, and one should not forget that details of many kinds, including the sort considered in this book, go to make up the whole. So this is a survey of a piece of territory. It has been surveyed before, chiefly at the end of the last century and at the beginning of our own, and it is now starting to attract surveyors again, myself among them. I believe I can claim that no one has taken the matter quite so far, over so wide a piece of the territory, as I have done here. Little of my material, however, is entirely fresh; much of it has been published before, albeit mostly in rather obscure places. My purpose has been to set all this into what I believe is a sensible order, in the hope that this will form an effective framework on which others can build.

The published work of a number of erudite Italian scholars working in the years around 1900 here deserves to be saluted. The inventories and commentaries they published have been much quoted in this book. I would particularly like to single out Curzio Mazzi, the soundest of them all, in my opinion, and a man I would dearly like to have met.[2] His name and those of a dozen others appear in the list of abbreviated titles that I have had to adopt because I refer to their works so often (p. 367). Such abbreviations are denoted throughout the text by an asterix.

It has been my good fortune to spend much of my working life on the staff of the Victoria and Albert Museum in London, first for eight years in the Department of Textiles and then for twenty-two in the Department of Furniture and Woodwork. This made it possible for me to become familiar with what is probably the finest and largest assemblage of Italian Renaissance decorative art anywhere in the world. The V & A's extensive collections contain many Italian objects that are super-stars by any reckoning but it is the range of the collections that is so astonishing. It would be difficult, if not impossible, to write a book like this without having worked on a daily basis with a large and rich collection of objects surviving from the age on which one has decided to concentrate. The interest – indeed the excitement – these objects generate soon stimulates study, the wish to know more about the circumstances in which they were created. This inevitably leads on to interpreting, or trying to interpret, the parallel surviving documentary evidence and to understand what is actually to be seen in contemporary pictures like those reproduced here. This fascinating activity has been part of my job – the part I have enjoyed most – during all the years I worked at the V&A (and before that at the Fitzwilliam Museum in Cambridge, and now at Sir John Soane's Museum in London which, although small in size, is in essence a great museum). I owe a great debt to these wonderful institutions which have provided me with a way of life among interesting and often beautiful objects, with excellent libraries close at hand, and colleagues working alongside whose interests have coincided sufficiently with my own to enable them good-naturedly to understand my enthusiasms and to guide me, every now and then, in realms of expertise adjacent to my own. My especial gratitude in this respect goes to Simon Jervis, Donald King, John Mallet, Lynda Fairbairn and Ronald Lighthown – the last, particularly for having introduced me, now many years ago, to John Florio's dictionary of Italian into English, published in 1611, a work that has been invaluable to me in my researches.

While at the V & A I was responsible, over a long period, for Ham House. This seventeeth-century building beside the River Thames at Richmond, still contains most of its original furnishings – a most remarkable fact which made the task enormously instructive. Much that I learned from this experience is embodied in two books[3] and it was because I had found the seventeenth century so fascinating that I later embarked on a study of developments that had taken place in the two centuries *before* 1600[4]. The result is the present offering. It greatly facilitated my understanding of Renaissance developments, incidentally, to have a good working knowledge of how matters were to evolve afterwards.

Among the foreign scholars who were attached to my department for some while were two who helped me launch into this study – Daniela di Castro (now Moscati) and Reinier Baarsen. The latter now occupies a senior post at the Rijksmuseum in Amsterdam; the former lives in Rome and has made a considerable reputation for herself as a writer on the decorative arts. I am grateful to them both for their assistance but my gratitude to Daniela di Castro is two-fold as she has also valiently read the typescript of the finished book and thus saved me from making a number of mistakes. From my time at the V & A dates also my reliance on Louisa Warburton-Lee (now Lawson) who has typed the manuscripts for all my books and has managed yet again to make sense of my atrocious hand-writing and confusing drafts. It has been good to have such skilful and patient assistance.

A large number of people in many parts of the Western world have helped me while I was preparing this book. In many cases their assistance is acknowledged in the relevant place. Others assisted me more widely; their names are listed below. A handful, however, have done such a great deal for me that they deserve very special mention. I am particularly grateful to the Marchesa Maddalena Trionfi Honorati whose studies of Italian Renaissance furniture have in recent years so greatly advanced our understanding in this field and who has communicated to me much information that has been extremely useful. It has been a privilege to talk to her and an encouragement to discover that our conclusions on many questions seem to coincide. I have derived much benefit from the published work of Dr Graziano Manni on the furnishings of the Este family during the Renaissance period and from his kindness to me subsequently. I am also greatly indebted to Professor Richard Goldthwaite, not only for presenting me with several of his most relevant essays that helped me the better to understand aspects of the background to my field of studies, but also for inviting me to stay in great comfort for a week or so at the Villa Spelman, a Florentine property belonging to the Johns Hopkins University at Baltimore, Maryland. The doctoral thesis of one of his pupils, Kent Lydecker, now at the Metropolitan Museum in New York, is the only serious large-scale survey in my chosen field to have been published since the 1920s[5], apart from the work of Graziano Manni to which I have already drawn attention. Janet Byrne, of the Print Room at the Metropolitan Museum, has also earned my sincere gratitude for helping me find interesting material in the collection which is in her care and for presenting me with a copy of her extremely useful guide to Renaissance ornament. The kindness shown me by Sabine Eiche, Caroline Elam, Gustina Scaglia, Nicolai Rubinstein, and Patricia Waddy[6] is also most gratefully acknowledged. To round off this list, I would like to record my appreciation of the work that Paul Gwynne, graduate of the Warburg Institute, did in chasing up for me elusive references in the last months before my typescript was handed in, and of Alex Barry's admirable sketch-plans which he prepared specially for me and which greatly help to clarify my theories on the planning of Italian Renaissance houses.

My wife provided the *cadre* within which, week after week and over several years, I could sit quietly and write; she did so by no means always encouraged by adequate expressions of gratitude from me, and I know she will not now mind my saying that the person to whom I am otherwise most of all indebted is our daughter Dora. She recently completed a doctoral thesis on a subject that touches tangentially on my own studies and was therefore able to help me in many ways, discussing aspects of what I was researching, bringing me many interesting pieces of information, most of which are incorporated in this book, and encouraging me generally. Although I was occasionally able to help her in return, the traffic was very largely in the other direction.

I was very fortunate to have been awarded an Emeritus Fellowship by the Leverhulme Trust which enabled me to travel rather more extensively in Italy than would otherwise have been possible, and to have been invited to spend a year at Oxford University by St John's College, which most generously offered me a Visiting Senior Research Fellowship that was not only an enjoyable experience but provided me with the opportunity of spending much time in four excellent libraries – the Bodleian, of course, but also that of the College itself, as well as those of the Taylorian Institute and the Ashmolean Museum where Mrs Eunice Martin was so exceptionally helpful.

My studies did, however, make me more fully aware of how much there was of a more general nature that I should have read before embarking upon the present enterprise, but I noted with some relief that even Jacob Burckhardt had had to confess that his pronouncements in one area touched upon 'only fragments of a great subject', that 'No one is more conscious than the author of the defects in his knowledge', and that 'Of the multitude of special works in which the subject is adequately treated, even the names are but imperfectly known to him'. I can only echo the words of that great scholar and adduce in my further defence the fact that this book has largely been written in my spare time, in moments when I was not performing my main task which is the running of a museum.

That this book covers the years between 1400 and 1600 has no particular significance; it is merely a convenient time-span which embraces the centuries known to Italians as the quattrocento and cinquecento, but which can only very approximately be labelled 'The Italian Renaissance Period'. This is what I sometimes ask the reader to regard as 'the period', referring to it thus in the text. I have retained the original spelling in all quotations from ancient documents (or the transcriptions given in the secondary sources that I have consulted)[7] and translations are given within square brackets. Since a number of inventories are cited frequently their titles have been abbreviated and a list of these is given on p. 363. Likewise, much-cited authors' works are denoted by an asterisk and their full titles are given on p. 367.

Of the many people who helped during the preparation of this book, I should like here also to mention:-

Italy
Candace Adelson, His Excellency Theodore Arcand and his wife, Jennifer, Piero Boccardo, Prof. Arnaldo Bruschi, Prof. Christoph Frommel, Annarosa Ceruti Fusco, Marzia Cataldo Gallo, Alvar Gonzalez Palacios, Gabriella Cantini Guidotti, The late Count Lionardo Ginori, Clare Hills-Nova, Pia Kehl, Maria Pia Malvezzi, Angelo Mazza, The late Professor Ulrich Middeldorf, Alessandra Mottola Molfino, Angela Montironi, Kirsten Aschengren Piacenti, Francesco Scoppla, Farida Simonetti, Marco Spallanzani, Prof. Simonetta Valtieri, Annamaria Zanni and Frank Zöllner.

France
Prof. Marie-Madeleine Fontaine, Prof. Jean Guillaume and Jean-Pierre Ravaux.

Germany
Arthur Haase and Andreas Tönnesmann.

Switzerland
Alain Gruber.

Denmark
Dyveke Helsted.

Sweden
Lis Granlund

U.S.S.R.
Tamara Rappe

United States
Glenn Andres, Elaine Dee, Prof. Josephine von Henneberg and Kristin Mortimer.

United Kingdom
Bruce Boucher, Peter Burke, Suzanne Butters, Edward Chaney, Robert Charleston, Howard Colvin, Wendy Hefford, Kristian Jensen, Amanda Lillie, Christopher Lloyd, Giles Mandelbrote, Lisa Monnas, Jennifer Montagu, Jean Schofield and Sir Keith Thomas.
I am deeply grateful to them all.

Finally as this book is about to go into page-proof, I would like in addition to thank those who have brought its production to this point – Michael Dover, who leads the Art and Illustrated Books division at Weidenfeld and Nicolson, my excellent and hard-working editor Suzannah Gough, the clever designer Andrew Shoolbred, and Ralph Hancock, whose index greatly extends the usefulness of this book. Many others were involved, to all of whom I am grateful, but particular thanks must go to Mira Hudson of the Witt Library who traced a great many of the illustrations that I had so carefully chosen. Her success in this exercise means a lot to me.

Sir John Soane's Museum   *Peter Thornton*
London
April, 1991

1 An opulent bedchamber in Ferrara, about 1470

Much rich detail is here rendered with meticulous care as if the client really cared that all this was shown. In the first half of the fifteenth century the subject itself, supported by minimal furnishings, had been sufficient. In circles connected with the Este court which the artist, Francesco del Cossa, served, they were particularly keen to show luxurious effects that look entirely convincing. Note the bed's lappeted valance of velvet, the fine carving of the bed-chest, and the carved stone table (clearly an object of display, with its curious column and gilded finial).

Francesco del Cossa, *Annunciation* (detail), before 1472
Gemäldegalerie, Dresden

INTRODUCTION

The so-called *kultur-historisch* introductions in textbooks contain a good deal that is ridiculous, summarizing long periods of time under concepts of a very general kind which in turn are made to account for the conditions of public and private, intellectual and spiritual life. They present us with a pale image of the whole . . .

(Heinrich Wölfflin).

'We waxed rich due to the barbarous ignorance and indolence of others.' This was how a Florentine in the eighteenth century, looking back on more prosperous times, accounted for Italy's immense wealth during the Renaissance period, wealth that was greater than that of any other European nation until well into the second half of the sixteenth century.[1] The fastest rise in prosperity had taken place already in the fourteenth century but substantial new fortunes could still be made throughout the fifteenth and sixteenth centuries, the centuries that concern us here, while 'old money' was for the most part being consolidated by fresh transfusions of capital. Indeed, by the sixteenth century, the rich on the whole seemed to be getting richer while the poor, with prices rising against them and the cost of labour falling away, found themselves increasingly impoverished.[2]

The censure formerly directed by the Church against those who were successful in making money (especially from usury, the lending of money with interest) had largely been lifted by the beginning of the fifteenth century,[3] as it became more widely recognized that many of the improvements and benefits which the community was now enjoying had only been made possible because the money to pay for them was readily made available, either through taxes or through private generosity. 'Whence are our houses and palaces produced? From riches. Whence the means to educate our children . . . [to build] the walls, the towers, the defences . . . the most noble buildings, the bridges, the streets, with what have you built them?' asked a Florentine rhetorically in 1427.[4] These things do not just happen, he asserted; they are all based on riches which someone has earned. Towards the end of the century Lorenzo de' Medici claimed that he had no regrets about the enormous sums of money he had spent on public works, on charity and on taxes, because 'I think the money well laid out in the promotion of great public objects.'[5] It was all right to make money, in fact, so long as you spent it well. A goodly proportion of it ought to be contributed to the common good – and Renaissance Italians had a strongly developed sense of social collectivity – after which it was acceptable that a man should spend it on himself and his immediate family, especially if he then proceeded to build himself a splendid mansion that could be seen as a positive ornament to the city in which he dwelt. By the middle of the fifteenth century, Alberti and Filarete, both authors of celebrated treatises on architecture, were insisting that expenditure on building was an entirely respectable and moral activity for a private person to undertake, not least when the building concerned was that which he himself would occupy. Three-quarters of a century later Michelangelo was saying that 'A noble house in the city brings considerable honour, being more visible than all one's [other] possessions.'[6] Thus encouraged, it is hardly surprising that men of business in many parts of Italy felt impelled to build fine houses for themselves. They were of course not oblivious to the fact that such a private residence would also tend to stand as a proud monument to its builder;[7] for, being of stone or brick, it seemed virtually indestructible – which is of course a most desirable quality in a monument. A gentleman who had just completed a house for himself in Rome did in fact have a plaque set into its façade stating that, in erecting this building, he was hoping to be remembered by posterity.[8] The attitude of many successful businessmen of the period is probably well summed up by Giovanni Rucellai when, towards the end of his life (he died in 1481), he said that 'I think I have done myself more honour by having spent money well than by having earned it. Spending gave me deeper satisfaction, especially in the money I spent on my house in Florence.'[9]

We have mainly been speaking of the upper-middle classes and what was novel in the fifteenth century was the fact that these rich people began to build splendid dwellings for themselves in such great numbers.[10]

This substantial wave of new building was added to the constant and habitual building activity undertaken by powerful rulers who felt compelled to build magnificently as evidence of their authority. Moreover, the numerous small states in the northern half of the country were gradually amalgamated during the Renaissance into a dozen or so relatively powerful political units, the rulers of which required palaces and country retreats of a grandeur and degree of opulence that would affirm symbolically their enhanced status. What is more, it was normal among princes and the nobility to modernize and generally do over the family's principal residence every time a new generation succeeded to the title. And, when such people got married, it was important that an apartment should be prepared that provided a worthy setting for the new consort, for the marriage will of course have been made for dynastic purposes (love rarely came into the calculation even if it sometimes blossomed) and a level of honour had in consequence to be paid to the bride (and, through her, to her illustrious family) roughly equal to that being commanded by her husband. The Este and Gonzaga accounts are full of items concerning the creation of new spaces – often complete apartments and sometimes an entirely new wing – to receive a bride.

Princes hoped to derive credit for improvements they had wrought through building activity. For example Lodovico Sforza (1451–1508) was greatly praised for the changes he made in the castle at Milan, the central seat of power in his Duchy of Lombardy. The same prince rebuilt much of Pavia, a small city which had been mean and filthy, according to a contemporary chronicler, but of which 'one could now truly say that it was indeed exceptionally beautiful'.[11] The Duke's achievement does him honour and is highly praiseworthy, the commentator added. Rich merchants, in building fine houses for themselves and hoping to reap

praise from their fellow men, were really only emulating their aristocratic and princely superiors – but, now, with society's full sanction.

Of the major Italian cities, Rome occupied a special position as the capital of Christendom. For much of the fourteenth century the Papacy had functioned in exile at Avignon but Gregory XI brought it back to Rome in 1377. It was, however, not until the time of Nicholas V (1447–1455) that a pope was able to start to create a political and cultural capital commensurate with the authority of the institution that was now once again based there. Much needed to be done. The city was small and shabby in the mid-fifteenth century.[12] Lavish patronage by successive popes during the Renaissance did, however, gradually turn the city into one of suitable magnificence and which, by the mid-sixteenth century, had become very impressive indeed. Cardinals were encouraged to build and many did so in great style, vying with each other to erect ever more splendid and up-to-date residences for themselves.[13] Many of the

2

3

2 Mid-fifteenth-century luxury indoors in Genoa

This painting of 1451 shows more objects than usual for this date, but the artist was not Italian and clearly delighted in the depiction of such detail. Nevertheless he would not have done so unless this kind of density of objects and patterns had been familiar to the contemporary viewers of his painting.

Giusto di Ravensburg, *Annunciation* (detail), cloister of S. Maria di Castello, Genoa
Photograph: Soprintendenza B.A.S. Liguria, Genova

3 Lying-in; Tuscany, about 1430

The convention of omitting to show one wall in order to depict a room is well exemplified here. The resulting aperture is often trimmed neatly with architectural detailing but we can be sure this Tuscan lady did not give birth in an open *loggia*. To this extent one has to make allowances when looking at many quattrocento pictures of interiors but the wealth of detail can for the most part be taken at face value, although here the bed-head is shown as far less tall than would have been the case in reality.

Central panel of a birth tray (see p. 252), Tuscan, *c.*1430
Ca' d'oro, Venice (CGF d. 85), (Photograph: Osvaldo Böhm)

4 Privacy and personal comfort

The *studio* [private study] was a small room in which a person could gather round himself (a few women also had such rooms) his most treasured possessions and could have the room's fitments tailored to his personal needs. There would normally be a concentration of objects in such rooms (this being so striking that it was often depicted); the density of loose objects elsewhere in the house was generally less great. This drawing of about 1400 purports to show Petrarch in his *studio* but in fact gives a wonderful impression of a learned man's study in the early quattrocento. It was in such small rooms that personal comfort in many guises was first evolved, as those who owned a *studio* tended to spend long hours there.

From a Paduan translation in Italian of Petrarch's *De viris illustribus* *Hessiche Landes- und Hochschulbibliothek, Darmstadt*

5 Another comfortable study

As with 'Petrarch's *studio*' such rooms of course had doors and were fully enclosed. Removing one wall to show the inside of a room was a common artistic convention, as other illustrations in this introduction show.

Lazzaro Bastiani (*c*.1425–1512), *St Jerome in his studio*, originally in the Bishop's Palace at Empoli, Apulia, late 1400s *Pinacoteca Provinciale, Bari (71) (photograph: Soprintendenza B.A.S. Publia. Bari)*

4

5

members of the Papal curia, the secretariat and the administrative body that supported the Papacy, also became sufficiently wealthy to enable them to build substantial houses for themselves. Some of the administrators and functionaries attached to the courts of principalities elsewhere in Italy found themselves in a similar position, incidentally, and likewise built notable houses for their own use. The famous poet and dramatist Lodovico Ariosto, who was attached to the court at Ferrara, neatly expressed the feelings of such people in the words he caused to be inscribed and put up on his own house in which he points out that the building was 'the fruit of my own earnings'.[14]

Once the building of private residences became an activity that was positively encouraged among wealthy people – and, just as it was considered bad manners to dress in a slovenly manner,[15] so it was important to build in a manner appropriate to one's station in life, neither meanly nor too grandly[16] – many among the 'building classes' began to take a great interest in the theory of building design, in the way that comfort and convenience might best be achieved, and in how the decoration and furnishing might be tastefully contrived. It was in answer to this new interest among people of an intellectual cast of mind that architects and architectural theorists began to write books on the subject which, especially once printing became a viable means of disseminating the written word after 1500, gradually ensured that a substantial number of people came to be rather well-informed about these matters. The

presence of such a critical body in turn had a considerable impact on the quality of new buildings that came to be erected.

The result of all this was that many Italian cities underwent what one can truly describe as substantial urban renewal during the Renaissance, a period in which many patrons of architecture can be said to have been possessed by a veritable passion for building. Building is a voluptuous pleasure, one great fifteenth-century architect averred, 'like being in love'.

Antonio Manetti, writing in the 1470s, said that people built not only to acquire fame and arouse admiration through the splendour and good taste of their houses, but also to achieve a higher level of comfort and security.[17] Most students of the Italian Renaissance would probably claim that, in the field of architecture, Italy's greatest contribution has been the devising of a manner of building private houses that embodied elegance and considerable magnificence. But no mean achievement was the establishment by Renaissance Italians of a concept of domestic comfort which laid the foundation for that which most of us enjoy today. Since this is of direct concern to most people living in the Western world, whereas being housed magnificently affects relatively few, this too must surely be reckoned a major contribution to civilized life. It is around the belief that this is true that this book has been written.

The pictures selected here to illustrate the various themes incidentally reveal much about comfort indoors in Renaissance Italy and suggest how much thought went into its creation, among those who could afford this

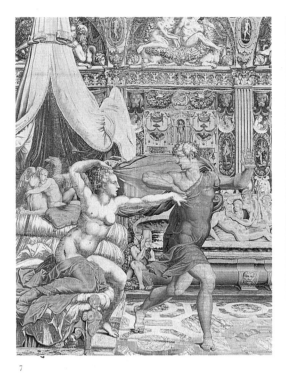

6

7

6 A luxurious setting in Naples, about 1355

Although artists working before the mid-fifteenth century always represented rooms in a simple manner, even rich people had fewer possessions than was to be the case later on. Sumptuous, however, in this painting are the clothes, the silk wall-hanging, the linen diaper cloth on the side-table and the silver (and gold?) vessels standing on it. The two dogs were no doubt also expensive items.

Unknown painter, *The Marriage Feast at Cana*, from an Angevin Bible
Bibliothèque Nationale, Paris (n. 9561)

7 Mid-sixteenth-century palatial splendour

By the mid-sixteenth century the density of ornament has greatly increased and one is given the impression that objects of many kinds fill the room, even though in fact we can here only see a long seat, three tapestries (depicted on the wall, between the columns) and a day-bed. Upholstery is now very evident (the rich bed-furnishings, the mattress and cushions on the seat; see diagram 22, p. 362) and we can be sure there were items like a mirror, caskets, small sculpture, chairs and a cupboard-like *credenza* elsewhere in the room – which, even though the scene is of Joseph escaping the clutches of Potiphar's wife, shows an artist's impression of a superb modern bedchamber (the tapestries depicted exist and were woven for Cosimo de' Medici, to hang in the Palazzo Vecchio).

Tapestry designed in 1549 by Bronzino, woven in the Medici workshops under Nicola Carcher
Photograph: Scala

8

8 Displaying the new-born in 1416

Not many items are represented here but those that are betray considerable wealth – enough to establish the credentials of St John the Baptist's parents, which was what was here required. Note the superb coverlet on the carved and inlaid bed, the fine tablecloth and sumptuously decorated cushion.

Giacombo Salimbeni, *The Birth of John the Baptist* (or, more correctly *The Lying-in and Circumcision*), Oratorio di San Giovanni, Urbino
Photograph: Scala

9 Florentine super-luxury in about 1470

This is an obvious exercise in perspective and realism, with much precise representation of decorative detail, and it is interesting to note that no loose objects are visible – if one excepts the superb bed which is so massive as to seem like a fixture. There would of course have been a few more items present in reality but not many; such pictures had to be plausible to contemporaries who knew precisely how their rooms looked. Some artistic licence was of course acceptable; a high degree of unreality was not. If we too accept this convention, we presumably here see something very like the best room and associated *loggia* of a luxurious patrician villa outside Florence (the viewpoint is apparently that from the Medici villa at Careggi).

9

Piero del Pollaiuolo, *Annunciation* (detail)
Gemäldegalerie, Dahlem, Berlin (73)

not inexpensive luxury. Of course, by comparison with the comfort enjoyed by Parisians of the seventeenth century, and those who closely followed their example, what was achieved in the preceding centuries in Italy was primitive but, during that earlier period, people were beginning to reckon comfort and convenience important ingredients of good building for domestic purposes. In Italy, this was certainly a comparatively widespread notion by the end of the sixteenth century but we can see evidence of it much earlier. Veronica Franco, a Venetian courtesan famed not only for her charms but also for her intelligence (her poetry was widely admired), specially mentioned the indoor comforts and arrangements of a luxurious villa where she had been to stay in about 1570.[18] Privacy is of course one of the principal requirements of domestic comfort, and great ingenuity was devoted to achieving it – once again, by those who could afford it, for privacy also tends to be expensive. One contemporary commentator was of course referring to privacy when he asked, 'What is the use of power and riches if one cannot have a few minutes' peace?'[19] He was in fact encouraging rich patricians to go and find – or build – a villa in the country outside the town, but 'a few minutes' peace' could equally well be achieved in people's city residences by means of clever planning, by distributing the rooms so that the owner, his family and his friends could enjoy privacy, and thus peace, away from the demands of public duty. Architects and their clients quite evidently thought hard about this question, as will be seen in Part Three. Indeed, even if bodily comforts were still only catered for in a fairly rudimentary manner by 1500, extremely sophisticated measures for securing greater privacy had already been introduced in a certain number of palatial buildings and villas, several decades earlier. Villas, incidentally, were a class of building where one could most easily experiment with ideal schemes in architecture. Out in the countryside adjacent buildings rarely restricted the building-site, so it was there usually possible for architects and patrons, trying to devise new solutions, to put up whatever shape of building took their fancy.[20] Italian Renaissance villas, it should be added, were for the most part places of relaxation for the urban élite.[21] Although vegetables, olive oil, wine and other provender, that could be enjoyed at the villa or in the main residence in town, might be produced on the estate where the villa was placed, relatively few of these small houses in the country were associated directly with agriculture. They were for the most part essentially urban dwellings set in the countryside, smaller than their city counterparts but often of considerable elegance.[22] In some cases they were what can only be described as palatial, embodying arrangements that were at most somewhat simplified versions of those pertaining in the owner's princely residence in town. They should most definitely not be thought of as farmhouses or country cottages.[23] People descended into the country in order to enjoy themselves, by and large; the country was otherwise thought of as a place where animals lived.

Even more fundamental than any contribution Italy may have made in the field of architecture during the Renaissance period, however, was the devising of a civilized pattern of life which still forms the basis of the good manners and social intercourse current in Western society today. This affected many aspects of life including domestic arrangements. As Jacob Burckhardt explained, it was the 'thoughtful study of all questions relating to social intercourse, to education, to domestic service and organization' that 'first brought order into domestic life, treating it as a work of deliberate contrivance'.[24]

The new styles of domestic life arising from this intelligent reappraisal brought about a need for different forms of domestic space (this, again, is discussed in Part Three), and led also to the development of new forms of furniture to meet new requirements – for example, the smaller sideboard to go in the private dining-room where husband and wife entertained only a handful of friends, great banquets no longer being the fashionable way of having a party; another example is the 'chest of drawers' which was developed shortly before 1600, by which time the practical advantages of

10

11

10, 11 When bad art is best

By far the best source of information on the subjects discussed in this book is the contemporary picture, for all its distortions and artistic editing. The work of the greatest artists, however, tends to be less helpful than that of the lesser practitioners and the two extreme examples reproduced here make the point to an almost grotesque degree. One is by a Greek artist working in Venice. Trained in Greek-Byzantine tradition, he struggled to master the current Venetian idiom with charming but curious results. But for all its technical incompetence (we are not talking about spiritual content) this painting provides a great deal of information – from the way the oil-lamp was suspended to the structure of a bed at that time (Joseph, the carpenter, is busy building one on the right). Plate 11 by Raphael, on the other hand, tells us much less although the discerning eye will see that even he, with his mind on greater things, incidentally tells us something about *tarsia* decoration on beds and the trimming of coverlets.

Teodoro Palaki (active in Venice in the seventeenth century), *The Holy Family at Home*
Museo Correr, Venice (1113) (photograph: Alinari Archive)
Raphael (and Perugino), *Birth of the Virgin*, 1497
Galleria Nazionale delle Marche, Urbino (photograph: Alinari Archive)

the robust and heavily-lidded chest had long since ceased to be of any consequence as the owner no longer needed to take it along too, when he or she went on a journey. The fact that the seigneurial classes, and those who sought to imitate them, no longer took with them much of their furniture when they travelled had a profound influence on the design of furniture, a great deal of which could now be expected to stand wherever in the room it was placed, for years on end.[25] Indeed, new classes of objects of many kinds were produced to meet revised needs.[26] An enormous expansion took place in the production of luxury goods as a result; indeed, even if there had been no stylistic innovation at all during the Renaissance in Italy, the scale of the economic activity that sprang from all this building and furnishing would in itself have been remarkable.[27]

Works of art, created consciously as such, first emerge as a clearly defined category of goods during this period. What is more, the intellectual élite became increasingly discriminating in their tastes and began to appreciate, and therefore to value, refined craftsmanship and

good design rather than merely the intrinsic value of an object. Put in crude terms, this meant that the emphasis was no longer on amassing in a strongroom great quantities of gold and silver plate, heavily bejewelled objects and a few expensive rarities like a porcelain cup or the horn of a narwhal; attention now came to be focused far more on the decoration and furnishing of the domestic setting with objects of refinement and beauty.

A strong sense of progress was undoubtedly felt by many Italians during the fifteenth century and well into the next, not least in the field of domestic architecture and the way people lived within the new buildings which had been going up everywhere.

How greatly things were changing during the middle of the period, for instance, is indicated by Isabella d'Este's remarks on seeing the new apartment in the castle at Mantua prepared specially to receive her future daughter-in-law, Margherita Paleologa (Pls 365, 366) in 1531. Isabella, who had herself been able to enjoy just about the highest possible degree of elegant comfort, claimed that Margherita's arrangements were infinitely more comfortable than anything she had been able to command in all her thirty years as duchess in Mantua.[28] Indeed, in cities all over northern and central Italy, what had seemed like an enormous and splendidly furnished palace in 1450 looked like a very ordinary large middle-class dwelling to people who were alive a century later.[29] Moreover, the pace of renewal was often very fast. A man returning to Rome in 1590, after an absence of only ten years or so, exclaimed that the place was unrecognizable, so great had been the changes that had been wrought in this short time.[30]

These changes are to a large extent reflected in the illustrations included in this book, even though the pictures are not organized chronologically (they are mostly grouped typologically or thematically). It has been claimed that such contemporary illustrations cannot be trusted, that they are distorted, inaccurate, edited pictorially to suit the artist's immediate purposes. In some measure this may be true but they are by far the best evidence that we possess concerning the appearance of rooms at the time, and once we ourselves have learned how to make certain allowances, they in fact reveal much, especially about details.[31] On more general matters like how much furniture there was in a room, how many other objects were present, and on the density of arrangement, these pictures can be misleading, if only because artists mostly included no more than was needed to make their point; they did not want to clutter up their pictures. On the other hand, artists often included details for fun, because depicting them gave delight – to the painter and the beholder. In other instances the artist put them in to fill a void.[32] But in virtually every case, these details are represented with considerable precision and it must always be remembered that contemporaries would have been quick to mock an artist who had depicted everyday objects in a totally unconvincing manner or who had included a feature that was absurdly improbable – unless the story being told called for such wild invention.

If we want to know how many items were to be found in, for example, a princely bedchamber in 1480, the most helpful indication will be found in contemporary household inventories but these too may not reveal the full picture because a whole category of items may have been omitted from a particular inventory on purpose.[33] That inventories, taken in isolation, could be a sterile and unbalanced source of information was noted by Shakespeare when he describes how a treacherous admirer of a woman climbs out of a trunk in her bedchamber in order to steal a bracelet off her arm as she sleeps. This is to be evidence that he has seduced her (untrue, of course) and, to back up his story, he needs to remember how her room looked. It was his intention 'To note the chamber. I will write all down./Such and such pictures. There the window. Such/th'adornment of her bed. The arras, figures;/Why such and such. And the contents o'th' story.' Then he looks at her sleeping form and adds despairingly, 'Ah, but some natural notes about her body,/Above ten thousand meaner moveables/Would testify, to enrich mine inventory.'[34]

The best way of reconstructing in the mind's eye an image of how Renaissance rooms looked is to combine a close study of contemporary pictures with an informed reading of contemporary inventories, together with a good knowledge of the surviving artefacts in museums and private collections. Examples of some classes of object – beds, for instance – do not survive at all[35] but the illustrations provide much evidence, to the extent that it is possible here to present a plausible visual survey of the development of the bed in Italy during the Renaissance period, backing this with documentary evidence largely culled from inventories. Because inventories are so important a key to our understanding, it is of course essential that we should be able to determine what the terms used by those who compiled the inventories are likely to have meant. A good deal of attention has here been paid to this problem in order to try and construct a more faithful model of how things actually were. In trying to envisage how our ancestors lived at any period, certainty is of course hard to come by and, all too often, one has to guess. Particularly difficult is to discover what people at the time took for granted, which is something they obviously do not bother to tell us.

This survey of the domestic interior in Renaissance Italy deals with what was to be seen *nelle case conspicue* [in houses that stand out] as an earlier historian working in this field described them.[36] Francesco di Giorgio, one of the most celebrated of all Italian Renaissance architects (1439–1502), spoke of *una degna casa* [a house of distinction] when wanting to describe the sort of house that interests us here.[37] Residential buildings of consequence are usually referred to as *palazzi* in Italy today, especially if they are large. During the Renaissance, however, a house was called a *palazzo* only if it was large and occupied by a prominent personage. Indeed, before that, the term seems to have been reserved for the residences of monarchs or princes.[38] This usage was retained in Venice well into the fifteenth century, other men's houses being called *case* [houses] or *case di statio*, if grand.[39] By no means all the buildings mentioned in this book should be classed as *palazzi*; many were smaller structures, notably the villas. There is no generic label that satisfactorily embraces all the sorts and sizes of building which concern us, but it will be evident from all that has been said above that we are dealing with buildings erected for, and often by, members of an élite – a well educated cultural, social and political minority. The domestic arrangements of the majority also merit study but they are not the subject of this book. Truly humble housing is characterized by lack of predictable and analysable form, while that of intermediate levels tends to be modelled on forms created for the upper class. This is not simply a question of mimicry; it springs also from feelings of insecurity which tend on the whole to drive people of intermediate status to draw on the cultural language of the dominant class, in so far as their means allow – in housing as in other matters. As a scholar writing about classical Roman housing put it, 'There is no one language for the rich and one for the poor: but a common language in which the rich are eloquent and the poor dumb.'[40] In order to study the housing of the poor and of 'the middling sort', it must therefore presumably first be necessary to understand how the élite arranged matters.

All Italians, and most students of the Italian Renaissance, whatever their nationality, will probably be shocked when they discover that this survey seeks to deal with Italy as a whole, for there is a commonly held view that the inhabitants of the different regions that make up geographical Italy each have their own distinctive culture and traditions, and that these are so strong that they must inevitably override any attempt to treat the geographical entity as a cultural one as well. Nevertheless, in so far as the matters treated in this book are concerned, it can be demonstrated that, to a very large extent, what was true of Genoa was also true of Florence, Naples, Ferrara and Venice – and of all the other chief Italian cities. This is because our survey concerns the arrangements made by and for what *The Times* used to call 'Top People', and because these people mostly had close links with each other that were not greatly affected by regional boundaries. It ought therefore not really to surprise the reader to discover that, for example, the forms of bed fashionable at any given moment at Mantua, Turin, Palermo and Milan (or, again, in all the other major centres) tended to be very similar. And the same goes for most classes of object, and most forms of decoration, to be found in *case conspicue* at each stage. Local traditions of course often affected the form and ornament of those products which were made by tradesmen working within a strong guild tradition – so that the standardized shapes of large chests varied considerably from one region to the next, for instance, and there were local preferences in the way the ends of long linen table-cloths were decorated. Private houses also generally followed local vernacular traditions because they were usually erected by builders with strong conservative tendencies. Innovative buildings of advanced character, on the other hand, usually had rather more in common with houses of similar status in the other principal cities, the Florentine patrician mode of the middle decades of the fifteenth century, for instance, having enormous influence on buildings of a similar superior class all over Italy,[41] while the later Roman version of the Florentine model in turn had a similar influence on building in many parts of the country.

What continually actually strikes the historian working in this field is not how marked are the regional differences but, rather, how prevalent was the artistic cross-fertilization across regional boundaries. This was of course recognized by many people at the time; we have only to think of Vasari's well known *Lives of the most excellent painters, sculptors and architects*, published in 1550, which includes artists from all over Italy, to be reminded that this is true.[42] When the architect Sebastiano Serlio, who came from Bologna, compiled his highly influential treatise on architecture (p. 339 and Pls 14, 60, 363), he was concerned with advanced practice wherever in Italy this was to be found. A room in Rome that had been newly decorated in 1515 was apparently judged by Isabella d'Este to be 'perhaps the most beautiful in all Italy' [*forse la più bella de Italia*].[43] She herself was a princess from Ferrara, married to the Duke of Mantua, with relations who linked her directly or through marriage to many of the leading families in Italy – as a whole. Political frontiers offered little or no hindrance to the interchange of cultural ideas on how to live in a civilized manner. Theirs was a common culture springing from a shared inheritance that went back, it so clearly seemed, to an heroic age when the united Italy of classical Antiquity had ruled a vast empire. For all the ferocity of their inter-state squabbles, this was in a sense a rivalry of siblings. When faced with foreigners from across the Alps, from Iberia or the countries of Islam, they were always conscious of being different. They were also convinced that their form of civilization was superior to that of others. Need any further excuse be offered for treating Italy as an entity in the present context?

The writer Pietro Aretino asserted that one can tell a man's character [*animo*] from his dwelling [*habitazione*].[44] A study of contemporary *habitazioni* must therefore reveal something about the nature of the Italian Renaissance.

12 Extreme luxury in Venice, 1490s

The walls of this bedchamber are entirely revetted with marble of two kinds. Such treatment would be pleasantly cool in summer, for a ground-floor bedchamber in the city or at the family villa out in the country, which is what we see here. The artist, Giovanni Bellini, was interested in perspective and in depicting textures but he did not bother to show the details of the window-shutters. On the other hand he shows the *lavoro di intarsio* decoration of Mary's desk with great precision. This is probably executed in bone, or just possibly in ivory, laid into cedarwood or cypresswood. The bed has red velvet hangings with borders embroidered in gold thread. The tent-like *cortinaggio* was probably suspended from the ceiling by a cord attached to its apex; there are no signs that the bed had posts (see diagram 1, p. 359 showing such a bed).

Giovanni Bellini, *Annunciation*, painted organ panel, 1490s
Accademia, Venice (photograph: Scala)

12

Part One:

THE ARCHITECTURAL SHELL AND ITS EMBELLISHMENT

Before discussing the furnishing of rooms, something has first to be said about the permanent features that affect a room's appearance.

It is not here the intention to survey those technical aspects of building which lead to the creation of a room – the wall surfaces, the ceiling construction, the materials of which floors are made – but rather to consider some of the more prominent architectural features of interior architecture and say something about their embellishment. In so far as the wall elevations are concerned, these features include the chimneypiece, the windows and the doors. Something also needs to be said about ceilings and floors. A few observations on matters like panelling, wall-painting, and floor-tiles are included by the way.

The Chimneypiece

Design

I Camini veramente sono di grande ornamento alle habitationi [Chimneypieces are indeed important ornaments of dwellings], wrote the architect Sebastiano Serlio in his famous treatise on architecture, the first volume of which appeared in 1537.[1] Once the fireplace had been moved to the side of the room, so that smoke and fumes could be conducted up and away in a flue,[2] it became necessary to decorate the surround of the opening, especially if this were fitted with a hood that projected into the room. When the fire was simply made up against the wall, the hood had to project well out from the wall in order to entrap the smoke; it thus constituted a large, dominant feature in a room. By setting the fireplace back into the wall, the hood did not need to project so far and could in consequence be made smaller although it was still a substantial feature. This, combined with the fact that a fireplace was anyway a focal point in a room, as the source of heat around which one might gather when it was chilly and, more important, as the chief source of light in a room after dusk, made the chimneypiece a feature that merited the attention of those with a talent for design, of those who could turn this ungainly great protrusion into the chief decorative accent in the room. Architects were considering this a challenge worthy of serious thought by the middle of the fifteenth century, if not earlier, and it is therefore curious how little has been written on this subject by architectural historians.

The earliest hoods were conical and purely functional (Pl. 84). If tucked away into the corner of a room (a solution only feasible in small rooms), the conical hood of course hardly protruded at all but the conical form was difficult to disguise or turn into a really attractive feature. More promising was the hood of pyramid shape – or perhaps one should call it wedge-shaped, with the flanks tapering to form a roof-like structure that was at least architectonic (Pls 13, 22, 23, 36) and did not possess the almost organic character of the conical form. Because the wedge-shaped hood [*nappa, cappa* in modern Italian] resembled a tent, it was called a *nappa a*

padiglione – pavilion-like. All the great architects of the fifteenth and first half of the sixteenth centuries turned their attention to the design of this class of hood, juggling with the proportions, trying to reduce its size, furnishing it with cornices and mouldings, adding decoration of various kinds (Pls 14–16).

When the hooded fireplace was in the main room, in the *sala* (p. 285), it was not uncommon to have the owner's coat of arms displayed prominently on its centre. These could be painted or carved in stone, in relief; sometimes they were neatly encompassed within a circular frame (a *tondo*). The architect Filarete, writing in about 1460, recommended that stories in which fire plays a central role should be depicted in this prominent position – Vulcan at his forge, Mucius Scaevola putting his hand in the brazier, Phaeton in his fiery chariot.

In the sixteenth century the *nappa a padiglione* took on a whole range of shapes, as the architects became more inventive. A truncated form was often adopted which could be made more graceful by making the sides curved or waisted. Scrolls, figures, mouldings and ornament of many kinds were added in different combinations until the chimneypiece became very elaborate, the hood-like character disappearing entirely by the mid-sixteenth century. The massive flanking brackets which had supported the heavy wedge-shaped hoods of the early period evolved as graceful forms, swaying down and back towards the wall, reaching down to floor-level (Pl. 15). They might also take the form of columns or even of figures that could be naturalistic or grotesque (Pl. 19).[3] In these ways the structure became increasingly architectural, in many respects resembling an altarpiece or a triumphal arch. With only minor changes, as Serlio* tells us in 1537 (*Bk. IV*; Pl. 363), such designs were often equally suitable for doorways or the surrounds of windows. Eventually the disguised hood above the bold moulding became a scrolled cresting (often flanked by vases or some other form of finial; Pl. 18), or degenerated into a cartouche (Pl. 19) or frame in relief that was sometimes actually separate from the chimneypiece underneath. The story is one of increasing complexity that cannot be followed in detail here (indeed, the information still needs to be assembled) and a glance at the illustrations in this book will have to suffice for our present purposes.

The pyramid-shaped hood of the early phase in this development came to be called the *nappa a padiglione* because it was tent-like (Pl. 13). It was the standard form in Italy (*al costume universale d'Italia*, as Serlio put it in the mid-sixteenth century in his Vol. VII). We have said something about its evolution but it should just be noted that some fireplaces, where the walls were thick, could be entirely encompassed in the wall, whereupon only a plain rectangular opening presented itself to the room. This could be trimmed with a moulding (Pl. 20) but in some cases was left unadorned; elsewhere it might be decorated with painted simulation of a chimneypiece that was architectural in character. Scamozzi called his type *alla Romana* [in the Roman fashion].

Chimneypieces varied greatly in size but were generally designed so as to be in scale with the room in which they featured. Once again Scamozzi helps us, urging that those in principal rooms should have openings

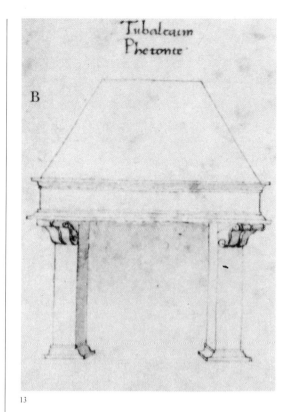

13

14

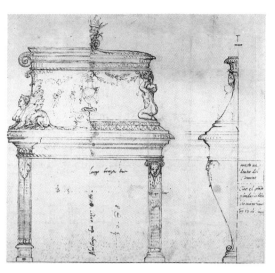

15

16

13 The characteristic fifteenth-century form

Used all over Italy, this type of chimneypiece with a huge pyramid-shaped hood – *a padiglione* – was so common that Filarete, in his treatise on architecture of about 1460, did not feel it necessary to illustrate any other.

From the original manuscript of Filarete's Treatise (*Codex Magliabechianus*) that belonged to Piero de' Medici
Biblioteca Nazionale, Florence

14, 15, 16 Making the *padiglione* more graceful

Plate 14 is a design by Sebastiano Serlio published in Venice in 1537. The pyramid form has been waisted and sphinxes further disguise the severity of the basic form. Serlio published ten designs for chimneypieces in Volume IV, the first volume of his great treatise to appear; each was couched in a different classical order. The present design employs the Composite order; it is for a small room and the fireplace can in this case be set into the wall so the hood scarcely projects.

Plate 15 is a design by Giulio Romano and his assistants working in Mantua, probably about 1530. Alternative schemes are proposed for this waisted hood, one with sphinxes, one with 'playing boys' at the corners. This elaborate ornament was probably to be executed in stucco. The side elevation shows how the supporting consoles are pulled back to give a lighter appearance.

Plate 16 is by a French architect visiting Rome in the 1560s who felt this chimneypiece in the Palazzo Massimi was so interesting that he drew it most carefully and recorded all the dimensions meticulously. The vertical line on the right shows the central axis so only half the design is shown; to the right is a side elevation.

From Serlio's *Treatise on Architecture*, Vol. IV, 1537
Courtesy of the Trustees of Sir John Soane's Museum, London
Giulio Romano, chimney design
Musée du Louvre, Paris
Unidentified French artist, Palazzo Massimi, drawing of an elevation and section of a mantelpiece, *c.*1560
The Metropolitan Museum of Art, New York. Gift of Janos Scholz and Anne Bigelow in Memory of Flying Officer Walter Bigelow, 1949 (49.92.83v)

17

18

19

20

17 The architectural surround

Once the hearth was set back into the thickness of the wall and no projecting hood was therefore needed, it became possible to make the chimneypiece architectural or sculptural, or both. This design can be dated very precisely, as Adrian VI's pontificate only lasted a few months (1522–3). The architect, Antonio da Sangallo, placed the pope's arms prominently on this project that was designed to a new formula which set a pattern for the future.

Antonio da Sangallo, design for a chimneypiece
Uffizi, Florence (Dis. Arch. 170) (photograph: Alinari Archive)

18 The most influential chimneypiece design ever published

The fireplace in the main bedchamber at the Palazzo Farnese in Rome of about 1560 which bears the name of Cardinal Ranuccio Farnese. This engraving was first published by Vignola in the 1563 edition of his *Regole delle cinque ordini*. Its inclusion in this celebrated and much-consulted work ensured its fame and led to its influencing architects in many parts of the world but particularly in England and America long after its earliest publication.

Vignola, design for a fireplace at the Palazzo Farnese, Rome, *c.*1560, engraving, from *Regole delle cinque ordini*, 1563 edition
Courtesy of the Trustees of Sir John Soane's Museum, London

19 The elaborate sculptural overmantel

The characteristic Venetian form of the later decades of the sixteenth century, although described as a hood *a padiglione*, this is a far cry from the ungainly and ponderous pyramidal antecedents of a century earlier (e.g. Pl. 13). The present hood hardly projects at all, as the side elevation shows; the overmantel is purely a vehicle for sculptural ornament. The scene in the opening is probably to be understood as painted on a chimneyboard inserted into the cavernous opening in summertime when the fireplace was not in use.

From Scamozzi, *L'idea dell'architettura*, *c.*1615
Courtesy of the Trustees of Sir John Soane's Museum, London

20 Encompassed in the wall

A design for a mural decoration centred on a fireplace with a simple moulded surround, surmounted by a framed overmantel painting, and flanked by doorways that seem to have sculptural ornament. The sculptural compositions may have been meant to be rendered in stucco or in *trompe l'œil* fresco, and one of the doors may also have been a *porta finta* (see p. 320).

Perino del Vaga, drawing, probably *c.*1540
Uffizi, Florence (No. 640) (photograph: Soprintendenza B.A.S. Firenze)

21 A mobile heater in late-quattrocento Florence

A brazier on wheels is in the foreground; one wheel can be seen end-on. It burns charcoal. A baby is being held by a woman while a nappy is aired, but attention is primarily concentrated on the young mother. One servant prepares to wash the mother's face and hands, proffering a basin and holding a ewer from which water will be poured when the mother is ready. A towel is draped over the servant's shoulder. Another servant brings bowls of nourishing broth while a covered basket of delicacies is brought in from the left. The pillow-case has tassels and its two halves are buttoned together, revealing the pillow inside. The sheet is turned down over the coverlet. On the deep cornice of the bed-head stand a glass flask and a maiolica jar. Note the keyhole of the bed-chest.

Antonio di Niccolo, *Birth of the Virgin*, miniature, 1474/5
Library of the Convento dei Servi all' Annuziata (choir-book 4f. 40v.)
(photograph: Scala)

22 The decorated mantel-shelf

The mantel-shelf on many forms of Italian Renaissance chimneypiece lent itself well to the display of decorative objects, as here where we see a pair of pricket candlesticks as well as a pair of ewers with a basin – all formally set out. Much of the time, however, items were simply parked on these shelves in an entirely casual manner. What looks like an iron fireback is fitted behind the hearth. The bed (a *lettiera*) has a suspended tester sporting handsome valances and there are two rustic chairs which will have had rush seats (see Pls 190 and 194). Painted between 1510 and 1519.

Boccaccio Boccaccini, *Birth of the Virgin*, Cremona Cathedral
Photograph: Scala

21

approximately as high as a tall man while those in small rooms [*camerini*] should not be above chest level.

A splendid chimneypiece of marble or some other attractive stone was an expensive item that was meant to be noticed by visitors, and sometimes such a feature is indeed recorded in memoirs and travellers' accounts. Evidently quite exceptional was the chimneypiece *tutto de marmoro de Carrara lucente come l'auro, lavorato tanto subtilmente de figure e de fogliame, che Prassiteles ne Fidia li potrebbero adjungere* [entirely of Carrara marble shining like gold, carved with great delicacy with figures and foliage, which neither Praxiteles nor Phidias could have improved upon]. This stood in the splendid bedchamber of a lady of the Venetian Dolfin family who had just given birth, in 1494, and was lying-in, receiving the congratulations of her friends.[4] It was the polished marble catching the light that made such an impression, and in this case the figures (presumably caryatids or some similar beings supporting the entablature) will have seemed to move and dance in the flickering firelight. Indeed, a chimneypiece only really came into its own by firelight. When the fireplace was in use and therefore strongly illuminated from the hearth, the surround came to seem almost liquid, and the otherwise heavy overmantel was to a large extent hidden in shadow. With the fire unlit, which was the case much of the time, a chimneypiece was essentially rather forbidding – cavernous, black, heavy and obtrusive. The task of architects in the fifteenth and sixteenth centuries was to make this great feature blend with the rest of the basic decoration of the room, to become a graceful and pleasing adornment.

Fire-irons, ornaments and other equipment

One way of hiding the cavernous opening of a fireplace when it was not in use was to fill the opening with a chimney-board, a panel that fitted

22

23

23 Continued popularity of the basic form

The pyramid-shaped hood *a padiglione* was still to be seen throughout Italy, right through the sixteenth century. This view of an artist's studio in Rome also reminds us that, after darkness had fallen, the chief source of light was the fire in the hearth, although a boy holds a small oil-lamp to illuminate the inside of the chest where the older man is searching out a drawing. Note the fire-dogs with hooks for spits, the tongs and shovel, and the bellows. A frying-pan and a skillet hang on the wall behind. The multi-leaf shutters are closed and a basket containing food is suspended by a cord running over a pulley fitted with a bell, presumably to protect the viands from mice (was the cat insufficient?). A boy grinds pigments on a slab lying on a box-stool.

After Federico Zuccaro, *An artist's studio*, Inv. 1027
Musée des Arts Décoratifs, Paris (Sully – Jaulmes)

precisely into the front of the opening. It usually had two handles close to the sides so one could lift and push it into position, or pull it out when a fire was required again. Such boards were not only decorative; they also cut out draughts from the chimney (often smelly in hot weather) and prevented dislodged soot from falling into the room. One could fit a chimney-board where the chimney opening faced into the room. It must have been much more difficult to close off the opening of a hooded fireplace.

An early reference to a chimney-board occurs in a Florentine document of 1427; *una piana di chastagno pel chamino* [a board of chestnut wood for the chimneypiece].[1] It is likely to have been essentially a functional object. The *quadro da fuogo* in the Odoni mansion in Venice in 1555 (Odoni Invt.), on the other hand, while presumably somewhat similar, may have been more decorative. It was probably of wood but in the same house was one of canvas (it must have had a wooden stretcher) with a depiction of Vulcan on it [*un quadro de tella davanti el foger con un vulcan*]. What must be a painted chimney-board is to be seen in Pl. 19. It has to be said, however, that references are not all that common. Alvise Cornaro, the erudite gentleman-architect who wrote a treatise on building in the late 1540s, describes the latest forms of chimneypiece which hardly project at all into the room (one and a half *piede* is perfect, he says) and how chimneypieces should have *le sue porte di legno per chiuderla l'esta* [doors of wood for closing it in summer].[2] Schiaparelli also cites references to doors, two in each case, in three quotations of the 1490s, calling them *sportelli*, which is the term used for cupboard-doors.[3] This implies hinges and, even if the doors could be lifted off, there would be no point in adopting this arrangement unless the doors were normally in place and stood open when the fire was lit. It would seem to be an arrangement that was only practical with a small fireplace.

There were also firescreens [*parafuoci*] and *scremaii* [i.e. *schermagli*]. These will have had feet of some sort so they could stand independently in front of the fire. The great architect Serlio claims always to have supplied a plate of iron or other metal [*una lamina di ferro o d'altro metallo*] mounted in some way so that the *fuoco non offendesse gli occhi di coloro, che sono al fuoco per scaldarsi* [the fire should not offend the eyes of those who are warming themselves at the fire].[4] Most firescreens were of wood, however, Cosimo de' Medici having, for example, one of walnut in his ordinary bedchamber (where he actually slept) at the Palazzo Vecchio in Florence in 1553 (Medici Invt.). Several *scremaii* are mentioned in the Este inventories of 1436 but with little in the way of description; one gathers they were simple boards set horizontally (one was seven *braccia* long, and a half deep). Later in the century firescreens became decorative. The most capable woodworker in Ferrara in 1481, Stefano di Dona Bona, made one for the young princess Isabella d'Este which was of carved walnut with ball-finials topping the uprights [*uno scremaio de nogara Intaiado ... come doe balle sopra li cantonali fo fato per madona Ixabela*].[5] Firescreens were not greatly used but were found in the best places. For the most part people shielded their face from a hot fire by holding a hand up in front (Pls 24, 239).

24

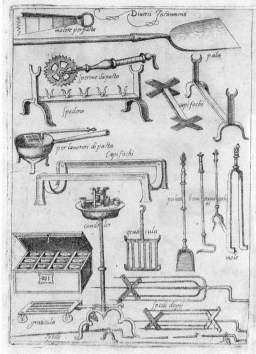

25

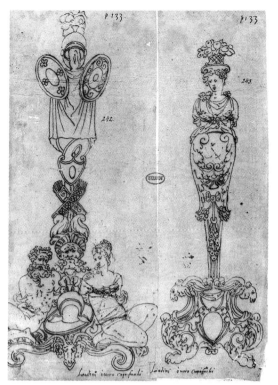

26

24 A kitchen dining-room

Cooking at a hooded fireplace in a kitchen where meals were evidently taken habitually, as the dining arrangements are by no means casual (note the wall-hanging, the handsome cloth with a woven border, glass drinking-vessels, etc.). Presumably this shows a modest citizen's house with not many rooms and where one normally ate in the kitchen – the kind of house of which many examples could be seen in every Italian city during the Renaissance. In a niche is a *lavabo* at which one rinsed fingers before and after a meal, or could perform minor exercises in washing-up.

From the *Contrasto di Carnescale e la quaresima*, a Florentine publication *c*.1495
British Library, London (B.L. IA 27918)

25 Equipping the fireplace

Page from a cookery-book of 1570 showing, amongst other things, fire dogs [*capi fochi*, here], rests for spits [*spedi*], and fire-irons (shovel, billet-hook, spiked poker for handling logs, tongs). There is also a candlestand, and implements for making *pasta*.

From the *Opera* of Bartolomeo Scappi, personal cook to Pope Pius V [*cuoco secreto di Papa*], Venice, 1570
Metropolitan Museum of Art, New York, Elisha Whittelsey Collection, Elisha Whittelsey Fund, 1952 (52.SAS.12[16])

26 Designs for splendid fire-dogs

Both inscribed *Landini overo capifuochi* [andirons or fire-dogs], these are tracings of design by Giulio Romano, presumably to be executed in bronze at Mantua for important Gonzaga fireplaces, during the second quarter of the sixteenth century. The billet-bar runs backwards from the central boss of the base, and the pillar rises at the front to form a purely decorative feature that acquired an exciting appearance when seen by flickering firelight.

From a collection of designs by Giulio Romano and his assistants (including some later tracings like these)
Strahov Monastery, Prague (Cat. Nos. 138/242 & 243)

27 Underfloor heating at Padua in the 1520s

One can see the flames under the floor of the domed octagonal room which was apparently where the owner of this *palazzo* in Padua held musical gatherings. Conventional fireplaces may be seen in the first-floor rooms. The house, known as the 'Odeo Cornaro', was designed by the brilliant Veronese architect Giovanni Maria Falconetto to the exacting requirements of Alvise Cornaro, himself an amateur architect of no mean talent. The house was built about 1524. In order to accommodate the tall Music Room (essentially a salon), the ceiling over the ground floor had to be set high; this enabled mezzanine rooms to be introduced on either side of the domed ceiling, interposed between the ground floor and the first floor (one can see the extra windows).

From Serlio's *Treatise on Architecture*, Volume VII, published posthumously in 1575 (he died in 1554)
Courtesy of the Trustees of Sir John Soane's Museum, London

27

It was found sensible to have a fireback of iron against the back of the fireplace and one occasionally sees these in sixteenth-century illustrations (Pls 363 a & b). On the hearth invariably stood a pair of fire-dogs, placed either side of the centre of combustion, across which the logs rested – to keep them off the ground so they burned better. These are frequently illustrated (e.g. Pls 10, 118). Called variously *alari, capafuoci, brandenali* and *cavedoni*,[6] these were basically iron tripods with two legs in front and a bar, reaching backwards, that formed a support for logs and ended in a downward-turned third 'leg' (Pl.132). Rising from between the two front legs was a pillar to prevent logs rolling forwards and falling into the room. The top of this pillar could be finished with some form of decoration – a scroll, a knop or a figure (Pl. 26).[7] On the grander sort of fire-dog, the finial was often of brass or bronze and was usually tall, sometimes of what one might call asparagus shape, sometimes with a ball-finial[8] or a mask.[9] Polished brass reflected the firelight in a cheerful manner. Additional advantage was taken of this when the brass finials took the form of human or near-human figures which danced in the firelight (Pl. 26). A particularly elaborate example of this kind must have been the pair in Alvise Odoni's house in Venice in 1555 (Odoni Invt.) which were tall, of bronze, and had *due figure in cima et oseletti [uccelletti] atorno* [two figures on top with birds all round]. The Venetian sumptuary regulations of 1562 were probably drawn up with this kind of thing in mind, when they prohibited citizens from furnishing their fireplaces with fire-dogs and fire-irons that were gilded, damascened or of bronze [*cavedoni, et suoi fornimenti da fuoco dorati, o di lavoro alla damaschina o di bronzo*].[10]

It will be noted that the sumptuary law just cited makes mention of fire-irons because, in a splendid fireplace of the sixteenth century, these would sometimes be *en suite* with the fire-dogs. For example, a Medici set had the family arms on each item, by way of ornament.[11] A set of fire-irons usually comprised a fork [*forchetta*], a pair of tongs [*molle*] and a shovel [*paletta*], to which was sometimes added a hook or two-pronged 'rake' for moving the burning logs [*rastrello da brace*]. Some fire-irons had handles of brass, which conducts away heat more speedily than iron. Lorenzo the Magnificent had a set *lavorate alla milanese* [worked in the Milanese manner] which suggests elaborately decorated steelwork, perhaps made by Milanese armourers (p. 269).[12] What, however, can have been the nature of *unum par alarium inghilesi* [a pair of English fire-dogs] which were to be seen in a Florentine mansion in 1417?[13]

A pair of bellows might be found near a fireplace (Pl. 23).[14] They were essential equipment for a forge or furnace but were also useful where cooking took place.

Although, by 1400, people of standing were no longer cooking in their main rooms, it was sometimes convenient or amusing to run up a light meal in a bedchamber or anteroom. Thrift was also a potent notion in most households during the period, especially slightly lower down the social scale, and it was clearly sensible to make use of a fire that was burning anyway, if one found oneself wanting a snack or perhaps needed to warm up broth for an ailing member of the family (Pls 24, 312, 316).

Most forms of chimneypiece during the period had a moulding somewhere above the opening of the fireplace. It was usually a bold feature that formed a shelf on which one might place objects of various kinds. In many instances it was merely a parking-place for whatever items needed to be set aside for a while (e.g. a candlestick, a small box, a jar) but one could also place objects there as ornaments. One can see an ornamental arrangement of this kind in Pl. 22. In the Medici town residence, Lorenzo the Magnificent had two red glass vases on his mantelshelf when an inventory was taken in 1492 (Medici Invt.) [*Dua orciuoli di vreto paghonazo sopra il chammino*]. It does not seem, however, that ornaments were specially made to go on mantelshelves until after 1600.

Other sources of heat

It was said that the famous palace at Urbino, the most advanced building of its time (*c*.1480), had 250 rooms but only forty fireplaces. It can be very cold in Italy during the winter, especially up in the hills, so there must have been some other form of heating in the 210 rooms that were not provided with fireplaces. Before discussing these other methods it should just be said that the room where a fireplace was present was sometimes called a *caminata*. This was especially the case with a large room where the chimneypiece was a dominant feature, most especially the main room of the house – the *sala*. Indeed, in Genoa and perhaps elsewhere, the word *caminata* was synonymous with *sala*. The *sala* in some great houses might have two fireplaces, as for example did the *Sala Bianca* in the Palace at Ferrara already by the 1430s.[1]

Since the chimneypiece was a fixture, it was not normally mentioned in inventories so one has to infer its presence where references to fire-irons, and other items usually associated with fireplaces, are listed. The absence of such references can probably be taken to indicate that the room concerned had no fireplace, although one can of course not be certain. Rooms where one dined, the *sala/caminata* and the *salotto*, would always have fireplaces with prominent chimneypieces. Bedrooms and the adjacent *anticamere* were mostly likewise equipped. Small rooms like the *studio*, on the other hand, rarely had a fireplace; they were easy to heat by more limited means.[2]

What were these means? The principal alternative form of heating was the brazier; one is shown in Pl. 33. Any large metal bowl might serve as a container for the burning charcoals (Pl. 270). It was a refinement to have a pierced lid on top. In Pl. 21 we see a small hearth on wheels which could be moved about at will like a modern electric fire – without the disadvantage of having a flex.

The charcoal-burner could be adapted for a multitude of uses. At the end of a long handle it served as a bed-warmer [*scaldaletto*] or warming-pan; one can be seen on the wall in Pl. 23.[3] On a small stand it served as a chafing-dish for warming food near the dining-table [*scaldavivande*]. Placed inside a wooden box with a pierced lid, the charcoal-burner (then usually in an earthenware vessel) became a foot-warmer [*scaldapiede*].[4] One could also have a small sphere of pierced metal, with a container for the coals inside, that could be carried about to warm the hands [*palla de scaldare le manj*; Acciaiuoli Invt., 1363]. Finally, of course, the charcoal-burner became a perfume-burner or censer, when you fitted a small pan above the container of the coals, placing on the pan scented pastilles and the like to produce sweet-smelling smoke (p. 249). A very handsome model is shown in Pl. 280.

People wore warm clothes during the cold months of the year and kept the fires burning brightly, if they could afford to do so. Hand- and foot-warmers helped a bit, if you owned such things. At night the amount of bedding could be increased and the truly rich, who may have owned day-beds as well as great 'standing beds', could move these lightweight structures closer to the fire for extra warmth (p. 152). Nevertheless, even when all such measures had been taken, the cold of an Italian winter could still be appalling. Many people must have echoed the feelings of the lady-in-waiting from Ferrara who, when staying in the castle at Milan in the particularly cold winter of 1493, lamented that she was so cold she feared she would never be warm again [*si freddo che temeva quasi non havere mai caldo*].[5]

Under-floor heating and hot-air ducts in the walls were by no means unknown although such luxuries cost a good deal to instal. They were mostly associated with bathrooms (p. 318) but a room in Padua had under-floor heating in the mid-sixteenth century (Pl. 27) and no doubt this was not a totally isolated phenomenon.

Alberti, in his important treatise on architecture written during the third quarter of the fifteenth century, explains that 'in Germany ... and other Places, where Fire is absolutely necessary against the extreme Cold, they make Use of Stoves'.[6] Stoves were certainly known to the Italians. They were to be found in bathrooms (Pl. 349) and might be found in the sauna [*stufa*, a word from the same stem as 'stove']. They never became part of the Italian tradition except in the Alpine regions. The Duke of Ferrara seems to have had a stove installed in his private study [*camara sechriecta*] in 1478; the services of a bricklayer were required to set it up.[7] At least two stoves, faced with tiles of maiolica, were to be seen in small rooms in Este residences in and around Ferrara in 1529.[8] These stoves must themselves have been quite small.

Windows

Glass

'The first charm of a house is light', said Pope Pius II when describing the new palace he had built at Pienza in the 1460s.[1] He was speaking for the generation which had realized that, while the supporters of rival factions might fight each other murderously in the street and the mob might occasionally rampage through the city, there was no longer any need to have one's town residence looking like a fortress. So long as unfriendly people could not too easily smash in the gates, and unwelcome callers – be it common thieves or importunate suitors for the daughter's hand – could not clamber through the ground-floor windows, the windows of a modern house could now be large and let in plenty of light. The problem now was how to fill such large openings to prevent draughts and keep out the weather, and how to mask the window during the heat of the day in the hot months of the year.

The only satisfactory way of dealing with the first problem was to fit the window with a framed glass insert – a glazed window.

Of course a few rooms, including important ones like Piero de' Medici's study in the family's house in Florence, built in the 1440s, had no windows at all,[2] but generally speaking the windows of important rooms in houses of standing mostly had glass windows by then. In a Bolognese inventory of 1335 (Belvisi Invt.) note is made of 'two glass windows' [*duas finestras de vitro*] as if they were then still something rather exceptional,[3] while at Genoa *fenestri iii vedrii* were installed in a house in 1368 by one Antonius de Rapallo who called himself *Vitrarius*, which suggests that he did a certain amount of this kind of work.[4] Indeed, by 1375, the Commune felt it necessary to take steps to protect glass windows, presumably because there were so many that the breaking of them had become a widespread nuisance. A Florentine inventory of 1391 also includes references to glazed windows,[5] but because windows could be regarded as fixtures, a lack of references to them in inventories of movable goods does not in itself prove they were uncommon in the late fourteenth century. On the other hand, the fact that a window was glazed seems still to have been worthy of note in many places in Italy, even at the end of the fifteenth century.

The Florentine inventory of 1391 refers to twenty-four *occhi bianchi di vetro* [white 'eyes' of glass]. *Occhi* was the term used for the roundels of glass commonly fitted in glazed windows,[6] mounted close-set with lead 'cames' (Pls 140, 218). The star-shaped space formed by the juxtaposing of any four *occhi* was in turn filled with glass, in some cases of a different colour to that of the *occhi* (Pl. 173).[7] The assemblage of *occhi* and lead cames was fitted into a wooden frame which opened inwards (in some cases they were fixed). Had they opened outwards, which would have been more convenient, they would have been buffeted by every wind and the flimsy assemblage would have been at risk. As it was, iron rods were fixed at intervals across the wooden frame, lying against the inside of the glass montage, to give it strength; one can see such rods in Pls 293, 349.

The rods might also be of brass or copper.[8] Glass *occhi* mostly came from Venice; there were, for instance, many payments made in the 1440s for *occhi* imported into Ferrara where a Venetian *fenestrato* installed what must have been a good many windows over a decade or so.[9]

Although *occhi* may have let light in, they were not truly transparent because of the method by which they were made. As Vasari said, in the mid-sixteenth century, *La transparenza consiste nel saper fare elezione di vetri che siano lucidi per se stessi; ed in cio meglio sono i franzesi, fiamminghi ed inghilesi, che i veneziani* [To obtain transparency it is necessary to select pieces of glass that are polished; the French, Flemish and English glass is better than the Venetian in this respect].[10] The better quality of the foreign window glass may also have lain in the fact that it came in panes, i.e. that the pieces were rectangular, not circular. In the building accounts for the Villa Medici in Rome, in the late sixteenth century, distinction was made between *vetri ordinari*, *vetri spianati* and *vetri cristallo* (Medici Invt., 1598). *Spianato* means flat so the ordinary glass must have been uneven and coarse but it will have been in panes; at that late date *occhi* had ceased to be used in new buildings of importance. The crystalline glass, which was of an exceptionally clear metal first evolved about a century earlier, also came in flat panes. Describing the *sala* at Belfiore, the almost legendary Este pleasance [*luogho di delizie*] on the outskirts of Ferrara, in the late fifteenth century, special attention was drawn to the way the room was being *perlustrata da cinque finestre de cristalino vetro* [brightly lit by five windows of crystalline glass].[11] It was painted with scenes of falconry; this implies that the glass consisted of large panes and was flat.[12] Remarkable about Belfiore at this date, anyway, was the fact that *all* the windows in the house were glazed [*tutte le stantie ... prendono lume per vitriate fenestre*].[13] That this struck the sophisticated chronicler[14] so forcibly that he felt impelled to remark upon it, suggests that it was not only the fact there was glass in each window which he thought curious but that the glass itself was in some way noteworthy – presumably because it let in more light than usual.

Stained glass was not an art much practised in Italy.[15] The Belfiore windows were 'painted' and one should probably take this literally (i.e. that they were painted with some form of oil-paint) but it seems there may have been a limited revival of the art of stained glass proper in the 1560s, for a certain Pastorino di Pasterini was paid for having *fatto ... finestre di vetro figurate e colorite* [made figured and coloured glass windows] in a loggia put up in some hurry in order to receive the Princess Barbara of Austria when she came to Ferrara in 1565 to marry Alfonso II d'Este.[16] Vasari tells us that Duke Cosimo de' Medici had two windows in the Palazzo Vecchio fitted *di vetro con li imprese ed arme sue e di Carlo V* [of glass with the Duke's emblems and arms on those of Charles V]. A painter from Arezzo, Baltista da Borro, was responsible; the work could not have been bettered [*non si puo far di quel lavoro meglio*].[17] This was in 1553.

It should be added that the introduction of windows with rectangular panes was held back so long as Gothic windows (whether single arched or biforate) remained fashionable. Dividing off the arched top(s) in order to create a rectangular area of window below was ugly; at the same time,

making the hinged window of a fancy shape was unpractical. It was only when the rectangular window became common on grand buildings that hinged windows of rectangular form with frames to match could readily be inserted. Such frames could be made stronger, could have larger areas of glass than the old form with *occhi*, and could therefore let in more light. This development was taking place in the third quarter of the fifteenth century.

Shutters and impannate

Before the introduction of glass windows, window-openings in Italy (as elsewhere) were closed with heavy shutters of wood. They might be single or in pairs. Some were divided horizontally so that an upper part could be pushed open while the lower remained shut, or vice versa. They were hinged at the side and opened inwards (Pl. 258). Occasionally a shutter would have its lower part top-hinged so that one could push it open and look down into the street.

Montaigne said what one might think was the last word on these solid wooden shutters. 'The windows [in Italy] are large and wide open, except for a big wooden shutter that keeps out the light if you want to keep out the sun or the wind.'[1] That was in 1580 but one can cite Baldassare Castiglione's *The Courtier** of half a century earlier by way of riposte. Castiglione has his courtiers gathered round their Duchess at Urbino, having discussed all night whether 'Women are as capable of divine Love as Men', when one of them realizes that dawn is already upon them and says 'It is Day already ... and shewed her [the Duchess] the Light, which began to enter through the Chinks of the Shutters'.[2] Even in the palace at Urbino, where some of the most capable woodworkers must surely have been on hand, it was evidently not possible to make shutters that totally excluded all light.

However convoluted the shape of a Gothic or an arched window might be, it was usually possible to fit rectangular wooden shutters inside that closed up against the back of the Gothic framework and fitted into a matching rectangular recess (Pl. 134). It was therefore not necessary to shape the shutters to the fancy form of the stonework. Once the windows themselves became rectangular, fitting shutters was more straightforward.

Wooden shutters were built like outside doors, with nailed faces towards the street, and ring-handles, bolts and hinges inside. By adjusting shutters to different settings one could alter the way light came into the room. The slatted form of shutter, so familiar to all travellers in Italy today, does not seem to have been introduced until after the Renaissance period. Louvred shutters [*gelosie*], when first introduced, served to prevent casual observation from outside while enabling the occupants of a room thus equipped to view discreetly what was taking place outside.[3]

If one wanted light to enter the room but did not want to suffer draughts and other nuisances that could attend the opening of the shutters, one could fit a *fenestra impannata*, a wooden frame over which a textile material was stretched. This was inserted into the window-opening

28 Window fitted with *fenestre Impannate*

Inserted into the openings are light wooden frames over which is stretched oiled white linen; this treatment made them highly translucent although not transparent. The nails securing the cloth are shown, as are the crossed wires inside that strengthen each pane. A rod holds the lower sections open.

Attributed to Fiorenzo di Lorenzo, *Miracle of S. Bernardino* (detail), 1473.
Pinacoteca, Perugia (photograph: Anderson)

28

and the shutters could then be closed up against it at night or in the heat of the day. The textile was usually linen which was soaked in turpentine to make it more translucent – although not transparent.[4] Such a panel resembled the canvas on which an artist paints a picture, and it is hardly surprising that *impannate* were not infrequently painted with some ornament a coat of arms, some device or formal motif, or sometimes a figurative subject (Pl. 119).[5] They opened outwards, usually with their lower half top-hinged to open (like some wooden shutters just mentioned) for ventilation and so as to allow occupants of the room to look down into the street (Pl. 28).[6]

Fenestre impannate no doubt needed replacing more often than glass windows but remained fashionable throughout the period. Only one is mentioned in the Este inventories of 1436 (Este Invt); at the Palazzo Vecchio in Florence in 1553 a great many are listed.[7] If the glazing of windows did not make as speedy a headway as one might expect, given the advantages glass would bring, it must have been because these *impannate* were effective and rather jolly. In the background of a portrait in the Palazzo Spada one can see a *fienestra impanata* from the inside and it is evident that one could not see through the material but that it let through plenty of light.[8]

Other optional window features

The wooden frames of *impannate* and glazed windows were probably varnished[1] in most cases, but sometimes ostentation got the better of 'top people', as when Alfonso II d'Este had the window-frames of his sumptuous study gilded in 1560.[2]

On ground-floor windows one might fit iron grilles outside. These still form a striking feature of the façades of many Italian Renaissance town residences. As they were fixtures, and anyway fitted outside the building,

they are not mentioned in inventories, except incidentally.[3] They took a certain amount of light away and were rather forbidding but they kept undesirables out (Pl. 29).

On the outsides of Italian Renaissance *palazzi* one often sees iron brackets ending in rings or loops (the opening facing upwards) that project from the façade in pairs, one on either side of each main window – on the floors above ground-level. These supported poles or booms, laid horizontally so as to cross in front of the window, slightly above head-height. On these booms one could hang washing to dry (p. 321) but they were primarily used for fixing up a *tenda*, an awning. If fixed at the top of the window and draped out over the boom, the *tenda* cut out a good deal of strong sunlight (thereby reducing the heat in the room) but, by being held open slightly, nevertheless allowed air into the room.

Tende actually came in many forms. Some were modified versions of the framed *impannate*, draped instead of framed. Many were coloured and this of course affected the quality of light that came into the room.

Window-curtains, as we understand them, hardly existed during the period and were essentially utilitarian, when present (Pl. 270).[4] If one wanted it to be dark when one was trying to sleep, one pulled the curtains that were around the bed. One might also close the shutters. There was no question of drawing curtains across the windows in order to exclude daylight; they might be used as sun-blinds to cut out the glare of strong sunlight. Yet, even if there is little direct evidence of the use of window-curtains before 1600 in Italy, the Venetian government introduced a sumptuary law in 1562 which specifically forbade the use *alle finestre panni di seda d'alcuna sorte* which must mean silk materials of any kind 'at the windows'.[5]

Once introduced, window-curtains also provided some measure of privacy. Hitherto this had either not been achieved or was produced by fitting wicker screens into the windows. One can see a pair of such screens in Carpaccio's famous scene of St Ursula's bedchamber – an indication, incidentally, that the room was on the ground floor because the screens, which only cover the lower parts of the window, are designed to prevent people looking in from the street (Pl. 140).

Doors

Most doorways were fitted with a single door but paired doors (i.e. with two leaves meeting in the centre of the opening) were certainly known at the beginning of the period (Pl. 31) and were recognized throughout the two centuries as being the most suitable form for settings of elegance and splendour.

Humble doors were of unadorned boards presenting a plain face into the room. In the kinds of room with which we are here concerned, however, the doors were mostly decorated, sometimes elaborately and in a manner consonant with the decoration of the architrave of the surrounding door-frame. In the first half of the fifteenth century fine doors were commonly decorated with borders of inlaid geometrical *tarsie* (Pl. 31) but this gradually evolved to become more complex, with borders of formal pattern surrounding formal, and finally figurative, *tarsia* in the centre. The highest achievements in the field of *lavoro di intarsio* [inlaid work] were produced during the later decades of the fifteenth century and the early decades of the sixteenth (p. 92). Some idea of how exciting such work seemed to the beholder when this genre was new can be gained from a poem about the wonders of the Palazzo Medici, written in 1459. It speaks of an intarsiated door [*Un uscio intarsiato*] which led to the Chapel 'which no one could ever tire of looking at' [*ch'alchun mai di mirarla non fu stancho*], and of another door decorated with such skill that one would think its subjects were in the round whereas it was in fact flat *intarsio* [*un uscio di tanta arte ch'il chonclud'io vero rilievo – et e pian tarsiato*].[1]

Such *lavoro di intarsio* was executed on doors that were panelled, each panel being framed by profiled mouldings. Many panelled doors were of course not *intarsiata*, however; they were left plain and their aesthetic quality lay in good proportions, handsome timber and fine workmanship. Towards the end of the fifteenth century mouldings came to be carved, at which stage *tarsie* started to fade from the fashionable scene. In the sixteenth century doors in important rooms relied almost entirely on carved mouldings for their embellishment. Serlio shows a whole page of illustrations of panelled doors in the fourth volume of his influential treatise on architecture which came out in 1537. Doors might also be painted, in the sixteenth century, often in keeping with the mural decoration of which they formed part.

The Renaissance architect's deep-seated need to impose symmetry on a room led to the installing of false doors to balance real doors that had, for reasons to do with planning, to be offset at one end of a wall (p. 319). The architect Pietro Cataneo discusses such *porte finte* in his treatise, published in Venice in 1554, but this device was certainly adopted well before that.[2] Doors became a major architectural feature when architects began to align them so that one could proceed in a straight line through a sequence of rooms. As the apartment system evolved (p. 300), the sense that each successive door opened into an increasingly important room carried its own magic and it is therefore evident why the entrances to such chambers should be suitably decorated – the more significant the room, the more impressive would be the doorway by which it was entered.

In rooms entirely decorated with fresco, *porte finte* were not built but were rendered in paint *en trompe l'oeil*, sometimes with servants shown naturalistically passing through the simulated doorway (Pls. 20, 299). In one such room, the Sala Paolina in the Castel Sant' Angelo in Rome, executed for Pope Paul III (1534–49), the *porta finta* is shown with a *portière*[3] hanging in front but being pushed up out of the way by a servant. This is a reminder that the *portière* was an important feature of many grand doorways during the period.

An early reference occurs in a Florentine inventory of 1449 where we find a *panno da uscio richamato* [a door cloth, embroidered] (Pucci Invt.). Another embroidered *covertina* [i.e. *cortina*] *overo usciaia di panno cilestro* [curtain or *portière* of sky-blue cloth] of somewhat later date had the family's coat of arms worked on it (Tura Invt., Siena, 1483). Coats of arms, indeed, were probably the chief ornament to be seen on *portières* during the period, but not a few *usciale* had one or more large figures worked on them. *Uno usale facto a figure* is listed in a Modena inventory of 1474 (Pico Invt.); a *portière* of *araza* [Arras, i.e. tapestry] on which was depicted a woman on horseback that is mentioned in a Florentine inventory of 1534 (Capone Invt.); and *dui portali figurati* appear in a Palermitan inventory of 1561 (Requesens Invt.) which must likewise have been of tapestry because the item follows immediately after a list of tapestry hangings.[4] A *portière* of verdure tapestry may be seen in the famous Ghirlandaio painting reproduced in Pl. 35. *Un portiera di damascho ... con frangie e pass[ama]ni doro e seta* [of silk damask with fringe and trimmings of gold and silk] was *en suite* with the wall-hangings, in a room at the Villa Medici in Rome in 1598 (Medici Invt.).[5] A *portière* of gilt leather painted with the family arms was to be seen in the Palazzo Correr in Venice in 1584 (Correr Invt.). During the second half of the sixteenth century, the hanging in front of the door sometimes matched the hangings on the bed, in grand bedchambers. At a humbler level, doorways might be filled or masked with a rush mat.[6]

The English word 'usher' derives from the French *huissier* and the Italian *usciere* – the man who wards the door [*uscio*]. Guarding an important door was a responsible job and, where the lives of great princes (and princesses) were at stake, such servants were armed. Among the trusted servants of Alfonso the Magnanimous, King of Naples in the mid-fifteenth century, were four *uxers darmes*. From a Spanish Ordinance of 1344 it is clear that these were armed soldiers who controlled access to the royal person at strategic doors. Later, this honour was entrusted to noblemen.[7] It is presumably because such splendid people did not hang about in doorways, except on occasions when their duties could be performed in front of an appreciative crowd of courtiers, that a supporting team of *porters de massa* [carriers of a mace (*mazza*)] were on hand who were more actively responsible for the king's person.

29

29 Protecting the daughters

Iron grilles in front of ground-floor windows were an effective means of keeping importunate young men away from the daughters of the household, although these features were primarily a defence against burglars and unruly mobs.

Milanese miniature from the *Paolo and Daria Codex* containing verses by the aristocratic poet, Gaspare Visconti, 1493–5. *Staatliche Museen Preußischer Kulturbesitz, Kupferstichkabinett, Berlin (photograph: Jorg. P. Anders)*

30 Two *impannate*

The lower portions of these windows are top-hinged and can be drawn upwards by means of a cord. The central window has nail-studded shutters. A drain in the centre of the courtyard may serve to collect rainwater in an underground cistern. Mary has a stake-legged stool with a scrolled back of unusual form.

Attavante, miniature, MS. 154 ff 13v 1480s
Reproduced by kind permission of the Syndics of the Fitzwilliam Museum, Cambridge

30

31

32

31 Paired doors with *lavoro di intarsio*

Although the artist has not bothered to show details like door-handles, locks or hinges, he has carefully delineated the inlaid geometric pattern on these fine doors. Similar decoration is to be seen on the seat, and on the bed which stands in the room beyond. The bed-curtain has a netted heading running on a rod.

Masolino, *Annunciation*, Florentine, *c*.1425/30
National Gallery of Art, Washington, D.C., Mellon Collection (16)

32 Real and imaginary doorways

The opening with a pair of panelled doors is the real doorway to this bedchamber. It has a deep cornice on which stand two maiolica vessels on display. The large arched opening is introduced by way of artistic license, in order to convey that the house was spacious and grand; it is inconceivable that any bedchamber would actually have had a large doorless aperture opening into it from a stairway in this manner. The object here was to make out that the parents of St John the Baptist were well-to-do citizens. The splendid bed is furnished with a massive tester suspended from the ceiling.

Master of the Apollo and Daphne Legends, *The Birth of John the Baptist*, *c*.1500
Howard University Gallery of Art, Washington, D.C.

33 The splendour of the late sixteenth-century upholsterer's creations

There must be a hook of some sort at the side of the door holding the heavy *portière* when it is pulled out of the way to admit visitors. The hanging may well have matched those of the splendid bed which is domed, with figures forming finials and with a rich, lappeted valance, each lappet bearing a tassel. In the background is a handsome chimneypiece. A woman sits on a rush-bottomed chair, perhaps of the kind termed *a pistolesi* (from Pistoia; see pp. 174–5).

Giovanni Caccini, *Birth of the Virgin*, relief in bronze, after 1595, Pisa Cathedral
Photograph: Alinari Archive

34 A divided *portière*

The Duke of Urbino passing through a doorway furnished with a *portière* that is in two halves. The two curtains are hitched up at the sides, the bunches of cloth being passed through two rings. The capping has a flame pattern and a fringe. This scene is rendered in *lavoro di intarsio* on the walls of the Duke's studio in the Palace at Urbino, created in the 1470s, quite possibly by the Florentine workshop run by Giuliano and Benedetto da Maiano (see pp. 94 and 342).

Photograph: Alinari Archive

33

34

The degree of respect due to the person controlling an important door is conveyed by a description in that romantic fantasy, the *Hypnerotomachia*, which was published in Venice in 1499 and, for all its fairytale quality, actually gives helpful insights into many aspects of life at the time. The hero and heroine, approaching the doorway, find a 'vigilant and innocent Damosel that is the keeper of the doore'. She holds up the *portière* to let them enter, and they note that it is *di artificio & compositione nobilissima* [of the very noblest workmanship and design]. As they pass on, he salutes the girl 'with proper reverence'.[8]

One could place objects of various kinds on the deep shelf that was provided by the top of the heavy projecting cornice of one of the common forms of Italian Renaissance doorway. Sculpture was not uncommonly placed there (Pls 140, 142, 312) and references to such arrangements are to be found in quite a few documents. For instance, when some small rooms in the castle at Ferrara were done over in 1518, *fra le altre cose La vedra sopra tutti li ussi depsi Camerini varie teste antiche e moderne de sculptori* [amongst other things you see above all the doors of these small rooms various antique and modern heads of sculpture].[9]

Walls

Woodwork

However much Renaissance architects may have planned ideal houses (see Part Three), in practice their schemes were invariably altered by subsequent generations – and sometimes even by the client himself – as fresh requirements had to be accommodated. Rooms were divided up in order to fit in more people, new groups of rooms were formed, secondary entrances were opened up to allow other families or tenants (paying what was often much needed rent) to come and go independently. The partitions that were put up to hive off part of a larger room in such circumstances were often simply made of boards. Even where such pressures were not present, however, walls faced with boards from the start were not unknown, if we are to believe the evidence provided by a famous painting by Carlo Crivelli in the National Gallery in London. Here we see the Virgin as a well-dressed young woman in a house that is

35

35 The decorative *portière*

A *portière* of verdure tapestry hangs in front of the door at the back. It is attached to a roller which drops into a pair of hooks set at the top of the doorway. The *portière* was probably *en suite* with wall-hangings – time (and restoration?) having obliterated their pattern. Pilasters with ornament that is *intarsiata* [inlaid] are fitted into the corners of this fine room which purports to show the birth of St John the Baptist although the setting is actually one of high patrician splendour in Florence during the 1480s. The superb bed, a *lettiera*, is made of a dark wood with black mouldings and gilded decoration. The coverlet is of the finest red cloth and has an embroidered border. A ewer and basin stand on an inlaid box.

Domenico Ghirlandaio, *Birth of John the Baptist* (detail), S. Maria Novella, Florence
Photograph: Scala

by no means humble. Yet, behind her bed is a wall made with bare boards set vertically (Pl. 40). Admittedly it has a gilt frieze at the top but the plain finish of the boards seems comparatively austere. Although it is possible that Crivelli was hereby commenting on Mary's character, he would not have included such a feature (most carefully depicted) if it had not appeared entirely plausible to his contemporaries, as a recognized form of decoration in a respectable house. In the castle at Milan, in the late fifteenth century, an important room was known as the *Camere de asse*, the Boarded Chamber,[1] and it may be that this, too, had walls revetted with vertical boards in a similar manner. It has been suggested that the woodwork was in fact panelled (i.e. with rectangular panelling surrounded by mouldings, e.g. Pl. 36 which shows what must be Milanese panelling of the 1480s) but *asse* means boards, not panelling, and one should at least consider the possibility that a boarded character was very evident and was therefore reflected in the room's name.[2]

When Pius II had finished building his country palace at Pienza in the 1460s, he had his own bedchamber lined with pine [he wrote in Latin, *hoc Pontifex habitavit, quod abiete iusserat incrustari*].[3] This was, he claimed, in order that 'the dampness of the new walls' should not trouble him but, although this measure was in the first place taken to ward off damp while the plaster was drying out, the word *incrustari* suggests that some degree of elaboration was involved, and that the Pope's bedchamber really was properly panelled. Indeed, the Pope was proud of his building and described its principal features with evident delight. The fact that this woodwork is mentioned, even if somewhat tangentially, suggests that it was rather special. Plain panelling, designed by a really talented architect, could be very elegant indeed, as Pl. 36 shows. The Pope's panels were quite probably inlaid as well – hence 'encrusted'.[4]

By the 1460s at any rate, some wall-panelling could have been decorated with *lavoro di intarsio*, inlaid ornament that was to be much used in the finest panelled rooms during the last quarter of the century. Pls 35 and 93 give a good idea of how glamourous such decoration could look.

Painted decoration

A few small rooms were faced with marble but to do this was very expensive indeed (Pl. 12). A cheaper and almost equally effective mural treatment was to 'marble' the walls with skilful simulation in paintwork (Pl. 38). It seems that mirrors may also have played a part in the fixed mural decoration of a few rooms during the second half of the sixteenth century (p. oo). Most walls, however, were plastered, in which case they would be painted – at least with whitewash or a colour-wash, or with more elaborate schemes of decoration executed in fresco, if something finer were required.

In the sixteenth century the walls of all important rooms were divided horizontally into several zones – usually comprising (working upwards) a base or skirting, a dado, the main field of the wall (the so-called 'filling'), and the frieze which was customarily surmounted by a cornice. The relative proportions of these zones varied considerably and an architect's judgement was revealed by the way he handled these relationships.

At the beginning of the previous century, walls of the better sort had almost invariably had a frieze, usually painted, but many walls were otherwise plain. The general introduction of dados and skirtings took place from about 1430 onwards, and Pls 37 and 39 exemplify the state of development in fine rooms at the end of the century. The frieze was normally the dominant band and could be very deep, and the decoration of the 'filling' would in that case be subordinate although, when the latter space was filled with large painted scenes or covered with great scenic tapestries, the frieze did tend to become overpowered. This stage was reached during the second half of the sixteenth century when mural and ceiling decoration in splendid rooms had become so complicated, that breaking the rules in a clever and tasteful manner must have been one of the artist's principal concerns.

So much has been written about fresco painting that little need be said about it here. Dickens wrote, more than a century ago, that there was scarcely a famous picture in all Italy 'but could be easily buried under a mountain of printed paper devoted to dissertation on it'.[1] The heap would of course be much taller today and would extend to many paintings which could by no means be called famous.

This welter of writing, however, usually fails to tell one that much fresco-painting was not pictorial at all. Regularly spaced repeating patterns of many kinds were spread across walls and ceilings, right through the period. In the fourteenth century the patterns might take the form of lozenges, chequers or stripes; and juxtaposed shields of arms, forming an all-over pattern, were greatly favoured. Another pattern, popular with Tuscan patricians, consisted of close-set simulations of miniver [or to be more precise, *vair vaio*], the winter pelts of northern squirrels which are white or greyish (Pl. 284). Cloaks and coverlets (and possibly even wall-hangings, although this would be incredibly expensive) made up with dozen of these small skins were an item of great luxury; to have representations of them on one's walls was evidently believed to be good for one's image.[2] Documents survive concerning the painting of rooms in the castle at Milan in 1469 with what must have consisted of all-over, regular patterns (e.g. *pinta tutta a zigli nel campo celestro, mettendo delle stelle tra luno ziglio e l'altro* [all painted with lilies on a blue ground and putting stars between one lily and the next]).[3] An important ceiling with a similar regular pattern, of about the same date, may still be seen in the building, now known as the Castello Sforzesco. It has doves centred on sunbursts, the device of Bona di Savoia, the wife of Galeazzo Maria Sforza (assassinated in 1476); they are executed in gold on a red ground. There must be quite a few other examples of regular-patterned wall decoration to be seen in ancient buildings in Italy but, in comparison with the number of pictorial frescoes that survive, the quantity is small. Not being expressions of High Art, few have been thought worthy of preservation. Nor have art historians paid much attention to this aspect of wall decoration although much information must be lying awaiting attention in archives.

36

36 Wall-panelling of exceptional elegance

Well-proportioned panelling with finely profiled mouldings in an elegant interior. This fresco in a Milanese church, executed in 1484, has been attributed to Donato Bramante and Giovanni Donato Montorfano but some authorities doubt whether Bramante himself was directly involved. Whatever the case, the artist would seem to have been familiar with the style of Bramante during the early phase of his career when he was working in Milan, before he moved to Rome to become the principal exponent of Renaissance classicism, deeply knowledgeable about the models furnished by Antiquity, and himself an inspiration to many generations of architects working in the classical tradition. A chimneypiece with a hood, *a padiglione*, that projects only slightly may be seen on the left.

Donato Bramante(?) and Giovanni Donato Montorfano, *Birth of St John the Baptist*, S. Pietro in Gessate, Milan

37 A sumptuous Florentine bedchamber, about 1480

This terracotta is by Benedetto da Maiano. Although today known chiefly as a sculptor, he and his brother Giuliano ran a workshop that executed much of the high-class woodwork produced in Florence during the last decades of the quattrocento, including fine carving, *lavoro di intarsio* and complete schemes of panelling like that shown here. Benedetto was therefore familiar with fashionable room-decoration executed in wood and this scene must show the kind of work his firm produced. Note the elegant pilasters set between the panels, the frieze carved with garlands in relief (perhaps gilded), and the great bed which was probably designed *en suite*.

Benedetto da Maiano, *Birth of St John the Baptist*, terracotta *Victoria and Albert Museum, London (7593–1861)*

37

Such over-all patterns, with regular 'repeats', can look very like depictions of textiles and, indeed, a common form of wall and ceiling decoration took the form of simulated figured textiles. Striped and sprigged materials were in favour before 1450 while very careful representations were rendered in fresco after that, usually in relatively small rooms. A fine example of such accurate depiction is the green and white silk damask painted in the Library of Sixtus IV in the Vatican which must date from the 1470s. This practice continued into the sixteenth century, a delightful manifestation being the simulated figured silk in a small *saletta* in the Palazzo della Cancelleria in Rome which may have been executed when the architect-decorator Baldassare Peruzzi was working there about 1511–14. The 'silk' has a lattice pattern and fills the space between simulated columns; there is a charming frieze above, very much in Peruzzi's style.[4] Furthermore, just as mid-sixteenth-century artists sometimes depicted doors fronted by textile *portières* (Pl. 20), so they could equally well represent large tapestries with figures which, when new, must have looked very like the real thing. A related expression of this fashion is the huge representation of a painted leather hanging on a wall of the *salone* in the Palazzo Farnese in Rome, presumably dating from the 1540s. This spectacular hanging has scalloped lappets at top and bottom, and one may presume that real hangings of leather thus painted were also produced at this time. It is at any rate exceptionally realistic, painted by members of the team trained by one of the foremost mural-painters of the mid-sixteenth century, Francesco Salviati (1510–63).

While it is not the intention here to add to the already vast literature devoted to figurative painting on Italian Renaissance walls, it is amusing to note why Alberti – humanist, polymath, and adviser to princes on architecture – urged that a husband, when considering how to decorate the bedchamber he and his wife were to share, should take care that 'nothing be painted' on the walls 'but the most comely and beautiful Faces'. This could, he explained, be 'of no small Consequence to the Conception of the Lady and the Beauty of the Children'.[5]

Alberti assured the readers of his treatise on architecture (written in the mid-fifteenth century) that, for the great reception room in a *palazzo* (the *sala*) 'the brave and memorable Actions of one's Countrymen ... are Ornaments extremely suitable' and this advice was frequently taken throughout the next two centuries. He also recommended that 'Upon side Walls no Sort of Painting shews handsomer than the Representation of Columns in Architecture'. In this he was seeking to revive a practice current in antique classical Rome when to introduce columns, part of the language of public architecture (e.g. in the *forum*), into the confined space of a private dwelling, was seen as generating a sense of splendour and great luxury.[6] A fine example of a room decorated with fictive columns is the Bibliotheca Graeca in the Vatican Palace, executed in 1454 for Pope Nicholas V, probably with Alberti himself acting as consultant.[7] The mural decoration of which columns there form a prominent part is entirely classical in style – an early expression of the full-blooded revival – but some decoration added later above the frieze has Gothic elements that would probably have offended Alberti's sense of decorum. A wall painted

with columns in the 1470s came to light recently at the Palazzo Altemps, also in Rome (Pl. 101), but rooms painted with such architectural features only really came into fashion in the sixteenth century, a particularly striking (and no doubt extremely influential) example being Peruzzi's *Sala delle Prospettive* in the Farnesina in Rome, painted around 1516.[8] There one sees views of the surrounding cityscape and suburbs depicted as lying beyond columns that make the room look like an open loggia. Elsewhere, complicated architectural fantasies appear between the columns (e.g. at the Villa delle Peschiere, Genoa, of 1556–8).[9] Whatever the permutation chosen, the aim was to produce the illusion that the room had no walls, or had large apertures (Pl. 44), and that one could see into the distance which was either delightful or impressive. A curious variant of this fashion was the depiction of a wall shown as if partly ruined so one sees a landscape beyond the tumbled masonry.[10]

Ruins provided a much more important source of inspiration in quite another direction, however. Excavations among the ancient ruins of classical Rome continued right through the period. At first this consisted simply of quarrying for marble for re-use in modern buildings or for calcining to produce lime. Gradually more excavation was undertaken to locate antiquities – sculptures, pottery and bronze artefacts – to satisfy the curiosity of antiquarians and the cupidity of those who were beginning to form collections for display in their houses (Pls 317, 319). Every now and then, as this activity proceeded, the remains of ancient wall-paintings came to light. A vast repertory of antique classical ornament became increasingly known to Italians during the Renaissance. Artists, and their clients, many of them already firmly believing that the classical past offered much that could suitably be imitated in their own times, soon also saw this great repertory of motifs as one from which they could borrow, either through direct copying or as a potent source of inspiration for compositions more directly suited to modern tastes.

The influence, for the most part, of this excavated decoration took three directions. The earliest centred round the form known as *la candelabra*,[11] which is a vertical and symmetrical arrangement of scrolls to either side of a central stalk, the scrolls being treated either fairly naturally with foliage or, on the other hand, with fantasy involving bizarre details of every kind (Pls 35, 40, 195). The *candelabra* was a versatile motif marvellously well suited for decorating architectural features like pilasters, portals and window-surrounds (Pl. 48). It could be rendered in relief-carving, or in paintwork simulating the former or rendered in 'naturalistic' colours. Suitably adapted its form could be used to form horizontal borders as well. And, finally, the detail motifs of *candelabra* might be lifted out of context to form ornaments in their own right.

The second direction in which antique classical ornament inspired the Renaissance artist-decorator concerned that strange form of decoration called *grottesche*[12] – because the form was to be found in *grotte*, the name popularly given to the excavated ancient ruins which, being mostly underground, could sometimes only be reached by hazardous routes down rickety ladders, along passages that might at any moment subside, and often in darkness requiring the carrying of flaming torches. It is

38

39

38 A marbled wall

In contrast to the mural treatment shown in Plate 12, this wall is marbled with paintwork. Otherwise it would not have been possible to hammer a nail into the wall to hold the ring of the frame behind St Ursula's head. Lines simulating the joints have been neatly drawn in to produce a convincing result. Under the bookshelf is a *spalliera* of verdure tapestry. The bed has hangings in the form of a *padiglione*. A Turkish rug draped over a chest forms a seat. On the wall is an *anchonetta*, a devotional painting of the *Madonna and Child* in tabernacle form, an almost obligatory item in Italian Renaissance bedchambers.

Carpaccio, detail from the St Ursula cycle from the Scuola di Sant' Orsola; 1490s
Accademia, Venice (photograph: Scala)

39 Top quality Florentine *lavoro di intarsio*, 1480s

The wall-panels of this fashionable room are decorated with *tarsie* organized on the *candelabra* principle that may also be seen as a very early manifestation of grotesque ornament (see p. 37). The panels in Pl. 37 might have been decorated in a similar way but there the ceiling is rather low. The arrangement shown here was the more usual formula. The painted simulation of sculptural reliefs skilfully sets the shadows away from the light coming from the small window. Some very important paintings that now grace the walls of major public galleries of art originally occupied a similar position above panelling in this manner. The bed-head appears to be built into the panelling; the bed was at any rate supplied along with the rest of the woodwork of this splendid room. Note the keys in the lock of the bed-chest.

Domenico Ghirlandaio, *Birth of the Virgin*, S. Maria della Maria, Florence
Photograph: Scala

40 The spurious humility of raw wood?

The walls of the Virgin's bedchamber, and the furniture in the room, are of untreated timber which may at first sight suggest relative poverty but almost everything else in the room suggests the opposite. At the top of the boarded wall runs a gilded frieze; the bed-curtain and coverlet are superb, as are the three pillows and valuable articles are to be seen everywhere. Indeed, Mary's surroundings support the preferred notion in Italy at the time, namely that she was a member of a patrician family who did not want for the good things in life, and especially not the material comforts and intellectual sustenance (note the fine book on the lectern). Was the raw timber of the walls an affectation? Was it supposed here to hint at her humility in spite of the richness of her surroundings? Or was the timber perhaps of some very costly kind that is not evident from the painting?

Carlo Crivelli, *Annunciation* (detail), 1486
National Gallery, London

OPVS·CARO
LI·CRIVELLI
VENETI

·1486·

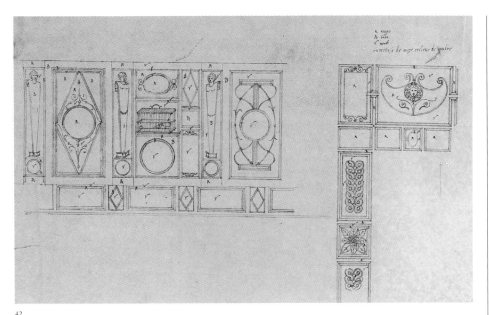

41 Characteristic grotesque ornament

'Grotesque' decoration was usually conceived as a symmetrical design but with the pairs of fantastic motifs varying in detail. The system was highly adaptable and could be stretched in any direction to fit any given area, however irregular in shape (Pl. 43). This engraving is one of about twenty plates published in the 1530s by an unknown designer who described them as 'Lighter and (as can be seen) extemporaneous pictures which in everyday language are called grotesques' [*Levoires et (ut videtur) extemporaneae picturae quas grotteschas vulgo vocant*]. This set of designs was copied by Enea Vico (published in 1541) who was to become a famous engraver and numismatist (Pl. 358). Such engraved patterns could be rendered line-for-line or used as a source of inspiration for a variant on this general theme, usable on walls in fresco, on book-bindings, maiolica, gilt-leather hangings or worked with a needle.

Unknown artist, from Levoires . . .
The Metropolitan Museum of Art, New York, Harris Brisbane Dick Fund, 1928

42 Roman mural scheme of the 1560s

When a French architect sketched this it was probably new and he must have thought it of interest. He was apparently in Rome in the 1560s. The colour-scheme was red, white and green with the Medusa head marbled. This, and the general style, show the strong influence of classical wall-painting of the kind later found at Pompeii and Herculaneum; one might almost regard this as a forerunner of the so-called Pompeian Style that came into fashion at the end of the eighteenth century.

Anonymous French wall decoration of the Palazzo Spada, Rome
Metropolitan Museum of Art, New York, Gift of Janos Scholz and Mrs Anne Bigelow Scholz in Memory of Flying Officer Walter Bigelow Rosen, 1949 (49.92.79 verso)

43 The adaptability of grotesques

Sketch for part of a scheme of grotesque ornament, probably for a cove uniting a wall to the ceiling above. This shows how flexible were *grottesche* as a means of covering irregular spaces with ornament. The sketch has been attributed to Perino del Vaga who certainly was responsible for a great many decorative schemes in this general style (notably in Genoa) during the second quarter of the sixteenth century. He had worked under Giovanni da Udine on the grotesque decorations in the Logge at the Vatican before moving to Genoa in 1527. On his return a decade later he became court painter to Pope Paul III.

Perino del Vaga(?), design for a grotesque wall decoration
The Metropolitan Museum, New York, Elisha Whittelsey Collection, Elisha Whittelsey Fund, 1959 (No. 59.605.5 recto)

44 Illusionistic scheme with columns

Although Alberti (d. 1472) had urged those decorating the principal rooms of palaces to have columns depicted on the walls, it was not until the next century that this form of embellishment was widely taken up. The single drawing must suffice here as an example of a vast repertoire of such illusionistic schemes in which vistas seen between columns are the main feature. Alternative proposals are offered for the sections to either side of the central aperture; that on the right would have the simulated columns continuing round the room while the wall in the left-hand scheme is treated in the more usual manner with a frieze at the top, a filling below and dado or base rising from floor-level.

Federico Zuccaro (1540–1609), drawing for fresco painting and probably a papal commission
Fondation Custodia (Collection F. Lugt) Institut Néerlandais, Paris

44

difficult to describe grotesque ornament but illustrations like those reproduced in Pls 41, 46, 47 and 356 make its character plain. It will be seen that it had a random structure and could be developed in any direction to fill any given space, although for the most part grotesque composition tended to be essentially symmetrical.

Candelabre and *grottesche* of course have many features, many motifs, in common but the two formulae served different purposes, the former mainly as border-decoration, the latter for large planes. The manner in which this class of ornament was taken up by Italian decorators has been admirably charted and need not detain us here, fascinating as the story is.[13]

The third direction this classical inspiration took lay in the overall schemes that were sometimes revealed and which offered an entirely fresh form of decoration, relying largely on a multiplicity of compartments, that could be adapted to modern ceilings and, to a lesser extent, walls (Pl. 42). Such decoration was a precursor of the 'Pompeian' style that became fashionable in the late eighteenth century; indeed, the two styles ought not really to be considered separately as they have the same roots, similar motifs and not dissimilar colouring. The compartmenting characteristic of this style was amalgamated, late in the sixteenth century, with other styles, notably moresques, and a form of Proto-Pompeian decoration with Islamic-type scrollwork was devised, mainly for small-scale items (p. 98) but also suitable for room-decoration.

Not all wall painting was executed in fresco on plaster. The plaster ceiling of the Sala di Psiche in the Palazzo Tè at Mantua is painted in oils for instance.[14] Wooden panelling was painted with some form of oil-bound pigment and the author of the *Hypnerotomachia* (1499) mentions walls *perfectamente picturata di Enchaustica opera* [painted with perfection in encaustic work].[15] Precisely what this last term meant is not clear but it was known that the Ancients had used an encaustic paint in classical times and perhaps this should only be taken as a fanciful reference to a marvellous and by then mythical form of painting.

Newly executed fresco-painting could be brilliant in its effect. Some idea of how bright the colours might be can be derived from representations of the paintings in Raphael's *Loggie* at the Vatican to be seen in an album now in Vienna, made when the frescoes were about forty years old – in 1556. The appearance of these unfaded colours is quite astonishing.

Painting, usually in fresco, was the commonest method of decorating walls throughout the Renaissance period but anything at all elaborate was expensive, so only the chief rooms in a house would be decorated in an ambitious manner. This in effect meant that the *sala*, the principal room in which guests were received (p. 285), was the first to be considered for decoration; next the *saletta* where the owner dined *en famille* or with a few chosen guests would be dealt with, and after that the owner's bedchamber. A room with such elaborate painted decoration was often referred to at the time as the *camera picta*, 'the painted room'. The famous 'Camera degli Sposi' in the Palace at Mantua, frescoed by Mantegna in 1474, was known by this name, as was the room in the Palace at Urbino which is believed to have been the meeting-place of Baldassare Castiglione's courtiers when they gathered round the Duchess for their teasing, gallant and charming philosophical conversations which are recorded in his famous book, *Il Cortegiano*, written between 1508 and 1528.[16]

45

46

47

45, 46 Colours unrestored

These two handsome compositions are to be found in a series of volumes presenting the armorial bearings of prominent families in Bologna. As they have always been protected by being in a book, they are relatively undamaged by light and wear, and thus give a good idea of how wall-paintings in this same style – current in the second half of the sixteenth century – were supposed to look. One is clearly dated 1580 and the other dates from 1583. The latter embodies a system of scrollwork developed from grotesques but rendered very freely.

From the *Insignia* series, Vols I (p. 202) and II (p. 40)
Archivio di Stato, Bologna (photographs: Scala)

47 Reminders of former brilliance

Borders from *The Farnese Hours*, a manuscript begun about 1535 and completed in 1546 for Cardinal Alessandro Farnese. Having been protected from the ravages of light, these delicate little paintings remain very nearly in pristine condition and are a reminder of how bright were the colours of much wall painting when they were new. Comparison between small paintings in tempera and large ones in fresco are not entirely valid but it does nevertheless give an indication of how much the latter have lost in brilliance with time – and sometimes also as a result of poor restoration. Painted by Giulio Clovio, adopting a style that owes much to the *logge* decorated by Raphael at the Vatican some thirty years earlier.

From *The Farnese Hours*, (M. 69, 104V, 105) *c.*1535
Pierpoint Morgan Library, New York

48 The useful *candelabra* formula

The grey walls of this room are much enlivened by a fresco-painted border forming a frieze and a window-surround. The verticals are based on the classical *candelabra* formula while the horizontals are composed with rows of motifs that are clearly derived from individual elements in the verticals. It looks as if stencils may have been used. This painting by Francesco di Simone of 1504 is one of the earliest representations of a posted bed of the massive form that has been conceived as a piece of architecture, complete with capitals and heavy architrave, evidently designed by someone familiar with the classical orders (see p. 137). Note the lappeted valance depending from the wooden tester, between the posts (which, being of square section, should probably be called piers). The ball-finial presumably caps an iron spigot rising from the top of the posts and passing through a hole in the tester to locate the assembly.

Francesco di Simone, *Annunciation*, 1504
Photograph: Accademia del Carrara, Bergamo

AVE·GRATIA·PLENA

FRANCISCVS·DE·SANTA
CRVCIS·FECIT·1504

48

49

49 *Trompe l'œil* of a garden

It has been suggested that this charming sketch by Martin van Heemskerck, executed at Mantua in about 1535, may show the view into the garden from a loggia at Marmirolo, a Gonzaga villa which was rebuilt by Giulio Romano after its destruction in 1530; but the scene is more likely to be imaginary even though characteristic of the kind of surroundings one could expect to see at princely villas in many parts of Italy during the second quarter of the sixteenth century and later. On the other hand it may be a sketch of a tapestry or of a fresco to be seen at that period in or around Mantua.

Martin van Heemskerck, mural decoration, c.1535
Staatliche Museen Preußischer Kulturbesitz, Kupferstichkabinett, Berlin (photograph: Jörg P. Anders)

50 Medici splendour reflected in tapestry

This handsome design by Bernardino Poccetti (1542–1612) was for one of a series of tapestries which appear not to have been woven. The series depicts scenes from the life of Scipio Africanus; here Sophonisba receives the cup of poison. The cartoons date from the end of the sixteenth or very early seventeenth century; this one shows how ambitious was the Medici tapestry-weaving establishment at the end of the sixteenth century. Poccetti was responsible for decorating many Florentine rooms with fresco-painting in this general style, to brilliant effect.

Bernardino Poccetti, from a series of tapestry cartoons depicting the life of Scipio Africanus
Uffizi, Florence (photograph: Soprintendenza B.A.S. Firenze)

Unless a room is called *la camera picta* or something that hints at painted decoration, inventories will not normally record the presence of painting as the compiler of inventories was primarily interested in moveables, not in fixtures. Sometimes it is possible to infer the presence of painted walls because no object that would occupy wall-space is listed (e.g. no hangings, no framed paintings, no tall furniture). Moreover, even when described as a *camera picta*, this in itself reveals nothing of the character or quality of the painting. Had there not been outside evidence, no one would have suspected that the *Camera nova terrena depinta* in the Medici villa at Castello, mentioned in the inventory of 1498, was probably the room that had been decorated by Botticelli, the year before.[17]

Wall-hangings

The common formula for walls in important rooms, where they were not painted all over, was to have a painted frieze at the top, while 'the filling' below (p. 44) was dressed with wall-hangings. These were removed when the room was not on display – when it was not being used or at any rate when no guests were expected – and the bare wall below the frieze was then left exposed or, alternatively, curtains of an inexpensive material might be hung on the walls instead.[1] Unfortunately we so often see such rooms today in an undressed state, with a splendid painted frieze and a bare wall below – naked and very unattractive. The intention was that walls should either be painted or should be clad; they should not be bare, which is a condition that gives a completely false impression. The 'softness' imparted by wall-hangings is lost when they are gone[2] and the rooms look unbalanced. Lacking the hangings underneath to hold it up visually, the frieze seems as if about to slide down the wall on to the floor. Some people can make the necessary mental adjustment and allow for the lack of this textile component (sometimes it was of gilt leather), while others are simply not aware that something is missing because that is how such rooms have looked as far back as anyone can remember.

51

51 A Gonzaga tapestry designed about 1470

Mantegna was asked by the Marquis Lodovico Gonzaga in 1469 to make some drawings of a cock and a hen peafowl 'to put on one of our tapestries'. The result may be seen here. If Mantegna had a hand in the design as a whole, the interpretation by the weaver has ensured that this is not now evident but the general conception must be of about 1470, even though the owners claim that the tapestry dates from the time of Duke Francesco (1506–19). The explanation could be that the weaving of this particular hanging was executed after an old design, or that the arms have been altered.

Courtesy of the Art Institute of Chicago. Bequest of Mr and Mrs Martin A. Ryerson (1937.1099)

52 Unity – wall to ceiling

The compartments of the barrel-vaulted ceiling of the great hall, the *sala*, in which this crowded scene is set match the divisions of the mural decoration, producing a unified effect. The double-tiered frieze is unusual but may have been introduced here in order to include more scenes than could have been encompassed in one. Note how the wall-hanging reaches down to the floor. Its pattern would never in reality have spanned such a width. In spite of the liberties taken by the artist (the far end of the hall was not wide open, either), this print is informative also at our level.

From the 1584 edition of Lodovico Ariosto's famous *Orlando furioso* (first published in 1516), a dynastic celebration of the Este family clothed in the legends of Charlemagne and even of King Arthur
The Houghton Library, Harvard University, Cambridge, Massachusetts (Mortimer 30)

53 The splendour of silk hangings

This wall-painting shows a rich silken material attached to hooks on the wall. Such a horizontal hanging would be called a *spalliera*. The *cielo* or tester suspended over the bed is of the same material, a silk which, if not actually from the Near East, is certainly of Eastern inspiration. The *cielo* was clearly constructed ready for suspension and must have three built-in rods so that only three points for attachment on the walls and ceiling are required. Pendant finials hang from the rods' extremities. The coverlet and covering of the chest that flanks the bed are of silk with two other patterns, and the floor-covering may be of yet another silk (it does not seem to be an Eastern carpet). Note the oil-lamp (night-light) hanging from the ceiling, on the left, and the ceiling itself which is of the shallow coffered variety, with painted quatrefoils.

Giotto: *St Francis appears to Pope Gregory IX in a Dream*, Upper Church, Basilica of S. Francesco, Assisi, *c.*1300
Photograph: Scala

47

It is anyway important that we here recognize that all walls in Italian rooms of any importance, during the Renaissance period, were either painted all over, or were partly painted and were clad with hangings where there was no paintwork. The only exception to this rule was where parts of the wall were faced with panelling or with tiles, and there were comparatively few rooms thus treated.

During the early part of the period two terms were being used to describe a wall-hanging – *capoletto* and *spalliera*. The *capoletto*, as its name implies, had at first been a hanging suspended on the wall at the head of a bed, rising vertically above the bed-head. Later, the term came to apply to wall-hangings generally but probably mostly to those that were taller than they were wide. When Boccaccio wants to describe a beautifully decked-out dining-room, he speaks of how delightful it is to see the *capoletti* hanging around the room [*e maravigliosa cosa a vedere i capoletti intorno alla sala dove mangiamo*], so already by the mid-fourteenth century they could be entirely dissociated from a bed and might be used in multiples.[3] A *spalliera* was a horizontal hanging that had at first been hung on the wall behind a dining-room bench so one could lean back against it. It derived its name from the fact that it was a person's shoulders [*spalle*] that touched it first.[4] As with the *capoletto*, this term likewise came to apply to larger hangings but *spalliere* were always 'horizontal', i.e. notably longer than their height.[5] A late example of this were the three *spalliere* with foliage and figures [*a foggiami et figure*] which formed a set of wall-hangings that furnished the room [*che fornisce la camera*] off the staircase at Alvise Odoni's house in Venice in 1555 (Odoni Invt.). This presumably meant that they covered all or most of the available wall-space. *Spalliere* and *capoletti* could be made of any of the materials used for wall-hangings at the time.

The term *capoletto* went out of fashion in the first half of the quattrocento and *un paramento* became the common term for a set of wall-hangings, although in Lucrezia Borgia's inventory of 1503 (Borgia Invt.) they are called *Aparamenti da Camara*. In the north of Italy, however, people also continued to speak of *una camera di . . .* (adding the class of material concerned, e.g. *una camera di tela de bruges* [of cloth from Bruges; Fieschi Invt., Genoa, 1532]) when describing the hangings of a room. The author of a report on the new furnishings of the Pitti Palace in 1576, when it had become the grand-ducal residence in Florence, makes special reference to the splendid wall-hangings but he confuses us greatly in doing so.[6] He uses the term *paramento* but also speaks of a *fornimento*, an *addobamento* and even (once) an *adornamento* in describing the hangings of some two dozen rooms. He may simply have wanted to 'ring the changes' so that his report (it was to the Venetian Senate) should not be too boring but there is probably more to it than that. In the seventeenth century it became common to have all the textile furnishings of a room *en suite* (e.g. walls, window-curtains, chair-covers, table-carpets, etc.; Pl. 367) and such unity was becoming fashionable in the 1570s in advanced circles (p. 341). One might suppose that one of these terms referred to this phenomenon, but this does not seem to be the case. Frankly, it is not clear what were the distinctions, if any, between these four terms and this question must for the moment remain unanswered. Another term relevant to wall-hangings was *arazzare* which, according to Florio*, meant 'to tapistry with Aras works', or to put it in modern English, to hang with tapestry [*arazzi*; see below]. The poet Aretino goes one better and speaks of a room being *tutta impannarazzata*, that is, totally hung with *panno arazzo* [tapestry cloth].[7]

Many classes of textile were used for hanging walls. In very splendid houses there might be hangings of a lightweight and light-coloured material, intended for use in summer; heavy woollen tapestries or the dust-trapping pile of velvet were understandably considered rather suffocating in hot weather. Some comments on the qualities and character of the various types of textile materials available at the time are to be found in Part Two and reference to these may help the reader the better to understand the passages that follow here. For example, if we know that *tela di cambri* was linen from Cambrai (i.e. cambric), we can be fairly sure that the *camera di tela di cambri*, comprising sixteen pieces, was a set of white linen summer hangings.[8] They were to be seen in the Fieschi mansion in Genoa in 1532 (Fieschi Invt.), at that time one of the most sumptuous palaces in that city of great palaces. The linen material painted with the story of Bacchus [*panno lino depintovi l'istoria Bacho*] that was fixed round the walls of an *anticamera* at the Medici residence at Fiesole in 1498 (Medici Invt.) probably served the same purpose, as Florentine patricians went up to Fiesole to get out of the great heat of their city during the summer months, and what could be more charming than a hanging painted with the frolics of the wine-god, catching any gentle breeze, as a backdrop to the langorous life one led in such places of retreat?

It is generally believed that the walls of all Italian Renaissance rooms of any consequence were hung with tapestry (unless the walls were painted all over) but this was not so, because tapestry was very expensive. This was especially the case with the kind of tapestry that the term today brings to mind – the type decorated with scenes [*istoria*] or human figures [*a figure*]. Lorenzo de' Medici owned a Flemish tapestry depicting *una chaccia del Duca di Borghona* [the Duke of Burgundy hunting] which was very probably similar to the famous 'Devonshire Hunting Tapestries' in the Victoria and Albert Museum in London. This single hanging of twenty *braccia* in length and six in height was valued in 1492 at 100 florins. That was one of the most expensive items in the house, by far, and this valuation was only exceeded by that of the set of six paintings by Uccello and Pesellino forming a frieze in Lorenzo's bedchamber – paintings which are now world-famous – and by seven bronze candle-holders which were no doubt elaborate and must have been created by an ingenious sculptor working in metal. The pictures were set at a total of 300 florins and the candle-holders at 160.[9]

Tapestry was expensive because the process by which it is woven is complicated and therefore slow to execute.[10] Tapestries also had to be brought a long way, to reach Italy, as they were almost all produced in the Low Countries. Both in England and in Italy the city of Arras lent its name as a generic term for tapestry; every schoolchild learns that Polonius was caught eavesdropping by Hamlet, hidden 'behind the Arras', and

Italians still speak of *arazzi*. Arras must have woven the finest tapestries for a while during the Middle Ages in order to have earned such a reputation but, during the Renaissance, tapestries of high quality were produced at a handful of centres in Flanders including Arras, but notably also at Tournai and Brussels.

Tapestry of course came in different qualities but all of it was intended for use in circles where people were fastidious and choosy. Indeed tapestry became associated in people's minds with upper-class tastes and a privileged way of life. It was actually a robust material which made it suitable for the customary seigneurial pattern of life that commonly involved much travelling, 'showing the flag' in the various parts of one's domains, visiting friends, and so forth. This occasioned frequent moves and, because princely owners tended to carry their furnishings around with them, tapestries were an ideal form of furnishing material. One could quickly rig up a colourful and striking setting in an otherwise bleak castle, tapestries made a room warmer (they absorbed a lot of damp which was useful, even in Italian castles), and one could not only hang them up fairly quickly (sometimes just by nailing them to the wall along the top edge), but one could take them down again just as easily – a process often carried out very roughly. Rolled up and bundled on to a cart, they were ready for the move to the next stopping-place. They might need beating with a 'carpet-beater' to get rid of dust and spiders, and sometimes the occasional tear needed mending, but otherwise they tended to remain bright and colourful – and a telling reminder of the owner's status.

Although the odd panel of tapestry had reached Italy earlier, it was not until the second quarter of the fifteenth century that hangings of this material began to make their appearance in some quantity in the inventories.[11] An early reference must be that in the Guinigi inventory of 1430 (Guinigi Invt.) showing that the ruler of Lucca owned *uno panno d'Arasso verde fiorito* [i.e. a panel of Arras with a green floral ground] ... *con figura d'una donna con arco et d'un homo ferito* [with the figure of a woman with a bow, and a wounded man]. Over at Ferrara, Niccolò III d'Este had rather more than a dozen tapestries with figures on them and one with his coat of arms (which must therefore have been specially ordered from Flanders). This was in 1436 (Este Invt.).

In the fifteenth century, tapestries were mostly used singly and, as they can rarely have fitted whatever wall they happened to be dressing at any given time, there would usually have been space that was not covered, at the sides, or above or below. It was probably not much before the beginning of the sixteenth century that rich people began to acquire *sets* of tapestry that covered the walls of a room entirely. An exceptional and very early manifestation of this took place in 1448 when the Medici's agent in Antwerp wrote to Giovanni de' Medici, father of the more famous Cosimo, about a set of tapestries that Giovanni required for the *sala*, the main room, in his house in Florence.[12] There was a question of which of two sets the agent should commission. Should it be that with the story of Samson which was rather a lugubrious subject, so the agent felt, and was anyway extremely expensive (700 ducats), or should it be the Narcissus set which was a much more attractive subject and cost less (only 150

ducats)? The agent asked Giovanni to decide and send the measurements of the walls they were to cover [*mi puoi solamente mandare la misura e la storia vuoi*]. Inventories, however, give the impression that sets of tapestries were far from common in fifteenth-century Italy.

Figured tapestries continued to be the most expensive and the most prized class of hangings of this material. The title of the *istoria* depicted on such a hanging is sometimes recorded in inventories (e.g. *de nabucdonosor* [Nebuchadnezzar] or *de biancafiore* [Blanchefleur, Fieschi Invt., Genoa, 1532]), but otherwise we only know that this class of weave is in question when a term like *a figure* or *di personaggio* occurs (Tura Invt., Siena, 1483). A rather less costly form of tapestry was that of the verdure class [*a verdura/verzura, d'herbaria, a boscagia*] which had clumps of flowers scattered over a green ground. We see a portière of this material in front of the door in the well-known painting reproduced in Pl. 35 but it is probable that the walls too were hung with this material, in fictive rendering, before time, or perhaps uncomprehending restorers, caused the flowers to disappear (the hangings are now plain green).[13] A *spalliera* of verdure tapestry may be seen in Pl. 73 and several paintings in which coverlets of the same material are represented, are also illustrated in this book. Verdure tapestry was a delightful class of material. It required no border but often, in the more expensive grades, had a small central feature like a coat of arms,[14] or sometimes a figure or a small scene.

'What I am saying about the clumsiness of painters, who make quite as many mistakes as scribes and copyists, is true not only of wall-paintings, but also of those tapestries from Transalpine Gaul you see hung on the walls. Certainly there is much skill in this kind of work, but the weavers and designers are far more concerned with opulence of colour and frivolous charm . . . than they are with the science of painting. Generally they depict popular absurdities, pandering to the extravagance of princes and the stupidity of the crowd.' This was Leonello d'Este's view on the aesthetic merit of tapestries in his time (he died in 1450) and one can hardly gainsay him. Only weavings from a handful of major centres are entirely satisfactory on all counts – design, execution, colour and subject.[15]

Fifteenth-century tapestry, both of the figurative and the verdure type, possessed a two-dimensional character; whatever was represented on them seemed to cleave to the plane of the wall on which such tapestries were hung. The weaving in Brussels, during the second decade of the sixteenth century, of a set of tapestry hangings depicting *The Acts of the Apostles*, after designs (cartoons, as they were called) by Raphael, was the single most important factor that changed the course of tapestry design fundamentally.[16] The rugged figures, and landscapes in perspective, of Raphael's designs were uncompromisingly three-dimensional and the scenes broke through the wall-plane, as it were, to show vistas beyond the room. Soon thereafter three-dimensional scenes became the norm for pictorial tapestry. Moreover, the fact that it was the Pope (Leo x) who had commissioned this series, and that they had aroused such interest and were for the most part greeted with such enormous approbation in discriminating circles, gave pictorial tapestry an amazing new lease of life

54

54 Dining backed by a *spalliera*

A *spalliera* of a striped woollen material (perhaps *celone*) suspended behind the bench on which the diners are seated. The scene is no doubt meant to be understood as taking place *in* the castle seen beyond. The servants attend the diners from the free side. Note the tablecloth of linen laid over the striped table-carpet. The table has two pillars rising from a wooden platform, all one great fixture in what is probably a *saletta* – a private dining-room for the master of the household and his immediate family or friends.

Anonymous Rimenese artist, *Herod's Feast*, c.1365
The Metropolitan Museum of Art, New York. Lehman Collection
(No. 1975.1.103)

and soon tapestries following the formula devised by Raphael were to be seen in all the best houses, so to speak.

Another feature of Raphael's creations was the manner in which they were to be seen, hung close together in a continuous band round the walls. This may have been done before, elsewhere, but here it was carefully planned in a scheme that quickly became famous because it was to be seen at the very centre of Christian power – on the walls of the Sistine Chapel in the Vatican itself. This was no casual dressing of a castle wall with a bright cloth; it was a permanent feature, in the sense that each hanging had its appointed place even if it was sometimes temporarily taken down for one reason or another. Henceforth much figurative tapestry was designed to hang in special locations[17] and, although tapestries were allowed to hang free (secured only at the top edge) until the end of the century,[18] their furnishing role was now not very different from that of wallpaper today. However, the connotation which tapestry had long carried, namely that it was something only 'top people' possessed, now

became even more firmly established and this notion maintained tapestry in favour among the powerful and the rich right through to the end of the eighteenth century. The practical qualities that had suited tapestry to a mediaeval way of life among the ruling classes was no longer of any consequence; it was the implication that the owner was a person of standing that now made it such a desirable possession. Anyone who felt they belonged to the higher echelons of society now tended to feel that it confirmed their status to own (and of course display) examples of this costly material which was (luckily, for this purpose) immediately recognizable, at any rate by those who mattered.

Verdure tapestries also changed character in the wake of the stylistic revolution wrought by Raphael and his followers. They became more pictorial and the verdure became larger in scale. Some became jungle-like, with huge exotic leaves and fronds; others turned into landscapes or gardenscapes. Their character was no longer two-dimensional.

A new class of hanging came into being around the middle of the sixteenth century, which met the demands of those who wanted 'flat' wall decoration in this medium. The new formula was tapestry bearing grotesque patterns (p. 40). These became very popular indeed (Pl. 7).

Most tapestries continued to be brought down to Italy from Flanders during the Renaissance[19] but not infrequently we learn of Italian artists designing cartoons that were then sent to Brussels or Antwerp for weaving. We noted that Niccolò III had his coat of arms on a tapestry already by 1436 (p. 49) and, as no tapestry-weavers seem to have been established in Italy by then, this must have been specially woven for him in the North after a drawing of his arms had been sent up there. In Ferrara, likewise, the artist-decorator Gerardo Costa in 1472 prepared a design for a hanging with the ducal arms of Este that was to be sent to Flanders for weaving.[20] We saw how tapestries for the Sistine Chapel were produced in Brussels from designs by Raphael (they were first put up in 1519) and it seems that designs by Giulio Romano were processed in the same way, for the Gonzaga court at Mantua.[21] Perino del Vaga, working in Genoa in the Raphaelesque style, provided designs for hangings to go in Prince Doria's villa at Fassolo, in the middle of the century,[22] and Luca Cambiaso and Lazzaro Calvi, both Genoese artists of rank, were likewise sending designs to Flanders for execution.[23] In Rome Francesco Salviati provided designs for a set of tapestries, commissioned by Pier Luigi Farnese in 1538, which were painted on large cloths and were then woven in tapestry in Flanders [furono poi in fiandra messa in opera di panni d'arazzo].[24]

Tapestry was woven in Italy, mostly in a small way, although a truly successful establishment was set up under Medici patronage in the mid-sixteenth century. In 1545 Cosimo I was writing to one of his wife's Spanish relations (she was Eleonora of Toledo, it will be remembered) that he hoped the workshop would soon be sufficiently productive to make it no longer necessary for his people and their neighbours to bring tapestries all the way from Flanders [che non sara piu necessario alli sudditi di questo stato et alli circumvicini ancora di venire a fornirsi in Fiandra di tapezzerie].[25] The workshop was headed by Nicola Carcher, son of a Brussels tapestry-weaver who had come to Italy to work for Paleologi lords at Casale Monferrato (d.1536). The son later moved to Mantua where he remained from 1539 to 1545, and then moved to Florence.[26] The first important products of the Florentine workshop was a set telling the story of Joseph (Pl. 7), the first panels of which appeared in 1549. The set was designed by Bronzino but a sequence of distinguished artists acted as designers for the manufactory during the second half of the century (Salviati, Bacchiacca, Allori, Stradano, with Vasari acting as artistic director much of the time).

Otherwise Italian tapestry production was really of no great consequence. Much of it consisted of small panels, at least in the earliest stages. For example a certain Alvise Pentor [i.e. the Painter] produced some designs for bench-covers [banchali de razo] at Venice in 1450[27] and a weaver from Arras was set up by the government at Siena in 1442 who is known to have produced at least forty-two panels that seem mostly to have been small; he later moved on to Rome and no more is heard of him.[28] At

Mantua, where Carcher was later to be active for a short while, an establishment existed by the middle of the century. In 1469 Lodovico Gonzaga asked Mantegna to provide a drawing of two peacocks in the menagerie for the weavers to render in tapestry [ritrarre due galine de India del naturale ... per metter suxo la tapezzeria].[29] A further burst of creativity occurred at Mantua in the mid-sixteenth century (Pl. 51). At Ferrara a more determined attempt was made to establish an effective workshop, using court artist-decorators as designers. For instance Cosmè Tura produced designs for the local weavers (that included uno maestro di franza [a French master; probably a Fleming, in fact) in 1457 when Galeazzo Sforza paid a visit to the Este capital.[30] Three-quarters of a century later we find Battista Dossi, brother of the more famous Dosso Dossi, made responsible for designing tapestries that Carcher was to weave in 1536.[31] Apart from a small establishment active between 1501 and 1509 at Vigevano, patronized by Gian Giacomo Trivulzio,[32] and the short-lived workshop set up by Vincenzo Grimaldi di Durazzo at Genoa in 1554 with a Brussels weaver, Dyons Martens, as its leader, there was little other tapestry weaving in Italy during the Renaissance.[33]

When tapestries were designed for a specific location, during the sixteenth century, they were usually intended to hang with their lower edge just above floor-level (see Pl. 52). The hanging showing Potiphar's wife clutching at the fleeing Joseph (Pl. 7) was thus seen at eye-level, which must have made it a far more engaging image than if it had been skied, well up the wall. There is evidence for this[34] but further confirmation is neatly provided by a description of the ceremonial entrance of Duke Alfonso II of Ferrara into Venice in 1572, when he was welcomed at the Doge's Palace. It was noted that the great sala was vestita di razzi dal tetto insino a terra [covered with tapestries from the ceiling right down to the floor].[35]

The poet Bandello published a series of Novelle in 1554. In the third of these short pieces of fiction he describes a richly appointed house mentioning the chief beauties of its furnishing. Of the bedchamber, he says that 'instead of tapestries, it was entirely hung with crimson velvet skilfully embroidered' [La camera, in luogo di razzi, era di velluto carmesino maestrovolmente ricamato]. This is a reminder that other forms of wall-hanging were available and that some of them were no less appreciated. Silken materials of many kinds were especially used for the smarter kind of hangings. The Venetian sumptuary regulations of 1476 forbade citizens to have wall-hangings of cloth of gold, cloth of silver, brocade, velvet, satin or tabi – all silk materials.[36] (The nature of the textile materials discussed here is explained in Part Two.) No mention is made of tapestry in the 1476 regulations; they are mentioned first among the prohibited hangings in the new law of 1562 when, however, much sterner condemnation was levelled at silks than at tapestries: Le spalliere et ogni sorte de tapezar: con oro a con argento, over di seda d'ogni altezza siano del tutto devedate ...; non si potendo alle mure ... panni di seda d'alcuna sorte [Wall-hangings and all other kinds of upholstery worked with gold, silver or silk of whatever size are absolutely forbidden ...; one must not hang on the walls ... silk materials of any kind].[37]

One can see wall-hangings that are evidently of silk in a number of the illustrations in this work (Pls 76, 92, 122, 309, 367) and references to such hangings occur frequently in the inventories. What is said later about bed-hangings, as far as silk materials are concerned (pp. 158–161), applies also for the most part to wall-hangings. When plain or not strongly figured materials were used (including those like *tabi* which were often watered), it was usual at least to apply gold, silver or silk lace or fringe to the seams and around the edges, but many more elaborate variations on this formula were adopted (e.g. Pls 159, 173).[38] Hangings of 'plain' materials might also have fairly wide borders of another material all round, with the same border being used between each width, thus forming a row of vertical panels, boldly framed.[39] Sometimes such borders were embroidered. Intervening 'borders' could be made more dramatic and architectural if they took the form of applied columns of pilasters.[40] A column of this sort might be cut out in profile, complete with a classical capital and base. Appliqué work on a smaller scale was also practised and some elaborate patterns might be executed in this expensive technique involving needlework. The cut-out pattern was usually trimmed with an applied (couched) silk cord.

In the case of woollen materials, the simpler forms of embellishment used with silks were often adopted. It should, in this connection, be remembered that the finest qualities of wool or worsted materials were very splendid indeed, fully worthy of display in the best circles (e.g. Pls 6, 54).

There was a class of woollen material with patterns that was specially intended for wall-hanging and the like. These stuffs are discussed later (pp. 75–7) but some at least may be the *celoni* of the fifteenth-century Italian inventories, and in Pl. 54 we see a handsome striped material in a setting that is scarcely humble. Cotton and linen materials were not much used for wall-hanging although some white linen was used for summer hangings, and painted linen hangings were to be seen in some houses (pp. 73–4).

Large hangings of linen painted with scenes similar to those on tapestries were produced in the late fifteenth and sixteenth centuries. Painted hangings are often thought to be tapestry designs but a class of summer hangings of this character certainly existed. In the bedchamber of the Valle house in Genoa in 1488 there were *Telle dipinte cum figuris.* This might possibly have meant pictures of some people painted on canvas[41] but it occurs among a list of bed-furnishings and is more likely, therefore, to refer to hangings painted with figures. *Tela* implies a cloth of linen or canvas.

Gilt leather hangings were also in great favour all over Italy during the sixteenth century (pp. 85–6). Extremely colourful (Pl. 89) and made up of skins that could be assembled to produce panels of any size, gilt leather was well suited to making hangings that fitted a wall precisely. However, the manufacturers usually turned out panels of a certain size that could be assembled side-by-side but with a wide ready-made strip set between each of the panels. The same vertical strips, together with others specially designed to run horizontally, were used to enframe the whole assembly. A hanging could thus be built up, the two outer panels being reduced equally in width, if necessary, so the hanging fitted the wall, leaving the whole neatly symmetrical. Hangings could be designed specially to fit walls of a known height, with a pattern that did not repeat vertically; such refinement was probably not practised much before the middle of the century and must have been expensive to execute (Pl. 90). Mostly, however, the designs followed those on contemporary textiles like velvets or gold brocades.

Gilt leather hangings had begun to make their appearance on walls in Italy at the end of the fifteenth century and Lorenzo di Pierfrancesco de' Medici owned some which must have been rather special. They were set above the wooden panelling and were themselves framed.[42] They totalled thirty *braccia* in length and came from Spain. They were valued at 180 *lire*. Botticelli's painting, today known as the *Primavera*, was fixed on the wall below and was valued at 100 *lire*.[43]

Wallpaper as such was probably not known in sixteenth-century Italy but small panels of printed paper may have been used for decorating rooms in various ways. Some very large prints, made up with engravings taken from several plates designed to produce a single scene, were made in Germany with a landscape based on a drawing by Titian (Pl. 55). Large prints by Dürer, and no doubt other artists, were also produced. Some years ago the remains of such a 'giant print' were found on the back of a door of an ancient building in northern Italy, when work was being carried out there. Sabba da Castiglione, who was amongst other things a collector and delighted to study his collection of engravings (particularly his Dürers), may have kept his prints in a portfolio or on a large shelf but no special furniture had by that time been devised for the collector of prints and it seems that some such people simply pinned them to the wall. Sabba da Castiglione, describing the different ways in which one might decorate personal rooms, states that some *le adorna con carte impresse in rame, & in legno in Italia, o altrove, & sopra tutto di quelle venute di Germania, & massimamente di mano di Alberto dureri* . . . [adorn them with prints, either copperplate or woodcut, made in Italy or elsewhere, but particularly those from the hand of Albrecht Dürer].[44] Paintings that were free-hanging (i.e. framed rather than set into the panelling or executed as frescoes) became common in the second half of the sixteenth century but it was still considered rather surprising, as late as 1615, when the walls of the *sala* at the Villa Medici in Rome were hung with pictures and sculptures so closely packed that there was no need for wall-hangings.[45]

Walls were sometimes faced with rush matting which could be very colourful although most was plain (and therefore straw-coloured) or had a pattern in black. There was a *stuoia per uso di spalliere in sala* at Poggio a Caiano in 1492 (Poggio Invt.) which was *tutto rotte* [a mat for the *sala* walls . . . in shreds]. In the Capponi mansion in Florence in 1534 was to be seen a *spalliera* of *gunchi di ispagna* [a wall-hanging of Spanish matting]. Twelve years later a Florentine master glassmaker was recorded as owning a patterned mat [*stuoia a fighura*] that served as wall-hanging and cornice, which had its pattern painted green (i.e. it does not seem to have

55

55 A precursor of wallpaper

A large print, suitable only for wall-decoration, made up from several sheets. Apparently printed in Germany but clearly after a drawing by Titian, as the inscription states – in Italian. A handful of such large pictorial prints are known to have been produced in Germany. This one dates from about 1511. It measures 79 × 107.6 cm.

Staatliche Museen Preußischer Kulturbesitz, Kupferstichkabinett, Berlin (photograph: Jörg P. Anders)

had an inwoven pattern).[46] In mid-fifteenth century Genoa something known as a *boida* was to be seen in many grand houses. They were to be found in the main room (known in Genoa as the *caminata*; p. 290)[47] and 'around the bed' in bedchambers. This last phrase could imply that it was on the floor or on the walls of an alcove. It has been suggested that a *boida* was a form of mat, which would explain why one from Genoa in 1458 (Lomellini Invt.) was described as *Buoa una vetusta jhonchis* [old, of rushes]; but another in the same list had a pile surface [*pilosa*] We should at any rate reckon with the possibility that matting was used on the walls, sometimes. We have already heard of matting used for filling a doorway (p. 30)

To sum up, it is worth citing Sabba da Castiglione again. 'Others adorn their rooms with tapestries and *celoni* brought from Flanders, decorated with figures or flowers, and some with verdure [tapestries], or with Turkish or Syrian rugs, or with covers or hangings from Barbary, and some with canvases painted by great masters, and some with leather hangings ingeniously worked and coming from Spain, and yet others with new things, fantastic and bizarre but cleverly contrived, brought from the Levant or Germany ...' [*Alcuni altri apparano & adornano le loro stanze di panno di razza & di celoni venuti di Fiandra, fatti a figure & a fogliami, & chi a verdure & chi con tapeti & moschetti turcheschi & soriani, & chi con carpette & spaliere barbaresche, chi di tele di mano di buoni maestri, chi con corami ingegnosamente lavorati venuti di Spagna, & alcuni altri con cose nuove fantastiche & bizarre, ma ingeniose venute di Levante o d'Alemagna ...*].[48] It will be seen that the choice was wide.

Ceilings

The Italians call a ceiling either a *palcho* or a *soffito*. The terms may derive from two distinct types of wooden ceiling that appear quite different when seen from below. The basic form is the *palcho*, formed with baulks of timber that we call joists and which in Italy are called *bordoni* or *bordinali* because they bear the main burden of the ceiling. They span the width of the room and are set at regular intervals down the length of it. The *soffito*, on the other hand, was a wooden membrane composed of framed panels, originally of equal size, suspended below the joists of the *palcho*, and it is suggested that, because it was *sub-ficto* (hence *soffito*), that was the name this form enjoyed. Unfortunately, Schiaparelli, who put forward this theory, had to admit that the documents he had studied did not disclose any evidence that fourteenth- or fifteenth-century Florentines used the two words with this distinction in mind, and that the words actually seemed to be interchangeable.[1].

Timber ceilings were to be found in all rooms above ground-floor level during the fifteenth century; the rooms on the ground floor, on the other hand, were usually vaulted with masonry.[2] In the sixteenth century, a few important rooms on the floors above were sometimes also vaulted, not so much with masonary as with a structure of lighter weight made with timber, plaster and stucco.

The *palcho* of exposed joists could be very impressive, with the heavy beams lending majesty to a large room. The width of a room was of course

56

56 The exposed *palcho*

The most basic form of beamed ceiling, unadorned (except for small areas of blue paint, in this case). The main joist rests on massive brackets. This house is not palatial (this could explain why the ceiling is not more elaborate) but is comfortable in a modest way. The bed in a niche is not a usual Italian form. The bed-curtains are of sober character, as is the coverlet. St Anne, who has just given birth to the Virgin, has spread out a small cloth to protect the bedclothes as she prepares to sip some of the broth a servant is about to offer her. The tabernacle, with a lamp in front and protected by a curtain, bears a Jewish inscription. The artist knew that St Anne was of that faith; obviously to depict a *Madonna and Child* or a *Crucifixion* in that position would have been an anachronism, for this purpose, but such would have been the two commonest subjects for devotional tabernacles in Renaissance Italy. Note the Turkish rug, and the decorative panel beyond which may be of gilt leather.

Vittore Carpaccio, *Birth of the Virgin*, Bergamo; 1504–8
Accademia Carrara, Bergamo

57 A beamed ceiling

The main beam spans the room, resting on brackets or corbels. Lying on the top, at right angles, are smaller beams. The spaces between the latter are divided further to form small panels that lend themselves well to painted ornament. The larger and smaller beams may also be painted but the surfaces suited to painted decoration are formed by boards set at an angle facing downwards above the main beam and between the smaller ones.

Illustration by Alex Barry

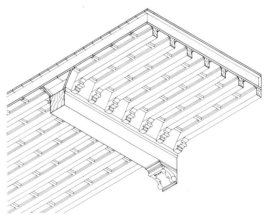

57

58 The suspended *soffito*

The common form of timber ceiling for fine rooms of the smaller kind, with a grid-like framing of shallow panels *a caselle*, shown in a little-known painting of 1470. The bed has two steps that continue round the sides of the room, incidentally forming a stand for an enclosed *credenza*. Note the elegant glass vessel.

Benvenuto di Giovanni, *Annunciation*, S. Bernardino, Sinalunga, 1470
Photograph: Scala

59 A splendid ceiling *a casselle*

This ceiling has exceptionally bold dish-shaped bosses. A large and fine Turkish carpet lies on the long table on which stands a woven straw box of amazing shape. The tops of the two arched windows are filled with panels of white glass with red glass fillings between each of the *occhi*. The windows can only be made draughtproof by closing the large wooden interior shutters. Mary's bed is in a niche.

Andrea Previtali, *Annunciation*, S. Maria del Meschio, Vittorio Veneto, Treviso, *c.*1508
Photograph: Weidenfeld Archive

58

59

60

61

60 The first published designs for ceilings

Serlio's treatise (1537) included several pages of ceiling-designs, some certainly being his own compositions. That in the bottom right-hand corner was to be seen in the Palazzo della Cancelleria in Rome where Baldassare Peruzzi, Serlio's master, had worked in around 1511.

From Serlio's *Treatise on Architecture*, Volume IV, Venice, 1559
Courtesy of the Trustees of Sir John Soane's Museum, London

61 The antique example closely imitated

Some antique classical exemplars provided sanction, if this were needed, for breaking up the regularity of panelled ceilings *a cassettoni* or *a caselle*. Perino del Vaga, one of the principal exponents of such imitations of the classical formula, created many fine ceilings in this idiom in which boldly-framed compartments of different sizes, filled with formal ornament, were combined with panels of figural subjects executed in paint or stucco relief.

Studio of Perino del Vaga, ceiling design
Christ Church, Oxford (491)

determined by the length of the timbers that were available (or affordable by the person who had to pay) and it no doubt added to a visitor's amazement, when viewing a room ceiled with enormous beams, to know that they must have been brought a long distance because such logs were no longer to be found in woods close to any of the principal cities of Italy, by the fifteenth, let alone the sixteenth century – for this type of ceiling remained in favour right through to 1600 and beyond. By the middle of the sixteenth century, however, beams of exceptional length might be contrived by means of splicing, with a complicated locking joint all held together with iron bands that were to some extent disguised by being sunk into the surface of the beam. Illustrations of such joined beams were included in Cosimo Bartoli's edition of Alberti's Treatise, published in 1550.

The main joists rested on massive corbels or carved brackets projecting from the walls and supported two subsidiary sets of timbers, each laid at right-angles to the set below. This produced rectangular frames for small panels deeply set up between the main joists (see Pl. 57). Painted decoration might be added to such a *travamento* [assemblage of beams], the main work being applied to the deep beams while subsidiary ornament was given to the smaller beams and panels above. A favourite space for decoration was the side faces of the main beams, which of course faced anyone entering from the ends of the room. Here it was not uncommon to paint profile portraits, stylized foliage, coats of arms or fantastic beasts. Sometimes, in these spaces, panels of wood were inserted facing

downwards at an angle so as to make the plane more easy to see from the ground, and these panels were then given the decoration that would otherwise have been put straight on to the beam (Pl. 57).[3]

The ceiling sporting great heavy beams could be rather overpowering (Pls 56, 291). The suspended ceiling with panels was much more graceful and, moreover, lent itself more readily to painted decoration because the structure was essentially all on one level. Indeed, in the fourteenth century, the panels were scarcely set back behind the level of the surrounding framework (Pl. 59) and this shallow form of coffering, if one can call it that, remained in fashion in rooms of small or moderate size right through to the early sixteenth century (Pls 8, 9, 37, 58, 59).

However, in the middle decades of the fifteenth century, a variant of the suspended ceiling was developed for use in large rooms, where the framing of the panels grew bolder to form ribs which became increasingly heavy. The result was to produce deeper coffers surrounded by prominent ribs or framing which was usually richly carved and sometimes had ornament executed in stucco. The rosettes at the centre of each panel became very prominent, and bosses or rosettes were also placed on the crossing-points of the heavy ribs (Pls 195, 372). Such boldly coffered ceilings are usually described as being *a cassettoni* (the suffix *-one*, in the singular, normally implies that the object is of large size). It seems wrong also to apply this term to, or to call 'coffered', a ceiling of the earlier type with only shallow depressions. Was a distinction made at the time? It may have been. When a new ceiling had to be installed over a passageway in the castle at Ferrara in 1471, the court painter-decorator was paid for embellishing thirty-four *caselle* '*per lo pezolo novo*'.[4] A *pezzulo*, according to Florio's dictionary of 1611*, meant a 'dangling or downe hanging' which one might think was an apt description of a suspended ceiling. *Caselle* meant 'pigeonholes' (although the term may later have been extended to embrace drawers – which fit into pigeonholes) and this would seem to be a far more appropriate term than *cassettoni* for the shallow form of coffering used in small rooms and private passageways in a 'secret' apartment, which is what the Ferrara commission concerned.

The first Renaissance ceilings with deep coffering had rectangular panels; this form had made its appearance by 1450.[5] By the 1470s, some ceilings of advanced design had octagonal coffers, inspired by some of the surviving classical examples that were now beginning to be studied, not just as curiosities, but as subjects for emulation. In every case, at this stage, the coffers were all of equal size.[6] Deep coffers were mainly to be seen in large rooms of considerable height, where the recesses produced deep shadows. These enormous wooden ceilings were left mostly unpainted but some were decorated with a single colour (sky blue was in particular favour) and a few had details picked out in gold. They relied chiefly on carved decoration for rich effect although a few had inlaid ornament as well.[7]

Serious antiquarian interests among the leading architects and their clients in Rome, from about 1515 and through to the middle of the century, centring around Raphael and his followers, saw the adoption of antique classical ceiling formulae which encouraged the use of more adventurous relationships between sizes and shapes of the panels of a coffered ceiling. No longer did they have to be equal in size, nor did they have to remain rectangular. At first angular panels of various kinds (crosses, diamonds, oblongs, triangles, etc.) were favoured (Pl. 60); later the shapes became more fanciful, heralding the arrival of the Baroque style (Pl. 62). They also tended to become larger because, from the middle of the century onwards, the panels would normally contain paintings and the artists did not like being cramped.

In the case of the vaulted type of ceiling, in the fifteenth century, the preferred form was *a lunette* or *a nicchio*. These terms refer to the shape of that arched area at the top of the wall which is scribed by the ceiling as it meets the wall. This could either have a semi-circular head or one with a point like a Gothic arch. These spaces were at first treated separately, but generally the tendency through the sixteenth century was to blend the ceiling with the walls, in rooms of importance. This was contrived by carrying the stucco relief ornament, which became ever more exuberant, down from the ribs of the vaulting on to the walls below. At the same time the wall-decoration crept up to integrate with that of the ceiling.

These developments made it increasingly important to ensure that there was a correspondence between the separate areas or panels of the ceiling-decoration and the intervals of decoration, or features like windows, on the walls below (Pl. 52).[8] In the second half of the sixteenth century fresco-painting took over the ceilings of important rooms, to the extent that the ceiling became the dominant feature of the room, and painted room-decoration was now often conceived as an integrated scheme, working from the ceiling downwards rather than vice versa, as had previously been the case.

62 A ceiling with spaces for Tintorettos

Irregular schemes like this became fashionable in the late decades of the sixteenth century. Although very grand, this design is fairly characteristic of the Venetian variant of this style. It is for the ceiling of the Senate Chamber [*Sala dei Pregadi*] in the Doge's Palace; it is by Cristoforo Sorte, an erudite Veronese artist who was famed as a map-maker and wrote a treatise on painting, *Osservazioni nella pittura*, published in Venice in 1584. This drawing, dated 1578, bears the signature of the distinguished woodworkers who were to execute it, Andrea da Faenza and Francesco da San Moise, who thereby agreed to follow the design faithfully, and in fact the actual ceiling differs little from this design. In 1595 the *lacunae* were fitted with paintings by Tintoretto and others.

Cristoforo Sorte, design for the ceiling of the Senate Chamber in the Doge's Palace, 1578
Victoria and Albert Museum, London, (E.509–1937)

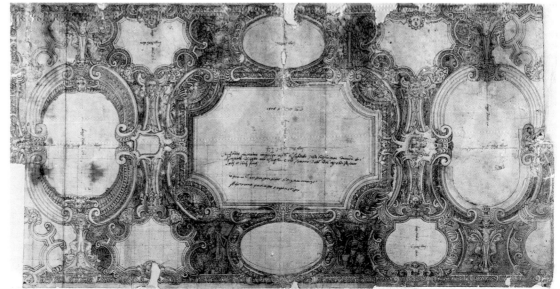

62

These are large subjects and cannot be discussed in any detail here but others have dealt with them and the reader is referred to such specialized surveys.[9] Nothing fruitful can here be said about illusionistic paintings, for instance, or about the charming schemes devised to look like a *pergola* or a bower of foliage, or indeed about the way stucco was used to form ribs for compartments and subsequently became increasingly sculptural, so that figures painted on the ceilings had cousins nearby executed three-dimensionally in white stucco, all of which produced ebullient effects completely different from the severely geometric schemes of a century before. Fortunately, such matters have received much attention elsewhere.

At Pesaro there are some details of ceilings still to be seen which are unlikely to have been isolated phenomena. A beamed ceiling of a *sala* at the Villa Imperiale, dating from the 1470s, is decorated with coats of arms and *imprese* [insignia] of the Sforza family printed on paper from woodblocks and then painted before being pasted in position.[10] At the same villa are two ceilings of the second quarter of the sixteenth century decorated with 'tiles' of card stamped with relief ornament, in the first instance taking the form of *imprese* and monograms, painted and partly gilded, all held in place with strips of white stamped card in the form of bands of oak leaves with gilded acorns,[11] and in the second instance stamped with more elaborate ornament secured with double lines of white petals, each nailed in position separately.[12] Down in the city itself, in the Palazzo Ducale, some elaborate domed ceilings created under the direction of Bartolomeo Genga in the third quarter of the century have elements that look as if they were executed in stucco but turned out to be of *carta pesta* [an early form of *papier mâché*] during recent restoration work.[13] The forms are of almost Baroque exuberance.

63

63 Florid grotesques; proto-Baroque

A fresco ceiling in a late sixteenth-century Florentine *palazzo* embodying an advanced form of grotesque ornament that lacks the rather wiry character of earlier manifestations of this genre. This ceiling in the *sala* of the Palazzo Orlandini, originally the Palazzo dei Gondi di Francia, so-called on account of the family's prominent role in French political and diplomatic life, notably at the time of Queen Catherine (de' Medici). Although their principal residence was then in Paris, they did over their Florentine property in the 1590s, perhaps with the aid of Bernardo Buontalenti. The present ceiling was painted at this stage, in the style of Bernardino Poccetti (see Pl. 50). The arms are those of France, and of the Grand Duke Ferdinand I of Tuscany and his wife, Christina of Lorraine, recording the family's dual allegiance. Ferdinand married Christina in 1589.

Fresco ceiling in the Palazzo Orlandini
Photograph: Monte dei Paschi di Siena

64
65

64 A *spinapesce* floor

Bricks or thick tiles laid in a herringbone pattern [*spina-pesce*] shown in a manuscript made for Giangaleazzo Visconti, Lord of Milan. Ostensibly representing the birth of the Virgin, the scene is presumably set in a late fourteenth-century Milanese bedchamber of some splendour. The bed (*lettiera*) has the characteristic upward curving, northern type of headboard. It also has flanking benches, not chests. The bedclothes are of the most sumptuous kind.

Giovanni dei Grassi, *Birth of the Virgin*, miniature, *c*.1388–95
Biblioteca Nazionale, Florence (photograph: Scala)

65 Inlaid tiles

One can just see the inlaid tiles behind the Madonna. They are of the mediaeval kind, impressed with a pattern while the clay was still soft, whereafter the depressions were filled with a white slip (a clay of creamy consistency) and the whole was covered with a transparent lead glaze prior to firing. The stunning appearance of rich textile materials is admirably shown here. The chest forming a seat is covered with a superb figured velvet.

Gentile da Fabriano, *Madonna and Child*, about 1425
National Gallery, Washington, D.C. (1939 1 255)

An important point to bear in mind about Italian Renaissance ceilings is that one could rarely have seen them at all clearly because, at night-time, relatively little light reached up there from firelight and candles at or near floor-level (Pl. 301), while in daytime the shutters were often closed to keep out the strong sunlight of summer or the cold of winter. So all the boldness of decoration we have been considering, especially in connection with large rooms, where the ceilings were high above the ground, was essential or one would have seen nothing at all, most of the time.[14] Of course, today, when such ceilings are often floodlit by means of extremely powerful electric lighting, much of their mysterious opulence is lost and they tend to look rather crude. The student of painting may want to be able to see every detail, and the artist also may have hoped the viewer would be able to do so, but such lighting upsets the balance of the room. It was not the intention that the ceiling should be thrust at the visitor, so to speak, to the exclusion of all else in the room, even when ceilings had become the dominant feature of rooms. They were, even then, part of a carefully orchestrated whole. Of course, in so many cases, much of the 'whole' has been lost – there are no longer any hangings and the furniture has been dispersed. Nevertheless, it does not help to make the room top-heavy.

Some ceilings were covered with a textile material. We could be sure this was the case if only because a few rooms survive in which such a treatment is simulated in fresco.[15] The material was pasted to the undersurface and could thus follow curves; indeed, this form of decoration will only have been used with vaulted ceilings. There would be no point in using it on a timber ceiling. Galeazzo Maria Sforza (d.1476) wanted a ceiling of a great hall [*sala*] in the castle at Milan to be covered with red velvet, which must have been a telling example of conspicuous expenditure.[16] The eminent scholar who tells us this mentions at the same time that this tyrant ordered that the room in which his precious gyr falcons were kept should be garnished with green velvet embroidered with his arms. He does not actually state that the velvet was on the ceiling but it could well have been. Nothing but the best would have been good enough for these birds which had probably been brought all the way from Iceland, their natural habitat.

Awnings [*tende*] sometimes formed ceilings over open loggias, enclosed courtyards, bowers where suppers were to be given, and the like. In some covered loggias, like that at the Farnesina in Rome, *tende* have been represented in fresco on the ceiling to make it seem as if the loggia was open to the skies. The pair of *tende* on the Farnesina ceiling are painted with figures of gods and goddesses which should be understood not simply as a way for the artist (in this case Giulio Romano) to tell his story but as a faithful representation of a real *tenda* of the grander sort, many of which are very likely to have been painted in such a manner.[17]

Floors

Surfaces

Vaulted ceilings, constructed of stone or brick, could of course support tiled floors or floors laid with marble. The huge beamed ceilings of the Renaissance were also capable of holding up a tiled floor but were probably not thought sufficiently strong to uphold marble. Tiles were laid on a substructure of earth or sand, or of *terrazzo*; this layer was in itself heavy but provided a virtually inert underfloor.

Floor-tiles were of brick [*mattoni*] and might actually be brick-shaped and as thick as our standard bricks today but were also made like thick versions of modern tiles.[1] A late fifteenth-century Pisan document refers to *mattoncetti strettissimi ossia di quadrucci* [very narrow bricks, or rather tiles].[2] *Quadrucci* was the normal word for tiles and the term indicates that they were originally square rather than rectangular. Unless one used tiles of more than one colour, there was nothing one could do to make patterns with square tiles. However, floors covered with bricks or oblong tiles could be laid in patterns of various kinds, notably in a herringbone pattern [*spinapesce*] which may be seen in Pls 64 and 253.[3] The patterns devised for such floors were later taken up by those who had to lay parquet floors with oblong strips of wood. Brick tile floors were polished and provided a very practical unbroken surface (the grouting of the interstices also received the polish) that could be seen in the best houses and in the best rooms. Pius II spoke with pride of the floors of polished brick in his new mansion at Pienza, built in the early 1460s, which were 'without any unevenness whatever'.[4]

Earthenware tiles, which are of course related to brick tiles but were glazed and mostly came from the kilns of potters rather than brick-makers, were also used for floors in the mediaeval period (p. 109). Some were inlaid with patterns in a contrasting colour, usually white on the natural colour of the earthenware squares (Pl. 65). The inlay was produced by stamping the surface with a pattern using a mould, and filling the resulting impression with a white slip; thereafter the tile was glazed. It seems that such inlaid tiles were still being used in Tuscany and Umbria (and probably elsewhere), well into the fifteenth century, judging by a painting by Domenico di Bartolo which is in the city art gallery at Perugia. Tiles with a pattern in relief, the production of which must also have involved a special mould, are to be seen on several floors in the Villa Imperiale at Pesaro dating from the mid-sixteenth century (p. 109).

Maiolica tiles were used on particularly splendid floors during the fifteenth century, in Naples and elsewhere in the Aragonese kingdom of southern Italy where tiles were brought in from Valencia.[5] It may be that Valencian tiles are to be seen on the floor in Pl. 210. A class of tile of Spanish origin which was apparently brought to Italy in some quantity, perhaps mostly via Genoa, was that known as *cuerda seca*. On these, the various colours of a maiolica glaze were separated by ridges of clay produced by impressing the surface with a mould. The ridges served also to protect the vulnerable glaze from wear. Some are to be seen on the floor of rooms in the Borgia Apartments in the Vatican, dating presumably from the time of Alexander VI (1492–1503) who was of course of Spanish origin, and also at the Casina of Pius IV in the Vatican gardens dating from 1561.

By the second half of the fifteenth century polychrome tiles of maiolica were being made in several places in central Italy, including Florence, and glazed terracotta tiles were also being produced in Florence at the Della Robbia factory (p. 109). These colourful tiles were not only used locally but were exported in some quantity to other provinces. For example, there were floors laid with Florentine tiles at Poggio Reale, the royal villa outside Naples, designed by Giuliano da Maiano in the late 1480s, and such floor-decoration came to be described there as being *ala usanza fiorentina* [in the Florentine fashion].[6]

One sees many paintings of the Annunciation showing Mary receiving the astonishing news in a splendid setting where a floor faced with marble quarries is a principal feature. Such floors may still be seen in many an Italian church but were probably not so common in private houses (Pl. 69). Marble may be beautiful and opulent but it is not a particularly sympathetic surface to have continually underfoot. In introducing a marble floor into a painting of the Annunciation, an artist may have wanted thereby to underline that Mary was an exceptionally fine lady, for whom only the best was good enough.

One speaks of marble but several other kinds of expensive stone were also used for such decorative floors – serpentine, porphyry and granite, for example – and marble of course came in a wide range of colours and patterns. These stone floors were laid on a sub-floor of *terrazzo*. While most patterns were composed with square pieces, circles and triangles were common, as were oblongs. Early fifteenth-century marble floors tended to be made with relatively small pieces (Pl. 68), the pieces getting larger through to 1600. Patterns of a complicated nature, like *lavoro di intarsio* [intricate wooden inlay; p. 92] but rendered in stone, were carried out in some small rooms, and details like coats of arms might be executed in this medium. Actual mosaic work (i.e. with small *tessere*) was practised to some extent throughout the Renaissance,[7] but was not as popular as it had been before 1400. Vasari states that it was a suitable form of floor for bathrooms and saunas [*per bagni e per i stufi*] and mentions some representations of fishes with scintillating scales [*pesce ch'anno la pelle lustra*] that looked alive when covered with water.[8]

The Italians have for centuries been expert in laying floors of *terrazzo*, and they still are. This is a compound of stucco with small pieces of marble and ground-up stone, built up in layers (each well compacted) and then polished.[9] Giovanni Antonio Rusconi[10] devotes several pages to the technique of laying this kind of floor, with illustrations of the work being carried out.

Many floors, of course, were of wooden boards. The best floors of this kind were laid on a sub-floor of boards which will have minimized movement resulting from shrinkage. Palladius Rutilius Tauro, an aristocratic Roman architect of the late classical period, wrote a book

66 A roll of matting

An illustration from a cookery-book of about 1570 showing of some of the equipment a pope needed when travelling. Several items have locks, including the large jars. The tool-kit no doubt came in handy. The two iron-bound chests are covered in cow-hide that still sports its hairs.

From the *Opera* of Bartolomeo Scappi
Metropolitan Museum of Art, Elisha Whittelsey Collection, Elisha Whittelsey Fund, 1952 (52.592.2[24])

67 Cutwork patterns for the domestic embroideress

This manual of about 1545 directed at *Belle et Virtuose Donne* includes *varie sorti di frisi con li quali si potra ornar ciascuna donna, & ogni letti con ponti tagliati … & ogni altra sorte di ponti …* [various kinds of border with which every woman and every bed may be decorated with cutwork … and all other kinds of needlework].

From Giovanni Andrea Vavassori, *Fior di gli essempli …, c.*1545
Victoria and Albert Museum, London (95.0.28 Pl. 13)

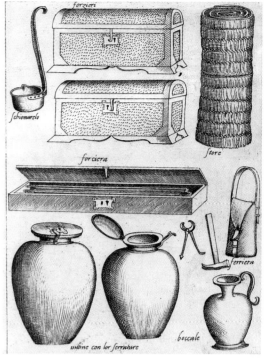

66

67

68 Small-scale marble patterns

A floor laid with small pieces of marble to form a rich overall pattern. This form of floor-decoration was used from classical times and right through the Middle Ages. Handsome examples, now much worn, are to be seen in many Romanesque and Gothic churches in and around Venice, for instance. Here St Luke is painting a portrait of the *Madonna and Child*, employing an easel very like those still used by artists today. St Ambrose has the equivalent of a modern peg-board attached to his desk, on which he has hung up his writing-case with its inkwell, and a bottle (of ink?). He has a small platform to keep his feet off the cold floor; it is painted with a pattern more or less like that of the floor.

Unknown artist, *St. Luke and St. Ambrose*, Atri Cathedral, third quarter 15th century
Photograph: Autostrade

69 A floor fit for Salome's dance

A particularly splendid floor composed of five kinds of marble is the most prominent feature of Filippo Lippi's scene of *Herod's Feast*, painted between 1452 and 1466. The scene has great charm in spite of its gruesome subject. The severed head of St John the Baptist is presented on a charger as if it were the principal dish of the meal – like a stuffed peacock, a sturgeon or a sucking-pig. An escutcheon hangs on the wall above the principal diner bearing the arms, presumably, of the person who commissioned the painting.

Filippo Lippi, *Herod's Feast* (detail), Prato
Photograph: Scala

68

69

70 Exotic rush matting

Matting with a pattern in red and black setting off the natural straw colour of the fine rushes of which it is woven. Such matting probably came from North Africa or Spain.

Sassetta, *Virgin and Child* (detail), Museo Diocesano, Cortona, Tuscany, 1432–6
Photograph: Scala

71 Florentine luxury, around 1400

The floor appears to be covered with quarry-tiles impressed with a pattern. On the floor lies a fine Turkish rug which must surely be included to indicate that this is no humble home. The message is further underlined by the coloured *lavoro di intarsio* of Mary's seat and the sprigged pattern executed in gold on the summer hangings of her bed. The reading-stand might easily be mistaken for a nineteenth-century confection, if it were to turn up in an auction-room today.

Agnolo Gaddi circle, *Annunciation*, S. Maria Novella, Florence, early quattrocento
Photograph: Scala

70

71

about villas – how to site them, how to build them, how to organize the work on their land – which was translated into Italian and published in Venice in 1560 as a useful handbook for modern Italians seeking to emulate the Ancients in the matter of living in the country.[11] Palladius tells us that the best floors should be made of oak, holm oak or beech.

It was common to provide wooden floors for studies and other small private rooms where the owner might sit for long periods, reading or writing – or otherwise passing the time of day (Pls 210, 255). For the same reason platforms often formed the base on which stood a desk, and sometimes also a seat, which items might be fixed to the platform (Pl. 261). The great seats in which Mary is often shown seated, in pictures of the Annunciation, were commonly constructed with a raised platform, as were many *lettucci* (p. 149). The point of these platforms was to keep the feet off the cold floor of the room itself which would usually be of brick, tile or (occasionally) marble.

Such wooden floors were mostly utilitarian and of a plain character but Leonello d'Este had a floor laid in a small chamber next to his bathroom, in 1485, where the floor was of black and white squares laid on a sub-floor of maplewood.[12]

Just as in important sixteenth-century schemes of decoration, it became customary to relate the divisions of the ceilings to those of the walls, so it also became important to make the design of the floor-decoration correspond with the compartments of the ceiling. Correspondence of this kind seems first to have made its appearance in Rome in the mid-sixteenth century, and was to be seen, for instance, at the Villa Giulia, of which the architect Bartolomeo Ammannati actually stated, in 1555, that *i pavimenti di mattoni intagliati ... rispondono a' palchi* [the floors of cut bricks correspond to the ceilings] which were elaborate.[13] This could mean that bricks (or, rather, tiles of brick) were trimmed with a chisel to fit the patterns required; but some tiles were probably specially made of an irregular non-standard shape for such purposes. A floor with the owner's coat of arms in the centre, at the Villa Lante at Bagnaia, seems to have been created with such shaped tiles, each in one of three earthy colours; this presumably dates from 1596. The floor of the reading-room in the Biblioteca Laurenziana in Florence, dating from 1549, has a very complex pattern (echoing the ceiling, incidentally) which is executed by carving into the tiles to produce an intaglio effect. Into the excavated channels was then poured some form of composition based on stucco which was lighter in colour than the ground. Surely the *mattoni intagliati* of the Villa Giulia floors must have been made in this way – that is to say, they were decorated 'in *intaglio*', as we put it in English, rather than trimmed or carved in the ordinary sense.

Floor-coverings

The commonest way of insulating the feet from a cold floor was to introduce some form of wooden platform, as we have just seen. In wealthy households one might lay some form of carpet on the floor.

The English word carpet meant any covering of a pliant nature that was made to lay on a flat surface, be it the floor, a table or a dais. The same may have been the case in Italy although no instances have been noted of a *carpeta* described as lying on the floor; on the other hand, the term *carpeta da tavola* [a table-carpet or table-cloth][1] is not uncommon and it is perhaps worth noting that Florio* tells us that *carpeta* does indeed mean 'a table-carpet', and gives no other meaning. A Near-Eastern carpet could be used as a table-carpet, as many illustrations show (e.g. Pls 59, 346), and this is also indicated by an entry in a Venetian inventory of 1562 reading *Una carpeta da tavola morescha* [i.e. Moorish, which meant Islamic].[2] Mostly, however, table-carpets were of other textile materials; green cloth was widely favoured for this purpose.

The common term for a textile or leather floor-cover – i.e. a carpet – was *un tappeto* which was often spelt with one 'p' and could be rendered as *tapedo* or *tapeyda*.[3] Florio* seems to get it right when he says that the word meant 'any kind of carpet' and it is therefore noteworthy that we occasionally come across a *tapedo da tavola* [table-carpet][4] or one which *serve il descho* [goes on the desk] or *sul descho da scrivere* [on the writing desk],[5] while some were laid on the bed (*tappeti da letto* were among the goods on which an import duty was paid at Siena in the fifteenth century)[6] or on the *lettuccio* (p. 149; *uno tappeto da lettuccio di turchia* was a Turkish rug used in this way).[7]

While most *tappeti* were of Near Eastern origin, as we shall see, and this normally meant that they were carpets with a pile, some *tappeti* were of silk or woollen cloth and must have been Italian products of various kinds.[8] The *tappeto senese* [from Siena] mentioned in a Florentine inventory of 1404 cannot have been Near Eastern and was probably of a locally woven woollen material.[9]

By and large, however, a *tapedo* or *tappeto* will have been a Near Eastern carpet, which is to say that it was made of wool and had a hand-knotted pile surface. A few Near Eastern carpets were made with silk but it really was not many.

Dante makes references to *tappeti tartareschi* [from Tartary] in the *Inferno* (c.1310) and we find mention of *tappeti* which were *turchiesco* [Turkish] in quite a few inventories.[10] In the sixteenth century references occur in Venetian inventories to *tapedi a moscheti* or *tapedi moschetti* which is thought to refer to prayer rugs bearing an inwoven representation of an arched prayer-niche.[11] Ten such rugs mentioned in a Venetian inventory were evidently small because they were for laying on chests [*da cassa*] and this was probably always the case, as prayer-rugs are by definition not large; Muslims customarily carry them about and unroll them when the time for prayer arrives.

Italians did not distinguish between the place of origin of Near Eastern carpets until well into the sixteenth century. When they are described as *turchesco* it does not necessarily mean that they came from Anatolia although most of them will have done so. Only towards the end of the century is a distinction made in some inventories between Turkish carpets and other types – notably Persian and Cairene (i.e. from Cairo).[12] An inventory from Venice of 1584 (Correr Invt.) includes references to *un tapedo da tavola persian, un tapedo cagiarin da tavola quadra* (the Cairene table-carpet was square so was probably designed specially for use on a table) and *un tapedo turchesco da tavola*, not to speak of nine carpets described as *simiscasa*, eight of them for laying on chests (i.e. they were small), and one for a table which was *longo* seven and a half *braccia*. *Simiscasa* must refer either to a place of origin, or a port of exportation or transhipment,[13] or to a clearly recognizable pattern or form. It seems just possible that it is a corruption of Circassia, which lies east of Anatolia in the general area of the Caucasus – a major carpet-making territory.[14]

So the principal source of knotted pile carpets was Anatolia while a certain quantity may have come from the Caucasus. Persian and Cairene carpets were not unknown but probably only came to Europe in small numbers. To this we should add Spain where carpets of Near Eastern type were woven at several centres during the fifteenth and sixteenth centuries.[15] Some of these must have reached Italy, and especially the Kingdom of Naples which had such strong affiliation with Spain. It would seem that a few carpets were actually woven in Naples, for in 1456 one Francisco de Perca, *mestre de fer catiffes de casa del S. Rey* [master of carpet-making to the royal household], was listed as being among the current court appointments.[16] Carpets may also have been woven for a short while at Ferrara where, in 1493, Sabadino Negro, *m[aestro] de tapidi*, set up a manufactory using wool from North Africa [*lana barbaresca*] and a loom that was constructed on the spot.[17] He was black, as his name implies, and was also known as Sabadino Moro [the Moor]. Ercole I d'Este provided him with a house and looked after him in other ways, presumably because he was an effective producer of *tapedi*. He at any rate produced one because Alfonso I bequeathed it to the Queen of Poland, or so we are told, and it must therefore have been an object of some importance.[18] Nevertheless, few carpets were made in Italy; they were probably small and they affect our story not at all.

While some entries in inventories mention the origin of a carpet, it was more common simply to describe salient features of the pattern but usually in such vague terms – with circles, squares, with a Moorish pattern [*a ruote, con quadrature, alla moresca*] – that it rarely gives us an idea of how that particular carpet looked. However, we can be fairly sure that a carpet was Near Eastern if it is described as being *pelosa* [piled, or with a pile surface].[19] Apart from the carpets made in Spain (which were anyway made by Moors or in a Moorish tradition), carpets with a pile were not woven anywhere else, to all intents and purposes.[20] One type of Persian carpet, made for the Shah's court in the sixteenth century,[21] had a pile of silk that was so finely woven and of such short length that one might think it had no pile at all. It is possible that the *tappeto raso alla moresca chon quadrature* [flat carpet with a Moorish pattern with squares], and another described with the same words in different order, might be Persian silk carpets of this kind. They were among the carpets belonging to Lorenzo de' Medici on his death in 1492 (Medici Invt., Florence). We know that the Shah was in the habit of sending fine silk carpets to important foreigners as diplomatic presents and there is no reason why one should not have been conveyed to the leading figure in Florence at the time. If this carpet did really not have any pile at all,

however, it must in fact have been a *kilim* which was a tapestry-woven carpet (which, by definition means that it had no pile) that was decorated with patterns of unmistakable Near Eastern character. A Medici carpet which will almost undoubtedly have been of this latter kind is mentioned in an inventory of 1456 (Medici Invt., Florence) where it is described as *Uno tapeto grande sanza pelo* [a large carpet without pile]. It is just possible that this carpet was one of the two mentioned in 1492. The *tapeto raso* was ten *braccia* long which would certainly qualify it for being called *grande*.

We can be certain that a carpet listed in an inventory was placed on the floor when the terms *in terra* or *da terra* are used in the description but otherwise we cannot be sure. Judging from the evidence provided by contemporary illustrations, it would seem that they were customarily laid on the floor in the fourteenth and early fifteenth centuries, following Islamic usage, although they were not used for sitting upon to any great extent (Pl. 71).[22] For some reason, they seem rarely to have been used on the floor from about 1430 until early in the sixteenth century; instead they were used for throwing over tables and covering seats. Once carpets became relatively common, after about 1500, it again became common-place to spread them on the ground (Pls 167, 318). Of course, all really large carpets had inevitably to go on the floor, whatever the date, because they could go nowhere else.

Cloths of various kinds were sometimes laid on the floor. Some striped materials seem to have been deemed sufficiently respectable to lie at the feet of the Virgin Mary and are to be seen, for instance, in a Ghirlandaio Annunciation in Lucca Cathedral and in the famous Giorgione of about 1504 reproduced in Pl. 80. Woollen velvets were being made in the Low Countries, anyway by the sixteenth century (p. 77) and robust versions of such weaves, later called *moquettes*, were suitable for floor-covering. It may well be that the *oeuvre sarrasinoise*, a material woven at Tournai apparently already by the 1360s and certainly by 1410 when regulations governing its production were issued, was in fact a tough woollen velvet.[23] Its very name [in the Saracen manner] implies a similarity to Near Eastern materials, and a feature that was particularly striking about an easily-recognizable Near Eastern textile product was the pile. These northern imitations of materials with a pile surface, if that is what they were, probably did not reach Italy in any great quantity during the Renaissance period but it is worth noting a reference in the lists of belongings of the Florentine Acciaiuoli family in 1363 (Acciaiuoli Invt.) to *uno tapeto saracinesho picholo* which could well have been a small *tapis sarrasinois* from the Low Countries or France rather than from the Levant.

Matting was laid on the floor – probably mostly on stone floors in summertime. The matting was made of thin rushes and seems mostly to have come from North Africa (Pl. 66). Mats could be decorative. The learned doctor of medicine, Bartolo di Tura, had one on the floor which was black and white [*Una stoia di gionchi, grande, figurata, bianca e nera*][24] and we see floor-matting with two colours in Pl. 70. Elsewhere we have considered the meaning of the word *boida* which indicated something to be found in many mid-fifteenth-century Genoese houses (p. 66). They

72

72 A magnificent 'animal carpet' on the floor

A large carpet imported from Asia Minor is spread on the floor for this important occasion – the Coronation of the Virgin. It has octagons alternately filled with addorsed eagles and stylized plants. A scene on the predella of the same altarpiece shows another carpet with octagons encompassing figures of eight with a star within each loop.

Sano di Pietro, *Coronation of the Virgin*, La Collegiata, S. Quirico d'Orcia, Tuscany, *c.*1470
Photograph: Scala

were to be seen 'around the room' or 'around the bed', in some cases, but whether this meant they were wall-hangings or floor-covering is not clear.[25] If a *boida* was some form of matting, as seems possible, we have a parallel reference in a Florentine inventory of 1510 where there were two mats around a bedchamber in the family villa [*dua stuoie intorno alla camera*].[26]

Verdure and sweet-smelling herbs were cast upon the floor on festive occasions, probably not so much in the main rooms of elegant houses as in garden-rooms, *logge* and at the country villa. For example, Petrarch writes of a small house [*casetta*] out in the wilds, far from the madding crowd [*lontan da la gente*], where greenery was strewn on the floor [*di verde frondi ingiuncha*]. And, in the *Hypnerotomachia* of 1499, in which are described arrangements that are no doubt exaggerated but not entirely fanciful, we are told how, after all the diners at a banquet had drunk from the loving-cup and the company had temporarily withdrawn, the floor was cleared of flowers and was seen to shine like a mirror. Apart from telling us something about a charming practice of the time, this shows that the Italian ideal was to have one's floors well polished.

73 The charm of *arazzo a verdura*

Textiles played an important role in furnishing Italian Renaissance rooms. A *spalliera* of verdure tapestry forms the backing to a bench on which the diners at the table will shortly sit. One can see how this long hanging is nailed to the wall. The table consists of a long board laid on a pair of three-legged trestles [*trespiedi*], the front legs of which are braced with a web carved as a Gothic arch. On it lies a linen cloth.

Cristoforo de Predis, miniature in the *Libro della fine del mondo*, 1474 (MS.VAT 124, f. 100)
Biblioteca Reale, Turin (photograph: Chomon, Torino)

73

Part Two:

FURNISHINGS

Materials and Techniques

No attempt is here made to provide a balanced survey of the materials and techniques used in the confection of household furnishings during the Italian Renaissance. I believe that one should write about what interests one or on matters about which one is tolerably well informed. Having at one stage long ago worked with historic textiles, I have in the meantime kept up my interest and gathered a certain amount of material which is now set forth here in the belief that it may be helpful to some readers. As is explained below, some sort of a guide to the confusing field of Italian Renaissance textiles is required if one is to understand the terms that are found in such profusion in the inventories of the time and which are so frequently cited here. Much less needs to be said about the woodwork of the period as that has mostly been covered satisfactorily by others and is therefore already fairly well understood. The same can be said of ceramics, while I have to admit to being largely ignorant about Renaissance metalwork although here, once again, I believe the subject is to a great extent covered by existing literature.

The need for a glossary of textile terms current in the Renaissance period has long been recognized but so far nothing really helpful has been forthcoming. Several scholars made the attempt in the nineteenth century but their experience lay on the archival side; they were rarely familiar with collections of historic textiles or with the technical distinctions between the various classes of material, so their pronouncements are not of all that much value. In the twentieth century the archival scholars have scarcely ventured into this territory at all, but the textile historians have surveyed it and fallen back baffled by the complexities and apparent contradictions of the problem. Heroic work with the microscope enabled them to bring some order to this new discipline in that, by studying the construction of fabrics and stitches, it became possible to contrive an acceptable categorization with an agreed vocabulary which has made it possible for them to talk to each other about the surviving materials. Unfortunately this has not greatly helped the rest of us, and particularly not those of us who want to know what the terms in the documents mean, or meant to people at the time. We still need help to envisage what all these materials looked like, as a simple matter of interest and because we should like to try and relate the descriptions to the materials that we see in so many pictures of the period.

Textile historians, knowing how complex a field this is, have tended to hold back from the attempt, but the need remains and the present small offering should be seen as a stopgap 'until the real thing comes along'.[1]

A person faced with the task of drawing up an inventory of objects in a room will use terms, to describe each item, that are familiar to him and which he expects will be readily understood by contemporaries with the same general level of intelligence and experience as himself. He will not usually inspect items very closely, and the features he chooses to describe, or which help him to select what he considers the appropriate term, will probably be obvious to any beholder. This was always so, just as it is today.

Those compiling inventories during the Renaissance could make mistakes. Subtle technical distinctions were usually beyond them. In deciding what terms to use in a particular case, they almost invariably chose ones that were current generally; they did not normally adopt the technical terms of the artisan or the tradesman – and when describing a textile object, they certainly did not have recourse to a microscope in order to give it a name. Nevertheless they probably only felt they had real difficulty when they came across an unfamiliar object – a novelty or an exotic import. In such cases they often 'straddled' it by explaining that it was 'a such-and-such, or rather, a so-and-so', using *ovvero* as the conjunction.

Collectors of rarities – exotica, antiquities and the like – were in a position to be more discriminating and might recognize differences that the average inventory clerk would not appreciate. They might sometimes advise the clerk on what to write; this is of course invaluable – when it happens! Generally speaking, however, the inventories of the Renaissance record obvious features that were readily visible.

There was therefore plenty of room for confusion and this was compounded by the fact that the terms used in each region were not necessarily the same for any given object, and even if the identical term were used in two regions, the spelling often differed – sometimes considerably. Patience and real familiarity with contemporary inventories will, however, show that the matter is not quite so confusing as it at first seems and that a framework of sorts can be established. What follows here is an attempt to provide just such a framework.

Textiles

These are usually described in three or four words. The raw materials of which woven fabrics were made are hardly ever mentioned. The fact that a material was of cotton [*bambagia*] is often noted, for some reason, but otherwise one mostly has to infer of what raw material a fabric was made. A silk is usually so described if it has no particular distinguishing features, if one cannot immediately say that it is a light taffeta [*cendalo*], a velvet [*velluto*] or a watered silk [e.g. *tabi*], all of which are of course terms describing technical features but terms that were widely used in general parlance as well.

The Italians use three words for 'cloth', in the most general sense of a piece of textile material – *tela*, *drappo* and *panno*. *Tela* was usually employed in reference to linen cloth and to canvas, ticking and that general class.[1] This is a fairly sure guide if it occurs in a description (e.g. *tela di renso* was linen cloth from Rheims). *Drappo* was much vaguer; it might be used for a silken material but some fine woollen materials were probably also embraced by this term.[2] *Panno* was often used in connection with woollen cloth but a linen might be called a *panno lino*. Sadly, therefore, these last two terms offer us little help.

Quite often the decoration is noted (e.g. it was striped or with figures) and usually the predominant colour is given. Some common materials seem to have derived their names from their colour [e.g. *panno bigello*, which was grey]. Generally speaking the names given to colours were subjective and imprecise, as is of course still the case today, unless a standard colour-code is ready to hand.

Within the textile trades and commerce, all kinds of niceties might be noted (technical, pattern, colour) that would be reflected in their specialist terminology. This was readily understood within the business but was far too subtle to be adopted generally.

Many materials derived their names from their provenance. Thus *celoni* came from Châlons and there were *perpignani* from Perpignan in southern France, but both *celoni* and *perpignani* were imitated in Italy and were sold under the same title, so that the term became generic – like 'Genoa velvet' which describes a class of material largely woven in Genoa in the seventeenth and eighteenth centuries that was also made elsewhere (e.g. at Lyons and in Spitalfields in England).

Silks

In 1476, as a means of controlling luxury consumption, the city fathers in Venice decreed that it was absolutely forbidden for citizens to have hangings and similar furnishings made from cloth of gold, cloth of silver, brocade, velvet, satin or *tabi* – that is, from very expensive materials made largely of silk – but that it was perfectly in order to use *taffeta*, *zendado*, and *ormesin* for the purpose.[1] Few Venetians took much notice of these regulations even though a fresh set was issued every few years but the list gives us some idea of which silk materials were considered sumptuous and which were relatively inexpensive. We still have taffeta today; it has a

74 A rich silken canopy

This sumptuous backcloth of silk may be of Near Eastern origin but is more likely to be an imitation of an Eastern silk, woven in Venice. The bowl of the canopy is of cloth of gold, lined with what looks like a velvet that is decorated with a pattern executed with applied gold braid. Small glass drops hang from each lappet.

Bergogone, *Madonna Enthroned* (detail), northern Italian, 1490
(*photograph: Fotowerkstatt, Staatliche Museen, Berlin*)

75 A Venetian silk canopy?

The artist who painted this picture had links with the Guild of Silk Weavers in Venice (he painted an *Annunciation* for their chapel in 1495) so he was presumably well aware of what the Guild's members could produce and will have noticed when a particular pattern was outstanding in design and quality. The silk shown here may look Turkish but is probably a *tour de force* of the Venetian silk-weaver's art of about 1512, which is when the picture was painted.

Cima de Conegliano, *Madonna, St John the Baptist and Mary Magdalen*, 1512
Musée du Louvre, Paris

74

75

plain weave and is usually of a single colour but could be striped, checked, or 'shot' which the Italians called *cangiante* because the colour changed as the material moved or was draped.[2] *Zendado* or *cendalo* was a lightweight form of taffeta much used for linings[3] while *ormesino* (the Venetians always tend to drop the terminal vowel) was a stouter material, probably with a small pattern (sprigs, stars and the like, maybe self coloured). Related to *zendado* was *terzanello*[4] which was often given a watered or *moiré* effect. *Tabi*, which was one of the prohibited materials and therefore was clearly altogether richer, could also be watered (indeed, it probably was in most cases as the word originally implied a wavy effect, which is why we still speak of 'tabby cats').[5] *Ormesino* might evidently also have a watered effect, as a reference in the Florentine records to *ermesino a onde* indicates.[6]

Some silks, probably taffetas, were apparently given a glaze which was imparted by applying a dressing of diluted gum arabic. If these were forerunners of the French *taffetas lustrés* (English 'lustrings') of the seventeenth and eighteenth centuries, the process will have been completed by drying the material over a mobile brazier while it was stretched on a frame.[7] The best *zendado* came from Florence while Bologna was famed for its taffetas but such materials were woven in many other places.

More costly than the silks discussed so far was satin [*raso*] which was and is also a plain material; it has a special weave which makes it exceptionally shiny. It was at first known by its Near Eastern name, *zetano* [hence our 'satin'] but soon came to be called *zetonino raso* and then simply *raso*. The satins of Milan and Lucca were widely admired at the end of our period.

Silk damask [*domaschino, damasco*] was a striking material somewhat higher up the cost-scale than satin to which it was and is related; the figure is produced by the contrast of satin with the reverse of satin weave. In 1450, at the Aragonese court at Naples, it was still necessary to list the material as *drap de seda ceamat domasqui* [silk cloth called *domasqui*].[8] It was usually of a single colour but could be of two. Silk damask came primarily from Venice and Genoa. Although it was available in the fifteenth century it was not until the sixteenth century that it came into wide use in the furnishing field, or so it seems (Pl. 313).

Gold and silver thread were naturally very expensive and, in order to save on these threads, it was sensible to insert the thread precisely where needed (i.e. not to have it spanning the whole width of the material, hidden away in the weave and only coming to the surface where the pattern demanded; this was wasteful). The expensive thread was wound on a broach or bobbin [*broccia*] and was then inserted into the silk at the appropriate places as the material was being woven, as an operation separate from the main weaving action of shuttle and loom. The process is known as brocading and is in a sense akin to embroidery; it has always been slow and therefore costly. Because at first brocading was chiefly carried out with gold or silver thread, the resulting 'brocades' were mostly embellished with these expensive effects. So *broccati* or *borcati*[9] could justifiably be called 'cloth of gold' (or 'silver', as the case may be) in most instances, and certainly seem to have been in general parlance, even though brocading might also be carried out with coloured silks as well. A particularly rich silk, which was frequently brocaded with gold, was *baldechino*, known in France as *baudequin* ['bodkin' in English]. The material was a speciality of Lucca in its heyday, when it was the chief centre of silk-weaving in Italy – during the fourteenth century[10] – but it continued in favour on into the sixteenth century. Both satin and damask could be brocaded with passages of pattern in gold thread,[11] as also could velvet, as we shall see.

In the second half of the sixteenth century a silk material called *brocatello* was developed which often had a strengthening weft of linen in its make-up. This of course made the material rather stiff, less pliant than other silks of comparable weight, so it was not suitable for draping but was excellent for hangings that were suspended flat against a wall. The patterns were commonly quite large for that reason. A list of Venetian silk products of 1587 includes *brocatello di due colori* [with two colours] and we find a *carpetta de brocadello di piu collori uxada* [a table-cover . . . of several colours, used; i.e. old] in an inventory of 1590.[12] A fine table-carpet of this date would often have been made for a particular table so that the main field fitted the top precisely, while four flaps fell down the sides – for all of which a stiff material was eminently well suited.

Camoca was also a rich figured silk, current before the beginning of the Renaissance and apparently a lightweight relation of *baldechino*.[13] The term seems to have fallen from use early in the fifteenth century but we find the word *camocato* instead.[14] What the relationship can have been is not yet clear but the term would seem to imply that the latter material had a *camoca* effect. If so we should probably be looking for a lightweight silk with a pattern of several colours that was *not* brocaded, either with gold or silver thread, or with coloured silk. The woollen (or, rather, worsted) material called camlet could have a similar colourful effect; in a Genoese bathroom of the 1450s was to be found a quilt of *ihameloti acamocati*.[15] Wardrobe lists of the time of Alfonso I of Aragon (d. 1458) show that at the Neapolitan court *chamocato* was a very expensive material.[16]

Velvets of silk [*velluti*] came plain or figured (Pl. 80), and some of them were among the very richest materials woven during the Renaissance. Florio*, writing in 1611, tells us that there were four classes of silk velvet – *alto basso, figurato, peloso,* and *riccio*. *Alto basso* must have been the kind with two depths of pile which allows the pattern to be stepped to produce a subtle modelling in relief. This material is one of the great *tours de force* of weaving.[17] *Peloso* velvet presumably had an especially long pile, which would make it the forerunner of what the French called *peluche* and we came to know as plush. Some very rich velvets had small loops of gold in the ground or peeping through the pile at intervals (Pl. 76); these formed the class called *riccio*, which means a loop although the word was of course easily confused with *ricco* [rich], a source of confusion the dealers did nothing to minimize. These looped effects were also stated to be *alluciolati*. Many velvets had a pattern executed in pile on a satin ground while a rather more elaborate type had a damask effect in the ground – *zetani vellutati* and *domasco vellutato*.[18] The patterns of some velvets were

76 Portrait showing no fewer than four, and maybe eight, silk materials

Behind the sitter hangs a superb silk velvet with a huge pattern that would make it suitable only for furnishing purposes, as here. It has a ground of silk damask, two heights of silk pile, and small gold loops in the pile. What may be a green watered silk hangs behind. The man's sleeves are also of velvet as is the covering of the X-frame chair (one can only see its armrest; see Pl. 199). Whether the table-carpet and his cap are also of velvet is unclear. Also of silk (taffeta) are the small pillows, while his embroidered doublet is of satin. In passing, one should also note his voluptuous gown of lynx-fur.

Moretto da Brescia, *Portrait of Count Sciarra Martinengo Cesaresco, 1526*
National Gallery, London (299)

76

stamped onto the pile by pressing it between a heated metal plate and a woodblock on which the pattern had been carved out in *intaglio*. Some bed-hangings at Perugia in 1582 were made of such a *velluto stampato* which was probably made locally by the small velvet-making industry established there.[19]

Velvets were also made on a small scale at Modena but the chief centres of production were Venice, Milan and Genoa. The term 'Genoa velvet' became generic for all velvets, wherever they were made, decorated with a large pattern, right down to the end of the eighteenth century, and it was widely recognized that no other centre could match the excellence of the black velvets woven there.[20] Velvet weaving was first practised in the Near East and it continued to be woven there right through the period. Much velvet came from or through Alexandria in the fourteenth and fifteenth centuries;[21] subsequently Turkey provided a great deal of the Near Eastern import into Italy. The latter largely came through Venice and must have been brought in chiefly for its novelty value, as Venice was perfectly capable of producing enough velvet on its own to meet the local demand and much more. The Doge Tommaso Mocenigo claimed that his native city made an annual profit of no less than two million ducats from its silk industry and that, already in 1423, there were sixteen thousand weavers in the city.[22]

Also of silk was *posta* which Florio* tells us was a narrow material suitable for women's garters but one may imagine that it had other uses – like making edgings, for instance. Borders could be contrived with silk lace [*trine*] which was an openwork strip laid onto a hanging, cushion-cover or table-carpet, either close to the edge or so as to disguise a seam (Pls 86, 216). Most fringes [*frangie*] were also of silk (or mixed with gold thread, in the more expensive varieties) and invariably had straight 'hangers' making the actual fringing, but the hangers could be of widely varying lengths; fringe with especially long hangers might have the latter gathered and then knotted to form spaced tassels (Pls 198, 203). Proper tassels [*fiocchi*] were likewise mostly of silk but once again could incorporate gold thread. Silk cord [*cordone di seta*] was used for suspending the bowls of *padiglioni* (p. 121) and for tie-backs, among other things. *I passimani* [trimmings] only became complex, however, in the later decades of the sixteenth century and, even so, were simple compared with those of the next century.

Veiling, an ultra-light material resembling fine netting, could be made of silk or linen, and the finest silk veils came from Bologna and Modena, with Perugia as runner-up. Such material was primarily used for dress purposes but we can see some very fine veiling thrown over the back of a *lettuccio* in the Botticelli painting reproduced in Pl. 161 and the hanging shown in Pl. 78 seems also to be of fine veiling which one can see through. It has a black stripe but veiling could be completely coloured while some silk veils were worked with gold. Thomas Coryat, visiting Venice in the early years of the seventeenth century, writes of the veils worn by Venetian women. 'These vailes are eyther blacke, or white, or yellowish'. The material was 'so thin and slight, that they may easily look through it. For it is made of a pretty slender silke, and very finely curled [spun].'[23] Pietro Aretino put it more charmingly. '*Sotto il nero trasparente velo*', he wrote of Venetian women, '*veggonsi in carne gli angioli del cielo*' [Beneath the black transparent veil are the angels of heaven incarnate].[24]

It should be noted that taffeta could be painted. Some bed-curtains of *taffeta bianche dipinte* were listed among the wall-hangings and bed-furnishings in the Palazzo Medici in Florence in 1456 (Medici Invt.).

77

77 A local weave

The inwoven band of blue stylized ornament betrays the Italian origin of this long tablecloth which had a similar band at the opposite end. Cloths with such unmistakable borders are often thought to have been woven in Perugia but they were certainly woven in more than one place and are usually described as being of *tela nostrale*, woven 'in our country', in contradistinction from the linens that came from the Low Countries – which were considered to be generally finer. This cloth, however, is fine enough to be used for the *Last Supper*, associated with some handsome refectory seating and delicate glass vessels that presumably come from Venice and were not cheap.

Domenico Ghirlandaio, *The Last Supper* (detail), S. Marco, Florence, *c*.1480
Photograph: Alinari Archives

Linen, cotton and hempen materials

Prodigious amounts of linen are listed in the inventories of great Italian houses in the Renaissance period. Having quantities of fine linen, and being able to display it at the table and on the best beds, was clearly a telling symbol of status because it was expensive and had to be brought from far afield – from northern France, Flanders and, later on, Holland.

The best linen came from Rheims (or, rather, was made in the surrounding province and sold through that city) and the inventories frequently refer to *tela di renso* or *di lenso*. Cambrai was almost as important a centre of this trade, hence the *tela di cambri* or *di cambraia* of the inventories. These terms became generic for the finest class of linen cloth, much of which may well have been woven elsewhere, by the late fifteenth century.[1]

Wherever it was woven, most of this fine material was plain but the cloth used for table-linen often had an all-over, regular pattern of lozenges (Pls 184, 237). This was called 'diaper' in England but it seems likely that the linen described in Italian inventories as being *alla parigina* [in the Parisian manner] was of this class, although one cannot at present be sure.[2] Much more elaborate were linen cloths with patterns produced by a damask weave (p. 70). Linen damask had certainly made its appearance in Italy by 1430 as it is mentioned in an inventory of that date (Guinigi Invt.) The illustrious Paolo Guinigi, tyrant of Lucca, had fourteen *tovalliole domaschine* [damask napkins], each four *braccia* in length, in a small room near his dining-room, and there were many rolls of material, stored in linen-chests, awaiting cutting up and making into napkins, all described as being French and *lavorata alla domaschina*.[3] In France, incidentally, much fine linen is described as being in the *façon de Venise* but such a term does not occur in Italian documents and linen was not woven in Venice. It may well be that the first linen damasks reached Europe through Venice, however.[4]

Linen was woven elsewhere in Italy, on the other hand. Some of it may have been of fine quality, sold under the intentionally misleading names of *tela di renso* or *di cambraia*, but most was never quite as fine as the Flemish or Burgundian products. When not masquerading as imports from northern Europe, these Italian weaves were simply called *tela nostrale* [of our own making] or *paesana* [from the countryside]. If it was actually woven on the premises, it might be described as *tela di casa*. The better qualities of Italian linens came from Florence, Siena, Cremona, Perugia, Pozzuoli near Naples, Viterbo and no doubt several other places. Some of the more elaborate Italian products often had a stripe across each end, mostly blue but sometimes brown, sometimes taking the form of a formalized design of animals or flowers (Pls 81, 237). These are today often called 'Perugia towels' but they must have been made in many places and they are *tovaglie* [i.e. napkins] rather than towels in the English sense.[5]

Rather coarser was *tela di revo* which, however, came in *sottile* and *sottilissime* [fine and very fine] qualities; it was used for bed-linen of the rougher sort. *Tela di sorenghine* seems to have been an even coarser material perhaps related to buckram, which is today a very coarse linen material stiffened with glue. In the sixteenth century, on the other hand, it does not seem to have been stiffened as it was used for clothes and other purposes requiring it to be drapable. It was also rather more classy, it seems. Florio*, writing at the end of the century, says '*Bucherame* [was] anciently ... taken for the finest linnen cloth'. He also tells us that it was called *Tela di Sangallo*.

Mattresses and the like had to be made of a stout material which the quills of feathers or the straw used for stuffing could not penetrate. Canvas [*canevaccio*] was used for the roughest variety but finer materials like *boldro* or *bordo*, which we would now call ticking, was more commonly used for this purpose in houses of some standing. Such materials were often striped (Pls 111) and seem to have come from Naples and from France, thirty-one Medici mattress-covers of 1553 being made with *tela di rovano* [from Rouen]. *Pignolato*, also frequently met with in the inventories, was a hempen or flaxen material of similar character, used for mattress-covers.

Some materials were made with both linen and cotton yarns. Once such mixed fabric was *boccaccino* which seems to have come from North Africa (Tripoli); it was much used for linings.[6] So was *cotanino* which came from Naples and Spain (Aragon) and could be mistaken for a silk material. A fine ivory casket lined with green *cotanino* was noted in a Milanese inventory of 1420 (Trivulzio Invt.). *Dobletto* or *dobretto* was another such mixed stuff. It was clearly a rather pleasing material; the *padiglione* of a Medici bed in 1553, of red velvet with a satin ground, had a lining of red and green *dobretto di Napoli* [from Naples; Medici Invt., Florence, 1553]. Another Medici bed of some forty years later had hangings made entirely of *dobretto*, again showing that this material must have been quite presentable.[7]

Materials made solely of cotton were also to some extent used for furnishing purposes, particularly for summer bed-hangings and coverlets, since cotton fabrics tend to be light and cool. Plain cotton cloth was called *bambagina* (from *bambagie*, cotton 'bombast'). Cotton tended to be left white to preserve its cool appearance but dimity [*dimito*], which we may associate with white bed-hangings, often came coloured.[8] *Bambaxina*, as it was sometimes spelt, could have a pile which made it a cotton velvet like modern velour and presumably therefore related to those 'fustians' (also a cotton material) which had a pile,[9] notably the 'Naples fustian tripp' which was being imitated at Norwich by the 1550s (although probably in worsted rather than cotton, making it a woollen velvet which is what most *trippes* were).[10] *Fustagni* did not by any means always have a pile, as we all know from 'jeans' which was 'Jeans fustian' (i.e. from Genoa). The finest fustians came from Milan.

Cotton materials came to Italy, from the Near East and even from India. The *padiglione* of *mussolo biancho* mentioned in the Correr inventory from Venice in 1584 is likely to have been a muslin, used here as a mosquito-net. A very splendid quilt in the Medici collection in 1553 (Medici Invt., Florence), had a ground of *tela di Portogalo dipinta* [painted Portuguese cotton, or possibly linen but definitely not a woollen

78

78 Silk veiling used for furnishing

Normally associated with dress, veiling might also be used for making mosquito nets or for protecting mirrors from flies. In this case the sitter has a canopy made of this fine material which is almost transparent. It has undoubtedly been included in this portrait to inform the viewer that Anna Eleonora Sanvitale, the sitter in this portrait, is a very fine lady. Note also the trimming of her skirt.

Gerolamo Mazzola-Bedoli of Parma, Portrait of Anna Eleonora Sanvitale, *c.* 1540
Galleria Sabauda, Turin (photograph: Scala)

or silken material]. This was almost certainly an Indian *chint*, or painted cotton, a class of material that first reached Europe in any quantity in Portuguese vessels, passing through Portuguese ports on its way to rich and discerning customers, seeking rarity and exotica, right across the Western world. However, *chints* could also come to the Mediterranean via Egypt, and some Medici beds hung with *tele banbagine dipinte* which had been captured in some Alexandrian galleys in 1592 are very likely to have been materials of this kind which were still at this time regarded as amazing as well as delightful.[11]

We noticed that lace might be made of silk, or of gold or silver thread (p. 72); but it could also be made of linen and, indeed, since the early seventeenth century, most people have understood the term to mean this variety even though laces of silk or metal thread continued to be made, albeit in relatively small quantities, right through to modern times.

Linen lace evolved during the late decades of the fifteenth century although lace recognizable to us as such was not developed much before the middle of the sixteenth century and only really came into its own as a major form of fashionable trimming shortly before 1600 (Pl. 367).[12] It was in the main developed from cutwork which involved cutting small apertures in the woven ground of a linen cloth (e.g. a sheet, pillow-case, handkerchief or napkin), the apertures being excised so as to form a pattern. The apertures were then trimmed and ornamented with needlework executed with white linen thread. This 'needlepoint' might be further embellished with work built up into relief ornament. The net-like patterns worked in these techniques were given the name *reticella* which, as Florio* tells us, meant 'any fine or small net or caule worke' (*rete* being the Italian for net while 'caule' was the English term for the kind of net used for women's coifs).

Cutwork patterns could be worked in the middle of a large piece of cloth or might be worked as borders or inserts.[13] Where two or more pieces of linen had to be joined, the seam was sometimes filled with such a strip of openwork. In the sixteenth and early seventeenth centuries ornamental linen borders often consisted of a row of tooth-like projections which the Spanish called *puntas*. These *ponti*, as the Italians called them, were first formed by cutting such an indented border from a strip of linen, excising the apertures, and working it all up with a needle. Patterns for such cutwork 'points' were published in some quantity in sixteenth-century Venice (Pls 67, 223, 289). One was by Giovanni Andrea Vavassori (about 1545) on the title-page of which it was explained that the gentle reader (it was directed at *Belle et Virtuose Donne* [beautiful and virtuous ladies]) would find inside 'various types of edgings with which one may decorate any lady or any sort of bed with *ponti tagliati* [points of cutwork] or any other kind of point'.[14] An important class of needlepoint lace came eventually to be known in France as *point de Venise* [Venetian point] but already in the sixteenth century *reticella di venezia* formed a recognizable class of such proto-lace. Dentilated borders were however used long before this. Mention is made in the Este inventories of 1436, for instance, of sheets trimmed with *vergadi a dentexelo* [borders of *denticello*].

The points or tongues were next worked entirely with the needle, no longer relying on a woven ground for a basis. Such lace was worked on a parchment pattern but was in a sense created in the air, hence the term *punto in aria*.[15] Lace could also be produced by means of bobbins, usually made of bone.[16] In modern Italian the generic name for all linen laces is *merletti* which, as Florio* explains means 'little battlements' (once again a reference to the points, which can also be said to resemble the crenellations topping a castle wall) but 'also a kind of bone lace', he adds. Strictly speaking bobbin-lace should indeed be called *merletti* whereas needlepoint-laces should more probably be called *dentelli* – from the word *denticelli* that was current already by the 1430s, as we have shown.

Laces might equally well have been discussed under the heading 'Needlework' but, because many came as strips of ornament ready for attaching to other materials, we have preferred to include them here.

Woollen materials

If we were vague about the character of many of the named varieties of silk and linen materials, our bewilderment is even worse when it comes to trying to identify the different types of woollen cloth, especially the less expensive varieties. For an enormously wide variety of woollen stuffs was available in Renaissance Italy and only the drapers who dealt in them will have been able to recognize for sure the different kinds on the market.

Woollen cloth was made in most parts of Italy, much of it for local use. Materials of higher quality were woven principally in the north – in Tuscany, on the Lombard plain, and among the foothills of the Alps. In 1402 Florence went to war with Pisa over the wool trade and came out victorious; a very high proportion of the Florentine citizenry was engaged in the cloth trade in all its branches, including working over and improving upon cloth that had come in from France and Britain. The products of the Lombard centres were mostly sold through Milan which also handled woollen yarn brought from all over Europe before passing it on to the weaving centres that included Parma, Firenzuola, Pavia, Brescia and Cremona down on the plains, and Bergamo, Como, Udine and Pordenone up country. Verona and Vicenza were also important in this respect and Venice became so in the sixteenth century. A kind of cloth much referred to in the inventories was *panno romagnuolo* which came from the Romagna and was presumably therefore marketed through Bologna although the name may have become a generic term for a relatively coarse material that was easily identifiable.

Woollen cloth was also imported from places as distant as Turkey, the Algarve, Britain and North Africa. Some seats described in that romantic fantasy, the *Hypnerotomachia*, were covered in *erythreo* (P. 215). In the English translation of a century later this is given as 'tawny' and Florio, in his dictionary of 1611*, tells us that *Erithrea* was 'a kind of red wooll that sheep beare in Asia', so perhaps those Venetian seats, which in this respect can not have been entirely imaginary, were upholstered in a red cloth brought all the way from Eritrea, which admittedly is in East Africa but had to be brought to Italy either through Egypt or Asia Minor.

Apparently easy to recognize were cloths from Perpignan which must have been the product of an extensive area of south-western France; *pirpignano* is certainly mentioned often in the inventories, primarily in connection with garments. No doubt it was imitated in Italy once it had become a sought-after class of material.

A cloth known as *bigello* or *panno bigello* was a commonly used coarse material of a grey colour.[1] *Scotto* was a material like frieze, and *botana* was like flannel; both were occasionally used for bed-hangings in sixteenth-century Venice.[2] A robust worsted material also much used for furnishings in the sixteenth century was camlet, known in Italy as *ciambellotto* (the first letter in some spellings being 'z' or 't' instead of 'c'). This had a marked ribbed effect which could be given a *moiré* or watered finished; a Florentine treatise of 1453 actually refers to this process, explaining that *Ciambellotti . . . e tessuti se gli da l'acqua che fa il marezzo, e poi si da il mangano* [a material which is watered to make it shine and which is then put through the mangle or callander].[3] This was the process to which the silk called *tabi* was also subjected (p. 70). Indeed, camlet sometimes looked very like silk, to such an extent that children and slaves in Genoa, in 1504, were forbidden to wear various materials *comprehendo lo ihameloto lo quale se intende esser seta* [including camlet which is meant to look like silk].[4] It should be added that some 'camlets' were actually made with silk, in Venice, during the fifteenth century,[5] but Venetians otherwise spoke of *zambellotto o panno simile di lana* [or similar materials of wool].[6] The material originally came from Asia Minor and Venetians had produced them at their trading stations in Armenia. Camel-hair may have been used in the earliest camlets but other forms of hair (notably that of the Angora goat) came to be used later and, by the sixteenth century, most camlets were made with worsted yarn. Materials with a *moiré* effect are depicted in numerous Flemish tapestries of the late fifteenth and early sixteenth centuries at which stage it was primarily used for costume. Some camlets seem to have had an in-woven pattern (i.e. they were figured), if a reference to *ihameloti acamocati* of 1459 can be taken to mean that this particular piece of camlet was decorated in a *camoca*-like manner (p. 70).[7]

Very common, and often of high quality, was 'say' [*saia*], a material for which Norwich became famous in the sixteenth century but which was principally a product of the Low Countries, notably Bruges [*saia de broza* in some Italian inventories].[8] It also came from Orléans [*de orliensi*] and was imitated in Florence [*sagia di Fiorenza*] (Requesens Invt. 1561 and Odoni Invt. 1555). Say was a fine cloth with a twill weave that produced a distinctive diagonal ribbing. We are now faced with the difficulty that *una saia* was clearly the term used for some sort of furnishing item and, moreover, that such were not necessarily made of 'say' or, indeed, of wool. A *saia* of purple and white silk [*di seta paonaza et biancha*] lined with linen in a Sienese inventory of 1483 (Tura Invt.) is a particularly good example of this transposition of the word which, on the analogy with *sargia* (discussed below), was probably a form of coverlet or blanket.

Serge [*sargia*] was essentially a heavier version of say, also embodying the distinctive twill weave. It clearly came as a cloth (in a roll or 'bolt') but must also have been made up as a furnishing item, presumably rectangular and therefore once again taking the form of a blanket or coverlet – in the first place, at any rate – as it is so often associated with beds. A Florentine inventory of 1424 gives us *1 sargia al letto* [on the bed] several times, for instance (Uzzano Invt.), and Boccaccio has a character raise the *sargia* off the bed to reveal the sleeping forms of his daughter and her lover, in one of his steamier novels [*levo alto la sargia della quale il letto era fasciato*].[9] The French, who were the principal weavers of serge, spoke likewise of *sarges de lit* [for beds] and it is probable that such were distinctive furnishing items; Italian inventories show that they were colourful and that some were striped or checked[10] but it may well be that some *sarge* were quite elaborate and highly decorative, which would explain why they so often seem to receive special mention.

Which brings us to the question of *draps de haute lisse*. Textile historians explain that there are two kinds of tapestry (a well known form of figured woollen furnishing material already discussed, that woven on the upright loom [*haute lisse*] and that woven on a loom lying flat [*basse lisse*]. The position of the loom makes very little difference to the appearance of the resulting fabric, which is distinctive. At Tournai, which is the key city in this question, all the famous weavers of tapestry called themselves *tapissiers* and the *tapissiers* of that city marched, on festive occasions, under a different banner to the *hautelisseurs* who must therefore presumably have been making something that was not tapestry.[11] The 1408 regulations for the Tournai weavers make specific reference to *draps nommés haultliche* [cloths called *hautelisse*] which had to be made of good linen (for the warps, presumably) and good wool, and were to be twenty-eight Tournai ells in length.[12] Proper tapestries were made of wool only and did not necessarily have to be of a standard *length* (implying something long and narrow) even if in practice they were often woven to standard *sizes*. Moreover tapestries proper were not referred to as *draps*, which implies lengths of cloth.

Regulations of 1491 show that the Tournai *hautelisseurs* wove cloths that could be striped [*draps royés*], decorated with *oeillets* [eyelets which probably meant small octagons, each with a fleuret in the centre], or chevrons [*quievrons*].[13] Furthermore (and here we start coming back to serge and say), in 1524 the *hautelisseurs* began to march with the say-makers in street parades, while the *tapissiers* went with the dyers. By the 1530s, however, the say-makers were getting too big for their boots, according to the *hautelisseurs*, who complained that the former were now also making figured materials which required a loom of some intricacy.[14] That the *hautelisseurs* already used such a loom is proved by a reference to one of their number in 1505 having some looms and some *harnas* [harness] and the last is only required for a draw-loom, a machine necessary only when regular repeating patterns of some complexity are to be woven.[15] So the *hautelisseurs* must have been users of the draw-loom, a piece of machinery on which elaborate repetitive designs could be produced. It should therefore not surprise us to find references in the Tournai archives to figured *hautelisse* products – six cushions *à hommes sauvages* [with wild men: 1400], a dozen more *ouvret de personnages* [worked with human

figures; 1438] and six *ouvrez de chierfz* [with stags], not to speak of cloths with coats of arms on them.[16]

Among the products of the *hautelisse* weavers were *sarges*. A man bequeathed, in 1460, *une chambre de haulteliche, le sarge, xii coussins, iii banquiers et ung drap de couche qui sont d'un ouvrage* [the hangings for a bedchamber as well as a *sarge*, twelve cushions, three bench-covers and a coverlet for a couch with are all of the same work, i.e. *en suite*].[17] The *sargiers* and the *hautelisseurs* sided together against the *tapissiers* and *marcheteurs* (another group of weavers) in a dispute in 1491.[18] That *sarges* could also bear intricate patterns is borne out by the report of a weaver who had died in 1481 while making *une sarge de l'histoire de Nabucodonosor* [with the story of Nebuchadnezzar], a design that must have involved a complicated weaving process.[19] French *sarges* were attractive objects, it is clear, suitable for cheerful occasions. Boccaccio, for example, had a master of ceremonies prepare a location for a rather private party out of doors by setting up beds in bosky dells and surrounding them with hangings including some of French *sarge* [*letti … di sarge francesche e di capoletti intorniati e chiuse*].[20]

By 1534 there were over 600 looms active at Tournai weaving *hautelisse* products that included *sarges*, as well as looms worked by the *sayetteurs* whose products could be sufficiently elaborate to seem like a threat to the *hautelisseurs*, or so they claimed. By 1550 other centres rivalled Tournai in this trade – notably Brussels, Lille, Amiens and Bruges. Much of the export trade from these centres, and many smaller places nearby, went through the city of Châlons-sur-Marne and this lent its name to a distinctive material that came to be known to the Italians as *celone*.[21]

It would seem that the Italian term *celoni* embraced the more glamorous forms of the imported *sarges*.[22] Under the Milanese sumptuary regulations of 1498, citizens could no longer arrange for their wives to lie-in, after the birth of a child, in a bedchamber furnished with hangings of silk. They were, however, allowed hangings of *celone* worked with silk [*exceptis celonis etiam seta laboratis*],[23] which suggests they came next down the scale of furnishing fabrics, in richness and therefore expense, after the silks and were themselves quite elaborate. Although *celoni*, like *sargie*, could lie on a bed,[24] they evidently also served as wall-hangings. For instance, round a bed in Genoa in 1456 was suspended a sky-blue *celone* with the arms of the family [*pecium unum claroni telle cellestie circa lectum cum armis*; Vivaldi Invt.] and in the very same year a Florentine inventory recorded *une sargia da muro* [for the wall] which was embroidered with the family arms.[25] Several inventories of the period refer to their being *diversorum colorum*, as if they were striking on this count. Indeed, so much in favour were these handsome cloths that they eventually came to be imitated in Italy. Looms for weaving *zaoloni* were set up at Ferrara in 1436;[26] they seem also to have been made in Venice and in Siena, while a large table in the Palazzo Medici in Florence in 1532 was covered with *un celone nostrale* which must have been a local product (Medici Invt.). Already in 1335 the Florentine statutes were listing *celoni* together with *sargie* but that does not of course mean they were woven there at that stage.[27] In trying to identify the *celoni* that figure so prominently in Italian quattrocento documents, therefore, we should be looking for a large panel of material, big enough to cover a bed, decorated with a regularly repeated pattern of some size, colourful and perhaps furnished with an integral woven border (Pl. 91).

Some cloths of this class bore painted decoration, like the *sarza rossa dipinta in fiandra* [red sargia painted in Flanders] which was to be seen in Pierfrancesco de' Medici's room at Cafaggiolo in Tuscany in 1498 (Cafaggiolo Invt.). It is perhaps worth recalling that, at Hardwick Hall in Derbyshire in 1601, there was a set of tapestries for hanging on the walls of the great *sala* on the *piano nobile* but that, for summer use, was provided a suite of 'eight peeces of woollen cloth stayned [i.e. painted] with frett and storie and silk flowers'.[28] These were very large hangings with a strapwork border embellished with silk floral ornament, with figure subjects in the main field. Pierfrancesco's hanging could well have been a forerunner of such sumptuous furnishings.

Another class of woollen material, one that was to become important in the seventeenth century and virtually epitomized the High Victorian period, was woollen velvet – commonly called plush (or, today, quite misleadingly, mohair). This was mainly produced in the Low Countries and was not all that much used in Renaissance Italy for furnishing purposes, it seems. It was of course admirable for seat-covers and cushions except in hot weather.

The English name for this material was 'mockado' and a list of import duties in 1582 gives it as 'of Flanders making'.[29] An Italian reference to *muchiardi larghi di Lilla* would seem to concern just such a material, from Lille.[30] The fact that these were large, and perhaps therefore had large patterns, suggests they could have been a furnishing material. In French the term was rendered as *moucade* and later as *moquette*. Another term for woollen velvet was *trippe* (French) which became *trippa* in Italian.[31] This was one of the materials produced by the *hautelisseurs* of Tournai.[32] Knowing that many of the materials woven by this class of weaver were made on a draw-loom, we can be fairly certain that many *trippes*, and the closely related *moucades*, had quite elaborate patterns and were extremely colourful.[33] *Muchaiardi* were also woven in North Africa [*di Barberia*],[34] and *muchiari* of silk were for a while woven at Ferrara.[35]

Plushes tended to have longer pile than normal woollen velvets, if the term were being applied correctly. Sigismondo Chigi had a garment of some sort of *panno peluccio* in 1525.[36]

Among Lucrezia Borgia's *Coperte da leto* [coverlets] in 1503 (Borgia Invt., Ferrara) was one of red *Lanna pelosa* [wool with a pile surface, or a hairy woollen material]. This could have been a woollen velvet but was more probably a rather shaggy bed-cover often called a *bernia* or *shernia*. The word is derived from the name for Ireland, Hibernia, and, as Florio* explains, it meant 'an Irish rug or mantle'.[37] Such coverlets are discussed with other bedclothes (p. 162) where we note that a *schiavina* was another form of shaggy coverlet that could be very attractive, coming from Slavonia, the modern Yugoslavia.[38] Another pile material associated with a bed would seem to have been '*savastina*'.[39] Shaggy coverlets of this general class are to be seen in Pls 119 and 174.

Related to these long-haired materials are pile carpets, which were discussed in connection with floor-coverings (pp. 64–5). Their general conformation is familiar to everyone and it is appreciated that they consist of a ground-weave onto which the pile is knotted by hand. Compared with a *sberne*, the pile of 'a carpet' is relatively short and, in the finest weaves, very short indeed. Most such carpets came from the Near East; a few came from Spain; and it seems that small workshops producing carpets were established at Naples and Ferrara for a while. In the Near East, carpets were also woven with patterns similar to those of pile-carpets but using the tapestry-weaving technique instead. These, now generally called *kilims*, may have been known in Italy during the Renaissance.[40] Carpets were commonly used as table-covers as well as floor-coverings, especially in the sixteenth century.

This brings us to tapestries, the last major group of furnishing materials that we need include in this brief survey. We have already considered this important class when discussing wall-hangings (p. 48) but it must be remembered that tapestry-woven materials were also used for seat-covers, coverlets or made up into cushions. It remains merely to remind readers that the tapestry-weaving technique is different from that of other weaving systems. No shuttles are shot from one side of the material to the other to form a weft; the material is built up in patches to suit the design and the result is an easily-recognizable fabric with which most people are familiar. The technique has nothing to do with embroidery.

Tapestries were often listed separately, in Italian Renaissance inventories, and anyway usually are among the first items mentioned in any group of furnishings where they were present. But it needs to be said that they represented only a small portion of the textile component of a household's furnishing. They were only to be seen in some principal rooms and many other textile materials were visible at the same time in the same surroundings; moreover plenty of textiles were to be seen in all the other rooms where tapestries had no part to play. This present survey seeks to some extent to redress the balance, to show that many other classes of textile material played an important role in the furnishing of a great Italian Renaissance household.

Needlework

Decoration wrought with the needle played a far greater part in the embellishment of Italian Renaissance rooms of the better sort than is generally realized. It might be seen on textile furnishings of many kinds. Most fine linen, for instance, had needlework decoration of some kind, be it a neatly hemmed edge, a worked border, a band of embroidered ornament near the ends, or cutwork trimming. This was particularly the case with bed-linen (notably pillow-cases and sheets; Pls 64, 175, 216) but a certain amount of table-linen was also decorated in such ways (particularly napkins and table-cloths but also *guardanappi* and other forms of hand-towel; Pls 104, 223). The cloths that were thrown over tables used for purposes other than dining (i.e. table-carpets) might also

79 Turkish rug used as a table-carpet

St Jerome sits writing in his comfortable study with his treasured possessions massed around him. The rug will also have been a prized item. This painting by Domenico Ghirlandaio of 1480 clearly shows an Anatolian rug but it is not of a very common pattern.

Domenico Ghirlandaio, *St Jerome*, Ognisanti, Florence
Photograph: Scala

80 Do we here see a *celone*?

The nature of the woollen (or rather, worsted) material known as *celone* has still not been determined to the satisfaction of textile historians but it was striking and was not inexpensive. *Celoni* were often striped but the richest varieties could be figured (see p. 76): They at first came from the Low Countries but, later, imitations were woven in Italy. Perhaps the striped material shown here is an example of such a home-grown product. Seen here in association with two superb silks, and used under the feet of the enthroned Madonna herself, this material must at any rate have been considered rather special by the artist.

Giorgione, *Castelfranco Madonna* (detail), Castelfranco, Veneto, 1500–02
Photograph: Scala

80

have an embroidered border or a needleworked edge (Pls 186, 217, 376) and some were 'worked' all over, no doubt. A favourite vehicle for the display of embroidery was the cushion (Pl. 179); the same applied to its un-stuffed relation, the bench-cover. Bed-hangings, too, were often sumptuously decorated with fine embroidery, particularly the valances hanging down from the edge of the tester; as beds played such a dominant part in decoration of smart bedchambers, their hangings were often remarked upon (Pls 148, 156, 172, 283). Wall-hangings were likewise not infrequently decorated with embroidery which could be very rich indeed, vying with woven tapestry as the most splendid form of wall-decoration.

Some idea of the application of skill that might be brought to bear on an especially sumptuous suite of embroideries can be gained from the case of two complete sets of embroidered silk bed-hangings [*recami de apparamenti di seda*][1] which were commissioned in 1457 for two Este bedchambers at Ferrara. The task was given to a couple of Milanese 'master-broderers' brought in specially to work on these two suites [*lavarare in li ricami di dui apparamenti da leto*]. The two men, Zohanne di Corri and Gabrile Bolate, both of Milan, had a host of assistants (all men)

including one from the Low Countries (Giacomo d'Olanda) and one from Burgundy (Antonio da Borgogna). The well-known artist, Cosmè Tura, had to provide designs for the Este court embroiderers, but these particular sets may have been designed by Gerardo Costa, a second-line designer-painter much engaged in drawing ornament, but who also executed full-scale schemes for the Este residences.[2] Exactly a century later Ercole II d'Este visited Venice where he kept a town house in which there were some embroidered hangings that were clearly quite exceptional. They were described as being very large 'of gold, silver and of silk worked with the needle' [*grandissimi panni … d'oro, d'argento et di seta lavorati ad ago*] with human figures, animals, trees and plants – all of such an incredible richness that the viewer was stupefied at the sight of such beauty and the delicacy of the workmanship which had been that of a large number of hands [*richezza inestimabile … da stupore a vedere la bellezza del' opera et la sottilezza del lavoro …*].[3]

Really sumptuous embroidery was executed in professional workshops, and no doubt much routine decoration of a regular character on table- and bed-linen was also produced in similar but less ambitious establishments.

81

Making a fine show

Two Turkish rugs are draped over the balustrade of the *loggia* and its approach on a festive occasion. They were probably otherwise laid over tables but, at around this time (the fresco was painted about 1511), carpets began once again to be used on the floor – as they had been when they first reached Europe and until the second quarter of the fifteenth century, it seems. Carpets of this type are called 'small-patterned Holbein carpets' by textile historians; the pattern was very popular and some experts believe they may have been woven in the Ottoman territories in southern Europe. On this occasion the family were dining in their open *loggia* when someone dropped a tumbler over the edge. The miracle, for which St Anthony was evidently responsible, was that the glass remained intact after hitting the ground. The diners view the occurrence with suitable amazement. Note the classical head in its roundel and the iron tie-bars that strengthen the arcade.

Follower of Girolamo da Santa Croce, fresco in the Antisacrestia, S. Antonio, Padua
Photograph: Alinari Archives

But needlework could also be done in the home, and inventories quite often reveal evidence of such activity. For example there were *dui barri per ricamari* [two bars (rollers?) for embroidery] which may have been embroidery-frames (or parts of such) in the Palermitan house of Don Berlinghieri Requesens in 1561 (Requesens Invt.). We can see an embroidery-frame in use in Pl. 375. If the frame were large it could be rested on a pair of trestles, as the woodcut reproduced in Pl. 83 shows.

Evidence that needlework was thought an entirely suitable pastime for high-born ladies is provided by an early fifteenth-century bronze medallion on which Paola Malatesta, the wife of Gianfrancesco Gonzaga, first Marquis of Mantua, is shown working with a companion at an embroidery-frame.[4] A certain Caterina Cantona of Milan, described as a *nobildonna*, was renowned for her ability to work a pattern so that it appeared identically on both faces of the material [*cuce con tale arte che il punto appare dall'una come dall'altra parte*], according to a sixteenth-century historian.[5] That such activity was widespread, if not quite so proficiently executed, is implied by Anton Francesco Doni when, explaining the function of a *sala*, he says that women often stand in the widow-embrasures of these large rooms as the light there is good and it is an ideal place to execute delicate work with the needle [*la Donne si stanno a piedi delle finestre, si per vedere a lavorare con l' Agole cose sottili*].[6]

It was presumably in the first place in order to assist such domestic embroiderers that pattern-books with designs for needlework began to be published in the sixteenth century. Perhaps the earliest printed Italian pattern-book for embroiderers was Giovanni Antonio Tagliente's *Opera*

nova . . . intitolata esempio di raccami [A new work . . . entitled examples of embroidery], first published in Venice in 1527. The second edition of 1530 actually states that the intention was to teach women to embroider [*che insegna a le donne a racammare*]. In the same way, Domenico da Sera goes so far as to claim, in his handbook of 1543, that he seeks to teach all noble and delightful young ladies how to embroider [*si insegna a tutte le nobile & leggiadre giovanette di . . . reccamare*].[7]

Such pattern-books were probably of little use to professional embroiderers; the designs are likely to reflect the sort of work they had been executing for some years. Nevertheless, some of these books contain designs that it would require considerable skill to carry out. For example some of the patterns in Giovanni Ostaus' *La vera perfettione del disegno di varie sorti de recami* [The true perfection in the design of various kinds of embroidery] of 1567 are very elaborate and would require great dexterity in terms of modelling and shading to execute.[8] Osthaus was a German printer and publisher working in Venice. Although he claimed the patterns in this book were *fatto nuovamente* [newly made], he had in fact copied several German and Italian designs as well as devising a number himself. His publication reminds us that many patterns of this sort could be useful to artisans in other fields, not just to amateur embroiderers. By the same token, designs of all kinds (e.g. for inlaid woodwork) could be helpful to a professional embroiderer who would usually be perfectly capable of adapting a design to suit his own purposes. As we shall see, patterns were also provided by professional designers (including sometimes artists of considerable stature) to satisfy specific commissions in the field of embroidery. We have mentioned Cosmè Tura, working at Ferrara; Perino del Vaga also designed embroidered bed-hangings and Vasari mentions Raffaelino del Garbo in connection with needlework.[9] The ability of Antonio Pollaiuolo in this direction can be judged from a glance at Pl. 175. The best part of a century later (1584), Jacopo Ligozzi, painter and designer attached to the Medici court, supplied embroidery designs for Bianca Capello to execute; she was first the mistress and then, by this time, the second wife of the Grand-Duke Ferdinand.[10] Does any of her work survive?

It is the professional workshops which interest us more, in the present connection. The outstanding centre for fine embroidery was Milan which reached the height of artistic and technical achievement in the sixteenth and early seventeenth centuries. Brantôme spoke of *les bons brodeurs de Milan*, and when Andrea Doria (d.1560), the chief citizen of Genoa, was to welcome the Duchess of Lorraine to his house, he ordered from Milan an especially sumptuous bed which sported wonderful carving, and silk hangings decorated with extremely rich silk trimmings and striking tassels of gold and silver thread – its richness owing much to the skill of Milanese embroiderers.[11] An embroiderer named Girolamo Delfinone is known to have worked for Doria and perhaps made this astonishing bed; he was active in the 1530s. His son, Scipione, worked for the King of Spain and for Henry VIII of England; he flourished around 1550. We have

already mentioned Caterina Cantona, a Milanese woman of noble birth, who is said to have invented a special stitch which produced the pattern on both faces of the ground material. Her praises were sung by Torquato Tasso in his famous *Gerusalemme liberata* (1581). Charles VIII of France (d.1498) called Milanese embroiderers to work for him in Paris – including one Pantaléon Comte [Conti?], *ouvrier en broderie*, and his wife. In 1530 there was published in France *La Fleur de la Science de Pourtraicture, Patrons de Broderie, Façon arabique et ytalique*, [patterns for embroidery in the moresque and italic style], written by one Francisque Pellegrin.[12] It is usual to equate the author with Francesco di Pellegrino, the Tuscan painter who assisted Rosso at Fontainebleau and is mentioned several times by Vasari. But it is worth noting that one Antonia Pellegrini, established in Milan, was so accomplished an embroideress that she was given the task of working the altarcloth for the Cathedral, and it seems rather more likely that our Francisque was an expatriate member of an important Milanese family of embroiderers, some members of which would certainly have been able to draw such patterns with ease.[13]

In the Doria inventory (Doria Invt., Genoa, 1561) there are many references to linen sheets and pillowcases with embroidery executed in Milan [*recami fatti a Milano*] which could be black, red or blue. There is also mention of Spanish embroidery and Florentine, the last being white on white [e.g. *lenzoli di tela d'olanda con li recami bianchi di fiorenze novi –*

82 Setting out embroidery patterns

The frontispiece to a Venetian manual on embroidery of 1527(?) aimed at women working in domestic cirumstances. It is clear that the ladies depicted here, although not professional embroideresses, were advanced and skilful practitioners of the art. The woman at the bottom left is pouncing a design through a pricked pattern onto the textile ground to be embroidered while the others seem to be drawing patterns with a pen directly onto the ground-material. When it is not possible to use daylight to make the pattern show through, a candle placed under the work served the same purpose. In two scenes patterns hang on the wall behind.

From Alessandro Paganino, *Il Buratto. Libro de recami*, Venice, 1527
Victoria and Albert Museum, London

82

83 Ladylike accomplishments

Italian Renaissance artists and their public held the Virgin Mary to be a well-born young woman fully accomplished in all activitities a lady of her class was at that time expected to master. From the rather cramped scene of the *Annunciation* in the background it is evident that Mary can read, while in the foreground she is shown working delicately at an embroidery frame resting on trestles. An angel is being useful, laying the table, while another prays. Note the circular side-table.

Unknown artist, *Annunciation*, Atri Cathedral, third quarter 15th century
Photograph: Autostrade

84 Tooled leather cushion

The small dog sleeps curled up on a cushion [*carello*] covered with red leather that has a tooled pattern executed in the so-called *cuir ciselé* technique that involves incising the outlines, stamping the ground and punching it to leave the pattern standing proud and smooth. This was a popular form of decoration for leather in late Gothic times. The cushion lies on the bed-chest which also provides a seat for the old lady with the cat. The bed-head has fine *tarsie* and the walls are frescoed with a regular pattern. St Anne takes refreshment from a tray (the scene is yet another *Birth of the Virgin*) while the jolly servants assist her. Top marks go to the reader who spots the nesting swallows at first glance.

Unknown artist, *Birth of the Virgin*, Atri Cathedral, third quarter 15th century
Photograph: Autostrade

these sheets were new, with Florentine 'white work']. Florence was indeed an important centre for embroidery, notably in the fifteenth century after which it yielded pride of place to Milan.[14] Some embroidered orphrey-panels in the Museo dell'Opera del Duomo in Florence, designed by Antonio Pollaiuolo between 1469 and 1480, show the high standard reached by the principal Florentine needleworkers in the second half of the fifteenth century.[15] The Florentine Broderers' Guild included among its masters several foreigners, in 1466 including one Coppino de Melina [i.e. Malines or Mechlin, in Flanders] and a Piero da Venezia.[16] At this time the painter Parri Spinelli provided twenty designs with scenes from the life of San Donato which his sister was to work, and she was reckoned an excellent embroideress. Raffaellino del Garbo, according to Vasari, was providing designs for Florentine embroiderers around 1525. Perhaps the high point of Florentine achievement in this field was the provision of a bed for Eleonora de Toledo on her marriage in 1539 to Cosimo de' Medici. This was designed by Francesco Bacchiacca and executed by his brother Antonio, who was apparently a very skilful embroiderer [ottimo ricamatore].[17] The bed was extremely elaborate and its embroidery included pearls in its make-up.

Although most of the early needlework pattern-books were published in Venice, Venetian needleworkers do not seem to have enjoyed such a high reputation as their rivals in Milan and Florence, but we should not forget that needles were also used for making reticella and needlepoint lace, specialities for which Venice was renowned. Whatever the case it is perhaps worth noting that an embroideress named Perolla was praised in a contemporary Latin poem for her skill, as if this were widely appreciated.[18] Moreover Andrea Doria felt it worth bringing a Venetian embroiderer over to work for him in Genoa.

Excellent needlework was produced in Ferrara, as we have already noted. In the inventory of the Este castles in 1436 (Este Invt.), we find a special room set aside for the court broderers [la chamara da li rechamadurj] in which there were ten embroidery-frames [telari diexe de rechamare] and twelve trestles which probably served as supports. The Marchioness, Parisina Malatesta, had her own personal quilter and embroiderer, known as Niccolò da la Coltra [quilting], in the 1420s.[19] Likewise in Naples, at the Aragonese court, there was a perponter among the court officials in the mid-fifteenth century.[20] He too was a quilter, a pourpoint being the French term for a quilted doublet. Florio, in 1611,* tells us that trapunto meant 'quilted or counterpointed or embroydered'. In Palermo, in 1561 in the Requesens establishment (Requesens Invt.), a linen quilt was repuntata di sita ialna [quilted with yellow silk]. Quilting with yellow on white is rather more striking than the commoner white on white form.

Most of the stitches familiar to modern needleworkers were known to Italians in the Renaissance period. They seem to have believed that punto serato was an innovation of around 1500; it enabled a skilled worker to 'paint with the needle'. Floss silk came to be much used in the sixteenth century to produce naturalistic effects. A good deal of gold thread was employed for the more sumptuous classes of work and a favourite technique was to couch such thread, or silk cord, onto the surface of the ground-material. It was said that the special technique of working oro velato was particularly difficult and required much patience and skill [comanda piu di pazienza e di intelligenza]; it was a Florentine speciality in the fifteenth and sixteenth centuries. A cord edging, sewn or couched to the surface, was often laid round the edges of the cut-out elements of material used for appliqué work, to disguise frayed edges and keep the pattern distinct. The Venetian sumptuary regulations of 1562 prohibited the use of such seda intagliati [cut-out silk] for wall-hangings and the like.[21]

Among the many moschetti [i.e. padiglioni or suspended bed-canopies of lightweight material, for use in summer] in Andrea Doria's possession (Doria Invt., Genoa, 1561), one was of blue satin with borders of cloth of gold intagliati di veluto, which must mean that it had cut-out (decoupé in French) pieces of velvet forming an appliqué pattern. This, and indeed many of the other moschetti listed in the same inventory, is a reminder that the padiglione was among the most striking, and often the most sumptuous class of object that Italian Renaissance embroiderers produced (Pl. 130). The broderers of Florence, Venice and Genoa banded together in guilds, which should not surprise us of artisans labouring in these republican cities; but the broderers of Milan also had a guild even though their city was in a dukedom. This was presumably because there were so many of them, only comparatively few of whom actually worked for the court while the rest were engaged in commercial enterprise like their Florentine, Genoese and Venetian rivals. At any rate, the Florentine broderers called themselves baldicuarii, not because (as has been averred)[22] they wrought their patterns on a ground of baldachino, a rich silk material, but surely because their most splendid confections were baldachini or, to use the commoner term for such canopies, padiglioni.

English readers may ask why no mention has been made of opus anglicanum, which some may claim has been England's greatest contribution to High Art of all time, an art form which was regarded as an appropriate gift among the most discriminating princes and prelates in the fourteenth century. By the fifteenth century, however, the quality of the workmanship had declined and while old specimens of opus anglicanum needlework might still make handsome presents,[23] no great effort seems to have been made on the Continent after the beginning of the century to acquire English embroidery. No references to such items were noted in the inventories surveyed for this study.

Anyway, from about 1450 the finest European needlework was probably being executed in Italy, first in Florence and then in Milan. Italian embroidery could be exquisite on the one hand or imposing on the other. A superb example of the latter is the throne canopy in the castle at Stockholm which is probably Milanese work of the early sixteenth century (Pl. 85).

Leather

Gilt leather

Stunning effects could be produced in a room by hanging it with gilt leather, as we have already noted when considering wall-hangings. Here it merely remains to explain how these were made and where. Hangings of gilt leather came into fashion during the sixteenth century, in Italy, but had long been used in Spain.[1]

These hangings were made up to the desired size by sewing together 'skins' (rectangular panels) of leather[2] to one face of which metal foil had been applied. The foil was usually of silver, the gilt effect being contrived by coating the silver with yellow varnish. The surface was often tooled with punches or metal combs, and a pattern might be printed in outline on the skin, using an engraved wooden block and black ink. The pattern could then be painted in with one or more colours. The embossing of gilt leather, so greatly favoured in the late seventeenth century, does not seem to have been practised before 1600.[3] The silver has usually tarnished on old gilt leather hangings, and the leather has usually darkened and become stiff. The original striking and brilliant appearance has as a result mostly been lost but some idea of how these once resplendent panels looked may be gleaned from a glance at Pls 89 and 231.

According to Fioravanti, a native of Venice writing in 1584, great use was made of gilt leather hangings [corami d'oro, lit. gold leathers] in that city, as well as in Rome, Naples and Bologna.[4] He was probably wishing to imply that they were *produced* in those cities. Certainly Venice was the chief Italian centre of production in the sixteenth century and Venetian gilt leather was exported all over Italy in substantial quantities. The walls of many rooms in the Palazzo Tè, the Gonzaga summer palace at Mantua which was being decorated about 1530, were hung with Venetian gilt leather. Early in the sixteenth century there were about sixty workshops engaged in this industry and at some later point this had risen to seventy-one; the masters of the trade formed a branch of the Painters' Guild.[5] In 1591 the Procurators of St Marks ordered, from one *mistro Piero dalli cuori d'oro*, some hangings with patterns *a brocadi* and *alla grotesca* [i.e. with brocade-like patterns, and with grotesques].[6] A courtyard in the San Fantin area of Venice is still called the Corte dei Cuoridoro.

Nothing much so far seems to be known about the industry in Rome beyond the fact that Isabella d'Este in 1516 thought Roman gilt leather better than that made in Ferrara.[7] The hangings of *corame dora di Spagna* and the *quoio d'oro mezano di Spagna* in the Villa Medici in Rome in 1598 (Medici Invt.) may possibly have been local products rather than imports from Spain. As for Bologna, the other city mentioned by Fioravanti, it is evident that an industry existed there because a maker of gilt leather from that city named Pietro Ruinetti had established himself in Ferrara by 1554.[8] He was presumably related to Giacomo Ruinetti who, in 1590, provided gilt leather hangings both for the Castle and the smart new apartment being furnished for Virginia Medici (newly married four years

earlier to the future Duke of Modena) in the Palazzo dei Diamanti, a building which survives. Ruinetti was described as *mess[ere] Jacomo rovinetti m[aest]ro da corami d'oro* and he produced *alcuni paramenti da camera* [several sets of hangings for rooms] of this material.[9] Two prominent painter-decorators at Ferrara, Ludovico Settevecchi and Leonardo Brescia, supplied hangings of some sort to many leading families in the Duchy in the 1570s. They ran a leather-working establishment at the same time, presumably producing gilt leather hangings.[10] The ambitious design for a gilt leather panel decorated with grotesques shown in Pl. 90 might well be an example of the kind of work they produced, working as they did under the learned Pirro Ligorio, the architect and antiquarian who had arrived at Ferrara from Rome in 1565. He was particularly clever at composing designs for grotesques and this pattern is very much in the style he had long espoused. Brescia and Settevecchi executed many schemes under his direction and will have been entirely familiar with his style. At any rate, in the time of Alfonso II d'Este (d.1597), gilt leather was the height of fashion at Ferrara and it seems that most of it was made locally. Because the city lay at the centre of an area principally devoted to stockbreeding, leather-working had always been a speciality so it should not have been too difficult to develop this new branch when demand began to develop in the late fifteenth century. Late sixteenth-century inventories of the palace at Urbino show that most of the fine rooms were hung with gilt leather, which is likely to have come from Ferrara, given that there were such close liks between the two cities.

Thomas Coryat saw some 'very faire hangings' of this material at Padua when he stayed there in the 1590s[11] but they were probably Venetian products. On the other hand gilt leather was produced at Genoa, and at quite an early date, for in 1510 the Signoria found it necessary to impose a value-added tax of fifteen per cent on ninety-seven pieces of *coreorum* which had just arrived from Cadiz, presumably in an attempt to protect the local industry.[12] This reminds us that gilt leather continued to be made in Spain throughout the Renaissance[13] although importation no doubt dwindled during the sixteenth century as the Italian industries became more accomplished. We have already noted that some gilt leather hangings in the Villa Medici in Rome in 1598 were apparently from Spain and Thomas Platter, a year later, reported on the beauty of the leathers then being made in Barcelona.[14] The Spanish must have continued to enjoy a high reputation in Italy, judging by the fact that a design for some hangings of gilt leather, together with the necessary number of blank skins, were sent from Pesaro to Spain in 1546, presumably to be decorated. It would seem that the Venetian products had been found to have shortcomings.[15] The centres springing up in the Spanish Nether-lands at this period, which were to become so important in the seventeenth century, were also probably able to support a sizeable export trade before 1600 although no reference to such north European products has been noted in the documents we have surveyed.[16]

An item that was probably not of gilt leather although it has a connection with Italy was the *parement ... de lict* which was provided for the bed of the Queen of France in 1496 – an object which will certainly

85

have been in exquisite taste.[17] It was made of *ung grant cuir de bueuf blanc* [a large white oxhide] which had been specially prepared for the purpose by a master-craftsman at Tours and then delivered to *ung painctre que le Roy avoit fait venir d' Ytalie*. No gilding is mentioned but this Italian artist must have possessed some special skill in order to have made it imperative to bring him so far in order to fulfil this task. Painting on leather involves a technique not dissimilar from that of painting on textiles, which was a branch that excellent artists were prepared to undertake in fifteenth-century Italy, as we have seen (p. 72). Even though the ox was large, one skin would not have been large enough to provide a set of bed-hangings, which would be the usual meaning of *parament de lit*. In this case a fine coverlet must have been the subject on which so much care was to be bestowed. One can imagine that such a delicate and attractive item was for throwing over a luxurious daybed rather than for display on a bed of state.

Other types of leather

Corame and *cuoio* both meant dressed leather and there does not seem to have been any distinction other than regional preference in the use of these terms; they embraced leather with a wide range of finishes and very rarely do we find greater precision in the inventory descriptions. Occasionally reference is made to *montanina* which seems to have been an exotic hide made of sheepskin [*montone*], imported from afar. Leather produced in the great Spanish city of Cordoba was famed all over the Western world, particularly the red variety which was dyed with madder. The *quoio rosso grande di Spagna* mentioned in a Medici inventory of 1456 must have been of this material. Cordovan leather was imitated in other countries with varying degrees of success, the London City Company of Cordwainers having derived their name from the making and marketing of this beautiful material which was their original activity. Although it has been claimed that the term 'Spanish leather' was also used in reference to hangings of gilt leather, this does not seem to have been the case in Renaissance Italy.

Items of dress of many kinds and numerous household objects were made of leather during the Renaissance but few need detain us here.

Leather was of course also used for book-binding but was mostly of a utilitarian nature until well into the sixteenth century when decorative leather bindings came into fashion. Before that, fine bindings were usually covered with a silk material, in the most splendid instances, helped out with goldsmith's work.

Wooden boxes and chests of all sizes, from charming caskets to hold trinkets and keepsakes, to large trunks and travelling-coffers, were covered with leather which was afterwards strengthened and protected at vulnerable points by metal mounts – brass or delicate ironwork for the small pieces and straps of iron for the larger ones. The leather thus used was sometimes dyed but much was given painted or gilded decoration.

Cases of all kinds were made of leather covering wood but a favourite material for the making of cases was *cuoio cocto*, which in English is called

85 Milanese professional embroidery at its finest

One of the most splendid surviving examples of Italian Renaissance embroidery is a canopy (shown here is the backcloth) in the Royal Castle at Stockholm. It shows the heights to which the best Italian professional broderers could rise at that period. The canopy is believed to have been brought to Sweden in 1562 by Katarina Jagellonica, when she came to marry the future Johan III of Sweden. Her mother was Bona Sforza who married Sigismond I Jagellon, King of Poland in 1518 and whose father was Giangaleazzo Sforza, the famous Duke of Milan. It seems unlikely that it was made as late as 1562 (i.e. for Katarina) but could well have been made for her mother, Bona Sforza, while she was still in Milan – perhaps when she married Sigismond or when she was created Duchess of Bari on the death of her own mother in 1524. If one wants to push it back further in date, the date of her parents' wedding in 1500 may be relevant. In any case such a superb object must have been made for an important occasion by a top-class Milanese broderer. The arms and cipher were added later, probably in Sweden.

Swedish Royal Collections, Stockholm Castle

86, 87 Dynastic pride

Princely babies in their finery, proudly shown to the world by their parents. Thus specially dressed, the child would be placed in a superbly embellished cradle (Pls 281, 282), the point being to underline the fact that, particularly in elevated social circles, the birth of this child set a seal on the dynastic union between two powerful families – an achievement that called for widespread celebration. Here we see fine silk materials embroidered richly with coloured silks and gold thread, handsomely trimmed. Similar work was to be seen on exceptionally luxurious furnishings like the beds of popes, grand dukes and their consorts – and of the leading courtesans.

Tiberio Titi, *Prince Leopoldo de' Medici*, 1617
Pitti Palace, Florence (photograph: Scala)
Frederico Barocci, *Prince Federico d'Urbino*, 1617
Galleria dell' Accademia, Florence (photograph: Scala)

86

87

88 A *cuir bouilli* knife-case

The *colteller[i]a* on the left is a case for knives, probably for a carver of viands at table. A case like this would today be made of a plastic which would need to be rendered strong in much the same way – by forming ribs that were created when the leather (pliant when being worked) was being moulded. The lid slides on the cords which also serve for attaching the case to the bearer's belt. The other implements are skewers, a fork, a syringe, and a roller for cutting pasta into strips.

From Bartolomeo Scappi *Opera*, Venice, 1570
Metropolitan Museum of Art, New York, Elisha Whittelsey Collection,
Elisha Whittelsey Fund, 1952 ([52.595.2]13)

89 The stunning effect of gilt leather

The hangings of this striking material seem here to consist of wide panels with narrow borders between them. This votive painting, presumably recording the recovery of the man in the bed from some misadventure, dates from 1501, at which time gilt leather was probably still not all that common in Italy. At any rate the artist was clearly impressed by it and recorded the leather's bold effect for us to see. The bed does not seem to have posts; the rectangular tester was probably suspended from the ceiling by a cord which is not here visible (see diagram 1, p. 359). The chest by the wall is much taller than the chests round the bed which had to serve as steps and seats.

Attributed to Gian Francesco de' Maineri
Said to be in Columbia, Missouri, but efforts to contact the owner have
failed (Photographed from the Catalogue of the Kress Collection)

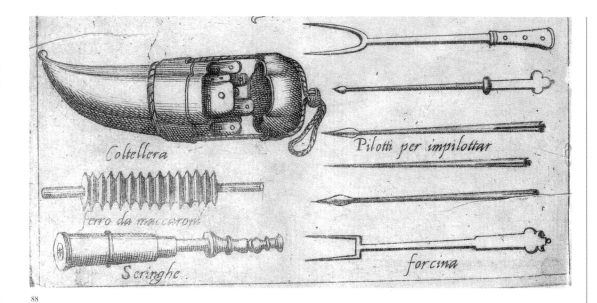

88

89

cuir bouilli, using the French term.[1] Sheaths for knives, cases for a personal set of cutlery or for a carver's set of carving-knives and forks,[2] cases for writing implements or for the tools needed by the needleworker, cases for the wax seals hanging from documents, and much else were made of this lightweight but strong material which had much the same properties as the stout cardboard of which rolls for posters and the like are made today (Pls 5, 88, 227). *Cuir bouilli* could be left plain, or it could be decorated with paintwork or gilding. It was often decorated with relief-ornament worked up when the leather was soft, before the material dried and set into its finished state of rigidity.

The seats and backs of chairs were sometimes of leather; this was rare in the fifteenth century but became common in the sixteenth. At first the leather was used in the form of wide straps stretched across the framework to form a seat or a back-rest. Later, stuffing was introduced so the leather came to form a top cover. No doubt various types of leather were used for this purpose, as in later centuries, but distinctions do not seem to appear in the inventories. Cushions were frequently made of leather – sometimes of gilt leather (p. 85) and sometimes, it seems, of scorched leather which was a technique much favoured in seventeenth- and eighteenth-century Italy but was certainly used earlier. The scorched patterns were executed with heated irons; in the seventeenth century (and perhaps before) a hot iron plate was used and the leather was pressed against this by a wooden board (block) into which the pattern had been carved in *intaglio*.[3]

Leather was of course also used for book-binding but was mostly of a utilitarian nature until well into the sixteenth century when decorative leather bindings came into fashion. Before that, fine bindings were usually covered with a silk material, in the most splendid instances, helped out with goldsmith's work

Woodwork

Timbers

The names of various timbers occur in inventories. *Albero*, meaning a tree, was also the generic word for wood but this gave way during the sixteenth century to the modern Italian word *legno*. The term *legname* meant members of wood or the parts of a wooden framework (e.g. a bedstead that was dismantled). *Albero* also meant poplar wood which was, and still is, a tree much in evidence in the Po Valley. It was used for everyday furnishings of no great value.

Abete meant pinewood or fir; it came in many qualities and both simple as well as fine furniture was made of it. One class of such pinewood was called *pezzo* which means 'a piece' and carries exactly the same meaning as the English word 'deal', which comes from the Scandinavian word *del*, a piece. Among the relatively common timbers that were used in the manufacture of modest furnishings were chestnut, elm, ash, larch and willow [*castagno, olmo, frassino, larice, salice*].

Most high-class furniture was made of walnut, however. Called *noce* in most of Italy and *noghera* in the Veneto, it was regarded as sufficiently special for the Venetian woodworkers' guild to have a separate division for 'workers in walnut'. Walnut can have a very beautiful grain and takes a polish well.[1]

Rovere, the word used to describe timber taken from an oak tree [*quercia*], is rarely mentioned in the inventories. Cypress wood [*archipressa*], on the other hand, was much used, especially for making clothes-chests, as the strongly-scented wood effectively warded off moths.[2]

Pearwood and limewood [*pero* and *tiglio*] lent themselves well to carving, being soft yet dense, and the latter was also much used for inlay [*lavoro di intarsio*] as it is almost white and produces a striking contrast with the ground which was mostly of walnut. *Silio*, which we call spindle wood, was used for a less costly form of *tarsia*.[3] Today it is known as *fusaggine* and Florio* in 1611 called it *fusano*. The contrast between these white timbers and the ground into which they were set by inlaying is today no longer apparent, both now being brown, but this contrast in new *lavoro di intarsio* may be seen in Pls 91 and 93.

Of the exotic woods coming from far afield, ebony [*ebano*] was the chief. This striking black timber was greatly prized and was of course expensive. It contrasted well with walnut and might therefore be used for mouldings on walnut furniture but it was also used on its own, particularly for picture-frames. Towards the end of the sixteenth century it was used as a veneer, sometimes in conjunction with ivory. One Federigo Curelli had a workshop by the Rialto bridge in Venice and there, probably some time in the 1570s, he made a bedroom suite comprising bed, chests, tables and other furnishings of ebony and ivory [*un guarnimento di lettiera, di case, di tavole et d'altri arnesi . . . d'ebano e di avolio*].[4] It was ornamented with gold, presumably painted on the black ground, and was so amazing that it was impossible to describe [*che e impossibil cosa a narrarlo*].

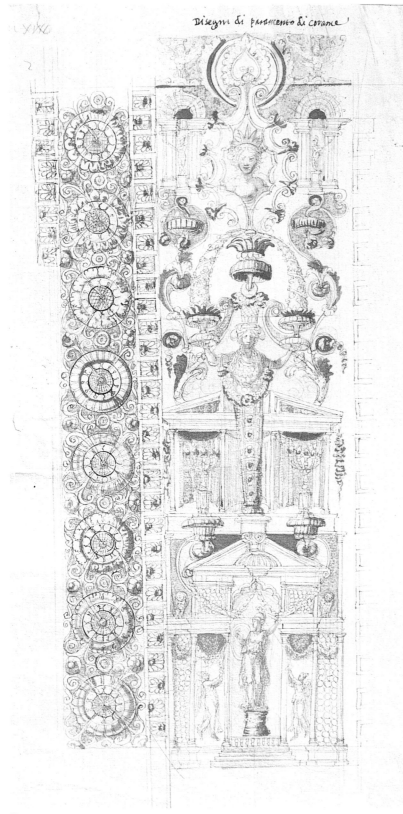

Disegni di parumento di corame

90

90 Custom-built gilt leather hanging

This has been specially designed for a room of known height; there are no repeats in the design of the main panel. Normal ready-made hangings of gilt leather had the same pattern repeated up their whole height (e.g. Pl. 89). The intention here was that the main panels with developed grotesques should alternate with borders decorated with bold rosettes (shown on the left). The design may well have to do with a factory producing gilt leather at Ferrara in the 1570s which worked under the influence of Pirro Ligorio, the architect with strong antiquarian leanings who favoured grotesque ornament in this general style (see p. 37). As the drawing is in the Este Archives, the design will have been connected with some scheme of decoration being contemplated by that family.

Archivio Estense, Modena (photograph kindly provided by Dr Graziano Manni)

91 Showing how striking *tarsie* were when new

The contrast between the white wood commonly used for the inlay, and the ground into which it was set, was vivid when the work was fresh. After five centuries most of this differentiation has disappeared under layers of dirt and polish coupled with fading: now all tends to be a uniform brown. We see the original effect on Mary's reading-desk and seat, and on the various parts of the bed and on the headboard of the *lettuccio* behind it. The book Mary was reading lies upon a book-cushion. A splendid coverlet with a woven pattern is cast over the bed.

Filippo Lippi, Annunciation, c.1465
Galleria Nazionale, Palazzo Barberini, Rome (photograph: Scala)

Ebony probably did not make its appearance in Italy much before 1500. Some gamesboards veneered with ebony and inlaid with simple geometrical patterns executed in ivory and coloured woods seem to date from the late fifteenth century and are related to what looks like an ebony and ivory chest or cabinet that stands on the floor next to the bed in one of Ghirlandaio's famous frescoes in Santa Maria Novella, which date from the 1480s (Pl. 35). Some tripod tables carved from ebony [*tripodi di Hebeno* and *le eburnee mense* are the phrases used] with circular tops 'of gold' are described as wondrous items in the *Hypnerotomachia* which was published in Venice in 1499 (Pl. 240). Isabella d'Este acquired some combs in 1500 which were made of ivory, horn and *legno da ebano*, the last being inlaid with ivory.[5] In 1506 a *tarsia*-worker at Ferrara obtained *certo ligname negro* which should probably be translated as 'some pieces of a certain black timber', in order to carry out some task for the Este court, and in 1518 a maker of musical instruments at Ferrara was acquiring *ebano* and other timbers in order to make an instrument of some sort for the Duke which was no doubt exceptionally ornamental.[6]

The poet Pietro Aretino is said to have had a large room 'lined with ebony cabinets' in his house in Venice where he lived between 1527 and 1533 but the source of this information may not be all that reliable.[7] However, among the treasures at Villa Giulia, the suburban *vigna* of Pope Julius III, was an ebony table inlaid with agate and other semi-precious stones; it was later removed by his successor, Pius IV, presumably on account of its importance.[8] The base for Cellini's famous salt-cellar, made for François I in 1541, was made of a block of ebony, and a casket set with plaques of cut rock-crystal, made in Milan in 1560 for Duke Albrecht V of Bavaria, had members of ebony.[9] Perhaps of greater influence was the ebony cabinet inlaid with precious stones designed by Bernardo Buontalenti in Florence in 1568 for Francesco de' Medici who became Grand Duke in 1574. This sumptuous object no doubt impressed all who saw it and several will have wanted to own something similar made with this attractive wood.[10] Indeed, it was soon to become the fashionable wood for cabinets (hence the French name for a cabinetmaker – *ébéniste*) and Buontalenti was to design an even more imposing cabinet of this timber in 1584, made to stand at the focal point of the Uffizi Gallery in Florence. Another exotic timber was that used for making some beds to be seen in 1531 at the Palazzo Medici in Florence (Medici Invt.) (p. 154).

Graining, that is the painting of an inexpensive wood to make it resemble a more costly kind, was by no means unknown during the Renaissance, and the practice no doubt went back a long way. One might think graining was only to be found in relatively humble surroundings but there was a picture-frame in the splendid Villa Medici in Rome, in 1598 (Medici Invt.), which was of *legno finto di noce* [wood feigned to look like walnut]. Alongside was a frame *tinto di nero* [stained black] which must have been of black-stained pearwood, the usual counterfeit for ebony. The cabinetmakers of Augsburg were so concerned, around 1600, to convince their customers that the cabinets that they had for sale were not made with such stained wood but were of the genuine article, that their guild ordered its members to stamp their wares with the word *eben*.[11]

Techniques

The Italian word *cornice* connotes not only a cornice but also a profiled moulding which can be used as a straight run of wood or, with mitred corners, as a frame for a picture (then *also* called a *cornice*) or for a panel which is then *incorniciato*. These applied mouldings produced a framing in high relief. Well made and well proportioned panels could produce an elegant effect and this might be heightened by making the mouldings of a wood of contrasting colour to the main body of the structure (Pls 118, 379). Sometimes panelling with such rectangular framing was described as being *quadrato* or *riquadrato*.[1] The fact that a piece of furniture or panelling was embellished with finely profiled mouldings was sometimes thought worth noting at the time. Isabella d'Este, for example, was provided with a walnut table with fine mouldings of the proper sort [*una tavoleta de nogara cornexada*] in 1484, made by the exceptionally skilful joiner and inlayer, Stefano di Dona Bona.[2] A much simpler form of decoration was produced by nailing strips of moulding to the plain surface of a piece of woodwork. This was presumably what *regolato* meant. It was apparently discouraged by guild regulations.[3]

As for joints, dovetails were developed in the fourteenth century and were common by the fifteenth. Truly neat dovetailing was required by the makers of caskets [*cassette*] and small boxes of fine quality for dressing-tables and the like, and became important to the cabinetmaker when, towards the middle of the sixteenth century, he began to make rather glamorous furniture, finely finished inside, especially in the many drawers with which such pieces of furniture were usually fitted.

Lavoro di intarsio, or inlay,[4] consists of setting into the ground-timber ornamental forms cut with a fretsaw from one or more other sorts of wood. Space for the pattern is gouged out, and sometimes very complicated designs of several sorts and colours of wood, forming motifs that resemble assembled pieces of an old-fashioned wooden jigsaw puzzle, were sunk into these declivities. A charming example of such work is shown in Pl. 95. Where only one sort of wood is used for the inlay, it is usually of a very light colour (often *silio*, now called *fusaggine*) which produces a striking effect (Pls 91, 379). The inlaid pieces are usually about four millimetres thick (about four times as thick as the veneers of eighteenth-century furniture) but even cutting wood into panels of this thickness required special sawmills, it being almost essential, and certainly quicker and less laborious, to use a water-driven saw. There was a water-driven saw-mill at Augsburg already by 1322 but such machinery did not become common until the fifteenth century and Augsburg only acquired a saw-mill capable of cutting truly thin veneers in 1587.[5] It was only after the introduction of such a machine that the craft of the cabinetmaker could really develop. The *intarsio* workers did not have this facility in their day.

Lavoro di intarsio was at first, in the second half of the fourteenth century, confined to small panels and the patterns were geometric, made with small pieces of wood in a style derived from the Near East (Pls 31, 92, 303). This is today called *alla certosina* work but not, it seems, for any very good reason.[6] These panels got larger in the early fifteenth century but, in

92 High-quality woodwork in early quattrocento Naples

The silk hanging at the back is depicted with uncanny realism, the pattern being distinct as are the rings running on a rod, and the pseudo-Kufic inscription of the border. This is almost certainly an expensive material from Lucca and it indicates that the other items in the room are also likely to be high-class articles. The desk is prettily inlaid with geometric *tarsie*, there is a carved panel at the side, and the back has blind arcading. Mary's seat (this is yet another *Annunciation* where she has been disturbed while reading in her study) is also inlaid – *en suite* because the seat and the desk are probably fixed to the platform on which they stand, so the whole ensemble was a fairly substantial item.

Attributed to Ferrante Maglione, *Annunciation*, c.1419
Casa dell' Annunciata, Aversa, north-west of Naples

93 Exceptionally fine *lavoro di intarsio*, 1490s

Note the paternoster beads suspended as ornaments. The throne seems to be integral with the wall-panelling.

Bergognone, *Madonna and Child*
Borromeo Collection, Milan (photograph: Alinari Archives)

92

93

the meantime, figurative ornament began to be executed in this medium and the patterns became ever more elaborate and ambitious as the century wore on. An early example of figurative *tarsia* ornament will have been the coat of arms of Leonello d'Este inlaid on a table-top in 1441 by one Pantaleone da Cremona.[7] At about this time the most accomplished craftsman in wood working at Ferrara was Arduino da Baiso, *magister lignarum subtilissimus* [a very skilful master of woodwork]. He was both a carver and a worker with *tarsie* and he made a beautiful inlaid table [*uno desco belissimo*] for the chapel at Belfiore, one of the Este pleasure-palaces; it was regarded as something of a wonder and was usually shown to important visitors.[8] Another brilliant *tarsie*-worker at Ferrara was the above-mentioned Stefano di Dona Bona who, in 1485, made some doors for the palace decorated with some stoats and two monkeys.[9] An example of this kind of pictorial inlay may be seen in Pl. 95. A rather different sort of figurative *intarsio* was that in which perspective views of architecture were rendered, several striking examples of which may still be seen to this day on doors in the palace at Urbino. These probably date from the second half of the 1470s and may have been designed by Francesco di Giorgio Martini although this is by no means certain.[10] Early manifestations of such perspective *tarsie* were executed between 1436 and 1445 for the Duomo in Florence by Antonio Manetti and Angelo di Lanzero, but it was the brothers Lorenzo and Cristoforo Canozi da Lendinara who brought this art-form to a state of excellence. They came from Modena but worked mostly in Ferrara during the middle of the fifteenth century. Apparently they were friends of Piero della Francesca at a time when he was much preoccupied with the rendering of perspective pictorially, and he may have provided designs for them when they were faced with the task of making some panelling in the cathedral at Modena in 1477.[11] It was said of Cristoforo's son Bernardino that he also *lavora de prospectiva*; he was still actively employed in such work in 1502.[12] A fine example of this class of inlaid work is to be seen in Pl. 94. By 1530, however, pictorial *tarsie* had gone out of fashion and we find one Paolo da Modena, *intarsiadore* at Ferrara, inlaying eight walnut armchairs 'in the new fashion'.[13] These chairs were very probably inlaid all over with roundels and runs of small-scale inlay recalling the *alla certosina* work of a century earlier – a form of decoration that can be seen on certain X-frame chairs which survive in various collections and seem to date from about this time. A portrait in the Palazzo Spada in Rome (museum no. 62) attributed to Gerolamo Siciolante da Sermoneta and painted in about 1550, shows a cardinal (perhaps Gerolamo Veralli, d.1555) seated in such an inlaid X-frame chair.

While the *tarsie*-workers of Ferrara and Modena were undoubtedly very skilful, their rivals in Florence were no less so. In 1474 there were said to be eighty-four workshops executing this kind of work in Florence. No doubt much of it consisted of regular and repetitive ornament but some establishments carried out brilliant work and the most important workshop of all was that of Benedetto da Maiano (better known to us now as a sculptor) and his brother Giuliano who seems to have been more the businessman of the enterprise.[14] The stalls in the chapel of the Palazzo Medici in Florence are probably by them as certainly are those in the cathedral at Perugia,[15] and what must have been some superb *tarsie*-decorated furniture by them is discussed here on p. 149.

Excellent inlay was of course also executed elsewhere in Italy, and one gets the impression that some *tarsie*-workers moved around the country quite readily. For example the splendid doors in the Stanze della Segnatura at the Vatican are by Fra Giovanni, a native of Verona, while the delightful choir-stalls in S. Giovanni in Monte in Bologna were made by Paolo Sacca who came from Cremona; they were executed in 1527 – rather a late manifestation of this technique which has largely survived in churches but was certainly also adopted in secular decoration, most of which has disappeared.[16]

Lavoro di intarsio was accomplished with relatively thick pieces of wood laid into the surface of the ground-timber but, as it became possible to cut thinner sheets of wood, so the task of the inlayer became easier and he could produce more delicate patterns. He also came to realize that he need no longer lay the wood *into* the surface; he could lay it *on* the surface of the ground-timber; indeed, he could cover the entire surface with a sheet of veneer which could be plain or made up with a pattern composed of woods of several colours – but all cut thin. When this stage has been reached, the result is called marquetry but there is no definite point at which inlay becomes marquetry and it was clearly not obvious while this development was taking place. Vasari, who lived at that very time, explained that the term *rimesso*, as applied to woodwork, meant *una specie di tarsia con legni tinti e ombrati* [a kind of *tarsia* accomplished with woods that are tinted and shaded],[17] but he certainly had in mind complicated patterns, probably figurative, in which pieces of wood that were shaded were used to produce three-dimensional effects and modelling. Shading, which was achieved by scorching a piece of wood by dipping it in heated sand, could only effectively be done with thin veneers. The tinting, on the other hand, will have been carried out with stains but pieces of naturally-coloured woods were also specially chosen for the purpose. Once the joiner had learned to make neatly finished drawers and cupboards, and could decorate the outer surface of his furniture with marquetry, he was well on the way to becoming what the English came to call a 'cabinetmaker'.

Even though a clever woodworker could execute both carving and *tarsie*, in practice the two techniques required very different skills. What is more they rarely went together. So while woodcarving had always existed, it yielded to *tarsia*-decoration while this was fashionable (it also yielded to painted decoration) but re-captured the ground, as it were, once this fashion ran out of steam. So carving became the principal means of decorating woodwork in the sixteenth century. There is nothing much one can helpfully say about work in this technique, which followed the current styles in sculptural ornament. A piece of carving [*intaglio*] that would be interesting to find on several counts is the walnut firescreen made for Isabella d'Este in 1481 by Stefano di Dona Bona, the highly skilled craftsman working in Ferrara for the Este court, who has already been mentioned.[18]

Relief ornament was also worked in gesso, which could be applied in a

94

95

94 *Un prospettivo intarsiato*

A favourite medium for perspective exercises was *lavoro di intarsio*, and townscapes like this lent themselves well to representation in this medium. The results were often something to wonder at and comment upon.

Panel in the choirstalls in the Abbey of Monte Oliveto Maggiore, near Siena, *c.*1500?
Photograph: Scala

95 A charming example of naturalistic *lavoro di intarsio*

Because they are black the markings of the cat still contrast strongly with its other colours but the colouring of the landscape has almost entirely disappeared.

Panel on a lectern in the Abbey of Monte Oliveto Maggiore, near Siena, *c.*1500?
Photograph: Scala

96

96 Carved walnut furniture becomes fashionable

Furniture that was *intarsiata* [inlaid] or painted boldly gradually went out of fashion in Italy around 1500 and walnut decorated with carving took the place of these earlier forms of embellishment. The desk of fanciful shape shown in this rather battered fresco by Pinturicchio of the 1480s is an early example of the fashion for walnut carved in relief which was to become dominant in the next century. Mary's desk has a revolving lectern mounted on it. She continues to be absorbed in her reading, seemingly unaware that the room is full of angels. Note the shelves for books set just above shoulder height.

Pinturicchio, *Education of the Virgin* (detail), S. Maria del Popolo, Rome, fresco, 1480s
Photograph: Alinari Archives

thick coat to a wooden ground and then carved into shape when dry. Gesso ornament could also be cast in moulds and applied to the ground-surface. In most cases the intention was to provide a fancy ground suitable for gilding. Cennino Cennini, in his *Trattato della Pittura* of about the 1390s, has a good deal to say about this matter as well as about the delicate gesso ornaments that were cast in moulds and separately applied. For smaller items like caskets, relief ornament was also made in small moulds in which *pastiglia* was cast. This white paste would seem to have had the consistency of masticated chewing-gum but was rather more white. It took moulding well, rendering sharp edges and details clearly. When dry it was glued to the prepared face of a box, mirror-frame or similar small item. Often the whole thing was gilded but sometimes the *pastiglia* relief was left untreated and it then stood out in white on the gilded, or sometimes coloured, ground. What had not been realized until recently was that *pastiglia* was scented[19] and that it was principally used in conjunction with articles associated with the *toilette*. The scents used in *pastiglia* were musk-based, hence *pasta di muschio* with which, for instance, four circular mirror-frames were decorated for the personal use of Duke Ercole d'Este in 1466.[20] It seems that a French parfumier, Jean-Charles di Bretagne (also called Carlo di Monlione), who was established in Ferrara, fashioned the scented reliefs[21] while no less an artist than Cosmè Tura saw to the gilding of many of the items the Frenchman was to embellish.[22] One may presume the Breton had learned his trade in Paris where, already then, attention was being paid to the production of delightful articles that would be pleasing to women. It is a nice thought, therefore, that the Duchess Eleonora d'Este had a special frame (for a looking-glass?) *lavorato de moschio* made to give to her daughter Isabella

in 1485 and that five years later two caskets likewise *lavorate con pasta con muschio* were produced for her younger daughter Beatrice.[23]

Fine furniture incorporating elements turned on a lathe did not make its appearance until such machinery was sufficiently perfected to produce work of the required standard. This did not really take place until after 1500 when we begin to find mentioned in the inventories balusters and finials that must have been made in this way.[24] However, there were turners [*tornitori*] in the Este service already by the 1460s when several *magistri de torlo* [masters of the lathe] are recorded including an Antonio *del tortoleto* [i.e. *tornietto*, a small lathe] and Domengo *tortolero*.[25] In the sixteenth and even more in the seventeenth century, it was regarded as a suitable activity for princes to execute delicate work on a lathe. Alfonso I d'Este must have been one of the first to do this, causing a lathe to be installed in his private workshop in 1503. Paolo Giovio, who wrote a biography of the Prince in 1552, actually mentions that he made flutes on his lathe (to banish boredom he would *lavorare atornio flauti*, games-boards, boxes and much else).[26] Once beds acquired posts and these had not to look too massive and heavy, it became imperative for woodworkers to make use of a lathe and they quickly learned to produce complicated forms with this new mechanical tool (Pls 142, 146, 151).

We often associate 'bentwood' with the nineteenth century because it was then that the technique was adopted on an industrial scale, but the technique was known long before. If we can believe Fioravanti, it was used more to straighten a bent piece of wood than to bend a straight one,[27] but it did of course work both ways. This technique must have been employed for creating several pieces of furniture shown here (Pl. 206).

Finishes

The painting of chests, of the finer sort, has received a fair amount of attention from art historians because, as Vasari pointed out, in the fourteenth and fifteenth centuries, 'the most excellent painters' were prepared to carry out this kind of work, which they did 'without shame, as would be the case today' – that is, in the mid-sixteenth century.[1] This matter is discussed in connection with chests (p. 193) but, as Vasari also said, the artists of those times were likewise prepared to decorate beds, panelling, the friezes around rooms and, he could have added, expensive boxes, caskets, birth-trays, chairs and cupboards.

As a general rule the most important commissions of this kind would be given to those artists with the highest reputation at the time but these artists were of course the heads of workshops and will certainly have given much of the more humdrum work to their assistants, only adding the finishing touches to important passages where their own intervention would tell. There were of course also specialist painters of decorative work, like the *pictor cofanorum* [painter of chests] mentioned in a Florentine document of 1384,[2] but a painter like Apollonio di Giovanni who, with Marco del Buono, ran the largest of the Florentine workshops producing painted chests in the mid-fifteenth century, also painted miniatures in books (Pls 123, 219).[3] His work has considerable charm but his was not one of the great talents of the time. Many of the Italian Renaissance paintings on wooden panels that grace art galleries today originally formed part of the embellishment of a fine room in which the furniture was decorated *en suite* with the mural decoration. The panel forming a bed-head, the front of a chest or the back of a *lettuccio* (p. 149), once cut from its original setting, would usually be indistinguishable in character from those decorating the walls. Indeed, in the case of Botticelli's famous *Primavera*, it is really not certain whether it was suspended directly above a *lettuccio* or whether it formed the panel in the back of such an imposing piece of furniture (p. 149).

Most of the studies in this area have concentrated on Florence but recently we have learned much about Ferrarese painters working on furnishings and interior decoration.[4] Most of the Florentine painter-decorators were independent artists whereas those working at Ferrara, of whom we now have information, were mostly attached to the Court and their commissions and accounts are documented in the Este Archives. A court painter, who owed his livelihood to the princely family for whom he worked, had to be even more versatile than his independent co-practitioners. For example, Jacopo Sagramoro, who had a high position in the Este service and of course had a number of assistants, was not only involved with important room-decoration in fresco but also painted and gilded important chests for Leonello d'Este including two marriage chests for a state wedding in 1434, and in addition had to paint a private altarpiece for Leonello in 1439, as well as doors and friezes, playing-cards, banners and hangings. In 1443 we find him re-painting some old chests which were no doubt rather splendid or he would not have been given this task.[5] Another court painter at Ferrara was Andrea Costa of Vicenza who died in 1454. The year before he had been engaged in painting a superb cradle which Borso d'Este was to send to his sister Isotta who was married and living in Croatia, and was expecting a baby. It was an elaborate Gothic confection which Costa gilded; it was then painted with stars on a blue ground, the Madonna and Child, St Francis, an Annunciation, and St George and the Dragon, not to speak of foliage and the arms of the Duke Borso.[6] Gerardo Costa, Andrea's son, played perhaps an even more important role as designer and painter of decoration. In the year 1471 he decorated the state barge [*bucintoro grande*] a number of important chests, numerous coats of arms, protective cases for musical instruments, the face of a clock and the clock-case, and much else including panels for a ceiling and ornaments in a church.[7] He even saw to the white-washing of some offices.

A sketchbook of coloured drawing on vellum in Sir John Soane's Museum contains details of architecture, ornament in wide variety, drawings of furniture (Pl. 264), tabernacles, centrepieces, decorative vases and parade helmets. The sketches probably record things seen rather than design proposals; they would be a useful source of inspiration for a designer-decorator who could perhaps also show some of the drawings to prospective clients, to help them make up their minds as to what kind of thing they wanted to commission. Opinions differ as to the provenance of this early pattern-book; some suggest it may be Milanese and others say it comes from Ferrara. The name of Gerardo Costa, just mentioned, has been put forward[8] although some of the designs seem to be rather too late in style (they must date from the 1480s and even 1490s, whereas Costa seems to have died in the early 1480s). Whatever the case, Costa was a designer-decorator of the second rank, the primary position in Ferrara at that time being occupied by Cosmè Tura (1429–95) who had a supervisory role, overseeing a host of artists and craftsmen, providing the necessary designs and, in special cases, executing them himself.[9] Previously all this had been a fairly casual procedure but it became institutionalized in the 1470s. In 1487 Ercole de' Roberti took over this important co-ordinating function which did so much to place Ferrara and its court right in the forefront of fashionable taste at that period. Nevertheless, he himself attended to the gilding of a cage for a parakeet[10] and to the gilding of a cherub that topped a canopy [*padiglione*] which was to go over a Madonna and Child carved in relief by Stefano di Dona Bona (see p. 94); these must have been important commissions.

In the sixteenth century painting played a much less important part in the decoration of furniture (this word is here used in its widest sense). It was not so much that no painted work was now required but that it was now purely decorative and the split between Fine Art and Decorative Art becomes apparent to us, with hindsight, although it may well not have been so clear-cut at the time. So the Princess Anna's lovely new four-post bed in 1534 was merely gilded and the finials on top were painted – all no doubt most delicately, but it will have been a far cry from the pictorial splendours of the previous century.[11] Ambitious paintwork was principally to be found on musical instruments, particularly keyboard instruments which have large lids that provide an extensive surface for

97

97 Subtle effects with lacquer on gold

A magnificent wooden throne, carved to look like stone but too delicate to be the real thing; lacquered with a transparent red varnish over gilding, the arabesques being reserved (see p. 99). The small plaques carved in relief may be of ivory, inset. As the patterns on the silks are entirely plausible, one can presumably also trust the representation of the woodwork and may assume that something along these lines, even if a little less elaborate, was to be seen in splendid settings – in great churches or at the courts of princes.

Stefano Veneziano, *Madonna Enthroned with Child*, 1369
Museo Correr, Venice (photograph: Scala)

98 Delicate paintwork around 1500

Several favourite techniques are to be seen here including marbling and gilding, as well as skilful infilling with moresque patterns.

Emilian artist working about 1510
Museo Poldi-Pezzoli, Milan (No. 1589)

decoration. In 1536 the Duke Ercole II's sister Leonora, who was mother superior of the fashionable convent of Corpus Domini, had the case of her harpsichord [*clavicembalo*] painted with floral decoration 'touched with gold' [*fatta foiami tochatti doro*].[12]

Indeed it was floral ornament (usually formalized rather than natural), arabesques or moresques, and grotesques that now held the stage. Any human figures that are present tend to be small. The man who gilded and painted the Princess's bed in the same year also decorated two benches with arabesques [*due bancheti fatti da rabesco*] and the Duke's arms.[13] A superb harp was ordered in Rome in 1581 for the Duke Alfonso II's private orchestra, the *musica secreta* where the performances by three of his wife's ladies-in-waiting excited the greatest admiration. Anna Guarini played the viola, Livia d'Arco the lute. The harp was intended for Laura Peperara who was the most talented of them all.[14] This instrument was decorated at Ferrara with carving by Oratio Lamberti who was Flemish, and with delicate lacquered effects on a gold ground by Giulio Marescotti in a miniature arabesque style, this master receiving payment in 1587 for having done the work *de miniare con colori et oro un' Arpa d'ordine di S[ua] A[ltezza]*. The harp is today one of the great treasures of the Galleria Estense at Modena.[15]

The Venetian virginals that belonged to our Queen Elizabeth, dating from about 1570, are decorated in the same lacquered technique with miniature arabesques or moresques.[16] The lacquer (red, green, blue, black) is painted over the gold ground and is translucent, rather like some types of modern nail-varnish, so that the gold shows through. But the pattern is chiefly rendered by leaving its lines exposed (i.e. not covered with lacquer) so it is the ground that is lacquered while the pattern is 'reserved', as it is called. The effect can be stunning and was much favoured in the second half of the sixteenth century and into the first half of the next century, for particularly sumptuous furnishings. Caskets and other small boxes might be decorated in the same way, a certain class of Venetian work being executed on a ground of mother-of-pearl which shone through the lacquer in the same way as the gold. Of course moresque patterns could equally well be painted with gold or opaque pigments, in the normal way, without the ground showing through.

Clearly there were exciting new developments in paint technology and painting techniques during the sixteenth century. These are reflected in descriptions like that of 1575 concerning some beds that were silvered and somehow coated with *Lacha di grana* [which may well have meant red-stained lacquer of the 'nail-varnish' kind that figures so prominently on the harp and the virginals just mentioned] and with *verde ramo a olio con vernice di Mastici* [copper-green in oil with a mastic varnish],[17] and another bed of 1589 finished with *lacha di cremese con vernice a oglio pure* [crimson lacquer with oil varnish as well].[18] Probably such work *aminiato* with delicate arabesque patterns that clearly derive from the Near East was sometimes called *alla damaschina*, for when the harp got damaged and Lamberti was asked to carved a new finial for it (in 1591), it was described as the *Arpa damaschina*.[19] The question of whether a few discerning patrons of talented craftsmen were familiar with Oriental lacquer, at the

98

very end of the century, and in consequence may have had imitations made in Rome, is discussed on p. 157, incidentally.

The work of Renaissance artists practising at Crema and in neighbouring cities has been the subject of a study[20] which stresses the range of talent or capability among painters in that area at the time and has many illustrations showing the different levels of achievement. The author has drawn attention to whole dynasties of artists, each successive generation being trained in the parents' workshops, some carrying out fine work but many performing repetitive tasks like painting household Madonnas for hanging in bedchambers (p. 216) of which many thousands were produced as virtually every household required at least one. Moreover, most families with pretensions to gentility wanted their coats of arms or *imprese* painted wherever they would catch a visitor's eye.

If excellent quattrocento painters were not ashamed to carry out ornamental work, by the same token men of rank did not consider it undignified to be painters. One of the sons of the Marquis Niccolò III of Ferrara was engaged as a painter.[21] At Castelleone, Ilario Rodiani, a man of noble birth, was a talented painter who was assisted by his daughter Honorata, in the fifteenth century.[22] Several noble families at Crema produced painters or artists capable of decorating a wide range of objects or acting as designers. In the sixteenth century, however, the high-born became more self-conscious and could no longer allow themselves to take part in what then came to be regarded as a trade.

Something has already been said about graining (p. 92). The same technique is used for 'marbling' which was by no means unknown in the fifteenth and sixteenth centuries. Indeed, no other nation has ever excelled the Italians in this realm. The fact that a nail has been driven into the wall in the picture by Carpaccio reproduced in Pl. 38 shows the wall cannot have been of marble but must have been marbled (i.e. with paintwork). Once printing had become well established, some printers ran off sheets with grained patterns on them, or decorated with moresque borders and the like; Pl. 99 shows a sheet of printed borders. Such papers could be pasted onto furniture and coloured up to produce a simulation of a painted wooden surface. At Kloster Wienhausen near Celle in northern Germany, there are some ceilings entirely faced with elaborate grained and ornamented papers and it would not be surprising if similar papers were used in northern Italy which was in such close touch with Germany. *Tarsie* might also be imitated in paintwork. Lorenzo de' Medici had several pieces of rather grand furniture which were of walnut with simulated *tarsie* [*cholorito di noce e dipinto di silio*].[23]

Painting and gilding went hand in hand during the fourteenth and fifteenth centuries, and were practised in the same workshop even if, no doubt, there were those in each establishment who specialized in one or other of the two very different techniques. Gilding is of course meant to look like solid gold, a fact that we tend to forget when we today see gilded antiques where the gold is damaged, filthy and often actually coated with a toning varnish to give it a *patina*. It was always an expensive finish and only the most glamorous furnishings were gilded. As the Venetian sumptuary regulations of 1530 warned, nothing is guaranteed to consume a person's cash so effectively as gilding [*non essendo cosa nella qual più si*

99 Paste-on ornament; 1470s

The strips and squares of ornament printed on this sheet were intended for cutting out and pasting on wood or card to produce an effect of carved decoration. The patterns might then be coloured by hand. Such prints were mostly used by frame-makers but might also be pasted around prints pasted directly on a wall (see p. 52). This is believed to have been engraved by Francesco Rosselli in the 1470s. He was a member of a family of painters that included Cosimo Rosselli, executor of *cassone* panels, who became a successful print-maker and maker of maps. Whatever its precise date, this is an early example of printed paper ornament intended for woodwork, a form of embellishment much used in the late sixteenth and early seventeenth centuries in Flanders.

Francesco Rosselli(?), designs for a picture frame, engraving
Metropolitan Museum of Art, New York, Harrison Brisbane Dick Fund, 1927 (29.16.3)

99

perda et si consumi il danaro che in questa].[24] The painted front of a quattrocento chest, now considered worthy of being hung, suitably framed, in a museum, will often have cost less to execute than the gilded areas which surrounded it originally.[25]

Gilding was executed on a gesso ground applied to the woodwork.[26] Added interest was commonly provided by applying gesso ornaments or figures in relief prior to the gilding (p. 96). These reliefs, produced from moulds, could be assembled in a different order on each chest, to produce variety, although an expensive chest might have a carefully designed and integrated pattern of gesso-relief overall.

Gilding, like painting, was of less consequence in the sixteenth century when carving was the principal form of decoration. In Italy at this time carving was usually executed in walnut, but it was not uncommon to add touches of gilding to scrollwork, borders and the like. Moreover gilding came back in a new guise as a background for lacquered decoration, as we have just noted.

Craftsmen

The woodworkers [*marangoni*] of Venice were divided into four groups by the mid-sixteenth century. The least refined craftsmanship was that of the *Marangon de Fabrica* who ran up the wooden structure of buildings and carried out ordinary carpentry. The *Marangon de Noghera* worked in walnut [*noghera*] and other fine woods, but were working in the solid; they were joiners. The *Marangon de Soaze* made picture-frames and tabernacles. And then there were the *Remesseri* who executed inlay and, later, marquetry (p. 92); these were 'cabinetmakers' in our parlance.[1] There were also carvers, and there were painters. In early times the painters also carried out gilding; later gilding was often done by the carvers or, rather, in their establishments. And finally there were the turners who worked with a lathe.

Woodworkers at Ferrara and Modena called themselves *marangoni* as well but in Milan they were called (in Latin, in official documents) *Magistri a Lignamine*, a title they acquired in the fourteenth century but were still enjoying when the Emperor Charles V gave them fresh Statutes in 1554. At Genoa, in the late fourteenth century, mention was made of *Cassiari, bancalari e caseleri* which one might suppose meant the makers of chests [*casse*], those who made benches [*banchi*] and probably also tables, and those who made small-scale items of some delicacy [*caselli, cassette*], but the distinctions may have been otherwise.[2]

Another group of workers principally in wood were the musical instrument makers. They needed to be skilful in various ways. Those making wind instruments used a lathe and had to work with considerable accuracy. Keyboard instruments required a great deal of technical expertise, and those who made stringed instruments like lutes and viols had to have a good eye for shape and a delicate touch. Moreover, instruments made for rich customers or patrons were commonly decorated and quite a lot of this work was probably done 'in house', in the instrument-maker's workshop, although particularly ambitious work no doubt was sent round to specialists. We saw how the decoration of a fine harp at Ferrara was farmed out to several specialists (p. 99).

Italian keyboard instruments were mostly made by Italian craftsmen, judging by the names inscribed on their productions, but many of the best lutes were made by Germans working in Padua, Bologna and Venice,[3] and it is striking how many craftsmen coming from the Low Countries and the Rhineland (and therefore usually called *fiamingo* or *todesco*) were active as skilled woodworkers all over Italy during the Renaissance, not just as makers of musical instruments but in all fields of the craft. Already in 1450 we find three Germans working for the court at Ferrara – Leonardo, Simone and Augustino da Alemagna, who are described as *intagliatori de legname* [carvers in wood]. They were working on an important commission alongside Arduino da Baiso, the principal woodworker in Ferrara at that time (p. 101).[4] We noted how a Flemish carver worked on a fine harp used in the private orchestra under Alfonso II d'Este in the late 1580s (p. 101) and we find another Fleming, Jacobus Fiamengo, working as a cabinetmaker at Naples in the 1590s, executing superbly veneered cabinets and tables.[5] In the documents he is described as a *scrittorista di avolio* [maker of scriptors (or cabinets) of ivory], his work being distinctive on account of his use of ivory in the contriving of intricate designs decorated with fine engraving.

Germans as a whole have long excelled at woodwork but it has been particularly the peoples living in the Lower Rhineland, and in neighbouring Flanders and the adjacent Low Countries, that have produced many of the world's outstanding craftsmen in wood – many of whom left their native country in order to practise their trade in foreign parts. Abroad, they often came to occupy highly regarded positions, the famed seventeenth- and eighteenth-century Parisian cabinetmakers Boulle, Oeben, Van der Cruse and Weisweiler being outstanding cases in point, but one could list many others, not only among Parisian cabinetmakers but in most of the principal cities of Europe. It is interesting to note, however, that this pattern was already becoming established in the fifteenth century in Italy.

Metalwork

For the purposes of this book it will here suffice to clarify the basic metalwork terminology in order the better to understand what the descriptions in the inventories mean.

One might expect that the names of the chief metals would present no difficulty and, in the case of silver and lead [*argento* and *piombo*] they do not do so. But *stagno* meant both tin and pewter. The later is an alloy that, admittedly, contains a high proportion of tin and, as tin was not used to any great extent unalloyed, it is probably safe to say that all references to

100

stagno during the Renaissance in fact concern pewter. In the same way *ramo* meant copper but it could also mean brass, which is of course an alloy of copper with some zinc.

Bronzo meant bronze but Florio* confusingly tells us that it meant 'brasse, or bell-mettle', the latter being akin to bronze. Further confusion arises when we discover that a *bronzo* was a ewer, many of which were in fact of bronze including some of the most handsome, although they could also be made of silver or pewter. For example the Bishop of Ferrara in 1494 had *tri bronzi* [three ewers] of silver[1] and the Duchess of Urbino offered to sell two silver-gilt basins with their ewers to Isabella d'Este in 1516 when they were described as *dui bacilli con dui bronzi da mano* [*da mano* implying that they were for the ceremonial washing of hands at meals].[2] Fortunately for the scholar struggling with inventories, the commoner word for a ewer was *bronzino*, so we find mention in an inventory of 1474 of four bronze basins with their *bronzini*.[3] The same kind of transference of meaning from metal to vessel occurred with *stagno* (tin or pewter, or a jug/ewer, as we noted) which was also sometimes extended to become *stagnono* or *stagnara*, where a vessel was concerned.[4]

A fine kind of pewter was known as *peltre*. It was alloyed with copper and/or antimony, and occasionally with bismuth. In a Venetian inventory of 1592[5] there is a list headed *Peltri* which clearly refers to the household pewter. Pewter cannot be hammered so it has to be cast. Relief ornament can be imparted to the surface during the casting process. In former times pewter was always polished, in which state it closely resembles silver. Most pewter was plain so this bright effect was particularly important. There are no deposits of tin in Italy so little or no pewter was made there; it all had to be imported and was therefore comparatively expensive.

Bronze is an alloy of two soft metals, tin and copper, which fuse to become a hard one. It was not suitable for tableware as it might, in the presence of acids, produce substances harmful to human beings if ingested with food or drink. This presented no problem with ewers intended for water and the rinsing of hands at mealtimes, or for purely decorative vessels to stand on a *credenza*, for instance, and the talents of considerable artists were sometimes directed into designing and fashioning such objects. Bronze was also much favoured by sculptors who made small figures – true sculpture – and utensils of an ornamental kind including inkwells, hand-bells, candlesticks and the like. Some of these utensils are delightful works of art in their own right as well as being items of practical use. So greatly were the small 'bronzes' sought by collectors and people of taste that imitations in less expensive materials were made, not with intent to deceive, merely to satisfy a demand. Plaster of Paris or terracotta figurines might be given a convincing bronze-like finish; discerning collectors owned such objects (p. 269).[6]

An important class of object often made of brass (the cheaper sort was of stone) was the mortar [*mortaio*] which, together with a pestle, was used for grinding all kinds of things. The mortar was not merely an essential tool of the trade for the apothecary; it was also needed in the kitchen or wherever the often expensive spices were ground up prior to use in the preparation of food. They were moreover sometimes needed by a

100 Bathing the baby

Prominent is a large bronze ewer and a deep basin that is here being used for washing the new-born Virgin Mary. The nurse tests the temperature of the water with an age-old gesture. St Anne lies on a bed [*lettiera*] which has a separate tester and curtains suspended from the ceiling. Note how indistinct is the deeply coffered ceiling, even when daylight is coming from the window on the left, and how strong is the light from the fire in front of which a woman airs a nappy.

Domenico Beccafumi, *Birth of the Virgin*, 1540–43
Pinacoteca, Siena (photograph: Scala)

101 A *credenza* dressed with plate, about 1480

This is a fresco that came to light during recent restoration showing a table serving as a *credenza*, with two stages at the back, with silver and parcel-gilt plate displayed in a symmetrical arrangement (see also Pl. 236). Three dishes covered with napkins lie in front. Behind is depicted a delightful verdure tapestry of Flemish origin, shown as if hooked up to form a *spalliera*. Painted in the style of Melozzo da Forlì in the *sala* of the Roman residence of Girolamo Riario and his wife Caterina Sforza, probably around 1477–81. The building is today known as the Palazzo Altemps (see Pl. 329).

Photograph: by permission of the Soprintendenza Archeologica di Roma

101

householder who had to prepare powders and potions for his family (especially if staying beyond easy reach of a doctor, during the summer recess), or by persons with a scientific bent who wanted to carry out experiments of some kind. The mortar could indeed be seen as an adjunct of learning and professional status. A version of bronze used for some objects of this general class was 'latten', in Italian called *latone*.[7]

Brass is an alloy of copper and zinc but it was not possible to isolate the latter metal until long after the end of the Renaissance, it being added to the copper as a compound known as calamine before that. Brass conducts heat well and was therefore used for the handles of fire-irons of the better sort. It takes a polish exceptionally well which explains why it was used for the finials of fire-dogs that reflected the flames in an exciting manner. When it was used for such purposes it was frequently called *ottone*.[8]

Like bronze, brass could give off poisonous compounds if used for cooking or tableware, but it was fine for water-vessels and other essentially utilitarian items. Brass was much used for scientific instruments and clocks, on the other hand, in which form it was to be seen in very exalted circles.[9] It lent itself well to engraving.

Brass vessels (mostly large dishes or basins) could be inlaid with silver, a process called damascening. This was a Venetian speciality but vessels *alla domaschina* may well have been made in several places and some of them may have been imported from the Near East whence the technique and original inspiration had undoubtedly come. Such objects were evidently prized and their presence among household furnishings was usually noted specially.[10] In the middle of the sixteenth century Vasari could speak of how in his time great advances had been made in this particular field [*in cio grandemente gli (moderni) hanno avanzati*] and that there were now being made *cose lodevoli e tenute maravigliose* [by which he must mean that they were highly praiseworthy objects that were considered truly marvellous].[11] The Venetian sumptuary regulations of 1562 tried to forbid citizens sporting such glamorous confections in their houses.[12]

Iron was of course widely used and was at this time always wrought (although cast 'pigs' of iron were used as a first stage in the manufacturing process). Prominent in many houses were window-grilles that prevented people climbing through windows on the lower floors (Pls 29, 291), sheet iron that was nailed to many outside doors, and nails which could have highly decorative heads and were to be seen studding doors, shutters and furniture. The thin straps of iron used to fortify chests in the fourteenth and fifteenth centuries were usually tinned and so had a silver-white appearance which was itself decorative, but the primary purpose of this treatment was to ward off rust (Pl. 226).

Steel is a modified and hard form of iron; iron can be filed or engraved with a steel implement. Steel was not to be seen much around the house, except where there was armour, but carving-knives and cutlery were of steel. By the sixteenth century some locksmiths were executing delicate mechanisms in steel and occasionally made jewel-caskets and safes of this strong material. Moreover, when armour was going out of use, towards the end of that century, some Milanese armourers turned to making decorative objects of steel inlaid with brass and silver, just like the showier kinds of armour.

Steel mirrors, which were much used in the fifteenth and early sixteenth centuries (p. 234), were of a steel to which copper, tin, antimony and arsenic were added. They took a fine polish but the polished surface had to

102

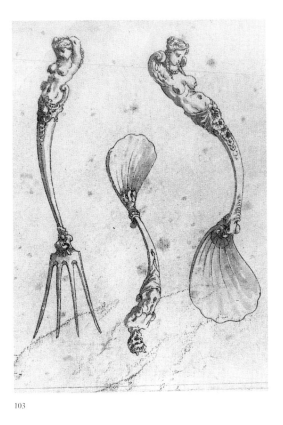

103

102 A Medici wine-fountain of about the 1550s

A shield with the Medici arms is attached to the collar round the horse's neck that bears the word 'Arezzo' (precisely why is not at present known). Probably intended to be made of silver, gilded. Wine from the central reservoir spews from the masks on the rim into the large dish which has figures in relief that show through the liquid. The effect would have been particularly delightful if red wine were used, the gilding showing through in flashes. The three tripod stands sketched below may have been ideas for a support for the vessel although stands like this normally supported basins for hand-washing, and one would expect a wine-fountain to stand on the dining-table, rather than to be separated from it.

By courtesy of the Trustees of Sir John Soane's Museum (photograph: Ole Woldbye)

103 'Designer cutlery', about 1545

Delightful drawing attributed to Antonio Gentili who worked in Rome during the middle decades of the sixteenth century. One should envisage these designs as being executed in silver, perhaps gilded or partly so – or, just possibly, with the figures coloured with enamels.

Cooper–Hewitt Museum, New York (1938–88–7848)

104 Polished pewter on display

On a *credenza*, of the later type with a cupboard base, is set out a service of pewterware. Well polished, this almost resembles silver and certainly makes a brave show, as we see here. The elegant ewer and basin, probably of brass, stand ready for the largely ceremonial rinsing of fingers before and after meals. On this occasion they will be needed on practical grounds as the company is about to eat asparagus.

C. P. Cavagna, The Last Supper (detail), S. Martino, Treviglio, near Bergamo, 1602
Photograph courtesy of Banca Poplare di Bergamo

Ceramics

104

be well protected against anything that might scratch, pit or tarnish the reflecting surface. Eventually steel mirrors were ousted by mirrors of glass.

Little need be said about silver. Because it was such an expensive metal it tended only to be entrusted to talented craftsmen and it was towards the workshops of silversmiths and goldsmiths that the cleverest craftsmen gravitated. As a result wonders were often created in this medium, but most of it has long since been melted down. Silver plate is commonly listed separately in the inventories, which underlines its value and its special character.

Vessels of earthenware are depicted in fifteenth-century paintings but references to such items are not all that common in the inventories of the time that we have consulted. This could be explained, perhaps, by our having only scrutinized the household inventories of rich or relatively wealthy people who tended to use vessels of metal rather than earthenware.[1] Pottery vessels of whatever kind were at any rate chiefly to be found in kitchens and other service areas; most were essentially utilitarian and need not detain us here. On the other hand, vessels used for hand-washing at the dining-table, or for early morning ablutions in the bedchamber, had to be finer, even showy, as they might be seen by guests and other visitors. In addition there was a class of vessel that was made entirely for display, for which reason a good deal of trouble was taken over its decoration. Refined ceramics suitable for such purposes were not produced in Italy much before the middle of the fifteenth century, and any ceramic ware used in elegant surroundings before that will have been imported. In the sixteenth century references to pottery vessels become commoner and it is clear that wares of the finer sort were now generally acceptable for polite use in the higher echelons of society.

We do of course come across the occasional reference to vessels of earthenware [*di terra*][2] in fifteenth-century inventories but in most cases the items concerned are exceptional in some way or are being contrasted with other vessels. For example there was an oil-jar in a Genoese mansion in 1459 that was green [*jarra uno pro oleo terra viridis*] (Spinola Invt.) while five more oil jars are listed in the Este inventories which were of middling size [*orne ... de terra da olio mezane*] but they were standing alongside some jars of marble (Este Invt., Ferrara, 1436). The green jar will have had a lead glaze that was coloured green. The other colours then available for this purpose were a pale yellow, various shades of brown, and a smoky blue.

Among the lead-glazed wares was one class that was undoubtedly made for display. This was a refined sort of incised slipware, the decoration of which was accomplished by scratching the design through a cream-coloured slip that covered the entire ground so that the ground (usually a reddish brown) showed up as brown lines on the cream forming a background. In the more ambitious examples the slip was scraped away leaving areas of pattern, not just lines. This 'scratched ware' could be further embellished by tinting the subsequently applied lead glaze in the manner just mentioned. Handsome *sgraffio* ware was produced at various centres north of the Apennines (notably at Ferrara, Bologna, Venice and Padua) and in Florence, during the second half of the fifteenth century[3] but we have not noticed any references that would seem to refer to such pottery in the inventories and it could well be that high-class *sgraffio* ware was really not at all common; indeed, relatively little survives, quite probably because very little was made, and it must be admitted that it is a much less attractive material than maiolica – to which references are quite common.

Maiolica is one of the several names that have been given to tin-glazed earthenware; that is to say, earthenware with a lead glaze to which tin oxide has been added so that the glaze becomes opaque and white. A particularly imposing and attractive form of tin-glazed ware was made in Spain, first at Malaga and Murcia and subsequently at Manises near Valencia, which was decorated with patterns painted on the glaze that has a lustrous metallic effect as a result of a third firing in the kiln. Spanish lustreware was eagerly acquired by rich Italians in the fifteenth century, not a little of it specially commissioned with the arms of the Italian owner painted on it.[4] It was mostly imported through Majorca and it is believed that the word maiolica is a corruption of the name of that island (the Spanish of course pronounce Majorca with a soft 'j'). It would moreover seem that all references to maiolica in Italian inventories before about 1520 are likely to concern the Spanish tin-glazed lustreware although, later, the term was applied to tin-glazed wares made in Italy, whether lustred or not. This glamorous Spanish pottery was certainly made primarily for display or ostentatious use and it figures in many of the inventories of fine houses, in the best rooms. At Udine the Monticoli family had twelve small flat dishes of this ware and twelve bowls, in 1413, while the De Fece in Siena in 1450 had no fewer than twenty-seven pieces.[5] In both cases these treasures were kept in a chest. Sometimes such ware is actually described as being *de Valentia*[6] but in one Genoese inventory (Lomellini Invt.) the ware is called *terre de Malica* which is presumably a corruption of maiolica rather than of *Malaga* even though, in Valencia, lustreware had at first been called 'Malaga work' [*obra de melica*] because that was where it had initially been made. Attempts were made to produce lustreware of the Spanish type at Siracusa in Sicily and maybe also in the Aragonese kingdom of Naples, but perhaps not with any high degree of success as discriminating people at the time could apparently distinguish between *li veri da mursia* [the real things of Murcia?] and the south Italian imitations.[7] Late in the fifteenth century lustreware was being made at Deruta, in Umbria, and the technique was soon adopted elsewhere in that province and in the Duchy of Urbino. On the back of a lustre plate made at Gubbio in 1532 is painted the phrase *fini di maiolica* [finished in maiolica],[8] a reminder that this term had for more than a century implied that a piece of pottery was decorated with this greatly admired finish.

Tin-glazed ware of a primitive kind was being made in several parts of Italy by 1400. The glaze was not very white and the decoration was of a simple kind.[9] As tin glaze was in fact a lead glaze with tin oxide added, there was no great technical distinction between the opaque white tin-glazed wares and those glazed with the transparent lead glaze although they appear very different. At any rate, during the fifteenth century, both were described perfectly correctly as being *di terra*, of earthenware. Even as late as the 1570s, elaborate vessels made at Urbino were described as *vasi di terra* although they were outstanding examples of tin-glazed pottery, decorated skilfully with grotesques.[10] So, although during the sixteenth century Italian tin-glazed ware was sometimes referred to as maiolica (even though it was not lustred),[11] *di terra* remained the normal

term throughout the Renaissance. Thus early Italian maiolica from important centres like Siena, Montelupo, Viterbo and Savona must be masquerading behind this neutral label, or occasionally behind descriptions like *lavoro da Montelupo*.[12]

Italian maiolica, the home-grown tin-glazed ware, became increasingly sophisticated in potting, form and decoration, so that, by the third quarter of the fifteenth century, the best qualities were considered acceptable in discriminating circles, if not for the grandest use, then at least by grand people when they felt they could be informal. The level of acceptance in polite circles can be judged by the prevalence of vessels bearing family coats of arms or *imprese* which become common after about 1470.[13]

The question of how and where maiolica was used deserves a little attention even though it is never possible to hazard more than an informed guess about such matters. A pointer is to be found in the commentaries of Pope Pius II who tells us that Antonino, the Archbishop of Florence who died in 1459, lived very humbly and expected his household to do the same. He used only vessels of glass or earthenware, we are told, whereas of course everyone knew that such prelates normally dined in splendour off silver, with drinking-vessels to match. A few pages later Pius speaks of Borso d'Este, then recently created Duke of Ferrara. Borso liked to surround himself with the richest kinds of furnishings and 'even in the country he used gold and silver dishes'.[14] The implication would seem to be that, when relaxing at their villa or country seat, most people tended to use some less costly form of tableware. It is therefore interesting to find Eleonora della Rovere, Duchess of Urbino (a city where some of the very finest maiolica was made in the 1520s) writing to her mother, Isabella d'Este, telling her that she had commissioned a set of vessels for a sideboard [*una credenza de vasi di terra*] which she was now having sent over to Mantua, hoping these would be acceptable for use at Porto, one of Isabella's villas, 'because it is a villa thing' [*cosa da villa*].[15] Here, it seems, a distinction is being made between what was suitable in the country and the more expensive services that a person like Isabella would be expected to use in her city residence. A somewhat similar notion would explain why a member of the Medici family in 1470 commissioned another sideboard garniture from the Montelupo potters which was intended *per la caccia* [for the chase].[16] Like Isabella's service this was no doubt highly decorative – rather like our own 'cottage china' – and, if it got broken, that was not too serious a matter. Anyway, it saved the silver from the rough and tumble of the hunt and country picnics. When Clarice Strozzi ordered a service of eighty-four pieces from the Montelupo potteries in 1517, it was for her villa, Le Selve, near Florence; and Giovanni Batista Barpo, writing of *Le Delitie e i Frutti dell' Agricoltura e della Vina* (Venice, 1634), said that at your villa you should have – according to your means – several spoons and forks of silver and some plates of beautiful maiolica in order always to retain a measure of civility and to show that you are well born [*alcuni piatti di bella majolica, per conservar sempre certa civiltà, e dimonstratione d'esser ben nato*].[17] So, by the early seventeenth century, a set of *maiolica* could show that your credentials were in order but it was nevertheless essentially 'a villa thing' – for informal occasions.

111 All-over painted maiolica dish

The arms are those of Julius II, the della Rovere pope (1503–13). The white tin glaze of the ground has been reserved so as to form the figures and principal ornaments. This composition was evidently intended to be seen standing upright, as it would be if displayed on a *credenza*. Perhaps this dish formed part of a service for use at a papal villa or on hunting picnics.

Giovanni Maria, workshop, Castel Durante, 1508
Metropolitan Museum of Art, New York (1975.1.1015)

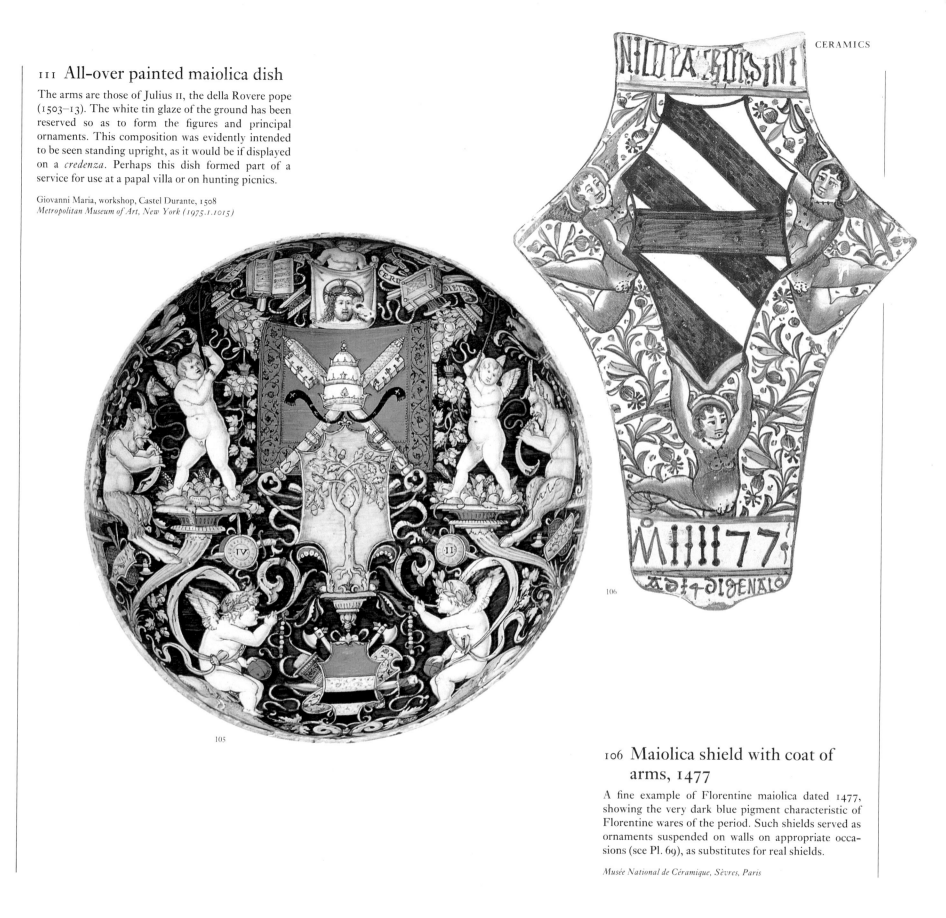

105

106

106 Maiolica shield with coat of arms, 1477

A fine example of Florentine maiolica dated 1477, showing the very dark blue pigment characteristic of Florentine wares of the period. Such shields served as ornaments suspended on walls on appropriate occasions (see Pl. 69), as substitutes for real shields.

Musée National de Céramique, Sèvres, Paris

BENEDICTVSDOMINVSDEVSISRAELQVIAVISITA

107 Glazed terracotta ornaments

On the bed-head stand two vases of flowers. Full-sized vases of flowers or baskets of fruit were executed in polychrome glazed terracotta at the Della Robbia factory in Florence, in the early sixteenth century, for use as ornaments like this. The scene is the birth of St John the Baptist and it was made of Della Robbia ware in 1511 when the establishment was under the direction of Giovanni della Robbia.

S. Leonardo, Cerreto Guidi, near Florence
Photograph: Alinari Archives

107

While even the finest qualities of maiolica made in Italy between, let us say, 1480 and 1530 were regarded as of humbler status than silver plate (it was much less expensive, for a start), it seems clear that it gave pleasure to many discerning people who did not need to have it offending their eyes if they had not approved of it. Pope Sixtus IV and Lorenzo the Magnificent both expressed thanks for gifts of maiolica, saying that they valued it more than if it had been made of gold or silver – which not only seems to imply considerable approval but shows that such ware was considered suitable for important gifts. A little later, we find Isabella d'Este having a piece of maiolica repaired, which she would not have done unless she had valued it. And we find her nephew, the Duke of Ferrara, asking Titian to supervise the making of some maiolica in Venice, which indicates that this ware found favour with the Duke and that, in his estimation, it was worth engaging an artistic consultant of high reputation to ensure that the commission, whatever it was, came to be executed in the best possible manner.[18]

The painted decoration on Italian maiolica had become ever more skilful and ambitious as the fifteenth century advanced. By the early sixteenth century it often covered the entire surface so that none of the white ground was visible. Eventually there was a reaction to this and maiolica that was entirely white or with only sparse painted decoration came into fashion. This was known simply as *maiolica biancha* or *terra biancha* and was first developed at Faenza.[19] Montaigne, travelling through Tuscany in 1581, encountered this earthenware 'which is so white and clean … that it seems to me pleasanter for the table than the pewter of France, particularly what one finds in inns which is squalid.'[20] Food looks more appetizing served on a white plate. An important commission was given in 1563 to Bernardino Cattolo di Faenza, then established in Ferrara as maiolica-maker to the court. This was for *due credenze di Maiolica Biancha* and was ordered by Cardinal Ippolito II d'Este.[21]

One can imagine that it required the talents of considerable artists to design important services, as the technical skills of the potters increased and important patrons grew to accept maiolica for prominent display. Already by 1520 or so, the well-known painter Dosso Dossi was providing designs for the *bochallari* at Ferrara. Of course he was not only a painter at the Este Court; he had to undertake the designing of all kinds of decoration for his demanding masters.[22] Much later Battista Franco and Taddeo Zuccaro, both well-established painters, could be found design-ing maiolica services.[23] No doubt the resulting pottery was highly accomplished but there was a tendency to imitate the forms of metalwork vessels which led in consequence to the loss of the satisfying character that pottery conforming to ceramic tradition possesses. Much of it was decorated with small-scale grotesques, the best of which was produced at the Urbino factory of the Fontana family; Cardinal Ferdinando de' Medici, the future Grand-Duke of Tuscany, in 1573 received from Flaminio Fontana an imposing group of vessels *di terra d'Urbino, lavorati a grottesca*.[24] The Cardinal made presents of such flamboyant pottery to high prelates of the Church and, it would seem, also to a lady, no doubt high-born, who was expecting a baby. This would seem to be the implication of the entry in the same list that reads *uno credentino da donne di parto* [a set of the kind given to women who have given birth].

Another class of object made of maiolica that could have a notable effect on the appearance of the interior of fine buildings was the tile. Bricks and lead-glazed tiles had of course been available long before the Renaissance, and many of the forms were suitable for flooring. It was not until well into the fifteenth century, that tiles of the colourful maiolica were produced.

In 1441 the chief court painter at Ferrara, Jacopo Sagramoro, and his assistants obtained pigments from Venice in order to decorate glazed tiles [*quadri di preda in vedriati*][25] which were almost certainly of a tin-glazed ceramic ware of the kind also produced by the Della Robbia firm in Florence by the 1450s and probably before that.[26] The Della Robbia product is usually described as being of terracotta, but for our purposes it is the visual effect that matters, and in this respect there is little difference between tin-glazed terracotta and maiolica. If there is a difference, it may be that terracotta lends itself more readily to modelling. Sagramoro provided designs on paper for the Ferrara tiles which were to be used for re-facing benches or edgings round the flowerbeds in the Fountain Court of the castle. Della Robbia tiles were used for facing small areas of wall more than on floors (Pl. 108). However, beautiful maiolica tiles from Faenza are still to be seen on the floor in San Petronio, Bologna (1487), and others from Pesaro of about 1494 are to be seen in the Victoria and Albert Museum.[27] Painted tiles were not in much favour in Italy, the maiolica tiles laid in the Logge at the Vatican in around 1519 being among the last important manifestations of the genre. When such tiles were used in 1516 to pave Sanmichele's Petrucci's chapel (S. Domenico, Orvieto), they were mostly plain. The effect is pretty, in a 'farmhouse manner', but nothing more ambitious than some simple coats of arms was attempted in what must have been quite an important commission.

Brick tiles continued to be made, on the other hand, and there are some glazed terracotta tiles at the Villa Imperiale at Pesaro which have designs impressed or ornament in relief; they must date from about 1530. Tiles of terracotta with relief ornament were made in the fifteenth century. Some were glazed with a single colour, some were gilded all over.[28]

The making of reliefs with the Madonna and Child, or some similar holy subject, of the kind that was to be found in almost every bedchamber in fifteenth-century Italy (e.g. Pls 311, 374), was often achieved by series-production methods involving the use of moulds. Some of these tabernacle-figures were fairly crudely executed but the best reach quite high levels of artistic accomplishment and a few are outstanding. Among the last were the works in this line brought out by the Della Robbias. The first member of the family to take up series-production methods was Luca Della Robbia (1399–1482), a talented artist, when already well established as a sculptor in marble and bronze. He was presumably also producing run-of-the-mill tabernacle-figures in his workshops and, at some point, began to coat them with a glaze containing the tin oxide used for maiolica, but of a dense, opaque kind, thickly applied. So attractive were the results that he also used this technique for large one-off creations, some of which are sculptures of high artistic worth. The firm's activities in the field of repetitive sculpture and architectural ornament continued under Luca's successors well into the sixteenth century. Although much of the production took the form of reliefs, many items were three-dimensional – not merely angels and saints but also fruit and foliage. A useful form of Della Robbia ornament was a vase or basket of flowers which could stand as an individual piece of decoration on a cornice, for instance, or as a pair mounted as finials on a bedhead (Pl. 107). Two *vassi della Robbia con frute* [two vases . . . with fruit] were to be seen in the *sala* at the Capponi house in Florence in 1534 (Capponi Invt.); they may have graced the *credenza*.

Tin-glazed ware of great beauty was made at Isnik in Turkey from the late fifteenth century onwards and was certainly known in Italy because imitations of it were made there.[29] Persian tin-glazed ware of the sixteenth century, much of it decorated in imitation of Chinese porcelain, must also have reached Italy and may have been taken for the real thing by many of those who saw it. It will anyway have helped fuel the already strong desire, felt among Europeans of standing and discrimination, to own specimens of Chinese porcelain – true porcelain.

It was not until the late fifteenth century that Chinese porcelain reached the West in any quantity. Until well into the second half of the sixteenth century, indeed, it was still regarded as an exotic treasure, to be kept in a special place, be it a private study or a cabinet of curiosities, where it could be shown to those who would appreciate such a wonder.[30] For example, in the 1550s, Cosimo de' Medici kept most of his collection of Chinese porcelain in his Private Wardrobe [*Guardaroba Secreta*] at the Palazzo Vecchio, where the pieces were stored in cupboards. One contained a large number of items, mainly of blue and white porcelain but including some (green) celadon wares and some *a fiori rossi e verdi a uso di zucchetta* [with red and green flowers in the form of a gourd], while in another cupboard, amongst a lot of silver, was a wine-cooler (usually a large item) of blue and white porcelain and various smaller pieces. One item, in Florence, had a fitted leather case showing that it was considered worthy of special protection (Medici Invt., 1553). In the collector Alvise Odoni's house in Venice, we find him keeping his porcelain in his study where he had his most precious belongings. A reference to *porcellana* did not always mean that a genuine piece of Chinese or Japanese porcelain was

in question, even at this late date, but in Odoni's case we can be sure he knew the difference between the real thing and imitations in Italian maiolica (or Turkish or Persian imitations, for that matter), as he also listed actual maiolica items (specified as such) in the same room (Odini Invt., 1555). Venice, along with Faenza, was in fact renowned for its white maiolica which had some resemblance to porcelain. This is reflected in a letter of 1550 concerning *terraglie veneziane* [Venetian earthenware or maiolica] that Eleanora of Toledo, Cosimo de' Medici's wife, had ordered. Two kinds were available, the writer explained, 'one with many colours, the other without, but both closely resemble porcelain' [*ma ambidue tirano asai alla porcellana*] (Medici Invt., 1553). By the 1570s collectors like Cardinal Ferdinando de' Medici owned large quantities of porcelain. Its general shape is usually described but rarely is anything said about its decoration. Most of it was no doubt blue and white; some was gilded, we are told, and a few pieces were of celadon [*porcellane verde*].[31]

Although the makers of maiolica in sixteenth-century Italy had often painted their white wares to resemble Chinese porcelain, the character of the two products was entirely different – in weight and substance as well as appearance on anything like close inspection. This was apparent to the discerning and several attempts were made in Italy to invent a ceramic body that was like true porcelain. The basis was usually ground-up glass with an admixture of white clay. The first attempt that met with some success was made in Florence under the patronage of the Grand Duke Ferdinand between 1575 and his death in 1585.[32] The designer Bernardo Buontalenti seems to have been in charge of the project and was presumably responsible for the shape and decoration of this attractive ware. However, very little 'Medici Porcelain' was made.

Among those who were also seeking to imitate porcelain was the Duke Alfonso d'Este who had set up a certain Camillo d'Urbino in the castle at Ferrara with orders to perfect this precious material. Unfortunately the arcanist was mortally wounded in an explosion when a new culverin was being demonstrated by the Master of the Ducal Ordnance in 1567 (the gunner had been careless with a lighted candle). Quite unseemly were the steps taken to extract from the dying man the secrets of his process, which may not have added up to much, anyway. At any rate nothing came of the venture and the kilns were dismantled in 1570.[33]

108

108 The vivacious effect of Della Robbia ware

Tin-glazed terracotta tiles painted with coloured glazes at Luca della Robbia's establishment in Florence. Small areas of wall, floor or ceiling could be covered with such tiles in especially sumptuous surroundings.

Lucca della Robbia, detail from a Cardinal's tomb, S. Trinita, Florence
Photograph: Scala

Beds, Canopies and the *Lettuccio*

The basic structure and simple beds

A bed is a place to lie on and you need a bed of sorts when you want to sleep. A mat laid on the floor can constitute a bed, albeit a very simple one, but a bag filled with straw or feathers – a mattress – is more comfortable. You can insulate the mattress from the floor by placing it on a simple platform, and if you raise this sleeping-surface off the ground and place supports under it you have a bed of the kind that most people today would recognize as such. In Italian such a structure is called *un letto* (sometimes spelt *lecto* during the Renaissance) but this word could also be used to describe a mattress.[1] A similar usage existed in English at the time, the word 'bed' being used in reference both to the structure (usually of wood) and to the mattress. Thus a 'feather bed' was a mattress filled with feathers and a 'dust bed' was one filled with woollen flock of poor quality.

The base-board or *fondo* of a simple bed could be contrived with several planks [*assi*] assembled side by side; these could be joined together to form *una tavola* [lit. a table, which was of course a flat surface before it became a piece of furniture with legs]. The *tavola* (in Ferrara it was called *un tolado*, a corruption of *tavolato*) or the *assi* rested on a pair of trestles [*trespoli*, *trespidi*, *cavaletti*]. Thus a Venetian inventory of 1534 (Marcello Invt.) gives us *un par de cavaletti con le sue tavole da dormir suso* [a pair of trestles with their table to sleep upon], and a Genoese inventory of two years earlier (Fieschi Invt., 1532) has another pair *cum le tavolle suso per un lecto* [with the table upon them for a bed]. A bed of this basic form may be seen in Pl. 111 which reproduces a painting showing a girl sitting on a bed consisting of a mattress lying on a boarded base that rests on trestles. The picture dates from the early eighteenth century but the form of her bed is an ancient one, and the beds of many servants and most poor people during the Renaissance period must have looked very like this.

The trestles had to be sturdy and easily came to resemble a school bench or form (e.g. *uno letto su le panchette basse* [on low trestles, or small benches; Medici Invt., Florence, 1553, p. 23]. See diagram 13 on p. 361). The wife of the Lord of Ferrara had a bed that was new in 1436 (Este Invt.); it comprised a *tolado* that was accompanied by *Banche doe da trj arlotj per caschaduna … per lo dicto tolado* [two forms, each with three supports/legs …, for the said *tavolato*].[2] A *fondo* for a large bed might have eight planks (*panchette con otto pezzi d'asse*; Medici Invt., Florence, 1553) but a small one in Bologna was described as being *solum de quatuor assidibus* [only of four boards; Belvise Invt., 1335]. Although such arrangements may sound primitive, here we see the highest in the land sleeping on such a confection, and Montaigne, visiting Italy in 1580 could still say that the beds in Rome 'are wretched little trestles on which they throw planks' on which, surprisingly, 'you are very well lodged if you have a canopy'. 'I have no need for bedsteads. One is very comfortable', he adds.[3] By bedsteads he means proper beds with integral legs (discussed below). Although the gentry came across the simpler forms in rented

accommodation, inns and other temporary lodgings, they were otherwise by that time to be found in the rooms of relatively humble people only.

All but the most primitive beds had a headboard [*capezzale*, *cavezzale* – which, however, could also mean 'a bolster']. The headboard was also known as *una testiera*, as a *capoletto*, and as a *capuzzario* or *capellinaio*. These terms are discussed more fully in connection with the *lettiera* (p. 114). As footboards were less common, they were sometimes referred to as 'headboards at the foot-end' (e.g. *capezzale da piedi*; Este Invt., Ferrara, 1436).

Although some supporting trestles were decorated and therefore must have been intended to be seen,[4] it was normal on the better sort of bed to enclose the sides with boards set on edge; and, if there were no *capezzale da piedi*, no footboard rising well above the level of the *tavola*, a further board tended to be needed at the foot-end. A board flanking the *tavola* was called a *sponda*, a word that therefore corresponds to our 'bedside'. Up against the sides of such a bed could be placed benches or chests, and a chest might also be placed at the foot-end as well. The Ferrarese poet Matteo Boiardo, explaining how Islamic peoples were wont to sit on carpets spread on the floor, remarked that they did not sit on benches nor on the edge of the bed (*banco nè sponda*), which was to say 'not as we Italians do'.[5]

Exactly how the various boards were held together is not clear, in the case of a bed resting on trestles, but it must have become evident quite early on that a much more sturdy structure could be produced if vertical pieces of wood of square section were set at the corners, to which the vertical boards could be fixed with a pegged joint. It needed the skills of a joiner to construct, set up or dismantle such a bedstead which might be quite a massive piece of furniture. We can see pegged joints in Pls 114 and 115; such a joint requires skill to construct. If the corner-pieces were extended downwards, they came to form legs. When chests were standing against the sides of a bed one could not see such legs although they must have been present in most beds of the better sort during the Renaissance. Nevertheless, some quite grand beds continued to rest on trestles well into the fifteenth century. By the sixteenth century, however, this must have seemed a very old-fashioned arrangement, only fit for the humblest settings. When the inventory of a grand house in Palermo was taken in 1561 (Requesens Invt.), one large bed was found to have trestles and was in consequence described as 'very old' (*una lictera cum soi trispidi, vechissima*). A bedstead without its bedding may be seen in the view of a market-place in Bologna (Pl. 112). The corner-pieces forming legs are quite clear, one can see the planks forming the base inside, and the boards forming the sides are in fact panelled – a form of construction requiring a fair amount of skill. The three hospital beds to be seen in Pl. 121 are of the same type. The only reason one can see their legs is that, in hospital, patients do not require much storage-space so there was no need to place chests alongside, and they would anyway have got in the nurses' way.

Beds of simple conformation, especially when not fitted with great headboards and other heavy features, were known in France as *couches* (or, if very small, as *couchettes*).[6] People who had plenty of space and could

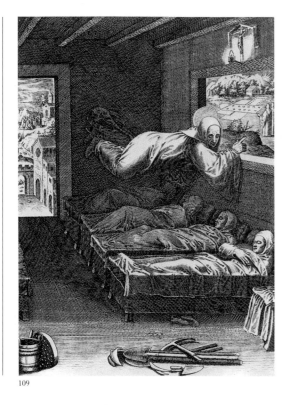

109

110

109 A monk's dormitory in the sixteenth century

A row of simple beds with plank sides fixed to corner-posts of square section that form legs. There apppear to be head-boards. These beds are simple versions of the *lettiera* (Pls 114, 118) which had however long gone out of fashion by the time this engraving was made to illustrate a book about St Benedict, published at Rome in 1579. The saint hovers over the sleeping monks, inspiring them to build yet another abbey. Note the crucifix with draped cloth and an oil-lamp fixed in front, burning all night.

From Bernardino Passeris, *Vita et Miracula Sanctiss'mi patris Benedicti*, Rome, 1579
Houghton Library, Harvard University, Cambridge, Massachussets
(362)

110 Set in the wall

The opening of this bed is fronted by a curtain that has a special peg over which it can be looped when pulled back. A seemingly rather narrow shelf or chest is fitted below the opening; this forms a seat for Mary who is reading at a desk. She rates two pillows!

Bartolomeo Vivarini, detail from a triptych, third quarter 15th century
Metropolitan Museum of Art, Robert Lehman Collection, 1975
(1975.1.82)

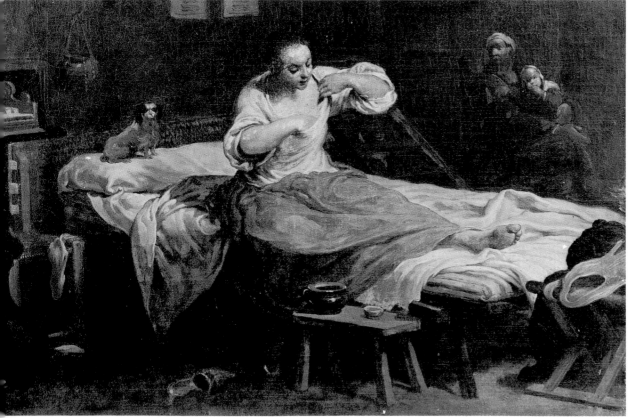

111

111 Simple bed on trestles

The striped mattress lies on a board made up with planks, and laid on trestles, one of which is clearly visible. A piece of rush-matting nailed to the wall serves as a head-board. Such beds were common during the Renaissance but, as this early eighteenth-century painting shows, they remained popular into modern times. Although her bed is simple and is placed in the kitchen, the girl is thought to be a courtesan (not a fine one, it would seem), the presence of a spinet (left), a lap-dog and an elegant slipper being cited as evidence – as indeed is the putatively erotic subject (she is searching her shift for fleas).

Giuseppe Crespi, *Ragazza che si spulcia*, c.1725
Museo di Capodimonte, Naples

afford the luxury of having a secondary, private bedroom or a small room to which one could retire for privacy during daytime, might have such a small bed standing in such a retreat. The *couche* served as a secondary bed or as a daybed – a couch, in fact. This simple and apparently humble form was to play an important part in the development of the bed in the sixteenth and seventeenth century, as we shall see.

Furnished with small wheels, low and small versions of the *couche* became truckle beds (also sometimes called trundle beds) that could be pushed out of the way under a great bed during daytime. *Soubz ledit charlit a una petite couche roulante*, under the aforesaid bed, is a small rolling bed, a French inventory of 1471 tells us.[7] Such wheeled *couches* or *couchettes*, also known in France as a *chariolle*,[8] were perfectly familiar to Italians throughout the Renaissance and many references to *una carriola/caruola* occur in their inventories, rarely with any explanation of what it was because that was unnecessary. However, Bartolo di Tura (Tura Invt.) had a great bed at his villa in Siena which had *una cariola con sachone, sotto a la decto lettiera* [with a straw mattress, under the said bed], and when Eleonora of Aragon described the bedchamber prepared for her reception in Rome in 1473, she mentioned the bed *et socto quisto lecto e una carriola*.[9] Truckle beds were usually occupied by personal servants of the great person who slept in the main bed; indeed, in one case we are told that two members of the household staff were sleeping in a single truckle bed [*e due famigli furono nel letto della carriuola*].[10] At Ferrara, in the earlier part of the fifteenth century, such a bed was called a *chariola da fioleto* and sometimes simply a *fioleto* which seems to imply use by a child – *figlioletto* (Este Invt., p. 43).

No doubt the beds described in inventories as simple [*semplice*] or as *salvatico* [rough, rude, savage][11] were sometimes of the same elementary form of construction as the basic *couche*, rather than of the type resting on trestles or benches. Servants and the less important members of a household slept on such beds which had few if any distinguishing features and attracted little attention as the inventory-writers went their rounds and recorded what they found in each room.

The wooden parts of a bed, as an ensemble, were usually called the *legniame* but in Genoa the term used was *un torchio* (sometimes with *da letto* or *del letto* added). Genoese inventories written in Latin, as was still the common practice there in the mid-fifteenth century, render this as *un torcular*.[12] Either way, this was the equivalent of our 'bedstead', or 'bedstock' as it was commonly called in sixteenth-century England.

A form of bed which does not get mentioned directly in inventories but was sometimes present in a room was that in a recess in the wall. Because the recess was part of the structure of the building (usually set into panelling), it would not be mentioned in a list of 'moveables', of furnishings, although one might expect the bedding and a curtain across the opening to be listed. Such beds do, however, appear in a handful of illustrations which all date from the last years of the fifteenth century and are associated with Venice (Pls 56, 110, 292). In the Venetian examples the opening is flush with the wall, so the bed must have been boxed in behind the façade but 'box-beds', as they were called in England in the

seventeenth century, could of course also be built out into the room, in which case they looked more box-like. The development of this type of bed is not, it seems, well understood. It was certainly popular north of the Alps, especially in rural areas, in the seventeenth century. It must surely have been too stuffy and airless a form to enjoy great popularity in Italy except perhaps in mountain areas. But Carpaccio and the illustrator of the *Hypnerotomachia*, who also depicted this form of bed, were interested in settings of high status; so, at least for a short while, this claustrophobic form of bed must have enjoyed a certain amount of fashionable favour in northern Italy.

Some Florentine bedsteads of the fifteenth century are described as having a trestle [*trespolo*, always in the singular] and *un cannaio* or *canario*.[13] Florio* does not help us with this word but Torriano (1659 edition) explains that it means 'a kind of hurdle or lettice [lattice] to dry fruit on' and the Accademia della Crusca Dictionary tells us that these objects were large. It was, in fact, of cane [*canna*]. The only position in which one could use a large hurdle in connection with a bed would be to form a base for the mattress; in which case this must have been a 'bed-lattice' introduced to form a springy *tavola*, an early attempt to create a sprung bed. The single trestle associated with such a 'bed-lattice' was presumably to support the centre so it did not sag too much. Whatever its purpose, the feature seems only to be found in connection with the large form of bed known as a *lettiera* (p. 113). Moreover its use seems to have been confined to Tuscany and apparently ceased after the beginning of the sixteenth century. But it appears in the inventories of some very grand houses, on *lettiere* in the best bedchambers, as well as elsewhere in the building. The Florentine writer and official, Alamanno Rinuccini, apparently had three beds in his house, each described as being *con cannaio e trespolo*. In his will of 1499, he left his beds, *lettucci* (p. 149), trestles, benches, *cannai et trespoli* to his wife and two daughters.[14] As these items are specifically mentioned, he must have regarded them as important.

The lettiera

The *lettiera* was the standard form of bed used in Italy during the fifteenth century. It was a massive piece of furniture and must always have dominated the room in which it stood. It came in a wide range of qualities, from the simple *lettiera salvatica* made of untreated chestnut-wood (e.g. Uzzano Invt., Florence, 1424), to elaborate versions with carved decoration, inlay, paintwork or gilding. Although humbler people slept in simple forms of bed of the kinds just described, anyone of substance reposed on a *lettiera* and this imposing form is represented in countless illustrations of the time (Pls 114, 118, 123).

The general conformation of the *lettiera* was established during the 1300s (e.g. Pl. 113) and this type of bed then reigned supreme in Italian bedchambers for the best part of two centuries, only being gradually superseded by new forms after 1500. What distinguished the *lettiera* from simple beds was its tall headboard which was usually capped by a massive cornice that projected well forward over the bedhead to provide a deep shelf on which objects of various kinds could be placed (Pls 35, 107). Although the headboard was a striking feature, it was attached to the basic framework of the bed (the *fondo*) and so was not mentioned specially in contemporary inventories unless it were in some way extraordinary. It seems that it might be called *un capoletto*[1] but that it was more commonly called *una testiera* (e.g. *lectera una cum la textera pincta* [a *lettiera* with its painted headboard, or 'testerne' as the English called such a component; Sforza Invt., Milan, 1493]). Some *lettiere* had a vertical board at the foot-end as well, less tall than the headboard but mostly likewise capped by a substantial cornice (Pls 137, 311). In Tuscany, during the late fifteenth century, at any rate, such beds with foot-boards were sometimes described as being of a Venetian type. This we learn from Bartolo di Tura's house in Siena (Tura Invt.) where one large *lettiera* was *chiusa da piei a la venitiana* [closed at the foot-end in the Venetian manner]. With their deeply projecting cornices the boards at head and foot resembled the standard hat-rack or hood-rack of the period (Pls 164, 228) which was called a *capuzzario* or *capellinaio*. When a lady's *lettiera* in Verona in 1408 (Aleardi Invt.) was described as being furnished *cum una capuzaria ad pedes* [lit. with a hood-rack at the feet], it did probably not actually have such a rack at the foot-end but was simply provided with a footboard capped with a cornice that resembled a hood-rack, and we can be fairly sure that the same was the case with two *lettiere* in the Medici villa at Cafaggiolo, near Florence (Medici Invt., 1498), which were *con el caplinaro apichato da pie* [with the 'hat-rack' fixed at the foot-end]. While the form was evidently not confined to Venice, many of the contemporary illustrations of beds with footboards do stem from northern Italy.

Lettiere were not all of the same size. One from Florence in 1424 of six *braccia* in length was described as 'large' whereas in the same house the wife's bed was half a braccia shorter (Uzzano Invt., cf. pp. 13 and 17). In anothr Florentine inventory (Pucci Invt., 1449) mention is made of a pair of *lietteruccie piccine* which presumably means that they were a small variant of the standard form. The lists also include many *lettiere* described as being low [*bassa*]. As a new *lettiera* was commonly acquired when a couple got married it was not infrequently occupied by them both throughout their conjugal life; this was certainly the case with the 'beautiful bed' [*pulchram lettieram*] in the Parisi residence in Bologna (Bologna Invt., 1313) and many other instances could be cited (see also Pl. 184).

Early versions of the *lettiera*, made in the fourteenth century and anyway before about 1430, often had what amounted to a small overhanging hood at the top of the headboard. While always supported by brackets (usually carved) at each end, the projecting part could take various forms – from a simple flat board, to one canted upwards from the back edge and in some cases fitted with a fancy apron-piece along the front edge, or to a vaulted version which curved up over the sleeper's head. Every area may have had its preferred variant of this hooded form which is depicted in many illustrations of the period (Pls 113, 114).

Another characteristic of the *lettiera* was the cluster of benches or flat-topped chests that were normally ranged around its flanks – usually against all the three exposed sides of the bed, for of course the *lettiera* habitually stood with its head against the wall, projecting out into the room. These accompanying chests and benches were mostly designed for the purpose so fitted neatly up against the sides of the bed itself and, with a complete set of such ancillary furniture, the *lettiera* came to look like a huge platform occupying much of the centre of the room (Pls 116, 118). The flat shelf formed by these accessories, which were almost obligatory, had many uses. One could sit on it when conversing with the occupant of the bed, for instance, and it offered a convenient perch for someone pulling on their stockings or hose. Wash-basins and what was required for light meals could be placed there (Pls 226, 275). It was not clear whether the chests were always loose items, separate from the bed, or whether they were sometimes built together with the bed as a single integrated structure, but some illustrations show a mitred joint (i.e. at 45°) between two chests at each corner at the foot-end of the bed (Pl. 114) which suggests that these particular chests at any rate were an integral part of the bed. It will have required the assistance of a joiner to set up a *lettiera* in a bedchamber and he could have assembled the various components including the purpose-designed chests (which tended to be shallower than normal chests) that may have had some means at the back for fixing them firmly in position against the sides of the bed – probably with the aid of pegs.

These *panche* (also *banche*, or *banchali*)[2] did indeed often take the form of benches, especially earlier on (e.g. Pl. 64, 186), but mostly they were box-like, for which reason they were sometimes called *cassa panche*, usually as one word (e.g. *una lettiera grande . . . colle cassapanche dinanzi et da lato* [with its box-seats in front and at the sides, i.e. on all three sides] which is mentioned in the Uzzano Inventory, already cited. But while the flat tops of such *casse* were sometimes fixed,[3] they mostly had hinged lids so that the *casse* could serve as chests to provide highly convenient storage. That many of these 'benches' were in fact chests is revealed by the fact that locks are often mentioned (e.g. *torcullar unum cum sua bancha circumcirca dictum torcullar, clavata* [a bed with its bench around the said bed, with locks], Italiano Invt., Genoa, 1451) and, anyway, locks are clearly visible in numerous illustrations of such beds (Pls 114, 179). In some cases the chests are actually described as such (e.g. *tre goffani . . . intorno al letto* [three coffers around the bed]; Tura Invt., Siena, 1483).

While these chests usually formed a broad unbroken ledge around all the three exposed sides of the *lettiera*, sometimes the flat-topped chests were confined to the sides only and some other form of chest, not necessarily with a flat top, was placed at the foot-end of the bed. The Uzzano Inventory yet again furnishes a good example; here a *lettiera* had a *cassapancha* on each side and a pair of *cassoni* at the foot-end. This same bed also had a *pancha dietro al letto* [a bench at the back of the bed]. This must mean 'behind the headboard', a position that could only be thus occupied if the whole bed were pulled out from the wall so that there was a gap between the wall and the headboard (Pl. 134), but this was not a common arrangement. In cases where a *lettiera* was furnished with a

112 Market-place in Bologna, 1411

In the centre of this colourful and instructive scene stands a *lettiera* with a curled-over head-board, which has no mattress so one can see its construction with boarded base, panelled sides and squared uprights at the corners forming feet. Other furniture stands about including a close-stool with back and arms and a pierced seat.

From the records of Bologna's Drapers' Guild, miniature showing the market in Piazzo di Porta Ravegnana
Photograph: Museo Civico Medievale, Bologna

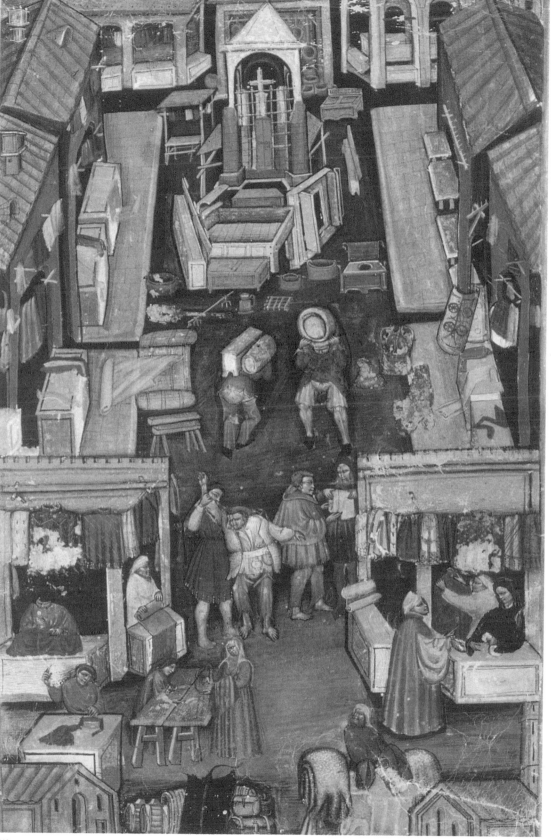

112

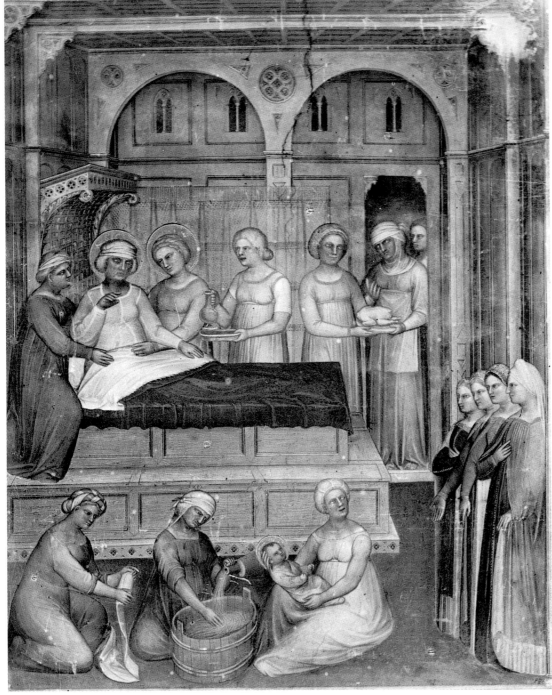

113

114

113 An early form of *lettiera*, about 1370

This piece of furniture is extremely well made with neat and well-proportioned panelling. A problem, however, was how best to deal with the two corners at the foot-end where the bed-chests had to meld at right-angles. Here the joiner has adopted an arrangement that produces squared chests whereas the bed in Plate 114 has a mitred junction at the corner which looks neater but produces chests of an awkward shape. That this present joiner knew all about mitred joints may be seen on the moulding running round the base. The arched-over bed-head is characteristic of early *lettiere*, especially in the north of Italy; it is finely carved and is faced with delicate small panels. A woman supports St Anne while sitting on the bedside with her feet on the step formed by the bed-chest. Note the baby-bath and swaddling band.

Giusto de' Menabuoi, *Birth of the Virgin*, The Cathedral Baptistry, Padua
Photograph: Deganello Padua

114 Early *lettiera* with neat corners

Compared with the bed shown in the previous Plate, which is of roughly the same date, the junction between the two bed-chests at the corners has been better managed even if not so neatly. The edges appear to be bound with metal straps fixed with large nails. Note the locks. St Louis is offering his bed to the leper who evidently smells so offensively that the courtiers have been unable to remain polite.

Unknown artist, *St Louis and the Leper*, fresco, Oratorio Visconteo, Albizzate, Lombardy, last quarter of the 14th century

115 The construction of a *lettiera*

The pegged construction is visible, showing how the flanking boards were attached to the tall bedhead. The tray-like structure of such a bed may be seen more clearly in Plate 112. The flanking bed-chest is in one piece but has three lids, each with a lock, and therefore undoubtedly with divisions inside. The women on the right are seated on substantial and clearly very solid cushions; the other woman has adopted the time-honoured position for swaddling a baby. Cooking, using a pot-hook and chain, is taking place under the projecting hood over the fire.

Stefano da Zevio, active in Verona and the Tyrol in the early 15th century (d. 1434), *Birth of the Virgin*
Albertina, Vienna (24.015)

116 The bed-head becomes increasingly architectural, 1490s

The finest beds could now require the attention of a designer prior to construction and then the skills of first-class carvers and inlayers to embellish the joinery which had to be well-proportioned and neat. The bed was after all the dominant feature of a bedchamber (especially in this case where the chimneypiece, the only other rival for attention in a bedroom, hardly projects into the room at all). This picture (once again, of the birth of the Virgin) must show a fashionable bedchamber of the 1490s; it is by Francesco di Giorgio Martini who was also one of the best architects of his day (see Pl. 348) and knew well how to design a stylistically integrated interior like this. Note the deep frieze painted with festoons.

Francesco di Giorgio Martini, *Birth of the Virgin*, Bichi Chapel, S. Agostino, Siena
Photograph: Soprintendenza B.A.S.Siena

115

116

117

117 A crested bed-head

This Lombard *lettiera* has a cresting of addorsed dolphins with a central finial. Between the carved pilasters is a pattern executed in *lavoro di intarsio*.

Minature in the Arcimboldi Missal, 14
Biblioteca Capitolare, Milan

118 The fully-developed *lettiera*

Although the artist may have exaggerated the height of the bed-head, by the late decades of the fifteenth century this feature often dominated the bedchamber in which it stood. This bed rests on a platform; it does not have bed-chests in the usual way. If you were sufficiently grand (and this illustration comes from the Duke of Urbino's personal Bible so probably reflects the kind of furnishings he possessed), you probably had no need of bulk storage in your bedchamber; clothes, bedclothes and the like would no doubt be removed by servants to some other room for safe-keeping, cleaning and mending. Near the bed-head, a box-like superstructure on the platform serves as a seat but would also have been handy as a rudimentry bedside table. Note the pretty coverlet of verdure tapestry and the white summer curtains. The joinery seems to involve two contrasting kinds of wood enhanced with gilding. The fireplace has no hood so must be set deep into the wall; it is furnished with fire-dogs (only one is visible) and fire-irons. Against the wall leans a warming pan.

Francesco di Antonio del Chierco, *David receiving Bathsheba* and *Solomon*, miniature from the Bible of Federigo da Montefeltro, 1476–78
Vatican Library

118

119

120

119 A humble *lettiera*

This bed of unadorned wood is a reminder that beds of the same general shape came in many qualities. Note how the deep cornice of the bed-head serves as a parking-place for objects of various kinds. One could only have used the shelf in this way if the bed were built in a very substantial and rigid manner, and it will be noted that the two sleeping monks clearly have faith in the excellence of the joinery and do not fear that the heavy candlestick will fall on their heads. The coverlet has a shaggy pile (see p. 162). The window is fitted with a *fenestra impannata* which has religious emblems painted on the linen panes. There are shutters below.

Sodoma, *St Bendedict appearing to the Monks*, Monte Oliveto
Maggiore, near Siena, 1505–8
Photograph: Scala

120 Independent bed-curtains

Suspended from a wooden framework with rings running on rods, two curtains can enclose the sides of the bed. The bed is of a simple type but it probably had a head-board even if this is not shown. No chests or benches are placed alongside. Note the striped coverlet or blanket.

Giotto, *Birth of the Virgin (detail)*, Scrovegni Chapel, Padua, 1305–6
Photograph: Scala

121 Mid-fifteenth-century hospital in Ferrara

The beds are of the *lettiera* type but, since patients do not usually have many belongings with them in hospital, they do not need much storage-space, and it was not necessary to provide bed-chests to fit alongside these beds in the otherwise customary manner. Besides, with no flanking chests, nurses could tend the patients more easily. An *orinale* in its case of plaited straw hangs on the wall. The surgeon has a stake-legged stool with a back which must be fixed with a strong mortise-and-tenon joint.

Mid-15th-century Ferrarese miniature
Biblioteca Laurenziana, Florence, (MS. Gaddiano 24)

truckle bed that could be pushed under the main bed when not needed, this would clearly only have been possible when one side, or the foot end, of the bed was left open, without a chest hindering access from that direction.

Bed-hangings: the early forms

The *lettiera* had no posts so the bed-hangings, required on all but the humblest beds, had to be suspended either from hooks driven into the ceiling or the walls, or on rods somehow attached to ·the interior architecture. Prior to the end of the fifteenth century, bed-hangings were virtually never attached to the bed itself.[1]

The aim was to produce a cubicle round the bed but the curtains did not necessarily hang close to the bed; in some cases they seem to be well clear of the sides so one could probably move about inside the enclosed space quite easily. Illustrations of the period show that there were many possible arrangements (Pls 122, 275, 278). A common formula was to hang a curtain across the room, towards one end, so as to form a niche or alcove, the three walls of which might then also be hung with curtains. Curtains forming a cubicle round the bed standing out in the middle of the room were another commonly adopted arrangement. Free-hanging curtains (i.e. those not forming wall-hangings) could be drawn back during the day to reveal the bed and could be drawn across in front of the bed at night-time to provide privacy. In winter the curtains could be of a heavy material that excluded draughts and helped create a snug compartment with the bed at its centre.

Such dissociated bed-hangings were commonly called *cortine*, a word sometimes confusingly spelt *coltrine* although these hangings were in no way related to the *coltre* or *coltrone* which were bed-quilts (p. 165). Lorenzo de' Medici's bed at Careggi (Medici Invt., 1492) had *una cortina che ricigne il letto* [which surrounds the bed] and a bed in Genoa in 1451 (Italiano Invt.) had *cortina una circa lectum telle cellestris* [a curtain round the bed of a blue material] while a Veronese bed in 1408 (Aleardi Invt.) had *una coltrina nova . . . et unum ferum pro dicta coltrina* [a new curtain . . . and an iron (rod) for the said curtain]. Whenever one comes across references to *cortine* associated with a bed, at any rate prior to about 1480, they are likely to concern independent hangings of this kind, and it is evident both from the inventory-descriptions and the contemporary illustrations that they were often extremely decorative and costly items. The Veronese example just mentioned, for instance, was *picta a lionpardis cum armis Aquile et Baynerie, tele todesche nigre* [of black German cloth painted/decorated with lions (leopards?) and the family arms]; Astorgio Manfredi, member of a grand family in Faenza (Manfredi Invt. 1469), had *una cultrina da lecto cu la historia di Sansone* [with the story of Samson depicted on it]; and around a *lettiera* in the well-appointed Florentine residence of Niccolo da Uzzano was a *cortina* described as being *di tovaglie capitate* which means of linen that was therefore almost certainly white, while *capitate* probably indicates that it had a heading or capping decorated distinctively. We can see what must have been something similar in Pl. 122.

In the 1483 inventory of the late Bartolo di Tura's house in Siena are at least four references to *tende* in apparent association with beds. It seems that these were also curtains, late versions of the *cortina da letto*. As *Florio** explains, a *tenda* was not only a tent or pavilion but could also be a curtain because *tendere* means 'to extend, to spread, to reach, to display'. One of di Tura's *tende* had a *ferro da tenerla* [an iron to hold it – presumably a rod to hold it up] and these hangings were no doubt also well worth displaying, some of them being trimmed with *reticella* (p. 74) and fringe while others were decorated with the owner's arms (e.g. *Due tende de pannolino dipente con l'arme di casa, in torno al letto* [two hangings of linen painted with the family arms, around the bed]. The term *boida* (*boyda, boeda, boiha*) that is met with frequently in mid-fifteenth-century Genoese inventories may also refer to dissociated curtains of the type under discussion. For instance in the Spinola mansion (Spinola Invt., 1459) there was *boida una circa lectum . . . cum armiis de spinulis et de Vivaldis* [around the bed, bearing the arms of Spinola and Vivaldi]. However, it is more probable that a *boida* was a form of matting that lay on the floor (p. 66).

There was a form of hanging called a *capoletto* which, by Boccaccio's time, the mid-fourteenth century, was evidently a wall hanging (p. 48) but must originally have been a hanging suspended at the head of a bed, as the word implies. Of the many fourteenth- and fifteenth-century Italian illustrations of beds surrounded by hangings in the way already described, hardly any have distinctive hangings at the head so presumably the coining of the word *capoletto* goes back to an even earlier time when any hangings that were associated with a bed tended to be concentrated at the head-end. However, the origins of the term need not delay us; suffice it to say that it was no longer commonly used by the fifteenth century and, where it occurs in inventories, it probably refers to wall-hangings rather than a form of bed-hanging. The great exception is found in the Este inventories (Ferrara, 1436), where half a dozen splendid sets of bed-hangings are listed, each of which includes a *capoletto*.[2]

The beds of popes and other important people, long before 1400, were sometimes furnished with a hanging suspended horizontally to form a flat 'roof' over their bed (Pl. 53). This, together with the curtains, completely boxed in the bed. By suspending the cloth from points inset from its edges, the sides could be made to fall down to make the hanging more roof-like and eventually these hanging sides were made as separate strips called *pendenti* [pendants or 'valances' in English]. The main cloth, because it formed a firmament, was called 'a sky, a heaven' – *cielo*, *capocielo* or *sopracielo*.[3] If the Italians who compiled inventories had left it at that, all would have been simple; but there was no consensus at this early stage in the development of the 'hung bed', so several terms came to be used to designate the same item.

Particularly confusing is the word *testa* (or variants like *testale* and *testiera*) which was used in reference both to the *cielo*, because it was suspended above the sleeper's head, and to the headcloth which was suspended against the wall *behind* the sleeper's head.[4] Thus a bed of red serge among the belongings of Piero de' Medici (Medici Invt., 1456) had *uno sopralecto . . . et pendenti* [lit. an over-the-bed with valances], *uno drieto a lecto* [lit. a behind-the-bed], and *una testa da lecto* which must here surely refer to a *cielo*, the *drieto* being the headcloth which does indeed hang behind the bed. It might be thought that the *sopralecto* was the *cielo* in this case, because it sounds as if it were high above the bed and because it had valances which the *cielo/sopracielo* by this stage commonly possessed. However, while *sopraletto* may have been used to designate a *cielo* in some cases,[5] here it must mean cloth lying on top of the bed and its bedclothes (the *letto* proper; p. 162) which could of course also have *pendenti* that fell down on the three exposed flanks to cover the sides of the mattresses and other bedding. So in this case *testa* apparently meant the *cielo*. On the other hand, the term *testa* – or *testale* which was the Latinized version – clearly meant 'headcloth' in the case of the splendid cloth of gold and crimson bed-hangings that Bianca Maria Sforza took with her in 1493 when she went off to marry the Emperor Maximilian (Sforza Invt., Milan, 1493). These comprised *capcellum, testale et culcitra* – a *capocielo*, a headcloth and a quilt or coverlet [*coltre*]. Since there was already a *cielo*, the *testa* here was clearly something different.

The lack of consensus among inventory-clerks (and why should one expect consensus?) produced many other sources of confusion for the modern students of these matters. The valances, for instance, were usually called *pendenti*, as we have seen, but in Genoa they were called *fenogieti* and in Ferrara *bandirolle*.[6]

Whatever the various parts were called, the complete ensemble was usually called *un fornimento* or *un paramento da letto*;[7] and, because a set of hangings formed a sort of roof over the bed, the ensemble also seems to have been called *una volta* [a vault or roof] in some areas.[8] *Fornimento* fell out of use towards the end of the fifteenth century, it seems, but at about the same time, the word *cortinaggio* comes in instead.[9] Although this word might seem to have general application (i.e. as 'curtaining'), it probably was chiefly used in reference to a rectangular, box-like form, as we shall see (p. 129).

The padiglione *and the* lit à la romaine

Another means of encurtaining a bed was to suspend a *padiglione* over it. This consisted of a cone-shaped or domed cap, hanging by a cord attached to a hook in the ceiling, with curtains fixed to its lower edge that spread out to surround the bed below (Pls 126–32). In fact the *padiglione* looked like an old-fashioned tent and, with a central post inside to hold it up, did indeed serve that very purpose when military gentlemen were out on campaign or when festivities were arranged in the open (Pls 229, 353).[1] The *padiglione* could equally well be used as a canopy or 'cloth of estate' when it served as a mark of high rank (p. 177); it could also serve as

122

122 Room within a room

Independent curtains with rings running on iron rods that are attached to the architecture. The curtains appear to hang well clear of the sides of the bed. They have a richly embroidered frieze-like heading trimmed with a three-colour fringe. They are of a lightweight white material – undoubtedly they are summer curtains – with a star pattern executed in gold thread. The chequered coverlet has a star pattern in each square; could this figured material be a *sargia*? The bed-chest is inlaid. The women are engaged in the usual activities associated with the birth of the Virgin. The girl entering from the left carries a basket which is presumably the ancestor of the birth-tray [*desco da parto*]; see plate 284.

Paolo di Giovanni Fei, *Birth of the Virgin*, 1380s
Pinacoteca, Siena (photograph: Scala)

123 Curtaining a *lettiera*

Separate bed-curtains depend from an iron rod bent into a 'U' shape, attached to the ceiling. The arrangement would suggest that the foot-end of the bed was open, uncurtained; in which case the light illuminating the carved figure on its bracket on the wall would have served also as a comforting night-light. Note the large chest. The artist who painted this miniature ran a workshop in which he and his assistants also painted furniture, including chests (see Pl. 219).

Apollonio di Giovanni, illustration to *The Aeneid*, *c*.1460
Biblioteca Riccardiana, Florence (MS. 492)

124 Separate curtaining; an unusual arrangement

Here summer curtains of white linen are draped over rods from a central point under the ceiling from which they spread out over the bed. This is essentially a *padiglione* (see Pls 127, 132) that will not cause claustrophobia. Note the bold *tarsie* of the bedhead.

Predella showing *Birth of the Virgin*, Sano di Pietro, S. Quirico d'Orcia, Tuscany
Photograph: Scala

125 Side-screening only

A small curtain hangs from a rod projecting from the bedhead which is of the curved-over variety popular in northern Italy during the late Gothic period. On the bedside bench and under the bed are items associated with a sick-room (the scene is of Christ healing the sick woman); an *orinale* in its case hangs by the bedhead.

Romagnola School, *Christ healing the Sick Woman*, 1473
The Badia, Pomposa (photograph: Scala)

123

124

125

126

127

126 The *padiglione* as mosquito-net

Suspended from a hook in the ceiling over a standard *lettiera*, this hanging is of white veiling which served as a net to exclude flies and mosquitoes in summer.

Francesco Granacci, scene from the *Life of John the Baptist*, *c*.1500 *Metropolitan Museum of Art, New York, Gwynne Andrews, Harris Brisbane Dick, Dodge, Fletcher and Rogers Funds, funds from various donors, Ella Morris, Dekeyster Gift, Mrs. Donald Oenslager Gift, and gifts in memory of Robert Lehman. (1970.134.1)*

127 Likened to a sparrowhawk

When tied back to hooks in the wall, the hangings of a *padiglione* assumed the appearance of a hovering bird of prey – hence its alternative name, *sparviero*, which in English became 'sparver'.

Sodoma, *Birth of the Virgin*, refectory at Sant' Anna in Camprena, near Pienza, Tuscany, 1503 *Soprintendenza B.A.S. Siena*

curtaining for a bath, and various other purposes, as we shall see (Pl. 276).

This structure was normally suspended at a point between the bedhead and the middle of the bed, so it was more or less over the sleeper's head. In order that the curtains could properly envelop the entire bed – including reaching out over the foot-end – they had to be so long that they would have dragged on the floor, when not extended, unless they were hitched up in some way. This hitching was usually aranged so that the curtains were pulled back and bunched on either side of the bedhead (Pls 127, 132). During the daytime the *padiglione* thus came to resemble a hovering bird of prey, especially when it swayed, as it so easily did; and for this reason the Italians often called it just that – *un sparviero* [a sparrowhawk].[2] Where there was uncertainty as to the purpose a particular *padiglione* or *sparviero* was intended to serve, a writer of inventories might give an additional clue (e.g. the Acciaiuoli Invt., Florence, 1363, *un sparviere da letto* [for a bed]).

The English term for a bed with a *padiglione* was 'a canopy bed'[3] and the word 'canopy' derives from the Greek word for a mosquito-net – *cōnops*. Indeed, it was as a mosquito-net that the *padiglione* formula first appeared, and it must have done so long before the Renaissance. References to *zenziere* (from *zenzara*, a gnat or mosquito) are found in numerous Italian inventories of the fifteenth century but, because the *zenziera* was also useful for keeping off flies, the term *moschetto* (from *mosca*, a fly) became more commonly used after about 1500.

Pardi draws attention to some items called *staze* which were of ash painted red and were in some way associated with mosquito-nets.[4] He suggests they were rods to support the net but they may equally well have served to spread the net out over the bed – some form of light framework, perhaps.

The *zenziera* or *moschetto* was effective if it was made of net, keeping the insects out but letting air in (Pl. 126), and occasionally inventories seem to describe such items – like that in the Acciaiuoli house in Florence (Acciaiuoli Invt.) where there was a *sparavero di tela sutila a maglia* [of fine linen net?], and one mentioned in a Genoese inventory (Fieschi Invt., 1532) which was of *seta verde fato a rete* [green silk net]. A *padiglione* was provided for the Grand Duke's bed by the Medici *Guardaroba* in about 1590 which was *di velo* [of veiling or net].[5] However, *zenziere* and *moschetti* were more frequently made of white linen that does not seem to have had an open weave, and much of this came from Cambrai, if the inventories can be trusted, but also from Rheims or, later, from Holland.[6] These white *padiglioni* had a cool appearance which made them popular for bed-hangings in summertime. The *zanziere di cotonina* mentioned in a Florentine inventory of 1496 (Gaddi Invt.) was probably also white, but of cotton not linen. Many *zenziere* and *moschetti* were decorated, sometimes richly – *uno zenzariere richamato d'oro e di seta* [... embroidered with gold and silk, i.e. in colours], *un altro paviglione moscheto di tela biancha cum le porte et la capelina de velute cramesito* [... of white material with the opening and dome of crimson velvet] (Medici Invt., Florence, 1463, and Di Challant Invt., Turin, 1522).

There was, however, a limit to the amount of ornament these summer hangings could bear if they were to remain light and airy in appearance –

but no such inhibitions held back the upholsterers and their customers when it came to decorating other kinds of *padiglioni* and some highly flamboyant confections were the result (Pls 171, 283). They could be made of the very richest materials, with elaborate trimmings (p. 84), and it is clear that the intention in such cases was to impress visitors to the splendid bedchambers in which these amazing pieces of furniture were displayed. It must of course also be remembered that the canopy always carried with it the implication that the person above whom it was elevated was of high rank; so princes, who may have had a right to such symbols of estate, liked to have a *padiglione* over their beds, but so did many other people who merely had aspirations towards princely status. In the inventory of Lucrezia Borgia, taken in 1503 and reflecting her exalted position as a princess of Ferrara, a special section is devoted to listing her *padiglioni*, and very splendid they must have been – of white brocade and crimson velvet arranged in stripes with a crimson taffeta lining and gold and silk fringe, for instance, and of gold and crimson silk net with swathes of purple silk and blue and gold fringe [*de brochato biancho piano e di veluto Carmexino fato a liste, fodrato di tafeta Carmexino ... con fanze de oro e seda Carmexina*; and *de rede doro e seda Carmexina con le falde ... de Cendale pavonazo con franze doro e seda Celestra ...*]. Bianca Maria Sforza (Sforza Invt., 1493) carried with her three *sparviere* when she left Milan to marry the Emperor Maximilian, and one of them was proudly decorated with the Sforza coat of arms; likewise when Vicenza Moncada, a Sicilian noblewoman, got married in 1598 she brought with her *un pavaglione de tela de landa* [of Holland linen] which was no doubt an elegant and costly object.

Padiglioni became generally more elaborate as the sixteenth century wore on (Pls 131, 171, 217), the height of richness and complexity being reached in the seventeenth century when an elaborate form of couch (p. 113) topped by a *padiglione* was in France called a *lit à la romaine*.[7] The term must reflect some association with Rome, either because this had previously been a form in favour in opulent circles in that city or because it was believed that the ancient Romans of classical times had used beds of this type, perhaps with some sort of a hanging suspended over them. In fact both notions are probably true. It seems evident that the form was popular in Rome during the second half of the sixteenth century, expecially in circles where a degree of ostentation was thought acceptable (Pls 171, 217); but the form also had a link with the couches of classical Antiquity.

Of course, in its essentials the form was not unlike that of the simplest beds used in the Renaissance, nor indeed was it so very unlike that of the French *couche* which, as we noted (p. 113), could be simple or quite elaborate, although elaboration was mostly contrived through providing it with richer forms of hanging. Awareness of the character of the classical couch, on the other hand, was sharpened by the discovery, during excavations that took place in Rome in 1506, of a wall-painting that became known as 'The Aldobrandini Marriage'. This event caused great excitement in antiquarian circles in Rome at the time. Raphael produced his own rendering of the scene which, partly through engravings, quickly made the picture widely known. It shows what was thought to be a Roman marriage ceremony, and part of an elegant couch is visible behind the central figures. Soon couches inspired by this and other ancient paintings were being depicted, with elaborations to suit modern tastes, by artists working in various parts of Italy. Many of these new scenes illustrate episodes in some well known story from classical mythology, or from classical history, in which a bed plays a part. One might suppose the beds shown in such pictures were meant to look like those used by the ancient Romans but some of these beds are rendered in an extremely realistic manner and seem to be perfectly plausible if rather fanciful pieces of sixteenth-century furniture (e.g. Pls 170, 378).

The 'Aldrobrandini bed' has no hangings and it was by no means clear to those who were interested, early in the sixteenth century, how classical bed-hangings looked, or, indeed, if they had had bed-hangings at all, in classical times.[8] Those faced with the problem of creating a modern couch in a classical style therefore had to invent a suitable form of bed-hanging for this newly fashionable form. For this purpose the *padiglione* lent itself to perfection. It could be made as elaborate as was desired, it had an exotic air, it looked right. Perhaps it was also known to Italian artist-designers of the early sixteenth century that the French *couche* had often been furnished with a *padiglione* (French *pavillon*) in the fifteenth century; if so, their eye was already attuned to the proportions created by such a combination.

At any rate, what is here suggested is that beds like those shown in Pls 7 and 171 could well have existed and that, anyway, elaborate couches with richly decorated *padiglioni* were to be seen in some Italian bedchambers of the second half of the sixteenth century, and that these stood as prototypes for the astonishing *lits à la romaine* for which several sets of designs were published in Paris in the middle decades of the seventeenth century.

One piece of evidence exists which strongly suggests that such beds were fashionable already by about 1550. It appears in the plan of a Venetian house by Serlio who died in 1554. It was to have been included in the sixth volume of his famous treatise on architecture, a volume which was never published (not until 1978, that is). On the plan he shows the location of two bedchambers with alcoves, then rather a novel feature in Italy, and he explains that these rooms are for the ladies of the house. What is of particular interest to us in the present connection, however, is the small sketch he includes of one of these alcoves from the front (Pl. 172) and it will be seen that it contains a couch, with a pillow at one end, surmounted by a large *padiglione*. So it would seem that Serlio wanted to suggest that such a bed was entirely appropriate for a great lady by that time.

The Serlio couch-bed is relatively plain but some of the beds of this class were extremely elaborate. They had rich carving at their heads and beneath the *tavola* on which the luxurious mattresses lay, and their legs often took the form of some beast. Above this ensemble hovered a great *padiglione*, with a richly decorated dome, a valance of fancy shape, and a billowing tumble of curtaining held up out of the way, when not needed, by tasselled cords and tie-backs. Presumably not everyone would have felt

128

129

130

128 A bed with a *padiglione*

Drawing of a handsome *padiglione* which matches the deep valances of the bed it accompanies. The domed *capelletto*, with its finial, is suspended by a cord attached to the ceiling. Note the netted fringe trimming the bowl and the curious wisp-like tassels on the seams between the alternating widths of white and purple materials. One of a series of bed-designs which appear to be associated with the post-Sforza court at Milan, possibly during the time that the Marchese del Vasto was governor (1538–46) or, more probably when his successor, Ferrante Gonzaga, held power and his daughter Ippolita was the centre of a cultivated circle responsible for high artistic achievements.

Unknown draughtsman
Fondazione Querini Stampalia, Venice

129 The *padiglione's* decorative character

This summer-hanging has a conical *capelletto* with fancy trimming and an opening edged with flounces. The *lettiera* appears not to have the usual tall bed-head but has bed-chests that provide Mary with a seat. Note the maiolica jar.

Miniature from a Florentine Book of Hours, *c* 1500
Victoria and Albert Museum, London (L.2386–1910)

130 A square *padiglione*

Its cord shows clearly. It hangs over a bed with an unusual head-board and no flanking chests. One curtain is knotted and bundled up, out of the way (see diagram 5, p. 359). The valances are richly embroidered. The husband sits on an X-frame stool with arms but no back. The new-born child (the Virgin Mary) has been tightly swaddled.

Rodrigo de Osona the younger, a wing to an alterpiece by Bartolomé Bermejo, *c*.1481–6
Cathedral, Acqui Terme, Piedmont (photograph: Scala)

131 Pillows indicating status; about 1540

A splendid green silk *padiglione* with a 'soft' bowl. Mary has at least two pillows lying on her bolster; they diminish in size to form a pyramid. She has a carved and gilded reading-desk. The arms of Cardinal Alessandro Farnese appear in the magnificent border of this miniature which is by Giulio Clovio, working here under the influence of Francesco Salviati who was active in Rome at this period, decorating churches and palaces with vast frescoed schemes in a style very similar to this but of course on a huge scale.

From *The Farnese Hours*, folio 4v, completed in 1546
Pierpont Morgan Library, New York

131

132

at ease having such a flamboyant piece of furniture in their house; indeed, such outrageous ornamentation cannot have been favoured by those sensitive about their dignity, and one must have had to be rather daring and none too conventional to sleep in a bed of this kind. One group of people who might have found such expensive and eye-catching beds to their tastes were the great courtesans and maybe a scene like that reproduced in Pl. 171, although purporting to show an episode in the story of Mars and Venus, actually gives us a fair idea of how the bedchamber of a famous Roman courtesan was furnished (p. 355). A succesful courtesan, of course, had to keep up with the very latest fashions; everything in her surroundings must be showy, evidence of her power to attract the highest in the land and of her patron's power and ability to foot the bill. An astonishing bed like this, topped by an amazing *padiglione*, would surely have been one of the most potent symbols of such a young woman's success in an age when the foremost courtesans enjoyed widespread approbation among influential people.

We shall return to consider these forerunners of the *lit à la romaine* when considering this and other forms of day-bed (p. 152).

Whatever the purpose of a *padiglione*, whatever the materials of which it was made, it invariably had a capping which was sometimes called *un capello* [a cap][9] but more often the diminutive was used, *capelletto*.[10] This last was not infrequently spelt *capoletto*[11] although it had nothing whatever to do with the wall-hanging of that name already discussed (p. 48). Other terms for head-gear also lent their names for the purpose – *capuccio*, *capuzzo* and *scapucin*, all meaning a hood or a cowl,[12] with

capuccini of course being the name given to Capuchin friars on account of the cowls they wore.

At the top of the *capelletto* was a finial called a *pomo* [apple] which in turn had a ring on top to which the cord [*cordone*, *fune*, or *cordello*] was attached for suspending the whole affair to a hook in the ceiling.[13] Around the lower edge of the *capelletto*, on all but the simplest versions, was fixed a valance, a strip of material like a modern pelmet, hiding the top of the curtains.[14] We have already seen that valances were commonly called *pendenti* but might also be called *fenogieti*. In the sixteenth century the term *tornaletto* came into use to describe a valance which did indeed 'go round [*attorno*] the bed'. The term might be used for the valance that depended from the *capelletto* of a *padiglione*, or from the *testa* of a conventional set of bed-hangings, but it was also used to describe the valances that could be fitted between the legs of a bed – the 'base valances', as they were called in England. But the *tornaletto* is perhaps best discussed in connection with the posted bed (p. 135).

In the Cosimo de' Medici inventory (Medici Invt., 1553) there are many references to *pendalgi* in connection with bed-hangings of different sorts including *padiglioni*, and it is clear that these were some form of *pendente* or valance. *Uno cappelletto da padiglione con pendalgi* and *Un cortinaggio . . . con sua pendalgi* are two examples. Looking at illustrations of the sixteenth century one sees that the valances of *padiglioni* particularly, but also of rich bed-hangings in general, had become much more elaborate, often with shaped lappets, sometimes with tassels, and frequently with added appliqué decoration (Pls 1 and 128). Indeed the valances are usually the most striking component in a set of bed-hangings. Could it be that using the term *pendalgi* was the Florentine inventory-clerk's way of describing a rather early manifestation of this elaboration? Florio, 1611*, tells us that a *Pendalgio* was 'any pendent or downe dangling things as of a Trumpet'.

Sleeping in a bed furnished with a *padiglione* must have been rather claustrophobic, with its mass of material gathered up to the hovering *capelletto* above.[15] This would especially have been the case in winter when heavy hangings were fitted. Managing the curtains from inside cannot have been quite easy, moreover, although grand people no doubt had an alert personal servant in attendance, ready to spring to their aid in this matter, as in much else. Even so, bed-hangings where the curtains ran on rods, following the outer edge of the bed, would clearly be much easier to manage, whether from inside or out. We shall see that such hangings were becoming common in the first years of the sixteenth century and one may therefore wonder why the *padiglione* continued to enjoy such favour throughout that century and well into the next. At any rate, many people who could well afford whatever form of bed-hanging that was available at the time were still prepared to put up with the *padiglione's* inconveniences and to spend very large sums of money on these amazing objects. Lorenzo de' Medici, for example had a very fine *lettiera* at his villa at Careggi, decorated with elegant mouldings and elaborate *Tarsie* (Medici Invt., 1492). It was a luxurious piece of furniture, valued at four florins, but the *padiglione* suspended over it was apparently worth three times that sum. We are always being told that Lorenzo took some trouble not to appear ostentatious to his fellow citizens, even when he was *de facto* ruler of Florence. If so, we must presume that other Florentine patricians had similar furnishings. However, in this context is is worth noting that, in his town residence in the Via Larga, Lorenzo's bed was also valued at four florins but the *padiglione* of linen was appraised at only ten florins (the same sum, incidentally, as a portrait by Pollaiuolo hanging in the room). An astonishing fact then comes to light; the main bed-hangings of Lorenzo's *lettiera* were assessed at no less than sixty florins. They were made of saye, a worsted material, in this case embroidered with falcons and dormice.[16] Perhaps any lack of ostentation that may have been present lay in the fact that the hangings were of wool and not of silk. It might be more true to say that Lorenzo was ostentatious in a fairly subtle manner!

Some idea of the trouble taken to create a rich *padiglione* may be gained from the fact that Cosmè Tura, the painter and designer in charge of all decoration executed at the Este Court at Ferrara at the time was, in 1472, commissioned to design the canopy that was to hang over the nuptial bed of Ercole I when he married Eleonora of Aragon. He made a full-scale model which he erected with the aid of a pair of tall trestles; the accounts mention *dui Trespidi alti per m. ro Gosme dipintore che depinze uno esempio de uno aparamento da Leto . . . .*[17]

The suspended cortinaggio.

With bed-hangings of the old-fashioned, detached form (pp. 170–71) it was difficult for the occupant of a great *lettiera* to manage them from the inside. On the other hand it was a nuisance if one had to call in a servant to help every time one wanted to adjust a curtain in order, for instance, to let in more air or less light, or to get out of bed. Having a servant come in inevitably destroyed one's privacy and privacy of course constitutes an important aspect of comfort. If one *did* want to manage things on one's own, it meant climbing out onto the *cassapanca* or stepping down to the floor so as to be able to reach a curtain. With a *padiglione* it was perhaps even more difficult. To get out from under all those folds of material encompassing the bed must have been awkward and could not have been made easier if the *capelletto* was apt to swivel and sway.

To be able to manage one's own bed-hangings from inside the bed must therefore have come to seem highly desirable to those seeking to increase their creature comforts in the second half of the fifteenth century. Once one could do this, not only was it simple to make small adjustments at will; it also allowed one to move about more freely to quench one's thirst from the flask provided, to use the *orinale*, to go and talk to one's spouse, or simply to walk about one's own room if one were sleepless all without calling in even one's personal servant.

To achieve this desirable state of affairs one needed to be able to reach the curtains easily. They also had to remain in the position to which they had been adjusted; it was no good if they swung back into their former position or if they suddenly dropped down from some hitched-up arrangement. By far the best scheme was to hang the curtains from rings running on rods. This was not a new idea (Pl. 92) but it provided the most practical solution to the problem. The curtains, for their part, needed to be brought close in around the bed, so they could be reached without difficulty, and this necessitated having them depend from a rectangular frame set horizontally above the bed and covering roughly the same area as the sleeping surface below. The frame could either be suspended from the ceiling or it could be supported by posts rising from the bed itself.

Fitting a bed with posts to hold up the hangings, usually called the *cortinaggio* in the sixteenth century, turned out to be the more satisfactory of the two methods. Posted beds began to make their appearance in Italy towards the end of the fifteenth century (p. 135) but various forms of suspended *cortinaggio* were tried out at the same time and, because they were developed from earlier forms of curtaining, they are here dealt with first.

Pl. 127 shows a *lettiera* with a *padiglione* suspended over it with the normal single cord rising from a *capelletto*, but this particular *padiglione* has a built-in rectangular frame that, once the curtains were closed, formed a rectilinear cubicle round the bed with a pavilion-like top.[1] It must have been difficult to prevent such a confection from twisting out of alignment with the bed below and the next stage in the development was to have four cords attached to the corners of the frame, as may be seen in Pl. 134 which shows a Milanese miniature dating from 1493–5. The

133 Bed testers; the French solution

In France and Burgundy, and no doubt elsewhere in northern Europe, the textile testers of beds were often suspended by cords attached high up on the walls, as here shown in a painting of about 1460. Such a system does not appear to have been adopted in Italy where testers always seem to have had a frame to make them rigid.

Rogier van der Weyden, *Annunciation*, c.1460
Alte Pinakotek, Munich

133

134 Bed testers; the Italian solution

The frame from which the curtains hang is suspended from the ceiling of the room with cords. The frame has its own 'ceiling' and thus becomes a tester; it is a development of the ceilingless form shown in Pl. 136 but must be made of wood or one could not have attached valances to it (i.e. it could not have consisted solely of an iron rod as does the frame in Pl. 136). Italian valances were very shallow at this early stage. The four curtains are bundled up out of the way (once again this is a birth scene). Although the bed is a *lettiera*, it is not furnished with bed-chests. Chests stand against the wall instead. The bed does not have its head against the wall. Note the interior shutters, and the tabernacle with paired doors on the wall.

Gasparo Visconti, *Birth of Daria*, miniature from the *codex of Paolo and Daria*, Milan, 1493–5
Staatliche Museen Preußischer Kulturbesitz (photograph: Jörg P. Anders)

135 Il Moro in bed, about 1495

An ultra-modern bed with the new lightweight suspended tester which has a frame with its own 'ceiling' and a two-colour fringe serving as a shallow valance. The capitals behind are stone consoles supporting the vaulted ceiling and have nothing to do with the bed. Ludovico Sforza (Il Moro) sits up in bed, talking to the Virgin who has appeared outside his window. One of his personal *imprese*, a clothes-brush [*setola*], hangs on the wall, more by way of identifying the Duke than as a realistic feature.

Madonna appearing to Lodovico il Moro, c.1495
Poldi-Pezzoli Museum, Milan

134

135

136

137

138

136 Not yet a tester

The old frame formula consisting of an iron curtain-rod suspended from the ceiling of the room (in this case, by means of long iron hooks) is here neatly contrived but the frame at this stage, the mid-fifteenth century, still does not have its own ceiling. One curtain is hitched back over the tall bed-head of a standard *lettiera* complete with bed-chests.

Attributed to Benozzo Gozzoli, *Antiochus and Stratoniche* (detail)
Musée Cluny (E. CL. 1744)

137 Suspended wooden half-tester

Suspended over a *lettiera* (getting old-fashioned by this stage) at a time when beds with posts had for some while been commonplace. This was not a very practical form and fell from favour in the second half of the

sixteenth century; it could be elegant, however. Objects stand on the deep cornice topping the wall-panelling and the door has a *portière*. About 1535.

Bartolomeo Neroni, *Birth of the Virgin*
Musée du Louvre, Paris

138 Suspended heavy tester; 1470s

This massive wooden tester is not supported by posts so must be suspended from the ceiling. It is architectural in character and has narrow valances, with net curtains below. Note the very tall foot-board and bed-head; the latter is painted with a female figure. The massive *candelabra* is present purely as a device for separating this scene from that on its right which is not shown here.

Master of the Stratonice Panels, *Antiochus and Stratonice* (detail), 1470s?
Henry E. Huntington Library and Art Gallery, California

139 The suspended *cortinaggio*

This was still used occasionally, long after the introduction of beds with posts that supported a tester and
the hangings. This sketch is from the Medici Wardrobe Archives [*Guardaroba*] and calculations written
on the original seem to have to do with the amounts of
material needed. Some of the other sketches in the
group bear dates between 1582 and 1593. Note the two
lengths of fringe and the location of the opening up
towards the head.

Unknown draughtsman
Archivio di Stato, Florence (Guardaroba 143)

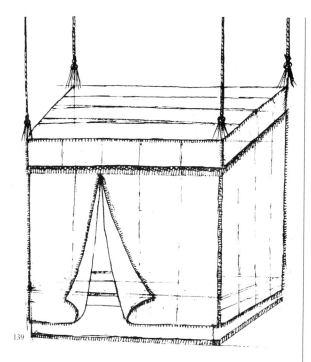

curtains of both these beds have here been knotted and bundled out of the
way, as they often were during the day (diagram 6, p. 360). What is more,
neither bed has *cassapanche* set against its sides. This must have been
because such chests or benches got in the way of the curtains, forcing
them to be hung well out from the bed (unless they were made very short).
This would have defeated the new requirement that the curtains should
be easy to reach from the bed.

A Milanese bed of similar type to the last-mentioned is shown in
Pl. 135. This reproduces a miniature in a book celebrating the marriage of
Lodovico Sforza (Il Moro) of Milan to Beatrice d'Este in 1491 and shows
him sitting up in bed on the miraculous occasion when the Virgin and
Child suddenly appeared to him in the sky outside his window.
Lodovico's bed seems still to have *cassapanche* but this picture must
represent what was very much a transitional phase. The testers of the two
Milanese beds are flat, the wooden frame being hidden by fringe, and it is
clear from the way the curtains have been gathered that they run
horizontally on rods with rings that must also be hidden by the fringe.
Each bed seems to have four curtains.

Could the form of *cortinaggio* represented by these two Milanese
miniatures be a *travacha*? The term occurs fairly often in inventories
about the turn of the century and is found here and there in documents
throughout the sixteenth century.[2] The *travacha* must have been an item
of some importance as a separate list of *Pavaglioni e travache* is given in
Lucrezia Borgia's inventory of 1503 (Borgia Invt., 1503) and the textile
materials of which *travache* were made do not seem to differ from those
used for *padiglioni* of the richer sort. That the *travacha* was probably a
suspended framework is suggested by a reference in a payment made in
1493 to the important carver Stefano di Dona Bona, working for the court

at Ferrara, who had made *2 telari da travacha* [2 *travacha* frames] that were
associated with fine linen from Cambrai, which suggests some form of
canopy.[3] The listing of *padiglioni* and *travache* together in the Borgia
inventory, moreover, suggests they were in some respect similar, and as
the feature that distinguished a *padiglione* from other clearly identifiable
types of bed-hanging is the fact that it was suspended, could not the same
apply to the *travacha*?

That there was cause for confusion at the time is borne out in several
documents. In the Borgia inventory a cradle is described as having *una
travacha o pavaglion*. When the Neapolitan authorities framed yet another
set of sumptuary laws, in 1596, they ordained that citizens were not
permitted to decorate with gold, silver or silk embroidery *paviglioni,
travache, sopra tavole e qual si voglia altra cosa di casa*.[4] It may be thought
that the mention of table-carpets [*sopra tavole*] and 'other household
items' may weaken the argument that *padiglione* and *travache* were related
but the relationship seems to be confirmed by the Venetian sumptuary
laws of 1644 where a similar prohibition was applied to *trabacche, o
pavioni, o tornaletti, o con qual altro nome si possano chiamare* [here
tornaletti (i.e. valances, a prominent feature of *padiglioni*) are added to the
list but the lawmakers then gave up and ended 'or whatever other name
you may choose to call them by'].[5] It may be objected that the *travacha* of
1644 was not necessarily like that of the 1490s but presumably they had
some feature in common and it is suggested that it was that they were
suspended rather than supported.

It is curious that the Italians do not seem to have adopted suspended
bed-hangings forming a box-like cubicle before the last decades of the
fifteenth century. No illustration of such a bed seems to exist, at any rate,
nor are there references in Italian inventories prior to the end of the

140

140 An early posted bed

This famous painting by Vittorio Carpaccio, dating from the early 1490s, is perhaps the earliest picture of a posted bed that could undoubtedly have existed and probably did so. It is essentially a *lettiera* with an insubstantial superstructure of slender posts, ceiled tester and shallow valances. No curtains are shown but they would surely have been present; the point of having posts and a tester was to hold up the curtains. Among the many details worth noting are the wicker screens in the window, the figure over the doorcase, and the elaborate armchair.

Carpaccio, *The Dream of St Ursula*
Accademia, Venice (photograph: Scala)

141 A mid-fifteenth-century *lettiera* with an integral tester

Entries in the Este inventories of 1436 suggest that beds like the one shown here existed (see p. 137). It is in fact a *lettiera* with a wooden tester supported by an exceptionally tall head-board and an equally tall board at the foot-end. It does not have posts and is very different in character from the early posted beds which made their appearance about 1490.

Miniature from the Bible made for Borso d'Este, executed between 1455 and 1461
Biblioteca Estense, Modena (Vol. 1.139r)

142 With very fancy posts, about 1507

There is still nothing architectural about this bed. The slender posts must have been produced by a very skilful turner using a large lathe. The bed cannot really have stood on such a tall platform from which it would have been difficult to descend. The valance is still very shallow but has tassels on each lappet. Note the details of the chimneypiece with the brass fire-dogs, and of the doors above which bronze figures are placed. This *Birth of the Virgin* has been attributed to Girolamo da Santa Croce and to Giulio Campagnola and its date is disputed. The bed is unlikely to date from after 1510.

Birth of the Virgin, Scuola del Carmine, Padua
Photograph: Scala

fifteenth century. Yet beds with such hangings are commonly shown in Burgundian and French miniatures from the 1430s onwards (Pl. 133) and it is surprising that this formula was apparently not imitated in Italy until the best part of half a century later. Perhaps further study will reveal that such bed-hangings *were* in fact used in the north of Italy, in territories strongly influenced by France (in the Savoy, for instance), by the middle of the century. Whatever the case, even when they had begun to suspend their bed-hangings, the Italians seem to have made their *cortinaggi* lower in their proportions than their North European counterparts (Pls 133, 134). It was not until well into the sixteenth century, or so it seems, that Italian bed-hangings acquired the tall proportions that had long been the tradition north of the Alps.

Quite early in the sixteenth century the design of beds took on an architectural character. This development is more easy to follow in the history of the bed with posts (pp. 135–46) but was evidently echoed in that of the suspended *cortinaggio*. Pl. 32 shows an early sixteenth-century *cortinaggio* with a massive wooden frame that must be hanging from the ceiling. A more famous example of the same type of tester is reproduced in Pl. 165; this has two curious concentric rings adorning the underside of the *cielo*. These two wooden testers, and some later examples all seem to hang below the ceiling but a few other testers of this sort seem to be be constructed so as to fit up under, and form part of a wooden ceiling. At any rate none of these testers are supported by posts.

Beds with half-testers might be treated in the same way, as Pl. 137

shows. This has two curtains pulled back to the wall exactly as would be done with a regular *padiglione*. There is a finial at the apex of the roof-like tester at which point the structure is attached to the ceiling. A Sicilian inventory of 1508 includes the item *Una trabaccha di once torniata* [presumably it had a walnut surround] which was *dorata in parte* [partly gilded] and had *soi fornimenti con due ordine* [cortine?] *et quattro pomi indorati de oro lavorati in vasi, nova* [its hangings with two curtains(?) and four gilded finials in the form of vases – and it was new].[6] Although the tester in the last-mentioned illustration has only a single finial, in other respects this description might very well seem to fit the tester shown in the picture. Most *travache*, if that is what they were called, were however full testers. In the history of furniture this form has been neglected and it was admittedly a form without a future. It did, however, not simply disappear from the scene once the bed with posts had become popular. Pl. 139 shows a Medici bed of about 1590 not very different from the Sforza bed of a century earlier (Pl. 135).

The bed with posts and the camp-bed

If the aim was to contrive a form of *cortinaggio* which allowed the occupant of a bed to control the curtains with ease, this could best be achieved by hanging the curtains from a rectangular frame set above the bed. If the frame were slightly larger in plan than the bed below, the curtains hanging from it would fall neatly past the edges of the bed,

141

142

143

144

143 The characteristic Italian shallow valance of the late fifteenth century

In this instance the structure is a canopy over a throne but it has much in common with the posted superstructure of St Ursula's bed (Pl. 140). The painting, which was destroyed during the war, also comes from the Veneto and was dated 1489. The ball finials shown here are a neat feature which was not obligatory on early posted beds.

Cima da Conegliano, *Coronation of the Virgin*
Formerly in Kaiser Friedrich Museum, Berlin

144 Resembling a camp-bed?

Another famous illustration of an early posted bed. The posts are more elaborate than St Ursula's (Pl. 140) but are scarcely less slender, and the valances are shallow. The bed itself is quite different from any standard pattern of Italian Renaissance bed; it is of a form that points to the future but may perhaps have been derived from contemporary camp-beds or travelling-beds which could be dismantled. The chests placed alongside are reminiscent of a *lettiera's* bed-chests; on the other hand, if this is a camp-bed the chests may possibly be containers used for transporting the posts and other slender members. The triangular object is a *spera* – a convex mirror and frame with three pegs which were to hold a small protective cloth (see

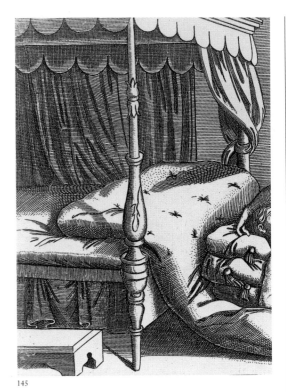

145

p. 236 and Pl. 267). Once again the bed has no curtains; the illustrator must have omitted them for the sake of clarity.

From Francesco Colonna, *Hypnerotomachia Polifili*, Venice, 1499.
Courtesy of the Trustees of Sir John Soane's Museum, London

145 Suitable for an afternoon's dalliance

Giulio Romano drew this bed while he was working in Rome; he cannot have done so later than the early 1520s when he moved to Mantua. He was a keen observer and a first-class designer of furnishings so this representation is likely to be fairly accurate. It shows a lightweight bed, a late version of the early posted beds of the 1490s. These must have existed, perhaps as furniture suitable for villas, *maisons de plaisance* and the rooms of the more lively courtesans. At any rate, it is included in this engraving (we show a detail) by Marcantonio Riamondi after one of sixteen illustrations by Giulio Romano showing positions for love-making.

Marcantonio Riamondi, eleventh position from his *Modi* (detail)
Albertina, Vienna

146 The massive posted bed with hangings; 1519

Not an entirely plausible representation. Almost certainly the head of the bed would have been against the wall and St Anne would not have lain diagonally across the bed as here shown; nor would she have lacked a mattress! The way the curtains have been tied up out of the way is entirely convincing, on the other hand.

Baccio Bandinelli, marble relief executed in 1519; *Santuario della Santa Casa, Loretto, (photograph: Alinari Archives)*

147 Sketch for the bed shown in Plate 146; about 1518

The posts, with their massive balusters, are here clearly shown. The putti holding festoons are probably larger than would have been normal for decoration topping a tester (the draughtsman, Bandinelli, was of course a sculptor so would have laid stress on such a feature) but there is an obvious likeness between these and the putti on the Farnesina bed (Pl. 148) which must in reality have been more formal than those cheerful little beings depicted by Sodoma.

Bandinelli, design for a bed
Ashmolean Museum, Oxford (P. II, 80)

146

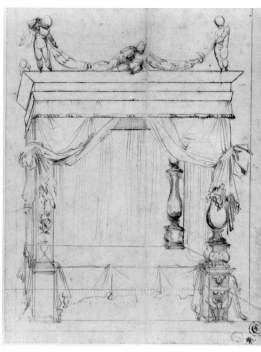

147

enclosing it in a box-like cubicle. We have seen that such a *cortinaggio* could be suspended from the ceiling (p. 129). It could also be held up by bed-posts rising from the corners of the bedstead. This was of course to be the successful variant, in Darwinian terms.

The posted bed had a precursor that was furnished with a tall headboard and an equally tall 'foot-board' that supported a wooden tester. We see such a bed in Pl. 141 which reproduces a miniature in the Bible of Borso d'Este, a work in preparation between 1455 and 1461. Several entries in the Este inventories of 1436 could refer to just such a bed. The most relevant would seem to be the *lettiera* which had *sponde de chapo et piedj et cielo de asse lavorada a capiteli* [side-pieces at head and foot and tester of boards decorated with capitals]. This stood in a second-grade bedchamber, but in a fine room, the *chamera da lj imperadurj* [Chamber of the Emperors], stood a *lettiera* with *cielo da asse churnixada bella antiga* [fine ancient tester of boards with mouldings] and in a neighbouring fine room was one of *asse cum el cielo et capoletj de asse curnixada* [of boards with a tester and headboards (note the plural) of boards with mouldings]. If our reasoning is correct, we have here several beds with a wooden tester supported at each end by tall wooden 'headboards' and the conformation may well have looked like the bed shown in Pl. 141 which in itself looks plausible enough and may therefore represent a form current between the mid-1430s and mid-1450s. Such beds were a variant form of the standard *lettiera*; they were not posted beds but they showed the way forward. The first posted beds, as we shall see, were quite different in character and cannot have been derived from this rather cumbersome formula.

The earliest illustrations of posted beds date from the last years of the fifteenth century, one of the earliest being the Venetian painter Carpaccio's famous picture of the mid-1490s showing St Ursula lying in her bed. This is a lightweight affair with slender, turned posts and an insubstantial tester with scalloped valances (Pl. 140). Such beds must have had curtains but Carpaccio has not shown them. A rather similar confection is to be seen in an illustration in that strange romance, the *Hypnerotomachia*, which was published in Venice in 1499 (Pl. 144). A bed with posts that are only slightly more robust than those of the first two beds is to be seen in a painting in Padua of about 1507 (Pl. 142).[1]

With their shallow valances and lack of finials, the supported testers of these posted beds differ in no way from suspended testers of the same date (Pls 134, 135). However, it was soon realized that the posted formula was the more practical of the two systems and, no doubt because powerful people were quick to see the advantages and wanted to possess such a bed and place it in their best bedchamber, architects and other capable designers do not seem to have been slow in turning their attention to its design. At any rate, very early in the next century, posted beds with architectural features begin to make their appearance in contemporary illustrations. The earliest manifestations of this concern with the design of important posted beds is to be seen in the way the posts are formed like architectural piers (they were probably called columns) with capitals which support bold cornices forming the edges of the tester (Pl 48).

All the illustrations of early posted beds mentioned so far have come from Venice or its neighbourhood but this type of bed, while it may have been seen in that part of Italy earlier than anywhere else (we consider its

148 The architect-designed bed
par excellence

This famous painting by Sodoma of about 1511, executed in Rome on a wall in the Farnesina, shows what must surely be the most splendid bed ever represented in a notable work of art. It foreshadows the development of the posted bed for the next two centuries and must clearly have been designed by someone conscious of the problem of how the massive presence of this class of bed might best be made to blend pleasingly with the decoration of a splendid bedchamber. Although Sodoma himself may just possibly have been capable of designing such a bed, one should probably be looking in the direction of talented architects like Raphael, Peruzzi or a member of the Sangallo circle in order to find the creator of this astonishing piece of furniture which, even if no bed exactly like it existed, must be of the kind that was to be seen in one or two grand Roman *palazzi* by about 1512. Note the plinth-like base, the fine fluted columns, the massive entablature, the embroidered valances, and the multiple mattresses. A convex mirror hangs at the head of the bed (Roxana, or the artist, must have shifted her bolster round to one side of the bed) and the tasselled object hanging from the tester seems to be a night-light.

Sodoma, *Alexander visiting Roxana*, Farnesina, Rome
Photograph: Scala

149 Hive of activity around a splendid bed, late 1560s

The woodwork of this bed seems exceptionally fine. It is architectural in character and has a vase finial topping each post. Angels hold up the bed-curtains in this scene of the birth of the Virgin by Cesare Nebbia who worked for many years in Rome and may here be depicting the kind of bed to be seen in the best houses of that city in the mid-sixteenth century. Note the *portière* with a lappeted valance and the hooded chimneypiece with ball finials.

Cesare Nebbia, *Birth of the Virgin*, Orvieto Cathedral, 1567–9
Photograph: Scala

149

150

150 Roman bed-posts; late sixteenth century

Drawings by Giovanni Battista Montano (1534–1621), an architect who seems to have executed many designs for woodwork and became professor of carving and painting at the Accademia di San Lucca in the 1590s. He was himself a craftsman and was said to be able to work wood 'with the fluidity of wax'. A close friend and associate of the architect Giacomo della Porta, Montano moved in intellectual circles and made a study of Augustan antiquities. He worked for Clement VIII, the Medici Pope, and Camillo Borghese who became Paul V in 1605. What is probably the Borghese eagle forms a finial to the right-hand column and another eagle decorates a capital on the column centre-left. Note the lappeted valances and the curtain-rings. These posts would all have been first turned on a lathe.

Giovanni Battista Montano, designs for columns from Chinnery Albumn, 42
Courtesy of the Trustees of Sir John Soane's Museum, London (Photograph: Courtauld Institute of Art)

151 True bed or day-bed?

In contrast to bed-posts turned on a lathe (e.g. Pls 148, 153), a fashion came in during the mid-sixteenth century for carved posts of which those seen here may be early examples. All four posts are carved to form terminal figures that watch over the occupant of the bed – in this case Danäe. The story of her seduction by Jupiter was sufficiently racy to allow the artist to show her on a bed that is rather small and delicate (of the same class as the Giulio Romano bed shown in Pl. 145), and perhaps in that case resembling the day-bed of a contemporary courtesan. The sides of the bed rise up alongside the bolster in a boat-like manner more associated with day-beds than with the sober furniture of a respectable citizen's bedchamber. The presence of the vessel under the bed is not easy to explain; was it for ablutions?

Giulio Campi, preparatory sketch for a fresco in the Palazzo Aldegatti, Mantua
By kind permission of Thomas Le Claire Gallery, Hamburg

151

origins below), was soon being made elsewhere in northern Italy. A carved stone relief by Baccio Bandinelli, executed in 1519 and set up in the Santuario della Santa Casa at Loreto, near Ancona, shows a fully developed four-poster with massive cornice and robust baluster-shaped posts (Pl. 146). The famous Sodoma scene of Roxana receiving Alexander the Great, painted on the walls of the principal bedchamber in the Villa Farnesina in Rome in about 1511 (Pl. 148), is an even more telling expression of carefully integrated design – if not by an architect, then at any rate by someone well versed in the mysteries of classical architectural idiom. The Farnesina bed has posts in the form of classical columns with a massive entablature above. The *putti* playing on top may look realistic but there were probably carved figures set on top of actual beds of this class, as ornaments, as is suggested by the Bandinelli drawing (Pl. 147). Already early in the century finials had been set above testers, over the points where the posts came up through the tester-frame. On beds with flat-topped testers, which was always the commonest form, it became the norm to have a finial at each corner and, although ball-finials were the favourite type, finials could be elaborate, running from simple ovoid shapes, through vases and urns (Pls 143, 150, 160), up to human figures like the playing children already mentioned. Cosimo de' Medici's partly gilt walnut bed in the Palazzo Vecchio in Florence (Medici Invt., 1553) had gilded pine-cone finials [*quattro pine dorate*], while elsewhere in the same building were beds with finials in the form of *vasi* and *vasetti*.

This new form of bed, with posts, must have made a strong impression on people who came across it in fashionable bedchambers around 1500,[2] and it must soon have acquired a name to distinguish it from the massive *lettiera*. A term that begins to appear in about 1520 is *una cuccia*. Lydecker* (thesis, pp. 292 and 294) cites a reference of 1518 to *una chuccia* and another of 1520. Both had *balaustri d'ulivo* [balusters of olive wood] which must refer to baluster-shaped columns similar to those to be seen in Pls. 144, 145, 146. A drawing of 1592 shows the wooden parts of a posted bed, the assemblage being described as a *legniame da cucia* [a wooden frame or bedstead of a *cuccia*].[3] An associated drawing shows the same *legniame* fitted with its *cortinaggio*. Another drawing in the same group as these two, likewise a bed made for the Grand-Ducal Court in Florence around 1590, shows that the posts were called *colonne*. But these beds date from the end of the century. The inventory of the Palazzo Medici in the Via Larga, taken in 1531 (Medici Invt.), shows that the Grand Duke Alessandro had only beds described as *una cuccia* in the best rooms (sometimes they are called *uno letto grande a uso di cuccia* [a large bed in the form of a *cuccia*] or of the *cuccia* type, as if the term were not yet generally accepted) while in store were XIII *colonne da cuccie inorate* [thirteen *cuccia* posts, gilded]. Moreover, one *cucia* had *soui fornimenti di legname* [its wooden components] which suggests posts or parts of a tester, and another is described as *una cuccia di noce semplice con le colonne*. A later Medici inventory, that of 1553, amplifies these points; we there find *una cuccia di noce a colonne con sua fornamenti* and, in store, *4 colonne da cuccia dorate, con 4 vasi dorati* [i.e, both it and its finials were gilded].

What may be an early reference to a *cuccia* occurs in a Piedmontese inventory of 1512 (Frossasco Invt.) where we see, written in notarial Latin, *tres cogias postium albre cum banchetis*. The editor publishing this inventory claimed that *cogia* here meant *couchette* but it would have been more to the point if he had written *couche* which, as we have seen (p. 111), was the French term for a simple bed – as opposed to a grand bed, *un lit*. When in 1380 the French king Charles V lay dying, he was transferred from his everyday bed in his private bedchamber to his state bed where he could die in dignity, surrounded by his sorrowing courtiers. *Porté fu le Roy de sa couche en son lit* [The King was carried from his *couche* to his *lit*].[4] As we noted, the *couche* was a simple structure with low posts at the corners forming legs and hardly rising above pillow-level. By extending the posts upwards, the *couche* could acquire the essential framework needed to support a *cortinaggio* and it is here suggested that this is the stage reflected by the Piedmontese reference; the *cogias* had wooden posts that were in some way distinctive, presumably because they were taller than those of the standard *coggia/couche* of the time that everyone could recognize. However, these beds were described as being accompanied by 'benches' [*cum banchetis*] which we know was a term that embraced the chest-like seats fitted alongside the standard *lettiera* (p. 114). The early posted bed shown in the *Hypnerotomachia* of 1499 (Pl. 144) likewise has small flanking chests. All grand beds in Italy had hitherto had such chests fitted alongside but, to take advantage of the close curtaining, it was best to be rid of the chests and this indeed was the next step. The bed with posts soon presents itself in a trimmer guise, completely enclosed with curtains that reach almost to the ground. The base might be box-like but it did not project beyond the sleeping surface (Pl. 145).

Normally the tester (or *cielo*) was flat on top, apart from the four finials, and this must have been the form of a bed in the Villa Medici in Rome (Medici Invt., 1598) described as a *letto con sua cuccia piana* [presumably a bed with a *cuccia*-like flat *cortinaggio*]. In the same building stood a *letto con Cuccia a Cupola*, which must mean that the tester was domed.[5] Among the sketches of beds provided by the Medici Guardaroba in the 1590s is another *a cupola* and one *guarnito . . . d'uno cortinagio a chupole*. Such a bed might have five finials (one on the very top) as equally well might a tester of pyramidal shape like a simple roof, although these mostly had no finials at all. Beds *a cupola* are also called *a tribuna* on other drawings in the same collection (Pl. 159).[6] One of these drawings, incidentally, tells us that already in the 1590s some very grand beds had posts fitted with sheaths of material (presumably *en suite* with the other bed-hangings); they were called *guarda colonne*. The flat-topped tester of course produced a totally box-like or cuboidal *cortinaggio*. Beds of this common type were therefore sometimes described as being *facto a cuba* [made like a cube] (Requesens Invt., Palermo, 1561) and later simply as having *un fornimento a cuba* (Correr Invt., Venice, 1584).

When the posted bed supplanted the old-fashioned *lettiera* as the bed one could expect to find in the best bedchambers, and the *lettiera* as a result became obsolete, the term was bestowed on substantial bedsteads in general. For example, *una lettiera di noce a colonne* must simply mean 'a large walnut bed with posts' and *un lettiera de noghera con la Cuba* in the

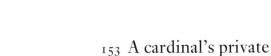

152

153

152 A fine carved bed; mid-sixteenth century

A bed with gilded figures in the form of *canephorae* (maidens carrying baskets on their heads), all facing forwards. The hipped tester has six finials. The bed stands on a platform. Three mattresses, an enormous bolster and a scarcely less bulky pillow make up the bedclothes, along with a coverlet.

Attributed to Sarsellino, *Birth of the Virgin*, mid-16th century
Collection of Prince Ernst August of Hanover (photograph: Weidenfeld Archive)

153 A cardinal's private bedchamber; 1530s

In contrast to the architect-designed bed, a parallel development from about 1530 onwards concerned beds where all one saw was bed-hangings. An early stage in this development, where the posts are still very evident but there is otherwise nothing architectural about the form, is shown in this view of an unidentfied cardinal sitting in his study in which there is a small bed. With no cornice, the valances assume greater importance, as do the finials above.

Illumination by the brilliant miniaturist Giulio Clovio, probably executed at the monastery at Candiana, near Padua, about 1530 and certainly before 1534 when he moved to Rome
Royal Library, Windsor Castle; by gracious permission of Her Majesty the Queen (R.L. 13035)

154–7 The fully upholstered bed

Four Milanese beds probably dating from about 1540. Their posts are relatively slender and are not supposed to show from the outside. Three of these beds have frogged ties to keep the curtains closed at the corners. The curtains are not lined. Two materials are used for each bed.

Unknown draughtsman
Fondazione Querni Stampalia, Venice

154

155

156

157

158

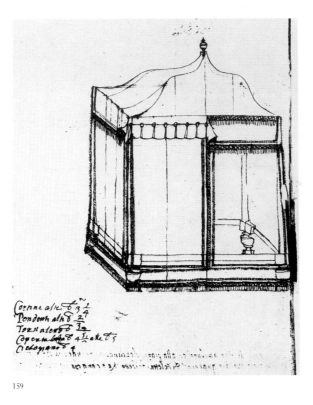

Corne alte 8 3¼
Pendenti alti 8 2¼
Torna letto 8 3¼
Coperta larga 8 4½ alte 8 5
Cielo piano 4

159

158 Fully sculptural carving; 1550s

Diagram 4 on page 359 shows how this bed looked. The four posts take the form of human figures; they stand on terminal consoles. There is likely to have been a massive tester, perhaps domed. Note the double row of lappeted valances.

Illustration to Giovan Francesco Straparola's *Le Piacevole Notti*, 1550–54

159 Medici bed of about 1590

The domed tester is described as being *a tribuna*. Drawn with a view to calculating the yardage of material required, this sketch shows how the wooden members are joined, how the curtains hang on tapes looped through rings (to save material as the tops of the curtains are hidden by the deep valances), and the several lengths of fringe. This form of bed was apparently of a kind which was made in Rome [*che si fanno in romo*, it says in an associated drawing]. The components are here listed – *Cortine, Pendenti, Torna-letto, Coperta* and *Cielo piano* [curtains, valences, base valances, coverlet and tester].

Unknown draughtsman
Archivio di Stato, Florence (Guardaroba 143)

main bedchamber in the Correr residence in Venice (Correr Invt. 1584) must likewise have been a heavy posted affair and not a *lettiera* in the old sense. By 1611, when Florio published his dictionary*, the word *lettiera* simply meant a bedstead, he tells us. The term *cuccia* also fell out of use eventually because, when all respectable beds were posted, there was no longer any need to distinguish this form. The bed with posts was then called *un letto*, a bed. When today Italians speak of a *cuccia*, incidentally, they are referring to a dog-basket – an ironic devaluation when one recalls that once every person of rank slept in one.

Judging from the pictorial evidence, such as it is, the earliest posted beds were lightweight structures and in this respect they may well have resembled the camp-beds of the period although we do not know much about the latter. A charming camp-bed of about 1580 is to be seen in the Bayerisches Nationalmuseum in Munich (see diagram 2, p. 359).[8] It has slender posts and a light tester of pyramidal form; it can be taken to pieces, as was essential with a camp-bed in order that it might be packed up and carried with the other baggage to the next resting place. This bed may not be very different from the camp-beds of a century earlier and certainly has much in common with the insubstantial bed shown in the *Hypnerotomachia*, for instance, while it is quite different in character from the standard, fully developed posted bed of the sixteenth century (Pls 144, 149, 158).

High-ranking officers in the field had to have camp-beds – for the sake of comfort and as a symbol of status, but other people of standing – cardinals, ambassadors and high-born ladies – were quick to see the advantage, in terms of comfort, in taking such a piece of furniture with

them on their travels. Too fastidious to put up at inns and wanting to ensure that, if they had to stay in some semi-furnished castle, they had their own comfortable bed with them in their baggage-train, they had the perfect answer in the lightweight camp-bed that could be dismantled. But a grand traveller could of course never be sure that the room in which the next night was to be spent would have the requisite number of hooks in the ceiling so that the hangings of the camp-bed could be suspended; and it was therefore a great advantage if camp-beds could have some in-built means for holding up the bed-hangings. Posts, or *colonne*, met this requirement.

When the Milanese noblewoman, Bianca Maria Sforza, went off to be married in 1493 (Sforza Invt.), she took with her one splendid bed with crimson and gold hangings, and a camp-bed which was described, in dog-Latin, as *Apparatus unus pro fulcra seu lectera una castensi*; which should mean 'the furnishings of a *fulcrum*, that is to say, a camp-bed'.[9] The word *fulcra* in Latin meant a couch or bed,[10] but with the probable implication that it was a lightweight structure and, anyway, the word here needed explaining – 'it is a camp-bed'. Clearly the form was not familiar to the writer compiling the inventory and the word *apparatus* was presumably his attempt to describe the framework required to support the hangings which, we are told, were of silk damask. At any rate, the bed could be taken apart as two bags were provided for transporting its dismantled components [*duobus valisiis*]. In the Medici inventory of 1553 mention is actually made of *una cuccia di noce da campo, da disfare in piu pezzi, con ferri et suo valigione di quoio* [a couch of walnut for the field, to take apart in

160 The upholstered bed by 1600

Somewhat taller in proportion, it seems, and with deep valances bearing eye-catching decoration hinted at even in this sketch, the now imposing upholstered bed was ready for launching as the chief form of bed used during the whole of the seventeenth century in polite circles all over Europe. A tabernacle hangs above the marble chimneypiece.

Ludovico Cigoli, *Birth of the Virgin*
Istituto Nazionale per la Grafica, Rome

160

several pieces, with irons (i.e. the necessary hinges, hooks, and bolts), and its large leather valise]. Elsewhere in the same inventory we find *7 valligione di vacca per portar letta* [7 valises of cowhide, for carrying beds].

The first undoubted reference to a camp-bed so far noted in Italian documents concerns one made in 1507 for the Duke of Ferrara by the court joiner, Paolo da Lolio, who was provided with the necessary metalwork (hooks, hinges, bolts, etc.) by a German smith – Zoane Tedesco – who was also on the staff. The bed was described as a *letera [lettiera] da canpo*.[11]

Camp-beds could be very splendid indeed. In the Fieschi residence (Fieschi Invt., 1532) a *Lecto da campo* had hangings of crimson satin lined with green taffeta, trimmed with silk and gold fringe. An inventory of the Farnesina in Rome, taken in 1526 (six years after the death of Agostino Chigi and therefore not necessarily reflecting the undoubtedly opulent arrangements he made at the villa) shows that, in each of three bedchambers, there stood *una lettiera da campo* and in another room was

una lettiera con li bastoni dorati.[12] *Bastoni* implies thin wooden members (battens or rods) but they are presumably only mentioned in connection with this particular bed because they were gilded. The other camp-beds no doubt also had their *bastoni* but they must have been unexceptional and there was therefore no need to mention them; all such beds had them – that is, if we assume that the *bastoni* were the slender posts that were needed in order to hold up a camp-bed's tester and its hangings. That this was very probably so is indicated in a French source of 1498 where a *lit de camp* had *Huit bastons* supporting the hangings, with four *pommettes* as finials.[13]

That camp-beds could be handsome objects is also implied in the advice given by Francesco Priscianese to the patrician readers of his *Del governo della corte d'un signore a Roma* of 1542.[14] Their *camerieri*, the servants whose main task was to look after the *camere* and *stanze* (i.e. the rooms of a *palazzo*), should also keep in good order *qualche lettiera bella di campo ad usanza di Germania o di Francia con suoi fornimenti* [several fine

145

camp-beds of the sort used in Germany and France together with their 'furniture']. From this it is clear that German and French camp-beds were admired in Rome around 1540,[15] and it makes one wonder whether perhaps the camp-bed had been brought to a state of perfection north of the Alps and was subsequently adopted in Italy, and whether the development of the posted bed had not likewise taken place in France or Germany – or perhaps, one might prefer to think, in northern Italy, because it does seem to be the case that the earliest representations we have of beds with posts stem from Italy and not from further north (Pls 140, 142, 144, 145). Whatever the case, it seems probable that the inspiration came from the camp-bed, which would account for the fact that early posted beds had a similar light-weight character.

Havard* (Lit, p. 423) noted that the earliest reference he had found in French documents to a lit de camp dated from 1472 and references become common towards the end of the century – just the time when the posted bed seems to have made its appearance. As Havard explained, the chief characteristics of the lit de camp were that it was light and could be dismantled or assembled with ease. If we have understood the course of development correctly, the posted bed proper differed from the camp-bed at first chiefly in the fact that it was not meant to be taken to pieces quite so readily.

It should be added that some camp-beds were furnished, not with a posted cortinaggio but with a padiglione.[16] Maybe this was the normal way of equipping a travelling-bed before the introduction of posts. But a padiglione required a hook in the ceiling for its suspension. Out in the field, or in a strange house, this could pose a problem.

The Italians do not seem to have published engraved designs for furniture in the sixteenth century but such designs were appearing in Germany from the second quarter of the century onwards, and in France soon after that.[17] Peter Flötner published a design for a posted bed in Nürnberg shortly after 1530; this still possesses some of that fragile character associated with early beds with posts although it is elaborately carved and has finials on top in the form of figures in classical armour. Flötner also published designs for beds of the old-fashioned lettiera type. By 1540–41, he had brought out a design for a strange posted bed which is strongly architectural in character. He had apparently visited Italy (about 1530, it is thought) and this design may reflect the impression made on him by important beds that he saw in that country.[18]

At any rate, it is evident that a number of Italian artist-designers of consequence had been quick to appreciate that the posted bed was a new class of object that could require their attention. It was not that the lettiera or the padiglione or the suspended cortinaggio did not need to be designed; they certainly did, although this could mostly be left to a skilled joiner or upholsterer with a good eye, after which it was largely a matter of ornament – intarsio, painted decoration, embroidery etc. – requiring a talent for designing in small, as it were. With the new posted form, however, one was dealing with a structure very like a small building and it was quickly realized that architectural principles could be applied to its design. The bed depicted by Sodoma on a wall in the Villa Farnesina

shows that, already by the second decade of the century, a good deal of thought had been given in advanced circles in Rome to producing well-integrated designs for this new class of furniture (Pl. 148). The whole concept is different from that of the bed illustrated in the Hypnerotoma-chia (Pl. 144) of 1499 although scarcely more than a decade separates the two representations.

Bandinelli's drawing of about 1718 (Pl. 148) shows another attempt to devise a formula for the posted bed, one rather plainer than Sodoma's with which it may, however, have some relationship, if one considers the way both artists have placed large figures of putti on top of the tester. Although Sodoma made his putti come alive, to dance around the tester trailing a garland, in all other respects there was no reason why beds like those he and Bandinelli depicted should not have existed. There were certainly craftsmen in Rome and Florence capable of executing such a piece of work at that period.

A bed of very satisfactory design is that shown in Pl. 190 which may have some connection with Vasari, in which case one might truly say of it that it had been 'architect designed'. Its proportions would seem to call for a domed tester but unfortunately the drawing has been cropped so we are left to guess its shape. Another handsome bed of architectural form is to be seen in a painting by Cesare Nebbia in Orvieto (Pl. 149). This artist worked a great deal in Rome so the form of this bed may well be based on one seen in the Holy City. Very different in character is the bed illustrated in a Bergamasque woodcut of 1550 (Pl. 158 and diagram 5, p. 359). Here the posts take the form of full-sized male nudes standing on brackets or of herms. Heavily carved posts were more of a northern feature, one which French and Flemish designers took up with enthusiasm,[19] but evidently this usually rather overpowering idiom enjoyed a certain amount of favour in Italy as well, perhaps principally in the north. Italians did not on the whole approve of bed-posts that were heavily carved, they seem to prefer rich but controlled ornament based on a lathe-turned column (e.g. Pl. 150).

The history of the early development of the bed with posts deserves to be studied with more care. It is a fascinating subject with wide ramifications. What has been said here is only a scratching of the surface. There must be scope in the subject sufficient to attract a serious scholar. It will almost certainly be found that quite a few artists of high calibre were involved; it is likely that beds of the most advanced design were destined to stand in bedchambers in some very important houses; and it seems that the early development of the posted bed in Italy took place in Venice but that it was left to Roman artist-designers to develop the form. At its best, the great posted bed of the sixteenth century could be a work of art.

161 Fit for the future Queen of Heaven. A *lettuccio*; *c.* 1490

Like so many Italian Renaissance artists, Botticelli liked to envisage the Virgin Mary as a well-educated young lady, daughter of a wealthy family who could afford the best available accommodation and furnishings. Here we see her well-appointed bedchamber in which stands a *lettuccio*, no doubt made by one of the foremost woodworking establishments in town – like that of Benedetto and Giuliano da Maiano. It has its own plinth and some of Mary's treasured belongings stand on the cornice. On the seat is a mattress and pillow. When the *lettuccio* was not being used as a day-bed, the small mattress and pillows lived in the chest formed by the seat which was hinged to provide a lid. To stress what a fine lady was Mary, the artist has draped a veil of the finest quality over the elegantly proportioned back.

Sandro Botticelli, *Annunciation* (detail) *c.*1490
Metropolitan Museum of Art, New York, Robert Lehman Collection
(1975.1.74)

161

162

163

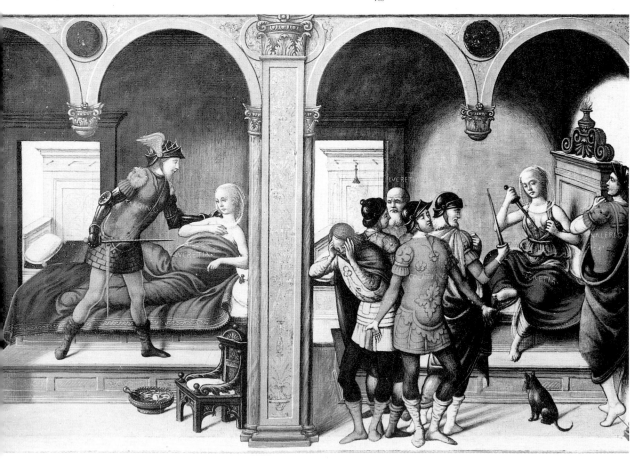

164

162 Dying well on a day-bed in 1496

This shows a *lettuccio*, that imposing piece of furniture to be found in many grand Italian bedchambers in the late fifteenth and early sixteenth centuries. The tall back of this characteristic Florentine model bears two large panels of *tarsie* with *candelabra* ornament and finials above the prominent cornice. This illustration from Girolamo Savonarola's *Predica dell' arte del Bene morire* [Sermon on the Art of Dying Well], Florence, 1496, shows a sick man lying on his *lettuccio*, with Death at the door and devils hoping to grab his soul; but a large *tondo* with Madonna and Child (an item often present in the best Florentine bedchambers of the period) will probably protect him, aided by the angels above who must have come through the window.

From Girolamo Savonarola's *Predica dell' arte del Bene morire*,
Florence, 1496
British Library, London (B.L. IA 27321)

163 *Lettuccio* as seat of honour

Serving here as a throne, the seat may be slightly narrower than that of the standard *lettuccio* but, even as a day bed, the form carried implications of grandeur.

Master of Apollo and Daphne, *Judgement Scene* in the *Story of Susanna and the Elders*, *c*.1500
Art Institute of Chicago, Mr and Mrs Martin A. Ryerson Collection (1933.1029)

164 *Lettuccio* with clothes-pegs

One can see the tall back-board in the room behind the bedchamber; it is fitted with pegs (or cloak-pins) on one of which hangs a clothes-brush. This was probably not a standard feature but it explains why the characteristic prominent cornice of the late fifteenth century *lettuccio* was sometimes referred to as a *cappellinaio* [a hat-rack]. Note the curious armchair.

The rape of Lucrece and consequent suicide, *c*.1500
Museo Correr, Venice (photograph: Osvaldo Böhm)

The lettuccio *and other forms of day-bed.*

Behind the curtsying Virgin in the painting by Botticelli reproduced in Pl. 161 we can see a *lettuccio*. It is an imposing and well made piece of furniture. It has an integral platform and stands in a recess in a sort of antechamber to the bedchamber beyond which contains, as we can see, Mary's *lettiera*. The *lettuccio* and the *lettiera* are decorated in the same manner, both presumably being of walnut with handsomely profiled mouldings. On the seat lies some form of overlay and we see a cushion at one end. Numerous entries in inventories concerning *lettucci* indicate that they were commonly furnished with a small mattress [*materassino*] and two cushions, together with a coverlet. The coverlet might lie on the seat most of the time but the mattress and pillows were usually kept in the chest formed by the seat, the top of which was hinged and could in many cases be locked.

The 'arms' of this piece are finely carved with scrolls in the form of dolphins, and we can see similar scrolls on the *lettuccio* represented in Pl. 163. Most *lettucci*, however, seem to have had horizontal armrests that were flat and unencumbered by scrollwork (Pl. 164) although sometimes a ball-finial was mounted at the forward end. The 'arms' were not so much arm-rests (although they could of course serve as such; see Pl. 162) but formed a head-rest when the bed was being used, with its mattress and pillows, as a day-bed.

A famous *Annunciation*, also by Lippi but earlier in date, shows a *lettiera* with most elaborate *intarsio* decoration and what must be a *lettuccio* standing behind it (Pl. 91). In fact, over and over again, in Tuscan inventories of the fifteenth century, we find a *lettuccio* listed as standing in the main bedchambers of great houses and villas, and the descriptions suggest that these items were commonly made *en suite* with the bed, as also seems to be the case in both the Lippi and the Botticelli paintings reproduced here.[1] The best were clearly objects of high quality and must have been eye-catching features of Florentine bedchambers of that period, and occasionally of antechambers as well. As we shall see, this class of furniture was by no means confined solely to Tuscany.

Modern Italians still have a saying that they are moving to and fro between their bed and their *lettuccio*, when they want to indicate that they are not feeling too well; but one can be sure that they do not actually own a *lettuccio* and few of them have any idea what one should look like. Indeed, the *-uccio* ending suggests the bed should be a poor one, of no consequence,[2] and the fact that this piece of furniture was once a thing of splendour has long since been forgotten and so has the fact that the *lettuccio* often stood quite close to the main bed so that it was but a few steps to totter from one's day-bed to the bed proper, as the fever took hold, or to move back again as one began to feel better. Only quite recently has the identity of this class of furniture been firmly re-established so that its former high status is now once again recognized.[3]

There is plenty of evidence that the *lettuccio* could be a luxurious object on which artists of considerable talent might bestow their skills. For example the well-known Florentine sculptor Benedetto da Maiano, who in partnership with his brother Giuliano ran the principal woodworking establishment in Florence, supplied a very splendid one to King Ferrante of Naples in 1473 and three years later they sent another to Naples for Ferrante's son, the Duke of Calabria.[4] The first was greatly admired when it was put on display in Florence – *una bella cosa e piace molto a ognuno, chosi dell'arte chome cittadini* [a beautiful object which gives pleasure to all, not only to artists but also to citizens; or, as we might say 'informed amateurs'. Sixteen or seventeen of the latter apparently returned more than once to view it]. The Duke's *lettuccio* was even more impressive. Not only was it decorated with carving and *lavoro di intarsio*; it was also painted and decorated with gold (no less than 2200 leaves of gold were required). It cost 210 *fiorini larghi*. No proper comparison can be made between the cost of an object as billed, and as an item in a household valuation (and especially not if it was made some twenty-five years later) but an idea of the comparative value of a *lettuccio* as against that of a bed can be gained from studying the inventory of Lorenzo de' Medici's town residence (Medici Invt. 1492). His *lettiera*, decorated with walnut mouldings and *tarsie*, was valued at four *fiorini* but his *lettuccio*, which was of cypresswood with panels of walnut decorated with *intarsio*, was set at forty-five *fiorini*. The bed of course had its quilts and blankets (thirty-six *fiorini*), a linen *padiglione* for use in summer (ten *fiorini*), and a *cortinaggio* for winter of embroidered red cloth valued at sixty *fiorini* (p. 129); and the *lettuccio* had its small mattress and a quilt valued at only three *fiorini*. Nevertheless, the elaborate character of the *lettuccio*'s woodwork, as against that of the bed, in what was one of the most splendidly furnished bedchambers in Florence, is striking.

The tall backs of the fully-developed *lettuccio* were frequently panelled, with surrounding mouldings, and there could be flanking pilasters and there might even be pilasters between the panels (Pl. 162). In some cases the backs were decorated with paintwork of a formal character[5] and sometimes the whole back was painted with a scene – flanked, no doubt, with pilasters at the sides.[6] It has been suggested that Botticelli's *Primavera* was originally set into the back of a *lettuccio* but this is no longer believed to have been so; it is now thought to have been fixed to the wall immediately above one but it was evidently regarded as belonging to it because, when the *lettuccio* in question was moved, the painting went with it and was fixed in the same relative position at its next resting place.[7] It is noteworthy that Vasari, writing in the mid-sixteenth century, relates how in former times Florentine artists had painted narrative scenes with figures 'not only on *cassoni* but also on *lettucci*, on wall-panels and friezes' [*non solamente i cassoni, ma i lettuci, le spalliere, le cornice che ricignavano intorno*].[8]

A characteristic feature of the fully-developed Tuscan *lettuccio*[9] was the massive cornice (strictly speaking it was a complete entablature held up, as it were, by the pilasters) which was not only decorative but provided a shelf on which one could place things (Pl. 161). In some instances, finials were fitted on top (Pl. 162). Presumably the *lettuccio*'s head-board might have a fancy cresting like that of the *lettiera* shown in Pl. 117.

165 A grand furnishing suite; 1513

The new-born Virgin's father sits on a splendid *lettuccio* that is *en suite* with the great *lettiera* – and probably also with the wall-panelling and other woodwork in the room. The bed has a massive wooden tester suspended above it, from the ceiling. Note the handsome chimneypiece.

Andrea del Sarto, *Birth of the Virgin*, SS. Annunziata, Florence *Photograph: Scala*

166 A happy Gothic tale; *c.* 1443

Another *lettuccio en suite* with a great bed; its hood is in the Gothic style. A drawer in the body of the *lettuccio* is open, presumably to show that the father has no money to pay for dowries for his three daughters, which explains why they are in despair. Luckily St Nicholas of Bari (not shown in this detail) is about to throw money through the window, so all will soon be well.

Francesco Pessellino, scene from the *Life of St Nicholas*, *c.*1443 *Galleria Buonarotti, Florence (photograph: Scala)*

166

called a *cappellinaio* because it resembled the standard cap-rack or hat-rack of the period (Pl. 228). We met with this same usage when studying the *lettiera*.[10] Some of these *cappellinari* were actually fitted with pegs or cloak-pins on which one could hang caps and other garments (Pl. 164) but this must have spoiled the look of an elegantly proportioned panelled back and the clothes must surely have got in the way, if one wanted to lean back; so one feels this cannot have been a commonly-adopted arrangement.

What are clearly *lettucci*, although they do not have a tall back, survive in some quantity in museums and are today all called *cassapanche*. This variant probably dates from the sixteenth century.[11] They do not seem to be represented in contemporary illustrations which may indicate that they were not rated very highly; those that survive are rarely so elaborate as the tall-backed form.

What must be a development of the older and more glamorous form is that shown in Pl. 7 which is of a Florentine tapestry designed in 1549. The scene is so busy that it is not easy to read but diagram 23 on p. 362 may be of help. We see Potiphar's wife springing from a very elaborate *lit à la romaine* complete with *padiglione* – the attributes of a fast woman, if we have read the signs correctly (p. 128) – while behind the fleeing Joseph we can see an equally elaborate couch furnished with a back that has openwork carving. Since the tapestry shown as hanging on the wall behind (its image, that is, woven into this actual tapestry) was itself actually woven and can today be seen on the walls of the Uffizi Gallery, one may assume that the couch also existed and was not simply a figment of the designer's imagination. If so, no doubt others were made and the

form may have evolved to become the double-ended couch (i.e. with outward sloping arm-rests at each end) that became a symbol of high status in northern countries.[12] The development of the relaxing day bed, on the other hand, went the other way round, as it were. It derived from the *lit à la romaine* and had a tall head-board at one end and no board at the foot-end; moreover, it could have a canopy.[13] Were the *letticciuolo basso di riposa* in a closet at the Villa Medici in Rome in 1598 (Medici Invt. 1598), and the *lettina da riposa* in another closet, examples of such day-beds? Did they in fact look something like that on which Venus and Mars are disporting themselves in Pl. 171. And was the asymmetrical ceremonial couch shown in Pl. 167 and diagram 6 p. 360 a link in the chain of development – that is, if such an object ever existed? It looks rather plausible as a stage in the evolution of the *lettuccio* on its way to becoming a day bed with a headboard, but at present it stands in isolation, unrelated to any inventory references that would seem to tally with such a form.

Attention has been drawn to the fact that Boccaccio, back in the mid-fourteenth century, mentioned a *lettuccio*, saying it was *da sedere* [for sitting upon][14] but he also makes one of his seducers put a *lettuccio* to more adventurous use (*con lei in un lettuccio assai piccolo si dormiva* [went to sleep with her on a very small *lettuccio*]).[15] The fully developed Tuscan *lettuccio* of the latter part of the fifteenth century could be a very glamorous luxury object and even the fairly plain versions cannot have been cheap. It must always have been seen as evidence of wealth and, by extension, a symbol of status, but it probably also carried a racy connotation of sorts as day beds always have. This is not to suggest that the Florentine magnates and their wives who owned such an object were

167

anything other than models of propriety, but possession of such a piece of furniture may have gone with risk-taking, cutting a bit of a dash, perhaps suggesting what might have been even if everyone supposed it had actually not. At any rate the *lettuccio*, while not structurally related to the form of day bed which became standard in the seventeenth century, with an elaborate head at one end, *was* related to it in function and to a large extent in spirit.

It is usually claimed that the *lettuccio* was essentially a Tuscan form, and certainly the evidence so far put forward here comes from Tuscan sources; but we have seen how two splendid examples were sent from Florence to Naples (some less elaborate ones went too) which cannot have gone unnoticed in the south and it is quite probable that local imitations made their appearance in Naples and perhaps also in Palermo in the late 1470s. Whatever the case in the south, *lettucci* were certainly known in Genoa, Milan and Ferrara[16] and it may be that the large seat with *cappellinaio* and pegs [*sedia grande con cappucciaio con caviche*][17] listed in the 1483 inventory of Bartolo di Tura in Siena may have been a *lettuccio* even if it was not referred to as such.

However, once one starts looking in the inventories for other terms that seem to refer to a large seat built up from a chest, the field quickly opens up and one gets the impression that one is recognizing both the contemporary relations of the *lettuccio* and its forerunners.

For example, that mediaeval piece of furniture known as an *archiban-cum* (to use the dog-Latin term) has been likened to a settle which is itself not so very unlike a *lettuccio*. Did it serve the same purpose? The word derives from *arca* + *banchus*, a chest and a bench. Many are listed in Bolognese inventories of the fourteenth century.[18] In Genoa they had something called a *bancale* which could have a mattress and two pillows lying on a chest-like seat with hinged lids, as did many a Tuscan *lettuccio*.[19] And there was the *archiscranna*, another large seat with a chest-like base (*arca* + *scranna*, i.e. a chest + a seat), the name of which was commonly corrupted to *ciscranna* and *iscranna*.[20] The *ciscranna*, however, was clearly not identical to the *lettuccio*, not in late fifteenth-century Florence, at least, because both terms are found in the same inventory and even concerning two pieces of furniture in the same room;[21] its nature is discussed below (p. 171). The point is that there were many variations on the theme of a seat formed by a chest with a back. They presumably all had a common ancestry in early mediaeval times (e.g. Pls 168, 169)[22] but it may well be that the *lettuccio* was its most glamorous variant.

Finally, there was a form of bed or couch called a *letirola* about which we can at present say very little. A *Letirola ... de asse vechia* [of boards, that was old] was to be found among a porter's (i.e. door-keeper's) belongings in the castle at Ferrara in 1436 (Este Invt.). It does not seem to have been an item of any consequence but this was certainly not the case with the *letirolla postiza, tutta dorata, cum quattro colonelle* which stood, together with a *letuzo* (i.e. *lettuccio*) in the private rooms of Beatrice d'Este, Duchess of Milan, in the castle of that city in 1493.[23] It will be seen that it was not only gilded but had four posts – perhaps among the earliest references to such features. It is not clear what *postiza* here means; Florio*, a century later, says this is part of a ship, so the bed may have been boat-shaped, but perhaps the word refers to the posts, also here called *colonelle*, as if they were slender in much the same way as the St Ursula bed (Pl. 140). A few years later (1507) we find Lucrezia Borgia acquiring a *letizolo* (also in the accounts called a *letera*, i.e. *lettiera*) which had four *colonelle*. This sounds very like the Milanese bed. The Ferrara bed (or was it a couch?) was a glamorous object, with rich carving in limewood (the capitals and bases of the *colonelle*), as well as gilding and painting by Tomaso da Carpi, father of the more famous painter Girolamo da Carpi. This evidently special confection stood in Lucrezia's private apartments.[24]

In the icy winter of 1493, special measures were taken to make life more bearable for the great who had foregathered in Milan to celebrate the birth of an heir to Ludovico Sforza. The Duchess of Bari had an immensely expensive bed, and also a second bed, presumably a day bed, set up close to the fireplace. It was *conza a la napolitana* which must mean 'rigged up in a style favoured in Naples', but all we are told is that it had mattresses (which must have been special in some way) and a *sparviero* of great richness, said to have cost no less than 3,000 ducats.[25]

The Duchess of Bari may have had to call in several menservants in order to move her day bed in front of the fire. How much easier it would have been if the bed had had wheels. Something of the kind seems to have been made for Isabella d'Este a decade later. An agent in Venice writes to her in 1502 saying that he is sending her a sketch of a *cariola* that he is having made for her [*ve mando un pocho de desegno della cariola la quale se à a fare per la Signoria Vostra*].[26] The characteristics of a *carriola* were that it was a small bed and that it had wheels; this made it easy for a servant or young person to push it under the great bed occupied by the owner of the bedchamber (p. 113). The ordinary *carriola* was a fairly simple affair but this one was carved, painted blue and subtly gilded, and had slender posts.[27] It must have been a day bed and was indeed to go in one of Isabella's small private rooms at Mantua, over the decoration of which she was taking so much trouble.[28] But, presumably because it was fitted with wheels so Isabella's maids could easily move it about, the agent called it by the name for the only type of bed with wheels with which he was familiar – the *carriola*. In fact, apart from the wheels, it was probably very like the *letirolla* with posts in her sister Beatrice's room at Milan and Lucrezia Borgia's *letizolo*, which have both just been mentioned. Indeed, the term *letirolla/letizolo* may possibly be a composite word like *archibanca* but in this case perhaps combining the word *letto* or *lettiera* with *rollare* to mean a fine bed that rolls. Maybe this is too far-fetched but there seems to be no reason to doubt that Isabella d'Este's small posted bed had wheels – otherwise it would not have been referred to as a *carriola*. When it was finally delivered, all of eighteen months later, she wrote to her agent expressing her delight with this luxurious object, and one senses his relief when he in turn writes back to this discriminating and often highly critical patron saying that her pleasure has given him *grandissimo contento* [the very greatest contentment].

A curiosity, perhaps a variant of the old settle/*lettuccio* form, was the bed Fynes Moryson saw in a small country retreat near Florence in 1594.[29] This was a 'Beddstead fitted with cushions of lether, and being narrowe it had a Cubbaard which drawne out inlarged it for a bedfellowe if neede were... The insyde was curiously paynted, but with Lascivious pictures...'. The description continues in this vein and Moryson explains that the owner, a member of the Buondelmonte family, liked 'to intertayne his Mistres or other frendes' in this hideout.

Materials and decoration.

The different ways in which beds could be decorated can best be understood by looking at illustrations of the period in so many of which beds are depicted, and no amount of quoting from inventories or other forms of description can convey anything like such clear information. Much of what has already been said in general terms under the heading 'Materials and Techniques' applies to beds and what follows here is intended merely to amplify certain points in the present context. The reader should therefore read this in conjunction with the general survey (p. 68 *et seq.*).

Many fairly ordinary beds were made of poplar which, when freshly cut, is nearly white (e.g. *i letiera d'albero bianca*; Capponi Invt. Florence, 1524). Chestnut was used for beds of the plainer sort (e.g. in the Uzzano family's villa in the country outside Florence stood *una lettiera salvatica di castagno*; Uzzano Invt., 1424). Rather grander, and common in fairly splendid surroundings, were beds of fir or pinewood. But the timber most commonly chosen for splendid beds was walnut.

In the sixteenth century, when exotic timbers were beginning to reach Europe in some quantity from the East or from the Americas, a few glamorous beds were made of such costly materials. For example, there

167 Can this piece of furniture have been real?

We see King Solomon giving audience beneath an elaborate canopy of state while resting on a day-bed – or throne – which is asymmetrical (see diagram 5, p. 359). The whole concept would seem to call for a seat with arms of the same height at each side but here one side is extended upwards to form a head-board as if this were a bed rather than a seat. As this is the direction that the main development of the day-bed was to take, and because so many other details in this illustration are plausible, it seems possible that such a piece of furniture did really exist. Note the striking clock, the convex mirror, the curious upholstered chair and the rug on the floor. Published in the 1490s.

From the Malermi Bible, Venice, *c.*1493
British Library, London (B.L. IB 23096)

168 A precursor of the *lettuccio*?

Painting of about 1340 from the Rimini area, showing the birth of St John the Baptist, in which an elaborate seat stands in front of a bed. It has Romanesque features but the lidded compartments with locks resemble those of the late fifteenth-century Florentine *lettuccio* and the general proportions are roughly the same – except that this seat does not have a tall back. *Lettucci* in other parts of Italy may not have been built on the Tuscan pattern and we should keep an open mind as to what constituted a *lettuccio* in other regions where this class of furniture was certainly not unknown (see p. 152).

Master of the Life of St John the Baptist, *Birth of St John the Baptist*, *c.*1340
National Gallery of Art, Washington, D.C., Samuel H. Kress Collection (1952.5.68)

168

169

169 The ample throne. The *lettucio*'s ancestors?

The Madonna is seated in a spacious box-like structure made sumptuous by being covered with a beautiful silk material. The front edges of the arm-rests are in fact decorated. Dated between 1345 and 1359.

Vitale da Bologna, *Madonna and Child*
Museo Poldi-Pezzoli, Milan (photograph: Scala)

170 The antique couch revived

Giulio Romano's representation of a day-bed appropriate for Cupid and Psyche reflects his familiarity with illustrations of such furniture in ancient Roman wall-paintings and carvings in relief. His fresco was executed in the late 1520s. This particular illustration was highly influential among those rich patrons of the Arts who were interested in having something of the sort themselves, at their villas or wherever they thought such classical trappings might be good for their image. Not only did a good many such people see the actual painting on its wall in Mantua but the picture was engraved (by Giorgio Ghisi) and prints bearing this image came to be widely disseminated during the middle decades of the century.

Giulio Romano, *Wedding Banquet of Cupid and Psyche* (detail),
Palazzo Tè, Mantua
Photograph: Scala

---

were three new posted beds of a timber called *verzino* at the Palazzo Medici in Florence (Medici Invt. 1531; *iii cuccie de verzzino nuove*) which the editor of the inventory glossed as brazilwood, a red timber from the East Indies (a form of rosewood). Ebony, which had been used for small items already in the early part of the century, was certainly being used for making the showy parts of a bed by the 1570s (p. 89)[1] and it is to be presumed that ebony beds were to be seen in a number of sumptuous Italian bedchambers by 1600 or so, by which time beds were being made of this timber in several other parts of Europe, notably Portugal and southern Germany.

The large flat surfaces of the *lettiera* lent themselves well to decoration of various kinds. Mouldings might be incorporated in the construction, as surrounds for sunken panels or in the form of bold cornices topping head-boards – and foot-boards, if these were present. Such mouldings might be made of a timber that contrasted with that of the field or the surrounds of the panel. For example, Lorenzo de' Medici had a bed of poplar embellished with walnut mouldings [*d'albero con cornice di noce*; Medici Invt., 1492] which, with is dark brown on white, must have been striking and may have looked somewhat like the bed shown in Pl. 118.

The *lettuccio* in Lorenzo's room was made of cypresswood with walnut mouldings and was further decorated with inlay [it was *intarsiato*]. *Lavoro di intarsio* in all the forms favoured during the fifteenth and early sixteenth centuries was used for decorating beds, from simple geometric inlays to bands of extremely complicated ornament[2] and even perspective views

(this last enjoyed favour towards the end of the period when *intarsio* was still in fashion; p. 94).

Lavoro di intarsio went out of fashion at about the same time as did the great *lettiera*. The bed with posts, which took the latter's place, tended to have quite a small head-board – and sometimes none at all, it would seem. In place of *tarsie* carved decoration became popular and we see head-boards acquire fancy outlines and intricate ornament in relief. The posts, a new feature, which now caught the eye, themselves became an important vehicle for ornament. Those which were of square section could be carved with sunken panels and ornaments in relief, like those on an architectural pier, while those which were of round section – the majority – could either be baluster-shaped or could take the form of an architectural column, complete with capital. Posts of round section were turned on a lathe, the columnar kind usually being further worked – often with fluting [*colonne scannelate*, i.e. channelled or grooved; Pl. 148]. Towards the end of the sixteenth century, great ingenuity was devoted to devising new formulae for the columns of the posted bed and important architects might become engaged in this activity when the necessity arose (Pl. 150).

Jumping backwards in time, it is to be noted that, during the last decades of the fifteenth century, some fine *lettiere* had their head-boards decorated with pilasters of classical form, likewise finished with delicately carved capitals and often fluted (Pls 116, 117). So strongly did this fashion establish itself in Florence at one stage that a young man, when preparing

170

171

172

171 The bed erotic

Showy beds of this sort were called *lits à la Romaine* in seventeenth-century France but it is not clear what they were called in sixteenth-century Italy although they were certainly known there (see also Pls 217, 378). Such beds had elaborately carved underparts (legs, apron-pieces, plinths, etc.) and a fancy head-board (not visible in this scene but it will have been on the left). They had no posts but a glamorous *padiglione* was suspended over them from which fell a frothy mass of curtainage. Artists commonly depicted a bed of this class when portraying an erotic scene set in a bedchamber – there was clearly something racy about such beds and it may be that the settings in which the great courtesans of the sixteenth century entertained their favoured admirers often had a bed of this kind as their focal point. The possible artist, Martin Fréminet, became court painter to Henri IV and spent some time in Italy (1592–1603).

Attributed to Martin Fréminet, *Mars and Venus*, drawing
Staatliche Kunstbibliothek, Charlottenburg, Berlin (Hdz. 3399)

172 A staid form of *lit à la romaine*

Detail from a design by Serlio for a bed-alcove in a house intended for a Venetian nobleman living in the city centre. The bed stands with one side against the back wall and has a bolster on the left, all being surmounted by a *padiglione*. Above the alcove was a more private chamber. There is no doubt that the bed shown here, which is imposing but not flamboyant, was entrely appropriate for surroundings of the utmost propriety like this. However, it is exceptional to find a bed of this particular type illustrated in such a setting; mostly they appear in scenes with plainly erotic content.

From Sebastiano Serlio's *Treatise on Architecture*, Volume VI, LII
Avery Library, Columbia University, New York

the main bedchamber of his family house to receive his future bride, updated what was presumably his parents' old *lettiera* – no doubt a handsome enough object in itself – by having pilasters with carved capitals applied to the head-board to bring it into line with modern taste.[3] Apart from the carved capitals of pilasters, the head-board of a *lettiera* might also have a carved cresting (Pl. 117). The same sort of ornament presumably could be added to the head-board of a *lettuccio*, a class of furniture which had arm-rests that could also sprout carved embellishment – like the dolphins to be seen in Pl. 161.

The finials on top of a posted bed were also mostly turned on a lathe although, once again, the most costly were further embellished with carving. The simplest were in the form of balls or 'vases' [*pomi, vasi, vasetti*]; slightly more elaborate were pine-cones.

Sixteenth-century day beds could have elaborately carved decoration, especially at the headboard but also sometimes on the legs or as open-work aprons between the legs (Pls 151, 171). Such carving could take the form, not merely of scrollwork or foliage, but of figures in relief or even in the round (Pl. 7). The most splended examples of this type of bed must be classed among the most sumptuous beds ever made anywhere, at any period.

Many fifteenth-century *lettiere* and *lettucci* were painted. Red and green seem to have been favourite colours. They may sometimes have been all of one colour but it is more likely that mouldings and other features were picked out in some second colour or in several colours. Certainly some beds were painted with graining on a ground of inexpensive timber, in imitation of more expensive timbers or elaborate woodwork effects. For example, at the Medici *palazzo* in Florence (Medici Invt., 1492) there was to be seen a *lettuccio* made of poplar – a very ordinary wood – that was panelled and grained to resemble walnut [*uno lettucio d'albero . . . riquadrato e cholorito a noce*].[4] In the panels were representations of *lavoro di intarsio* executed in spindlewood which is almost white when newly cut [*dipintove di piu chose di silio*; p. 92]. Not a few *lettiere* seem to have been painted with simulations of expensive silk materials, as if they were close-covered in such fabrics. In the Tura house in Siena (Tura Invt., 1483) for instance a fine bed was *dipenta ad drappo d'oro* [painted like cloth of gold] while a Sforza bride in Milan in 1493 (Sforza Invt.) was provided with a bed that had its head-board *pincta a brochato* [painted like a brocade, which here probably implies a silk brocaded with gold]. More elaborate still will have been the beds painted with the owner's coat of arms, a practice that was by no means uncommon.

As Vasari said (see p. 97), a great deal of furniture – including beds and *lettucci* – had been painted in the fifteenth century, not just with formal ornament but also with scenes or views. We have elsewhere considered (p. 149) whether Botticelli's *Primavera* could have been painted actually as the back panel of a *lettuccio* or was mounted as a panel above such a piece of furniture. Whatever the case, this now famous painting was undoubtedly associated with a *lettuccio*, as it was removed together with that piece of furniture when the latter was later transferred to a Medici

villa out in the country. A *lettuccio* which formed part of the furnishings of the famed painted room in the Palazzo Borgherini likewise had a picture fixed above it but the bed that dominated the room was itself decorated with painted scenes – on the head-board and on the faces of the associated bed-chests.[5] Maddalena Trionfi Honorati, discussing the decoration of *lettucci*, illustrates a bed (a *lettiera*) with a head-board bearing a painted landscape[6] and we have already noted how Francesco Guicciardini acquired a painting of St Michael which was cut from a *lettuccio* (presumably from its head-board). We must not imagine that such painted decoration was confined to Tuscany, by the way; Belgrano, the historian of Genoese social life and usage, mentions a pupil of Mantegna who painted a frieze for a bed in 1498 for one Genoese magnate (Belgrano*, p. 82; see Pl. 138).

Painted ornament on beds that was comparatively large in scale (and could include whole scenes, as we have noted) went out of fashion quite early in the sixteenth century but painted decoration with small-scale ornament (*miniato*) came into fashion instead – around the middle of the century. Indeed, there was presumably no hiatus in the development but the general picture suggests there was a lull in the century's second quarter. Belgrano also mentioned two Genoese painters who decorated a bed with gilding and polychrome arabesques. He gives no date but the *miniato* form of decoration often took the form of arabesques executed on a gold ground (p. 99) and Belgrano was probably referring to an event taking place around 1570. Arabesques might also be executed in gold on a black or a coloured ground, or (less expensively) in white or black on a coloured ground. The cradle shown in Pl. 289 has white arabesques on red. However, by and large, the ornament has by now become so small in scale and applied so generally, that inventory clerks tended just to describe the decoration as 'painted' rather than to qualify this in detail. The bed made in 1534 for Princess Anna of Ferrara, which was no doubt a delightful confection, was simply described in the Este accounts as being painted blue and gilded (p. 97).

A few beds were simply described as 'gilded' and no doubt the gilding in such cases was a dominant feature and probably covered the whole visible surface, or most of it. There was a gilded bed in the sumptuously appointed Palazzo Sanuto at Bologna (now known as the Palazzo dei Diamanti) at the turn of the century that was much remarked upon at the time,[7] and in the Fieschi residence in Genoa in 1532 (Fieschi Invt.) there stood *el torchio del lecto dal re dorato* [the bedstead of the King's bed, gilded] which was evidently particularly splendid; it may have been that prepared for Louis XII of France when he stayed in Genoa during his campaign in northern Italy in 1499 or that of 1509. A curiosity seems to have been the gilt bed that was to be seen in the Villa Medici at the very end of the century (Medici Invt., 1598). This was described as *Una lettiera dell' Indie tutta dorata co[n] mezze colonne* [an Indian bed, entirely gilded, with half-columns, i.e. short posts that did not support a tester]. Was this really from the Indies or was it an early expression of chinoiserie? Its embroidered silk coverlet may well have came from the East but that does not mean the bedstead was also imported. However, the room contained other furniture which was certainly of exotic character. There were three chairs which seem to have been of ebony and of Eastern origin [*indiane di legname nero*] which had some feature that was also 'in the Indian style' [*all'indiane*],[8] while a small table would seem to have been an imported item as it described as *Un tavolino de Chine del indie* ... It is possible that this last phrase describes a lacquered table with the word *china* connoting Far Eastern lacquer (just as we were later to use the same word to describe porcelain) and *del indie* meaning 'from the Indies'. This explanation might carry more force if it were not for the fact that in the room was also a chair *di cina dell Indie* that was, however, described as being *alla francese* [in the French taste]. It is difficult to conceive that a Chinese (or Japanese) lacquered chair would at this early date be formed in a French manner. All one can therefore say is that the Villa Medici 'Indian' gilt bed appeared exotic but we cannot say why. An Oriental bed of some sort was, incidentally, to be seen at the house of Ludovico Capponi in Florence at about this time. It was of exceptional workmanship [*di artifizio grandissimo*] and highly prized [*divaluta*].[9]

Much carved walnut furniture, including many beds, had details picked out with gilding [*tocca d'oro*] but walnut was too valuable a timber to cover totally with gilding. If that was the intention, a cheaper timber like pine was used, coated with gesso to form a foundation for the gold. The finials set on top of bed-testers were quite often gilded (e.g. four *vasi dorati* and four *vasetti di legno dorati* on two beds; Medici Invt., 1553) and some were gilded and painted as well – probably to match the decoration of a rather splendid bed, as no doubt was that at the Villa Medici in Rome (Medici Invt., 1598) which has *Cinque pomi dorati e depinti* [five balls, gilded and painted]. A tester with five finials must either have been hipped or *a tribuna* (Pls 155, 159) where four were set at each corner and the fifth topped the apex.

There is a mysterious reference in a Florentine inventory of 1424 (Uzzano Invt.) to *una lettiera ...ingessata*. This might seem to imply that it was coated with gesso but the bed in question stood in an unimportant room and a second bed so described was in a room used by servants or junior members of the family [*da famiglia*] and was anyway *chattiva*, in a nasty state. What is more, in the same house was also present a writing-desk [*tavola da scrivere*] that was likewise *ingessata*. Gesso was usually applied to woodwork in order to provide a base for gilding or paintwork but this cannot be why two relatively humble beds were gessoed, if that is what the term meant. Could this have been done in order to fill up joints and cracks so as to deny fleas and other vermin a lodging? Ridding beds of such undesirable residents was a perennial concern in former times and coating woodwork with a hard substance would seem a sensible measure to take. However, it is not a procedure mentioned in any other document scanned by the author and frankly we have no idea what the term meant.

Because bed-hangings were at first rigged up separately and not attached to the bed, they were listed separately in inventories during much of the period. Once beds had acquired posts, on the other hand, and the hangings came to be seen as integrated with the bed – and, indeed, were the bed's most prominent feature – it gradually became the practice to describe a bed by the type of material used for the hangings. Thus when a Venetian visitor to Florence went through the rooms at the Palazzo Pitti in 1576 he noted the presence of *uno letto di veluto verde* in one bedchamber and in another stood *uno letto di tela d'oro tirato in seta rossa, a nodi di Salamone* [a green velvet bed; and a bed of cloth of gold with salamonic knots in red silk] (Pitti Invt., 1577). By the end of the century it was not uncommon to list the set of hangings first and then the bedstead. Some of the splendid beds in the Villa Medici in Rome were described in this way, in 1598 (Medici Invt.). For example in one room there was *Un cortinaggio di damascho verdi guarnito de frangie pass[ama]ni doro e seta con arme de pezzi 13 fatto a cupola* together with *Una lettiera di noce co[n] colonne* and *Cinque pomi dorati co[n] flamme* [a set of green damask bed-hangings trimmed with fringe and gold and silk lace, with a coat of arms, comprising 13 pieces, (with a tester) of cupola form; a walnut bedstead with posts; five gilded finials with flames, i.e. flaming vases].

Most textile materials could be made up into bed-hangings but, in practice, the heaviest and stiffest were not much used for this purpose. The bed-curtains, at least, had to be of a material that could be pulled back and gathered freely or even bundled up (if the curtains were on a *padiglione*, for instance) and for this reason curtains were not infrequently made of a material of lighter weight than that used for the tester and valances. Niccolò III, Lord of Ferrara early in the fifteenth century, had several beds with hangings of *razo* [i.e. *arazzo* = tapestry] which must have been very splendid but only the parts that did not move were of this material (i.e. the *cielo, capoletto, coperta* and *parete*, i.e. the tester with its valances, the headcloth, the coverlet, and cladding of the walls alongside) while the *cortine*, the bed-curtains, were of *zendale verde* (green cendal, a thin silk) in one case and of a *saia verde* (green saye, a worsted cloth), in another. In fact tapestry was rarely used for bed-hangings although it was quite commonly made up as a coverlet (Pl. 123). 'Cloth of gold', which was basically a silken material where the coloured silk ground showed through the expensive patterns executed in gold brocading, was certainly heavy but was more pliant than tapestry. The same could be said of heavily brocaded velvet. Most silk materials were in fact suitable for bed-hangings although those of lighter weight were easier to manage. They were also cheaper and when city authorities were issuing sumptuary regulations (p. 324), they anyway tended to forbid citizens to use the richer silks for bed-hangings while use of lightweight materials was permitted. The Venetian authorities, for instance, in 1476 forbade the citizens to *tegnir a leto alguna cortina, ne coperta, ne covertor, ne tornaleto, ne altro ornamento ... de panno d'oro, de panno d'argento, de brochado, de veludo, de raso et de tabi* but allowed the use of *zendado, de taffeta, de catasamito et de ormesin* [to plenish a bed with any curtain, coverlet, counterpane, valance, or other ornament ... of cloth of gold, cloth of silver, brocade, velvet, satin or watered silk (but allowed) cendal, taffeta, catasamito and ormesine; see p. 69].[10] Similar regulations were issued again and again, right through to the mid-seventeenth century.

It will have been noticed that valances [*tornaletti*] were mentioned among the parts of the bed that were not to be richly decorated or of

173

173 The well-dressed *lettiera*

The curtains that can enclose this bed appear to be of a woven silk with elaborate stripes executed in gold thread. The coverlet is of silk velvet trimmed with gold lace that serves as a heading for tasselled fringe. The bolster has a white linen cover but the pillow is of a red material, possibly a silk taffeta, and has tassels at each corner. The woman airing a nappy over a brazier sits on a rush-bottomed rustic chair. Note the coloured glass infills between the *occhi* of the windows.

Pinturicchio, *Birth of John the Baptist*, Siena Cathedral
Photograph: Scala

174

174 Expiring on an Irish rug?

The dying monk lies on a bed covered with a rug, a shaggy coverlet that was evidently favoured in monastic circles (see Pl. 119) and probably also quite widely among less well-to-do people. Such long-piled coverlets seem to have had several names, the chief being *una bernia*, from Hibernia, the Latin name for Ireland. Note the window-shutters and the towel-rail.

Niccolò Giolfino (1476–1555, active in Verona), *Death of the Blessed Filippo Benizzi*
Museum of Art, Philadelphia, John G. Johnson Collection

175 Papal pillows; 1493

Close-up of the head of Pope Sixtus IV on his bronze tomb which is inscribed 'The work of the Florentine Antonio Pollaiuolo, famous in silver, gold, painting, bronze, 1493'. He might have added embroidery as he was also a masterly designer for the professional needleworkers, and the pillows under the pope's head give an idea of his skill in this direction. The heavily-embroidered pillow-cases are closed by means of large buttons in such a way as to allow the quilted pillows within to show through the gaps. Note the pattern of the silk mattress-cover.

Antonio Pollaiuolo, effigy of Pope Sixtus IV, bronze, 1493
St Peter's, Vatican (photograph: Alinari Archives)

175

expensive materials. Valances, which hang from the edges of the tester, were prominent features rather above eye-level and were therefore frequently more elaborately decorated than the rest of the hangings of a bed. Several of our illustrations show this clearly (Pls 154–7, 160). When bed-hangings had essentially been extensions of the wall-hangings, their top edges had commonly been furnished with a richer border (Pl. 122). The hanging then appeared to have a frieze, in fact. This concept was reinforced when designers, steeped in classical architecture, began to consider the design of beds which, as we have seen, occurred once beds had acquired posts so that the whole structure lent itself more readily to an architectural treatment. The Farnesina bed of about 1511 shows an early stage in the development (Pl. 148). Its valances are still shallow but they are embroidered with a pattern as rich as that of the *lavoro di intarsio* frieze above.

At all stages bed-hangings could be made from a patterned material but most hangings were plain, though in many cases embellished with a fringe or some sort of border and, in the sixteenth century, with silk or gold lace laid down over the seams. A way of enlivening a hanging was to make it of alternate widths of two materials of different colours. Another method was to embroider patterns on the material. In the fifteenth century, embroidery was mostly confined to borders (Pls 141, 173) although Lorenzo de' Medici's principal bed (Medici Invt., Florence, 1492) was embroidered more richly – with falcons and dormice, as we noted – and we can see some fairly ambitious embroidery in Pl. 148. In the sixteenth century, however, embroidery of intricate character could be seen on many beds in grand settings. At the Pitti Palace in 1576, for instance, there was a bed with embroidered hangings [*un letto di ricamo*] which was *fatto a ago con seta, e oro, e di piu sorte sete, di tutti i colori* . . . [executed with the needle in silk, gold and silks of every colour; Pitti Invt.]. More astonishing must have been the bed at the Villa Medici in Rome (Medici Invt., 1598) which had a *cortinaggio* composed of *quadretti di retino di seta con figure di seta et quadretti di bambacina* [small squares of *reticella* work[11] in silk with figures of silk, and (presumably alternating) squares of cotton (which was very unlikely to have been plain and may have been a chintz)] which was further embellished with *lavoro di seta rossa* [worked with red silk, presumably in needlework]. Another set of *reticella* of gold thread and silk in the same sumptuous residence is stated to have been made in Portugal [*fatto in portogallo*] whence perhaps the first set also came. Chintz was apparently not unknown in Italy in the 1590s, incidentally; a bed made up in the Grand Ducal wardrobe in Florence was of *bambagina dipinte* (painted cotton, which would describe chintz correctly).[12] It was made of material which came from Alexandria, captured from galleys (presumably Turkish) in 1592 (*di alesandria di quelle channo predato le ghalere Anno 1592*). It is entirely conceivable that a consignment of Indian chintz was on board a Near Eastern galley at this date. Expensive goods like this were precisely the kind of lightweight cargo that was sent in fast galleys by maritime powers trading in the Mediterranean, hoping that the great speed of which these ships were capable would keep them safe from the kind of danger this Alexandrian vessel clearly failed to avoid.

If bed-hangings were lined, in the fifteenth century (and some must have been, one would think), the fact does not seem to be mentioned in inventories but the presence of a lining is sometimes noted in the next century. In 1503, for example, a set of bed-hangings belonging to Lucrezia Borgia (Borgia Invt., 1503) was described as *Uno fornimento [da letto] de veluto Clestro . . . foderato de tela verde . . .*[of blue silk velvet lined with green material, perhaps of linen but anyway not of silk]. Another set of crimson satin had two curtains that were *desfodrate*, that is to say, unlined, while its *cielo* was lined. The curtains were left unlined so as to leave them easier to handle and drape. As no lining, or lack of it, is mentioned in most of the other sets listed in the same inventory, one must suppose that linings were then still uncommon; but by the end of the century linings seem to have become the norm, whether they were mentioned or not. By that time the practice may sometimes have been adopted, as it increasingly was in the seventeenth and eighteenth centuries, of using the lining material not only for the 'insides' of the curtains but for the faces of all the components within the *cortinaggio* – the headcloth, counterpoint, the underside of the tester and the inside valances (if there were any). The Farnesina bed (*c.*1511) already had this last feature, incidentally. Paired valances hid the tops of the curtains, with their rings and rods, from observers outside the bed and also from the occupant of the bed. A good example of attention being paid to such details is found in a Genoese inventory of 1532 (Fieschi Invt.) where a bed with a *padiglione* of gold brocade with a valance (*fenogieto dalto*) was lined with turquoise silk damask, whereas the *fenogieto da basso*, which was fitted between the legs of the bed, had a lining of *tella*, an unspecified material of no great distinction because it could of course not be seen (unless for some reason you were hiding under the bed).

When one had spent a very large sum of money on a bed with splendid hangings, it was natural that one should take precautions to ensure that the delicate materials did not get damaged by dust, rough handling or strong light. Hangings would be removed and stored (inventories drawn up some while after the death of the owner often list bed-hangings separately from their beds, presumably because they had been removed for safety), or they could be protected by throwing a cloth over them. What must have been a very splendid bed made for Ippolita Sforza had hangings of crimson satin embroidered with crests and other ducal emblems in silver thread [*zetonino raso cremesile racamato de argenteria come le cimerii et altre devise ducale*] and also *tre copertine de intorno de sendale de cremisile* which may simply have been meant to describe three *cortine* of crimson cendal but, if the word *copertine* is not a misspelling and we can take it to mean 'small covers', we may here have a reference to protective covers for the fine embroidery which went *around* the latter – hence *de intorno* (Trivulzio Invt., Milan, 1465). If this interpretation is correct, one should imagine some sort of bag with ties that totally enclosed the expensive hangings.

Bed-covers and bedclothes

We here deal first with the items which showed most, the coverlets (from the French *couvre-lit*) and other classes of bed-covering that formed the uppermost layers in most circumstances.

The Italians used the same term, *copriletti*, and also spoke of *coperte da lecto* while variations like *copertoio*, *copertone* and *copertore* are found in different regions. Attempts to discover a commonly agreed distinction between a *coperta* and a *copertore* or *copertoio* seem to have been fruitless; all one can safely say is that, while many coverlets formed part of a set of bed-hangings (i.e. they were of the same material as the curtains and other components), others were quite separate items that likewise served as the uppermost covers of a bed.[1]

In any case, coverlets could be very splendid and very expensive. In the drafting of sumptuary laws, the *coperte* of beds were singled out as items which should not be made of excessively costly materials or be too richly decorated, which is proof enough that they were frequently showy in the extreme. We get some idea of this from the *Coperte da leto* listed separately in the inventory of Lucrezia Borgia's belongings in 1503 (Borgia Invt.). Her grandest was of gold brocade with a grey ground, with a valance or border of black figured velvet appliqué patterns on blue satin, all lined with black cloth [*de brochato doro bertino con una balzana entorno de veluto negro frapato posto sopra raxo turchino fodrato tella negra*]. Several others were less elaborate, of a single silken material (damask, velvet, silver brocade or embroidered satin) or of two combined (yellow and purple damask, polychrome taffeta and white damask, green taffeta with crimson silk worked with gold), which must all have been striking enough but particularly luxurious must have been her coverlet of crimson velvet with a central panel and border of silver brocade, all lined with lynx fur [*de Veluto carmexin con una fassa atorno e in mezo de brochato dargento fodrato de lupi Cervieri*]. More than a dozen lynxes must have given up their pelts in some distant part of Europe to furnish that lining. Fur-lined coverlets are occasionally mentioned in other inventories; Cosimo I de' Medici had one lined with the fur of pine-martins [*di martire*] in 1553, for instance.

A commoner but still very expensive type of coverlet was that made of tapestry [*arazzo*]. These are shown in many illustrations and must have been greatly admired (Pls 118, 123). They seem mostly to have been decorated with clumps of flowers. Niccolò III's sets of tapestry bed-hangings (Este Invt., 1436, see p. 158) comprised matching *coperte*. Pierfrancesco de' Medici ordered three *copriletti* of tapestry from Bruges in 1454.[2] By the end of the century there must have been a notable export-trade from Flanders of such coverlets, not only to Italy but to many other parts of Europe including England. Edmund Spenser, wanting to depict a bed of splendour, mentions 'arras coverlets' as if they were familiar objects of luxury – or, at least, had been so, because tapestry coverlets seem to have fallen from favour towards the end of the sixteenth century. They were colourful, exotic (in Italy, at any rate), and evidently expensive but they were also heavy. At a time when people often slept with their coverlet still on the bed, a covering that was warm but not weighty must

have been what those wanting real comfort sought to obtain. A quilted covering was the answer, and these do indeed become increasingly common during the sixteenth century, as quilting techniques became more subtle. In 1526, at the Villa Farnesina (Medici Invt.) in Rome, a *coperta* of crimson *tela* (presumably a linen or cotton material) was *imbotita in mando[r]le* [quilted with almond-shaped patterns, i.e. ovals]. The nine *coperte bianche a botocini* in the Capponi mansion [white, with small buttons (Capponi Invt., Florence, 1534)] must also have been quilted, like a thin mattress or overlay; there can be no other reason for the presence of small buttons in this context.

If tapestry coverlets were uncomfortably heavy, Near Eastern rugs (i.e. with a pile surface) would have been even more so and they were probably very rarely placed on beds. However, textiles with a long pile that had some of the properties of a fur were used on beds (Pls 119, 174). The modern Greek *floccati* is such a material and the Finnish *rya* (rug) was another that was in common use until fairly recently. Irish rugs or mantles were early manifestations of this need to produce such warm coverings. The Irish used them as cloaks and no doubt also on their beds. In great English houses of the sixteenth century it was the practice to place 'an Irishe rugge' on the beds of important guests[3] and it would appear that the same was done in other parts of Europe; indeed, there must have been a notable export trade in these goods from Ireland. In France they were known as *ibernes* (from Hibernia, the Latin name for Ireland), *sbernes* or *bernies*, and similar terms occur in Italian inventories. Thus Florio* tells us that a *Bernia* was 'an Irish or Seaman's rugge' while a *Sbernia* was 'an Irish rug or mantle'. In fact, by the sixteenth century, the *bernia* had become a luxurious article of clothing, Toriano (in his 1659 edition of Florio's dictionary) explaining that it was 'a woman's garment in nature of a cloak but [now] no more in use'. It could be made of silk velvet or satin, it might even be set with pearls or mounted with silver.[4] However, when used as a bed-cover, a *bernia* was undoubtedly a woven material of wool with a long shaggy pile (Nicot's French dictionary of 1606; *Bernie. Gross mante velue faite de rude laine dont les Irlandais usent pour vesture*) and this must have been the character of the *bernia grande d'irlanda per coperta de lecto* which lay on a bed at the Medici residence at Fiesole in 1498 where there was also a *coperta [di] lecto di frigio d'irlanda*.[5] Although most fifteenth-century references to *bernie* in Italian inventories may well concern items of dress, some may be shaggy coverlets to lay on beds. Related to them must have been a *fargana* which, in a Sienese inventory of 1450 (Fece Invt.) was described as being *pelosa* [hairy – with a pile]. In 1388 a tarif of import-duties payable on the introduction of various good to the city of Siena mentions *Farghane de lletto, di lana* ...[for beds, of wool] and *Charpite overo farghane de lletto* equating these objects with covers [*carpite, carpette*]. In this connection should also be mentioned *schiavine* which were placed on beds.[6] Pardi (p. 112) suggests that these coverlets came from 'Schiavonia' (Yugoslavia) and may therefore have been the ancestors of the Greek *floccati*; that is with a pile, but maybe they were simply rather a glamorous type of blanket. One was anyway to be seen at Ferrara, among the Este possessions, and of it was said that *non se*

176

176 Conjugal bliss in San Gimignano in the late fourteenth century

Two coloured pillows lie on the bolster of this double bed. The sheet is turned down over part of the chequered coverlet or blanket. The woodwork of the bed seems to be untreated but the bed-chests are painted red and have tinned iron straps. A servant is pulling the plain curtains which must be attached to the architecture. There are striped wall-hangings behind. From a cycle of frescoes depicting the joys of married life (although why the wife in that case has turned her back on her husband is puzzling).

Niccolò di Segna, scene from *The Joys of Married Life*, Palazzo Comunale, San Gimignano, Tuscany
Photograph: Scala

po vedere, per la soa bonta, which would seem to imply that it was something very special, either in quality or appearance.[7] By the late sixteenth century, however, *schiavine* may have become plainer, if still fairly attractive items of bedclothing, judging by a reference to two which were white, hairy and handsome, [*bianche, pelose, buone*] in the Urbino Inventory of 1582.

Many pictures of the period show people in bed with the coverlet still in place (e.g. Pls 116, 173, 275). That this was the normal practice is also shown by one of Matteo Bandello's short stories in which the hero, with the help of a servant, gently removes the coverlet from a bed in which a young woman is sleeping, so as to reveal her 'smoothe and delicate forms which the very fine sheet did little to conceal' [*levo soavamente via la coperta dal letto, di modo che la donna resto solamente coperta da un sotilissimo lenzuolo, che nessuna parte del delicato e morbido corpo pienamente nascondeva*]. Bandello does not leave it at that, of course, but readers who want to know what happened had better read the complete tale.[8]

While the *coperte* of grand beds were frequently left in place even when the bed was occupied (with the top sheet simply turned down over the top edge of it), one gets the impression that in many instances the *coperta* was removed – in which case the next layer down was revealed. This would usually consist of a *coltre*, a quilt, or of a woollen cover like a blanket, or both.

Even the simplest blankets tended to be colourful objects, especially in the fifteenth century when they were anyway more in evidence. Many were boldly striped, others were striped both ways to form a tartan pattern (Pl. 176), and some were said to be chequered [*scaccato*, although this may simply have been the way of describing a tartan]. Blankets were made in many parts of Italy and used locally but some kinds were sent further afield, like those of the Romagna which must also have been distinctive as their origin is sometimes specified (*panno romagnuolo*; see the Uzzano Invt. and the Tura Invt.). But the most prized blankets came from Catalonia. They were often red (*5 panni da letto, di Catalognia, rossi*; Medici Invt., Florence, 1553); or *un catelano rosso ... per il lecto* (Di Challant Invt., Turin, 1522) but a white one is recorded in a Milanese house in 1529 (Trivulzio Invt.). Some had a long pile (*Ung tappis à hault poils de Cathelongne*, is noted in the Savoy Invt., Chambéry, 1497–8), and one at least was lined and quilted (*raddoppiato et imbottito*; Medici Invt., Florence, 1553).

What was clearly also a distinctive class of woollen bed-cover was *una sargia*. This may well have had a twill weave like modern serge but must have been a more luxurious material, in the fourteenth and fifteenth centuries, than it is today. *Sarge* were mainly imported from north-eastern Fance.[9] When Boccaccio wants to describe some particularly delightful retreat in the countryside, he speaks of a small valley where beds have been set up by a discreet steward who has rigged up hangings round them and furnished them with *sarge francesche*.[10] That they were used as top-covers on beds is also proved for us by Boccaccio who makes great play with a *sargia* in one of his more salacious tales, describing at one point how it was removed from the bed which it covered.[11] But that was in

the mid-fourteenth century. By the sixteenth century the *sargia* had gone out of fashion. These blankets, if that is how they should be described, could be red, green, yellow or white. Many were striped and one on a Florentine bed was embroidered (Pucci Invt., 1449). The material must have been fairly smooth because quite a few *sarge* are described as being *dipinti* which one would suppose meant painted (p. 75).[12] Whatever the character of this decoration, it was presumably applied where these cloths were made – in Northern France – but one late specimen of a *sargia dipinta* was specified as being *di bargelona*, from Barcelona. It was at the Medici Villa at Castello (Medici Invt., 1498) and was probably a striking object but it may well be that the technique used was imitated from the French product.

An even more eye-catching form of material often used as a coverlet, but also as a wall-hanging, was the *celone* which took its name from Châlons-sur-Marne whence the best specimens came.[13] We see the link in a Piemontese inventory of 1512 (Frossasco Invt.) where it lists some bedclothes *et chialono*, and in a Neapolitan inventory of 1400 where we find *chalone due*.[14] In northern Italy, the word was often written *zalone* and sometimes as *clarone*, and even as *telone*.[15] While the best came from Flanders, *celoni* were also produced in Italy; Pardi* (p. 49) states that there were looms weaving *zaoloni* at Ferrara in 1436. The local products were called *celone nostrale* ['ours', in fact]. Florio* tells us that *celoni* were 'course [coarse] hangings of rugged clothes [cloth]' and it seems likely that the material belonged to that large class of striped or figured woollen materials with a linen or hempen warps (the Aleardi Inventory of 1408 mentions the two sorts of yarn, *unus zalonus fili et lane*) which were known in Flanders as *hautelisse* (p. 76).[16] When 'figured', these materials were woven with the aid of a draw-loom, their figures or patterns being repetitive and mostly fairly simple, alternate motifs often being reversed. A *zalonus magnus cum figuris* [large, with figures, (here meaning human figures] is mentioned in a Paduan inventory (Alvarotti Invt., 1460). The highest grades had passages woven in silk but it is unlikely that they were totally of silk, in spite of the entry in the Florentine Capponi inventory of 1534 which reads *1 celone vecio alla turchesca di seta di braccia 6 et 2* [old, in the Turkish manner, of silk, 6 × 2 *braccia*] which, if it was a true *celone*, perhaps had passages of pattern worked in silk – unless, of course, this was a Turkish silk hanging in some degree resembling a *celone*. These materials came in widths which could be stitched together to make up a cloth of the desired size (*unus zalonus de tribus pettiis de pano turchino* [of three pieces of blue cloth]; Barzizza Invt., Padua, 1445). In the Capponi inventory just mentioned we find listed together *Tappeti e Cellonni*. The first word means a textile cover to lay on something and two of them were indeed covers for *cassoni*. The context makes it clear that the *celoni* here listed are also covers, presumably for beds. Elsewhere *celoni* are sometimes specified as being for beds [*da lecto*] and Milanese ladies, if they took any notice of sumptuary regulations promulgated in 1498, were not supposed to lie-in on a bed with a coverlet of silk, or one woven or embroidered with silk; they were only allowed to sport a *celone* worked with silk (*exceptis celonis etiam seta laboratis*), which gives us an idea of the standing of such cloths – handsome but not splendid.[17] A Florentine statute of 1335 lists *sarge* and *celoni* together.[18] Both were woollen stuffs and both came from Flanders but they may have had more in common (there were no doubt many grades and one class may, as it were, have shaded into the other). Certainly the distinction was not always readily apparent, as we see from a Genoese inventory in 1456 (Vivaldi Invt.) where listed is *claronum unum sargie vermilie*, and Schiaparelli (p. 227) cites references to *una sargia overo celone* and *celoni o sargie* (1418 and 1402) that betray the evident confusion these materials engendered even at the time.

We noted that some coverlets [*coperte*] were quilted but there were also quilts [*coltri*] that were so fine one could use them as coverlets, exposed to view. Once again the distinction was blurred, as Florio* reveals by explaining that a *coltre* was 'a counter point [counterpanes at that time were quilted] or quilt for a bed'. Most *coltri* were apparently of linen and therefore white but some were of thin silk (taffeta and cendal [*zendado*] are mentioned) which could of course be coloured. Others were of cotton [*bambagia*]. Sometimes the quilting was executed with a coloured silk (e.g. in the Requesens inventory from Palermo in 1561 one of white linen was quilted with yellow silk [*repuntata da sita ialna*]). Quite often the designs formed by the quilting are mentioned – with squares, waves, herring-bones, birds and flowers, circles and lilies, ovals, and no doubt many other patterns. An unusual quilt must have been that in the New Apartment at the Palazzo Vecchio in Florence in 1553 (Medici Invt.) *di tela di Portogallo pinta*, that was almost certainly of Indian chintz, most of which at that period came through Portugal. By definition quilting involves two layers of material but these usually form a sandwich with an inner layer of stuffing, albeit often a very thin one especially if a summer quilt was being made. This inner layer could be of cottonwool – or perhaps of wool, if a winter quilt was involved.

Next, working downwards, came the sheets which were employed in much the same way as they are today. Sheets were mostly of linen and the best linen sheets came from Rheims[19] or Cambrai (p. 73) and were sometimes further described as being *sottili* or *sottilissimi* according to the degree of fineness. There were less fine qualities right down to the coarse sheets of canvas used by servants. Some sheets were made of wool, one set being red and white. In the earlier part of the fifteenth century, many sheets were striped. In the sixteenth century the best linen came from Holland (*tela de landa*) and in a Sicilian inventory of 1598 this fine material is distinguished from coarser sheets of *tela di casa*, made locally (Moncada Invt. Sicily, 1598). Sheets often had fancy borders at the top [*orli*] – and might also be embroidered round the edges [*verghe*]. A very splendid pair in a Florentine villa was made of net or veiling, that was edged with gold thread (*di velo fregiato doro*; Uzzano Invt.). Sheets were of different sizes, made up with two, three or four widths. Some people, incidentally, slept naked in bed; most wore a night-gown of some kind. It was not uncommon to wear a coif or night-cap, as many of our illustrations show.

Beneath the sheets were mattresses of various kinds, those who could afford it having three and sometimes more (Pls 177, 231). Bandello, describing a grand bedchamber, lists four mattresses filled with cottonwool [*quattro materazzi di banbagio*; this must refer to the stuffing as it is unlikely that the mattress-covers were of a cotton material].[20] The usual arrangement seems to have been to place a *saccone*, a coarse canvas bag containing straw, on the wooden *fondo* or *tavola* of the bed. On top of this was then placed a mattress [*materazzo, stramazzo*] that might contain wool flock or, sometimes, feathers of a coarse kind. This was a more presentable object than the *saccone*, being made of ticking [*boldro*]. On top of this again it was normal to have a *coltrice*, a quilt filled with feathers of a finer sort, as a soft overlay. The sculptor Benedetto da Maiano (Da Maiano Invt.) had a *coltrice piena di piuma buona* [filled with good feathers] on his bed, laid on top of a *materassa* and *saccone*. One could of course adopt various permutations in these arrangements, and the rich usually had more and generally softer layers. Niccolò III, Lord of Ferrara, in 1436 (Este Invt.) had his *saccone* filled with cottonwool rather than straw, and his mattress filled with down instead of ordinary feathers.

Finally a bed required a bolster [*cavezale, piumaccio/primaccio*] to which it was not uncommon to add pillows [*origlieri, guanciali*] both of which were usually filled with feathers, the finer the better (Pl. 176). The actual pillows (i.e. the filled bags) were sometimes called *intimelle* (also *lentima, emptema* and the like) and they were encased with a covering that could be buttoned or laced at the sides, a pretty way of arranging this being to allow the bag, suitably covered in an attractive material, to show through gaps in the fastening (Pls 175, 219). The Venetian government, in several of its sumptuary laws, forbade the use of silk *entimele* worked with gold or silver thread or ornamented with jewels of pearls, all of which would only have been required if these stunning effects could be seen and admired.[21] The pillow-cases [*sonie, federe*] could be exquisite objects, in which case they were more suitable for decoration than practical use and we do indeed sometimes see them displayed at the foot-end of the bed – on the important occasions, no doubt – where anyone entering the bedchamber would be bound to notice them, while they would be out of the way of the occupant of the bed who would be sitting up at the other end (Pl. 173). In the inventory of the Fieschi residence in Genoa, taken in 1532, some *sonie* were recorded as being embroidered with black silk; and, once again, we can cite Bandello, this time describing another splendid room where were to be seen two exceptionally beautiful pillows of purple silk embroidered with gold thread.[22]

For a *lettuccio* two large and quite robust pillows were needed, one for each end, to lean against the arm-rests. Lorenzo de' Medici (Medici Invt., Florence 1498) had two of Spanish leather [*cuoro facto in Spagna*] for this purpose. At this point pillows cannot really be distinguished from cushions, which are here discussed under 'seat-furniture'.

177 Three mattresses, a red quilt and a pillow

This Venetian Mary, surprised by the annunciatory angel diving in from the left with a weaving escort of cherubim, has a solid bed with a fine *padiglione* of red silk. Three mattresses was the customary number for a bed in polite circles during the sixteenth century and the partly gilded ceiling shows that this bedchamber was indeed fairly grand. Moreover, Mary reads an expensive little Book of Hours. Curious, therefore, is the shabby and rough rustic chair in the foreground. Note how dimly one perceives the ceiling.

Jacopo Tintoretto, *Annunciation*, Scuola Grande di San Rocco, Venice, *c.*1570
Photograph: Scala

178 Three-mattress status under a half-tester

A coverlet lies over the top mattress. The bed has stump-like corner posts while tall posts at the head support a wooden half-tester (see diagram 3, p. 359).

Domenico Passignano, *Birth of the Virgin*, S. Maria, Impruneta, Tuscany, 1602
Photograph: Scala

179 The decorative pillow

Some pillows seem to have been made specially for display, exceptionally rich materials and fine workmanship having gone into their creation. It seems to have been the custom to display such pillows at the foot-end of the bed, on special occasions. This practice remained fashionable, in England at any rate, well into the eighteenth century. The hand-washing ceremony is here clearly shown. Note the keys of the bed-chests.

Miniature by Monte di Giovanni, *c.*1510
Vatican Library (MS. Barb. Lat. 610, 307v)

178

179

Seats and Seat-furniture

Stools

Scagno, sometimes *scanno/schanno*, was the Italian for a stool during the Renaissance. If the stool was rather smaller than usual it might be called a *scannello* or *scannetto* which very easily became *scabello/sgabello*. A particularly small stool might qualify for the term *scannelino* which was sometimes rendered as *scamelino*.

Stools could be of two basic types. The first and presumably the oldest was constructed like an old-fashioned milking-stool which had a solid wooden seat through which three or four holes were bored. Into the holes were driven rough-hewn and slightly tapered stakes that formed the legs. If the tips of the stakes projected above the seat, they were trimmed off. Stools of this type are often to be seen in the paintings of Fra Angelico (Pl. 278). On the finer variants of this class of stool, the legs were turned on a lathe and looked rather like lengths of broomstick. The seats could be round or octagonal for the type with three legs, and square or oblong for those with four (Pl. 180). The legs of staked stools tended to come loose and fall out of the bore-holes into which they had been jammed. Driving a small wedge into the top end was a means used later with the milking-stool and was probably already known to rustic stool-makers of the fifteenth century. Another method was to fit a web-like board between the legs. This required the skill of a proper joiner and was particularly the case when stools of this sort became elaborate at all. Very occasionally, the staked stool was fitted with a back (Pls 121, 182) but it must have been difficult to make this strong enough to lean back against. If the legs were made taller, stools of this class became tables. Illustrations of staked tables show them in kitchens, workshops, gardens, market-places and the like and only rarely in polite settings (Pls 8, 348).

The other basic form of stool was in the form of a box, open at the bottom, with four boards forming the sides that tapered inwards towards the top where the board forming the seat (overlapping at the edges) braced the whole structure (Pl. 318). 'Feet' were formed at the four corners by cutting away arched shapes at the lower edge of the four flanking boards (Pl. 299). When intended as a stool a slot was often cut in the seat so one could slip one's fingers through and carry the box to where it was needed. This type of stool, made slightly taller, could also serve as a writing-desk, or as a supper-table for a single person; if made taller still it could serve as a candlestand or support for busts or vases. Thus Lorenzo de' Medici had *uno descho d'albero* [which was presumably a desk to write at] with *uno deschetto di noce choperto di quoio da sedervi su* [a small desk of walnut covered with leather on which one can sit]. In Pl. 252 we see a writing-desk and stool of this kind although the desk is called a *banchetta* and the stools are *banchette per sedere* [small benches on which to sit]. We shall be discussing benches in a moment but, where the construction was the same, there is actually no great difference between a stool and a small bench. There would, incidentally, have been no sense in making Lorenzo's stool of walnut if it were to be totally covered in leather so we

must suppose that only the seat was thus covered – in fact, that it was upholstered, no doubt with padding under the leather. With regard to candlesticks, we can be fairly sure the six *sghabeloni a piramidi ... da candelieri* at the Villa Medici in Rome in 1598 (Medici Invt.) were of this form although of course the tops of the pyramids would have been cut off to provide a seating for the platform on which the candlesticks were to stand. Made very low, a stool of this construction also served as a footstool (Pl. 166).

Stools that are described as being painted were almost certainly of this box-like type which presented nice flat planes, ready for decoration. The two *sgabelli verdi* with the Duke's arms on them in the Palazzo Vecchio in Florence (Medici Invt., 1553) were clearly painted as were undoubtedly also the eleven *sghabelli ordinari dipinti* at the Villa Medici (Medici Invt., 1598). Stools stated to be decorated with *intarsio* must likewise have been of box form. Such ornament required a flat surface (e.g. *uno scagno quadro intersiato da camera* [a square stool]). This may actually have been a close-stool, of box form, as the term *da camera* often seems to imply (p. 248). The same may be the case with the *scamelino intersiato da camera quadro* which was in the daughter's bedchamber in the Fieschi mansion (Fieschi Invt., Genoa, 1532) whereas the *scagno* just mentioned was in a closet next to the mother's room. A close-stool is illustrated in Pl. 279; it had a lifting lid and a pan and ring-seat inside.

Tarsio, and to some extent paintwork, went out of fashion soon after 1500 and carved ornament became the paramount form of decoration. We noted how this affected the decoration of beds; it also affected the appearance of seat-furniture, even stools. The staked stool fell out of use in favour of the box form, in polite circles, and the latter was soon to be seen embellished with carving – first with a rim round the cut-out at the bottom edge and then with increasing amounts of scrollwork, masks and festoons. At some point early in the sixteenth century joiners began to make two opposed sides more prominent while the other two sides were reduced in size to become mere inset bracing pieces. Stools of this type then sometimes were furnished with a back fixed into a rearwards extension of the seat with a substantial mortise and tenon joint (Pl. 183, and diagram 9, p. 360). As such backed stools were mostly used in entrance halls or in large formal rooms like the *portego* of Venetian palaces, where they stood against the walls in rows, only the front face of the back and the fronting board below the seat were carved. The seat was usually octagonal and had a dish-shaped depression on top, presumably to help keep a cushion in place.

This backed stool, with its characteristic shape and bold carving, is today called a *sgabello* by collectors and dealers although at the time this term, as Florio* tells us, simply meant 'any kind of stoole' and the word probably ought not therefore to be used to distinguish this particular type. But if it was not called a *sgabello*, what was its appellation? As the carved decoration was usually executed in walnut, so we should probably seek the correct term among references to stools made of this timber. For example, could the twelve *scagni de nogara intagiade et doradi col pozo* in a Venetian *palazzo* in 1590 (Pollani Invt.) be such seats? They were of carved walnut,

180 The rustic stool

This, the ancestor of the milking-stool, is simple and easy to make. Stake-like legs are hammered into holes bored in the seat, whereafter any protruding ends are cut off. As we observe here, they could be seen in highly respectable houses and could be brought in from the back regions when needed. A popular woodcut engraving showing Lucretia's suicide. She seems to have taken a seat on the 'serving side' of the dining-table. She has jumped up, knocking over the stool, and plunged the dagger into her breast.

From *La historia e morte di Lucretia Romana*, Suicide of Lucretia, woodcut
Biblioteca Trivulziana, Milan (H. 270)

181 A versatile model

A development of the kind of stool shown in Plate 180, this has a circular seat and the holes for the legs are not drilled right through it. Making this refined model requires rather more skill. This drawing is one of a group showing 'stools' in use. This standard sit-upon model can also be used for doing up one's sandals. Taller models can serve as tables (see Pl. 8) and even as writing-desks. Tables with rectangular tops as well as benches, all constructed on this same principle, served often as secondary forms of furniture throughout the Renaissance.

Attributed to Antonio Pollaiuolo, *Man with stool*, drawing, c.1460
Uffizi, Florence (177F) (photograph: D. Pineider, Florence)

182 Board-back stool

In the right foreground a doctor(?) sits on a stool with a tall board-back. Behind him lies a patient under a suspended tester of netting which has a valance at the top; it must have had a lightweight wooden frame.

From an edition of Avicenna's famous work on medicine, the *Canon Maior*, first half of the 15th century
University Library, Bologna (photograph: Roncaglia)

183 The *scagno da poggio*?

This stool is constructed with boards; it has a board-back attached to the seat with a mortise-and-tenon joint like the stool shown in Plate 182. Its appearance as a whole is shown in diagram 8 on page 360. Many examples of this class of 'back-stool' exist although not a few are probably nineteenth-century reproductions. Today often called a *sgabello*, which merely meant a stool of any kind in Renaissance parlance, this is likely to be what in some places was called a *scagno col pozzo* or *da poggio*, which implies that it had a feature one could lean on, or back upon. The hard seat usually has a circular depression on top and was no doubt, as in this picture, often used with a cushion. Although often to

180

182

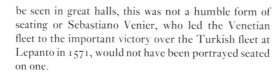

181

be seen in great halls, this was not a humble form of seating or Sebastiano Venier, who led the Venetian fleet to the important victory over the Turkish fleet at Lepanto in 1571, would not have been portrayed seated on one.

From Giacomo Franco, *Habiti Huomini et Donne venitiane*, Venice, 1610
Victoria and Albert Museum, London

183

184 Fixed benches as part of the architecture

These Apostles attending the Last Supper are represented as monks in a very splendid refectory of an important monastery where only the best was fine enough in the service of God. Thus the walls are revetted with marble of several kinds in a very expensive manner and a strip of costly Flemish verdure tapestry forms a seat-back and seat-cover. The seats themselves are of wood with inlaid decoration and a relief-carved ornament on the panel. The table is fixed, supported on columns rising from the platform which is built-in with the seating. Note the cloth of linen diaper on the table.

Andrea del Castagno, *The Last Supper* (detail), S. Apollonia, Florence, 1445–50
Photograph: Scala

partly gilded, but what did *col pozzo* mean? Could it mean 'with a back'? No dictionary seems to help us here but the term is not infrequently found in late sixteenth-century Venetian inventories. In the Zarlino inventory of 1589, for instance, we find some *scagni de nogara* six of which were *col pozo* and six *senza pozo* [without the feature]. Since chairs are also sometimes described as being *col pozzo* and, as chairs by definition have backs, it seems reasonable to suppose that the term must refer to the back-support. In fact the term is probably a corruption of *d'appoggio* [something to rest or lean against], for in a Ferrarese inventory of 1598 we find some stools *da Poggio* which should probably not be interpreted as a reference to their place of origin but merely as a description of their form – with a back.[1]

A fourth type of stool must have made its appearance in Italy, towards the middle of the sixteenth century as it did elsewhere in Europe. This had a square seat, often upholstered, and had four legs, one at each corner. The legs were usually turned on a lathe (so these stools were mostly made by turners rather than joiners) and had stretchers near the floor to brace them.[2] It may be that such stools were at first called 'German stools' in Italy, as a turner at Ferrara in 1582 provided eight turned legs for a pair of *schani . . . alla todescha*.[3] The nine *scagni di noghera con la coperta di veludo* [covered with velvet] mentioned in a Venetian inventory of 1584 (Correr Invt.) are also likely to have been of this new class. A variant of this type was the circular upholstered stool with three legs of which some examples were to be seen at Ferrara by 1598.[4]

Beyond what has been said, we cannot usually at present be sure, therefore, which type of stool is being referred to in an inventory entry but, before moving on, it is just worth noting two curiosities. In the Fieschi inventory from Genoa in 1532, mention is made of a *scanello d'archipresso polito* [small stool of polished cypresswood; perhaps a footstool], and of no fewer than twenty-five *scamelini* which were to be found in the bathroom. The Fieschi bathroom was no doubt a mod. con. of great splendour and capaciousness but it is still difficult to imagine why quite so many small stools were required there.

Benches and the ciscranna

In his dictionary of 1611, Florio* explains that the Italian word *banca* meant 'any bench or forme'. To a sixteenth-century Englishman, a form was a bench without a back but Italians did not make this distinction, as is shown by a reference in the Medici inventory of 1553 to *una panca d'albero, con l'appogiatoio* [of poplar, with a back-rest].

Although usually a movable piece of furniture, the *banca* could also be a fixture attached to the wall of a room. One frequently sees fixed benches in fifteenth-century scenes of the Last Supper which is shown as if taking place in the refectory of a monastery (Pl. 77). These fixed seats might simply consist of a shelf but often they were boxed in underneath, in which case the space thus contained could serve for storage (the seat had then of course to be hinged to form a lid allowing access to the container). Benches were also placed round beds, as we have already noted (Pl. 64, p. 114), and these could likewise be boxed in to form chests, then

sometimes called *cassapanche* – a sensible description that was unfortunately not always used. Furthermore, in scenes of scholars in their studies, we often find them seated on a box (a book-chest) rather than on a proper bench or chair (Pls 186, 260, 362). In other cases, the scholars are seated on a settle (Pl. 257), which is essentially a bench with a high back (Florio*, prefectly aware that *banca* and *panca* were the same word and that both meant 'any bench or forme', said of the latter that it also could mean 'a settle'). Comfortable places where one could read a book were also sometimes contrived alongside a bed, or close to it, with a reading-desk set out in front of a settle (Pl. 379). The latter is sometimes fixed to the wall and, indeed, may be an extension of the panelling. For their special comfort, women were sometimes provided with benches that were rather lower than the standard height, and children might also be furnished with seats that were truly small in scale.[1]

In some parts of Italy, notably Genoa, benches were called *bancali* but elsewhere the word meant the cloth that was laid on a bench. This confusing fact is confirmed by Florio*[2] but quite often some qualification is added which makes the distinction evident, for instance where a *bancale* is described as being decorated with *tarsie* or as having a lid with a lock, or (on the other hand) where it is known to be of tapestry or worked with silver and gold embroidery.[3]

Free-standing benches with a back do not seem to have been much in favour during the Renaissance period in Italy[4] even though they had been relatively common during the Middle Ages. However, settle-like seats with very tall backs are sometimes to be seen in pictures of the time, their seats being long enough to qualify as benches, while some throne-like seats seem to have existed which we can class either as high-backed benches or as chairs (Pl. 261). The *lettuccio*, of course, was a rather splendid variant of the settle but its seat was sufficiently deep for it to be used as a day-bed, which is why this class of furniture is here discussed along with beds (pp. 149–53).

There was also a type of seat called a *ciscranna* or *archischrana* which is presumably a composite word deriving from *scranna* or *scharanna*, an armchair (p. 174), and *archi*, either meaning large or with a box-like seat.[5] A *ciscranna* in a Medici residence in 1498 was described as *per sedere al fuocho* [for sitting by the fire]; somewhere in its make-up it had balusters (Fiesole Invt., 1498). Half a century later another Medici *ciscranna* was described as being *con la spaliera a balaustri rossi* which seems to mean that it had balusters or turned spindles set into the back, probably in a row (Medici Invt., 1553). At the beginning of the present century, in the countryside around Siena, the term *ciscranna* was still being used for a form of seat that was hewn out of a tree-trunk, which presumably means it was long, low and rather chunky. One of the Medici pieces was four *braccia* wide so the Renaissance *ciscranna*, it seems, was a long seat with arms and a low, pierced back, used by the fire. This brings to mind a class of seat not infrequently seen in Burgundian, French and German illustrations of between 1450 and 1525 which had a back that could be swung up and over to face the opposite way so as to allow the sitter to face the fire or to turn his back on it, and these northern benches are always

185

186

185 A hunting picnic?

Benches constructed like the stool shown in Plate 180 serve as seats for the majority of this boisterous party but the three important people at the back, who all wear hats, may have individual chairs of some sort. In front stands a portable *credenza*. The table has been set up in some primitive roofed structure that provides hooks for the two lamps which, with their large flames, may perhaps be more for warding off insects than for illumination. No other lighting is visible.

From a cookery-book of 1549 by Cristoforo de Messisburgo (a German, presumably from Merseburg), Banchetti, Compositione di vivandi, published at Ferrara
Biblioteca di Ferrara

186 The architectural bench

The carving at the front corners seems vulnerable but would to some extent be protected by the base-board (see diagram 7, p. 360). The seat is probably hinged to provide chest-space inside; St John the Evangelist is using the seat in his study where a chest was always useful for storing books (see Pl. 225). A table-carpet is spread on his writing-table.

From Andrea Spinelli, Evangelia (in Greek), Venice, 1550
Victoria and Albert Museum, London

187 Well constructed bench, handsomely covered

This fourteenth-century bench belongs with the bed that is largely hidden by the curtain. It is made with planks like that shown in Plate 64. Later, this position was usually occupied by chests, made not too tall so that they could likewise serve as seats or as a step-up to the bed. Here one sees how adaptable was this furnishing formula; a cloth thrown over the bench or chest at once made it an acceptable seat – even for a king, as here. Note the curtain-ring, the pillow-case, and the overhanging bed-head.

Guiron le Courtois, a Milanese manuscript of the 1370s
Bibliothèque National, Paris (MS Fr. nouv. ac. 5243.3v.)

187

placed in front of the fireplace – indeed, there could have been no other reason for designing them in this manner.[6] Could the *ciscranna* be an Italian version of this kind of seat? That this is a strong possibility is suggested by an entry in another Medici inventory, also of 1492 but of their town house, not a villa. Here we find a *ciscranna cholle spalliere che si volge et con balaustri* [with the back which can swing and with balusters], which would seem to describe the swing-back bench quite well. No Italian illustration of such a piece of furniture seems to have come down to us but a very handsome pair of benches of walnut with swinging backs is today to be seen in the Florentine church of Santa Maria della Carmine. Each has a low pierced back containing a row of turned balusters that would not have impeded a view of the fire from further back in the room. The swing-over back is particularly neatly designed (diagram 7, p. 360). In the inventory of the Capponi mansion of 1536 (Capponi Invt.) (a house not very far from the Carmine, incidentally) mention is made of *una bella ciscranna*, implying that it was a showy object. If we are looking for a splendid piece of furniture – long, low, with pierced back and balusters – that could stand alongside the fine *lettiere* and *lettucci* of the late fifteenth century, the Carmine benches would seem to be good candidates.[7]

Loose seat-coverings and cushions

Chests were primarily for storage but those that had flat tops and were not too tall often served as seats as well (Pls 126, 220); indeed, one may regard such chests as boxed-in benches, and Renaissance Italians treated them alike in this respect. Both benches and chests were commonly placed alongside beds in the fourteenth and fifteenth centuries, while chests were frequently ranged against the walls throughout the Renaissance, where they could be used as seats (Pl. 144). It was a widespread practice to place on the bench or chest-top a cloth of some sort in order to provide some small degree of comfort. Such *bancali* ['bench-carpets', Florio* calls them] could be of plain cloth but almost any kind of textile material might be used, right up to the very richest, with resilient materials like velvet or pile carpets being especially appreciated (Pl. 218). Many were of tapestry, often of verdure type with *milles fleurs* (Pls 73, 184). Some *bancali* were *en suite* with a *spalliera*, a long cloth forming a back-rest against which one could lean one's shoulders [*spalle*]. We see such a set in Andrea Castagno's *Last Supper* on the walls of Santa Apollonia in Florence (Pl. 184). The *bancale* in this case is sufficiently broad to hang down the front of the seat. A very handsome set like this was in the dowry of Ippolita Sforza when she came to marry Alfonso of Aragon in 1465. Among the rich furnishings of a complete room were *Bancali xiij et spalliere viiij ... Lavorato de seta[,] argento et oro ...* [worked in silk, silver and gold, i.e. embroidered; (Trivulzio Invt., Milan, 1465].

For a more comfortable seat one placed a cushion on the bench or chest-top. The Virgin Mary depicted on the early sixteenth-century Ferrarese tapestry actually has two cushions (Pl. 51) while, in a Tuscan painting of the late fourteenth century, Mary has used her cushion, which is *en suite* with the *spalliera* behind her, as a prop for the book.

Cushions offered a convenient way of making a hard seat comfortable and they were to be found in some quantity in the grander houses.[1] They were mostly square but could be oblong, while a few were round.[2] Many were covered in leather but other materials like silk velvet or woollen cloth were often used and some were covered in tapestry – perhaps, in some cases, with square panels specially woven for the purpose. Cushions usually had elaborate decoration around the seams, and tassels at the four corners. Indeed, some cushions were very costly items, intended more for display than comfort – like those in the Palazzo Borromeo in Milan in 1487 described as *dui cosini doro cum le fodrete de terzanelo* ['two cushions of gold with linings of tiercenel' which means they were covered with cloth of gold and that the case of the actual cushion was of this light-weight silk]. In the same house a suite of tapestry comprising two *spalliere*, two *bancali* and a pair of more ordinary cushions was valued at thirty ducats in all whereas two separate cushions were alone estimated at forty-five ducats. They must have been very splendid indeed.

Some cushions were described as *carelli*[3] which must be the equivalent of the French *carreaux*. These were square squabs placed on the floor like the modern *pouffe*. We see Mary is sitting on one in Pl.188 while two enormous round versions are to be seen in the drawing reproduced in Pl. 115. A round squab covered in cut leather lies on the bedside chest of a *lettiera* to be seen in Pl. 84, serving as a resting-place for St Anne's lap-dog.

In the mid-seventeenth century, the French considered the *carreau* – the large floor-cushion or squab – to be a Spanish form, of Moorish origin,[4] and we do indeed see such an object in the charming Spanish painting of Mary receiving all her suitors, reproduced in Pl. 189. To what extent the Italians took up this practice is not clear but it probably became especially fashionable under the Borgias, who were of course of Spanish origin. When Lucrezia Borgia was married at the Vatican in June 1492, all the ladies who followed the bride into the Sala Reale were 'all ... found places on the cushions scattered around the platform'. There were about a hundred cushions, incidentally, 'in various colours' but the chronicler, Johann Burchard, tells us that 'Donna Giulia Farnese, the pope's concubine, and many other Roman ladies, numbering in all about one hundred and fifty', followed Lucrezia into the room. Burchard often relates how ceremonial arrangements went awry, due to bad timing, simple confusion or, not infrequently, the truculence of a cardinal, but he does not suggest there was any problem, on this occasion, in getting 150 ladies to sit on one hundred cushions. Their behaviour seems to have been truly ladylike.

Just occasionally cushions (*cosini*) are called *origeri* (pillows or 'ear-rests') in Italian inventories, and of course there is not all that much difference between the two; but to speak of *origeri da sedere*, as did one inventory compiler, *is* something of a contradiction in terms (Fieschi Invt).

As they were mostly placed on the floor, *carelli* probably had to be more robust than ordinary cushions. A set of eight covered with leather is mentioned in the Uzzano inventory from Florence , in 1424 where there were also six with tapestry covers [*di panno di razo*]. In the same house was *uno pezzo di tappetto per quattro charelli* which would seem to have been a piece of material ready to be used for covering four squabs. A *tappetto* was a carpet in the sense of a cover for a flat surface. It is unlikely in this case to have been a Near Eastern carpet; more probably it was a stout upholstery material made in the Low Countries – perhaps a woollen velvet, anyway of wool – and here seemingly specially made for the purpose. How otherwise did the inventory-clerk know that this piece of *tappetto* was for making *four* cushion-covers?[5]

Chairs

For the most part it is seemingly impossible to relate the nomenclature of chairs to the different types of chair to be seen in Italian pictures of the Renaissance period. The pictures reveal that there were several fairly clearly defined types but that there were other forms of which only a single representation seems to exist, suggesting that the type was uncommon. Of course the spread of illustrations that has come down to us may not give a balanced impression of Italian chair production at the time but it does look as if some types were the product of localized effort which was not imitated elsewhere or thereafter.

Seat-furniture at the beginning of the fifteenth century consisted mainly of benches and stools, and the occasional chair with arms which was throne-like, both in form and in its symbolism as a seat of honour. Chairs without arms were rare. The number of chairs of all kinds gradually increased and, by the end of the sixteenth century, they were to be found in most rooms while grand dining-rooms might have whole sets of armchairs for the diners.

Large armchairs were symbols of high status and were reserved for the person, on any given occasion, to whom the greatest honour was due – be it the master of the household on ordinary days, or some guest he wished to honour on a special occasion. The master's armchair would be bigger than any other seat in the house; his wife's chair would be slightly smaller, and there might be other grand chairs for members of the family who rated honouring to a lesser degree. Niceties of this sort were not confined to princely courts where ceremony was firmly established; they also affected arrangements in patrician families whose fortunes were based on active commerce, and indeed in any circles where people were sensitive about their status.

Since women tended to spend much more time in the home than their menfolk, attention was paid to providing seats tailored to their requirements. Special chairs were made *pro muliere* or *da donna* [i.e. for women] which were rather smaller than average, while the actual seats were made more comfortable – either by fitting chairs with rush seats or by providing plenty of cushions (Pl. 194). During the sixteenth century a certain amount of padded upholstery was being applied to a relatively small number of chairs but this was not, it seems, specially for the benefit of women. At that time degrees of comfort were more a reflection of status than of the sitter's gender; grander people had more comfortable seating

than others and men benefited from this as much as women (Pls 213, 215).

The word *sedia*, sometimes rendered as *seggio*, could simply mean a seat but it was also a term used to describe a chair, with *seggiola* being used for this purpose most frequently.[1] An imposing *arm*chair might be called a *scaranna/scranna* in the fifteenth century[2] but more often it was called a *cathedra/catreda*, with was often rendered as *cariegha*.[3] *Cathedra* was a term used in northern Italy already early in the fifteenth century but was gradually adopted everywhere.[4] In the Sicilies the old French word *chaire*, rendered as *chiera/chiara*, was still being used in the sixteenth century to describe an armchair.[5]

One type of chair which is frequently illustrated in Italian pictures from the mid-fifteenth century onwards is low, rather roughly made, has a 'ladder-back', and is furnished with a rush seat (Pls. 191, 192, 194). Larger versions were made (Pl. 191) but the common model was small and therefore seems to have been used mostly by women, as the pictures suggest. Such chairs vary greatly in detail which indicates that they were made in many different places, probably as a sort of 'cottage industry' although there is no reason why they should not have been the product of small workshops in most Italian cities.[6] As time went by more refined versions were made. The previously rough-hewn members were now turned on a lathe as a result of which some gained pretty finials (Pl. 271). The turning gradually became more elaborate, with baluster forms and spindle-like stretchers making these later chairs much more sophisticated and therefore acceptable in smart surroundings (Pls 192, 249). This was especially the case when the chairs were stained, usually black, and polished. The later versions tended to be closer to normal size and were thus the ancestors of the 'country chairs' made all over Europe and, finally, of a type of chair greatly in favour with the Arts and Crafts Movement.

What can this sort of chair have been called? They are so distinctive that one feels they – or at least the more refined versions – ought to have had a special name. One might think the rush seat would have been mentioned but references to such a feature are rare.[7] Could at least the more refined versions be *seggiole di Pistoia*, of which there were sixty assembled in a room in the Palazzo Vecchio in Florence (Medici Invt., 1553)? Judging by the numerous illustrations of such chairs they were clearly produced in large numbers so it should not have been too difficult to procure sixty. In the same building were six more *seggiole pistolesi da donna* [Pistoia chairs, for women], so at least these six were small. Havard, in his great work on (primarily) French furnishings, cited a Marseilles inventory of 1587, that of a man called de la Setta whose name sounds Italian. It includes an entry concerning *Huit cheres de paille, servant à femmes, à la fasson de Pise* [eight chairs of straw (the usual way of describing rush-seated chairs at the time), for use by women, in the Pisan fashion].[8] This suggests the type was familiar in southern France and it may well be they were imported from Pisa. However, no corresponding references to chairs *alla pisana* seem to occur in Italian inventories and one may therefore wonder whether de la Setta's chairs were not perhaps from Pistoia rather than Pisa. If so Pistolese chairs were low, had rush

188 The large floor-cushion

A huge cushion on the floor serves as a seat for this Madonna. Tassels at the corners can be seen although partly obscured by the dazzling golden rays which emanate from her. The patterns of two rich silks are shown with care.

Francesco Ghissi, *Madonna and Child*, 1374
Pinacoteca, Vatican (photograph: Scala)

189 The Spanish tradition

The Virgin Mary greets her suitors, having risen from a large cushion lying on the floor of a wooden dais. The top face of the cushion is made of a brocaded silk velvet; the lower face is probably of red leather which would withstand constant abrasion better. Although the scene is Spanish, and the use of floor-cushions was much more common in Spain than elsewhere, their use in this way was certainly not unknown in fifteenth-century Italy (see p. 173). That Mary had so many suitors is revealed in the Apocrypha.

Pedro Berruguete, *Suitors of the Virgin*, part of a cycle, 1485
Museo Sta Eulalia, Paredes de Nava, Palencia

189

188

190

191

192

190 A turner's embellishment

Between the cresting and the rail below, on this 'woman's chair' with its rush seat and turned stretchers, is a row of turned spindles forming a band of ornament. This may possibly be an early example of a Pistoia chair (see p. 174 and Pl. 249). The posted bed is very finely made and was perhaps domed.

Tommaso Manzuoli, active in Florence between 1536 and 1571, *Annunciation*, drawing
Musée du Louvre, Paris

191 The rustic chair slightly refined

One can just see a corner of the rush seat. The frame of the seat and the stretchers have been turned on a lathe and fit into holes drilled through the uprights; one can see where they come through the timber. The uprights of the back are slightly curved; this must have been achieved by steaming the wood before bending the members – the bentwood technique was certainly not new even in the fifteenth century. A chopper-shaped cresting fits into slots at the top; this was a characteristic Lombard form, a curved cresting being favoured in Tuscany (Pl. 190). We see the poet Bernardo Bellincioni in his study, reading at a rotating lectern. Note the framing of this vignette which dates from 1493.

Unknown Lombard artist, *The Poet Bellincioni*
Victoria and Albert Museum, London

192 The refined rush-bottomed chair

All the members of this rush-seated chair, except for the cresting and the rail below, are turned and have quite fancy profiles. Gone are all traces of rusticity. It was almost certainly stained black. This Venetian woman is blonding her hair, seated on her balcony in the sun. She uses a wide-brimmed straw hat that lacks a crown. The hair was spread over the brim after being dampened with the appropriate preparation that would bring about the desired effect with the sun's aid. Frequent combing was essential. A box-stool serves as a dressing-table. On it stands a small dressing-mirror.

From Pietro Bertelli, *Diversum Nationem Habitus*, Padua, 1589
British Library, London

193 The armed rustic chair

Occasionally armed versions of the rush-seated chairs are illustrated in contemporary paintings. This detail from a picture by Gentile da Fabriano, completed in 1425, shows a Florentine example; a Lombard painting of 1475 shows one of a different shape.

Pinacoteca, Vatican (photograph: Alinari Archives)

seats, and were made in quantity. That list of characteristics could well suit the chair shown in Pl. 249, and it could well be that *sedia alla pistolese* was the term used for the better sort of chair of this class. What the cruder editions were called is still far from clear.

Another much-illustrated type of chair was that which folded, for which reason it was often described as being *da campo*, because you could carry it in the field, on campaign (Pls 196, 199, 203). A common version had a leather seat and back-rest. Some were decorated with inlay on the arms (p. 94). Thus in the Palazzo Vecchio in 1553 there were *2 seggiole da campo con tarsie con sedere et spalliera di quoio* [2 inlaid chairs with seats and beckrests of leather]. Chairs described as *desnodata* must be of this same class that could be folded because *disnodare* means 'to unjoint', according to Florio.*9 From the drawing reproduced in Pl. 203, we also know that *sedie alla napoletana* [chairs in the Neapolitan fashion] belonged to this class. The same may be true of some chairs in Lorenzo de' Medici's house, described as being *alla cardinalescha* [of the sort that cardinals use] but we cannot be certain.[10] Pl. 199 shows a *sedia* of this folding X-frame type. It has a low back, the back-rest being formed by a wide strap of material, be it leather or a textile. The seat was of course of the same material. Such chairs were sometimes carved. Late versions could be decorated with *tarsie*, as we have just noted (see also p. 94), or they might have their arm-rests close-covered with velvet (Pl. 198). There were backless versions which one might call 'stools' (Pl. 130) and there were grand versions which were seats of honour (Pls 197, 198), but while the latter must have been symbols of high status – chairs of state – not all X-frame chairs can have carried such a message. The multi-slat version (Pl. 196; see also diagram 9, page 360), seemingly favoured by scholars in their studies, cannot have been ceremonial seats as such in that setting, yet honour was of course due to such men of learning, they were masters in their own houses, and some were indubitably of high social status as well Pl. 200 shows an X-frame, high-backed chair of great elegance, made of metal – apparently bronze and brass. If such a chair existed, and one feels it must have done, was it a curiosity or was it a seat of high status? How did it come to be in this picture, anyway?

Chairs that folded fore-and-aft, as it were, instead of by bringing the sides together, were a good deal less common but certainly existed. An early version is to be seen in Pl. 202, and this is related to the strange chair, said to have belonged to Petrarch and still in his house (Pl. 201). It is interesting now chiefly as the ancestor (and what precisely was the link?) of the so-called 'Glastonbury chairs' to be seen in so many English parish churches.[11]

The well-known revolving chair, close-covered in red velvet, depicted by Carpaccio in his scene of St Augustine in his study (Pl. 317), is so strange that one may wonder if it actually existed. It may have done but the question is of no great consequence since it was probably an exceptional and perhaps a unique object – which could be why it was in his *studiolo* among his other treasures and curiosities. Antonella da Messina's equally familiar picture of St Jerome in his study shows the saint sitting in a barrel-like chair with multiple upright slats (Pl. 210).

193

194

194 The plain rush-bottomed chair

The chair's seat is obscured by a cushion with heavy tassels at the corners but the rushes can just be seen at the sides. Such fairly crude and undecorated chairs were to be seen even in houses belonging to people of elevated rank – as here where Mary is depicted in the glamorous surroundings of a splendid new house in Rome or Tuscany, in a fresco by Filippo Lippi, painted between 1488 and 1493. A curtain screens the entrance to her study (it is operated by a cord running over a pulley) in which a shelf set high on the wall supports various treasures. Note the *candelabra* ornament carved in relief on the pier.

Fra Filippo Lippi, *Annunciation* (detail), S. Maria sopra Minerva, Rome
Photograph: Scala

195 The folding chair as a throne

This well-known portrait of Sixtus IV by Melozzi da Forlì, painted in about 1477, shows the Pope seated on an X-frame chair that is clearly a throne, meant to emphasize his high estate. The painting celebrates the Pope's achievements in the cultural field, showing him in the fine room he built to house the Vatican Library that he had greatly enhanced. The inscription, to which his librarian, Platina, points, praises Sixtus' efforts to rebuild Rome and restore the city to its former glory. Sixtus also founded the papal collection of antiquities but today he is primarily famous as the builder of the Sistine Chapel.

Melozzi da Forli, *Sixtus IV Enthroned*, Pinacoteca, Vatican c.1477
Photograph: Scala

TEMPLA DOMVM EXPOSITIS·VICOS·FORA·MOENIA·PONTES·
VIRGINEAM·TRIVII·QVOD·REPARARIS·AQVAM·
PRISCA·LICET·NAVTIS·STATVAS·DARE·COMMODA·PORTVS·
ET·VATICANVM·CINGERE·SIXTE·IVGVM·
PLVS·TAMEN·VRBS·DEBET·NAM·QVAE·SQVALORE·LATEBAT·
CERNITVR·IN·CELEBRI·BIBLIOTHECA·LOCO·

196

197

196 Lightweight folding chair; Milan, 1503

Of X-frame construction with multiple slats, the hinge-point formed by a long pin threaded laterally through the intersections. At the back of the arm-rest are similar pommels (not visible here); a back-rest links the two arm-rests so the chair is not able to open up further than shown here (see diagram 9, p. 360). While this was a practical piece of mobile furniture, it was taken up by scholars because the form was recognized as being derived from antique models – a symbol of dignity – and this fitted in with their ideals. It came again to confer dignity among the learned. The candlestick has a slot in its nozzle, for clearing candle-ends when they have burned low – by prising out with a knife-point.

Frontispiece from Bernardino Corio's work on Milanese history, *Viri clarissimi mediolanensis patria historia*, 1503
Houghton Library, Harvard University, Cambridge, Massachusetts

197 Truly throne-like

Mary seated in an X frame chair with a tall back topped by large brass finials that are echoed by the pommels on the arm-rests. Above is a canopy of state with exceptionally long fringe in two colours. A similar fringe is used on the chair which is close-covered in velvet. Battista Dossi who painted this picture, and his brother Dosso Dossi, worked as painters, decorators and designers to the Este court and are most likely to have got their inspiration for this representation of a chair of state from what they saw, or perhaps helped to create, at Ferrara in the 1530s.

Battista and Dosso Dossi, *Conversazione*
Pinacoteca, Ferrara (photograph: Soprintendenza B.A.S. Bologna)

198 The fossilized form

A portrait of the late 1560s showing Pope Pius V seated on a throne of X-frame configuration that could probably not fold at all. It was purely a symbol of his high status and there was no call for it to fold. However, all the arts of the mid-sixteenth century upholsterer have been brought to bear on the embell-ishment of this magnificent seat which is covered with velvet, trimmed with gold braid and fringe. The finials (only one is visible) display the Pope's arms surmounted by the papal tiara and the keys of Heaven, crossed.

Bartolomeo Passerotti, *Portrait of Pope Pius V*
Walters Art Gallery, Baltimore, Maryland (37.453)

198

199

199 A seat denoting high rank in the 1550s

This chair probably could fold although it is unlikely that it was folded very often. The arms are close-covered in red velvet; the back rest and seat will be of the same material which is attached with gilt-headed nails and fringed. The legs and supports to the arms are left bare, however. The sitter is Isotta Brembati, a poet who married twice. This is likely to be a marriage-portrait.

G. B. Moroni, 1553–5. Still in possession of the family, the Counts Moroni at Bergamo
Photograph: Scala

200 Something rather special

An X-frame chair that seems to be made of steel – or, anyway, of metal – shown in a painting of 1482 by Filippino Lippi. It is too precisely depicted to be imaginary (note the accuracy with which the artist represents two Hispano-Moresque vessels on the shelves, and the clock alongside) so Lippi must have seen it and included it as something exceptional. A column rises from the desk and presumably forms a screening for the bed beyond.

Filippino Lippi, *Annunciation*
Museo Civico, S. Gimignano (photograph: Scala)

200

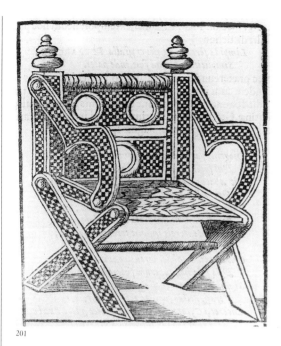

201

202

201 Petrarch's chair

This chair is constructed on the same principle as that shown in Plate 202 and would fold if pegs were removed. This illustration was published in 1635 in a book about Petrarch where it was said to be his. The chair may still be seen in his house at Arqua. Whether it actually belonged to him is uncertain but the form looks ancient and the tradition may well be correct. English readers will recognize it as the ancestor of the so-called Glastonbury chairs that mostly date from the nineteenth century and which are to be seen in so many English churches today. The 'breaks' in the arms form arm-rests.

From Giacomo Filippo Tomasini, *Petrarcha Redivivus*, Padua, 1635
British Library, London

202 A different model

Unlike the common form, this chair, and that above, folds fore-and-aft (if one takes two pegs out) and must have been regarded as a throne because the artist provides it as a seat for Pharaoh when he gives audience to Sarah. A seat of similar construction, but made of metal, is illustrated in a painting by Lorenzo Costa.

Marco dell' Avogaro, from a Bible of 1455–61
Biblioteca Estense, Modena (MS.VG12. Vol. 1, f.9)

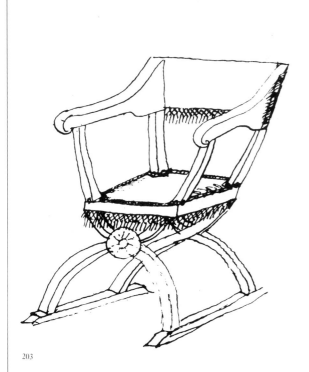

203

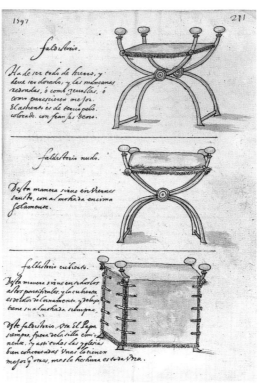

204

203 A Medici set of folding chairs of about 1590

This document concerns an order for a set of eight such chairs commissioned by the Medici Guardaroba. As several other such commissions were given, it would seem that these particular chairs were used in sets and did not embody any substantial symbolism of rank. They are described as being *alla napolitana* for reasons that are not evident but the seats were stuffed with feathers which may have been unusual. The backs and seats were covered with black velvet trimmed with a netted fringe. From the same source as Plate 139.

Unknown artist, chair design
Archivio di Stato, Florence

204 How to dress a folding stool

A Spanish drawing dated 1597 showing how a *faldistorio* can be clothed to make it box-like, in which form it was used by the Pope, the inscription tells us. The *faldistorio nudo* only has a cushion.

Bibliothèque Royale, Brussels (MS 11.1028, f.211)

This depiction had a powerful influence on chair designers around 1900, but the type does not seem to have been a common form during the period. Indeed, it looks thoroughly old-fashioned. Was Antonello perhaps trying to depict a Romanesque chair of the sort St Jerome might actually have used in his day?

The Madonna, as well as the literary Saints Matthew, Mark, Luke, John, Augustine, Jerome and Gregory, were often depicted by Italian painters of the fourteenth and fifteenth centuries – and even in the early sixteenth – enthroned in seats of astonishing elaboration which may in some cases be figments of the artists's imagination (Pls 259, 261). However, many of these illustrations seem plausible and, although such thrones can hardly be classed as domestic furnishings, details are often depicted with such loving care that they presumably tell us something about the styles and appearance of decoration at the time (e.g. Pls 205, 207).

Presumably an imposing seat of this kind was called a throne [*trono*] but some might be classed as *cathedre* which were large and impressive chairs with arms, as we have seen. It would seem, however, that the distinguishing feature of a *cathedra*, from about 1470 onwards, was that it was upholstered. For most of the period this meant that its wooden members were covered with a rich textile, commonly velvet, nailed and probably pasted onto the timber so as to 'close-cover' it (Pl. 195). There was no padding between the textile and the timber. This was the commonest form of decoration for the most splendid chairs right through the sixteenth century; it looked glamorous and it made the hard wooden members superficially soft. If seats and backs were sometimes padded, this is only very rarely to be seen in the contemporary illustrations and one must conclude that stuffed upholstery only made its appearance to any marked degree very late in the century (Pls 211, 216). However, some padded forms (benches) are illustrated in the *Hypnerotomachia* of 1499 (Pl. 215) and are described as being covered in bright green velvet [*ricoperto di veluto verdissimo*] secured with gilt galloon [*uno argenteo . . . nextrulo*]. They were apparently stuffed with flock to form a soft and moderately domed seat.[12] The early sixteenth-century portrait shown in Pl. 213 also has a representation of a stuffed seat, secured with nails. In the Sforza Inventory of 1493 is listed a *cadrega armata*, the property of a princess. Presumably this was a close-covered *cathedra*. The state of the art of seat-upholstery in 1518 is shown fairly clearly in Raphael's famous portrait of Pope Leo X. His velvet-covered chair has a padded seat and back-panel built on (presumably) girth-webbing or some other form of canvas – or leather straps, and with close-covered arm-rests and vertical supports to arms and back.

The problem with fixed padding is that it can shift about within its retaining cover. During the Renaissance period the people who had most experience of keeping shaped padding securely where it was needed were the makers of saddles. Indications that saddlers were involved in the early development of upholstery can be found in various places[13] but an Italian source is provided, once again, by the Este Archives which shows that in

205 Seat of honour fit for a king

This late Gothic throne has turned members reminiscent of the common rustic chairs with rush seats (Pls 191, 194) but the back and the spaces between the arms have been filled in with boards and some carving including a handsome cresting. The seat was probably boarded. The enormous pattern of the hanging depicted on the wall seems incongruous but a glance at Plate 76 shows that its scale is not inconceivable.

Giusto di Ravensburg, active in Genoa and Piedmont about 1450, *Biblical Figure*
Museo Correr, Venice

206 Robust joinery and bentwood

Apart from the nasty spiked tips of the uprights, this must have been a comfortable and sturdy armchair. It is the work of a competent joiner working in Piedmont using pegged mortise and tenon joints. The boards of the back curve down to form a seat; these must have been produced by the bentwood method (see p. 96) as were presumably also the uprights and the arm-rest supports

Follower of the Piedmontese artist Giacomo Jacquerio, *Evangelist* (detail), S. Sebastiano, Pecetto, in northern Piedmont, 1440s
Photograph: Museo Civico, Turin

207 Portrait of a learned man, 1547

This purports to be a 'naturalistic portrait' of the musician Gaspare de Albertis and, indeed, the details are rendered with meticulous precision so we can assume this monumental throne actually existed even if we have never seen anything quite like it in other contemporary illustrations or among surviving Renaissance furniture. The seemingly archaic design may be based on a Romanesque *cathedra* shown in some fresco or relief-carving. Note the arm-rest with its ball-finial, the spectacles, the stacks of musical scores, and the watered silk or camlet gown.

Giuseppe Belli, *Portrait of Gaspare de Albertis*
Accademia Carrara, Bergamo (911)

205

206

207

208

209

208 A *seggiola di Spagna?*

This term was used by Italians to describe what must have been a distinctive type of chair in the middle of the sixteenth century. In an English inventory of the period is listed a 'Spanyshe chair' that was decorated with coloured wood and coloured bone (which is white but could be colour-stained), perhaps like the decoration on this chair shown in a portrait of King Sebastian of Portugal (1557–8) in the third quarter of the century. That Spanish chairs of some kind were exported in notable quantity seems evident, and they must have been elaborate or this would probably not otherwise have been worth the trouble. This chair may be an example of such high-class Iberian export goods.

Cristobel de Morales, *Don Sebastian of Portugal*
Patrimonio Nacional, Madrid

209 A young Bergamasque lady; about 1589

Probably a wedding portrait, this young woman is dressed superbly; note her jewellery, the silk flowers, the ruff, the fine couched embroidery, and the indented lace which is of the sort also used for trimming pillows and the like. Her chair has a tall back with two backrests and is clearly a seat of honour (see diagram 10, p. 360). The woodwork is bare; close-covering of the wooden members went out of fashion towards the end of the century, probably because wear on the vulnerable edges speedily rendered such upholstery unsightly.

Attributed to Francesco Zucco or Gian Paolo Lolmo, *Portrait of a seated Lady*
Accademia Carrara, Bergamo (1224)

210 An archaic seat for an historic personage

St Jerome's seat in this well-known painting by Antonella da Messina of about 1460 was almost certainly based on a form current during the Romanesque period and may go back to classical prototypes. Learned people in quattrocento Italy would have been familiar with the form from illustrations in ancient manuscripts and it is interesting that the artist should have depicted the erudite saint, who died in about AD 420, as seated in the kind of chair that might well have been present in the fifth century. Of course it may be that this pattern appealed to Italian humanists in the middle of the fifteenth century, some of whom may have had chairs of this kind especially made for their personal use (see Pl. 227), in which case the form may have become associated in people's minds with learning and high thinking. Certainly most of the other details in the picture are shown with great verisimilitude.

Antonella da Messina, *St Jerome in his Study*
National Gallery, London (No. 1418)

1531 a Master Zoanni (Giovanni), calling himself a *selaro* [saddler], was paid for some special nails in order to make a *scaranna*; presumably they were showy items, probably gilded, to hold the outer cover of the upholstery.[14] The sketch of an invalid's chair used by Philip II of Spain in his last years (d. 1598) shows stuffing held in place by quilting in a diamond pattern (Pl. 212). We are told that the stuffing was of horsehair, a material that is easy to secure and, when well curled, provides a yielding form of padding, better than flock or wool.[15] Once again, horsehair is a material with which saddlers are familiar. Andrea Doria's armchair may also have had a certain amount of padding, judging from the portrait taken during the last years of his life (1560; Pl. 214 and diagram 12, p. 360). Once again, this may be an invalid chair and it is reasonable to suppose that it was in such furniture, made for the rich, that the greatest strides towards seat comfort were made[16] although it was left to seventeenth-century chairmakers to develop fixed upholstery that was truly comfortable, in a way that we today would understand. 'Sleeping chairs', a class occasionally mentioned in the inventories,[17] were also a form in which presumably a high degree of comfort was desirable. Incidentally, Philip II's chair had castors which were spherical; a Perugian inventory of 1582 (Vitelli Invt.) has a reference to a *sedia con quattro rote sotto* [seat with four wheels below]; for day-beds with wheels see p. 152.

It remains for us to list various types of chair mentioned in the inventories about which we at present seem to know little or nothing.

What, for example did the Bolognesi understand by the term *alla veneziana* [in the Venetian fashion], which is how the principal chairs in the dining-room at the Palazzo Sanuti, the most splendid building in town, were described in 1505 (Sanuti Invt.)? And what did the six seats *alla romana* [in the Roman style] covered with turquoise velvet, included in a rich Sicilian lady's trousseau in 1598, look like (Moncada Invt.)? The same question can be asked about the *sedia alla francese* [in the French taste] that was to be seen in the splendid Villa Medici in Rome in 1598 (Medici Invt.) which was of walnut covered with turquoise velvet, and about the *scarana de legno mantovana* [in the Mantuan style] that was made in Ferrara in 1451.[18] A *catedra de Constantinopoli* is listed in a Genoese inventory of 1461 (Busarini Invt.); that, too, must have been something rather special. We could cite several more examples.[19]

In the Medici inventory of 1553, mention is made of some chairs *di Genova* which are described as being of walnut, with red leather, and *semplice*. Lydecker (Thesis*, p. 314) noted four more in a document of 1574, also of walnut with red leather, which a member of the Martelli family had *fatta venire da Genova per la mia casa* [had ordered from Genoa for my house] in Florence. This suggests they were of good quality and that a distinctive form of chair of walnut was produced in Genoa and exported in some quantity. They could, at any rate, be recognized in Marseilles (which is a short sea-journey from Genoa) where, in 1556, there was *une petite chaise faite de marquetterie à la genevoise* [a small chair with marquetry in the Genoese style].[20] The Medici chair may have been 'simple' but it could well have had marquetry decoration and this could have been the distinctive feature of 'Genoese chairs'.

In the same Medici inventory we find a reference to some chairs which could be dismantled [*che si scommettono*][21] which are called *alla portoghese* [in the Portuguese manner] while nearby are some *seggiole di spagna* [from

211

211 Seated Venetian dignitary

This late sixteenth-century portrait shows a Procurator of St Mark's, one of the highest offices in the Venetian administration, seated in a high-backed chair that is throne-like and has a curtain behind it which may be hanging from a canopy – a further indication of his exalted position. Diagram 11 on page 360 shows how this chair will have looked. Although the arms are not padded, the seat will have been. The deep valance is trimmed with an indented fringe of the sort that was to be greatly favoured in Venice for the next century or so. Note the gondola.

From Giacomo Franco, *Habiti Huomini et Donne venitiane*, Venice, 1610
Victoria and Albert Museum, London

212 Chair for an ailing monarch

The invalid chair of Philip II of Spain who died in 1598. Both the back and foot-rest are adjustable, held in position by ratchets that presumably remained in position when downward pressure was exerted on them. The back, seat and arm-rests are padded with quilted upholstery stuffed with horsehair. It is fitted with ball-castors. Although this drawing of 1595 is Spanish, as probably was also the chair itself, it is likely that chairs built on similar lines were to be seen in Italy and elsewhere by 1600, in the houses of wealthy invalids.

Bibliothèque Nationale, Brussels (MS.II.1028, f.157)

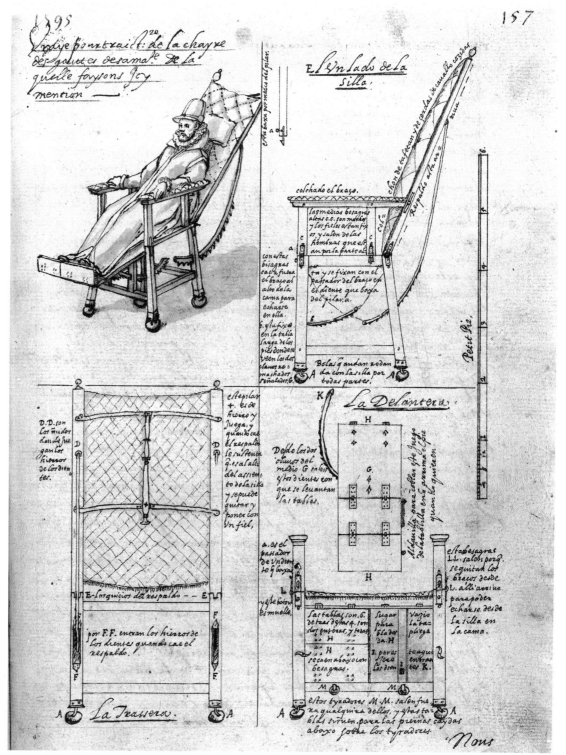

213

213 The state of expensive seat-upholstery in 1516

This cardinal sits in an X-frame chair (see Pls 197, 199), as befits his rank. It has a substantial amount of padding rising from the line of the affixing nails to form a domed seat. The panel below the nails must be a skirting.

Sebastiano del Piombo, *Portrait of Cardinal Bandinello Sauli* (detail)
National Gallery of Art, Washington, D.C. (Kress Collection)
Collection (1961.9.37)

214 A wealthy old man in his invalid chair; 1550s

The powerful Prince Andrea Doria died in 1560. Infirm but able to afford the most up-to-date equipment to ease his declining years, this comfortable reclining chair was probably specially made by a leading Genoese chairmaker. It has a well-sloped back and padded arms. It seems also to have had some form of support for the legs (see diagram 12, p. 360). Such invalid chairs were to point the way towards comfortable seating that eventually everyone could enjoy. The cat must somehow be very special. Note the fine clock.

Unknown artist, *Portrait of Andrea Doria*
Palazzo Doria Pamphilij (photograph: Soprintendenza B.A.S. Liguria)

215 Early upholstery of seats

The long wooden benches shown here (they should rightly be called 'forms', in English) are said to be upholstered, in the text of Francesco Colonna's *Hypnerotomachia Polifili* of 1499, in which this illustration appears. They were, we are told, filled with flock heaped to form a slightly convex covering that 'yielded extremely accommodatingly to sitting'. The cover was apparently of velvet fixed around the sides with gilt-headed nails passing through an edging of plain silver braid. Although Colonna's narrative is fantastic, the descriptions and accompanying illustrations of palatial rooms and furnishings mostly reflect advanced ideas of the time and only sometimes are greatly exaggerated.

From *Hypnerotomachia Polifili*, 1499
Courtesy of the Trustees of Sir John Soane's Museum, London

216 The way ahead in 1586

A chair that could have been made at almost any time in the seventeenth century, with curving lines and scrolled ends to arms, legs and back-rest – a complete breakaway from the X-frame formula and the standard upright armchair (Pls 197, 199).

Alessandro Allori, *Birth of St John* tapestry
Photograph: Soprintendenza B.A.S., Florence

214

215

216

Spain] that were decorated with *tarsie* and had seats and backs of cloth of gold, so were clearly grand items. A 'chayre of Spanyshe making … garnyshed with collored wood' is mentioned in an English inventory of 1556, in which another is stated to have been 'garnished with collored boone'.[22] Could such chairs have looked like that shown in Pl. 208 which shows a portrait of King Sebastian of Portugal, dating from the late sixteenth century? It is clearly inlaid with coloured woods and a white substance which could be ivory or bone.

Chairs were sometimes sent as diplomatic presents. In 1452 Borso d'Este, presumably wanting to curry favour with Cosimo de' Medici in Florence, sent him four chairs specially made for this gesture, produced in Ferrara by the court joiner. A century later Duke Ercole II ordered a handsome *scaranna*, upholstered in black velvet embroidered with silver thread, which he wanted 'to send to France'.[23]

The general picture, therefore, is one which shows that most chairs were locally made but that many grand chairs, even though locally made, were in a style (either in shape or decoration) that was known to be Venetian, Genoese, French, or of some other style that was easily recognized in the locality concerned. However, a few very special chairs were received by prominent people as diplomatic gifts and occasionally the rich commissioned chairs from far afield – like those which were ordered in Milan for the court at Ferrara in 1492.[24]

Chests

The large furnishing chest

The large chests that were so noticeable a feature in the grander sorts of room in Italy during the Renaissance, particularly in the bedchambers, tended to be showily decorated in the most fashionable manner by highly capable craftsmen. At the very least, the joinery was excellent but further embellishment, first with painting or *tarsie* and later with carving, was often added. When painting was present, it sometimes rose to a level where collectors of later generations could become interested in it as Art and in consequence had the panel cut out of its original setting, had a frame put round it, and would then hang it on a wall, purely as a picture; its original function as part of a handsome piece of furniture was then soon forgotten. Such panels grace many an art gallery today.

Chests were primarily intended for storage but those that were made for placing in the chief rooms of a house also served other purposes as well. Those designed to stand against the sides of beds, and many of those ranged against the walls, often side by side, were long and low so they could serve as seats (Pls 144, 218). Such chests could be decorative but their purpose was essentially functional. A taller, more massive form of chest was also produced which was more consciously designed for show, its more ample dimensions making a larger surface available for decoration on front and sides (Pl. 219). Relatively small chests were likewise produced but all these furnishing chests were essentially large – large enough for many a woman to hide her lover in, if we can believe the stories of the time. A chest of this class is today universally called a *cassone*.

The word *cassone* meant a large *cassa* which in turn meant a box or chest. There is no doubt that many large furnishing chests were called *cassoni* at the time, but not everywhere – not in Venice, for instance, where the word was only used in reference to flour-bins. The term was anyway used much less commonly in the fifteenth than in the sixteenth century. In Florence and many other parts of Italy, the preferred term was *forziere* until the middle of the sixteenth century while, in the previous century, in Siena, they liked to call them *goffani* or *cofani* [coffers]. However, a *cassone* and a *forzière* were to be found in the very same room in one Florentine house in 1424[1] so, at least in that instance, there must have been an evident distinction and the distinction was probably no less clear when, in 1483, the inventory of a Sienese mansion was taken and not only *cassoni* and *forzieri* but also *goffani* were recorded as being present in the house.[2] Yet even if the distinction was apparent enough to the Sienese inventory-clerk, the nomenclature he had adopted would not necessarily agree with that used by his opposite number in Venice, Naples or Milan.

It has been suggested that the difference between a *forziere* and a *cassone* was that the former was essentially a strong-box, stoutly built, bound with iron straps and fitted with locks – all with security in mind. It is true that many *forzieri* were iron-bound but so were some *cassoni*, and also a few *goffani*.[3] Did the difference perhaps lie in the shape? For

instance it has been said that, in seventeenth-century England, coffers had vaulted lids[4] and it could well be that the same was true of Italian Renaissance *cofani/goffani* but the *goffani* associated with a bed in Siena, said to be 'serving as bedside benches' [*che servano per la banca da lletto* and *al piei da lletto* (Tura Invt., 1483)] suggest that the matter is not that simple; a chest serving as a seat ought to have a flat top, not a rounded one. That also a *forziere* could have a vaulted lid is proved by the illustration reproduced in Pl. 66.

Learned scholars have struggled with the problem and have usually in the end decided to continue using the word *cassone* as the generic term covering the class of large furnishing chests as a whole. Faced with the same confusing evidence, I have likewise accepted defeat and have finally decided to do the same.[5]

Before moving away from this problem, we should just consider what *cassoni* were called in Venice since, as we noted, the term was apparently never used there to describe chests of this class. The term that occurs so frequently that it must refer to chests of this general type (even if somewhat different in shape and decoration due to local traditions and preferences) is *cassa* and sometimes *cassa grande*. Pieces so described, often present in some numbers and evidently very showy objects, were to be seen in important rooms like the *Camera d'oro* in the Palazzo Correr in 1584 (Correr Invt.) where there were nine *casse* of walnut, a relatively expensive timber [*Nove Casse de noghera*], and not much else except a bed. Of the nine carved and gilded walnut *casse* listed in a Venetian inventory of 1590 (Pollani Invt.), six were apparently *en suite* with the bed [*con la littiera compagna*]. Earlier, in 1534, when painted decoration was no longer fashionable, the *do casse depinte bone* [two fine, painted *casse*] that graced a Venetian palazzo must surely have been of this same class.[6]

It may be that *cassoni* were also called *casse* in the Neapolitan and Sicilian territories but the readily available evidence is too slender for us to be sure. However, in one long and important inventory of 1561, the term *scrigno ferrato* [iron-bound chest or case] occurs frequently although the term *caxa di nuchi* [*Cassa* of walnut, i.e. *noce*] appears with about the same frequency (Requesens Invt., Palermo, 1561). *Casse/cassie* as well as *scrigne* also occur frequently in a Neapolitan inventory of 1399–1400 (Amato Invt.) in which no other terms for a large chest are to be found. With an example from the beginning of the period and one from near the end, it does not seem unreasonable to suppose that *cassa* and *scrigno* were the preferred terms in the south.

To complete the picture, even though it makes it yet more difficult to interpret properly, we should note that *una arca* was also a term used in reference to chests in the fourteenth century. Even an *arca* described as not particularly large [*non troppo grande*] was big enough to hide a person in, according to Boccaccio who, incidentally, made two young men carry it into a bedchamber.[7] However, Boccaccio also has a lover hide in a *cassa* which, certainly in that instance, was clearly also large. The sarcophagus-like chest shown in Pl. 228 is described as an *arca* and the word was still being used in the early sixteenth century in Piedmont and perhaps elsewhere, but not necessarily for describing a *cassone*-like chest.[8]

217 The sixteenth-century travelling-coffer

This has broad, thin iron straps over velvet or leather which shows through the small openings between the straps. They were fairly lightweight and hence easy to manage when travelling, yet it was difficult for thieves to break into them. They were perfectly presentable as indoor furnishing, as well. The subject is the story of Lucretia and is therefore here given a classical setting but it is not inconceivable that a fashion-conscious courtesan at the top of her career might have persuaded one of her lovers to establish her in a glamorous room with a rather dashing day-bed, complete with fanciful *padiglione*, and all couched in the classical idiom like this (see p. 355). Francesco Salviati, who executed this drawing in the middle years of the century, would undoubtedly have seen the splendid rooms of some of these young women.

Francesco Salviati, *Rape of Lucretia*, drawing
Musée du Louvre, Paris (8796)

217

Scanning some eighty inventories from all over Italy one gets the impression that *forzieri* were usually robust chests, strengthened with iron straps (often tinned; e.g. Pl. 226), and painted in one or two colours, or sometimes with the arms of the family. Only rarely were they painted with scenes although, when they were, the painted decoration could no doubt be elaborate and one might guess that this was particularly the case with *forzieri a sepultura* [sarcophagus-shaped] which is a form that required great skill to make, must have been expensive in consequence, and is therefore likely to have been carefully decorated.[9] The more utilitarian *forzieri*, notably those produced in the sixteenth century when the *forziere* was no longer fashionable, were often covered in leather.[10] *Cofani*, on the other hand, seem to have been generally more glamorous than *forzieri*. Many were painted and some were gilded.[11] In one case at least a coffer was painted with four large figures.[12] *Cofani* disappear from the scene after about 1500. *Cassoni*, for their part, were sometimes painted but far more frequently they were of walnut, both in the fifteenth and the sixteenth centuries, and one did not paint walnut; one might inlay it with *tarsie*, as numerous illustrations prove (Pls 91, 275) and one might partly gild it, a form of added ornament much in favour in the sixteenth century. As for *casse*, some were painted but many were of walnut (often carved and likewise sometimes partly gilded), and these will have been of what we today call the *cassone* class. However, it must be remembered that the term *casse* also covers cases of all kinds (e.g. for silverware, for books, for linen) so it is not surprising that we also find references to many *casse* that were purely utilitarian; they were then often covered with leather.

Although much is made of *cassoni* painted with figures and scenes [*storie*] in the collections of great museums today, references in documents from the time suggest they were relatively uncommon – they were very expensive, let us remember – and contemporary pictures rarely show chests of this type (Pl. 219).[13] They should be regarded as exceptional objects which were prized in their day and continued to have an air about them long after they had gone out of fashion; this would account for the fact that comparatively large numbers of them have survived.[14]

Vasari, in a much-quoted passage, probably over-emphasized the quantity of storiated *cassoni* that was produced in Florence during the fifteenth century. Writing in the mid-sixteenth century, he was in fact criticizing the Florentine painters of his own time who would feel it beneath their dignity as artists, he asserted, to execute decorative painting on *cassone*-fronts or other panels forming part of furnishing schemes, and he clearly deplored this new tendency, presumably because he needed able decorators to assist him in finishing rooms he had himself designed.[15] The fact that artists of talent were no longer quite so ready to take on commissions of this kind must have made his life as a co-ordinating architect more difficult, and this outburst against his contemporaries should perhaps be seen more as vexation with a notion that had recently begun to take root, namely that artists should express themselves rather than work to a tight brief and do what they were asked.

Whether storiated *cassoni* were common or not, the subjects painted on them – in Florence, at any rate – were often taken from classical

218 An exotic chest-covering

A colourful Turkish carpet is thrown over the bed-chest which would make it a comfortable seat. The bed-chest also served as a step up into the bed and as a bedside table. This long chest is a single unit specially built for the purpose; earlier, beds often had a pair of chests placed side by side (Pl. 224). A second Turkish carpet lies on the floor. The bed-curtains must hang from a frame suspended above the bed. A splendid ewer, apparently of pewter, but perhaps of silver, stands ready for filling the large brass basin on the floor which is to serve as a baby-bath.

Liberale da Verona (sometimes attributed to Girolamo da Cremona),
Birth of the Virgin, miniature, 1472
Libreria Piccolomoni, Siena

219 The great furnishing chest alongside bed-chests

The furnishing chest is larger than the bed-chests and has a domed top upon which it would be awkward to sit. Struts hold the lids open. The large chest is painted and gilded. This Florentine miniature is by Apollonio di Giovanni who also ran an important workshop that produced painted chests so he knew precisely how they looked and functioned. Two chests of a different kind are being loaded onto the ship. Detail showing Sichaeus visting Dido who rests on her bed which has a coverlet of verdure tapestry. About 1460.

Apollonio di Giovanni, *The Ghost of Sichaeus Visits Dido*, miniature,
Aeneid f. 67v, c.1460
Biblioteca Riccardiana, Florence

219

mythology and the stories of Ovid in particular. Savonarola, who was so vehemently critical of his fellow countrymen's ungodly ways, claimed that no merchant's daughter in his day got married without having for her trousseau a *cassone* decorated with pagan scenes. 'Thus the newly-wed Christian learns about the deceitful trickery of Mars and Vulcan rather than the marvellous deeds of saintly women as told in the two Testaments.'[16]

We know of one major mid-fifteenth-century workshop in Florence where painted *cassoni* were produced and to which it seems possible to attribute several surviving specimens but otherwise the information we have about this trade is sparse.[17] Uccello, who painted scenes on *lettucci* and beds and 'on other small items' which could be seen, Vasari tells us, in many Florentine houses,[18] probably decorated the occasional *cassone*-front. Baldovinetti records that he had to paint the coat of arms of a newly elected Podesta of Arezzo on *4 forzeretti*.[19] Domenico Veneziano painted a pair of *forzieri* for an important Florentine wedding in 1448 while Jacopo del Sellaio and Biagio d'Antonio painted and gilded another pair (with *spalliere*) in 1472, which may today be seen in the Courtauld Institute Gallery in London.[20] Three painters working at Ferrara, Sagramoro di Soncino and his assistants Niccolo Panizato and Simone d'Argentina, gilded boxes and *cassoni* and painted on them the arms of Leonello d'Este in the 1440s.[21] The painter Marco Zoppo in 1462 wrote to Barbara Gonzaga about some chests she had ordered from him, and Domenico Paris painted two *cassoni* for the wedding of Isabella d'Este to Gianfrancesco Gonzaga in 1490.[22] And in 1485 a certain Angelo della Lama decorated a *cassone* for the Duke of Calabria.[23]

In the sixteenth century *cassoni* with painted scenes went out of fashion (although coats of arms continued to be painted on chests, as on much else) but one famous ensemble that included two *cassoni* was the bedchamber of Pierfrancesco Borgherini commissioned in 1515 for his wedding to Margherita Acciaiuoli.[24] The *cassoni* were of carved walnut, following the new fashion, but had painted *spalliere* [horizontal panels] above them, conceived as part of a decorative whole to which several important artists contributed.[25] The two *spalliere* were painted by Andrea del Sarto and one today hangs in the Pitti Palace; it has of course long since been divorced from its chest. In Venice, the *casse* (which we have

220

221

The chest as a seat

If a chest was not too tall it could serve as a seat and chests were placed, with this advantage very much in mind, alongside beds and against the walls of a room, sometimes close-set to form an unbroken range of seating (Pl. 144). In the background is a *credenza* of cupboard form. Above hangs a glass lamp that can be raised or lowered by means of a cord. This chest may have been made of cypresswood (see p. 200).

From a breviary published in Venice in 1517 by Luc' Antonio Giunta for Leonardo and Lucas Altantse
Victoria and Albert Museum, London

221 **The large furnishing chest**

Although probably not quite as large as shown here, this chest was clearly a heavy object that was not going to be moved often. It is decorated with geometric *lavoro di intarsio* and has a cloth cast over it. Behind is a less tall chest with a slightly vaulted lid. The wall-niche cupboard and the tabernacle are noteworthy.

La rappresentatione di San Grisante & Daria, Florence, 1559 (however, several features indicate that the print must be taken from a woodblock cut before 1500)
Houghton Library, Harvard University, Cambridge, Massachusetts (427.A4r)

suggested was the Venetian term that embraced *cassoni*) in the chief bedchamber of the sumptuously appointed *palazzo* of Alvise Odoni (Odoni Invt., 1555), together with the bed and doors, were said to have been decorated by a pupil of Titian's named Stefano (possibly Stefan Calcar)[26] but no mention of such embellishment is made in the inventory so perhaps it was not anything very special in itself. It may have been the fact that a man who was later to become known as a pupil of Titian's had executed this work that seemed subsequently worthy of note.

A far more important form of decoration was gilding. This was executed on a gessoed ground but the most costly chests embellished in this way had patterns in relief that were cast in moulds and applied to the ground prior to gilding. Some of this work is exquisite; it is so delicate that there can be no doubt that such chests were primarily for show.[27] Although very costly, such chests were made in sufficient numbers in Venice (and probably in other cities) to cause the authorities to try and ban the 'making and using' of *chasse dorate* in a sumptuary regulation of 1489.[28] Although much relief ornament was shallow and delicate, some Florentine *cassoni* bear large figures, almost as tall as the fronts of the chest. Figures on this scale offered scope for excellent sculptors and Vasari even credited the young Donatello with having executed *Fighure di relievo* on a *cassone*. Donatello did no such thing, it now seems, but the fact that Vasari could make such a claim is an indication of the high quality the relief ornament on these chests could possess.[29]

Painted decoration was always present in some measure on gilded chests; it could be limited to a small coat of arms that is almost lost in the surrounding sea of gold; at the other end of the scale it could form the sort of large storiated panel already discussed. It should here be remembered that the gilded areas may have cost at least as much to execute as the painted parts and sometimes much more (p. 101). In the fifteenth century the two processes were usually carried out in the same workshop; this was certainly the case with Apollonio di Giovanni's workshop in Florence.

When carved ornament became the most fashionable form of embellishment for woodwork, around 1500, some heavily sculpted chests were entirely gilded but such effects were thought too flamboyant for sixteenth century tastes when the preference was for untreated timber, notably walnut, with some of the details gilded. Such limited gilding is rarely noted in the inventories.

In north Italian inventories of the fifteenth and early sixteenth centuries, quite a few references are found to *casse* and *cassoni alla veneziana*, as if this were a clearly recognizable type.[30] In one case we learn that the chest in question was of walnut.[31] What form of chest or what type of decoration can have seemed characteristic of Venice? Although walnut was worked all over Italy, making furniture of this fairly costly timber was something of a Venetian speciality, to the extent that a special branch of the woodworkers' guild called themselves the *Marangon de Noghera* [joiners working in walnut] although they in fact worked in all

222

223

222 A chest in the Antique taste, 1499

Described in the text as an *arca*, this chest is of a form inspired by classical sarchophagi, in consequence of which the form was sometimes described as being *a sepultura*. It has feet in the form of harpies' legs with leaf-scrolls [*dui harpiatici piedi in folliatura*, as the text quaintly puts it]. The two openings in the front are there to suit the bizarre narrative to which this illustration refers; they were of course not standard features of such chests.

From Francesco Colonna, *Hypnerotomachia Polifili*, Venice, 1499
Courtesy of the Trustees of Sir John Soane's Museum

223 Two handsome north Italian chests of the 1490s

The picture is not too distinct, with regard to the lids of these fine painted and gilded chests (see diagram sketch 18, p. 361), but they were so greatly prized that fine veils were thrown over them, perhaps to protect them from spotting by flies. Mary Magdalene has a handsome silver vessel for her ointment, while Martha lays a table covered with a fine linen cloth trimmed with indented lace edging. The legs are in the form of dolphins (see diagram sketch 15, p. 361). The panels on the walls are probably of cloth with embroidered borders rather than of gilt leather. On the cornice stand three flower-pots which can surely not have been so small. Christ has been provided with a throne and canopy of cloth of gold, an ensemble which looks incongrous in what is otherwise an entirely domestic setting, but the painter evidently felt that something more than a normal armchair was called for in the circumstances. Find the parakeet!

Pietro Paolo da Santa Croce, *Christ in the House of Martha and Mary Museo Vetrario, Murano*

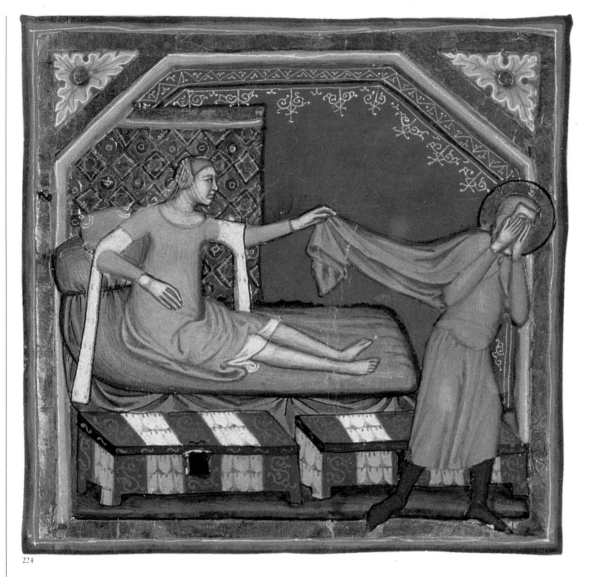

224

225

224 The elegant bed-chests of Potiphar's wife

The bed (or is it a day-bed?) is flanked by a pair of colourful chests that are simply placed alongside and are not, at this early stage, integrated in any way with the bed. The white bands are meant to resemble ermine (see Pl. 284); the lids have edges protected by iron straps.

Cristoforo Oriminia, *Joseph and Potiphar's Wife* in the so-called *Bible of Matteo di Pianisto*, Neapolitan miniature, 1343–5
Vatican Library (MS. Lat.3550.25)

225 The book-chest

Books were often kept in chests before book-cupboards and bookshelves took over the role. When even a learned person's library might only comprise a few books it was of course perfectly possible to house them in this manner. As books were precious, a stout chest with lock and key was a secure place in which to store them. This chest of a characteristic Gothic form has a 'till' at one end; this was a shallow compartment in which small articles could be placed so they would not get lost in the depths of the chest.

Follower of G. Jaquerio, *Evangelist* (detail), S. Sebastiano, Pecetto
Photograph: Scala

226 St Anne's bedside table, late fourteenth century

Having recently given birth to Mary, the mother now partakes of a refreshing meal served on a table seemingly made to stand on a bed-chest. The latter is painted green and the metal straps are tinned which produces a silvery surface. Note the curtains surrounding the bed, the large vessel used for bathing the baby, and the 'swaddling position' of the woman. Both the women in front sit on cushions laid on the floor.

Ugolino Ilario, *Birth of the Virgin*, Orvieto Cathedral
Photograph: Scala

227

227 Book-chests, bookshelves and a desk with shelving

A scholar's study with sturdy furnishings including two book-chests, one of exceptional size and depth. The chair is of the Romanesque type discussed under Plate 210. The placid lion looms large but there are also other fascinating details in this picture, including a mouse.

Colantonio, *St Jerome*, c.1436
Museo di Capodimonte, Naples (3303/2175)

228 Hiding in chests

Boccaccio has characters hide in chests for various reasons. Here we see two men climbing out of two bed-chests. Note the hat-rack on the wall.

Attributed to Rosello di Jacopo Franchi, a subject from Boccaccio's *Decameron* (detail), painted on the front of a Florentine chest, 1425–50
National Gallery of Scotland, Edinburgh (No. 1738)

229 The smart travelling chest

These usually came in pairs and could thus be strapped as a balancing burden on a mule or packhorse, their distinctive profile suiting them particularly well for this purpose (see diagram 16, p. 361). Being decorative, they could equally well stand in a fine room between journeys. Holofernes was sleeping in his splendid tent on a bed alongside which stood this chest (a table with his armour stands nearby) but brave Judith has just cut off his head. Note the handles at each end.

From the *Malermi Bible*, woodcut, Venice, 1490
British Library, London

the better sorts of wood. This branch did not apparently undertake *lavoro di intarsio*; that was the province of the *Remesseri*.[32] One striking class of chest which can only have been produced in a centre where numerous skilful inlayers were at work, as in Venice, is decorated with inlaid geometric patterns of Near Eastern inspiration executed with numerous small pieces of bone (i.e. white) and sometimes also with mother-of-pearl and coloured woods. Such delicate inlay is today called *certosina* work, for no very good reason. The patterns of this work are set in the walnut ground of these chests. Knowing how close were the links between Venice and the Near East, and how Islamic decoration was imitated in other classes of decorative art in Venice (notably metalwork), it would not seem unreasonable to assume these walnut chests with delicate bone inlay are the *casse alla veneziana* of the inventories.

In Milan, in the late fifteenth century, one type of chest was easily recognizable as a *casse alla ferrarese* [i.e. from Ferrara, or of Ferrarese shape].[33] Favoured at Ferrara at this period was a form of chest, straight-sided, with a heavily corniced lid that was 'square-domed', the whole affair standing on a substantial plinth (Pl. 234). Often the front was

divided into three or four panels. The decoration relied heavily on geometric *tarsie*.[34] It is a distinctive form, very different from the Florentine equivalent with which we are today more familiar. It is possible that this was what the Milanese had in mind when using the term *alla ferrarese*.

What of the cypresswood chests that are found all over Italy but which form a group, on the evidence of technique, and are therefore likely to have been made in a single locality? These chests were exported to many parts of Europe and some are so large that it would not have been possible to transport them other than by water, which suggests they were made in or close to a major port. Once again Venice suggests itself but it may be that they actually came from Crete which was a Venetian dependency (p. 89, fn. 2). Cypresswood chests are not only made of a timber which repels moths and so was prized for clothes chests, but are characterized by decoration with carving in intaglio, with punched work in the ground, and with inked detailing of the figures. Chests of *arcepressa* are mentioned every now and then in inventories. In one case the punched decoration is mentioned (*una casetta de arcipressa stampata*; Franceschino Invt., 1489).

228

229

Cypress chests have prominent dovetail joints at the corners, joints which, on early examples, are accentuated by the way the inked decoration is managed (Pl. 220). The earliest specimens bear Gothic ornament; those made in the sixteenth century have figural decoration that seem to be based on engravings. Inked and sometimes slightly coloured decoration is commonly executed on the inside faces as well, where designs stand out clearly on the pinkish ground of the unsoiled wood.

A form of chest that is quite often illustrated in pictures of between about 1440 and 1540 is long and low, with a shallowly vaulted lid, and a bellied front that curves down to a flared base; it has a flat, vertical back and handles at both ends (Pl 223 and diagram 18, p. 361).[35] Although they could stand in rooms as decoration, they were evidently designed as travelling trunks and a painting in a Russian collection shows a pair strapped to a mule, one on each side.[36] Pl. 229 shows one in use in a military encampment. When packed on a mule a special cloth was thrown over the animal's back and the two chests to keep out the dust. Such covers often bore the arms of the owner, so everyone could at a glance see whose was the baggage-train that was passing by. Could the *forzerette da soma* [small *forzieri* for mule-back[37]], mentioned in two inventories of the 1420s, be of this type? One might suppose that the pair of *goffanetti da cavalcare* [small coffers for cavalcading] in a 1450 inventory were not too dissimilar.[38] While dealing with travelling, mention should be made of the *capsia un magna pro navigando* listed in a Genoese inventory (Spinola Invt., 1459) and one may speculate on how this large *cassa* 'for going to sea' differed from other chests. For a start, a sea-chest made for a member of the Spinola family would probably be rather grander than those made for the average Genoese sea-captain.

The large chests we have been discussing were used for the storage of clothes and household goods of many kinds – bedclothes, linen, books, silverware, and much else. Small objects were put into boxes or caskets and then placed in these larger receptacles. A 'till' was sometimes built into the structure; this was formed by two boards set at right angles to each other, running across the depth of the chest, at one end, so as to create an open box that could hold small items (Pl. 225); for one of the drawbacks of the large chest was that small things were apt to slip to the bottom and be difficult to find and that, in order to reach the lower layers, it was necessary first to remove all the layers on top. One also had to bend over and reach down into it to get at those lower layers. Unless one were very supple, this meant kneeling on the floor, if the chest were a low one. Placing the chest on a plinth made kneeling unnecessary but all the time there was the added hazard that the heavy lid would come crashing down on one's hand. Although one might use a stick to hold the lid open (Pl. 219), the invention of the chest of drawers was indeed a great step forward! This was really a seventeenth-century development. Some sixteenth-century chests had been furnished with drawers inside, accessible only when the lid was opened. The idea of setting drawers into the front of a chest so that they could be reached without lifting the lid probably did not occur to anyone much before 1600.[39]

Some of the large *cassoni* of the fifteenth century were made on the occasion of an important wedding. In some Florentine inventories they are actually called *forzieri da spose* or *nuziali* [marriage chests].[40] In such cases they would bear the coats of arms or other insignia of the two families involved, either on the front, or on the sides if the front were otherwise elaborately decorated. In the fourteenth and early fifteenth

230

230 A very special chest

There is no knowing how large was the chest shown here but it belonged to the Perugia Guild of Money-changers in the late fourteenth century. As it is finely decorated and only has one lock, it is unlikely to be the Guild's big strong-box; it is more likely to be rather small, made to contain their charter or similar items. It seems to be painted green with stylized floral ornament and has decorative ironwork mounts.

Matteo di Ser Cambio, miniature
Photograph: Collegio del Cambio, Perugia

231 The chest's drawbacks

Practical as it was for those who had to travel, as a static piece of furniture the chest had grave disadvantages. To reach into it, and especially to reach the lower layers, one had to bend double or go down on one's knees. To get to items at the bottom, those on top had to be lifted out. Add to this the hazard of having one's fingers crushed by a heavy lid, and it will be appreciated why the 'chest of drawers' was so eagerly welcomed when it appeared around 1600.

Titian, *Venus of Urbino, c.*1538
Uffizi, Florence

231

centuries the bride brought part of her dowry in these chests which were carried proudly through the streets in ceremonial procession when she moved from her parents' house to that of her future husband. Such chests often came in pairs, but apparently – in Florence, at any rate – the financial burden of providing these marriage chests later tended to fall on the husbands. Kent Lydecker*, who first showed that this is what happened, in his study of Florentine patronage and the furnishing of grand houses, suggests that this may account for the preference for battle scenes and tournaments on late painted chests rather than subjects more readily associated with love and marriage which, he says, were more commonly found on earlier chests.[41] In Rome, on the other hand, around 1500, it was apparently the custom for the mother of a bride to enter the bridal chamber on the second day after the wedding and throw open the nuptial chests in order to show the assembled well-wishers that the girl had been provided with all the things that were appropriate for the occasion.[42] Furthermore, when a leading Ferrarese architect married off his daughter in 1502, the most expensive item in her dowry, for which *he* paid, was the gilding of a pair of marriage chests [*uno paro de case do spoxa metute a oro*].[43]

When chests were designed as pairs, their decoration was sometimes organized so as to be complementary. Painted scenes could relate to each other, *tarsie* could be left- and right-handed to produce symmetry.

Most chests were lined; the lining is sometimes mentioned in inventory entries. Mostly the material was strong and serviceable but the finest *cassoni* were often lined with splendid materials.[44] Sometimes painted imitations of rich brocaded silk materials are to be seen inside or on the backs of surviving *cassoni*. They may have been so executed in order to save money, the talents of a painter usually being much cheaper than the products of the silk weavers, but it may also be that such painting was applied to areas that were especially vulnerable, where it would be foolish to expose an expensive material, reserving the real thing for the parts that were better protected. Such a practice was certainly adopted for close-covered chairs in the seventeenth century. Some lids of *cassoni* survive decorated on the outside with superbly painted imitations of gold and crimson velvets, incidentally, and one must presume that this imitation was carried on over the whole exterior. In a Venetian inventory of 1547, mention is made of *casse depinte da pani di seta* which must mean 'painted with an imitation of a woven silk'.[45] In this respect they will have resembled the *lettiere* decorated in a similar manner (p. 157).

Very expensive *cassoni* were provided with specially-built cases, if they had to travel. When Paola Gonzaga set out in 1477 to marry the elderly widower, the Duke Leonhard von Goerz [Gorizia], she not only travelled in a carriage that was gilded inside and out but she had in her baggage-train four superbly decorated *cassoni* which were protected by wooden outer cases painted green.[46] These four chests survive and it was supposed that Mantegna had had a hand in their design but this is no longer thought to be so.[47] Their protective outer cases have long since disappeared.

Smaller chests and cases

A wide variety of boxes and cases must have been present in Renaissance houses, just as there is in houses today. Lucrezia Borgia, for instance, had a number of boxes [*scatole*] containing, amongst other things, nineteen feather fans, shoes, and some ermine pelts. She also had several caskets or small *casse* [*cassette*], one for jewels, one a small version of a *cassone a sepoltura*, one of carved ivory which came from Rome and contained small articles of clothing, and several of amber.[1] People might also have a *scatola* for their medicines, or *cassette* to hold a mirror or combs or chessmen. The purposes to which such small containers might be put are legion but what matters to us here is that many were highly decorative and meant to be seen.

Particularly attractive were the caskets that ladies tended to acquire as gifts either from a suitor, or from their husbands when they got married. These were the *cassette da sposa* or *capsiete una pro domina* which one finds so frequently in inventories.[2] They could be richly decorated and made of expensive materials.[3] Like their big sisters, the *cassoni*, these *cassette* were highly ornamental objects that must have stood on convenient shelves and tables where they could be seen by those who were likely to be delighted or impressed by them. Some took the form of miniature chests, with hinged lids and small locks.

The makers of these delicate little pieces of furniture had to be especially skilful since all the joints and fittings had to be on a small scale, because they had to bear close inspection, and because they were intended to contain valuable articles that needed cosseting. It was out of this tradition that the craft of cabinet-making evolved. Cabinets had also to be neatly, even exquisitely, finished for exactly the same reason. The first cabinets, as we understand the term, must have made their appearance shortly before 1500. Cabinets are considered again here, in relation to desks, in 'Studies'. A proper history of the early development of the cabinet is still awaited.[4]

When discussing woodworking techniques, we considered boxes decorated with *pastiglia* work (p. 96). It will have been noticed that this composition, made of powdered rice, was scented (*pasta de odore*).

In the Vitelli inventory of 1582 (from Venice) mention is made of *Una scatola della Cina* [a Chinese box]. Could this perhaps have been of Oriental lacquer?

Tables

Tables for meals, and the simple credenza

The standard form of dining-table in Italy during the fifteenth century was that contrived with an oblong board or *tavola* resting on two or more trestles (*trespodi, trespoli, trespiedi, cavaletti*).[1] If the board were very long and could seat a large number of diners, more trestles were required to support the longer span.[2] Like the *tavola* that formed a base for the mattress of most beds of the period, the *tavola* for a dining-table was made up with several boards set side by side and united underneath with two or three cross-pieces. The boards were usually of an inexpensive wood, kept scrubbed, no doubt, but the *tavola* was always hidden by a tablecloth when in use. The trestles, on the other hand, could be seen, unless the tablecloth reached down to the floor, so at least the lower parts of the trestles had to look decent. Some were quite elaborately decorated (Pls 233, 238).

Trestles could take the form of an inverted 'V' but a more stable form was one that was bench-like, with a horizontal board on top (Pl. 82). In order to brace the pairs of spreading legs a web was fitted between them, the lower edge of which was frequently shaped into a Gothic arch (Pls 237, 238). 'V'-shaped trestles were sometimes hinged at the top junction [*trespiedi desnodate*][3] so they could be folded for storage when not in use.

It will have been noted that one of the terms meaning 'trestle' was *tripodi* or *trespiedi* which seems to imply that the structure had only three legs and, if one looks closely at the relevant pictures, one does indeed see that the trestles supporting dining tables often have three legs (diagram 13, p. 361), the single one placed on the side where the diners are to sit.[4] A single leg of course gets in the way of the diners' legs far less than would the more regular inverted 'V' form of leg: it also, as a tripod, accommodates itself to unevennesses in the floor, which a four-legged conformation would not. Nevertheless, it seem unlikely that all *trespiedi* had three legs: it is more probable that, once the tripod form became common, the term was used for all trestles, irrespective of the number of legs. Conversely, the term *cavaletto* would normally, one supposes, be used in reference to a trestle with four legs (i.e. like a small horse) but this too seems to have become generic.

Some trestles were formed as a single column with a cross-piece at the top to support the *tavola* and with a cross-shaped foot. The French term for this was a *tréteau/traicteau à pied de grue* [like a crane's foot].[5]

The trestle-table was an eminently practical piece of furniture, ideally suited to the mediaeval way of life. The fact that it could easily be dismantled meant that it could be removed from the room once the meal was over, enabling the room to be used for other activities. When even very grand houses still had only a few rooms and each had to serve more than one purpose, the flexibility this provided was of course greatly prized. We see this in action in the *Decameron* where Boccaccio speaks of the tables being taken up after a meal [*Finito il mangiare e le tavole levate*][6] and elsewhere makes the person presiding over a day's proceedings order one of the ladies of the glamorous company to dance for them [... *come levate furono le tavole, cosi commando che Lauretta una danza prendesse*].[7] In a period when the seigneurial classes were always on the move, moreover, and tended to take their furniture with them, a table that could be taken down or set up anywhere was obviously useful. By bringing together several such tables it was also a simple matter to rig up different patterns for seating varying numbers of people (Pl. 234).

So useful was this type of table that it was still much used in the sixteenth century even though other forms had become fashionable.

232 The trestle-table as a desk

The trestle-table was primarily used for dining (see Pl. 233). The three legs of the trestle on the left are shown distinctly. Over the table lies a patterned table-carpet on which stand a pair of book-wheels and an inkwell. The master, whose study or classroom is here depicted, has an imposing *cathedra*, a dignified seat for a learned man. On a high-mounted shelf behind him is a row of volumes with heavily studded bindings.

From Marianus and Bartolomeous Socini, *Consilia*, Venice, 1521
Victoria and Albert Museum, London

232

233

233 The standard fifteenth-century dining-table

This had a table-leaf [*tavola*] lying on a pair of trestles which were often called *trespiedi* because they did in fact have only three legs (see Pls 232, 247, and diagram sketch 13, p. 361), as in the present case. The single leg back interferes only minimally with the legs of the diners who almost always only sat along that side and at the two ends of such tables. The inverted 'V' of the front legs is braced with a web, here carved with a shield. Unlike the linen tablecloth shown in Plate 77, the cloth on this Lombard table has bands of ornament woven with black as opposed to blue thread.

Giovan Pietro da Cemmo, *The Marriage at Cana*, Church of the Annunciation, Borno, late 15th century
Photograph: Scala

Montaigne, who visited Italy in 1580, reported how in Rome, in the house of the Cardinal of Sens – a Frenchman who 'observes more of the Roman ceremonies than any other' – the table was removed 'immediately after grace, and the chairs promptly arranged along one side of the room' on which the company then sat themselves and were apparently entertained with music.[8]

A development of the trestle-table had a pair of 'H' shaped legs-with-stretchers attached by means of hinges to the underside of the table-top, close to the two ends. The 'trestles' were braced in position by two long hooks, locked diagonally when in use. Such tables were known in England and elsewhere as 'Spanish tables'[9] and the term occurs occasionally also in Italian inventories (e.g. *un tavolino con il pe alla spagnola*, i.e. a small table

with its leg[s] in the Spanish fashion) made for the Este chancellery in 1581.[10] The same joiner, one Mathia Moreto, made what must have been a similar table two years later which was actually described as having folding legs and iron rods (*con il pe a compasso con due stange*).[11]

In rooms used habitually for dining the table might stand permanently in position. This was especially the case where there were benches fixed against the walls and the table stood in front of them – in great halls and in refectories – and with such an arrangement it was not uncommon to place the table on a dais, the wooden platform being pleasanter underfoot than a stone floor which was the norm in large rooms (Pls 77, 238). A trestle-table standing on such a platform presented something of a hazard because, if a trestle accidently shifted and one end fell over the edge, the whole structure would collapse, bringing down with it everything on the table-top, so it was soon realized that a better arrangement was to have fixed supports, since the table was anyway not to be moved, and the supports could grow out of the dais, as it were, and be totally rigid (Pl. 184).

Whether the dining-table was fixed or removable, one or more tables was needed nearby for the service of the meal – a surface on which to carve meat or from which wine could be dispensed. Most of these 'sideboards' were fairly small and probably also much narrower than the main *tavola*; so we find *tavole da parecchiare numero sei* [six tables for preparing (food)] in the Perugian Vittelli residence in 1582 (Vitelli Invt.), *una tavoletta nova per il trinc[i]ato* [a new small table for the carving of meat] in a Medici residence in 1531 (Medici Invt.), and in another Florentine mansion (Pucci Invt.) in 1449 the *2 tavole con trespolj* in a dining-room were backed up by *4 deschettj di nocie* [four small tables of walnut]. It will be noted that a distinction is here made between a *tavola* and a *descho* (or *deschetto*, in this case). It may be that *descho* was the term commonly used for a table with attached legs while *tavola* implied that the table-board had separate supports in the form of trestles, but this was certainly not invariably the case.[12] As will be seen, *descho* was also a term applied to desks and tables for writing [*descho da scrivere*] many of which had a box-like construction and it may well be that, during the fifteenth century, the term came to be used for tables with a frame supporting the table-top and providing rigidity for fixed legs at the corners. Later, when trestle-tables had gone out of fashion, the word *tavola* came to signify tables in general while *descho* was used in reference to more truly box-like structures. Is this too far-fetched? Essentially a *tavola* and a *descho* both present a flat surface of some size, lying as a horizontal plane. Was the distinction merely one of size?

In circles where people were particularly conscious of their standing, a table had also to be set aside – in rooms where one dined – for a display of wealth, evidence of the family's 'credentials', as it were, and a lot of attention was paid to the appearance of this *credenza* which had of course to be as imposing as possible. The family's most precious vessels were placed on show there on important occasions and, in great houses, special items were specifically set aside for dressing the *credenza* – *cose apartenenti alla credenza*, as one inventory has it.[13] These would include the most flamboyant pieces of silver plate, and sometimes also vessels of crystal or agate or other types of expensive stone, or of Chinese porcelain if the family happened to own some pieces. A brave effect could also be contrived with pewter, less expensive than silver but, when polished, looking very splendid (Pl. 104); and in certain circumstances a delightful confection could be achieved with maiolica (p. 109). And all was customarily placed on rich table-covers, often specially designed for the purpose. If then a family had a great number of objects to display on the *credenza*, it was necessary to fit staging at the back to raise the hindermost rows so that the whole dazzling array could be seen properly (Pls 236, 314). The number of steps was also an indication of the owner's rank, in court circles and noble households. One or two stages were not uncommon but a greater number might be arranged in special circum-

stances, like the occasion on which the Florentines wanted to impress the sons of King Ferrante of Naples in 1476 and, at one banquet, the end of the great *sala* was taken up by a *credenziera grande con viiij gradi, tutta fornita di argenti assai et belli* [i.e. large, with nine stages entirely furnished with much splendid silver], as well as some gold vases, *in tutto furono pezzi 80* [which consisted of 80 pieces in all] – not to speak of the silver on the dining-table which numbered some 300 pieces.[14] Lodovico il Moro, in Milan, heard about a particularly magnificent set of silver 'sideboard-vessels' [*vasi grandi da credenza ... bellissimi*] which had been made for Duke Ercole d'Este and, in 1483, he wrote and asked the Duke if he could have drawings of this wonderful service. He had to wait for two years before the drawings arrived because the service had been pawned in Florence when, for a while, the Este family had found themselves rather short of money.[15]

The *credenza* might be contrived with the aid of a trestle-table forming the base and with the staging superimposed,[16] or a special *descho per lla gredenza* (Pucci Invt., Florence, 1449) might be provided which was presumably a table with fixed legs and perhaps also with attached staging. Some *credenze* might be quite elaborate structures, as we shall see. As for the smaller *deschetti* nearby, the sideboards serving practical purposes, they not infrequently had a board at the back, against the wall [a *spalliera*], presumably to protect the wall-hangings from damage by splashed food or drink.[17]

Free-standing tables with attached legs were also sometimes used for dining, in the fifteenth century and even back in the fourteenth (Pl. 69), and eventually trestle-tables yielded totally in fashionable use to such tables which became the common form in the sixteenth. No illustration is included in this work but see diagram 13, p. 361.

A late sixteenth-century picture by Jacob van der Straet (Stradanus) shows a table which in his northern homeland would almost certainly have had leaves at each end that could be drawn out to extend the table-surface to double its normal, closed area, so that more people could sit at it. No draw-leaf tables seem to be mentioned in the inventories consulted for the present study although it is inconceivable that the Italians were unaware of this northern invention and that examples were not to be seen in Italian houses. The earliest printed designs for draw-tables were published at Orleans in about 1550 (Pl. 235)[18] and the formula must have been invented some while before that, in France or the Netherlands.

In the Villa Medici inventory (Medici Invt., Rome, 1598), several tables are described as being *con piedi alla francese* [with feet in the French style/manner]. A characteristic French form, evolved in the mid-sixteenth century and also adopted in the Netherlands, had stout supporting pillars at each end, rising from cross-pieces that formed feet and with a stretcher at floor level joining the two end-supports that lay on the central axis. Between the two main supports was set a row of turned balusters. This ensemble cannot have failed to catch the attention of anyone who had not seen such a table before, and one would have described it in special terms if it were not the common form. Common in Italy it certainly was not, but the form must on the other hand have been

234

236

234 *Al fresco* table-arrangements

Trestle-tables combined to form an L-shaped dining-table laid for a large company, using both sides of the table. Behind is a simple *credenza*, with three stages, all covered with a linen cloth and decked with plate. An inscription on the tablecloth indicates that the artist was working at Ferrara. The style is indeed close to that of Lorenzo Costa and the large chest on the right is of a type favoured in that duchy. Note the fine armour on display and the travelling-coffer in front.

From the Longleat Collection (photograph: Courtauld Institute)

235 The French draw-leaf table

The double layer of leaves, visible when the leaves are not extended, can be seen here, shown from one end. There was of course a matching support at the opposite end, while the stretcher between could be very elaborate. Designs by Jacques Androuet du Cerceau, published at Orléans, about 1560. He apparently became architect to Princess Renée of France, who had married Ercole II, Duke of Ferrara (d. 1559); he later dedicated his chief work on architecture to Catherine de' Medici, Queen of France, so it is unlikely that his publication went totally unnoticed among well-informed Italians, and Italians travelling in France will certainly have seen examples of this form of table there. Nevertheless, in spite of the advantage which the draw-leaf formula offered, it does not seem to have been widely adopted in Italy.

Jacques Androuet du Cerceau, designs for tables, c.1560
Victoria and Albert Museum, London

78

235

236 The simple *credenza*

This shows the stages placed on the table-top that formed this sideboard, with its rows of plate on display. While a linen *spalliera* is nailed up behind the staging, the latter is not covered with a cloth in the usual way.

Maso Finaguerra, Susannah and the Elders, c.1460
British Museum, London

237 A circular table for the Last Supper

An unusual form of table, mounted on trestles. The linen damask tablecloth seems to be made circular as well.

Antonio Vivarini (c.1440– or 1484), The Last Supper
Museo Ca' d' oro, Venice (Photograph: Osvaldo Böhm)

known there. Such a supporting frame was commonly associated with a draw-leaf top but could also support a plain top. One of the tables with *piedi alla francese* at the Villa Medici served as an altar.

A scene of the Last Supper of the early fifteenth century shows Jesus and his Disciples seated at a large round table supported by trestles (Pl. 237) but this was probably a rare form; at any rate, it is not commonly illustrated. On the other hand, depictions of small round tables are not uncommon. They are usually shown being used for intimate meals for two or up to four persons (Pls 242, 243), and they were quite frequently found in bedchambers. For example, in the master's bedchamber in the Palazzo Spinola (Spinola Invt., Genoa, 1459), stood *tabulla una rotonda ligni* [a round wooden table] while an engraving (Pl. 244) showing a small round table with a meal being set out on it has an inscription explaining that here we see how, after making love, Cupid and Psyche rose and dressed themselves (Cupid only had to don his quiver of arrows, judging from the picture) and *Al bel tondo a tre piei s'asside a cena* [sat down to dine at the beautiful three-legged round table]. The legs are zoomorphic – a puzzling cross between a lion and a chicken – but the *tondo da mangiare*, as many such small dining-tables are called in the inventories (Pl. 244), has legs that are rather more plausible. It has four of them which may have been a less common variant; they mostly seem to have three.

A small square dining-table is shown in Pl. 315 where it is seen forming the centre of a *triclinio* (p. 291). It has four scrolls set diagonally on a base-plate diagram 21, p. 361). Tables with scrolls or balusters forming a single, central support became common in the mid-sixteenth century, in

grand settings, and some were used for dining. A table with four nose-diving dolphins conjoined to form a central support may be seen in Pl. 223 (see also diagram 15, p. 361).

During the later decades of the fifteenth century and right through the sixteenth what amounted to enlarged box-stools (p. 168) served as tables for various purposes including dining but a *descho* of this type was inevitably fairly small (Pl. 192).

A small table being used for serving a bedside meal is to be seen in Pl. 226, and a small cupboard forming a bedside table is to be seen in Pl. 249.

Tables for show

'The Italians, and especially the Venetians, excell in the Art of setting Jewells, and making Cabinets, tables and mountings, of Christall, corall, Jasper, and other precious stones, and curious worke of Carving . . . And as Italy hath yealded many rare workemen in these Artes of paynting, Carving in stone and brasse, Architecture, setting of Jewells [,] composing these Cabinetts[,] tables and mountings . . . So the Princes and States of Italy are Curious in gathering and preserving the rare peeces of these workemen . . .'. So said the English traveller, Fynes Moryson, who was in Italy from late 1593 to the spring of 1595.[1] He draws particular attention to the tables and cabinets which were 'composed' by the Italians. He probably had in mind the Italian word *commesso* which was at this late stage of the sixteenth century applied to the bringing together of coloured stones or of different sorts of wood to compose patterns, often of great elaboration and beauty, the panels thus contrived being mounted as facings of veneers on cabinets, tables and other kinds of furniture. Such things were collected by 'Princes and States' when new, and those that survive are still collected and prized today. This means that scholarly attention has usually been turned on them and the literature of Italian furniture history tends to concentrate on such, for the most part, unique items.[2] And because they are mostly unique it is of course difficult to make generalizations about them.

As far as such tables are concerned, these were designed to stand in prominent places in the principal rooms of palaces, the most elaborate specimens being placed with other amazing treasures in princely cabinets of curiosities.

Often they were what today are called 'centre tables' which means that they were designed to be seen from all sides and would therefore normally be placed out in the middle of the room – the only kind of furniture designed to be so treated during the Renaissance, incidentally.

In the fifteenth century, tables had generally been made to look splendid by casting over them a rich cloth, a 'table-carpet', of some expensive material (see below, p. 266). The top of the actual table did not therefore need to be decorated but, as woodworking skills increased, some rich people began to order tables with inlaid tops as well as handsomely carved supports. The small round table with a central pedestal-support shown in Pl. 1 is presumably a representation of an actual table that could

237

238

238 Dining at a trestle table

The front legs of the two trestles can just be seen; they are braced at the top by a web. It stands on a dais of wood with parquetry decoration which is laid under the table to raise the diners' feet off the stone floor. The king has a foot-cushion in addition. Note the glass tumblers and the three handsome silver-gilt cups. Instead of being executed in fresco, the repeating pattern on the wall is produced with tiles decorated in relief. Such tiles might be gilded or could be painted; both effects are shown here where one pattern is used to simulate the mural decoration of a dining-room.

Francesco Zavattari, assisted by his two sons, *Wedding of Theodolinda and Agilulfo*, Church of St John the Baptist, Monza, Lombardy, 1444
Photograph: Scala

239 Another trestle table

This table surely once had legs which must have been lost during restoration, but they were undoubtedly of the trestle type. Note the silk hanging. The walls are decorated, probably in fresco rather than with tiles. At a fireplace furnished with a hood *a padiglione* a servant sqats, shielding his face as he turns the spit.

Unknown artist, Atri Cathedral, third quarter 15th Century
Photograph: Autostrade

be seen, about 1470, in some particularly splendid house in Ferrara. Already in 1441 we find the exceptionally skilful craftsman, Arduino da Baiso, making a table to stand in the chapel at Belfiore, one of the Este *delizie* outside Ferrara, which had a very beautifully inlaid top [*uno desco belissimo*] that, over the next few decades, all important visitors to the Este court were taken to admire.[3] In the same year, the scarcely less skilled craftsman Pantaleone de Marchi provided for the personal use of Leonello d'Este a table inlaid with the Marquis's arms [he was paid for having inlaid *le arme de lo illu. n. S.* [our illustrious lord] *de tarsie in una tavola de lo ill. n. S.*[4] Giacomo Sanuti, in his magnificent house in Bologna, likewise had a table inlaid with his own arms and those of his wife, Nicolosa Castellani. This was noted in an inventory taken shortly after his death in 1505 but the table will probably have been made at the time of their marriage, well back in the fifteenth century (Sanuti Invt., Bologna, 1505). It was described as a dining-table, as should probably also have been that of Leonello d'Este.

Mention has already been made (p. 92) of some tripod tables with elaborate stands of carved ebony or bronze with tops 'of gold' that are described in the *Hypnerotomachia* of 1499 which should be perceived as only a slight exaggeration of what was to be seen in exceptionally grand settings at the time (Pl. 240). The same fabulous tale continues to describe a further series of tables, most of them covered with superb table-carpets of silk (the attendant nymphs and waiters being dressed in the same materials, *en suite*). The seventh table, however, had no such cover because it was of ivory inlaid with 'the wood of aloes', worked with knots, foliage, flowers, vases, 'little monsters' and small birds inlaid with a black composition mixed with musk and ambergris – in fact, it was scented.[5]

Tables designed for show only really became a feature of furnishing arrangements in splendid Italian houses during the sixteenth century. Occasionally they are shown in pictures towards the end of the century and one must recognize that they were never common in any sense. On the other hand a form that is mentioned relatively often in the inventories is *un ottangulo* which had an octagonal top, and while these could serve utilitarian purposes, they could be handsomely decorated (Pl. 368). Eleonora da Toledo had *Un ottangulo d'ebano et avorio col piei di noce* [an octagonal table of ebony and ivory with walnut legs] in her apartment at the Palazzo Vecchio in Florence (Medici Invt., 1553). Across the Arno, in the Capponi family's *palazzo*, a few years earlier there was another,

239

240 A tripod-table for show

This base for a tripod-table must be made either of bronze or of ebony. According to the fanciful description its top was of gold but that is inconceivable; on the other hand, a marble slab decorated with gold could well have lain on this sturdy support. Illustration from the *Hypnerotomachia Polifili* (1499), in the narrative of which fantasy is given free rein although the glamorous settings described seem to be more or less within the bounds of possibility – so this table-stand may not be very different from the kind of thing one might have seen in splendid buildings in and around Venice in the late fifteenth century.

From Francesco Colonna, *Hypnerotomachia Polifili*, Venice, 1499
Courtesy of the Trustees of Sir John Soane's Museum

240

described as *1 desco bello otangolo in su 2 piedi di lioni di taglio comesso di nero* which seems to mean that it was very handsome, with legs in the form of carved lions.[6] The words *commesso di nero* may indicate that some pieces of black marble were set into the table-top which was a form of decoration in some favour during the sixteenth century, although the inlay may have been of ebony rather than stone in this case. A very handsome *ottangulo* survives in the Palazzo Guicciardini in Florence which has recently been identified as that presented by the monks of the San Michele in Bosco monastery, Bologna, to Franceso Guicciardini, the well-known historian, when he was governor of Bologna in the early 1530s.[7] It was made by Fra Damiano Zambelli who is famous for having produced the *lavoro di intarsio* panels in San Domenico, executed a few years later. The top surface and edges of the table-top are handsomely decorated with *tarsie* of a geometric pattern with a border of fruit amid foliage. The supporting pedestal has three faces, finely carved, with lion's-paw feet. It is said to have been designed by Vignola.

Tables with tops of marble or some other stone are quite frequently met with in inventories of the second half of the sixteenth century but not much before that. The Medici family appear to have been very much in the forefront with this fashion which was to loom so large in the seventeenth and eighteenth centuries. The Venetian diplomat who went round the Pitti Palace in 1576[8] noted the chief features of the principal rooms and a number of tables caught his eye, presumably because they were striking; so we see, for example, *primo vi e un tondo di marmo nero* [first there is a round table of black marble] in a bedchamber and in the next room he comes across one of porphyry fourteen *braccia* in diameter.

Another porphyry table had an edge-moulding of ebony as well as a border *di pietre di valuta di piu colori* [of valuable stones of many colours]. This brings to mind the Medici interest in table-tops decorated with patterns composed of semi-precious stones of many colours – *lavoro di commesso di pietre dure*, as they called it. A Grand-Ducal workshop was established at the Uffizi in 1599 to produce works in this technique but an earlier establishment had existed at the Palazzo Vecchio,[9] a product of which must have been the table in the Grand Duke's bedchamber at the Pitti, seen by the Venetian diplomat, which had a slab of alabaster *nella quale sono commesse pietre di gran valuta, che servono per tavolieri, e scacchieri, e per la tavola del 12* [into which is set a composition of stones of great value, which serves as a board for backgammon, for chess and for nine men's morris]. At the Palazzo Vecchio (1553), incidentally, the *sala* contained a long dining-table (of 9 *braccia*) requiring three trestles to support it; in the same room stood another table described as *Un quadro* [i.e. a square, or anyway rectangular, slab] *commessovi di piu sorte pietre mistie in su dua trespoli* [composed with many kinds of stones intermixed, supported by two trestles]. Clearly here too the Medici liked to have a *pietre dure* table for show, perhaps with a handful of splendid vessels standing on it – no doubt making a very brave sight indeed.

However, craftsmen working for the Este family at Ferrara seem to have been producing elaborate inlaid marble tables before the Florentine workshops really got going. A very splendid table with a circular marble top (of the expensive *breccia* marble called *mischio* – here *marmoro meschia*) was produced in 1519, the top being inlaid by the skilled marble-worker Domenico Segapietra [literally meaning 'sawyer of stone'] with porphyry, serpentine and *diaspro* in a pattern designed by a painter named Pietro da Mirandola who, the year before, had executed a picture of a tiger and a panther for the same patron, namely the cardinal Ippolito d'Este who was furnishing his palace in the diocese of Strigonia, in distant Hungary.[10] A whole string of commissions was issued in this connection; no doubt some of the items, like the pair of scissors for manicuring the Cardinal's nails, made an impression on the Hungarians. That, at least, must have been the intention.

A heavy stone slab, whether plain or inlaid with a pattern like that in the Palazzo Vecchio, would not in fact be safe lying on ordinary trestles, and the *trespoli* mentioned in the inventory were almost certainly hefty supports of a type inspired by antique classical tables. These supports, in their most elaborate form, resemble two brackets or consoles addorsed (i.e. back-to-back) rising from a narrow plinth with a bold moulding (see diagram 14, p. 361). In modern Italian such supports are said to be *a trapezofori*, which derives from the classical Greek word for a table-support, but the term does not seem to have been used in Renaissance Italy.[11] A magnificent table with a massive inlaid marble top, made for the Farnese Palace in Rome between about 1565 and 1573, has three superbly

carved supports of this kind with winged sirens chestily taking the huge weight on their shoulders.[12] Animals could perform the same service.[13] The Farnese supports are of stone, as were their classical predecessors, but supports of this form executed in wood became a common form for handsome tables in Italy during the latter decades of the sixteenth century; they usually had stretchers between the supports to brace the structure. Eventually quite ordinary tables were fitted with such supports where merely the fancy outline was retained, bereft of carving on the faces, which were left plain. Tables with such supports in some respects came to resemble the so-called *sgabello*, or box-stool with a back, where the front 'legs' often had a similar fancy outline (see diagram 8, p. 360).

The sirens, or whatever formed the curving outlines, could also be made free-standing, in which case the supports were more like legs. This form enjoyed enormous popularity in the later seventeenth and first half of the eighteenth centuries, but existed in the sixteenth. The *tavola di pietre negra* [of black stone] at the Palazzo Correr in Venice in 1584 (Correr Invt.) had *piedi d'orati* [gilded legs] which we may suppose were at least four in number and may have been of this bracket-like form, rising from a slab-like base.

241 A bedside table

The bedside table or 'pot-cupboard' was not invented before the second half of the eighteenth century but the need to have a surface close to the bed on which one could place articles of various kinds had existed long before the late fourteenth century when this picture was painted. The bed-chests of a *lettiera* were fairly handy in this respect but were a little too low for convenience. A special small table might be placed on the lid of the chest (Pl. 226) but a better solution is shown here. It consists of a small cupboard specially made to fit against the side of the bed, the bed-chests being made shorter than usual to accommodate it. The details are so clearly shown (note the keyholes and the panelled construction) that this modification of the standard *lettiera* assemblage is unlikely to be a figment of the artist's imagination even though the form may have been uncommon.

Giusto de Menabuoi, *Pharaoh's Dream*, The Cathedral Baptistry, Padua, *c.*1370
Photograph : Deganello/Padua

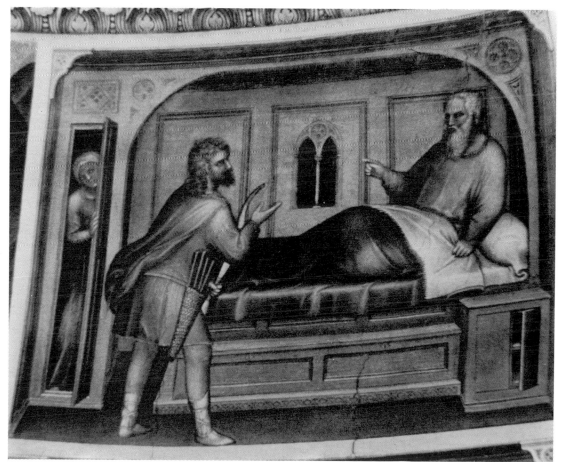

241

The inlaid marble slab of the Farnese table must have been made in Rome, where there was a manufactory rivalling that in Florence by the mid-sixteenth century. Was there also such an establishment in Venice? Alessandro Ram, who died in 1592, had a table in his *portego* – the principal room in his *palazzo* – which was *lavorata con pietre diverse* [worked with various kinds of stone]. It was somehow arranged in two pieces which seem to have lain on a supporting table. In the same house stood a table *con piet[r]a miniata* which could mean inlaid with a pattern composed with very small pieces of stone, or that it was painted delicately with ornament.[14]

Finally, attention should be drawn to the two small tables of *cina dell'Indie* [literally 'China from the Indies'] which were in the 'Indian' room at the Villa Medici in 1598 (Medici Invt.) and may have been – indeed, probably were – of Chinese or Japanese lacquer (p. 158). They both had *piedi a scranna*, in one case described as being *di cina* like the table-top. Chinese tables could have cabriole legs; but whatever the shape of these legs, they brought to mind legs on some form of Italian armchair (*scranna*).

In *Les Blasons Domestiques*, published in Paris in 1539, Gilles Corrozet speaks of the *Table tous les jours bien frotee* which must mean that table-tops should be well rubbed every day. He is probably speaking of the boards of trestle-tables which would need scrubbing daily unless they were of an expensive wood, in which case polishing would be in order. But Corrozet also speaks of a *Table comme ung miroir polye* [like a polished mirror] which is presumably how fine table-tops were meant to look, although modern Italians speak of a table-top being *pulito a specchio* which simply means very clean. In the circumstances of which are written here, this comes to the same thing.

Tables of other kinds

When members of the upper classes travelled, during the Renaissance period, they tended to take a certain amount of furniture with them, and a whole range of items came to be designed specially for the purpose. We have already discussed beds for travelling and chests for slinging on the backs of mules (p. 144 and p. 201). There were also tables *da campo* or *da campagna* – for the field, for the campaign, for of course a military gentleman needed such things more than anyone. But ladies could have them too. Eleanora da Toledo had two, *una tavoletta da campo con sua piedi* [a small camp table with its legs] and another with legs of walnut *con sua catene* [with its chains] (Medici Invt., Florence, 1553). Presumably these were tables with X-frame stands that had two chains at the top or bottom to prevent the hinged stand from opening too far. An illustration of such a table is reproduced in Pl. 246. The first table was probably not quite such an utilitarian object as its bald description would suggest because it stood in the Duchess's favourite room at the Palazzo Vecchio. It was probably useful as an easily movable occasional table and may never have been used 'in the field'.

Another form of table which had legs that folded was known in England

242

(and perhaps elsewhere) as a 'Spanish table'.[1] We have already discussed this development of the trestle table (p. 206), with its two long iron hooks that reached diagonally up from the stretcher to lugs set at the centre of the underside. No sixteenth-century illustration of an Italian table of this kind has come to light but a picture of about 1675 shows three in a room in Naples while two tables of this kind, with marquetry of ebony and ivory, survive in Italian collections and can be ascribed to a Neapolitan workshop active in the 1590s and into the early seventeenth century.[2] Such tables were very probably a Spanish invention, as the English, Dutch and French name for them would seem to imply, and specimens may still be found in Spain. It should not therefore surprise us to find them in Naples, given that city's strong connection with Spain, but it is unlikely that the form was not adopted elsewhere in Italy before 1600. Most tables of this kind were plain and essentially utilitarian. As their legs were not really very strong, they were easily broken and, once damaged, the whole thing tended to be discarded. Many of those that survive have had their hooks replaced by wooden struts, fixed rigidly so the hinged legs can no longer fold.

Back in 1461 a Genoese gentleman had some tables which apparently served to make his cabin at sea more habitable – *certe . . . tabule pro faciendo cameram in nave* (Busarini Invt., Genoa, 1461).

242 Dining *à deux*

A *tondo* in use. This rather charming maiolica group
was made in the Fontana factory at Urbino late in the
sixteenth century. It was in fact associated with an ink-
well and should be seen as an inexpensive version of
similar groups executed in bronze, produced as objects
for collectors of small works of art and curiosities to
keep in their their private studies (see pp. 268–9).

Urbino maiolica
Museo Civico, Pesaro (No. 233)

243 Dining in private in an *anticamera*

This small circular table used for dining seems to have
'stake legs' like the stools shown in Plates 180 and 181
and the small square table shown in Plate 8. A circular
linen cloth with a black border is spread over it. A small
credenza of the cupboard type stands nearby; its
'cupboard cloth' has a similar border. A *spalliera* hangs
behind San Savino whose bedchamber may be seen
through the doorway.

Giovanni Boccati, scene from the *Life of S. Savino*, for Orvieto
Cathedral, 1473
Galleria Nazionale delle Marche, Urbino (photograph: Scala)

243

Apart from tables for travelling, a Renaissance house had numerous tables in the service areas, in the kitchen, in the stores, in the stable, the garden, the laundry.³ These were mostly sturdy, simple structures consisting of a table-top made up with the requisite number of boards placed side-by-side and linked with cross-pieces. Into holes drilled in the 'table-board' [*tavola*] roughly hewn legs were then hammered in so that they jammed tight, on the 'milking-stool' principle mentioned here when dealing with stools (p. 168). Indeed, only size distinguished such tables from stools and benches all made in precisely the same way (Pls 8, 181).

Merchants had 'counters' in their shops just as they do today (Pl. 321). The English name derives from the fact that merchants counted money on them and some were even marked out on their table-tops so that coins of different denomination could be piled together in the appointed square – or whatever other convenient system was being used. Some 'counters' were surprisingly grand, however, and could be found in the smartest settings. Once again Eleanora da Toledo provides an example: she had in her own apartment *Uno tavoletto da contar denari di noce* [a small walnut table for counting money]. In a setting that was only slightly less grand, the Palazzo Correr in Venice in 1584 (Correr Invt.), we find, in the owner's well-appointed mezzanine office, a *tavola da contar soldi intarsiata d'avoglio* [for counting cash, inlaid with ivory].

As has already been said, box-stools could serve as small tables (e.g. for dressing; Pl. 271) and large ones were made as tables proper, rather than stools for which purpose they would be too tall (Pl. 252). The confusion that could arise from this is shown by the reference in the Badoer inventory (Venice, 1521) to *Uno scagno de nogara zoe desco* [a walnut stool, or rather, table].

Table-covers

During the Renaissance, most tables were largely hidden by some form of covering if the house where they were standing was in occupation. That is to say, tables in an outlying castle which was just being maintained against the time when the lord might turn up, would probably be left bare (if not stacked away), and those at the family's villa out in the countryside might be unadorned in winter. The same must have applied to tables in disused rooms in a large *palazzo* or castle, but otherwise tables were normally covered. When the trestle-tables were set up in the *sala*, they were covered with a long linen table-cloth (Pl. 233). The smaller dining-tables also had cloths (Pl. 243). So usually did the serving tables and the *credenza* (Pl. 234). The more splendid tables in the private dining-room of the owner would be covered first by a 'table-carpet' and then, during meals, by a linen table-cloth. The same kind of dual covering is to be seen on a table, that must have been in some way special, that stands in a *sala* – a great dining hall – shown in Pl. 69.

Even show-tables might have their own rich table-carpets and anyway all show-tables would have had coverings to protect their delicate and expensive tops when they were not 'on display'. Costly table-carpets were also protected, either by being removed to a wardrobe room [*guardaroba*]

or by having a covering of their own. There was, for example, a *sopra panno* of red leather lying over a *panno* of red taffeta with furbelows and fringes [*con cascate e frangie*] that in turn lay on a fine table, in the Villa Medici in Rome (Medici Invt., 1598).

A carpet, to an Englishman in the sixteenth century, was a cover lying on a flat surface, be it the floor or a table. The usual term used in Italy for such a cover was *tappeto* or *tapedo*¹ which could be *da terra* [to lie on the ground or floor], *da scagno* [on a stool], *da cassa* [on a chest], and *da tavola*.²

Tappeti da tavola could be made of a great variety of materials, from plain cloths to richly worked textiles. When Matteo Bandello, writing in the mid-sixteenth century, is describing an exceptionally well-appointed bedchamber, he mentions a splendid table, placed out in the middle of the room, which was *coperta d'un tapeto di seta* [covered with a silk table-carpet]. Lorenzo de' Medici had a *tappeto da tavola* of satin with a border of *palle*, the family's blason, probably embroidered on the silk. He also had one *chol pelo lavorato alla dommaschina* [with pile, decorated in the Damascus (i.e. Near Eastern) style] which must have been an Anatolian carpet. It was fourteen *braccia* long and five and a half wide.³

Anatolian carpets seem not to have been used as covers on tables much before Lorenzo's day (Pl. 79) and the practice only became common, in luxurious surroundings, during the sixteenth century (Pls 59, 81). They were marvellously showy objects and, with their sides falling down over the edges of a table, produced a colourful effect. What is more, to own such an exotic object – let alone several – was evidence of the possessor's wealth. However, one can by no means always be certain that table carpets described in inventories as *alla domaschina* or *alla moresca* were always of Near Eastern origin, although when the descriptions include a reference to a pile surface [*col pelo*], the most striking feature of such carpets, or to patterns characteristic of Near Eastern carpets (e.g. *con uno compasso* [a roundel], *con tre ruode* [three wheels or roundels])⁴ one may reasonably presume this to have been the case.

Quite often, in Italian sixteenth-century inventories, we find the word *carpetta* used, mostly in relation to table-covers. It seems probable that this did actually signify a Near Eastern carpet; at least, no reference to a *carpetta* noted while preparing the present study would seem to contradict this statement (although one should note that the term *corpetta* meant a form of bodice or gown and this word was sometimes rendered as *carpetta*⁵).

We surveyed the various types of Near Eastern carpet (p. 64) and all of them could serve as table-covers if they were not too large. Thus we have *tapedi da tavola persian*, *cagiarin* [from Cairo], *turchesco*, and *simiscasa*, the last almost certainly being Near Eastern although it is not evident what particular type of carpet was meant by the term.⁶

In the Florentine Capponi inventory of 1534 (Capponi Invt.) one list is headed *Tappetti e Cellonni*. We have considered the term *celone* and decided it was a rather heavy woollen material with stripes or regularly repeated patterns, coming in many qualities and widely used for a variety of upholstery purposes (p. 76). While mainly used on walls and on beds,

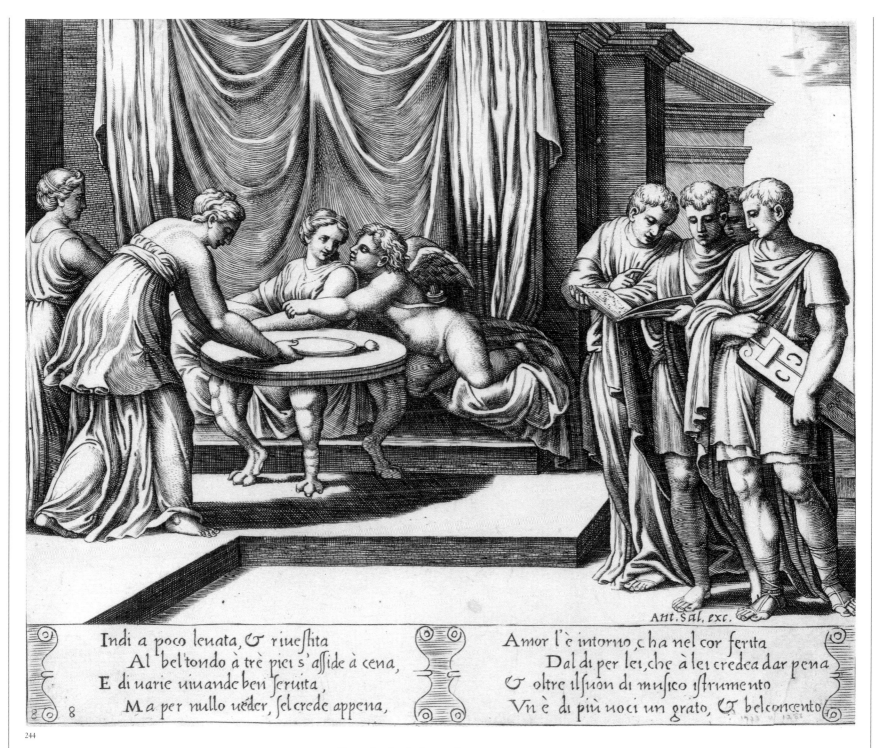

Ant.Sal.exc.

Indi a poco leuata, & riueſtita
    Al bel'tondo à trè piei s'aſſide à cena,
E di uarie uiuande ben ſeruita,
    Ma per nullo ueder, ſel crede appena,

Amor l'è intorno, c ha nel cor ferita
    Dal di per lei, che à lei credea dar pena
& oltre il ſuon di muſico iſtrumento
    Vn è di più uoci un grato, & belconcento

8

244

244 Psyche's *bel tondo*

The inscription tells us that this handsome circular table [*bel tondo*] with three legs [*a tre piei*] is being prepared for a meal to be enjoyed by Cupid and Psyche who have just risen from the couch in the background.

Engraving after Antonio Salviati; about 1545
British Museum, London

245

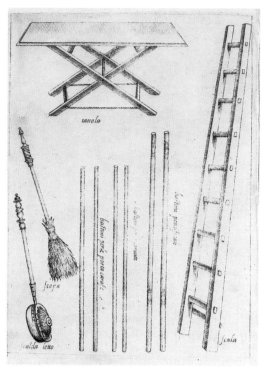

246

245 Table or chest?

This seems to show a chest of sarcophagus form being used as a table-top, but a closer look suggests that we may here see a table made in this form. Another engraving of 1523 shows a poet seated at a table of roughly similar shape. Did the *bombé* shape allow sufficient room for the knees or was there perhaps a knee-hole on one side? Whatever the case, some scholars evidently liked to have their furniture couched in a classical form.

From Bernardo de Granolachs, *Lunare*, Florence, 1491
British Library, London (B.L. 1A 27828)

246 A useful folding table

Instead of being held open, braced by clips, as such tables are today, the sixteenth-century version had cords at the bottom that prevented the legs from spreading open any further. It is here illustrated in a cookery book that lists items that would be useful in a great household, especially that of a pope. It will be seen that these include a warming-pan (see Pl. 118), a besom, a ladder, carrying rods for travelling-cases containing vessels for picnics, and staves of office painted with the papal arms.

Bartolomeo Scappi, from *Opera*, Venice 1570
Metropolitan Museum of Art, New York, Elisha Whittelsey Collection, Elisha Whittelsey Fund, 1952 (52.595.2[25])

celoni could also be thrown over a table, and some may have been specially made as table-covers, complete with borders.[7] The four *teloni da tavola* mentioned in the Della Rovere inventory (Della Rovere Invt., Bologna, 1493) might have been of this kind. They were all probably what are called 'double cloths', technically, which means they were reversible – quite a useful characteristic for a table-cover. As we have seen, while *celoni* in the first place came from the Low Countries and northern France (the name derives from Châlons, it will be remembered), they were also produced in Italy. In the Medicis' chief residence in Florence, in the Via Larga, in 1531 (Medici Invt.) there stood in the *salotto* a large trestle-table covered with a *celone nostrale*. It was probably rather a glamorous product of 'our' local looms. It is very likely, incidentally, that the *coperta roana* on a walnut table in the Correr residence (Correr Invt.) was also a *celone* and that it came from Rouen where this class of material was also made.

The heading in the Capponi inventory was 'Tappetti e Cellonni'. A dining-table of the better sort would normally be covered by its *tappeto* but when it came to serving a meal on it, the showy covering was in turn covered with a linen cloth. In such cases it was a good idea to have the cloth rather smaller than the table-carpet so that the edges of the latter could be seen (Pl. 69). There was, after all, no need to be modest if one owned a handsome table-carpet but clearly the Venetian government felt its citizens were overdoing it, by the late fifteenth century, and in 1489 introduced regulations governing banquets and feasts in which they

sought to prevent the use of *tappeti* under the *tovaglie* [table-cloths], such usage being a *superfluita vana et non necessaria*, a sentiment that needs no translation.[8] Only the finer qualities of carpet can have served for this purpose, one must suppose; a carpet with a long or coarsely-woven pile would not provide a firm base for glasses and other delicate but rather unstable vessels. When no table-carpet was being used under the table-cloth it was, incidentally, the practice to have a linen table-cloth that fell as far down the sides and ends as possible. This of course then posed a problem at the corners where long tails would trail on the floor – with obvious attendant hazards – but these were avoided by knotting the corners.

Florio*, in his dictionary of 1611, informs his readers that *una tovaglia* (also *tovaia*) meant 'a table-cloth, a board-cloth'. The latter simply meant a cloth to lay on a 'cup-board', the *credenza* on which cups and other vessels were displayed. We return to this point below (p. 219). However, a *tovaglia da mano* or *tovagliola* (or other diminutives of the word) meant a napkin. In the linen-cupboard the difference was purely one of size; it was only at the table that a difference in the way these cloths were used became apparent.

We surveyed briefly the various classes of linen cloth available in Italy during the period (p. 73). A lengthy inventory, that of Paolo Guinigi, Lord of Lucca, taken in 1430 (Guinigi Invt.), mentions many chests of linen and their contents comprised numerous *tovallie*. Some were *alla*

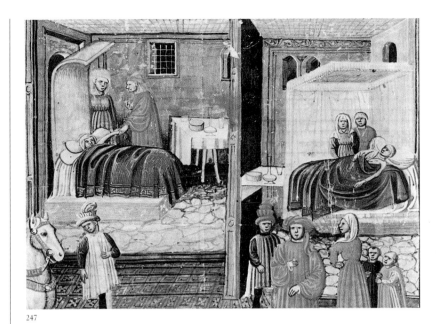

247

In the background we see one of the trestles that supports a table on which a doctor has placed his medicines. A female patient extends a very limp arm in order that he might take her pulse.

From an edition of Avicenna's famous work on medicine, the *Canon Maior*, first half of the 15th century
University Library, Bologna (photograph: Roncaglia)

parigina (i.e. in the Parisian style or actually Parisian, but in any case probably 'diapered', that is to say with a lozenge-pattern all over; p. 73, Pl. 243), others were *alla senese listata sottile* [fine, in the Sienese style, with stripes – but, more probably, with blue bands running across the width, near the ends of the cloth; Pl. 77]. The finest were some *tovalliole domaschine* [damask napkins], fourteen of them, each four *braccia* in length. However, there was an entire roll of this material which is described as being French [*uno cavesso di tovaglia francescha lavorata alla domeschina*] awaiting cutting up into napkin-lengths and hemming. Linen damask had not been woven in Northern Europe for all that long, by 1430, the date of the Guinigi Inventory.[9]

Very little relatively coarse linen cloth is listed in the Guinigi inventory but a length of *tovalla grossa occhiellata* is mentioned; this will have been a linen with a simple all-over diaper pattern, like eyes [*occhi*, presumably lozenges with a dot in the centre of each; Pl. 237]. Lacking from this particular inventory is linen *da rensa* meaning 'from Rheims' but this is present in other Italian inventories throughout the century. In the sixteenth century we find table-cloths of *tela d'Olanda* [from Holland] and *di Flandina* [from Flanders].[10]

Occasionally table-cloths of silk are mentioned like that in a Palermitan inventory of 1561 (Requesens Invt.) described as *una tovaglia murischi di sita laburato di oro* [literally Moorish, of silk worked with gold; it was probably Levantine and embroidered].

Just as a small *tovaglia* served *da mano*, as a napkin, so a *mantile* could both be a table-cloth or a napkin, but *mantile* is a term met with less frequently in the inventories.

Occasionally table-cloths that were intended to lie on round tables are mentioned. Among the Guinigi linen were some French *tovallie* that were circular [*tonda*], presumably for just this purpose.

Table-cloths were also needed on side-boards and especially on the *credenza* (Pls 234, 250). Because these tables, and their shelves or stages, were usually narrower than dining-tables, narrow cloths were often required for this purpose. So we find not only *togalie due a credentia*, for example, in an inventory from Pavia of 1449,[11] but also *liste da tavola* [narrow widths, strips] in one from Turin of 1522 (Di Challant Invt.). Among Cosimo I de' Medici's *Robe e masserite della Credenza di S. Eccza* [vessels and furnishings for His Excellency's credenza] were two *tovaglie* (Medici Invt., 1553) twenty-four *braccia* in length and four of forty *braccia*. Even allowing for a drop of a couple of *braccia* down over each end, this shows that Cosimo's *credenza* was an impressive affair but few such 'cupboard-cloths', as the English called them, were anything like so long. Cosimo's are described as being *alla perugina* which means that they had bands of formal decoration in a single colour woven into the material at each end. One can see bands of this type on the table-cloth in Pl. 77. The bands did not have to be blue; cloths were also produced with dark brown and black bands (Pl. 233). Moreover, Perugia was certainly not the only place where *tovaglie* thus decorated were made; above, we noted a Sienese cloth with a band or stripe, listed in the Guinigi inventory, while the black-banded cloth shown in Pl. 233 is probably a Lombard product.

A delightful way of decking out a dining-table or a *credenza* was to do so with verdure and flowers. This was of course chiefly done in connection with country entertainment – at the villa, at a pause in some pleasant location during a day given over to hunting, and so on. More is said about this on p. 260 and p. 261.

Cupboards, Desks and Cabinets

The elaborate credenza

The simple *credenza* (pp. 205–9) was merely a table which could be fitted with staging at the back for the better display of a fine array of silver or gold plate (Pl. 236). Although simple in structure, this form played an important part in courtly ceremonial. Before it was decked with plate it was usually either totally draped with a splendid cloth, or a narrow *tovaglia* might be laid along its length, specially designed for the purpose.

Many *credenze* are mentioned in the Este inventory of 1436 (Este Invt.). Most would seem to be of the simple type but a few had locks and keys, which indicates that the form embraced an enclosed space, presumably in the form of a cupboard which must have been underneath the table-surface. In a large room at the castle in Ferrara occupied by some ladies-in-waiting were two *credenze*, both new, one with two stages at the back, the other *aserada* [enclosed with panels] and with two locks and keys.[1] In a room of no great consequence stood a *credenza* with locks that is described as being *fata a la moderna* [made in the modern style].[2] Was there something special about this piece or could one say of all the pieces with lockable compartments that they were therefore of this new type? The enclosed form existed already at the beginning of the century, for a Verona inventory of 1408 (Aleardi Invt.) has a *credenza* with two cupboards with locks and ring-handles [*cum duabus clasariis (clausari) et clavibus et duabus anelletis*], but the standard form right through the century remained the 'simple' type.

These early Italian *credenze* with cupboads beneath were probably fairly plain, in most cases, but illustrations seem hard to find (Pl. 250); they may well not have looked all that different from the *credenzone* shown in an engraving of 1570 reproduced in Pl. 252. We would call such an object a cupboard but one has to remember that this English word became attached to the enclosed space, fronted with a door, that had formed the lower part of the characteristic Renaissance 'cup-board', the 'board' or table on which cups and other precious vessels were displayed. In Italy such a piece of furniture might sometimes be called *un armario* but this term was usually reserved for taller forms like a wardrobe rather than a piece on the top of which you could rest an elbow.

A few Italian *credenze* of the fifteenth century were far from plain, however. Niccolò III, the lord of Ferrara, had a very splendid *credenza* in his private dining-room in 1436 (Este Invt.). It was decorated with openwork carving [*a traforo*] and with *tarsie*, and had carved human figures, probably as supports. It had silver-gilt mounts and four ring-handles, presumably for cupboard doors.[3] A Paduan inventory of 1445 (Barzizza Invt.) includes a reference to a *credentia parva sculpta* [small, carved] which one may presume concerns an object decorated with a fair degree of richness, not just a few carved details. It is curious that the Italians do not seem much to have favoured *credenze* of the elaborately carved type that was developed north of the Alps, particularly in France

and Burgundy, of which so many illustrations exist. This form often had a backboard and sometimes even a canopy, to add stateliness. Additional stages were frequently integrated into the design. The whole was then decorated with carving which could be intricate and of great delicacy. Indeed, such *buffets* or *dressoirs*, as the French called them,[4] became vehicles for the highest degree of craftsmanship. On no other class of secular furniture was such skill bestowed until the making of cabinets became a preoccupation for the best woodworkers, in the middle decades of the sixteenth century.

Being for the most part a good deal smaller than the great staged *credenze* that we discussed earlier and which were the standard earlier form, these comparatively delicate objects met a new demand that arose during the fifteenth century, namely for a compact sideboard that would not take up too much space and yet would look elegant in the smaller dining-rooms into which the powerful and wealthy retreated, seeking greater privacy, at mealtimes on all but the most formal occasions when they might still feel obliged to dine in their *sala*. Top people in Italy cannot have been ignorant of the new Northern form of mini-sideboard and examples must have existed in Italy; but they do not seem to be shown in Italian illustrations of the period so the form cannot have been widely accepted. If we are seeking Italian parallels for the Northern *buffet* or *dressoir*, we should perhaps look first to those parts of Italy lying closest to France. For instance, in the Duke of Savoy's bedchamber in the castle of Turin, in 1497–8, stood a round table that was obviously used for dining

248

248 The elaborate *credenza*, about 1565

This still has the staging associated with the simple type of *credenza* which was the earlier form (Pl. 236) but the table-support has been enclosed to form a cupboard with two doors in front, as well as two (or three?) drawers above the cupboard space. It is also smaller than the average simple *credenza* and was therefore well suited for use in the small dining-parlours that had become fashionable among the great during the quattrocento. By the time this drawing was made, the form had been rendered highly decorative with carving. There are differences between the left-hand and the right-hand sides of this design which must have been made for submitting to clients. Another design in the same album apparently has an association with Cosimo I de' Medici and dates from the 1560s.

Vatican Library (cod. Ottob. Lat. 3110) (photograph kindly provided by Prof. Jesephine von Henneberg)

249 Enclosed *credenza* serving as dressing-table

A small cupboard (note the keys in the lock), with a linen cloth laid over it, on which stand toilet items and a ewer and basin for washing the face and hands. The dish is standing upright in order to save space rather than in order that it may be seen. It is perhaps a little surprising that the aged and blind Jacob, here seen feeling the fleece on Esau's forearm, should have required such a battery of toilet preparations but perhaps some of the vessels contain medicines. The rush-seated chair with turned balusters in the back may be a *seggiola alla pistolesi* (see p. 174).

Jacopo Ligozzi (1547–1627) *Esau and Joseph*, drawing
Lugt Collection. Institut Néerlandais, Paris

249

because the next item is *ung dresseur servant a buffet* which, given the close links between the Savoy family and France, may well concern a *dressoir* in the French style – small and with elaborate carving.

Gilles Corrozet, in his *Blasons Domestiques*, published in Paris in 1539, illustrates a *dressouer* and makes it clear that such a piece of furniture could be used not only in the *salle* [*sala*] but also in the bedchamber where, with its *deux guichetz* [two cupboard doors] *bonnes choses* could be *seurement fermées & closes* [fine things ... securely enclosed and locked away]. He lists the kind of things he had in mind – jewels, and trinkets, buttons, chains, small cases and caskets full of precious treasures, and also cash. Clearly the *dressoir* served many purposes.

Pl. 51 reproduces a Ferrarese tapestry probably designed about 1470 in which is depicted a small and seemingly low, two-door cupboard with a back-board [*spalliera*]. This may well have been classed as a *credenza* (or *credenzotto*?)[5] but is no dining-room piece. It stands in a bedchamber and serves as a dressing-table; the bed is not actually visible but, at this stage, the Virgin is almost always shown absorbing the message of the Annunciation in her bedroom. Also in a bedchamber stands the even smaller cupboard to be seen in Pl. 249, a drawing by Ligozzi dating from quite late in the sixteenth century. This serves as a dressing-table although on it stand a ewer and basin, so it also served as a wash-stand where fingers could be rinsed and the face wiped when morning ablutions were being performed.

In Italy the small cupboard-like *credenza*, of plain form, was the standard model for use in bedrooms and small dining-rooms during the sixteenth century (Pl. 248) while the old-fashioned staged table-like *credenza* continued in use in the larger dining-rooms.

There seems to have been no Italian equivalent of the incredibly complicated designs for *dressoirs* invented by the famous French architect and designer, Jacques Androuet du Cerceau (Pl. 251). He brought out some twenty such designs in about 1560 at which time he was probably working at Orléans.[6] Most of the designs incorporate shelves on which vessels could be set out, many have integral cupboards, and several have drawers as well. All are elaborately carved. As far as one can make out, they do not seem to have inspired the Italians who probably found du Cerceau's mannerism altogether too undisciplined, too lacking in *misura*.

Cupboards for storage

Long before 'cup-boards' had acquired enclosed spaces fronted by doors as a common feature of their construction, there had been cupboards that anyone familiar with this English term would today recognize as such. They came in all sizes from small cupboards hanging on the wall to vast structures that must have been built *in situ*. The term used to describe a cupboard, irrespective of its size, was *uno armario* (sometimes written as *armaro* or *armadio*, but not often). Small cupboards might be called *armaretti*. However, quite a lot of small *credenze* would also today be classed as cupboards, as we have just noted (p. 220).

Most cupboards served essentially utilitarian purposes and so were undecorated, but a few were evidently handsome objects. For example, in the Palazzo Vecchio in 1553 there stood *Uno armario grande di noce con tarsie serrato* [a large cupboard of walnut decorated with *tarsie*, that could be locked], and in the study of a fine house in Verona in 1408 was to be seen *unum armarium Intaiatum picij* [of carved pine] which had a lock and seems to have been used for storing books, as were many cupboards during the Renaissance (Medici Invt., 1553, and Aleardi Invt., 1408). In a Venetian mansion in 1579, two *armadi* were present, one painted green and the other yellow and white (Pasqualigo Invt.). On the whole, however, free-standing cupboards did not form a class of furniture that added lustre to a room in Italy at this period; had they done so there would surely be more representations of them in contemporary pictures.

In many Italian pictures of the fourteenth and fifteenth centuries one does, on the other hand, see a niche in the wall, sometimes fitted with a shelf, which served as storage space or a place in which objects could easily be set aside (Pls 200, 291), and some of those niches are fitted with a cupboard door (Pl. 221). As such cupboards were fixtures, they are not normally mentioned in inventories.

Early cupboards mostly had single doors which are of course easier to make secure than the kind with paired doors; when more than one door was present, each was normally set within its own individual frame. It was not until the sixteenth century that paired doors, closing so as to meet in the centre of the opening, became common. An *armario* in the Medicis' Via Larga residence in 1553 (Medici Invt.) had four doors [*quattro sportigli*]; presumably they were arranged in two pairs.

The large cupboards still to be seen in many Italian church vestries were provided for the storage of ecclesiastical vestments but clothes in the domestic setting were mostly kept in chests, it seems, rather than in wardrobe-cupboards (Pl. 231). However, coat-hangers that could be hung on a wall or in a cupboard existed, at any rate by 1570, as Pl. 252 shows. Arms and armour might be kept in a cupboard, and Pardi notes that linen was listed as being stored in some cupboards in the Este inventories in 1436 (Este Invt.). It is of course easier to place linen in a cupboard than in a chest, and removing it is likewise simpler. Neverthless most linen was kept in chests, or so it would seem. Nobody bothered too much about convenience when it was only that of a servant that was at stake.

Desks for writing and reading

One can both write and read at the same desk but the two activities ideally require desks of different form. Most people prefer to read with the book inclined at quite a steep angle (anything from 15° to 70°) whereas writers during the Italian Renaissance liked their paper lying on a shallow slope of not more than 15°. Of course there were no rules about such matters and one not infrequently sees both books and writing-paper lying flat on horizontal surfaces. On the other hand, Fathers of the Church may sometimes also be seen penning their immortal words with their paper at what would appear to be an uncomfortably steep angle.

We have seen (p. 207) that *un descho* in the fifteenth century seems to have been a table with fixed legs or supports, and was a form quite distinct from the *tavola* which was a 'board' supported on trestles, although, during the sixteenth century, the term *tavola* came to be used for tables of all kinds. At any rate, the term *descho da scrivere* is met with continually in Italian Renaissance inventories and it meant 'a writing-desk' although this could take so many forms that the term hardly helps us envisage how a given piece so described may have looked. One can get some idea of the many possible forms from studying the illustrations that are scattered throughout this book showing studies or the Virgin Mary reading (which she is often doing in scenes of the Annunciation).

A *descho* used for writing was quite often a straightforward table providing a flat surface, sometimes quite large (Pls 232, 257). More massive tables, often architectural in character, seem also to have existed although we should perhaps not take the desks shown in all views of Renaissance studies, or of the Annunciation, absolutely literally because this is a class of furniture which seems to have tempted artists to display their talents for design, and some quite amazing confections are depicted that *may* never have existed even though it is by means inconceivable that they did (Pl. 261).

A sturdy table-top, handsomely carved round the edge, is to be seen in

250 An early enclosed *credenza*; late 1450s

This may be what was meant by a *credenza fata a la moderna* [in the new style]. It stands in the bedchamber where St Anne has just given birth to Mary. The chimneypiece is equipped for cooking (two chains for pot-hooks are visible) which may be why rows of pewterware and brassware are set out in this room. On the *credenza* is a 'cupboard cloth'. The bed has a very tall foot-board. On the right Mary, now grown up, is reading at a lectern taken out onto the *loggia* and the annunciatory angel (not visible in this detail) appears before her.

From the *Bible of Borso d' Este*, miniature, f. 14572
Biblioteca Estense, Modena

250

251 The French *credenza*

Two designs by Jacques Androuet du Cerceau for what in Italy would have been called *credenze*, published at Orleans about 1560. The Italians do not seem to have favoured *credenze* of such elaborate form, however, even though such engravings must have been known in Italy in circles interested in questions of design and fashionable furnishings.

Jacques Androuet du Cerceau, *credenza* design for *Dres soirs*, engraving, 1560
Victoria and Albert Museum, London

252 A useful cupboard; 1570

Called a *credenzone* [large *credenza*], the form has now become essentially utilitarian and could serve a variety of purposes. The two box-stools above have slots in their seats by which one could carry them about. An enlarged version serves as a writing-table complete with drawer and knee-hole. The drawer is called a *cassetta* (sometimes rendered as *cassella*). Below, a coat-hanger and an ink-well.

Bartolomeo Scappi, from *Opera*, Venice, 1570
Metropolitan Museum of Art, New York, Elisha Whittelsey Collection, Elisha Whittelsey Fund, 1952 (52.595.2 [26])

251

Pl. 253 showing St Jerome in his study – a scene dated 1451. This table is curious because its 'stake' legs are crude in comparison with the top and because one end is attached to the wall instead of having legs. It is reproduced here in order to show how a separate writing-slope could be placed on the flat surface to produce a second surface set at the desired angle. This was a common arrangement (Pls 257, 260). The portable desk could be simple, or it could be of considerable complexity (Pl. 254). On flat writing-tables could also stand the rotating reading-stands that, judging from contemporary pictures, were important adjuncts of a learned person's study (Pls 258, 259). These could also be separate units, in which case they resembled contemporary church lecterns in all respects other than in the iconography of their decoration.

Of far greater importance for the future history of furniture was the form of writing-desk which consisted of a large box-like 'table'. It could be used as it was or one could place a writing-slope on it (Pl. 260). If it was large enough, one or more rotating book-rests could also rise from it. Obviously the space contained by the box might as well be put to good use, so an opening was usually made on one or more sides to form compartments in which one could place books and documents (Pl. 255). It was but a small step to enclose such compartments with a door to form a cupboard (Pl. 259), and drawers were eventually added to these structures as well.

Another development was to make the top sloping (Pl. 255). If the desk was for reading, a small ledge was fitted along the lower edge to prevent

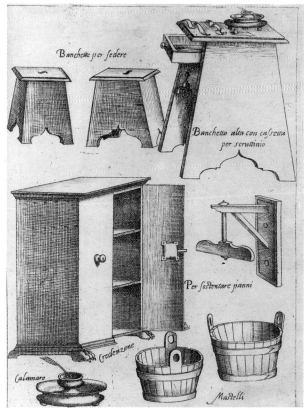

252

223

253

254

253 Writing-table and writing-slope

The terms *descho* and *deschetto* were sometimes applied to these two forms that both might be called a 'desk' in English but there was certainly no general agreement among Italians about the relevant terminology, either. *Descho* simply meant a flat surface and could be applied to a table, a tray or even a sloped writing-surface. The table here is attached to the wall and has a single 'stake leg'. The top is of framed construction with carved side-rails. St Jerome has a box-seat with a back that is braced by a side-piece (rising from the box) shaped to form a point on which the saint must surely often have banged his funny-bone. A *cuir bouilli* pen-case hangs from a nail.

Antonio da Fabriano, *St Jerome in his Study*, 1451
Walters Art Gallery, Baltimore, Maryland (37.439)

254 The enclosed 'desk' as a treasury

A French engraving showing a sloping-topped container constructed exactly like a writing-desk (see Pl. 310) but here used as a receptacle for small precious belongings. It is here called *un cabinet*. It stands on a large flat-topped chest. Had it been used as a writing-desk, it would have been called an *escritoire*. In Italian such an object might have been a *scrittoio*, but also a *descho* or *deschetto* – or, when containing valuables, as here, *un scrigno*.

From Giles Corrozet, *Les Blasons Domestiques*, 1539
Photograph kindly supplied by Simon Jervis

255

255 The block-shaped desk with sloping top, 1465

This desk is formed of a block-shaped base encompassing pigeon-holes at the side, constructed with an integral sloping top that must have an overhang above the writer's knees even if here St Augustine has one knee outside (see diagram 18, p. 361). An additional ledge is fitted along the front. The box-seat is associated with the desk; both stand on a platform to which they may be fixed. More pigeon-holes are set in the walls.

Benozzo Gozzoli, *S. Agostino*, San Gimignano
Photograph: Alinari Archives

256 A desk of 1492; a truly complicated piece of furniture

This desk has a tall superstructure with a cupboard for books and two rows of drawers below. The top is well on the way to becoming a cabinet. Beneath the overhanging writing slope is a further drawer and a niche in which several items are stored including a maiolica vase. From the revolving lectern hangs St Jerome's *cuir bouilli* pen-case. Note the spectacles hanging on a nail and the string of paternoster beads. Why does the writing- or reading-slope not have a ledge along its lower edge to prevent books sliding off?

Matteo di Giovanni, *St Jerome in his Study*
Harvard University Art Museum, Cambridge, Massachusetts
(No. 1966.3). Gift of Edward W. Forbes, in memory of his father,
William Hathaway Forbes

256

257

258

257 A desk worthy of a pope, about 1490

St Gregory is shown as if he were seated at a desk in a papal *studio* of the late fifteenth century that is furnished with great opulence. The furniture is decorated *en suite* with the wall-panelling, all being handsomely carved with classical ornament, as well as being gilded and painted. On the sturdy table stands a massive sloping-topped writing-desk, flanked by a revolving lectern with two faces and an arm above for an oil-lamp. The pope has an extra platform for his feet (not merely for comfort but as a sign of his superior rank) and a tall-backed seat draped with a width of cloth of gold. Costly objects stand on the deep cornices topping the seat and the panelling.

Giovan Pietro Birago, Milanese miniature from *The Hours of Bona Sforza* (Duchess of Milan, born princess of Savoy)
British Museum, London (MS. Add. 34294. fol. 196v)

258 Desk-unit on platform; 1482

Here shown transposed out into the courtyard, Mary would have had this unit within her bedchamber which can be glimpsed beyond. The space encompassed by the box-like desk is here utilized for shelving. A revolving lectern is attached.

Domenico Ghirlandaio, *Annunciation* (detail), the town loggia, San Gimigniano
Photograph: Scala

259 A North Italian writing desk of substance

Unless the artist's sense of perspective is faulty, this sturdy desk seems to have a sloping top. It probably has a deep overhang as well. Attached to either side are two revolving lecterns, each with four faces; their cranked supports enable them to be swung out of the way when not required. Having the cupboard doors on the front face can hardly have been convenient as it meant getting up and coming round if one wanted to find something inside. On the other hand, the writer's knees would have got in the way of doors opening towards the seat; once drawers became common, it was possible to have them on the inner side as drawers do not always need to be pulled right out and, generally speaking, they anyway take up less room than a swinging cupboard door. The amazing stone throne must be a figment of the artist's imagination for it is surely inconceivable that even a Father of the Church like St Anthony would have sat at his desk on a cold seat of such elaboration.

Gianfrancesco da Tolmezzo, *S. Antonio* Barbeano di Spilimbergo, Friuli
Photograph: Archivio-Foto Elio Ciol

260 A young Florentine scholar transcribing a text, 1480s

Built into his *studio* is a box-seat and box-desk both of which may have provided storage-space additional to that of the bookshelves. On the table-top stands his portable writing-desk, here with a hinged slope (note the lock) providing access to the inside which was no doubt fitted with compartments and possibly even small drawers. A lectern supports the large open book; it may be attached to the back of the small desk. Note the clock, and the filing-system for documents executed on slips of parchment – a sharp needle on a string.

Attavante, *Florentine Scholar*, miniature
Biblioteca Nazionale Braidense, Milan (MS. AC XIV.44f)

260

259

261

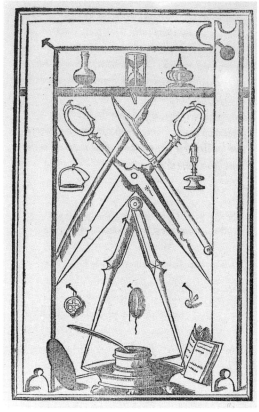

262

261 A superb desk-unit

A reading-desk and throne-like seat fixed to a wooden platform. Thus united and in a sense isolated, such an ensemble in many ways resembled a closet-like study although it was not totally enclosed. References to a *studio* in the inventory of a bedchamber may sometimes refer to such a furnishing unit. The carved and inlaid decoration of this Gothic confection is exceptionally fine and is rendered with such verisimilitude that one is inclined to accept that such a piece of furniture existed. However, it is unlikely to have stood out of doors, as seen here; it would have been placed in a sumptuous room, most likely a bedchamber.

Niccolò di Liberatore, *Annunciation*
Pinacoteca, Perugia (169) (photograph: Alinari Archives)

262 To be found in a *studio*

This shows the implements that a specialist in calligraphy considered were necessary if you wanted to write properly in 1525 (not drawn to scale; the candlestick was undoubtedly taller than the compasses in reality). The composition is framed by a set-square and a ruler. From top to bottom we see a bottle of ink, an hour-glass, a small container (for sand?), an oil-lamp that could be hung from an arm over the desk (see Pl. 292), a quill pen, a pair of scissors, a 'pen-knife' for sharpening pens, a candlestick, a pair of compasses, an ancient classical intaglio (?), some twine, a seal for impressing in sealing-wax, an inkwell with a pen in it, and a letter.

From Giovaniantonio Tagliente, *. . . la vera arte dello Excellente scrivere . . .*, Venice, 1525
British Library, London (B.L. C.31.f. 15)

263 Carved walnut reading-desk

Desk on a small platform that probably had a matching seat *en suite*. The carving in relief is characteristic of high-class Italian Renaissance furniture of the cinquecento that is mostly executed in walnut. The flowers are supported by a ring with upright sticks.

Carlo di Giovanni Braccesco, active in the 1470s until the early 16th century, *Annunciation*
Musée du Louvre, Paris

the book sliding off the sloping surface. Eventually some desks acquired a superstructure with cupboards and drawers; Pl. 256 shows a particularly elaborate example. The permutations were almost infinite; no two desks in contemporary illustrations seem to be alike and it is quite possible that a scholar or a merchant or a prince who required a desk might give rather precise instructions to a joiner as to how he wanted its various features disposed. However, there must also have been craftsmen in each great city who constructed desks to standard patterns, and one could probably buy such furniture ready-made, at least by about 1500.

The original box-like desks had no features breaking their uncompromisingly functional lines – that is, if we can trust the mostly rather primitive mediaeval pictures that show this early form – but, by our period, the box tended at least to have an overhanging cornice or moulding all round the edge of the writing surface and this grew in size to produce space underneath for the writer's knees (Pl. 255). The knee-hole desk as such was not invented until the very end of the Renaissance period (although see Pl. 245) but desks with a pronounced overhang, on one side only, were constructed well before 1500 (Pl. 310).

These developments are best shown by contemporary illustrations. They are hardly reflected in the inventories at all.

A common form of stool at the time was also box-like but with the sides sloping slightly inwards towards the top (p. 168), and this could be made taller to form a small table or a writing-desk of sorts, a *banchetto da*

263

scrivere. Such an item occurs in the Bartolo di Tura inventory of 1483 (Tura Invt.) and there is no reason why the form should have changed much in the next century so the *banchetto* shown in Pl. 252 probably gives some idea of how Bartolo's desk looked. It will be seen that it has a knee-hole and a drawer. An early version of such an elevated box-stool may have been the *scannum ad scribendum* of walnut mentioned in the Malvolti inventory of 1350 (Malvolti Invt.). In the splendid Fieschi mansion in Genoa, in 1532 (Fieschi Invt.) there was a study in which was to be found *Un scagneto . . . da scrivere* covered with red velvet. Whether this too was a small stool-like writing-desk or whether it was a writing-cabinet, as the learned editor of the inventory suggests, is not clear[1] but it was in any case a splendid object. A writing-table close-covered with red velvet is incidentally depicted by Carpaccio (Pl. 317). This has an X-type stand but seems to be fixed to a velvet-covered platform, so it could not fold. It is probable that a seat was fixed to the platform as well but this is hidden by the kneeling figure. Desks were often placed on platforms, usually with a seat *en suite*; the platform insulated the writer's feet from contact with the cold stone floor beneath.

Carving, inlay and complicated *intarsio* were all employed in the decoration of desks (Pls 12, 261, 263), and attention should be drawn to the amazing carved desk shown in a painting by Pinturicchio which is the kind of luxurious item that one might have found in a pope's study or in that of some cardinal with antiquarian interests; it must be one of the earlier expressions of revived classicism in furniture (Pl. 96).

Before moving on to discuss cabinets, what would seem to have been a splendid Medici desk should be mentioned. It stood in the family's house at Fiesole and is mentioned in the 1498 inventory (Fiesole Invt.). *Uno desco . . . grande da scrivere, con casse et spaliere, e uno armario con le cornice di noce et cassettine con tarsie* [large . . . with boxes (drawers?) and backboards, and a cupboard with a cornice of walnut with small drawers and *tarsie*]. This stood on a platform, and was fixed to the wall which suggests it was a large piece of furniture that needed steadying. One could imagine this being rather like a massive desk shown in a picture of 1492 at Harvard (Pl. 256). This has a heavily-corniced superstructure with cupboard doors and three small drawers, which would agree with the Fiesole description, as would the presence of a larger drawer under the overhanging writing slope. However, the Harvard desk has no feature that could be called a *spalliera*, let alone more than one.

While drawers had been known before the fifteenth century they were rare until the beginning of the sixteenth century but it was in the writing-desk, in its various forms, and in portable reading-stands, that drawers first became fairly commonplace (Pls 256, 295).

Cabinets

In the making of *cassette da donna* and related miniature chests and caskets (p. 204), Italian craftsmen had of necessity been forced to refine their skills to a higher degree than was required even for the finest *cassoni* and other types of large-scale furniture because, in order to create the smaller forms, much greater delicacy was called for. The joiners working in this exacting field learned to make more subtle joints, better-fitting lids and compartments, and more neatly finished interiors; the locksmiths discovered how to produce small-sized hinges and locks that worked more smoothly; and the decorators, be it inlayers, veneerers, carvers, gilders or painters, perfected their embellishing techniques. This process prepared Italian craftsmen for the challenge they were to meet in the sixteenth, when the making of a new class of furniture – the cabinet – came to be demanded of them. But before cabinet-making became a regular activity for the most skilful craftsmen, the making of another class of small-scale furniture had come to require a high degree of skill. This was the portable writing-desk.

We have already discussed these objects, with their sloping tops, and we noted how they were placed on a table or on the larger types of desk that stood on the floor (or, more commonly, on a platform). These small pieces of furniture tended to become more refined towards the end of the fifteenth century. They were better made, they were fitted out with useful compartments, and more attention was paid to their decoration (Pls 257, 260, 362). Their interiors were not only divided into compartments but were also fitted with small drawers.

Pl. 354 shows a large desk with a sloping top and with a level area at the back on which stands a small nest of three drawers. The writing-slope may have been hinged to form a lid over a shallow compartment but the details are not sufficiently clear to be sure. This picture was painted in 1488, a miniature in one of the most important commissions given to a Florentine book-illustrator at the time, and must reflect the most up-to-date ideas on how to furnish a smart modern study. If that is a reasonable assumption, then the little nest of drawers will have been in the newest fashion.

The small writing-desk was made right through the sixteenth and seventeenth centuries. It was useful because it could be used on any flat surface and it could be taken along on one's travels. Cleverly fitted out, it could even hold all one needed for normal correspondence. Because it was used so widely, not least among the wealthy, beautifully decorated versions were produced on which the utmost artistry was bestowed.

Gilles Corrozet, the Frenchman whom we have already met, describes what he calls a *cabinet*, in his work of 1539, and he illustrates it standing on a flat-topped chest. Corrozet's *cabinet* has a sloping top and is in fact of the same shape as the small writing-desks we have been discussing (Pl. 254). It happens to be filled with jewellery because, as he explains it is *remply de richesses, soit pour roynes ou pour duchesses* [filled with riches, be it for queens or for duchesses] and he enumerates the rings, precious stones, pearls, etc. that it contains. At the sides and front are small drawers. Having described the *cabinet* as an exquisite piece of furniture, he goes on to speak of the *cabinet* in the sense of a beautiful small room [*ce beau & petit lieu*] in which precious objects are kept. Among these he mentions *la gente escriptoire* [the elegant writing desk] which, by implication, because the other items are small, must also be of a portable type. It is because we think of pieces of furniture in a vacuum, as it were, as items which can be bought and sold by collectors of antiques for their own sake and without regard for their purpose, that we today find difficulty in conceiving how people in the past could use the same word to describe both a small room and a piece of furniture. But they of course thought first of an object's purpose. The small room was a private place in which precious personal belongings were kept. If you had fewer such objects, a piece of furniture serving the same purpose would suffice. It was simply a question of scale. Thus the terms *cabinet* (in French) and *scrittoio* or *studiolo* in Italian signified a housing for precious objects of a personal nature, irrespective of the container's size. This question is raised again when we come to consider studies and similar small rooms (p. 296).

Had the *cabinet* that Corrozet illustrates been shown used as a writing-desk, a purpose for which its shape was of course well suited – indeed, intended, as we see from many contemporary Italian illustrations – he would probably have called it an *escriptoire*, and when we come across the Italian equivalent, *scriptoro* or *scriptoio*, we can be fairly sure that, at least at this early date, it was to small desks of this type that reference was being made. Thus Alamanno Rinuccini had three in his house in Florence, one of which is described in the inventory of 1499 (Rinuccini Invt.) as *Uno scriptoio fermo* which was *con descho e pancha e palchetti* [a writing-desk that closes, together with a table, a bench and shelves], from which we can deduce that it lay on the table, that there was a seat for it, and there were shelves for books alongside.

The term *deschetto* was probably also used in reference to such small writing-desks. In a room called the *scriptoglio* [i.e. here the word means 'a study'] at Cafaggiolo in 1498 (Cafaggiolo Invt.) there were *Tre deschi da scrivere* and *Uno deschetto* which could here, on the other hand, mean a small table (as it would if found in a dining room; p. 207) but is more likely to mean the kind of small writing-desk we have in mind. The three *deschi da scrivere* were presumably altogether plainer items taking the form either of writing-slopes or of simple tables used for writing. The diminutive, *scrittorietto*, also occurs in inventories, at any rate from the mid-sixteenth century onwards, and may mean the same thing although, by that time, the word *scrittoio* had come to embrace an entirely different and new form of 'cabinet'.

This new form may first have been developed in Spain in the late fifteenth century, perhaps in Catalonia.[1] It consisted of a nest of drawers with a board, hinged at the bottom, that swung upwards to enclose and secure the contents (it locked at the top; see diagram 19, p. 361). Such cabinets could be placed on any flat surface at table height,[2] and when the 'falling front' was open, its inner surface provided a level plane on which one could write. This form, therefore was an extremely practical writing-desk *cum* document case. It could be made with a strong casing, with handles at the sides, eminently suitable for travelling; or it could be a delicate object, embellished with all the skills at the command of the 'cabinet maker'. The form must have become familiar throughout Charles V's Habsburg territories, and wherever else Spanish officials and their secretaries travelled. As far as Italy is concerned, one can expect to find the Spanish *escritorio* being used or imitated first in places most

264 An early cabinet?

A design executed on vellum in a book of patterns for ornaments and interior decoration, probably stemming from Ferrara or Milan and dating from the 1480s and 90s, and anyway of north Italian origin. The scale of the designs is not obvious but the object is an entity (i.e. it is not part of a scheme of panelling) and, if the six main rectangles are drawer-fronts, this then must be an early case of drawers or, if you prefer, a cabinet. There also seem to be two drawers in the base.

Courtesy of the Trustees of Sir John Soane's Museum (photograph: Ole Woldbye)

264

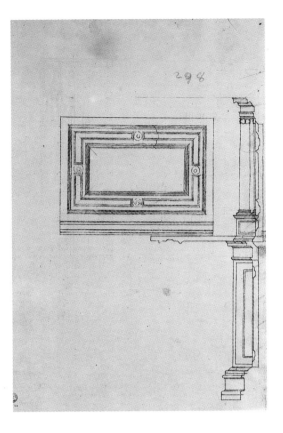

265

265 The cabinet as show-piece, 1560s

This cabinet on an enclosed stand is an imposing piece of furniture which would make it a decorative focal point of any room in which it was placed. It had a writing-leaf hinged at the bottom so that it closed upwards to cover the drawers and other compartments in the manner of all early writing-cabinets (see diagram 19, p. 361). The drawing is one of a group made by French draughstmen working in Rome in the 1560s, one of whom must have considered this object in some way remarkable, presumably because he recognized that the practical cabinet had here become a notable ornamental item.

Unknown French artist, drawing of an Italian cabinet
Metropolitan Museum of Art, New York, Elisha Whittelsey Collection, Elisha Whittelsey Fund, 1949 (49.19.39)

266 The truly ornamental cabinet, 1594

With its numerous drawers, the cabinet on the left was no doubt useful for the storage of small items but, with its cupboard-doors that could enclose the drawers or be decorative when open, this piece of furniture is primarily for display in a prominent position – which is why it appears in a drawing concerning Vanitas. Because such an object would be so conspicuous in a grand room, architects increasingly turned their attention to the design of cabinets and this specimen, strongly architectural in character, is of an advanced model that would not have seemed out of place in an early eighteenth-century drawing-room although some of the ornamental details might by then have seemed old-fashioned. Drawn by Giovanni Stradano, probably in Florence where he worked as a decorative designer for the Medici. He here dwells lovingly on the details of sumptuous furnishings which include rich vessels, boxes, baskets, a spinning-wheel and a winder for yarn, a bird-cage, a handsome chair, a portable dressing-mirror (with its shutter pulled out to expose the plate), a chest, a casket, a fine cushion, a viol, a lute, a framed picture which may be painted on glass and which probably had a mirror in its cresting and certainly has hooks along the bottom for brushes, etc. – which suggests it is an elaborate dressing-mirror.

Jan van der Straat (Giovanni Stradano), *Vanitas*
Teyler Museum, Haarlem

266

closely associated with Spain – in Genoa, Milan and Naples for a start – and what may be a reference to a writing-cabinet of this type is to be found in the Florentine Capponi inventory of 1534 (Capponi Invt.) which reads *1 iscriptorio alla napoletana dretovi [dentrovi] ischriture* [a Neapolitan *escritorio* with writings inside]. It may well be that writing-cabinets on the Spanish model were being produced in quantity in Naples by 1530 and that therefore the form was perceived in Italy as a Neapolitan product. Eleonora of Toledo, who was of course herself Spanish, had two *scrittoi alla napoletana serrati* [with locks] in her favourite room in the Palazzo Vecchio in 1553 (Medici Invt.). Had they been of Spanish manufacture, one feels the fact would have been recognized and recorded, given that context.

In the inventory of the Requesens mansion in Palermo, taken in 1561 (Requesens Invt.), mention is made of *uno scriptorietto di flandina picto*. Apart from the fact that it was painted (and for this fact to be mentioned, it suggests the painting was striking), what can have led the clerk to recognize this as coming 'from Flanders'? A variant of the fall-front cabinet, which was to become popular by 1600 and which was much produced in the Netherlands during the seventeenth century, had paired doors in front, hinged at the sides, instead of the single falling flap. Could the Flemish cabinet in Palermo in 1561 be an early example of this new form? Certainly by the 1590s cabinets of this type were being produced in Naples, as Alvar Gonzalez-Palacios, and subsequently Simon Jervis and Reinier Baarsen have shown.[3] There a 'Iacobus Fiamengo', described as *alemano scrittorista* [a 'German' maker of *scrittori*],[4] produced cabinets of both the fall-front and the paired-door variety. The earliest cabinet from his workshop known to us bears the date 1597. It has paired doors. The Fiamingo furniture described by the above-mentioned authors was produced from the 1590s and into the early seventeenth century, and is distinguished by being faced with very fine marquetry of ebony and ivory, the latter being exquisitely engraved. Fiamengo collaborated with an *intarsiatore in avolio* [a marquetry worker in ivory], at least during the 1590s and possibly later. The high level of craftsmanship exhibited by this group of furniture, which stands at the beginning of the great age of cabinet-making, shows that, by the 1590s, the craft must already have been well developed in Naples – and presumably also in Flanders. The Fiamengo group, incidentally, also includes folding tables that are of a Spanish type (p. 206), a form that may have been commonly associated with cabinets, as we have suggested above, because they too were portable.

Milanese armourers, when the need for superbly decorated armour began to fall away, started to produce other kinds of goods including cabinets in steel with fine damascene decoration. A very elaborate fall-front cabinet in this technique is dated 1567.[5] Some idea of the level of craftsmanship that could be achieved by Milanese cabinetmakers working in wood and ivory may be obtained from studying the superb spinet, dated 1577, made by Annibale de Rossi which is probably the instrument a member of the Trivulzio family kept in his cabinet of curiosities.[6] It is in the Victoria and Albert Museum in London.

These developments did not leave unaffected cities less directly influenced by Spain. In the *palazzo* of the late Lorenzo Correr in Venice in 1584 (Correr Invt.), there was to be found in his room *Un scrittoietto picolo coperto di cuoro* [a small writing-desk covered with leather] which was no doubt a handsome if small object, and may have been a local product.[7] Fynes Moryson*, who visited Italy in the 1590s, particularly mentioned the 'Cabinetts of mother of pearle' that adorned grand bedchambers in Venice at that time.[8]

Cabinets, both with fall-fronts or with paired doors (and sometimes without any front enclosure), were being made in Florence early in the seventeenth century and possibly before that.[9] They, too, were of ebony and often sported panels of *opera di commesso di pietre dure*. In the Villa Medici in Rome in 1598 (Medici Invt.) were several *studioli*;[10] one was of walnut stained black to resemble ebony, decorated with gilded arabesques, mounted with at least twenty-four gilt metal figures, and with six paintings forming doors. So precious was this object that it had a silk *padiglione* suspended over it for protection. However, by this date cabinets were no longer rare. Writing in the middle of the sixteenth century, Bandello did not mention *scrittoi* among the items of furniture one could expect to find in a splendid Italian room but, half a century later, Fynes Moryson* specifies 'cabinets' as being a characteristic feature of splendid Venetian bedchambers.

In Pl. 265 we see a drawing of a large piece of furniture that was probably to be seen in Rome in the 1560s. It consists of a cabinet with a falling front forming a writing surface, standing on a cupboard-like base. It has been given an elegant architectural form that would look handsome in any room, and was clearly not made to be moved about. It may have been two pieces of furniture on these lines that were to be seen in the *studio* and room next to it at Annibal Caro's house in 1578. Both were roomy containers, as we can see from the list of contents that is given in the inventory (Caro Invt., 1578). Each is described as a *studiolo di noce* [of walnut]: one had an upper and a lower part, inside which were kept precious objects and books, while the other held at least five boxes housing such diverse objects as some maiolica plates, a portrait of Caro, some sheets, a coverlet, and a pair of slippers. The drawing of 1594 by Stradanus, a Fleming who worked mostly in Florence, reproduced in Pl. 266 shows a large ornamental cabinet on a cupboard-base that is even more decorative.

The term *stipo* is much used by modern furniture historians in reference to cabinets like those discussed above but this word has not been noted in the inventories surveyed while preparing the present work.[11]

Mirrors and the *Restello*

Mirrors

During the Renaissance the reflecting plates of mirrors could be either of polished steel or of glass, silvered at the back. We are all familiar with the second type but mirrors of polished steel have long since ceased to be used in the domestic setting. However, during the fifteenth century and deep into the sixteenth, mirror-plates of steel seem to have been commoner than those of glass.

The modern Italian word for steel is *acciaio*. This was current in the sixteenth century, with variants like *acciale/azzale* being more common, the latter being the usual form in the fifteenth century. An especially handsome example of mirror with a steel plate must have been the *specchio de azalo con el fornimento de argento* [mirror of steel with its furnishing of silver] that formed part of the trousseau of a Trivulzio bride in 1420 (Trivulzio Invt.). Two other mirrors are listed in this inventory but the fact that this is described as having a *fornimento* suggests that it was something rather special. As Italian Renaissance mirrors normally had frames, this would not in itself be worth mentioning unless the frame were in some way distinctive (e.g. of ivory, richly carved, or painted with the family arms). *Fornimento*, therefore, may here mean that this mirror had a stand, in which case the mirror-plate may have been comparatively large. At that date most mirrors were small and could easily be held in the hand.

References to mirrors seem to be rare in Italian household inventories before 1450 or so. This could be on account of their normally being small objects, reckoned therefore among the personal possessions which were not usually included in such inventories. Mirrors were nevertheless familiar to most people of any standing by 1400 and even earlier. Dante (d.1321) knew he would be understood by his readers when, wanting to show how, some generations before his time, Florence had been an almost perfect place, he speaks of seeing a friend's wife 'come from her mirror with her face unpainted' [*venir da lo specchio la donna sua sanza 'l viso dipinto*].[1] Such natural behaviour would never be seen today, is what he is saying – and that it was in the early fourteenth century! What Dante says brings to mind Sabba da Castiglione's charming image of women using mirrors and painting their eye-lids so they looked like 'a mountain cat newly-arrived from India' [*un gatto mamone nuovamente venuto dall' India*]. Sabba was writing in the mid-sixteenth century.[2] In this respect little changed over the centuries except that mirrors became easier to procure as time went by. Women have always tended to need mirrors of some sort. Men on the whole need them less and this was particularly so during the Italian Renaissance when men were shaved by a barber.

Steel mirrors continued in use well into the sixteenth century by which time quite large plates were being produced for this purpose. One Francesco Zamberian still enjoyed the privilege, granted by the state, of making steel mirrors in Venice in 1572 and Isabella d'Este was ordering steel mirrors from that city in 1510 (she had not been satisfied with the Venetian mirror of glass that was sent to her in 1502).[3] Giuliano de' Medici sent her a steel mirror (presumably one made in Florence) in 1514 and, when thanking him, she claimed that it was 'one of the most prized of her possessions' [*una delle piu care cose che habbiamo*].[4] On the walls of a room in the Palazzo Sanuti in Bologna in 1505 (Sanuti Invt.) there were large steel mirrors. One cannot be certain what 'large' meant at that date but one might perhaps have used the adjective to describe a plate fifteen by eighteen inches. There was at least one large steel mirror in the Palazzo Vecchio in Florence in 1553 (Medici Invt.) and Sabba di Castiglione was praising the 'large and beautiful' steel mirrors made by a German, one Giovanni della Barba [Johannes Bart?]. Sabba thought one of these his

267

267 A *spera* with its *fazuol da specchio*; Venice, 1490s

A convex mirror [*spera* or *sfera*] in its frame with a fringed cloth [*fazuol*] draped decoratively over three pegs. The cloth would be pulled forward over the mirror when the room was not in use, in order to protect the plate which here is likely to be of glass. Such cloths could be expensive items that must have added a colourful note to a room. A similar mirror without its cloth is shown in Plate 144. Here an author is presenting his new work to his patroness who sits grandly enthroned and surrounded by attendants. That a mirror is shown in such circumstances is a reminder that mirrors were highly prized items which many people would think suitable for conspicuous display. This scene was first published (in reverse) in 1492.

Page from *Apocalypse*, published by Ferdinando Ongania in Venice, 1515

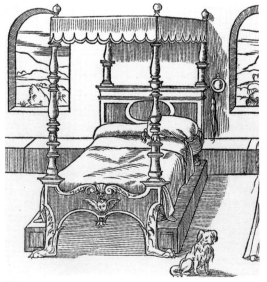

268

most prized possession.[5] It should be added that mirror-plates have been made of other metals in the past (notably bronze) but, when we read of *uno spegio de metalo* [a mirror of metal] in a Milanese inventory of 1487 [Borromeo Invt.], we can be fairly sure that it was of steel.[6]

Small glass mirrors were made in great quantity in Germany during the fourteenth and fifteenth century and many seem to have been exported. Such small objects would not necessarily be included in inventories of household goods, as we noted. A certain Vincenzo Redor, who had apparently come from Germany, is described in the Venetian archives as the *inventor fondator di specchi cristallini* [inventor and maker of crystalline glass mirrors?] in 1420[7] and it is evident that glass mirrors were being made in Venice (or, rather, on the nearby island of Murano) before the end of the fifteenth century,[8] although references to such items, specifying that they were of glass, have not been noticed in any of the inventories scanned during the preparation of this work.[9] However, in 1492 one Roberto il Franzoso [i.e. he was a Frenchman] obtained

permission to settle in Venice *e con una fornasetta far et exerciter l'arte soa zoe in far veri per specchi cristallini* [with a small furnace to exercise his art, namely to make glasses for crystalline mirrors].[10] Eleven years later the brothers Antonio and Domenico Gallo petitioned for a privilege to make mirrors *de vero cristallin, cossa preciosa et singular* [of crystalline glass, a valuable and singular material].[11] This was granted in 1507 whereafter the Venetian mirror-making industry became more firmly established, to the extent that Venice attained a dominant position in this field in the late sixteenth century – one that lasted to the end of the next century.

Nevertheless, inventory-makers often still felt it necessary to specify that a looking-glass was of glass [*de vero*, i.e. *di vetro*] until well into the middle decades of the sixteenth century. The compiler of the inventory of the important Palazzo Odoni, actually *in* Venice, the chief centre of production of such glass, did just that in 1555 (Odoni Invt.), for example. Even in 1590, in another Venetian inventory (Pollani Invt.), we find a reference to *Un specchio di cristal* but in this case the metal may have been

268 Dressing-mirror with comb-holder

A circular mirror, with its convex plate clearly shown, hangs alongside the bed and a *coda* of horsehair is suspended below, ready to receive hair-combs. This is a redrawn version of the illustration in the *Hypnero-tomachia* (see Pl. 144) which is included in the French edition of 1546. The bed has been made more robust, and has gained a head board and finials. On stylistic grounds, it seems unlikely that this was drawn as late as the 1540s: a date in the 1520s seems more likely – whatever bibliographers may say. An Italian edition of the work was published in Venice in 1545

From Francesco Colonna, *Hypnerotomachie de Polyphile*, Paris, 1546
By courtesy of the Trustees of Sir John Soane's Museum, London

269 Susanna after her bath, early 1560s

She regards her own reflection in a dressing-mirror that has quite a large plate which, by this time, will be of glass – especially as the painting is Venetian. The local glass-makers were fast learning how to make relatively large sheets of mirror-glass. Alongside the mirror may be seen a double-sided ivory comb, a bodkin (see Pl. 271), and a silver vessel that no doubt contains an expensive pomade.

Tintoretto, *Susanna and the Elders* (detail)
Kunsthistorisches Museum, Vienna

269

235

270

270 Dressing-mirror with shutter

Shown hanging on the wall (left), this mirror would have had to be set at a height in which a person could see himself – so here the figures must all be shown too small. The wooden shutter slides sideways and protects the polished plate (in this case probably of steel) when the mirror is not in use. For some reason it has been left open. Alongside hang a small dressing-case and a towel while what may be toilet-preparations stand on the shelf above. The window opposite has a curtain (one of the earliest representations of such a feature) while on the wall below is a strangely modern-looking hanging unit. In the left foreground stands a brazier and behind the bed is an occasional table with three legs. The scene is from a book on surgery and shows a trepanning operation when a hole is bored in the patient's skull. One woman looks on with fascination; another (the patient's wife?) sits weeping on a rustic chair which has a curious cresting. A small boy has also been allowed to watch and nobody has time to notice the rat (or outsize mouse) that seems to have found something to inspect well out on the floor.

From Giovanni Andrea dalla Croce, *Chirurgiae universalis opus absolutum*, Venice, 1596
Houghton Library, Harvard University, Cambridge, Massachusetts

of a particularly clear kind, that being the implication of the term *de cristal*.

The frames of 'looking-glasses' could be elaborate and of expensive materials. We have already noted a silver-mounted mirror of 1420. Three mirrors mentioned together in the Este inventory of 1436 (Este Invt.) had frames of gilded wood with the owners' coats of arms painted on them. One had a special box of painted wood to protect it. Another was described as being large and beautiful. Other Este mirrors of interest were the four made in 1466 with gilt frames which were decorated with scented pastiglia-work reliefs of *pasta de muschio et de Ambracha* [of musk and ambergris paste] for the use of Duke Lionello.[12] Such pastiglia-work was discussed on p. 96. In a Florentine bill of 1472 a carved wooden mirror frame is mentioned which was painted blue with gold decoration.[13] Mirrors with ivory frames are sometimes mentioned, one being carved with *una grillanda* [*ghirlanda*] *di figure intorno* which must mean a garland all round of figures, although whether this means human figures or some other kind of motif is not clear.[14]

Many mirrors made before 1550 were circular, or rather circular with a convex plate. This form must first have been adopted by glassmakers who were blowing glass by the so-called 'crown' process. The curved 'plate' of a convex mirror was produced by taking a section from a large bubble of blown glass. Mirrors of this form were also made of steel in imitation of the glass type. A circular convex mirror was sometimes called a *spera* because it was partially spherical; the term was mainly used in Tuscany, it

seems. The reflection to be seen in such a plate was fascinating; it enlarged, it distorted, and it enabled one to see all of the room in which it was hanging. In the Medici inventory of 1553 (Medici Invt.) mention is made of a mirror with an oval plate [*spera aovata*] which was no doubt also convex because it was claimed that it *mostra ogni lato* [shows each side, i.e. it had an especially wide reflection].[15] Once again Sabba da Castiglione makes an amusing observation on what an old man like himself sees when looking in a convex mirror that enlarges every detail. 'It gives such a magnificent reflection of the natural object', he says, 'that his eyelashes, hair and the hairs of his head look like the bristle of an old boar or the twigs of a besom, and the teeth resemble those of a Turkish horse, older than mine, which was fifty years old.'[16] Parmigianino painted his self-portrait as seen in a convex mirror (it now hangs in the Kunsthistorisches Museum in Vienna) which clearly shows the distortion; it is painted on a convex *tondo*. As can be seen, the image given by these mirrors was clear but rather dark. The character of this reflection can also be seen in the famous Van Eyck double portrait of Arnolfini and his wife in the National Gallery, London, painted in 1434. One can see a handsome *spera* hanging inside the bed depicted on a wall of the main bedchamber at the Farnesina in Rome, which was painted in about 1511 (Pl. 148).

The reflective property of a mirror was considered almost magical, even by people who were perfectly familiar with mirrors. One could not be quite sure that the astonishing capability to reflect light might not drain away or grow weaker. Did mirrors give off light? A mirror in a room, when

271 A Venetian courtesan at her toilet

She holds up a small dressing-mirror so she can see what her maidservant is doing with the aid of a bodkin [*scriminale*] to adjust the coiffure. A 'box-stool', without a slot in the top (see Pl. 252), serves as a dressing-table. She sits on a rush-seated chair of a sophisticated type with elaborate turned uprights; it was probably stained black.

Giacomo Franco, page from *Habiti d'Huomini et Donne venetiane*, Venice, 1610 (but probably first appeared in the 1570s) *Victoria and Albert Museum, London*

271

it is growing dark, will often seem to be brighter than the remaining daylight. A merchant, writing in 1396 in his study where he had just installed a mirror, could speak of 'The mirror or ray of sunlight which is a comfort to me', as if the mirror were akin to the sun and was actually a source of light.[17] This may be why Petrarch is shown as having such a mirror standing on his desk in Pl. 4. Great pains were at any rate taken to preserve mirror-plates from damage by scratching, corrosion (in the case of steel plates), spotting by flies, as well as the possibly hazardous effect of long exposure to light, about which no one was absolutely sure. For this reason we often find mirrors provided with curtains (Pl. 267), and expensive mirrors were housed in special cases, as we have seen. Sixteenth-century carved mirror-frames were quite often fitted with a shutter that masked the plate but could be pulled aside when the mirror was to be used (Pl. 270).

In his exhaustive study of the accessories of the Venetian *toilette* of the Renaissance period, Gustav Ludwig lists numerous references to the scarves or protective cloths associated with mirrors.[18] For example, one large mirror of 1530 is noted as being *con sua cortina* [with its curtain] but more often the cloth was called a *fazuol* (the modern word for a handkerchief is *fazzoletto*) and he cites many references to a *fazuol da specchio*. These cloths could be of almost any textile material; for example *un fazuol grando da spechio de Renzo* [of linen from Rheims (p. 73); 1530], another of *velle de Candia* [veiling from Candia in Crete; 1530], and one *de vello cum tremoli* [of veiling with sequins; 1513], not to speak of one *fazuol*

da specchio belissimo lavorado d'oro e de seda [exceptionally beautiful, embroidered with gold and silk thread; 1441].[19] One can see a *fazuol* draped over a mirror on the wall in the Venetian woodcut of 1492 reproduced in Pl. 268. This circular glass has pegs projecting above it over which the cloth lies; it would have been pulled over to screen the plate when the room was unoccupied. In Pl. 144 we see a simpler mirror with a triangular frame which has similar pegs set at each corner, ready to receive a *fazuol*. This was by no means just a Venetian practice; among the items in the dowry of a young Ferrarese bride in 1502 were *drapi dui di spechio* [two mirror cloths].[20]

Mirrors, then, were an adjunct of the *toilette*, they were curious (especially in their convex form), they could be used to direct light where it was needed,[21] and they were decorative. In the last category one should probably include the steel mirror *atacho alla ... spalliera* [fixed to the wall-panelling] in a room at Cesena in 1489 (Franceschino Invt.), and there can be no doubt that the circular glass mirror fixed in the middle of the ceiling [*a mezzo ditta camera sotta la trava dura*] in the Odoni mansion in Venice in 1555 (Odoni Invt.) was both decorative and curious. This brings us to mirrors used to enhance the interior architecture which was of course a practice that came to full fruition in the second half of the seventeenth century in France. However, its beginnings were to be seen in Italy which is where glass plates of relatively large size were being produced by the middle of the sixteenth century. The portrait of a four-year-old girl reproduced in Pl. 272 gives some idea of the size of mirror-plate that could be achieved by the 1560s. Clearly this mirror was considered exceptional or it would presumably not have been included in a portrait painting, an honour at that period only bestowed on items that were treasured or considered in some way marvellous.

Anton Francesco Doni wrote a book about villas in the countryside, published in 1566, in which he explained how they should be designed and arranged. He recommended that the owner should contrive to have a small room faced with large mirrors, on the ceiling, on all four walls and even, it seems, on the floor [*tutto sotto, sopra, et le quattro faccie, di specchi di piu gran quadri che trovar si potessino*].[22] Presumably a number of builders of villas took note of what Doni prescribed and actually had such closets built[23] but so far little seems to have come to light on the matter. However, it is worth remembering that Catherine de' Medici, Queen of France but an Italian by birth, had a closet that is described in the inventory taken after her death in 1589; it had no less than *Cent dix miroirs plains de Venise, enchassy dans les lambris* [one hundred and ten undecorated Venetian mirrors set into the panelling], while a portrait of her husband, Henri II, painted on a mirror was set into the chimneypiece (Medici Invt., Florence, 1589).

What is one to make of the fact that Niccolò III d'Este had a *Camera dal spechio* in the castle at Ferrara in the 1430s and that the Florentine official Alamanno Rinuccini, had a *camera degli spechi* (i.e. in the plural) in his house in the 1490s? (Rinuccini Invt., Florence, 1499). In neither case are mirrors mentioned in the inventories of these two rooms. Perhaps mirrors were set into the walls (or ceilings) or perhaps Niccolò had a scene with a mirror painted on the walls of his *camera* while Rinuccini, we know, had panelling decorated with *tarsie* and perhaps mirrors were depicted in this medium on the wall. The whole question of how mirrors came to be used as decoration deserves further study.

In the portrait of the little girl mentioned above the artist has enjoyed showing how virtually the whole figure is reflected in the large mirror. It is difficult for us to imagine how astonishing it must have seemed to our ancestors when it first became possible to see oneself reflected from top to toe in a single sheet of glass. Rabelais wrote of this after having hung a large mirror [*ung mirouer de crystallin*] in each of the closets attached to the main bedchambers of his house; he noted that they were so large that they could reflect the whole person [*de telle grandeur, que il pouvayt veritablement representer toute la personne*].[24] If Rabelais' mirrors came from Venice, as seems likely, this gives one some idea of the size of plate available around 1530.

The reflections to be seen in mirrors was a theme that provided many a writer of the period with virtually unlimited possibilities for being arch in a gently erotic vein, or for moralizing – or both. Gilles Corrozet's *Le blason du miroir* (one of his *Blasons Domestiques*, 1539) includes a long list of the charms of *la belle* who used a *Miroir de verre bien bruny/D'une riche chasse garny* [of well-polished glass, furnished with a rich case]. The author of the *Elegies de la belle fille lamentant sa virginité perdue* (Ferry Julyot, whose poem came out in 1557) makes his heroine reproach her parents for not having forbidden her to spend so much time looking at

272

herself in the mirror; obviously such indulgence, the author wishes to imply, could only lead to disaster. In a small book published in Milan in 1559 entitled *La Villa*, Bartolommeo Taegio gives his readers a dialogue between a devotee of the delights of country life and a man who greatly prefers life in the city. The latter thought everything was a bit too relaxed in the country, giving as an example the way a young woman of the city is apt to be much easier on the eye, 'made up and well turned out when she comes straight from her dressing-mirror, than when she has just got out of bed, all dishevelled and sleepy', as happens in the country [*una giovane donna e molto piu grata a gli occhi de riguradanti, quando ornata & polita se ne viene dallo specchio, che quando scapigliata & sonnachiosa esce dal letto*]. Ah, the women who live in villas are much more beautiful, charming and innocent than city women who are all artifice and mischief, he replies.

Rather a different note is struck by Giovan Francesco Straparola who, in his *Piacevole notti* of 1550–54, has a mirror insist that it loves the truth, that it never claims black is white, and has never learned to flatter. 'If

272 A mirror-glass plate of enormous size – for 1562

This little girl was four years old when her portrait was painted in 1562. Assuming that she was a normally developed child, the glass behind her must have been exceptionally large for that date and, indeed, was probably included in the portrait because the family knew it was something rather special, just as others might want a fine Turkish rug or a rare breed of lap-dog to be included in their portraits. The mirror-frame is also of interest; attention had now also to be paid to this component of what had become a conspicuous furnishing item. A large bronze figure stands on a side-table that is supported by winged sphinxes.

Girolamo Mazzola-Bedoli, *Portrait of Anna Eleonora Sanvitali*, 1562
Pinacoteca, Parma

273 A relation of the *restello*?

The tabernacle-like hanging shelf-unit houses some books, what may be jars of cosmetics, and a ewer for the washing of hands and face (the associated basin is not to be seen). Below are two pegs over which a cloth is draped; it may be a hand-towel or it could be a cloth to throw over the shelf-unit to protect the contents from dust. No mirror is visible although one might expect one to be present in association with the other toilet items. In Venice, a mirror with an elaborate framing and pegs underneath was called a *restello* (see p. 239). Andrea Sansovino, the sculptor who carved this relief in 1518–20, was a Tuscan who was called to Rome by Julius II in 1513. He may never have seen a Venetian *restello* but maybe this is a Roman or Florentine version of such a piece of furniture. Its prominence in this scene, which depicts a lady in a sumptuous bedchamber, suggests there was a connection, for the *restello* was also a very costly object made primarily for show.

Relief in the Santuario della Santa Casa, Loreto
Photograph: Scala

273

someone is happy, then I am happy too, it says; if they are sad, so am I. If an old woman looks at me, wrinkled, bleary-eyed, toothless and badly made up, tell everyone that I lie.'

The restello *and related forms*

In Italian bedchambers of the early fifteenth century there was a bed with chests all round it, there may have been more chests against the wall, and occasionally there was a table and a chair. Placing things in chests, or taking them out, is awkward and what was needed was somewhere to set aside articles in frequent use. For small objects like candlesticks, books, boxes containing treasured items, and articles connected with the *toilette*, one solution was to create a cupboard-like recess in the wall, usually without a door (Pls 200, 221, 291). These niches were often fitted with a shelf half-way up to provide an additional surface on which to place such things. Other possessions, particularly clothing, could hang on pegs driven into the walls or fixed in a row on a long board. Belts, cloaks, hoods, daggers, scarves, brushes (with a loop at one end), comb-holders, and caps

could all hang on such racks, and, because hats and hoods were the class of object most commonly seen there, such a fitment was usually called a *cappellinaio* or *capuseria*, that is a 'hat-rack' or a 'hood-rack'.[1] Because such a rack had a row of pegs (in England they came to be called cloak-pins) which in Italian are termed *caviglie*, it was sometimes called a *caviglaio*.

The *cappellinaio/cavigliaio* could be made more useful by fixing a shelf above it so that it in effect became an elongated console with pegs under the shelf (Pl. 228). When *lettiere* and *lettucci* came to have their headboards topped by a cornice that projected in a pronounced manner, as happened in the late fifteenth century, particularly in Tuscany, the cornice so resembled the contemporary hat-rack that it was sometimes actually called a *cappellinaio* even if it had no pegs (p. 114). In fact some *lettucci* with such a pronounced cornice did have pegs as well (Pl. 164).

The *cappellinaio/caviglaio* eventually became part of the 'bedroom suite'; indeed, together with the bed and the *lettuccio*, it formed the most spectacular furnishing ensemble of the time. For example, one of the major expenses connected with the wedding of Lotto di Gualfredi at

Pistoia in 1415 was a group almost certainly decorated *en suite*, comprising *una lettiera nuova intarsiata, con casse da pie, caviglaio et lettuccio* [a new bed decorated with inlay, with chests at its feet, a hat-rack and a *lettuccio*].[2] Even if they did not form part of an ensemble, such objects could be richly decorated.

Returning to the niche in the wall, it was but a small step to make this of wood in the form of a hanging cupboard. A very splendid example is to be seen in Pl. 273 which shows Sansovino's *Annunciation* at Loreto of 1518–20. Mary is using this to hold some books, a ewer and various small vessels or containers, perhaps for cosmetics. Underneath are two pegs in the wall over which is draped a cloth or a scarf. The pegs might just as well have been set into a board, in which case there would have been more than two pegs. A row of pegs set into a long batten resembles the old-fashioned wooden hay-rake which also had wooden pegs for teeth. In Italian a rake is a *rastro* and a small rake a *rastrello*. In the inventory of Poggio a Caiano (Poggio Invt.), taken after the death of Lorenzo de' Medici in 1492, we find *Dua rastelli d'albero chom pinoli che servono per chappelinai di br[accia] 2½ in circa* [two small wooden rakes with pegs (*pironi*) which serve as hat-racks of 2½ *braccia* or thereabouts]. No doubt Lorenzo's hat-rack was rather a handsome object but a *rastrello* (or *rastello*, as it became, and hence *restello* which we meet in a moment) could be an entirely utilitarian piece of furniture. In the larder of the papal kitchen shown in Pl. 347 one can see a shelf on brackets with hooks beneath, from which hang a ham, two hares and what may be *mortadella* sausages. The word *rastello* is actually inscribed on the depicted shelf.

Very different from this humble object must have been the *rastelli* which, together with *chasse dorate* [gilded chests], were the subject of a special clause in the Venetian sumptuary regulations of 1489. The citizens of Venice were forbidden to own, buy or cause to have made *rastelli* and *casse* that were gilded because such things had become *molto sumptuose et de valuta* [very sumptuous and costly], the subject of 'vain and superfluous expense' [*spexe . . . vane e superflue*].[3] Contemporary Venetian inventories confirm that the *restelli* of that city could be very splendid objects.[4] Take, for instance, a *restello dorato lavorado de relievo* [gilded and carved in relief; 1528], or another *con molte figure* [with many figures; 1512], not to speak of the many described as large, gilded and handsome [*grando e dorado bello*].[5]

One gilt Venetian *restello* in 1540 is described as being *con i suoi pironi* [with its pegs, or pins] as if these were a standard feature – which they ought to be if we remember that a *rastrello* is a small rake.[6] Many *restelli* also had a mirror built into their structure; for example, one gilt specimen in 1532 was formed *con uno spechio dentro* [with a mirror within, or at its centre] and another was described in 1534 as *Un rastrello grando indorado cum un spechio de vero dentro dicto restello cum algune figure* [a mirror of glass in the aforesaid *restello* (note the different spelling on the second mention) with various figures, (presumably carved on the frame)].[7] It did not take long before the mirror and the *restello* became integrated, so that one could not be quite sure how to describe such a combination (e.g. *uno spechio over restello de camera dorado con le arme Michiel in man di doi*

figurine [a mirror or *restello*, gilded, with the arms of Michiel, supported by two small figures; 1532]),[8] and commonly we find a *restello* described as 'with its mirror', as if this were normal (e.g. *cum el spechio* [1515], *col suo specchio* [1544], *col il suo spechio* [1560]).[9] The term *restello* disappears from Venetian inventories after the middle of the sixteenth century, by which time these wall-mirrors, with or without pegs, were simply being called *specchi*.

A single *rastelo* is mentioned in the inventories of the Este residences at Ferrara, taken in 1436 (Este Invt.); it had a shelf above two rows of pegs [*Rastelo uno de asse coverto de una asse* (i.e. one board fixed to the wall and one projecting as a shelf above) *cum doe tiere de chaichi* (*cavigli*)], and was presumably a purely utilitarian clothes-rack. The same may be said in connection with another early reference to such an object, a *restelo da calze* [for stockings] found in a Venetian inventory of 1461.[10] Also in a Venetian inventory, of four years later, is a *restelo da calze* which had a small curtain [*con la so cortineta*].[11] It would seem that other clothes-racks could also be furnished with 'curtains' or protective cloths – like the *rastellus a camera cum sua copertura parva* [a bedchamber-rack with its small cover] and the *copri capusorium* noted in a Genoese inventory.[12] Such cloths were presumably to keep away dust and flies (indeed, the last item was *pro estate* [for use in summer]). The Sansovino tabernacle-like hanging-shelf (Pl. 273) has a cloth hanging below which may well have served the same purpose. We noted that mirrors also commonly had protective cloths (in Venice, called a *fazuol* but elsewhere sometimes called a *cortina*), so when the *rastrello*, the small rake or board of cloak-pins, became combined with the hanging mirror, the protective cloth may be said to have been an optional accessory on two counts – to protect the mirror-plate as well as the objects hanging on the rack below.

The cloth needed a peg on which it could hang. Dressing-mirrors needed additional pegs for the articles deemed essential for the *toilette* – combs, comb-holders and brushes. We saw how the Venetian sumptuary law of 1489 forbade the use of gilded *rastrelli*. Similar regulations of only thirteen years earlier (1476) had forbidden citizens to have in their bedchambers *spechi, code, seole* or *peteni* of silver or gold or decorated with jewels or pearls or with embroidery.[13] These accessories to the dressing-mirror – the *coda*, the *setola*, and the *pettene*, which we discuss below – could all hang from hooks or pegs, so it is fairly clear that the *specchi* of 1476 were the forerunners of the *restelli* of 1489. Although no picture of a *restello* or *specchio* with a complete set of accessories hanging from it seems to be known, one can sometimes see one of these items hanging near a wall-mirror (Pl. 268).[14]

The *coda* [tail] was indeed tail-like, a gathering of long horse-hairs, bunched at the top, with a loop by which it could be suspended. It served as a comb-holder (*coda da pettene*); one simply dug the comb into it and for this reason it needed to hang close to a mirror (Pl. 268). One could also use the *coda* for cleaning combs by running the teeth down its length. The *coda* seems to have been a fashionable accessory in the second half of the fifteenth century and the first half of the sixteenth.[15] Instead of sticking the comb into a *coda* when one had finished combing one's hair, one could slip it into a comb-case [*busta da petteni*] which was an envelope of a textile material or leather. It could have several pockets to hold more than one comb or a small mirror, in which case it was longer and wrapped over several times before being tied up with an attached ribbon. It could have a loop by which it could be hung from a hook on the wall – or on a *restello*. The combs [*petteni*] of our period were short and broad, with teeth along both sides, one side being cut with finer teeth than those opposite (Pl. 269).[16] Combs were made of boxwood, ebony or ivory.[17] The *setola* was a brush (Pl. 302). It was usually fan-shaped, with a loop at the end of the handle. A clothes-brush, with bunches of bristles set in several rows into a rectangular wooden back, was also used. Gilles Corrozet (1539) illustrates both forms and explains the many uses to which brushes were put at the time, but those associated with mirrors were of course destined for the most delicate tasks – flicking specks of powder or the odd hair off bodices and lace collars, and so forth.

All these objects could be most beautifully made and quite often they came in sets with the dressing-mirror, as the 1476 Venetian sumptuary regulation implied. Undoubtedly forming a set were *Un spechio, una coda et una sevolla, tutti lavora di ricamo a la perosina* [all worked with embroidery in the Persian fashion, i.e. with moresques, probably in gold thread; 1529], while a fine group, described as old in 1569, was a *restello* of gilded wood with *Una sevoleta cum alchune perlete de onza atorno* [a small brush with several pearls around (its handle)] and the *Una coda de peteni con un petene dentro* [i.e. it had a comb stuck in it].[18]

There were other items associated with the *toilette* (notably the *scriminale*, a kind of pointer – in English, called a bodkin – with which women parted or fluffed out their hair) but these were usually kept in a special box or *etui* in which combs were frequently to be found. Corrozet illustrates such an *Estuy de chambre* with combs and other items in it;[19] it had a thong and could presumably be hung – on the *restello*. One is to be seen hanging on a hook next to a mirror in Pl. 270. Among the Venetian inventories we find many relevant entries, i.e. *una casseta de nogera da peteni da dona* [a woman's small walnut comb-box; 1544], *una peteniera con li sui fornimenti* [a comb-box with its equipment; 1557]; and *una casseleta de noghera da conzar la testa, scriminal d'arzento et altra cose de poca anzi niuna importanta* [a small walnut case for dressing the head, a bodkin of silver, and other items of little or no importance; 1579].[20]

Late in the sixteenth century such dressing-cases were getting so complicated that they began to require a stand, at which point we see the genesis of the dressing-table. The girl having her hair parted with a *scriminale* (Pl. 271) sits by a stool which serves as a dressing-table and on it stand cosmetics. Had all this been placed in a case, it would have resembled the *casselletta de nogara da peteni con un scagno de nogara sotto intagiado* [a walnut case for combs with a carved walnut stool underneath it] mentioned in a Venetian inventory of 1590.

At any rate, the *restello* was not really a separate class of furniture; it was simply the name given by the Venetians to a dressing-mirror that one could expect to find hanging on the wall of a bedchamber in grand houses in their city. Other people (e.g. Milanese or Genoese)[21] sometimes used the term but mostly called such an object *un specchio* – as indeed did the Venetians before the word *restello* was adopted with this particular significance for a period that coincided roughly with the first half of the sixteenth-century. Whether called *restelli* or *specchi*, they could be objects of stunning beauty.

We would, incidentally, have known without any doubt what a *restello* looked like if that which belonged to the Venetian painter Vincenzo Catena had not been destroyed. When writing a new will in 1525, he made a specific bequest of *el mio restelo di nogera con zerte figurete dentro depinto de mano de miser Zuan Belino* [my *restello* of walnut with certain small figures (set) in it painted by the hand of Master Giovanni Bellini]. The fact that the painter's name is actually mentioned shows that he was at the time regarded as an artist of renown, so the object he had thus decorated must also have been of considerable importance, as Catena's concern for its future safe-keeping implies. He would not have been pleased to know that this precious object was destined to be broken up so that the six small paintings could be shown separately. Five of them are now in the Accademia in Venice. No one knows what the *restello* was like and, delightful as the Bellinis may look on the gallery walls today, they have inevitably lost a little of their magic, for it is no longer clear to us what was the original point of their existence. Besides, to go with those paintings, the woodwork must have been of exceptional quality. This miserable piece of vandalism in the name of Fine Art must have lost us an outstanding expression of early sixteenth-century Venetian artistic creativity. Those who like to speculate about the value of works of art might care to guess what this little treasure would be worth today, had it survived.[22]

The Furniture of Hygiene

Wash-basins

The Italians, Fynes Moryson* tells us after a visit to their country in 1594, ' are neate & clenly about their bodyes, not enduring a sweaty shirte without present changing [i.e. presently changing it], and their wemen say they are not only more clenly but of sweeter complexion ... then the nations beyond the Alps'.[1] By Moryson's time this claim can have been no exaggeration. In the higher ranks of society, at any rate, where one was familiar with the pattern of polite behaviour encouraged by Giovanni della Casa's *Il Galateo* of the early 1550s and, more fundamentally, by Baldassare Castiglione's *Il Cortigiano* of some twenty-five years earlier, it was accepted that to attend to one's personal hygiene so as not to offend others was a necessary part of civilized manners. In this, as in so many other aspects of Italian life, a steady refinement had taken place during the previous century but Italians, as a race, were probably quite fastidious in this matter by the beginning of the period. People do not on the whole like being dirty or smelly. If they are taught how to keep clean, and if it is not too difficult to do so, they will mostly want to adopt a regime, practised fairly regularly, that leads to this end. At any rate, we ought not to suppose that people of the sixteenth century were much more dirty than most of us would be if we could not obtain as much hot or cold water as we please, simply by turning a tap. We also need to recognize that one does not need a bathroom in order to keep clean; it merely makes it easier.[2]

There is a certain amount of evidence that Italians of the Renaissance period were not as dirty as many people today believe.[3] Already in the fourteenth century, the *Regimen Sanitatis Salernitanum* included the recommendation that, on rising in the morning, one should wash one's hands and eyes in cold water, comb one's hair, and rub the teeth.[4] This treatise must have been familiar to all doctors of medicine and many other people of learning in the fifteenth century, as the work remained popular for a very long while. In a fourteenth-century treatise on cosmetics and on what today might be called 'beauty care', there was a section on how one should wash oneself.[5] Presumably this last was particularly directed at women, not because they were dirtier than men – far from it, one can be fairly sure[6] – but because the other information in the book must have been of primary interest to them. Ladies were enjoined to wash all over every few days with warm spring water [*ogni puochi giorni si lava tutta con acqua di fonte calda*] in *La Raffaela*, an influential manual of manners for women published in 1562. From another work we learn that the water was scented by boiling it first with some sweet-smelling substance in it [*fattore bollir dentro qualche cosa odifera*] and that the point of the whole exercise was that the resulting *delicatezza* would rejuvenate a woman's beauty [*è quella che rifiorisce la bellezza di una donna*].[7]

Women in Renaissance Italy must anyway have been forced to wash at least their faces, necks and hands frequently because they were continually washing their hair. Lucrezia Borgia, for instance, travelling from Rome to Ferrara to get married (for the third time) in the winter of 1502, had to make prolonged halts at least twice on the way, not merely because the journey was exhausting but because she wanted to wash her hair.[8] A good half century before, the Duke Francesco Sforza had advised his son Galeazzo Maria not to come back to Milan on a Saturday because on that day his mother, the Duchess Bianca, and all her ladies, would be entirely occupied in washing their hair.[9] Women, like men, wash their hair in order that it should be clean but in Renaissance Italy the washing process was in many cases connected with the far more time-consuming business of making the hair fairer, for in Italy, as the poet Firenzuola said,

274

274 A *lavabo*; late 1380s

To the left is a *lavabo* in a niche which has a sink and will have had a drain. Sometimes piped water was directly available through a tap but more often water was carried in and poured into a small cistern with its own tap, here visible suspended under the shelf on the left. Glasses and other vessels could be rinsed at the *lavabo*; ewers could be filled there with water and carried to seated diners when they were ready to perform their polite ablutions at table. A *lavabo* was more often to be seen in the dining-room; to find one in a bedchamber suggests that this house must have been exceptionally well appointed – as of course befits the parents of the Queen of Heaven. Note the vessels on the shelf above (including early maiolica?), the towels on a rail, the two cushions lying displayed at the foot-end of the bed, and the servant filling the baby's bath.

Attributed to Cennino Cennini, *Birth of the Virgin*
Pinacoteca, Siena (photograph: Alinari Archives)

275 Handwashing at the bedside in Siena; about 1435

St Anne has just given birth to Mary who is being bathed and swaddled. A servant has brought in a basin on three tall legs which seems specially designed for use alongside a bed, standing on the bed-chest. The servant pours water from a ewer over Anne's hands under which the basin catches the drops. The servant carries a long hand-towel or napkin over her shoulder. Refreshment is being carried in from the room beyond. Note the white summer hanging, the superb inlay of the head-board and bed-chests, and the lady visitor seated on one of the latter.

Sassetta, *Birth of the Virgin*
Museo di Arte Sacra, Asciano, Tuscany (photograph: Scala)

275

voi sapete che de' capegli il proprio o vero colore e essere biondi [as you know, where it concerns the hair, the correct or real colour has to be blonde]. The writer Sacchetti felt it necessary to explain that 'It is not as if Nature had made them all blonde without exception, but because brunettes have learned how to make themselves fair-haired.'[10] The process involved washing, tinting and exposure to strong sunlight. Achieving the desired shade of hair without at the same time acquiring a tanned skin – thought to be a most undesirable blemish at the time, as it may soon be deemed again – required some skill and a large straw hat without a crown known as a *solana*.[11] The manner in which this was used is shown in Pl. 192.[12] Indeed, it was a complicated business and, knowing this, we can better appreciate Isabella d'Este's apology to her absent husband for failing to write to him properly because 'having washed my hair today, it took so long to dry that the whole day just went on that' [*Havendome hozi lavata la testa, sono stata tanto a sugarla ch'el di è passato*]. That was in 1494.[13]

Apart from washing in the privacy of the bedroom or an adjacent closet, a great deal of washing of a more formal kind was associated with the taking of meals. In polite society, people invariably washed their hands before the meal and usually also did so afterwards. Although in the distant past this had primarily been done on hygienic grounds, now any serious hand-washing was done in private beforehand, and the process of washing the hands at table had long since taken on a ceremonial character, especially at banquets, and many are the descriptions of splendid festivities where this symbolic hand-washing is mentioned. The architect Filarete,* writing about an ideal palace, sometime before 1465, described the beautiful arrangements to be seen at meals there and how his lordship 'ordered water to be brought for our hands. Three young unmarried girls came in with three youths; they looked like angels. The girls were dressed in white with garlands of different flowers on their heads. Each had over her arm a white towel so that it floated as on a breeze when the arm moved a little. Each had a silver basin in one hand and a ewer in the other.' The youths were similarly equipped.[14] The normal procedure would then be for the servant to pour water (rosewater or water scented in some other way) from the ewer over the guest's hands while holding a basin underneath to catch the water. The servants whose task it was to *dare l'acqua* in this way had to be exceptionally dexterous, as was pointed out in the household instructions drawn up for the court at Urbino under Duke Guidobaldo (d.1508).[15] The normal procedure was to hold one end of the long towel, that was draped over the servant's arm or shoulder, under the basin to catch any drops that might be spilled; the towel was then used by the guest to dry the hands. Filarete wanted to go one better, however, and made the girls take the water from the basin in their mouths and pour it over the guest's hands – from their mouths, that is – which may well have seemed charming but might raise a few eyebrows if done at a banquet today. After the meal in Filarete's perfect palace the guests were able to wash their hands again, confections were brought in and later the company was entertained by girls who sang and danced. Shakespeare, in *The Taming of the Shrew* (1596–7), described the more conventional manner of extending such a courtesy to a welcome guest when the master

of the household issues order to his servants, saying 'Let one attend him with a silver bason full of rose-water and bestrew'd with flowers; Another bear the ewer, a third a diaper [i.e. a towel of linen diaper].' The washing of hands is clearly shown in Pl. 284 where a young mother is about to be served with a light meal soon after giving birth.

Any jug could serve as a ewer for the water and the basin could take many forms but tended to be a dish, quite wide in diameter so that it would catch all the water splashed over the hands. Already by the beginning of the period, in grander circles, ewers and basins were made *en suite*. One of the wedding-gifts at the Rucellai-Medici marriage of 1466 (Medici Rucellai Invt.) was *1 bacino e 1 misciroba collo smalto d'ariento* [one basin and ewer of enamelled silver, or of silver with enamelled decoration]. The common term for a ewer at the time was *una mesciroba* but, because many ewers were of bronze, one might also not infrequently call it *uno bronzino* (occasionally *uno bronzo*). Thus we find *bazile* [*bacili/bacini*] *quatro de bronzo, cum li bronzini: cum le arme de argento fin smalta nel mezo* in the Pico inventory (Pico Invt.) which shows that the basins and their ewers were of bronze with coats of arms of enamelled silver. The Duchess of Urbino offered to sell two silver-gilt ewers and basins designed by Raphael to Isabella d'Este, which no doubt attractive objects were described as *dui bacilli con dui bronzi da mano*.[16] When pewter [*stagno*] became more common, in the sixteenth century, and ewers therefore also come frequently to be made of this metal, such a vessel might also be called a *stagnara* or *stagnaria* even if it was in fact of some other metal. Among the silver in Sinibaldo Fieschi's great *palazzo* in Genoa in 1532 (Fieschi Invt.) was *Una stagnara grande d'argento facta a releva dorato* [large, of silver with gilded ornament in relief] with his arms as Governor of Corsica on it. Ewers and basins might also be made of brass or copper – *un stagnono col sui bacili de rame sotto* [with its basins of copper under it; Fieschi Invt.].[17]

The ewers and basins used in the dining-room would usually be rather large; indeed, they were often flamboyant objects that might be displayed with other silver on the *credenza* or on a sideboard when hand-washing was not in progress (Pls 101, 104). The sets used in the bedchamber tended to be much smaller, like the *baccinello* and *mescerobba* of brass mentioned in the Fece inventory of 1450 (Fece Invt.). Bedchamber sets might stand on any surface that offered itself – on a bedside chest, on a table (if one were present) or even on the floor. If a small *credenza*-like piece of furniture were in the room, this would be the ideal repository, but specialized wash-stands were rare and, where they existed, consisted of a tripod stand supporting a basin (Pl. 102). For example Niccolò da Uzzano had in his bedchamber in Florence in 1424 (Uzzano Invt.) *1 piedistallo di ferro con un bacino grande d'ottone* [a pedestal of iron with a large brass basin]. In the Uzzano villa outside Florence, one ewer with its basin was specially intended for washing the feet; indeed, references to *bacini da piedi* are not rare. Such basins will have been large and may have stood on the floor but some larger basins had tall feet (Pl. 37) and a few were so tall they looked rather like a font (Pl. 371). Smaller basins were made specially for shaving (*bacini da barbiere*) and must have been distinctive items.

Instead of the portable ewer, one could have a bucket-like vessel suspended on a hook above a basin for hand-washing. Such an ensemble had of course to remain in its appointed position, being sometimes built into a niche (Pl. 274). It must have been in such a setting that the *sechia d'ottone, con maniche e cuperchio e due buccuoli, da lavar mani* [brass bucket with handles, cover and two spouts, for washing hands] was to be used; it is mentioned in the Tura inventory of 1483 (Tura Invt.). Instead of a bucket a spouted vessel might be used for this purpose (Pl. 2). In some dining-rooms there might be a special room alongside, fitted with an *acquaio*, a fixed wash-basin often trough-like in form, which had running water fed through pipes. A splendid *lavabo* of this type, with several spouts, is to be seen at the famous Certosa at Pavia. In the Uzzano mansion, there was a hand-washing position in the *sala* that was provided with buckets [*secchie al pozzo di sala*] while an *acquaio* with a large bucket [*secchione*] is mentioned in the inventory's next entry; presumably this was for bringing in water from the piped source in an adjacent room.[18] A more sophisticated arrangement than the hanging bucket was a cistern with a tap; the *fontana da peltre* [pewter fountain] mentioned in the Ram inventory of 1592 (Ram Invt.) was probably such an item.

We saw how Filarete's girls carried not only a ewer and basin but also a towel for drying the rinsed hands. These *tovagli* or *guarda nappi* could be long, one end being hung over the servant's shoulder.[19] It no doubt required considerable skill on the part of the servant to manage the longer forms gracefully while at the same time holding a basin and pouring water from a ewer, but these ceremonial acts were of course almost like a ballet and without doubt required much practice (see above). The person whose hands were being rinsed was also given an opportunity to do this with graceful gestures and one can imagine that young ladies were shown how to manage these ablutions elegantly. It was not only the movements but also pretty hands, gorgeous rings, fine sleeves and much else that could be admired with perfect propriety on these occasions, as the basin made its rounds.

The washing of hands, or perhaps one should say the rinsing of fingers, before and after meals was part of the ceremonial associated with dining, but it played a more necessary part in the fifteenth century than in the sixteenth, by which time the use of forks for eating had become common in Italy[20] – although it still came as a surprise to many foreign visitors.[21] The use of forks of course made it unnecessary to dip the fingers into the dishes or to hold food while cutting it up, and this in turn meant that napkins did not get so soiled and hand-rinsing could be rather more perfunctory after the meal. The place-settings at the party shown in Pl. 309 include forks for each diner; the scene was painted in the 1480s. Some people liked to have their own personal set of cutlery. This could be kept in a small leather case which one's personal servant could make sure was delivered wherever one dined. Some charming designs for such cutlery may be seen in Pl. 103.

By the mid-fifteenth century water was being brought by pipes into houses of importance to provide at least one source of water, usually in the kitchen (Pl. 347 shows a late sixteenth-century kitchen *acquaio*). Careful

investigations in the palace at Urbino in recent years have uncovered a quite astonishingly intricate water and drainage system, with filtered drinking-water being taken to the kitchen and to the chief apartments, used but not very dirty water being taken through a network to flush drains, hot water being provided at strategic points, and rainwater collected from the roof being used to flush out major drains. The Urbino palace was certainly one of the most advanced buildings in the world when it was new, around 1480, but such complicated 'plumbing' could not have been devised unless an extensive background of experience and technical know-how had already existed. Filarete*, whose manuscript treatise on architecture is one of the very earliest of its kind (p. 338), hints at all this,[22] speaking of sewers, gutters, water running so that it cleans and carries away every foulness. It is all collected and runs away through subterranean channels. As for the places where water is delivered to the main rooms [*sale*], which is used 'for washing one's hands and the like' [*da lavarsi le mani e simili cose*], these can take various forms. In order to establish such systems a reliable and continuous source of water had to be present, and bringing water into cities was not straightforward. Aqueducts and other forms of conduit were required; it was not good enough to have to rely on barrels of water carried on mules (as in many parts of Rome) or by boat (as in Venice), or even on wells which were almost everywhere. A larger and steadier flow was needed if these systems were to work. Water on that scale must have been easier to obtain in the north of Italy.

In 1578 the wife of a high official in the German city of Halle received a present of two large boxes of Milanese soap for the hands. Soap produced in Venice was a luxury widely appreciated in the sixteenth century and perhaps before that.[23] On the other hand Anton Francesco Doni, a Venetian, writes in the second quarter of the sixteenth century of a man-about-town washing his face and hands 'with little pieces of Bolognese soap every morning',[24] as if that were the smart thing to do in his day rather than to use the products of his native city. Even sixteenth-century Venetians could evidently feel that the grass was sometimes greener elsewhere.

Close-stools

Latrines are smelly places, even if maintained in the best possible order, and tended therefore to be established well away from the principal apartments of a grand house – in the basement or across the courtyard, for instance. They were used mainly by the servants and there might therefore be several holes, set in a row, in the plank that served as a seat. A late mediaeval reference to a *locus communis* in a document relating to a house in Pisa probably concerns such an arrangement[1] and we can see multi-hole latrines of this sort on a sixteenth-century plan of the Palazzo dei Tribunali in Rome.[2] The owner and the chief members of his family or entourage would usually have more private arrangements, with an individual seat. Such a 'privy' could either take the form of a fixed seat set in a niche or small closet, or of a close-stool which was a moveable piece of

276

277

276 Conjugal bathing under a tent

This bath has a striped *padiglione* suspended over it. When the bath was enclosed by the hangings, a *sauna*-effect was contrived. Such a large bath is more likely to have stood in a bathroom; it us unlikely to have been brought into a bedchamber.

Niccola di Segna, scene from *The Joys of Married Life*, Palazzo Comunale, San Gimignano, Tuscany
Photograph: Scala

277 The standard bath-tub

Most people took baths in their bedchambers, as in this late fifteenth-century woodcut. The tub was rolled in and filled from jugs. After use it had to be emptied – laboriously. The lids on the bath at the rear helped to keep in the steam; this produced a *sauna*-effect of sorts. More effective was a tent suspended over the tub. Best of all was a special 'sweating closet' [*stufa*] of the kind shown in Plates 348 and 349.

From *Novelle di due preti et un clerico inamorati d'una donna*, Florence, 1500
British Library, London

278 An *orinale* at the bedhead; mid-fifteenth century

Its case is presumably of plaited straw (the *vesta* shown in Plate 279 is rather grand, being of leather). Besides meeting urgent needs at night, the *orinale* was also much used by doctors who required one for taking and studying urine samples. As the scene concerns the two saintly doctors, Cosmas and Damian, the *orinale* here serves both a practical purpose (for the sick man in the bed) and as an attribute for the medical men. They are incidentally performing that particularly spectacular miracle – transplanting the leg of a dead black 'donor' onto the amputated stump of a white patient who had contracted gangrene. Note the way the bed-curtains are arranged, quite separate from the bed; also the stool and the vessels standing on the bed-head.

Fra Angelico, predella of St Mark's altarpiece, *c*.1442
Museo di San Marco (Photograph: Scala)

278

furniture. Both forms were furnished with a removable pan, with a pierced seat that normally consisted of a padded ring, and a cover. When Machiavelli writes to a friend that 'I was on the privy seat when your messenger came, and just then I was thinking of the absurdities of the world', we cannot be sure on which type the great thinker was seated, although it is more likely that it was on a close-stool as these were mostly placed in the bedchamber or in a closet next door, where a messenger might well find the owner thus engaged; the messenger would not have pursued Machiavelli if he had retired to some truly separate retreat.[3] The matter would not have been worth mentioning if it had not been slightly ludicrous.

Gilles Corrozet (1539)[4] called a privy *La chambre secrete, ou retraict* [the secret room, or retreat] and one can often find such small spaces indicated on plans of houses (Pls 333, 335, 344). They could be in the thickness of a wall, or were often off one of those small spiral staircases (*chiocciole*) which were so popular with Italian architects and builders, but anyway tucked away, out of sight, and probably always furnished with a door (as is the one Corrozet illustrates). Architects paid some attention to the need to ventilate such places and a skilful practitioner, by the early sixteenth century, would be seeing if he could distribute the privies in such a way as to take advantage of the flushing potential of rainwater downpipes.[5] The plan reproduced in Pl. 344 shows groups of privies, set back to back in the thickness of the wall, presumably so that each group could benefit from a single downpipe from the roof.

However, a much pleasanter arrangement was to have a close-stool placed somewhere in one's apartment. If it were emptied by a servant immediately after use, the risk of it being smelly could be reduced. Nevertheless Alberti did not at all like the idea of having the close-stool actually in the bedchamber. Writing in the middle of the fifteenth century, he stated that 'there is one filthy Practice which I cannot help taking Notice of. We take Care in the Country to set the Dunghill out of the way in some remote Corner, that the Smell may not offend our Ploughmen; and yet in our own Houses, in our best Chambers (where we ourselves are to rest) and as it were at our very Bolsters, we are so unpolite as to make secret Privies, or rather Store-rooms of Stink. If a Man is Sick, let him make use of a Close-stool; but when he is in Health, surely such Nastiness cannot be too far off'.[6] But great people did not want to go to some distant part of the building every time Nature called; a much better scheme was to place the close-stool in a nearby room, a closet, a few paces from the bedchamber. If a personal servant also had to share the room with the close-stool, that was too bad. Thus Margherita Gonzaga, wife of Leonello d'Este, the heir to the throne at Ferrara, had her close-stool in her bedchamber in 1436, whereas her father-in-law Niccolò III had his in a *guardacamera* next to his bedchamber, a small room that seems to have served as a kind of dressing-room.[7] Although no doubt those who could afford to arrange matters with such refinement did so increasingly as time passed, it is to be noted that Eleonora of Toledo, Duchess of Tuscany, still had her close-stool in her bedchamber, in the Palazzo Vecchio in Florence in 1553 (Medici Invt.). This could be because it had not been possible to

devote a separate room, close by and yet sufficiently private for the purpose, when converting such an old building for her occupation. It could also be that her close-stool did actually stand in a niche, perhaps with a small door. In that case it might not have been listed as being in a separate room; for inventory-making purposes such a niche would be regarded as forming part of the room of which it was a mere extension. At any rate it is unlikely that she had this piece of furniture standing in an exposed position in her room, even though it was covered with red velvet.[8] Her husband, Duke Cosimo, had his close-stool in a servant's bedchamber – or so it seems, as none is listed among the contents of his own bedchambers (he had two, one formal and one private).[9]

The close-stool was normally called a *sedietta* in the sixteenth century but this was commonly spelt *seggetta/seggietta*. Pl. 279 shows one and it will be seen that this is box-like, heavily fringed, and will have been covered in a textile material or in leather.[10] Under the ring-seat inside was a metal pan (of brass or pewter). Sometimes the close-stool looked more like a chair that had the seat pierced with a large hole and provision for a basin underneath. Of this type may have been the *sedia da fare agio* [a seat/chair of easement] mentioned in a Sienese inventory of 1450 (Fece Invt.) and the *sedia di legna, bucarata, da camera* [of wood, pierced, belonging in the bedchamber] in another inventory from Siena (Tura Invt., 1483). In the sixteenth century armed chairs [*cathedre/carieghe* and so forth; p. 184] might also be thus pierced, in which case they might be designated *da camera*, which usually implies such intimate use. In the Fieschi mansion in Genoa (Fieschi Invt., 1532) there was *una cadrea da camera coperta di panno rosso* [covered in red cloth] while a *Cariega da far i suoi bisogni* [in which to do one's business] is listed in a Venetian inventory of 1584 (Correr Invt.). The *scharana ... da chamaroto* mentioned in the Este inventories of 1436 (Este Invt.) would also seem to have been an armchair that went 'in the small room' [*cameretto*]. An armed seat with a hole can be seen in Pl. 112.

We saw that *bucarata* meant pierced. *Forata* meant the same, as of course did *perforata*. These terms were applied to such seats. In the Bartolo di Tura mansion in Siena in 1483 (Tura Invt.) there were several *predelle bucarate* while in a Genoese house in 1451 (Negri Invt.) we find *bancheta una perforata*; both were presumably box-like seats, probably with lids – the ancestors of the form shown in Pl. 279. The *predella da catino* [with a basin] mentioned in the Florentine Uzzano inventory of 1424 (Uzzano Invt.) must have been a very early example, in that case. The pan or basin inside, incidentally, might be called *un catino, un cantharo, un pitale* as well as *un bacino/bacile*.[11]

We saw how Alberti conceded that a person who was ill might be permitted to have a close-stool placed near his sick-bed. In the house of a Tuscan glass maker, in 1546, was to be found a *predella da enfermj* which presumably was a box-like housing for pan and ring-seat (or simply a hole) used by an invalid.[12] Did this differ in any way from an ordinary close-stool?

Catherine de' Medici had several *pavillons* [Ital. *padiglioni*, tent-like canopies; p. 124] *pour couvrir une chaise d'affaires* [for covering a close-stool].[13] These pavilions will have been needed when her close-stool had to be set up 'in the field', on picnics or when watching tournaments and other outdoor activities. Presumably the equivalent was to be seen in Italy, in similar circumstances.

Even if the close-stool did not have to be seen by all and sundry, some could be very sumptuous. Particularly splendid must have been that of Sinibaldo Fieschi's wife (Fieschi Invt., Genoa, 1532) which was of box form decorated with *tarsie* [*un ascagno quadro intersiato da camera*]; it stood in a closet [*guarda camera*]. Most *seggiette*, however, even in grand establishments, seem to have been fairly plain – covered with velvet in the best apartments, perhaps, but more usually with woollen cloth [*panno*].

Rolls of lavatory-paper were of course not available during the fifteenth or even the sixteenth century. Square pieces of cloth were used instead.[14] Presumably these could be washed and used again, many times over – as with sanitary-towels which took the form of long strips of linen or cotton. The word towel, used in this connection, incidentally, suggests that some of the *tovaglie* mentioned in lists of linen during the period were in fact intended for such purposes.

The orinale

This piece of equipment is listed in inventories right through the Renaissance. It was clearly not simply used by doctors but served a common domestic purpose – namely as a vessel in which to urinate, kept near the bed, thereby saving its occupant from having to get up and go to the close-stool in times of need. Pl. 306 shows a lamp, the inner glass vessel of which is described as being like an *orinale*.[1] The vessel could be of glass, brass or even of silver.[2] It was housed in a case [*vesta*] that might be of leather (Pl. 279) or plaited straw (Pl. 278); it had cords by which it could hang.[3] Some clearly had a soft inner case as well as the *vesta*.[4] Sometimes they came in pairs, in a single container.[5]

Orinali sometimes came in a set together with a close-stool.[6]

It has been suggested that women might not find it all that easy to use as an *orinale* a vessel like that shown in Pl. 306. Be that as it may, it should be noted that the Queen of France was certainly able to use some sort of a vessel called an *orinal*, for in 1386 she received a case of *cuir boulli* (i.e. shaped leather) which was to *porter les orinaulx de la royne*; it had her coat of arms on it and could be locked with a key which suggests her vessels were valuable. This brings to mind the silver *pitale* of Biancha Maria Sforza mentioned above (p. 248) where it was suggested that this might not have been a close-stool pan but was perhaps a form of *orinale* more suited to female use. There is no reason to believe that women of high standing did not enjoy a similar level of convenience in the bedchamber as their menfolk.[7] The sick woman shown in Pl. 125 has what looks like a case for an *orinale* hanging at her bedhead but one cannot of course see the case's contents. Nevertheless, if our surmise is correct, this too seems to indicate that the *orinale* could be used perfectly well by members of either sex, and indeed many pictures exist showing doctors inspecting the contents of an *orinale* while a female patient stands by. This was a popular theme among Dutch seventeenth-century artists but Giotto depicts just such a scene in a relief on the campanile of the Duomo in Florence.

By the 1570s people began to use a euphemism for such terms as *orinale*. *Vaso dal corpo* [a vessel for bodily use, might be the translation for this phrase] was one such term. In a neighbouring room was kept *Una cassetta da tenerci il vaso dentro* [a small box to contain the vessel].[8] This vessel may of course have been more in the nature of a chamber-pot than the flask-like *orinale*. Chamber-pots were rare in Italy, judging by the few references to be found in the inventories.[9]

An item sometimes found in bedchambers or the adjacent closets was the clyster, used for administering an enema.[10] What looks like a primitive appliance for the same purpose lies under the sick-room bed shown in Pl. 125; it is constructed on the principle of a pastry-bag with which one ices a cake.

Perfume-burners

People may have been cleaner than we suppose – nice people, that is – but sources of bad smells abounded and every possible measure was taken to mask them with pleasing scents and perfumes. Bed-linen, fans, gloves and handkerchiefs were scented, sachets of sweet-smelling herbs were laid amongst stored clothing, the very name of rosewater indicates how this essential element of graceful hand-washing acquired its perfume. Scent played a prominent role in a lady's toilette; not only was it applied as it is today but scented substances were carried in special holders. Strong-smelling flowers and herbage were used to bedeck rooms on festive occasions, and herbs might be cast on the floor to give off their scent as people trod on them. But the principal weapon against evil smells was the perfume-burner.

The censer associated with religious rites is a perfume-burner and these have been in use since time immemorial to give off incense. To adapt the censer for domestic use was no great step for the householder although the clergy may have felt it somehow undermined the mysteries over which they presided. The perfume-burner was a brazier in which burning charcoal is placed; above the hot coals is a platform on which scented pastilles are laid and these give off scented smoke as the pastilles get hot. The word brazier comes from *bragiera* which Florio's* dictionary (1611) explains means 'a warming-pan [i.e. for a bed; see Pls 118, 246], a chafing-dish [i.e. for heating food]', but the Torriano edition of 1659 adds that it can also mean 'a perfuming-pan' and says the word can be spelt *braciera*.

Perfume-burners came in many sizes. A very splendid example, supported by female figures, is shown in Pl. 280. Lorenzo de' Medici had *uno profumatoio d'ottone grande et bello* [large and beautiful, of brass] at Poggio a Caiano (Poggio Invt., 1492) which had *uno fantaccino di bronze* [the small bronze figure of a warrior] either as a support or as a finial on the lid. An even more elaborate perfume-burner (or, rather a stand with six burners) is illustrated in the *Hypnerotomachia Poliphili* of 1499. Although the representation may be in part imaginary, it was probably based on an existing piece of late fifteenth-century Italian metalwork. The description

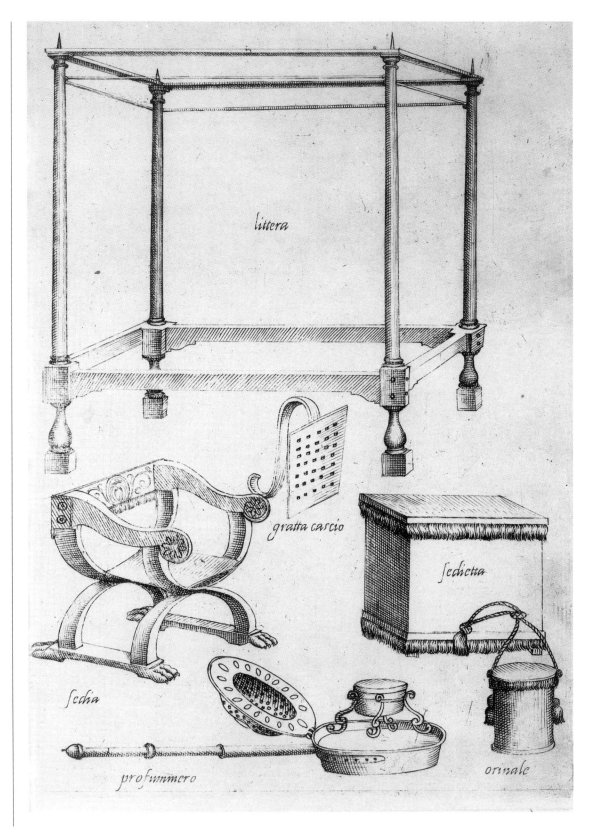

littera

gratta cascio

fedietta

fedia

profummero

orinale

279

280

279 The close-stool and the *orinale*

In the bottom right-hand corner is the carrying-case [*vesta*] for an *orinale*, a flask, usually, of glass, which looked like the vessel shown in Plate 306. Thus encased it could be carried about in a discreet manner or it could be hung up by the bedside ready for use at night (Pl. 278). Above it is a *sedietta* or *seggetta* – a close-stool with a padded ring-seat inside, under the lid, and a pan below which could be removed and emptied after use. The *seggetta* might be placed in the actual bedchamber but, where possible, was more often kept in an adjacent room. Although the *profumero* was for burning perfume, its long handle indicates that this model was for airing and scenting beds. The X-frame chair looks as if it was of the type that could no longer fold. The cheese-grater must in reality have been quite small. The rods for the curtains are clearly visible on the posted bedstead.

From Bartolomeo Scappi, *Opera*, Venice, 1570
Metropolitan Museum of Art, New York, Elisha Whittelsey Collection, Elisha Whittelsey Fund, 1952

280 An ornamental perfume-burner of about 1530

It is not quite evident how large is this object; if it was a table-ornament, one could conceive of it being about fifteen inches high but it could have been somewhat larger and have stood on the floor. The design must be by Giulio Romano and the engraving was published by Marc Antonio Raimondi in Rome about 1530.

Museum für Kunsthandwerk, Frankfurt am Main (LoA. 74/ref. 656) accompanying the illustration has it that the six boys each hold up a pan of burning charcoal which causes a sweet-smelling liquid in the small vessels above to give off a scented vapour.

A more workaday contraption is that shown in Pl. 279 which is described as a *profumerio* but it is in fact a bed-warmer [a *scaldaletto* which is also basically a brazier that has a long handle so that, when one pushes it between the sheets, all parts of the bed can be reached. But in this case it produced scented fumes as well as heat. Perfume-burners are not mentioned all that frequently in inventories of the period but Bandello, when listing the most striking features of a glamorous Roman house, makes mention of the *tanto soave odor* [the many delightful scents] to be enjoyed in this 'paradise', which was *profumata ... di legno aloe, d'augelletti cipriani, di temperati muschi e di altri odori* [with the wood of aloes, oil of cypress, wafts of musk, etc.], all of which probably were spread by perfume-burners.[1] According to Belgrano*, writing about life in Renaissance Genoa, mastic from the isle of Chios was imported for the making of pastilles to burn in *profumatoii* – or *perfumaroli*, as a Milanese inventory of 1488 (Gonzaga Invt.) also has it.

Musk of course has the amazing property of retaining other scents and so has always been a much-prized weapon in the perfumer's armoury. It was mixed with a paste and made into beads or small balls which might be held in a special spherical container that could be carried about or attached to the person (there was a chain and hook for the purpose). It was pierced so the scent could come out. The *balla de argento dorado alla venetiana con pasta de muschio dentro* mentioned in the Pico Inventory (Pico Invt., Modena, 1474) was clearly such a container, of silver gilt 'in the Venetian manner'. Necklaces and paternosters (made with beads, for telling one's prayers) could also be of a scented substance. *Pasta di Levante o Oldano* was used for this purpose but as apparently the beads were easily broken, they were often protected by a network of gold or silver thread.[2]

Musk and ambergris (also a scent-retaining medium) were added (together or separately) to a rice-paste that formed a composition from which small reliefs could be cast in moulds and used as ornaments, particularly on boxes and caskets, but also on dressing-mirrors and small chests. (See the discussion of such *pastiglia*-work on p. 96.) In the Pico inventory, just mentioned, there is also a reference to a *casete de pasta de muschio*. Such boxes survive in some quantity but it had been forgotten that they were originally scented; this was only rediscovered quite recently. Ercole d'Este had a French *parfumier* established at Ferrara in the 1460s, one of whose tasks was to fashion the scented reliefs that were to be used as ornaments on such gew-gaws.

Civet was yet another scent-retaining product reaching Italy from afar. Florio*, in his Italian-English dictionary of 1611, notes that a *Vaso di zibetto* was 'a Sivet-boxe'.

Amongst clothing or linen, or carried about wherever necessary, were what in Elizabethan England were called 'sweatebags', that is, *sachets* of lavender or other scented herbs or powders. These could be very elaborately decorated; indeed they were a vehicle commonly chosen by

ladies who wanted to demonstrate their skills with the needle on an object of small size. Such must have been the *Due piomacciuoli di baldacchino di grana broccato d'oro fino, con quattro bottoncini di perle alle nappe per ciaschuno, pieni di lavanda* [two small pillows (i.e. two *sachets*) of crimson baudekin (a silk material) brocaded with fine gold thread, with four small pearl buttons fitted to the tassels, filled with lavender] which are mentioned in the Guinigi inventory (Guinigi Invt., Lucca, 1430).

If one had failed to overpower evil smells with measures such as these, the final weapon that the perfumer could bring to bear on the problem was a scent-spray. A French inventory of 1328 mentions *deux esparjouers dorés, à gicter eaue-rose* which the erudite Henry Havard* (*Vaporisateur*) claimed was a vaporizer. It was gilded and therefore presumably of silver and was used, as the quotation indicates, for casting rosewater about the room. If the French had such devices, it seems unlikely that they were not to be found in Italy as well.

The Realm of Women

Birth-trays

Scenes of the birth of Mary, the future mother of Jesus, were a favourite theme with Italians during the Renaissance. Many hundreds of paintings of this subject must survive, dating from the mid-fourteenth to the mid-sixteenth century.[1] The theme became less popular during the later decades of the sixteenth century. In the majority of such scenes Mary's mother, St Anne, is seen sitting up in bed while the baby is being washed and swaddled. Often she is washing her hands over a basin, with water being poured from a ewer held by a servant, while another servant carries in refreshment for the young mother, a nourishing light meal to build up her strength – something to drink, some bread or biscuits, perhaps some nourishing broth, or a small bird from which to pick. The room, however, is tidy, the mother looks dignified and composed, and these scenes are not in fact of the birth itself, or even a short while after. What is portrayed is the lying-in of a mother some days after the event. In many cases friends and relatives are shown paying a visit to congratulate the mother and admire the child.[2]

The collation is usually shown being carried in by a servant, sometimes using a covered basket for the purpose but more frequently the restorative meal is being brought in on a tray (Pls 35, 126, 142, 284) which is often covered with a cloth and is occasionally carried rather daringly on the head (Pl. 37). Trays could be twelve-sided, circular or square (Pls 3, 36, 137).

The birth-scenes in which trays of various kinds are shown stem from all over Italy but trays made specially for this event, decorated with suitable subjects, seem to have been fashionable primarily in Tuscany[3] where they were so greatly prized that they were often suspended on the wall to record the birth long after the event, and passed on as family heirlooms. In Florence a tray of this kind was called *uno deschetto de parto* (1418) or *uno desco tondo da parto* (if it were circular),[4] the term reflecting its use *post partum* – after the birth. In the Uzzano inventory of 1424 (Uzzano Invt.) we find *uno descho tondo da donna di parto*, that is, for a woman in this situation, because these specially made trays were a present to her, marking this important occasion. In the inventory of Bartolo di Tura, the famous Sienese doctor, taken in 1483 (Tura Invt.), such a tray is described as *una tavoletta intarsiata da riscappate*[5] [a small table (using the term in its original sense), for a woman at childbirth, decorated with *tarsie*], which shows that they were not invariably decorated with painting, as is commonly believed today. In fact it is probable that the decoration of the *desco da parto* followed that of other classes of wooden furniture like *cassoni*; during the period up to about 1470 painted decoration was the most fashionable form while, after that, *lavoro di intarsio* became the smart thing. So Bartolo di Tura's tray with *tarsie* must have been in the very latest fashion when it was new, presumably in the middle of the century. Later, when carving became the fashionable medium for woodwork, this was obviously unsuitable for an essentially practical object like a tray, even of this special sort, which nevertheless had to present a flat surface. Women must have had meals served to them in bed after childbirth in the sixteenth century just as much as they had done in the fifteenth, and a tray of some sort must have been needed to carry it in, but we no longer hear anything about the tray and no special trouble seems to have been taken over the decoration of such objects after 1500 or so. We see trays used for this purpose in Pls 137 and 283, both of which are sixteenth-century illustrations.

Painted birth-trays vary greatly in quality. The best were produced in the same workshops as painted *cassoni* (pp. 193–5) and were decorated by the same painters. Members of the principal families in Florence, including the Medici and Tornabuoni, commissioned trays specially, prior to an eagerly anticipated birth, but others could no doubt buy trays ready-painted, with a blank space awaiting the adding of the appropriate coat of arms or some suitable emblem. Thus when the tailor Domenico da Pietrasanta bought a tray from the painter Neri bi Bicci in 1461, the painter told him it had been painted at his own expense [*dipinto a mia spesa*] which presumably means for stock, awaiting purchase.[6]

281

In the sixteenth century some potters made special sets of vessels designed for serving meals to mothers who were lying in. They were probably decorated with appropriate symbols and messages. Maybe these ceramic ensembles replaced the decorated birth-tray to some extent but references to such sets are not common.

Cradles

Cradles are often seen in pictures of the Holy Family and occasionally in scenes of the birth of Mary (Pls 283, 286). Most cradles were purely utilitarian objects, usually quite rugged and simple, but some cradles were much more elaborate because they were made for showing off the infant to visitors. In princely circles such cradles of state could be very sumptuous indeed, a vehicle for presenting to the world a child that was to continue a great family's line, if it were a boy, and which was anyway the result of a union between two prominent families. Certainly in Burgundy and in France the state cradles made in the late Middle Ages to celebrate such dynastic triumphs were very costly items[1] but the practice of showing off infants in splendid settings with a state cradle at the centre was also followed in princely circles in Italy.

A particularly handsome cradle formed a focus of the splendid arrangements that attended the birth in Milan of a child to Lodovico Sforza and Beatrice d'Este in 1493.[2] In a room dressed in the blue and white colours of the Sforza family stood a grand bed and nearby was the cradle [*cuna* or *culla*] which had been made in Milan, *assai elegante, tucta dorata, con quattro colonne cum uno sparvero galante* [very elegant, entirely gilded, with four columns and a splendid canopy].[3] The *sparviero* was of blue silk decorated with gold cords and trimmings. Alongside was a *lettuccio* which also had a canopy, and a coverlet of cloth of gold. Presumably the mother received the visitors who came to congratulate her, either lying in the bed or on the *lettuccio* which, as we have seen, was a kind of day-bed (p. 149). The aforementioned cradle was made in Milan and a Ferrarese lady attending the birth[4] admitted that it was indeed a *bellissima cuna* although the Este family had also had a cradle made for this important occasion (the child's mother was after all an Este princess) and sent over from Ferrara to Milan. The visitor wrote home loyally to say that 'our cradle' was also on display and was 'worthy of an emperor'.[5]

Half a century earlier the proud Duke Borso d'Este had sent off to his sister Isotta in Croatia another superbly decorated cradle when, in 1453, she presented her husband, Stefano Frangipane, Count of Segna, with an heir.[6] It was elaborately carved, with pierced work presumably in the Gothic style, and required gold leaf to the tune of twenty ducats for its basic embellishment, laid on by the Ferrarese court painter Andrea Costa da Vicenza, who then decorated it with appropriate scenes and the ducal arms (p. 97). It was of course a conspicuous piece of Este propaganda to the Croatians, reminding them of their dynastic connection with the proud little Italian dukedom. It seems that in order to get it to Croatia safely, it was carefully packed in cotton wool.

The Este family kept up the tradition of commissioning elaborate cradles for dynastic births in the sixteenth century. The painter Lelio Orsi, pupil of Giulio Romano and Michelangelo, designed a cradle at the request of Duke Alfonso in the 1560s.[7]

The Este were not alone in commissioning these expensive cradles. In the inventory of Lucrezia Borgia (Borgia Invt., Mantua, 1503) mention is

281 A dynastic cradle

In complete contrast to the cradles shown in Plates 283, 285 this spirited design by Giulio Romano is for a state cradle, commissioned in connection with an important Gonzaga birth – probably that of Francesco, born to Margherita Paleologa and Federico Gonzaga, Duke of Mantua, in 1533. While the design includes no family *imprese*, the general symbolism of water was one favoured by the Gonzaga family, established as it was on the banks of the River Po. A related design in the form of a boat with a sail forming a tester is in the Strahov Library in Prague. It must have been the intention that there should be four columns around the present cradle, supporting a tester or at least forming a framework for some kind of flamboyant enclosure. Presumably the cradle was to be carved in walnut with gilded details.

Giulio Romano, design for a cradle
Cooper-Hewitt Museum, New York (1911–28–169)

282 Another dynastic cradle

This design by Giorgio Vasari bearing the Medici arms surmounted by a crown must have been drawn in anticipation of an eagerly awaited birth among the most exalted members of the family – probably that of the children of Francesco de' Medici and Giovanna of Austria, the first of whom was born in 1567. Vasari, as court architect, had previously modified an apartment in the Uffizi for the couple and had designed the trappings of the bride's triumphal entrance into Florence prior to her wedding. So important were such cradles that one was preserved in the Terrazzino, a small room on a terrace at the family's Palazzo Vecchio where various treasures were kept. It was there in 1553 and had very likely been made for Francesco's birth in 1541. It was a large posted affair, of walnut, with gilded details.

Vasari, design for a cradle
Musée Bonnat, Bayonne

282

283 Sixteenth-century utilitarian cradle

Constructed with turned members like the rush-seated chair in front, this cradle will have been mass-produced and cannot have been very costly although it stands in a fine bedchamber (note the elaborate *padiglione* over the bed which has short ornamental posts). It was purely a practical piece of furniture, quite unlike the ostentatious display-cradles that are to be seen in Plates 281 and 289. The new-born Virgin can already stand up in her bath and pray, while her mother receives refreshment in bed, on a tray.

Calderari, 1532–5, *Birth of the Virgin*, St Roch, Montereale Valcellina
Photograph: Archivio – Foto Elio Ciol

284 A *desco da parto*

In this scene of the birth of the Virgin by Paolo Uccello, St Anne is rinsing her hands, assisted by a servant holding ewer and basin and furnished with a long towel. Another servant brings in refreshment set out on a tray, presumably a 'birth tray' [*desco da parto*] specially made for the occasion (see p. 252). A woman, seated on a bed-chest, is about to bathe the baby; a swaddling band lies rolled up alongside. Three ladies have come to pay their respects and a lively servant-girl hurries down the steps on the left, presumably bringing a present from a well-wisher. The regular repeating pattern on the wall, is in this case made to resemble miniver (*vaio*).

Paolo Uccello, *Birth of the Virgin*, Prato Cathedral, mid-15th century
Photograph: Scala

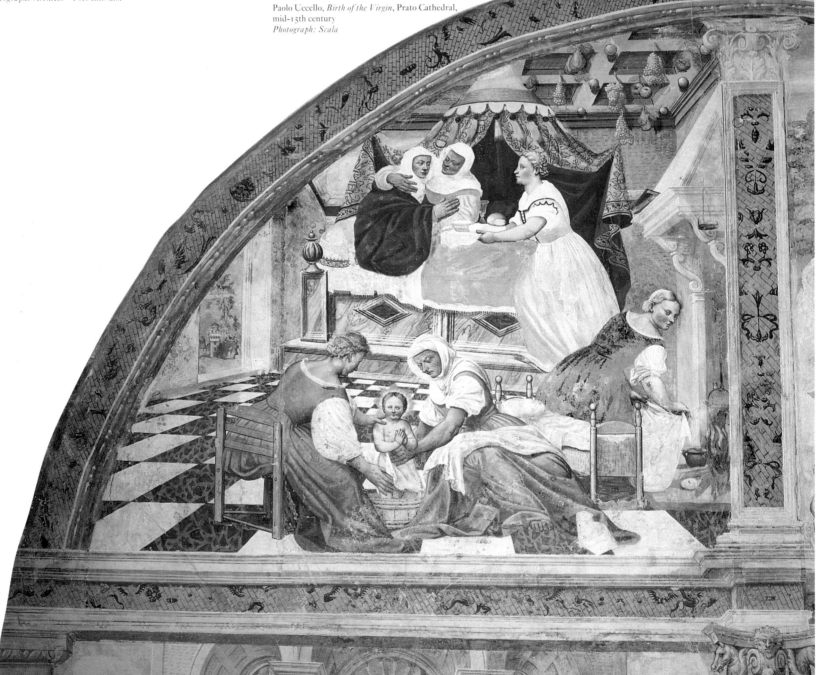

285

Not for ostentatious display like the ceremonial cradles, this is finely carved, probably in walnut, for daily use in a prosperous household (note the handsome carving of the foot-board of a large bed in the background). The semi-cylindrical form automatically produces a surface on which the cradle can rock. This shape was undoubtedly standard but Giulio Romano, who painted this scene in about 1520, has devised charming ornament for the ends. An interesting standard for an oil-lamp is in the background; it is based on Antique prototypes.

Giulio Romano, *Madonna and Child with St John and St Anne,*
c. 1520
Capodimonte Gallery, Naples (photograph: Alinari Archives)

made of a *coperta da cuna* [coverlet for a cradle] which was of an exceedingly rich gold and crimson brocade, lined with ermine. No actual cradle is listed but it can hardly have been a modest piece of furniture when its coverlet was clearly such a showy and expensive object. Designs for exceptionally elaborate Gonzaga and Medici dynastic cradles are reproduced in Pls 281 and 282.[8] Only slightly less decorative is the cradle shown in Pl. 286. It will be noted that these cradles cannot rock and are purely for show.

If it be supposed that lesser mortals did not follow the pattern set by the nobility, we should take note of the small coverlet of red taffeta lined with green silk *da culle da fanciulli* [for the cradles of children] listed in the learned doctor Bartolo di Tura's inventory (Tura Invt., Siena, 1483). Bartolo may have attended the Pope and was at home in grand circles but he was a successful professional man of the middle class with no pretension to noble, let alone princely, status. The silk coverlet for his family cradle (again, the cradle is not apparently listed) was not an inexpensive item, even if it did not have an ermine lining, and its purpose was evidently known to the clerk who compiled the inventory; that is to say, it was not just a small coverlet, it was for the cradle in which Bartolo's newly-born children were shown proudly to the neighbours – or whoever called at the house on these occasions. Dynastic considerations weighed

no less heavily with the middle classes than with the nobility; it was simply a question of how extravagant one was prepared to be when marking these important events. In order to hold back its ordinary citizens in this respect, the Milanese government introduced regulations prohibiting the use of gold and silver leaf in the decoration of cradles, as well as of *azurio fino,* the particularly expensive blue pigment from *ultramarino,* from far away.[9]

Quite a few cradles are to be seen in Italian sixteenth-century pictures. They are usually low and box-like, wider at the top than at the bottom, with vertical slab-ends that have a curved lower edge forming a rocker (Pl. 286). The slab-ends are made of quite a thick piece of wood carved in relief (in which case it is probably of walnut) and this in itself is an indication that a not inconsiderable sum has been spent on the cradle. One cradle, shown in a painting of 1579, depicting the birth of Mary, is a much more complicated affair on a tall sub-structure with large scrolled rockers (Pl. 288).

Some cradles were designed to rock fore and aft instead of from side to side. One would have thought this might have had an upsetting effect on the baby but the pattern was apparently favoured for quite a while. In the Palazzo Mansi in Lucca, carved in relief, painted blue and with details picked out in silver, is one that was rather splendid.

286 Elegant late sixteenth-century cradle

This has rockers at the base of the elaborately-carved ends and looks top-heavy. But a baby weighs little and the model was popular because one did not need to bend double to rock it. There were usually slots along the top-edge of the sides through which one could thread a tape that held the baby in place. A rush-seated chair with turned members stands on the left.

Carletto Caliari, *The Holy Family*, drawing, *c.* 1590
National Museum, Stockholm (NM1544–1863)

286

Cradles often had slots cut along the sides about half an inch down from the top edge. Into these one laced a long tape (in the manner used today for shoe-laces) so that the infant could be strapped in. The robe in which the new-born child was presented, and the cloth in which it was carried, could also be extremely richly decorated (Pls 86, 87).

Baby-walkers

These are small frames into which an infant is placed to help it learn to walk. The frame is cage-like, often wider at the bottom than at the top, and in the sixteenth century, might be fitted with wheels or castors. They may sometimes be seen in pictures (Pl. 375) but not in sufficient quantity to indicate whether there were common types. They were probably made to various standard patterns at workshops in the principal cities.

Children had leading-strings (tapes) sewn to the backs of their dresses by which a grown-up could hold them up while they were at the tottering stage. These strings also acted like a leash, helping to keep the straying child out of harm's way.

Weaving and needlework equipment

The actual weaving of textiles was an activity usually left to men except when the weaving concerned narrow-goods like ribbons, braids and the like. Indeed, women were in some places forbidden to work a loom as it was considered bad for them to be continually leaning over the warp-beam. But women were much engaged in the supporting trades, either where the weaving took place or in 'cottage industries' in the countryside nearby. The weaving of important classes of material was usually carried out at recognized centres where a large number of looms would be at work but individual looms might also be set up in private houses, especially on great estates. These domestic arrangements required a similar back-up locally, and this too was often left to women (Pl. 23). Spinning, carding, winding spools, even preparing warps, were all things in which women took a major part and sometimes the ladies of the household also became involved (Pl. 375). Certainly the mistress of the house would supervise such activities or would at least take an interest in them; they would form part of her household duties. For this reason the apparatus required for these activities was often to be found in the house (Pls 375, 376).

Another activity that occupied much time was needlework which, in the domestic context, was usually undertaken by women although the

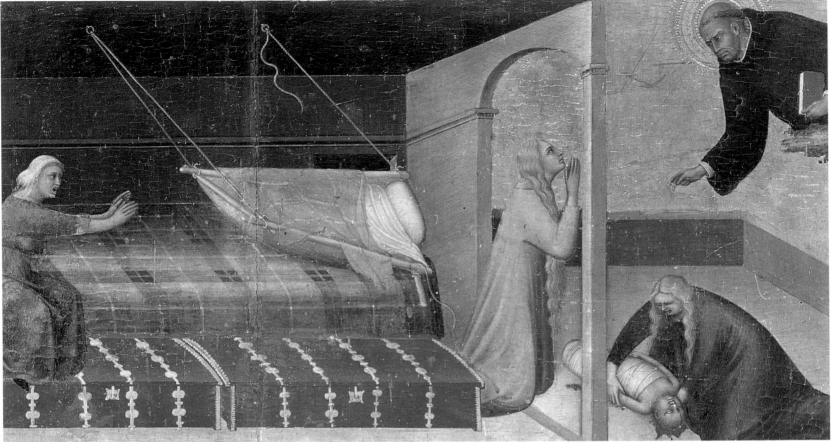

287

288

287 When the baby flew out of the window, early fourteenth century

Cradles suspended by cords from the ceiling (or a convenient branch) have been used in 'primitive societies' all over the world; the arrangement produces a particularly soothing rocking and swinging motion. The system is, however, not without its hazards, as this painting by Simone Martini shows. A cord has given way while the cradle was in full swing and the poor child has been propelled out through the window and down into the street below where, luckily, the Blessed Agostino (the scene forms part of an altarpiece dedicated to him) was at hand and the child was soon put right. Such cradles were purely utilitarian. They were probably used in humble households all over Italy right through the fifteenth century. Being very simple items, they would hardly be worth mentioning in inventories. Note the red bed-chests.

Simone Martini, *The Blessed Agostino*
Pinacoteca Nazionale, Siena (photograph: Scala)

288 A very tall cradle

Scrolls project from the rockers so that the cradle cannot swing too far over when rocking. The interior architecture of the room is unusually elegant. Note the *occhi* in the window which has a wooden frame of advanced form.

Dario Varotari, *Birth of the Virgin*, 1579
Museo Civico, Padua

289 Ceremonial cradle of the 1580s

Formed like a miniature posted bed, this cradle must have been specially made for showing off a new-born child, the fruit of a union between two powerful families. Note the small-scale arabesque decoration.

Lavinia Fontana, *Baby in a Cradle*
Museo Civico, Bologna

289

professional work produced in embroidery workshops for sale, or working to commission, was usually executed by men. Many ladies became very skilful with the needle (p. 77) and it was a matter of pride for a girl to be able to sew well. Household or other duties might occupy women for much of the day and it was anyway thought inadvisable to allow young unmarried women to be idle; that a great deal of needlework was executed for this reason of course had more to do with social convention and morals than any need for the product of such labour. However, when much of the clothing needed in a household had to be made on the premises, there was no doubt plenty of work to keep all the women occupied, when they were not otherwise engaged, on tasks to which their individual skills were equal (Pl. 299).

The making of cutwork, drawn-thread work, and *reticella* also required the use of a needle and might likewise be produced within a domestic framework (p. 84). The same applies to quilting; this too required a needle.

One sees apparatus connected with the making of textiles in quite a few pictures (Pls 23, 266, 375) and occasionally the inventories reflect the activities of women in the realm of embroidery and sewing generally (e.g. *Uno paio di forbici da donna, da cucire* [a pair of scissors, for a woman, for sewing; Tura Invt., 1483]. Embroidery of any but the smallest size requires a frame to hold the ground material stretched; we can see such a frame in Pl. 83. The *dui barri per ricamari* [two bars for needlework] mentioned in a Sicilian inventory (Requesens Invt., Palermo, 1561) were probably supports for a frame like this.

Pattern-books with designs suitable for execution by the domestic needleworker began to appear in Italy during the second quarter of the sixteenth century and a great number came out in the second half of the century. We have said something about these already and it will be remembered that most, if not all, were directed specifically at the ladies of the house (p. 80). Pl. 82 shows the first illustration of one such manual which shows four women preparing patterns for needlework – and it is clear that much skill is involved in what they are doing. Books of patterns intended for other crafts might also contain designs that could be adopted by the embroideress at home.

Flowers and Vegetation Indoors

Vases of flowers are sometimes to be seen in the contemporary illustrations but not commonly. It is probable that they were actually present more often than the illustrations would suggest, if only because we all know how much Italians take delight in flowers. Of course, a small vase of flowers does nothing to suggest an opulent way of life, which was what artists of the time were mostly trying to do in their scenes of the Birth of the Virgin, great banquets, the Annunciation,[1] etc. Rather more commonly to be seen, perhaps for that very reason, are handsome vases with pot-plants, sometimes taking the form of small flowering shrubs but more often small bushes, neatly trimmed into geometrical shapes (Pls. 48, 261, 263, 291).

More evident, at least on special occasions, seems to have been greenery of various kinds. The leaves or sprigs of sweet-smelling herbs were often cast on the floor where the servants crushed them underfoot while going about their business, thus ensuring a continual renewal of the pleasing scents.[2] The poet Pietro Aretino speaks of baskets of sweet-smelling herbs and flowers being placed in the corners of a room, presumably a dining-room; baskets were apparently commonly used for such highly ephemeral purposes.[3]

Rooms were often decorated with greenery made up into festoons which took the form of baggy compositions, either suspended at each end and looping heavily downwards or suspended at one end only and hanging straight down (Pls 50, 354). Festoons were often carefully made with leaves overlapping in a scale-pattern, sometimes studded here and there with flowers, and usually tied about with ribbon as if this were holding it all together – although it is more likely that the whole confection was built up on a core of hay to which the leaves and flowers were attached with thread or even wire. One writer in the late fifteenth century describes how one can decorate a dining-room in autumn with ripe bunches of grapes, pears and apples attached with thread [*In el autunno le uve mature, peri e pomi apicati cum filo . . .*].[4] At an important banquet at Milan in 1488, the room was decorated with festoons of juniper studded with oranges, which must have looked splendid.[5] The paintings of Mantegna often show amazing vegetal creations of this kind, composed with great refinement.[6]

Growing bushes and creepers could of course be trained up simple structures to form walls and enclosures, often with verdure forming a ceiling (Pls 49, 290). Such 'rooms' formed extensions to houses for many months of each year – they still do, as all travellers in Italy will know – but it needs to be remembered that these open-air enclosures can greatly increase the available residential space of a domestic building during the more clement times of the year.

We will not speak here of gardens[7] but these, with their general rather formal arrangement and small shady structures placed at strategic points, were in many cases seen as an extension of a house out into a controlled form of Nature. Indeed, architecture dominated Nature in Italian Renaissance gardens, even in those areas which were relatively wild and bosky. The sculptor Bandinelli, who executed a great many garden-statues which had to fit into such carefully-contrived schemes, insisted that in gardens architectural features ought to be superior to, and dictate the form of, those that are planted and grow [*le cose che si murano, debonno essere guida e superiori a quelle che si piantano*].[8]

In enclosures of foliage, a master of ceremonies in some great household might rig up an elaborate temporary arrangement of dining table, sideboards and *credenza*, all bedecked with foliage and flowers. Sometimes an entire small building was constructed in this manner for a special party. For example, Giovanni Battista Rossetti, the *scalco* [i.e. steward or senior officer] presiding over Lucrezia d'Este's household when she was Duchess of Urbino, described how he had organized a banquet for her at a villa, constructing a building of verdure with no fewer than four rooms which were provided with furniture including beds and small tables, all of verdure, while a beautiful table-arrangement round three sides of a rectangle stood in a nearby *boschetto* [bower].[9] On another occasion, Rossetti rigged up a dining-table within a space enclosed by an aviary so that the diners were surrounded by caged birds. Rossetti organized many such arrangements, but he was only one of many masters of households who were capable of creating similar temporary settings for jolly parties.

Not all flowers were natural. Flowers of silk might be used. The 'Nunnes, more spetially at Sianna [sic], Ravena, and Mantua, used to worke Curious flowers in silke, which our wemen of late have worne on their heads . . .' Fynes Moryson* tells us, writing of his visit to Italy in the 1590s.[10] Anna da Crema, one of Isabella d'Este's young ladies-in-waiting, received as a present *un mazzuolo di fiori di seta* [a bouquet of silk flowers] from one of her companions to mark some occasion in the 1530s.[11] Perhaps this was made by those nuns in the Mantuan convent that Moryson mentions. It was probably quite an expensive present.

Icons and other Wondrous Things

Certain classes of objects frequently present in Italian Renaissance rooms were sufficiently large or impressive to produce a notable effect, visually, and it therefore seems appropriate to say something briefly about them. Although all these items were small, compared with the more standard forms of furniture in the room, and could in most cases be carried and placed wherever required, they tended to remain in one position for long periods and thereby contributed to the overall appearance of the room concerned. Most if not all of these objects were kept there as rarities, curiosities or examples of especially skilful craftsmanship, but some were also functional. Their primary purpose, however, was to give delight to their proud possessor or to the occasional visitor who, it was no doubt often hoped, would, as a result of seeing these wonderful things, take away an enhanced perception of the owner's discrimination, erudition and – because we are talking about costly items – wealth.

Detached pictures

We have already said something about paintings that were executed on walls and other parts of the interior architecture (pp. 35–44) but some paintings were not integral with the structure; these were what we today call 'pictures', that is to say, loose items, usually framed, that could mostly be moved quite easily but were usually left hanging in the same position on a wall, year after year. Such detached paintings were rarely to be seen in a domestic setting at the beginning of the period but became commoner towards 1500.[1] Few rooms of any importance were without a single picture by 1600 and some rooms had a great number.

Images of the Madonna and Child, the Crucifixion, various saints, or the Annunciation were customarily hung on the walls of bedchambers; they were there for devotional purposes and varied greatly in quality. They mostly had a frame which took the form of a tabernacle; there was usually a pediment or cresting at the top and sometimes they were fitted with a pair of doors (Pls 138, 311, 374). There was, for instance, a *tabernacholo di nostra donna* in a bedchamber in the Uzzano's Via dei Bardi mansion in Florence in 1424 (Uzzano Invt.) while, in the Medici's residence on the other side of town, *Una tavola di Nostra Donna in uno tabernacolo con due sportelli dipinti* was to be seen in 1418 [i.e. it had two doors that were painted; Lydecker, *Ceti**]. The latter, incidentally, had a protective veil of silk [*con uno vello di seta innanzi*] as did another picture of this class in a neighbouring bedroom. In a ground-floor bedchamber, the doors on the tabernacle-picture could be locked [*una tavola di Nostra Donna da serare*] which suggests it was a valued item. The protective curtain could be a decorative object in its own right; one hanging in front of a two-doored picture of the Madonna in 1430 was painted with the owner's arms [*cortina dipinta a l'arme loro*].[2]

Another term for such devotional pictures was *una anchona*, which stems from the Greek word *eikon* (or icon); we see the link in a Sicilian

290

290 Extending the house with verdure

On the left the men sit at trestle-tables arranged in an 'L' plan, set up in the open just beyond a *loggia*, in a space enclosed by close-set poplars trimmed identically. On the right the ladies are dining together in a similar space framed by a hedge of rose-bushes trained to loop into an arcade against which a rich *spalliera* is suspended. With such vegetal screening, the house was as it were extended into the garden.

Filippo Lippi, details from a panel telling the story of Esther
Musée Condé, Chantilly

291 Mary's pot-plants

Inside the iron grille stands a drug-jar serving as a pot for a small shrub (box?); another plant grows in a jug in the window above, standing on a Turkish rug. The undecorated beams of the ceiling are clearly shown, and all Mary's furniture is of untreated wood – which may perhaps reflect on her humility, but she does nevertheless have no fewer than three pillows which betokens a fine lady indeed.

Carlo Crivelli, *Annunciation* (detail) 1482
Städelsches Institut, Frankfurt am Main

291

inventory of 1475 where is listed *yconectam unam veteram cum matri domini et eius unico filio domino nostro Iesu christo* [an ancient small icon with the Mother of Our Lord and Her only Son Our Lord Jesus Christ].[3] By the mid-sixteenth century, some Sicilians had abbreviated the term to *una cona* (Requesens Invt., 1561). Niccolò III, at Ferrara in 1436 (Este Invt.), had *Anchona una dipinta dorada bela de legno et cum el nostro Segnore incroxe denanzi a quela* [it was of wood, gilded and painted beautifully with Our Lord crucified fronting it]. The Marquis also owned an *anchoneta* [i.e. it was smaller than usual] with a Crucifixion scene painted on glass or modelled in glass [*lavorada de vedro*]. In Genoa an *anchona* was often called a *maiestas* (e.g. *maiestas una santorum*; Vivaldi Invt., 1456); again they were sometimes fitted with a curtain (*majestas . . . cum sua toaiolla*, Negro Invt., 1456).

By the middle of the fifteenth century, however, the tabernacle form seems to have begun to yield to the simple rectangular picture-frame with which we are today familiar. We find *Una madonna in tavolecta quadra* in a Sienese inventory of 1450 (Feci Invt.); this indicates that the picture was on a square or oblong panel and suggests that the frame was rectangular to suit it. It was housed in a painted chest and it too had a curtain [*con la tenduccia*].

These sacred icons were mostly small, made specially for a domestic setting, although some were no doubt exactly like church altarpieces, especially those 'with two doors' which very probably meant that they were triptychs, in most cases. But a new form appears towards the end of the fifteenth century, notably in Tuscany; this was the *tondo*, a circular painting, usually large, with a bold annular frame that was normally gilded. Most *tondi* depicted religious subjects like that which was *chon chorniccione d'oro di Nostra Donna e magi che oserfrono a Christo* [with a heavy gilded frame, of Our Lady with the Magi worshipping Christ],[4] but occasionally profane subjects were shown in *tondi*, an example being a 'Romulus and Remus' which is listed in the same inventory of 1498 from which the previous item was cited.

A large *tondo* is to be seen on the wall of a Florentine bedchamber in Pl. 162 and it is to be noted that *tondi* were usually hung in bedchambers, like other icons. Furthermore, they are commonly the first thing to be listed in inventories of the contents of such a room, which suggests they were prized objects.[5]

The tabernacle image might sometimes take the form of a lunette (i.e. a semicircular shape with its diameter forming the lower edge). This was known as a *colmo*. In spite of its shape, it might in some cases be housed in a rectangular case with a pair of doors that enclosed it. The *colmetto con dua sportelli* [small *colmo* with two doors] in the Palazzo Medici in 1492 must have been of this kind.[6]

Anchone printed and hand-coloured on white paper or card were available at least by 1440 in which year there is a record of their being produced in Padua. A year later the Venetian printers were complaining

292

292 Items one might find in a Venetian house around 1500

Part of a plate in a book for training the memory. No key seems to survive so we have to identify the objects ourselves. (1) Typical Venetian late-Gothic window. (2) Cupboard-type *credenza*, with cloth over it and a shelf above, together with a ewer and two wash-basins. (3) Convex mirror with its *fazuol* (see Pl. 267). (4) Flower-pot. (5) Trestle-table, with carafe and tumbler. (6) Wall-clock. (7) Devotional tabernacle with Madonna and Child (see p. 000). (8) Bed in a niche (see Pl. 56). (9) Bowl of fruit. (10) Paternoster beads. (11) Books in a study. (12) Revolving lectern with oil-lamp above. (13) Great chair or *catedra*. (14) Reading-desk in a library. (15) Desk. (16) Writing-desk and table (see Pl. 310). (17) Open books. (18) Parchment scrolls and an unidentified object. (19) Ink-well and hour-glass. (20) Pair of spectacles. The same woodcut was used in a book in 1533 on the same theme but many of the items would have been old-fashioned by 1520 (e.g. 3, 8, 13–15) which suggests the woodblock was cut even earlier – probably not later than 1500.

From Lodovico Dolce, *Dialogo nel quale si ragiona del modo di accresche en conservar la memoria*, Venice, 1562
Houghton Library, Harvard University, Cambridge, Massachusetts
(Mortimer 157)

293 A shelf with prized objects

This scholar in his *studio* keeps most of his prized possessions on the shelf that runs round the room. Apart from books, there is a flask which could be Antique, two candlesticks, several indistinct vessels, and a figurine which is probably of bronze. From the shelf hang geometric forms – a sphere and two polyhedra. In a niche fronted by a pair of doors are more books. Note the way the windows open, and the wires that brace the glass *occhi*. Precisely what the man is doing, holding up a pair of dividers at arm's length, is not too clear.

Vittorio Carpaccio, drawing *c.* 1502–05
Pushkin State Museum of Fine Arts, Moscow

293

of competition from imported printed and painted *anchone* which suggests they too were making such images.[7]

It was, however, portraits that formed the principal spearhead of the new development that took place during the second half of the fifteenth century and which was to place pictures on domestic walls and make them a common feature of rooms by the mid-sixteenth century.

Early portraits were small and tended to be of members of the owner's family. It was at first not illogical to keep such portraits in the same place as the family papers – in a secure or secluded room. It was only later, in the sixteenth century, that portraits were hung in reception rooms where they could be seen by guests, in which positions they served to remind visitors of the family's standing. Portraits, whether good or bad as art, came therefore to be a potent form of propaganda concerning the power of a family. But when, in 1466, Ippolita Sforza, Duchess of Calabria, wrote to her mother in Milan asking for portraits to hang in her private *studio* (p. 296), they were still seen as objects for personal enjoyment or, as she put it, to give her 'continual consolation and pleasure'.[8]

The identity of the sitter is quite often noted in inventory descriptions of portraits although frequently we are only told that the picture is 'the head of a man' – or of a woman. An important example of the latter is to be found in the inventory of Lorenzo de' Medici (Medici Invt., Florence, 1492) where the *colmetto* already mentioned is described as having *dipintovi dentro una testa di una donna* [painted inside it the head of a woman]. What is interesting about this little painting is that the clerk recorded it as being *di mano di maestro Domenico di Vinegia* [by the hand of Master Domenico of Venice – in fact, of Domenico Veneziano, who is of course an artist well known to students of painting in Italy].

Artists' names are rarely given in inventories, even as late as 1600, unless special circumstances prevail (e.g. listing a collector's possessions) and, even then, only star items are paid this honour – like the *quadro de san Zuanne de Titiano* mentioned in the Ram inventory (Ram Invt., Venice, 1592) which concerns Titian's *St John the Baptist*, now in the Capitoline Gallery in Rome. All other pictures in the Ram residence are identified by subject only.

294

This Titian is described as a *quadro*. As we have just noted, a mid-fifteenth-century *ancona* was painted on a *tavoletta quadra* (p. 264) and most portraits were oblong so also had frames of rectilinear form, which is of course today the commonest type of picture-frame and has been so since the early sixteenth century. Frames are mostly called *cornichi* in Italy but the Venetians called them *soaze* (e.g. there were four portraits *con le soaze d'orade et intagiade*, with carved and gilded frames, in the Pollani mansion in Venice in 1590; Pollani Invt.). While some frames were gilded all over, many more were carved in walnut and partly gilded, like much other furniture of the sixteenth century. Most were not gilded at all. Some frames were of a cheaper wood grained to resemble walnut (p. 92), and occasionally black frames are mentioned in late sixteenth-century inventories.

Although pictures might be painted on glass, like the portrait of Henri II in Catherine de' Medici's closet (p. 238; another example was mentioned above), pictures on other surfaces were probably not furnished with protective glass much before the end of the sixteenth century.[9] Glass was, however, used for protecting other precious items (in reliquaries, for instance) and the notion of using this medium for protecting paintings cannot have been difficult to conceive. Before this occurred valuable pictures had been furnished with curtains. Many instances could be cited but it should suffice to mention the portrait of Eleanora da Toledo, Duke Cosimo de' Medici's wife, which was hanging in the *sala* at the Palazzo Vecchio in 1553 (Medici Invt.; this was probably the well-known picture by Bronzino, now in the Uffizi), which had a curtain of green taffeta. At the Villa Medici in Rome in 1598 (Medici Invt.), a large painted canvas map of Europe also had a curtain of green taffeta as well as some *cordoni*. Were these cords for pulling the curtain aside or were they for hanging the picture from nails set high up on the walls so as to form a decorative

294 The contents of a cupboard; *lavorio di' intarsio*, 1521

Brilliantly rendered with inlays of different woods. Executed by Raffaele da Brescia, one of the great exponents of this illusionistic art. On the lower shelf is a box containing an ink-well and compartments for writing-implements. Its lid is propped open with a pen-knife while above hangs a bundle of uncut pens. Alongside are some letters and a small book, with an oil-lamp suspended from a pin. On the shelf above is a decorated box on which an hour-glass is balanced. The suspended vessel on the left may be an ink-well. The surround of the panel, and flanking pilasters, are finely carved with *candelabra* and trophies of woodworking tools.

Raffaele da Brescia, inlay, Chapel of S. Sacramento, San Petronio, Bologna
Photograph: Scala

295 Precious possessions of a learned man in 1480

St Augustine in his *studio* where are kept his most valued possessions, mainly on a shelf at just above shoulder height where they can be seen and may easily be reached, yet are safely out of the way. On the shelf are to be seen an armilliary sphere of brass, several books including one on geometry that is open, and a twenty-four-hour clock with weights. On the desk stands a four-sided reading-desk with a brass arm for an oil-lamp above (see Pl. 292) and drawers below (this is an early representation of such a feature). The desk must be able to rotate although this is not evident from the picture. The flat-topped desk has a carved base. The saint is using a loose board as a writing-slope, leaning it against the lectern. He holds his ink-well with a quill-pen projecting. The chequered cloth will have been woven locally (i.e. near Florence).

Botticelli, *St Augustine*, Ognisanti, Florence
Photograph: Scala

feature? This was to be a favourite method of hanging pictures in the seventeenth century. It produced a pleasing effect and made it unnecessary to hammer nails through the wall-hangings. Otherwise the usual way of hanging pictures was with one or more rings affixed to the top edge of the frame, and with a corresponding nail hammered into the wall for each ring. It should be added that at Urbino, in 1599 (Urbino Invt.), curtains on pictures were called *bandinelle*; they ran on iron rods.

We have already seen the *descho da parto*, the tray on which food and drink were brought to a post-parturient mother (p. 252). Many of these trays were painted and were kept as decorative objects, treated as pictures on the wall.

We noted that, at first, detached pictures were chiefly hung in bedchambers. Small pictures including family portraits were kept in the owner's *studio* or in his or her *anticamera*. Later, large paintings began to be hung in rooms of reception – the *sala*, *saletta*, halls and galleries. In an early seventeenth-century treatise on paintings, Giulio Mancini's *Considerazioni sulla pittura*, advice is given as to what sort of pictures should be hung where.[10] One should have landscapes and geographical subjects (e.g. maps and topographical views) in hallways to which the public are admitted. In the dining room [*sala*] should hang portraits or battle-scenes. In the bedchamber there should be religious pictures. In galleries off secluded gardens (i.e. in private spaces within an important person's apartment) it was all right to have mildly lascivious paintings but truly lascivious ones had to be kept in extremely private rooms.[11] If there were many pictures in a house, it was a good idea to build a special gallery for them, and to have them grouped according to subject and medium. It was not long before the groups came to be organized formally, set out in symmetrical arrangements with regular intervals. In some cases, by the early seventeenth century, pictures were being hung so close to each other that there was no need of wall-hangings (p. 52).

Sculptures in various media

Devotional icons might equally well be made by sculptors. Their products differed hardly at all from those of the painters except that they were rendered in high or low relief rather than on a flat plane. Indeed, many of these reliefs were painted in exactly the same way as the related paintings. Some, on the other hand, were gilded, or partly so, and others – those made of stone or terracotta, for instance – were for the most part left in their natural state.

One should here make a distinction between those reliefs which were directly carved by a sculptor as an individual work of art (if several copies were made, these too required the close attention of a sculptor) and those which were produced with the aid of a mould from which anything from, say, twelve to a hundred or more copies could be made. The former were obviously more expensive and were presumably made to order. The latter, on the other hand, while they could be delightful works of art in their own right, served the ready-made end of the trade.

In 1436 Niccolò III d'Este, the Lord of Ferrara (Este Invt.), owned an *anchona de preda viva* [i.e. of *pietra viva*, which meant of natural stone]. This must have been a carving in relief, presumably with a tabernacle-like frame. Lorenzo de' Medici, il Magnifico, had in 1492 *uno colmo di marmo* over the doors of his *anticamera*, which was *una Nostra Donna col bambino in braccio in mezzo relievo, con 4 agnoli, cio dua per lato* [Our Lady with the Child in her arms in high relief, with 4 angels, two on each side].[1] He also had, in his bedchamber, a Madonna *di mezzo relievo invetriata* which must refer to one of glazed terracotta that was almost certainly an example of the attractive products of the Della Robbia workshop (p. 109). Andrea Minerbetti, a year later certainly owned such an item, listed in his memoirs as *i nostra donna della robia murata* [on the wall, probably embedded into the wall's surface].[2] Very expensive must have been the *maiesta bella davollo cum la passione relevata* [beautiful tabernacle of ivory in relief, of the Passion] owned by a Sforza bride in 1465 (Trivulzio Invt.). In Minerbetti's *studio* was *i agnusdeo di cera* [a Pascal Lamb of wax] worked with gold which was probably also a relief, but was his little representation of St Bridget carved out of yellow amber [*i santa brigida d'ambra giallo*] a relief or was it sculpted in the round? The *Nostra Donna di gesso* mentioned in the Medici Inventory of 1553 (Medici Invt.) is anyway likely to have been a relief carving, since gesso lends itself well to coating a surface, ready for painting or gilding, rather than for working into three-dimensional form. Perhaps the least costly forms of painted reliefs of this class were those made of moulded *carta pesta* which was a form of *papier mâché*. A Madonna and Child in this medium may be seen in the small museum at Montalcino in Tuscany, which has a hole in it so one can see clearly that it is hollow behind. Could the *ancona carte cum multis figuris, vetus, posita super asseribus* [i.e. it was of paper or card, it was old and had many figures, and it was mounted on board] which was in the Aleardi mansion at Verona in 1408 have been an early example of work in this technique? *Carta pesta* is strong but needs setting on a backboard. Had this simply been a painting executed on paper, the presence of the board might perhaps not have been recorded; it would have been sufficient to describe it as a painting. The same would apply if it was printed on paper; if this were the case, it would be an early example, anyway (p. 264).

Turning briefly to sculpture in the round, so much has been written about this subject by art-historians that we here only need add a few comments.

Just as there were tabernacles executed both as paintings and in the form of sculptural reliefs, so too were there sculptural equivalents of the painted portrait. These were the portrait busts, an art form in which the Florentine masters excelled, and Vasari, writing about the sculptor Verrocchio (1435–88), actually states that portrait busts 'began to be seen in every house in Florence', placed on chimneypieces, above doors, in windows and on the shelf-like cornices that ran round panelled rooms. The finest portrait busts were executed in marble or terracotta; less costly were those executed in stucco which could be painted or gilded.

Statuettes, small sculptures of bronze or terracotta, were primarily intended for the collector who often placed them in their *studii* (p. 298) but small figurines were also to be seen in other rooms of a more or less private character.[3] The terracotta specimens might be painted to resemble bronze (e.g. the *testa di terra a bronzo* in the Minerbetti collection in 1545[4] or the set of twelve small busts of the Twelve Caesars to be seen in the house of the Venetian jeweller Antonio Fontana in 1583 which were of *stucho finse de bronzo* [stucco made to resemble bronze]).[5] Small sculpture of stucco was more common than is generally appreciated, even in the collections of discriminating connoisseurs. Alvise Odoni, for instance, owned *Un san Hieronimo de stucco* [a St Jerome] which stood on the cornice in his fine house in Venice in 1555 (Odoni Invt.). Although technically, in modern parlance, there is a difference between stucco and plaster – both were used for ceilings – it may well be that figures said to be of *stucco* were no different from those made of plaster of Paris elsewhere in Europe. When, on the other hand, a young Florentine patrician in 1472 traded in a small figure of Hercules 'of gesso' [*ercholetto di gesso*][6] in exchange for a mirror with a carved blue and gold frame (he was about to get married so it was probably part of the arrangements he was making for his future wife) it is unlikely that this was a figure in the round, as gesso was used as a covering layer in preparation for gilding or painting; it was not suitable as a modelling medium except for shallow surface-decoration. So, unless the Hercules was a three-dimensional figure with a wood or plaster core under the gesso, it must have been a figure carved in relief and thus coated. An entry in an inventory of 1546 helps us further. It refers to a *Nostra Donna di gesso* [Our Lady in gesso] in a *quadro* [a frame] which is how one would expect a relief to be presented.[7] Of course, inventory clerks may themselves have been uncertain about the difference between stucco and gesso, so we need not be too ashamed if we also are a little confused about the matter, now.

In the *quattrocento* sculptured busts might be placed in eye-catching positions, notably above doorways but also sometimes on the chimney-piece (on a mantel-shelf or a bracket).[8] It was probably not until after 1500 that special pedestals were devised to support busts at about eye-level. Such methods of display were originally associated with galleries in which an assembly of busts was to be seen.[9]

Ancient classical sculpture was of course also present – in considerable quantity, sometimes – in the houses of erudite people, or those who wished to appear so. It was placed in much the same places as 'modern' sculpture of the period but larger pieces were set up in courtyards (Pl. 319) and gardens. Much has been written on this question by others. What is likely to have been an important antique statuette was the *idolo di marmo* with a bronze base that stood in a small room in Paolo Guinigi's *palazzo* in Lucca in 1430 (Guinigi Invt.). The use of the word 'idol' indicates that it was a pagan object, which is how classical art was still viewed by Christians, back in the early fifteenth century. By the middle of the century, however, most educated people were regarding classical art as very much part of their own heritage, relevant in every way to their own thinking – and therefore constituting a class of object that was entirely suitable for the adornment of their own houses.

Arms and armour

'If by chance you were to ask me which ornaments I would desire above all others in my house, I would reply, without much pause for reflection, Arms and Books', said Fra Sabba da Castiglione, adding that the arms should be of fine quality, made by a first-rate Italian or German armourer, and they should of course be kept polished and bright.[1] Castiglione was a Knight of St John, a military order, and had been stationed for years on the island of Rhodes, in the very front line of defence against the Turks, so naturally regarded arms as especially important. Nevertheless, arms of high quality, finely decorated as the best specimens were, might be seen here and there in Italian Renaissance houses, kept more for specimens of superb craftsmanship than for use, and it is worth noting that Italian gentlemen did not on the whole walk about armed in the street.[2] That sort of thing was left to rowdies and hired assassins. Princes might have bodyguards, and the porter who guarded the front door of a great house would probably have a defensive weapon ready to hand to keep out undesirables. Moreover, military gentlemen and mercenary troops (who had largely superseded citizen-armies by the mid-fifteenth century) carried arms when going about their business.

By and large, then, Italians did not spend much money on what one modern authority has called 'ostentatious military gear'[3] and references to arms and armour do not loom large in Italian domestic inventories of the period. One finds a peg-rack for arms [*un cappucciaio da arme*] in the main bedroom of the Fece house in Siena in 1450 (Fece Invt.), and, in a Venetian house in 1592, there was another rack (apparently in the *portego* or *sala*; Ram Invt.) holding fourteen pikes and lances and some shields with the family's arms [*restelliera con picche e lanze . . .*] which would seem to have been more of a decorative feature than equipment set out ready for action.

Some officials had to carry arms ceremonially as reminders that they were appointed to uphold law and order. When a Florentine patrician was elected *podestà* of his city, for instance, he had to don military garb in order to parade through the streets on taking up office, but it was not unusual for him to borrow such equipment for the occasion. The three small shields carried as symbols of office [*tre targhette da portare in uficio*] in the Medici house at Fiesole in 1498 (Medici Invt.) must have been of this class; they were evidently more decorative than useful as they were kept in a lady's antechamber, along with a Moorish leather shield [*targheta moresca di cuoro*], and it is quite possible that they were arranged ornamentally. More serious, probably, was the sheathed sword hanging on the wall in the owner's bedchamber at the Venturini house in Venice in 1454 (Venturini Invt.). That may have been kept there just in case there was a need to drive off intruders at night. But it may equally well have been a badge of office.

Some weapons were of course associated with hunting. These were mostly to be found in country houses.

Clocks and scientific instruments

A careful study of the illustrations in this book will show that clocks are often represented. This does not mean that clocks were common in Renaissance Italy but rather that artists in the first place often chose to depict clocks among the objects that were to be seen in the private studies of learned men and that, later on, people with intellectual pretensions, when sitting for their portraits, sometimes asked the artist to include a clock among the props.

To possess a clock set one somewhat apart from one's fellow men. It indicated that one could tell the time and implied that one could make practical use of this information. Moreover, to most people clockwork seemed almost magical and, if the owner appeared to understand its workings, then he must indeed be clever. And, anyway, clocks were expensive items to buy and costly to maintain. But they were fun, especially if they rang bells, or if they worked ancillary mechanisms of various kinds, as was beginning to happen by 1600, especially in Germany. Indeed, the Germans were the best clockmakers in Europe, during the sixteenth century.

Clockwork driven by weights dragging on strings wrapped around a cylindrical barrel was probably first used for striking the hours in a city clock-tower, so that the populace within earshot would know the time. Hands and a clock-face were added later. The early mechanisms were fairly crude, mounted in cage-like frames, made of iron. A handsome version was in a special tower-room in the castle at Ferrara, early in the fifteenth century [*In la chamara de la tore e lo oreloio* (i.e. *orologio*), *Oreloio uno de fero belo in su la tore*; Este Invt., 1436] which was accompanied by a bell that was struck on the hour [*campana una da ore*]. Some poor fellow had to sleep up in the bell-tower; he had a bed that was described as old and small. Presumably he serviced the clock – an important function as everyone's day was governed by the chimes from that tower.

Small versions of such iron cage-clocks may be seen hanging on the wall in Pls 292, 295. The lead weights had to be able to fall freely. If a shelf or window-sill hindered their free fall, a hole could be cut in it to allow the weights to pass through this impediment (Pl. 298). The openwork movement easily became clogged with dust and clockmakers must have been kept busy cleaning these exposed mechanisms.[1] The answer, of course, was to fit the movement into a case. Already in the 1430s an Este clock had a painted case [*cum la soa chassa depinta*; Este Invt., 1436] but clocks mostly remained open until well into the sixteenth century. A neatly enclosed wall-clock of 1591 is shown in Pl. 296; an early clock-case may be seen in Pl. 260.

A spring-driven movement was invented early in the sixteenth century; this obviated the need for weights and soon quite small clocks (and also watches) were being produced. Table-clocks at first took the form of a small box which could stand on a table and had a dial on top. The next development was to make the case taller and put the dial on one vertical face. Much skill and good taste were brought to bear on the cases of these upright table-clocks and it is not surprising that, when Eleonora Gonzaga

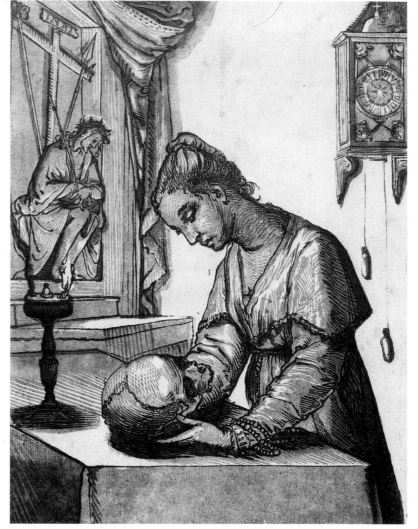

296

della Rovere, Duchess of Urbino, had her portrait painted in 1537, she made sure her valuable little table-clock was included in the picture. It was probably a German confection.[2] Andrea Doria's rather larger clock was undoubtedly included in his portrait with equal pride (Pl. 214). Alvise Odoni's *horrolloggio rotto in una colona* [its case was column-shaped and the clock was broken] was no doubt of a similar kind (Odoni Invt., Venice, 1555); and the same is probably true of the gilt clock *a Torre* [with a turret] which an Emilian clockmaker produced for Ercole II d'Este in 1540 as a present for the King of France.[3] The clockmaker concerned, Cerubino Sforzano, worked at Ferrara and was celebrated; presumably the Duke felt his work would even impress the French court. Clocks were evidently suitable diplomatic gifts. The connoisseur and collector, the Archduke Ferdinand of Tyrol, gave Alfonso II, Ercole's son and successor, a German clock which somehow incorporated a mirror (perhaps reflecting the dial) and had a black leather case; it struck the hours and quarters.[4]

296 A handsome wall-clock in 1591

Driven by weights but not yet regulated by a pendulum, this clock has a decorative case. The lady contemplates a skull by the light of a twin-spouted oil-lamp which has an enclosed reservoir. The altar tabernacle frames a figure of Christ, the Man of Sorrows; it can be totally screened by a curtain here shown bundled out of the way.

Andrea Andreani, a Mantuan working in Siena, engraving after a drawing by A. Casolani; dedicated to Eleonara Montalvi, a patron of Casalani and wife of a powerful Sienese politican
Gabinetto Nazionale delle Stampe, Rome (F.C.66429)

297 The making of music, a source of wonder and delight

Among the possessions an owner would treat with particular reverence were musical instruments, especially those which were decorated in a delicate manner, as is the small portative organ shown here which is ornamented with *lavoro di intarsio* that may include a white composition. Such an item would be kept with other personal treasures in a secure place, away from rough handling by the ignorant. This is one of the panels made by Antonio Barile (active about 1482–1502 and perhaps the most celebrated maker of *tarsie* in his day) for the Duomo at Siena, now to be seen in the Collegiata in S. Quirico d'Orcia, Tuscany.

Photograph: Scala

297

Two other Este clocks mentioned in the same document were French (one came from Lorraine); the finest was placed in a position of honour – on the table in the small Gilt Closet [*stava sopra la tavola del camarin dorato*].

None of these clocks was particularly accurate, even the best of them, by modern standards, and there was no agreed 'mean time'. The town clock was set by the rising or going down of the sun; how else could one do it? Clearly there was scope for improvement but the great step forward was achieved when clocks regulated by a pendulum were developed in the middle of the seventeenth century.

It should be remembered that the word *orologio* was originally applied to timepieces of all kinds including, of course, the relatively humble hour-glass which measures time in relation to fine sand dribbling through a small aperture in a waisted glass container (Pls 227, 294).[5] It also included sundials. There were two *horologii da sole* [sundials] in the Palazzo Vecchio (Medici Invt., 1553) in the time of Duke Cosimo I but they were in a store and were probably thought obsolete by then.

Terrestrial and celestial globes, and armillary spheres, were produced by instrumentmakers working in conjunction with mapmakers. The instrumentmakers worked in brass that was sometimes silvered and even gilded: their works could be extremely decorative as they had to stand in the studies or small galleries of discriminating people who would have been astonished to be told that Art and Science had nothing to do with each other (Pl. 295). The globes themselves were colourful but those that survive have become so ingrained with dirt that we can no longer appreciate how attractive they once were. A celestial globe in Medici possession in 1553 (Medici Invt.) had a special green taffeta cover, lined with kid, to protect it. The term *mapamundo* [map of the world] was usually applied to what we would indeed call a world map – a flat representation of the world – but was sometimes also, understandably, used in reference to a terrestrial globe. Such was the *bala da napa mondo* [i.e. it was spherical] in a Venetian palazzo in 1592 (Ram Invt.).

Maps of the world, or parts of it, were popular in the sixteenth century as wall-decoration in halls, galleries and large rooms of reception – either executed directly on to the wall-surface in fresco, or painted on wood or canvas, framed and hung up. Apart from being handsome, such maps might be a vehicle for all kinds of more or less subtle propaganda. A prince, for instance, could show the vast extent of his dominions (pencilling-in territorial claims where there was doubt); he could underline his alliances with powerful neighbours; or he could show how his intrepid seamen were opening up distant corners of the world. Maps, like portraits, could play a part in contemporary politics although the average visitor might simply see them as an attractive form of decoration.

Musical instruments

References to the presence of musical instruments in Italian Renaissance houses are to be found here and there in contemporary inventories. They mostly concern keyboard instruments. One would have expected to find mention of smaller instruments like lutes and recorders in most households but this is not the case. Were they omitted from the lists for some reason, or were they mostly the property of professional musicians whose inventories have not been perused here? Only a single lute was noted in the 1413 inventory to the Monticoli house in Udine (Monticoli Invt.), and we found Leonello d'Este paying for a special box in which to house two *chitarini* in 1443.[1] These were probably to be played by two of his court musicians who had earlier been described as *pulsatori optimo chitarini*. No doubt diligent searching would reveal more instruments of the smaller kind but they do not really concern us here, for the very reason that they do not loom large in the domestic setting. However, some instruments, particularly members of the lute family, were decorated most prettily and were by no means inconspicuous. The finest lutes came from Padua but those made in Venice between about 1590 and 1640 were undoubtedly the most decorative.

In describing the various ways that his contemporaries might decorate their rooms, Sabba da Castiglione tells us that 'some adorn them with musical instruments'.[2] They please the ear, they provide recreation for the mind, and they are easy on the eye in those instances 'where they have been carefully worked by the most excellent and ingenious masters, like Lorenzo di Pavia or Bastiano da Verona'.[3] Instruments came in several qualities – undecorated, for general use, and with ornament for those who could afford such luxuries. The ornamental specimens were kept among other household treasures, in the more private rooms where they would be safe yet might be shown to discerning friends, and played in pleasant company at intimate gatherings.

Although there were street-musicians entertaining the populace by playing on instruments of the cruder kinds, the owning and playing of instruments that produced sweet sounds was largely confined to people of learning and refinement. The ability to read musical notation, after all, required intelligence and as a result was largely the preserve of an élite. Studying the properties of strings under tension, and the sounds they could produce in various circumstances, was considered a proper activity for men of science as well as for professional musicians of the more intellectual sort. Against such a background, the making of music was not merely an activity that gave delight. It could also produce a sense of wonder since acoustic principles seemed to be anchored in mathematics and therefore appeared to reveal something of the underlying order that Renaissance man was convinced governed the workings of the world and, indeed, the universe. It is therefore not surprising that instruments which helped people to make music were treated with reverence and were seen as possessing almost magical properties.

An instrument known as a *manachordo* was present in several of the houses studied here. There was one in the Cesena collection in 1489 (Franceschino Invt.) and a *menachordo da sonare* [with which to make sounds, or for playing] was to be seen in a Trivulzio house in Milan in 1420 (Trivulzio Invt.). It has been supposed by some authorities that this was a 'monocord', by which is today meant a single-stringed instrument used for demonstrating acoustic principles and, what was perhaps commoner in Renaissance households, for tuning where several voices or other instruments were to perform together. It is, however, quite clear that one could play quite elaborate melodies on a *manachordo*. A description of a dinner party that Pope Julius II gave in 1511 in honour of his *de facto* hostage, Federigo Gonzaga (the son of Isabella d'Este who was kept in Rome under extremely polite restraint as a guarantee of good political behaviour by the state of Mantua) records 'After dinner was presented one who played the *manchordo* very well; then there came musicians and they played violins and sang . . .'.[4] It is evident that this was no scientific demonstration, nor was the *manochordo* being used simply for tuning. If we turn to Florio's dictionary of 1611*, we find the word *Monocordo* which, he says was 'an instrument with many stringes of one sound, which with little pieces of cloth make distinct sounds'.[5] Confusing as this may seem, it is in fact quite an accurate description of a clavichord where strips of felt are inserted between the strings (at one end) so as to dampen the sound as soon as the tangent of the key that had struck a note was released. The original monochord had a single string that could be struck by a tangent at various points to produce different notes. The clavichord was essentially a box containing a series of strings, all of the

298

299

298 Cage with parakeets, mid-1470s

Made of wood with bars of (brass?) wire, this cage is hanging from a hook in a window-opening – and the whole scene is rendered in *lavoro di intarsio*. Note the clock alongside; its weights descend into a hole cut in the window-sill. The birds have a feed-container decorated with his arms.

A panel in Duke Montefeltro's *studio* at Urbino
Photograph:

299 Sketch for a *porta finta*, 1587

Intended to be executed full-scale in fresco, this representation of a room seen through a doorway was to be painted on the wall of a room, probably in order to balance a real door elsewhere on the wall (see p. 320). A bird-cage of metal, with a water-container apparently of glass, features prominently in this composition. Both fictive doors have *portières*. In front of the girl who is sewing is what seems to be a basket of fruit standing on a box-stool. By Lelio Orsi, who worked mostly in the Romagna.

Lelio Orsi, *Girl Sewing*
Albertina, Vienna (57.255.C.)

same length and tuned alike (in a sense a series of monochords) that were struck each by a separate tangent and key at points that produced different notes. By the late fifteenth century the clavichord was fitted with paired strings for each note.[6]

The other keyboard instrument that was present in Italian Renaissance houses was a *clavicembalo*.[7] This was what we today call a harpsichord or, if small, a spinet. It operated on a different principle. Early specimens might have a single string to each key but most harpsichords have a pair of strings per key. This should in theory make it not too difficult for a taker of inventories to distinguish a harpsichord [*clavicembalo*] from a clavichord [*monochordo*] but of course, when faced with a large keyboard-instrument, some of them may well have plumped for whichever term first came into their heads. The taker of the Cesena inventory (1489) was evidently well aware of the difference for, after mentioning the *manachordo*, he lists *Uno chiavacembolo*.

The Cesena instrument was accompanied by a painted case [*cum la cassa dipinta*] which was almost certainly a separate item. Italian harpsichords and spinets of the sixteenth century were very lightly built and were in consequence delicate and vulnerable. In order to protect them, a more robust and usually lidded outer case was normally provided in which the instrument was kept and which defended it when it was being moved. It is probable that this practice was established long before 1500, as the Cesena entry suggests. On an inlaid panel in Isabella d'Este's *studio* at Mantua, dating from about 1500,[8] is represented a spinet with a separate outer case that is undecorated.[9] The instrument itself has elegant lineaments and was no doubt exquisitely made. Spinets and harpsichords were not inexpensive, especially if they were decorated. They were normally played in elegant surroundings by people with discriminating, not to say fastidious, tastes so it is not surprising that a good deal of attention should have been paid to the decoration of these instruments, which loomed fairly large in a room. Indeed, ornament of great delicacy was increasingly applied to their cases as the century wore on.[10] Outer cases were never so elaborately decorated and were presumably not brought into the room when the instrument was to be played – until harpsichords became so large and heavy that it became impracticable to remove the outer case and the instrument therefore had to live in its case *in* the room where it was played. It was then seen to be more practical to make the inner case stronger, fit it with a lid, and dispense entirely with the protective case. This did probably not occur before 1600.

Other types of instrument that might form decorative features of a room were harps (p. 99) and dulcimers, both of which could also have their own individual protective cases bearing ornament.[11]

Musical instruments are quite often depicted in Italian Renaissance paintings but mostly in those portraying religious subjects – St Cecilia, or groups of angels playing instruments for the entertainment of the infant Christ. Organs often appear in such scenes. They are usually of the small portable kind which could be held on the lap while being played. The small organ shown in Pl. 297, however, seems to be surrounded by secular images which suggests that such instruments were also sometimes to be

seen in domestic settings. Indeed, an *orghanetto* was present in the Cesena collection (1489).

The finest keyboard instruments became truly eye-catching pieces of furniture, towards the end of the sixteenth century, by which time some were being provided with stands. Particularly overpowering was a type of instrument today called an organ-harpsichord which consisted of a harpsichord mounted on an organ, the latter usually contained in a deep box-like plinth. The two were linked together mechanically. Such an instrument must have been the *istrumento da sonare co[n] corde e canni* [it had strings and pipes].[12] These combinations evidently fascinated the musical world between about 1580 and 1620 after which people seem to have lost interest in this cumbersome form which must have required a great deal of maintenance and continual adjustment.

A particularly elaborate spinet was made by a Milanese instrument-maker named Annibale dei Rossi in 1577. It is now in the Victoria and Albert Museum in London. It bears many cartouches of ivory and is set with plaques of coloured stone as well as some 1,900 semi-precious stones. For all its wealth of ornament, the design is so skilfully managed that it is an attractive object. It also sounds well enough when played. This is almost certainly the instrument that was bought, sometime before 1595, by 'the learned and refined gentleman' Carlo Trivulzio for 500 crowns.[13]

Another spinet, a Venetian instrument of about 1540, less glamorous than the dei Rossi but handsome enough in itself, bears an inscription which throws a witty sidelight on the then current Italian attitude to fine instruments that were also decorative. *Riccho son doro. et riccho son di suono. Non mi sonar si tu non a de buono*, which, roughly translated, means that 'I am rich with gold and rich in sound. If you do not have what it takes, do not play me'.[14]

Birds and their cages

Birds in cages are to be seen in a number of the illustrations in this book and it is not therefore surprising that references to bird-cages are quite often to be found in Italian Renaissance inventories. The word *gabbia* means a cage (sometimes spelt *cabbia* or *cheba*) and a bird-cage was therefore a *gabbia di uccello* or *da uccelli*. A Sicilian inventory in 1561 gives us *una yhagia di auchello* (Requesens Invt.) and later has *dui gagi di teniri papagla* which must have been a cage for parakeets [*pappagalli*]. In Venetian sixteenth-century inventories the term *una cheba da papa* is not uncommon. The spelling may be erratic but the meaning is clear; when not qualified, however, *gabbia* could also mean a meat-safe [*gabbia di carne*].

Bird-cages could be of iron (as was the first Sicilian example just given) and some were of wood with iron rods forming bars. But most were of brass which might be decorated with paintwork. Two brass cages painted red and gold are listed among Medici possessions in 1553 (Medici Invt.) and Eleonora d'Aragona, Duchess of Ferrara, had another made for her parakeet [*gabia da papagalo*] in 1493 which was gilded by Ercole de' Roberti.[1] An iron bird-cage mentioned in Bartolo di Tura's inventory of

1483 (Tura Invt.) seems to have been in the form of a ship or was boat-shaped [*cabbia da ucelljnj di ferro, ritracta ad navicella*].

When the Venetian nobleman Giorgio Ruzzini died on board a galley on his way to Alexandria, he had taken with him his parrot in a cage which had a curtain that seems to have been of canvas, a heavy material which may have protected the bird from spray while on board this fast-moving vessel [*Unus papagalus cum sua cheba coperta de chanipatia*].[2] In one of his sea-chests was a supply of bird-seed [*una cofa plena seminibus papagalorum*]. The Marquis of Ferrara had stands for his larger bird-cages (Este Invt., 1436); they are described as *cavaletti* and they supported the cages of his sparrowhawks and goshawks [*cavaliti . . . da gaibe da sparavierj et asturi*]. These must have been quite large structures.

Lighting

We all believe we have some concept of what it is like to live in a world where, after dark, light is not available merely by flicking a switch. Our experience comes from the occasional power-cut or perhaps from sleeping in a tent as a child, but always we know that our normal state is one in which light is obtainable where it is wanted, at once. In a world where no one had ever had such expectancy, the darkness of night seemed rather different – both easier to cope with because it was more familiar, and more alarming because it provided cover for a host of evils, real and imaginary. It was not a case of having to adjust to this state of affairs, we must remember; this was how it had always been and, although people had long striven to improve lighting, little headway was to be made until the Argand lamp was invented, late in the eighteenth century. The conditions under which our Renaissance ancestors lived can have differed little in this respect from those which had prevailed in the Bronze Age.

Providing artificial light was always costly, a notable item in a household's budget, and all but the most ostentatious people were thrifty with candles and with oil for lamps.[1] Indeed, there was very little light in houses after darkness had fallen except in very special circumstances, and then only in households where such conspicuous expenditure was a calculated part of overall splendour. On the few occasions when a great deal of artificial light was present, it was remarked upon with some awe. For example, when the Court at Ferrara wanted to entertain Isabella di Capua, Princess of Molfetta, in 1537, there was dancing in the courtyard of the Castle which had been turned into a huge ballroom for the occasion. So numerous were the lights that 'the night was turned into day' [*infiniti luminari che faceano la notte chiarissima*].[2] Most of the time, for most people, however, it was a question of making the most of daylight, of getting up early and, when twilight came, adjusting one's activities to it – and doing the same for the darker hours when candles and firelight provided the only illumination. That last phase was the time for talking, for card-games and the like whereas in the earlier half-light one could still manage certain types of handiwork, standing at the window. The tempo was different to ours, each phase being carefully gauged to the possibilities that varying degrees of light offered.

300 Once darkness had fallen

This picture is a reminder of how little light was present after dark in normal circumstances. As we see here, most of the light came from the fire in the hearth. This is here supplemented by a small oil-lamp which can be lifted off its perch and carried about, if one needed to light one's way in going about the house; one had to take care not to let the flame be extinguished. Normally the lamp was suspended over the hearth (a good safe place), always ready to provide a flame from which the fire or candles could be lit. With so little light, it is hardly surprising that people of a nervous disposition sometimes imagined there were devils lurking in dark corners. The task of preparing yarn, in which the three daughters are engaged, does not require a great deal of light.

Jan van der Straat (Giovanni Stradano), *The Generosity of St Nicholas*, 1585
Casa del Vasari, Arezzo

300

Darkness falls rather more suddenly in Italy than it does in the north of Europe. Paradoxically, darkness is also present indoors during the day, in many places, because Italians usually close the shutters or pull blinds and awnings across their windows during the heat of the day in the warmer months, so their rooms are then also dark although, outside, the light is brilliant. Much of the time, therefore, Italian rooms were (and still often are) seen in a state of darkness and this made a difference to the appearance of rooms and everything in them. How far this affected the design of rooms and furnishings is debatable but one could certainly not have seen much of elaborate ceilings in such darkened circumstances (that is, much of the time), and even wall-paintings and tapestries must have been hard to see. So boldness in colour and in relief-effects must have seemed desirable and certainly the many decorative schemes that we today see, with up-lighting and other forms of strong and steady modern illumination, must have looked very different to those who saw them when they were new, under such very different conditions.

The general lack of light also encouraged the introduction of shiny surfaces which would pick up and throw back into the beholder's eye any glint of light, from whatever source – the dying light from outside, light from the fire and light from candles and torches (see below). Gilding, of course, was one of the principal means of producing a reflecting surface. The gold of a picture-frame or a moulding on a piece of furniture will shine long after everything else in the room is lost to sight as darkness falls. The gilding of details on rich ceilings must have had just this effect, the gilded highlights being all that one could see much of the time. The brass of fire-irons and fire-dogs picked up the flicker of firelight in a delightful manner, and the polished marble of fireplaces did the same. Mirrors did not really come into their own until the seventeenth century but, where they were present in the Renaissance period, even the small mirrors of that time must have seemed wondrous in the twilight and after dark. When, towards the end of the sixteenth century, a few people began to fit small panes of mirror-glass into the panelling of a room, the effect would have been quite startling; after all, nothing like that had ever been seen before. But all shiny surfaces to some extent had this property of reflecting light even when very little light was present in a room. The polished marble of especially splendid chimneypieces are a good case in point; they reflected light, in the first place that of the fire in the hearth but also that of a mass of candles – when they were present. A Milanese gentleman visiting Venice in 1494 was struck by the shiny Carrara marble chimneypiece in the house of a noble lady who was lying-in after having given birth to a child. So brilliant were the illuminations on this important occasion that the marble glowed 'like gold'.[3]

After dark, the principal source of light in a room was the fire in the fireplace, except on festive occasions when a lot of candles might be specially introduced. This is an important point because it means that the main source of light came from low down, unlike modern lighting which mostly has sources high up, near the ceiling. So shadows fell quite differently and the ceiling was of course largely in darkness. So were many other parts of the room (Pl. 301).

The few subsidiary sources of light were also mostly placed low down; they needed to be because they had to be lit, trimmed during use, and extinguished afterwards. So portable candle-holders were placed on tables or shelves where needed. In grand rooms, there might be candle-branches attached to the wall (Pl. 309). Occasionally candles (or torches) were set on stands specially designed for the purpose but, again, at an accessible height (Pl. 305). Oil-lamps, when used in the better sort of room, were often suspended in the fireplace where they were safe and any smell would go up the chimney (Pl. 300). As for chandeliers, there were very rare (as always, until the nineteenth century). Like indoor lanterns, they were commonly suspended with a cord running over a pulley or hook, so that they could be lowered for servicing (Pl. 220), but no doubt some were fixed and had to be lit with a taper on a stick and extinguished with a small conical hood on another stick (the extinguishing of candles lower down was often achieved just with the fingers). As chandeliers are so rarely illustrated it is really not clear how they were managed, in fact.

Candles [candele] of the cheaper sort were made of tallow [sego or sevo]. This was smelly and did not produce as good a light as candles of wax [cera]. Moreover wax candles did not need snuffing so frequently.[4] Those who could afford the luxury had candles of beeswax that had been refined so that it was white and this fact is sometimes noted in contemporary documents. For example when Benedetto Salutati gave a dinner party in honour of the sons of the King of Naples in 1476, it was specially recorded that the candles in two large wooden chandeliers suspended from the ceiling were of cera bianca;[5] and the Tyrant of Lucca, Paolo Guinigi, had a large supply of candles in his residence at the time of his death, some of cerabiancha and some which were dyed red [vermiglia] (Guinigi Invt., Lucca, 1430). Describing rich rooms in Rome in the mid-sixteenth century, Matteo Bandello spoke of a little table or stand on which was a small lit candle of the very whitest wax [cera candidissima].[6] Venice produced the finest beeswax candles in the seventeenth century and had probably been doing so long before that. In 1499, Lucrezia Borgia's first child by her second husband, Alfonso of Aragon, was baptized in the Sistine Chapel. At that ceremony one of the papal grooms carried 'a great taper of white wax, some three pounds in weight, gilded and very beautifully decorated'.[7] No doubt this was something very special but painted candles were made from the Renaissance period onwards (there is a pretty example in the Victoria and Albert Museum, in London, among the woodwork collections); they may mostly have been for church use but there is no obvious reason why they could not have been used domestically as well. A very large candle was known as a torchio. Judgment was needed on the part of a candlemaker to choose a wick of appropriate thickness to go with a candle of a given girth; both had to burn down at the same rate. Too large a wick made the wax melt too fast and run down the sides; too small, and it easily got swamped by melted wax.

Candles of an ordinary size were held in a nozzle but candles of more considerable girth were pressed down on to the spike of a pricket-candlestick (Pls 305, 309, 317). All forms of candleholder were called candelieri or candelabre (these terms should not be taken as the equivalent

301

301 An evening party

Even on gala occasions when a lot of candles were present, the light fell unevenly. The ceiling was by no means clearly visible and, in really tall rooms, its details must have been truly indistinct. Deep coffering, heavy mouldings, prominent bosses must therefore have seemed far less overwhelming than they do under modern flood-lighting, while gilded areas took on a light of their own against a dark and mysterious background. The wall-hangings (in this case, woven tapestries) caught the light well, on the other hand, as they were suspended close to the source of light – candles on the table. This picture is not Italian and it dates from 1640 but is included because it makes the point so well.

Wolfgang Heimbach, *Evening Banquet*, 1640
Kunsthistorisches Museum, Vienna (549)

of the modern English words 'chandelier' and 'candelabrum', therefore, although they might in some circumstances have identical meanings; see below), and in most cases these terms referred to candlesticks of the kind that could be placed on tables or any other flat surface. When reference was being made to a *candeliere* that was suspended from the ceiling or fixed to the wall, this fact was usually stated. In the Uzzano inventory (Uzzano Invt., Florence, 1424), after listing some ordinary candlesticks of brass or bronze, seven iron *candellieri* are mentioned which were *da ficchare nel muro* [to drive into the wall, i.e. they must have had a spike at the back], while some *candellieri* in the loggia of the Pucci establishment (Pucci Invt., Florence, 1449) were likewise *al muro* [to go on the wall]. In the Medici inventory of 1496 (Medici Invt.) we find four iron *candeliera* fixed to the walls of a room at Fiesole [*apicato intorno ala sala*] and in the *sala grande* at Cafaggiolo there was *uno candeliero grande apicato a mezzo la sala* ['fixed in the middle' of this large room, so it must have been suspended]; it apparently had twelve nozzles [*con 12 candellieri apichati insieme*] although these last may just possibly have been separate wall-sconces. In the Guinigi palace at Lucca (Guinigi Invt., 1430) there were no fewer than 180 new candlesticks and many older ones, as well as a brass chandelier with six branches [*a sei rame . . . appicchato al sopracielo*] fixed to the ceiling. During Beatrice d'Este's state visit to Venice in 1493, there were one hundred large candles set in wooden chandeliers suspended from the ceiling [*100 torze sopra legni ataccati al celo*].[8]

Candlesticks could be placed on special stands although this was probably a sixteenth-century development. We noted Bandello describing a stand on which a candlestick was placed. There were six *sghabelloni a piramidi dipinti e tocchi d'ora da candelieri* at the Villa Medici in 1598 (Medici Invt.); these were presumably tall structures constructed like a box-stool [*sgabello*, p. 168] that were handsomely painted and gilded. A candlestand in the form of a boy holding a pricket-candlestick is shown in Pl. 305; this is a copy of an original drawing of the 1460s and, although we may have in mind that human figures in this role were a seventeenth-century phenomenon,[9] the notion simply springs from the fact that grand people had torch-bearers to escort them when they went about at night. If you were going to sit down in a room for a lengthy meal, however, you might as well make your torch-bearer of wood and give the man himself some other duties; there was little point in having him stand there throughout the evening. Such a piece of furniture was sometimes called a *torchiera* (e.g. Fieschi Invt., 1532). Lucrezia Borgia's two silver-gilt *candelieri . . . da torchie*, which had three nozzles each [*con tre bottoni*] and were *ala ganba* [with a leg or stand] (Borgia Invt., 1503), are described as being large and were very probably full-sized candlestands, rather than small items for use on a table. The silver satyr holding an oil-lamp [*uno satiro d'argento con una lucerna in mano*] in the Medici collection (Medici Invt., 1553) was more probably of the latter class, perhaps a small fellow some ten or twelve inches high.

Candle-holders, of whatever sort, could be made of various materials. Some were of wood, many were of iron which could be tinned or varnished black. Many were of brass and others were of bronze. More rarely they were of silver and exceptionally they were of rock-crystal mounted on a metal armature.[10] Some very special candlesticks were fashioned of brass inlaid with silver *alla domaschina* (p. 103).[11] Of these varieties, most will have had single nozzles but a few had twin nozzles. *Candelieri* with more nozzles are usually found to be chandeliers.

Short, stubby candles served as night-lights in bedchambers. Known as mortars in northern Europe, they could be placed in special holders that almost enclosed them and only let out a small amount of light, so as not to keep one awake but enough to see one's way about the room at night if necessary. The steward of the Palace at Urbino in 1587 recorded that his master wanted to have each night in his bedchamber a close-stool, a bell to call his personal servant, and a burning candle that was ready to hand but well screened.[12] In the *Decameron*, in the mid-fourteenth century, we find a request that a lighted *torchietto* be placed in a bedchamber at night (*torchietto* of course implies that it was a small and stubby candle).[13] That

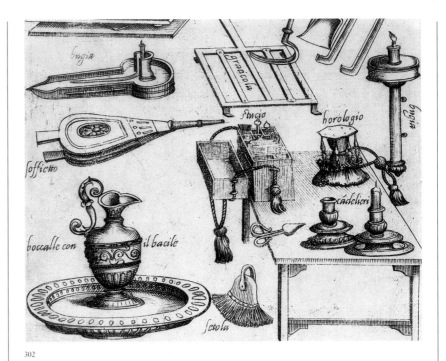

302

the practice of having a night-light in one's bedchamber was not uncommon is confirmed by the *Shorte Dictionarie for yonge beginners* of 1562 where the Latin term *lucerna cubicularis* is explained as meaning 'The lampe that burneth all night in the Chamber'.

It will have been noted that *una lucerna* was a lamp and one could of course have a lamp for a night-light just as well as a candle or mortar. An illustration of an antique classical oil-lamp in the *Hypnerotomachia* of 1499 has a text describing it as a *lucerna antiqua*. The learned writer Annibale Caro (d.1556) had, among the treasures in his *studio*, two *lucerne, una di bronzo et l'altra di terra antica*; the latter was certainly an antique classical lamp, as stated, while the bronze one could also have been antique but may equally well have been a modern production.[14] In the Medici inventory of 1553 (Medici Invt.), reference is made to a *lucerna* of *ottone di getto*, cast brass. The fact that the technique is mentioned suggests that its form was complicated. Maybe the oil-reservoir was shaped to produce a spout for the wick. Sometimes the reservoir was boat-shaped as a result, and this was specially pronounced if the container had two spouts, one at each end, which thus became prow-like. This may well be what was meant by a *lucerna a navicella*, a description to be found in the Gaddi inventory in Florence in 1496 (Gaddi Invt.). From the Medici inventory just mentioned, we learn that brass *lucerne* provided illumination on the staircase of the Palazzo Vecchio as well as in the *sala* [*3 lucerne d'ottone per lumiere in . . . sala, capo di scala et mezza scala*]. A light placed in a passage or on a staircase needs to have some form of glazed hood to ensure that the flame does not get blown out and so it becomes a lantern.

Another form of oil-lamp was the *lampada*, a word which could also be spelt *lampeda* or *lampana*. A silver specimen in Galeazzo Maria Sforza's

302 Candleholders, 1570

On the table stand two ordinary candlesticks. Behind them is a portable candlestick in which the candle is stowed in the handle and can be pushed upwards to protrude as much as is desired. A taper-stick is to be seen above the bellows; the long taper can be fed up through the nozzle as it burns down. The hour-glass is described as an *horologio*; it is housed in a leather case or bag.

From Bartolomeo Scappi, *Opera*, Venice, 1570
*Metropolitan Museum of Art, New York, Elisha Whittelsey
Collection, Elisha Whittelsey Fund, 1952 (52.595.2[23])*

303 Mary at her studies

A candlestick is parked on the window-sill. She has a small candlebranch that swivels above her lectern so that she can read in the evening. Her 'study area' is not a separate room but is adjacent to her bed, the head of which is just above her pillow. Note the attachment of the curtain-rod to the ceiling. The contrast between the two woods of the *lavoro di intarsio* of this throne like seat is clearly shown.

Giovan Pietra da Cemmo, *Annunciation*, S. Rocco, Bagolino,
Lombardy, 1496
Photograph: Scala

303

304 A wonderfully elegant chandelier

Looking as if designed in 1930, this metal chandelier is depicted in a painting by Carpaccio dating from the 1490s.

Carpaccio, *The English Ambassadors*, detail from the St Ursula cycle from the Scuola di Sant' Orsola; 1490 as (detail)
Accademia, Venice

304

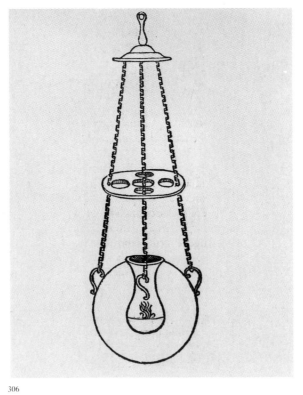

305 Ancestor of the *guéridon*

A candlestand in the form of a human figure, illustrated in Filarete's treatise on architecture of about 1460. Filarete says it was of bronze and was the size of a twelve-year-old boy so the candle (which fits onto the pricket) would have been at a height of between four and five feet.

From Filarete, *Codex Maglibechianus*, Vol. IX, p. 69
Biblioteca Nazionale, Florence

306 A special hanging lamp

This has two glass vessels, one inside the other. The smaller, which contained some oil and a wick, is described as being in the form of an *orinale*. The outer vessel is filled with distilled water which, as with a 'lace-maker's lamp', may have helped to concentrate the light. The device was clearly thought marvellous by the writer of the *Hypnerotomachia Poliphili* (Venice, 1499) who included many illustrations in his extraordinary work depicting ingenious or stylish items of various kinds which are by no means totally fantastic even though the descriptions sometimes seem far-fetched.

From Francesco Colonna, *Hypnerotomachia Polifili*, Venice, 1499
Courtesy of the Trustees of Sir John Soane's Museum, London

305   306

307, 308 Two designs for candlesticks

The one on the left is by Giulio Romano and bears an inscription telling us that it was to be executed in silver for Ferrante Gonzaga who became Count of Guastalla in 1539, which is likely to be the approximate date of this drawing. The engraving on the right is one of a suite of four published by Enea Vico in 1552. An erudite antiquarian and skilled engraver, Vico was certainly aware of what fresh stylistic developments were making their appearance in mid-sixteenth-century Italy. Such engravings were of course made for sale and helped to spread new styles – in this case, an uncomfortable form of Mannerism in strong contrast to the playful, even joyous feeling conjured up by Giulio Romano's drawing.

Giulio Romano, candlestick, c. 1539
Christ Church, Oxford (424)

Enea Vico, candlestick, 1552
Museum für Kunsthandwerk, Frankfurt am Main (Loz82/RF645)

307

308

309 Bronze candlebranches fixed to the wall

These are of the pricket type but, because this party is being held in daytime, the stubby candles that would be impaled on the prickets are not in place. Such branches could be very expensive (see p. 48). A handsome *spalliera* of silk forms a back-cloth for the diners to lean against. The table is formally set out, each place-setting being furnished with knife and fork, and a trencher (the dark rectangle which may be of pewter or wood).

Francesco and Raffaello Botticini, *Herod's Feast*, c. 1485
Galleria della Collegiata, Empoli (Photograph: Alinari Archives)

309

collection of plate in 1469 had three chains [*tre chadenelle*] which indicates that it was intended to be suspended from the ceiling. An illustration of a *lampada* (described as such) with chains for suspension was included in the *Hypnerotomachia* of 1499 (Pl. 306) but this seems to have been something very special, and the author describes it in some detail. It had two glass vessels, one inside the other. The space between was filled with *acqua ardente* [distilled water, in this instance five times distilled] which will have focused the brilliance like the water-filled globes used by lace-makers to concentrate the light of a candle on their work. In this case the light (an oil-lamp) was inside the inner container which was flask-shaped and of a very clear glass. It is interesting to note that Rabelais (*Gargantua and Pantagruel*, Bk. V, Ch. XLI, published in Paris in 1562) takes this description and embroiders upon it slightly, telling that the light produced by this amazing lamp was like high noon even if it was placed underground. He did of course have the French edition of the *Hypnerotomachia* to follow (1561). Two small glass *lampadini* are mentioned in a Milanese inventory of 1529 (Trivulzio Invt.) and a *lampanetta* of brass comes into a Sienese inventory of 1450 (Fece Invt.); if our interpretation is correct, these were small hanging lamps. The latter was in a bedchamber and may have been a night-light.

The word *cesendello* was also used for hanging lamps, usually of glass. Already in 1408 in Verona we find *unus cisendellus vitrey cum catenella ferri* [of glass with an iron chain] (Aleardi Invt.). Once again it was in a bedchamber and it may be that such hanging lamps, which were comparatively safe, could actually be suspended within the enclosure formed by the bed-hangings. One is visible in the shop shown in Pl. 321. A *cesendello* of glass was to be seen in the Odoni palace in Venice in 1555 (Odoni Invt.), hanging in the *portego* – the main *sala*.

Lanterns were fairly common. They were mostly made from thin sheets of iron, often tinned to counteract rust, with holes punched in them to let light through, or with larger apertures that were filled with horn, alabaster, paper or glass. A candle normally provided the light but an oil-lamp could be placed in a lantern equally well. A lantern protects the flame and prevents winds and draughts from blowing it out. Lanterns were therefore chiefly used for moving about in the streets after dark, but one could also use them in the loggia or in the entrance hall – or any other place where there might be a risk of the light being accidentally extinguished (Pl. 319). At the Palace in Urbino, early in the sixteenth century, a large lantern [*lanternone grande*] used to hang inside the front entrance and another on the main staircase. Indeed, the path from the entrance to the principal apartment [*de la porta fino a la stantia del signore*] was never to be totally in darkness [*non se vada totalmente a lo scoro*].[15] In a Florentine *palazzo* there is a small door opening on to a shaft in the thickness of the wall of the hall. Inside is a large hook. A rope used to run in the shaft up to a pulley in the ceiling of the hall, from which a lantern was suspended. The latter could be raised or lowered by adjusting the rope at the aperture in the wall. Looping the rope round the hook kept the lantern in place when raised.[16]

Most lanterns were utilitarian objects of no distinction but the Acciaiuoli, who were rarely to be found hiding their lights under a bushel, had two lanterns of silver (Acciaiuoli Invt., Florence, 1363). Incidentally, it became much easier to light rooms once windows came to be filled with glass panes. These kept draughts away from the candles a great deal more effectively than did shutters or even the rather flimsy *impannate* (p. 28). Once draughts has been excluded, lighting a room became altogether more rewarding.

310 **St Francis in his *studio*, 1504**

Sporting a magnificent cope and an unmistakable five o'clock shadow, the saint sits in his study, surrounded by his most valued belongings. The comfort and privacy that might be enjoyed in one of the small 'personal' rooms of an apartment is here evident.

Stefano Lunetti, Florentine miniature
The British Library, London (Ms. Harl.3229, fol. 26)

310

Part Three:

ARCHITECTURAL PLANNING

The Distribution of Rooms

An architect planning a house has to work out how best to distribute the rooms within the given ground-plan. He has to take many factors into consideration in doing so. He needs to take heed of the client's requirements; the house has to be convenient to live in, it has to offer comfort – and notably that most expensive of all comforts, privacy – and he may be asked to provide a certain degree of splendour as well. Furthermore, in periods during which classical principles prevail – as in late fifteenth- and sixteenth-century Italy – he may be expected to pay regard to symmetry and other factors that can produce harmony in a layout; he may also need to organize rooms so that their window-apertures coincide with a regular scheme of fenestration, when the building is viewed from outside.

These and many practical considerations need to be taken into account by the planner and it is therefore small wonder that, by the eighteenth century when the organization of a great house had become even more complicated than it was in the sixteenth, a French authority could claim that an architect's 'principal and most essential task', to which 'all others should be subordinated', was that of *distribution*. No matter how handsome the rooms, how splendid their decoration, 'what kind of success do you think will attend your efforts if your ground-plan is poorly distributed?'[1] Somewhat similar sentiments were expressed some two hundred years earlier by an Italian gentleman-architect of great talent, Alvise Cornaro, when he insisted that he greatly preferred a building that was only reasonably handsome but was supremely comfortable and convenient [*la fabrica honestamente bella ma perfettamente commoda*], to one that was extremely beautiful but lacked the other qualities [*bellissima et incommoda*].[2]

In primitive circumstances, where a house may only consist of two rooms, all this presents no problem but as soon as the number of rooms increases, as it did in houses of consequence all over Europe during the Renaissance period, the planner's difficulties begin. In Renaissance Italy, different solutions were worked out in each major city, thus establishing a range of vernacular traditions. To follow such a tradition, when building a new house, took no great skill but to improve upon it required considerable intellectual effort. In most cases the need to do so arose from a client demanding something extra – additional rooms, greater magnificence, more privacy, better services. At each stage, therefore, an Italian city would contain numerous old buildings, usually much adapted to suit new patterns of use, together with quite a few edifices that were more modern in character, built in the current version of the local tradition. In addition there would be a handful of innovative buildings which might set a pattern for the future. These buildings of an advanced character might be imitated not only in their native city but might also inspire architects or their clients who were visiting the city from other parts of the country. There was a good deal of cross-fertilization of ideas throughout Italy in the higher regions of architectural endeavour.

Such a kaleidoscopic picture is difficult to analyse fruitfully. It is anyway probably more helpful to survey the general principles that governed distribution so that one can judge how far a building matches up to the ideals that prevailed among discriminating people at each stage. It must always be remembered that the majority of houses, even of the better sort, were not in any sense advanced in character and that, within a generation or so, even a new building with innovative features in its layout was usually being used in a different way from that originally envisaged. Many factors could bring about such changes. The composition of the family might be altered, parts of the building might have been let to outsiders, changes in fashion might call for a fresh disposition of rooms. In real life, therefore, the distribution of rooms in a building cannot often have been more than an approximation of the ideal.

Nevertheless, the basic needs of human beings in this respect tend to be more or less the same at all periods. Most people, for example, want some degree of privacy in their houses, they want to be protected from the tiresomenesses and even dangers of the outside world, they want their possessions to be safe, and they expect their houses to provide a framework within which domestic life can be enjoyed and a measure of social life can take place. The great have additional special requirements in that they need both more space for representational activities or ceremonial, on the one hand, while on the other they need more elaborate arrangements to insulate themselves from the outer world when they are not 'on parade'. Sir Thomas Hoby, who translated Baldassare Castiglione's *Il Cortegiano* (1528) as *The Booke of the Courtier* in 1561, put it very neatly: 'Great men often times whan thei are privately gotten alone, love a certain libertie to speake and do what they please'.[3]

Some of the architects struggling to satisfy these demands felt urged to set down on paper their thoughts on the general principles. This no doubt partly sprang from Renaissance man's propensity for codifying knowledge but it must also reflect a wish to inform their clients, whether actual or potential, about the latest thinking on these matters. It was obviously easier and more satisfactory to work with clients who understood the problems in a general way and could, as a result of reading such treatises, readily appreciate some of the ways in which the problems might be resolved. This also helps us to appreciate the needs and aspirations, with regard to planning, that were of concern to Italians of an intellectual cast of mind from the middle of the fifteenth century, when Alberti* was writing the first of these treatises, to the end of the period which is effectively marked by Scamozzi's* treatise of 1615. Between those dates we have Filarete's* treatise of about 1460, Francesco di Giorgio Martini's* of about 1480, Serlio's* from the middle decades of the sixteenth century, and Palladio's* of 1570 (see pp. 338–40) Francesco di Giorgio was the first to speak of *le stribuizioni delle stanze* [the distributions of the rooms][4] but the general concept had obviously been understood by architects and most of their clients ever since the number of rooms had increased beyond two. This is implied in the texts even when no one felt it necessary to give the process a name.

The *Camera* and the *Sala*

The nucleus of the Italian Renaissance house,[1] whatever its size and importance, was the owner's bedchamber, his *camera*. It is in relation to this principal room that all the other rooms in the building should be seen because that is how the owner must have viewed his domain. The *camera* was a fairly private room during daytime and it obviously became more so when the owner retired to bed at night. The *camera* could remain relatively private because there were other rooms of a more public nature set between it and the entrance from the street or courtyard. The chief of these was the *sala*, a large general-purpose room in which one could dine and entertain, and where a host of other more mundane domestic activities could take place between times.[2] Moreover, associated with the *camera* there would usually be several more truly private rooms, placed yet further from the entrance. At the beginning of the period, however, while the sense of progression from public to private spaces was undoubtedly present, this progression was not organized in anything approaching a linear fashion. Such an intellectual rationalization of the ground-plan first made its appearance in the middle of the fifteenth century, as we shall see, and then for a long time only in a few buildings of advanced character.

The owner's *camera* and the *sala*, therefore, were the two essential rooms and there were many houses of a meaner sort that consisted of nothing more. On the other hand, in a large house there would be many *camere*, the bedchambers of the various members of the household. Some of these bedrooms would also be associated with one or more subsidiary rooms. A *camera* would normally have a bed standing in it (sometimes there were several)[3] although the term was occasionally also used simply to describe a room or chamber, in the sense of an enclosed space with no

311 The bedchamber as reception-room

The lady occupant of this bedchamber has invited three girl-friends into her personal room for a collation that is served at a table covered with an exceptionally finely woven cloth. Here they can talk and exchange confidences in relative peace but the furnishings are clearly intended to impress any visitors who might be permitted to penetrate so far into the apartment. Apart from the bed, which has a heavy wooden tester attached to the ceiling, a notable feature of the room is the devotional tabernacle.

Master of the Stratonice Panels, *Antiochus and Stratonice*, Sienese, 15th century
Henry E. Huntington Museum and Art Gallery

311

312

312 A relatively modest apartment, 1505–08

A private dining-room with a table laid for six. The bedchamber lies beyond and has a back door leading out to the garden. Cooking can be undertaken in the front room although there is no doubt a proper kitchen elsewhere. Note the poultry hanging from a nail, the bird-cage on the wall opposite, the bust over the door and the two hooks flanking the door ready to receive a *portière* (see Pl. 35).

Giovanni Antonio Sodoma, *Interior*, Monte Oliveto Maggiore, Siena
Photograph: Scala

313 A *sala* in use

Fresco of about 1520 depicting the banquet given in the main reception room at Malpaga Castle, seat of the famous *condottiere* Bartolomeo Colleoni, to King Christian I of Denmark in 1474. The king is seated on the left, separated from the rest of the company (even the host) to reflect his exalted rank. The carver prepares a small fowl for the king. A linen cloth lies over a large Turkish carpet. The walls are hung with two silk damasks, both of the same pattern but of different colours, used alternately.

Marcello Fogolino, *Banquet of King Christian of Denmark*, Malpaga Castle, near Bergamo
Photograph: Scala

313

314 Dining in a palace courtyard

Using all the trappings that would have been present in the main *sala* but here set up out of doors. The principal diners are seated at a high table under a canopy; the main company sits at longer tables below and in front. To the right is a *credenza* with a display of fine plate. A font-like wine-cooler on a stand is placed out in front. Four gilded statues are set in niches.

Apollonio di Giovanni's workshop, *Dido's Banquet*, part of a *cassone-*panel, *c.* 1460
Kestner Museum, Hanover

314

particular designation. More often, however, a room that was not a bedchamber, and was not specified in any other way, was commonly called *una stanza* (or sometimes *un luogo*). Of course a *stanza* might sometimes contain a bed;[4] a *camera* almost invariably did.

Husbands and wives normally had separate bedchambers. A wife's bed might stand in a room adjacent to that of her husband or she might, in a large establishment, have quite a separate apartment which, in a well planned house, the husband could reach without passing through any of the more public spaces. 'The Husband and the Wife should each have a separate Chamber,' Alberti explained in the mid-fifteenth century, 'not only that the Wife, either when she lies in, or in Case of any other Indisposition, may not be troublesome to her Husband; but also that in Summer Time, either of them may lie alone whenever they think fit. Each of these Chambers should have a separate Door, besides which there should be a common Passage between them both, that one may go to the other without being observed by any body.'[5] It seems that, in the Palace at Urbino, the Duke's apartment was connected to that of the Duchess by a covered passageway running alongside the secret garden that lay between them; at the Pitti Palace the Archduke Ferdinand could go and talk to his wife by traversing a cantilevered corridor that was attached to the outside of the walls of the chapel that separated their two apartments (Pl. 343). Less magnificent buildings will have had similar but less elaborate arrangements. There was of course nothing new in the idea of separate rooms for spouses but that their rooms should be so distributed that either could reach the other, without anyone except their personal servants knowing, was probably something of a novelty when Alberti was recommending it. As an indication that this may have been the case we can cite one of Boccaccio's stories, written a century before Alberti's advice was given, in which we are told how a king used to leave his bedchamber some nights and make his way to that of the queen.[6] In order to do so he would throw a cloak over his shoulders, rather as we might don a dressing-gown, and he needed a flaming torch so he could see where he was going; he then had to traverse the whole length of the great *sala*. There was evidently a lack of privacy in this arrangement as an admirer of the queen's was lurking in the shadows of the *sala*, noting how the king proceeded to knock on the queen's door with a wand, whereupon the door was opened by the queen's chambermaid. It is not difficult to guess how Boccaccio's tale continues, once the admirer had likewise equipped himself with cloak, torch and wand.

Alberti also advised those building on a princely scale to provide for themselves bedchambers both for summer and for winter, observing that 'it is not fit that a great Man should be worse lodged than a Swallow or a Crane'.[7] Since the principal rooms, including the main bedchambers, were almost always on the first floor, the *piano nobile* (except in villas in the country where there was often no storey above the ground floor), that was where the winter bedchambers were situated, and these would mostly do for the spring and autumn as well.[8] Summer bedchambers were normally placed on the ground floor, for which reason such a summer room was often called a *camera terrena*. In a city, with narrow streets and overhanging eaves, the sun could in many cases not reach down to the ground floor and make the walls hot; moreover the lower rooms were insulated from the heat by the rooms on the floors above. What is more, the outer and bearing walls tended to be thick and acted like storage-heaters, retaining heat if warmed up but also remaining cold if unheated. As Francesco di Giorgio explained, only a small thickness of wall suffices to keep out the cold but if you want to fend off the heat you need to build thick walls [*poca grossezza di muro e sufficiente a resistare al freddo, ma volendo ostare al caldo bisogna fare li muri grossi*].[9] So the rooms downstairs tended to be cooler than those above.

Although a principal bedchamber might be somewhat private, it could be used as a reception room for honoured visitors or as a kind of drawing-room for favoured friends. An instance of the latter use occurred at Mantua in the early years of the sixteenth century when Isabella d'Este, the Duchess, had her ladies-in-waiting, her daily companions, meet in the *camera di Madama* (i.e. in her bedchamber) where they would pass the time of the day in singing and other forms of music-making, in readings and story-telling, and in *alcuni giochi piacevole per passar il tempo* [various pleasant games to pass the time]. Each lady in turn was elected 'queen' or master of ceremonies for a week at a time.[10] Attending the Duchess could involve more than just sitting about, however, and one lively young lady, Barbara Soardi, writes to a friend rather charmingly of how *mi trovo tutta stanca havendo ballato quasi tutt'hoggi* which might be translated 'I am absolutely worn out, having danced almost all day'. But while such young women may sometimes have demonstrated a new dance-step to each other within the confines of a large bedchamber, that is not where they really danced. That would take place in a *sala* and, in this case, it was in the *sala* at the Duchess's villa at Solarolo.

Principal bedchambers also became rooms of reception on special occasions, usually when family pride was involved – in connection with weddings, for instance, or when a child had been born (Pl. 39). When a young mother was lying-in and the new infant was being presented to the world, she would receive the congratulations of her friends lying on her great bed and then it was of course important that the bedchamber and its furnishings should be as magnificent as possible. Many descriptions of such receptions have come down to us (pp. 23, 323).

In the houses of the great, the public pressure on the principal bedchamber, measured by the number of people who gained access to it, increased during the period to such an extent that, by the sixteenth century and sometimes even earlier, some great people arranged to have a much more private bedchamber somewhere behind the scenes, where they actually slept. When Cosimo I altered the Palazzo della Signoria in the centre of Florence so that he and his duchess, Eleonora of Toledo, could have up-to-date living quarters in this old fortress-like building, he contrived to have such a room within his own apartment. The room is not described as his private bedchamber in the inventory of 1553 (Medici Invt., 1553) where it is simply called his fourth *camera*; but we can see from the size of his bed (three and a half by two and a half *braccia*) and its relative simplicity that this was a subsidiary room to the third *camera* next

315 Dining in a *triclinio*

Couches are set alongside three sides of a square table; the furniture looks as if it was specially designed for the purpose (see diagram 21, p. 361). Purporting to show Christ dining with two Apostles, and based on archaeological knowledge of how people in classical times sometimes dined while reclining on couches, it seems that some late sixteenth-century Italians, wishing to emulate the Ancients, may occasionally have dined in this manner as well (see p. 291).

Paolo Farinato, *Christ and two Apostles*, drawing, late 16th century. *Art Museum, Princeton University, Loura P. Hall Memorial Fund*

316 A middle-class *saletta*?

Although of curious shape, this room appears to be rather grand, with its columns, handsome chimney-piece, heavy curtain and 'designed' bench. It can hardly be a kitchen but may perhaps be a *saletta* in which cooking can take place when the fire is lit (no point in wasting good heat). Such an arrangement was no doubt to be seen in many a middle-class house. The rush-bottomed chair with turned members is shown with such accuracy that one cannot believe the scene was otherwise imaginary to the point of implausibility.

Carletto Caliari (1520–96), *Madonna with her Child visiting the house of Zacharias and Elizabeth*, drawing
National Museum, Stockholm (NM1534/1863)

315

316

door where stood a magnificent gilded bed that was much larger (four by three *braccia*). That the fourth *camera* was Cosimo's and not a servant's is shown by the splendour of the bed-hanging (cloth of gold and red silk – although the hangings of the main bed were even grander) and the fact that the furnishings included four statues, one of them by Michelangelo, and that the walls were hung with gilt leather which is hardly the sort of material you would expect to find in a servant's room.

Privacy went hand-in-hand with security, and the bedchamber was therefore also considered one of the safest places to keep valued possessions (only important documents and greatly treasured items were kept in an even more secure room; p. 296). Alberti explains in an imaginary dialogue how the owner of a house could show his new wife where everything was in the building, adding that, 'At the end there were no household goods of which my wife had not learned the place and purpose. Then we returned to my room, and, having locked the door, I showed her my treasures ...'. Asked if that was 'because they were safer there', he answers that 'it is less difficult to guard a thing from a few persons than from all ...', adding that 'it is a good precaution to keep every precious thing ... well hidden'. 'No place seemed more suited to this than the room where I slept'[11]. Many of us would still feel this to be true today. Princes and other grand people would, moreover, often have a personal servant sleeping in the chamber with them – or in a nearby room – while those who felt the need might be further protected by having servants sleeping by entrance doors in the rooms 'out front', it then becoming necessary for an intruder to step over the sleeping attendant in order to reach the main bedchamber.

The second essential room in a house was the *sala*. It was the largest room in the building. At first it was the place in which the owner and his entourage dined and it continued to serve this purpose in the humbler sort of house right through the period,[12] but in houses of consequence, in some cases already by the early fifteenth century, the owner and his family would prefer to eat in a smaller, more intimate dining-room (see below). In large establishments, moreover, the senior staff might have their own dining-room, often referred to as a *tinello*.[13] The *sala*, being a large room, was also used for any activity that required considerable space, like banqueting, dancing, theatrical performances or games.[14] In a great house it would also serve as the major reception room and as the primary space given over to ceremonial. As the *sala* also tended to occupy a central position in an edifice, people were often passing through it on their way from one side of the building to the other. In hot weather, it was also usually cooler than other rooms as it almost invariably had a higher ceiling. So people would often pass the time of day there.[15]

In the time of Leonello d'Este (d. 1450), the main castle at Ferrara had a large hall with two fireplaces [*sala bianca grande dai due camini*]; it was evidently a white room and it must have been very large to require two fireplaces.[16] But a fireplace was essential in a *sala*, to the extent that in Genoa it was customary to call the room *la caminata* [the fireplace-room].[17] At first it had been the only room with a fireplace and of course, in houses of modest size, it was no doubt still common in the fifteenth, and even in the sixteenth century, to cook at the fireplace in the *sala*, so the room was then essentially a dining-kitchen with a single source of heat (Pl. 24).

The Venetians called this large room a *portego* (sometimes *portico*). In 1346, when it was still normal for people of standing to dine in their *sale*, we find Marco Semitecolo expressing the wish, in his Will, that his brother should always be allowed to enjoy his present status, occupying his own *camera* together with the rooms attached, and eating in the *portego* or in the *loggia* [*habere debeat suam habitationem in camera in qua nunc dormit, in quoquina ad quoquenda necessaria sua, et ad comedendum in portici vel lobia*].[18]

The story of architecture during the Renaissance period could be said to centre round the increasing proliferation of rooms in the houses of those who could afford to indulge themselves in this way. One notable cause of this increase was the demand in those circles for increasing privacy, which manifested itself both in the increased number of very private rooms created in the innermost reaches of great houses, but also in the provision of smaller and more intimate private dining-rooms where people of standing could eat with members of their family or with their friends – with their peer-group, as social historians might now put it – instead of in the great dining-hall, the *sala*, where all kinds of people – staff, strangers, poor relatives, and seekers of favours – might be present.

The smaller form of dining-room was sometimes called a *saletta* [i.e. a small *sala*] but equally often it was called a *salotto*.[19] The latter word today means a drawing-room or 'sitting-room' and this can colour our thinking when we try to envisage how such rooms were used in the fifteenth and sixteenth centuries. At that time there was no such room in a house. One dined in a *sala* (or in a *saletta* or *salotto*) and one slept in a *camera*. But one could sit and pass the time of day in either; there was no room set aside specially for sitting.

While a *sala* would virtually always be larger than either a *saletta* or a *salotto*,[20] there was no generally agreed distinction between the last two terms. Usage differed from city to city, from one person to the next, and perhaps also with each generation, so we cannot expect to offer a precise translation of these two words. Serlio does say that 'if anyone asks me what distinction I draw between a *sala*, a *salotto* and a *saletta*, I shall tell them that a *sala* should be twice as long as it is wide [i.e. 1×2; he says nothing about size but his plans all show the *sala* as larger than any other room], and I would also tell him that the proportions of a *saletta* should be three parts wide by five long [i.e. 3×5] but not less wide than one of the larger *camere* in the house. As for a *salotto*, it should be as broad as one of the larger *camere* and not more than one and a half times that in length [i.e. 1×1.5].'[21] In fact, he thought it a matter of proportion but Francesco di Giorgio* never uses the word *saletta* in his treatise, and speaks only of *salotti* which term appears on many of his ground-plans.[22] He recommended that there should be a *salotto* at each end of the *sala*, in a princely palace.[23] This sprang partly from his obsession with symmetry (in theory, although in practice he could be far more flexible) but it does seem, as Frommel points out, that the *salotto* was often placed next to the *sala*.[24]

This should not surprise us if we recall that both were primarily rooms used for dining and so, generally speaking, needed to be equally close to the kitchen.[25] Moreover, it must sometimes also have been convenient to have the large *sala* next door so that, when one had dined with one's friends in the *salotto*, one could move into the larger room for dancing or other activities requiring space.

Unlike Francesco di Giorgio, Serlio* often included a *saletta* in his plans. His *salette* are invariably smaller than his *sale* but rarely to any great degree. Sometimes they lie next to a *sala* which suggests they in that case served the same purpose as Francesco's *salotti*, but he often places them close to the main entrance of the building where one might expect to find the staff dining-room. Whatever the case, it is clear that these small *sale*, whichever name they were given, served primarily as intimate dining-rooms, the presence of a *credenza* (p. 220) being always a strong indication that meals were frequently taken there. For instance, in the richly appointed Fieschi residence in Genoa in 1532 (Fieschi Invt.), the lady of the household had her own *saletta* that was furnished with a trestle-table at which she dined and a second such table *per la credenza* [serving as a *credenza*], while next door lay another *saletta* for her ladies-in-waiting [*la saleta de le done*] likewise furnished with a trestle-table *damanzare* [for eating at] and a *credenza* on which stood a ewer and basin that would be needed for hand-washing at mealtimes. At the castle in Milan, perhaps the most splendid of all the princely residences in Italy in the years around 1500, we know there was a *saletta dove mangiava Madonna* [where My Lady dines] with two tables with folding legs for her personal use and a *credenza* dressed with a superb service of silver-plate.[26] Half a century earlier a special armchair was delivered for the use of Gurone d'Este and placed in the *salotto* 'where he eats' [*una scaranna . . . per uso de lo salotto dove manza Mess. Gurone*].[27]

There was also a *saletta da pranzo* [for meals] at Milan Castle which was very modestly furnished with nothing more than a table and eight stools. This must have been a dining-room for the senior staff, what elsewhere was often called a *tinello* (p. 291). Incidentally, the terms *saletta* and *salotto* are usually translated as 'dining-parlour' in English. In fact, when it comes down to it, the two terms could be applied to any room larger than the average bedchamber. Eleonora of Toledo had a *salotto* at the Palazzo Vecchio in Florence where her clothes were kept – in various chests and a walnut cupboard with brass ball-finials on top [*Nel salotto dove stanno le robbe della Sra. Duchessa*] (Medici Invt., Florence, 1553). It was situated on the floor above her apartment. Elsewhere such a room would have been called a *guardaroba* (p. 298).

Another term sometimes applied to a room used primarily for dining was *triclinio* from the Latin *triclinium* that, in its purest form, had consisted of a room with a square table in the centre, around three sides of which stood three couches on which three diners lounged as they ate. In fact many classical Roman *triclinia* could accommodate far larger numbers, which is why Renaissance Italians felt free to use the term to cover a dining-room of almost any size (e.g. Francesco di Giorgio* refers to *salotti over teclini* – they were the same thing).[28] However, the small

and truly intimate *triclinium*, suitable for only a very few diners (three or six), seems to have fascinated sixteenth-century Italians. Several pictures of the time show such rooms which may just be fanciful reconstructions of ancient Roman *triclinia*, although it is possible that a few such rooms did actually exist (Pl. 315). Is Scamozzi (1615) hinting at something of the sort when he writes that 'The Triclinij weare places to eat in, so called from the number of bedds wch. they were capable to containe . . . to lie upon, as now a dayes the Mastabei after the Moorish or Turkish fashion, now use in Italie also like your coutches whereon they leaned' [*I Triclinii erano luoghi da mangiare nominati da' letti che vi potevano capire . . . da corcarsi come hoggidì I mastabei all Moresca, ò Turchesca: introdotti anco qui in Italia: come letticelli dove stavano appoggiati*].[29] Does this mean that modern Romans lean on couches (or day-beds, as we might say) just as the ancients did, and as people in the Near East do, lying on a *mastaba* (a great couch or seat)? Or was there a group of people in Venice or Rome who called themselves the *Mastabei* and who dined in a *triclinium*? Was it perhaps some kind of private dining club to which Scamozzi was referring?

Yet another place where one might dine was the *loggia*, a space open to the air that could be covered or totally open like a terrace.[30] It was usually set back into the building, behind the façade, as it were; and it therefore often also served as a corridor linking adjacent parts of the building. In a free-standing house in the country, it was possible to have a *loggia* on each of the four sides so that one could dine in whichever *loggia* offered the most pleasant conditions at any given time – a south-facing sun-trap in winter, a cool space facing north away from the hot sun in summer and so forth. This was the ideal that could not necessarily be attained, but the *loggia* was very important to the Italians who, with their essentially trustworthy and felicitous climate, are able to spend so much more of their time out of doors than we less fortunate northerners. The *loggia* brings the out of doors conveniently within the walls of a building, and in many cases was actually connected with its surroundings – facing directly onto a garden, with steps leading down, for instance, or even doubling as an entrance foyer (in which case there would usually be another less public *loggia* on another side of the building).

Finally, while considering rooms where one might eat, it should be said that, in very splendid houses, there was sometimes a separate room next to the *sala* where servants could give finishing touches to the food – warming up a sauce, adjusting elaborate decoration, setting alight those dishes which had to be carried flaming into the *sala*, dealing with the wine. In especially grand buildings there was sometimes a special room where the *credenza* was erected. In papal circles, it was thought improper that the pope should have to look at the opulence of his own *credenza* so it was set out in a neighbouring room away from the Pontiff's view, it seems, and such fastidiousness may have been shared by other grandees.[31] There are many notions of this kind which we do not fully comprehend at present.

317 The inner rooms of an apartment, about 1502

This famous painting by Carpaccio probably shows the *anticamera* of a learned man, the personal room adjacent to his bedchamber from which presumably the viewer has just entered. The scholar's actual *studio* lies beyond, on the left. The right-hand door seems to be a *porta finta* (see p. 320). Careful study of this picture is rewarding. Apart from the strange chair with a reading-stand, and the scarcely less curious writing-desk, the shelf of small treasures that include bronze figurines and what look like classical spearheads and other antiquities is noteworthy. As this purports to show St Augustine, the artist has furnished him with an altar-niche, virtually a private chapel, that befits such a very holy person.

Carpaccio, *St Augustine in his Study*, Scuola degli Schiavoni, Venice
Photograph: Scala   317

The *Anticamera*

When it comes to personal space indoors, important people need more of it than others do. It is not simply that they usually have more possessions; it is also very much a question of dignity – ostentation, if you like. One has only to think of the average managing director's office today to recognize this truth; it is usually larger than that of anyone else in the firm. To occupy a great amount of space is evidence of wealth and/or standing. However, in so far as the Renaissance period is concerned, it was no good indefinitely increasing the size of the principal piece of personal space, the *camera*. Too large a bedchamber never gave a comfortable feeling (Pl. 152); besides, it was difficult to heat in winter. It was far better to add a second room next to the *camera* – an *anticamera* [from the Latin *anti* = next to or up against]. This was also a convenient solution because it enabled one to hive off from the bedchamber various activities, which thus left the *camera* more private. For instance, one could eat in some degree of privacy in an *anticamera* (and the bedchamber did not, as a result, come to smell of food), one could see friends there (or one could give audiences there, if that was one of one's duties), one could keep one's clothes there, and a personal servant could even sleep there at night. As the room might play an important presentational role, it was often decorated as splendidly as its adjacent and associated *camera*.

The idea of having a second room closely associated with a bedchamber caught on gradually as the fifteenth century wore on. When the learned educationalist Vittorino da Feltre arrived at Mantua in 1423 to establish his celebrated school under the patronage of Gianfrancesco Gonzaga, the house he was given had thirteen *camere* but only two had associated *anticamere*.[1] In the Florentine Palazzo Rucellai, designed by Alberti and begun in 1446, only the *camera principale* had an *anticamera* and this was described as being *allato alla sudetta camera* [attached to the aforesaid bedchamber], as if its purpose still needed explaining.[2] It has to be admitted that this phrase occurs in an inventory of 1548 and so might seem irrelevant to our case; but the writers of inventories commonly copy the sequence and descriptions of earlier inventories of the same building, so the wording very probably reflects the descriptions used in fifteenth century inventories. Besides, a sixteenth-century writer would surely not normally think it necessary to give such an explanation. By the mid-sixteenth century, at any rate, *anticamere* were common in great houses; Cosimo I had two in front of his main bedchamber in his apartment at the Palazzo Vecchio, created around 1550 (Medici Invt., Florence, 1553).

However, it seems that an *anticamera* was at first often called a *guardacamera*. No *anticamere* are mentioned in the Este inventories of 1436 although it is hardly conceivable that no rooms of this class were present in any of their many residences, as some of these buildings are known to have incorporated the latest thinking on such matters.[3] Indeed, at the delightful Este summer residence, Belriguardo, built in the 1430s and regarded as one of the marvels of its day, many of the elegant bedchambers were furnished *con le sue servitrice guardacamere* [with their attendant *guardacamere*], according to Sabadino degli Arienti who was writing some fifty years later but was presumably using the term then still current in Ferrara. But Sabadino also speaks of two *anticamere* which one must suppose were somehow different from the numerous *guardacamere* (one, frescoed with Sibyls, apparently had a bed in it).[4] Maybe Sabadino, when staying at Belriguardo, was always having his attention drawn to the strings of bedchambers with their smaller satellite rooms long known as *guardacamere* but that, when he himself came to describe two such rooms specially, he used the more modern term *anticamera*. Whatever the case, *guardacamere* usually seem to occupy the same position relative to a *camera* as did *anticamere*. For instance, in Verona in the Aleardi inventory of 1408 (Aleardi Invt.) we find listed a *sala* with a small bedchamber next to it, and a main bedchamber with a *guardacamera* which surely must have served as an *anticamera* to this important room. We have a description of some Neapolitan gentlemen waiting in a *guardacamera* outside the bedchamber of the gravely ill Isabella Sforza, wife of Alfonso II of Aragon, in 1473 at Naples, and greatly shocking a visiting Milanese court embroiderer with their loud laughter and what he claimed was uncouth behaviour,[5] just as we know that Isabella d'Este was kept waiting in an *anticamera* before being admitted to the Pope's bedchamber to have an audience with his Holiness in 1526.[6] She, incidentally, did not have an *anticamera* in her new private apartment in the castle at Mantua, built for her in the early 1520s, but she did have a *guardacamera*. Once again, it is inconceivable that she did not have the amenity of an *anticamera* built into this extremely comfortable suite of rooms, to the creation of which she devoted a great deal of attention.[7] It seems evident that what she called her *guardacamera* could equally well have been called an *anticamera* and it is probably safe to infer that this was usually the case. Presumably the prefix *guarda* was used in the sense of an edge or side, rather than to imply that this was a storage space (see *guardaroba*, p. 298); but *guarda* can also carry the sense of protecting or saving something from an unpleasantness or burden, so perhaps we should understand *guardacamera* as a room that allowed various activities to be removed from the bedchamber, thus preserving the latter. Nevertheless, *guardacamere* and *anticamere* were scarcely less splendid than the bedchambers with which they were associated in many cases.

In a Renaissance house of any great size a room's privacy tended to be greater the further it lay from the main entrance. As we have seen, the more public rooms – the *sala*, *saletta/salotto* – lay closer to the entrance than did the main *camere*. As the *saletta/salotto* was commonly the private dining-room of the occupant of a main bedchamber, it could serve as a buffer against the outside world if it were placed on the path along which a visitor had to proceed in seeking to reach the bedchamber. A second buffer could be provided by placing the *anticamera* on this path as well, between the *saletta/salotto* and the *camera*. However, the intellectual leap required to make this the standard practice, so that the *anticamera* was indeed 'a forward chamber', which is how Florio* translated the word in 1611, was not taken before 1500. We see Francesco di Giorgio*, probably the greatest architect of his day, recommending, already around 1480, that on the *piano nobile* of a princely house the *salotti* should be associated with *camare et postcamare et anticamare* (i.e. he wanted a room in front of and one behind the *camera*, making three rooms following the *salotto* or private dining-room).[8] Elsewhere he spoke of *salotto, camara e anticamara con studio e camerini* which clearly arranges these rooms in the order of their privacy,[9] from which it will be seen that the *anticamera* was to be placed *after* the *camera*. This was the common position for it throughout the fifteenth century and well into the sixteenth (Pls 336, 338, 341). Serlio* very correctly labels such rearward rooms *dietrocamere* [*dietro* meaning behind];[10] they were also sometimes called *retrocamere*.

In palatial buildings in fifteenth-century Tuscany, and probably elsewhere as well, the *anticamera* of an important suite of personal rooms – personal to a senior male member of the family, that is – seems often to have been occupied by his wife.[11] This would of course explain why *anticamere*, in such circumstances, were placed *behind* the master's bedchamber for it was only in these innermost rooms that a wife could be properly protected. Such an arrangement did of course not pertain when the wife had her own suite of rooms (p. 288). In aristocratic and princely families, marriages were commonly arranged for dynastic reasons – to forge alliances between great families, and increase a family's power and influence through such unions; love rarely came into it. Providing separate rooms for a consort was therefore simply a recognition of these circumstances. Could it be that, in republican cities like Florence, such aristocratic notions were not so freely entertained, at least not in the fifteenth century, so a couple could be presumed to have married out of love for each other – in which case it was no hardship for the husband to have his wife esconced in one of his own personal rooms? On the whole it is more likely to have been a question of what was customary in Tuscany where, for all their republican sentiments, their aspirations in such matters do not seem to have been all that different from those of other Italians of equivalent status. This was undoubtedly the case from about 1500 onwards, among the leading patrician families.

When a consort had her own apartment, it had to be as splendid as that of her husband because, in a dynastic marriage, equal honour had to be paid to her. Her presence, after all, symbolized the political alliance between two great families (or blocks of power) and the family she represented could easily feel insulted if the arrangements made for her were inferior to those made for her husband. At the end of the lengthy instructions drawn up for the running of the Court at Urbino under Duke Guidobaldo (1482–1508), it is laid down that the same arrangements are to be made for the Duchess [*Et el simile e da observare nella famiglia del Madonna Duchessa*].[12]

It remains to be said that there was often no great difference between a *salotto* commonly used for dining and an *anticamera* sometimes used for the same purpose. The distinction was not clear, for instance, in the ducal palace at Urbino where the *salottino* [small *salotto*] of the Duke was sometimes described as an *anticamera*.[13] In a papal palace, and subsequently in other princely residences, it was necessary to have a special room for giving more or less private audiences. Such a room might be in the position normally occupied by a forward-placed *anticamera* but an additional room might be introduced for this purpose, in which case yet a further buffer came to be provided, serving to protect the occupant of the bedchamber from tiresome interference from the outside world. It was desirable in such a case to have a private entrance and passageway leading from the street to this audience-chamber, so that favoured visitors could come and go without the less favoured being aware of what was happening. Alberti* had such an arrangement in mind when he wrote that 'the best Way will be to have several Doors to receive your friends at, [and] by which you may dismiss those that have had Audience, and keep out such as you don't care to grant it to, without giving them too much Offence' [*diverse porte, per le quali tu gli possa ricevere dall'una e dall'altre parte, e mandarne quegli che avranno avuta udienza, o tenere fuora senza contumacia quelli a cui tu non volessi dare*].[14] See plate 326.

The More Private Rooms

In the innermost reaches of the house, often tucked away behind the bedchambers, lay small rooms of various kinds. Some were independent rooms for servants, others were for storage, and yet others – the most important, from our point of view – were the private closets of the owners of principal bedchambers. All these small rooms, whatever their precise function, tended to be associated with a bedchamber,[1] just as were the *salotti/salette* and *anticamere/guardacamere* that lay in the more public areas 'out front'.

Such a small room was often simply a *camerino* or *cameretta/cameretto* [i.e. a small room]. It was the equivalent of what in England would be called a closet or, in French, a *cabinet*. Both these words in essence mean a very small room (think of a 'broom closet') but they have a glamorous ring about them because today they conjure up visions of those elaborately decorated little rooms, personal to a single individual, that played such an important role in fashionable social life in the seventeenth and eighteenth centuries. Many *camerini*, apart from being smaller, were probably indistinguishable from the *anticamere* and *dietrocamere* that lay *behind* a main bedchamber (p. 294). But there was one class of *camerino* which was very special and was indeed the ancestor of the seventeenth- and eighteenth-century closets or *cabinets* just mentioned. Very occasionally, mid-sixteenth-century Italians actually called them *cabinetti*, making it clear that they lay, along with the bedchambers, in the more private parts of the house.[2] For the most part, however, such a small room was called a *studio* (sometimes, but not all that often, *studiolo*) or a *scrittoio*.[3]

The English word 'study' does not really indicate that such a room possesses a delightful character but this was commonly the case with the *studio* in Renaissance Italy. This very special room was essentially a personal space and owners often refer to *mio studio* in diaries or letters to friends, sometimes adding a comment about the pleasure they derive from retiring into these intimate and private enclosures. Macchiavelli, for example, described how he would return home, cast off his everyday clothes and don special robes before settling down in his *scrittoio* where, he insisted, he could happily spend hours, forgetting all his troubles and without becoming in any way bored.[4]

The owners of these pleasant rooms tended to keep their most treasured possessions there – books, important family documents, and valuables of all kinds.

At first, in the early quattrocento, *studi* were furnished in a simple manner and housed few possessions. They in many ways resembled a monk's cell – from which, of course, they were derived. Indeed, many owners of *studi* were learned clerics, men familiar with meditation, the need for solitude and happy in a secluded place where they could read their texts, transcribe, translate, illuminate and write commentaries. *Studii* were to be found in papal apartments (e.g. at Avignon and in the Vatican) and no doubt most cardinals and other senior ecclesiastics had such an amenity as well. On the secular side, mediaeval monarchs and other men of standing often had treasuries in which they kept costly plate, jewellery and the odd curiosity, and these strongrooms were usually located in some withdrawn part of a castle, easy to defend and often quite small. The two traditions, of the cleric's cell and of the secular treasury, came together in the fifteenth century *studio* and, by the end of the century, the treasures housed in such rooms had become much more numerous so that it became necessary to provide special shelves where they could be displayed and enjoyed, and cupboards in which more items might be stored.[5]

It was principally the learned who wanted a *studio*, during our period. There is no doubt that many a *quattrocento* scholar sought to emulate the Ancients in this respect, as they turned to the works of classical authors which contained references to the use and decoration of private studies and libraries. It was probably the writings of Petrarch that gave real impetus to this development and the illustration reproduced in Pl. 4, based on a fresco of about 1370, shows the great man (d. 1374) in his *studio*, handsomely furnished and with valued objects all round (an exceptionally rich assemblage for that date, it would seem). He referred to his little study as his *solitudo*.[6] Petrarch's example was followed by others who were not clerics and, by the early decades of the fifteenth century, many 'secular closets' were to be found in Italian houses – as we can see from inventories and contemporary descriptions. In some great houses there was sometimes more than one *studio* or *scrittoio*, one for each main apartment and located close to a principal bedchamber.[7] Moreover it was not merely the learned and the powerful who required this amenity; men of business needed them as well, in the first place as offices but later (notably where the rooms were handsomely decked out) as rooms that inspired confidence among those whom it was deemed desirable to impress. The writer of a handbook for merchants first urges his reader to have a *studiolo* in a remote part of the house but close to the chamber where he sleeps, a place where one can easily read late at night [*poter commodamente studiare quando il tempo gl'avanza*],[8] but he then goes on to recommend that a merchant should have a *scrittoio* separate from the rest of the house so as not to disturb the family 'on account of the strangers who come to the house to contract business with you'.[9]

Such solicitude for the welfare of the rest of one's family may not have been all that common; a wish for privacy, or even secrecy, was probably at least as powerful a motif and some particularly sensitive scholars likewise sought to be right away from all disturbance. Erasmus describes such a man, whose study lay in the innermost part of the house, had thick walls, double doors and windows, and all cracks carefully sealed 'so that hardly any light or sound can penetrate even by day, unless it's a very loud one like quarrelling women or blacksmiths at work'.[10]

While most *studi* were hidden away at the back of an important bedchamber, a few were located off staircases – which might amount to the same thing because the staircases concerned were usually those at the back of an apartment (backstairs). In the Palazzo Rucellai (designed, probably with Alberti's help, in the 1440s) there was a *camera a meza schala overo scriptoio* [a chamber, or rather a study, half-way up the

318 *Studio* in the bedchamber, about 1520

Quite a large room serving primarily as a bedchamber, but this scholarly cleric has turned one end of the room into a study. The bed is screened by a wooden partition fitted with a projecting shelf that supports some large vessels and utensils hanging from hooks. To the right is an *étagère* piled high with books and an assortment of other objects. More items are spread on the table. The cardinal's lap-dog has its own cushion while he himself is seated in a high-backed X-frame chair that betokens, if it were not otherwise evident, that he is a person of consequence.

Lorenzo Lotto, *Cleric in his bedchamber*, drawing
British Museum, London

319 An antiquarian's courtyard, 1535

Sketch made by Martin van Heemskerck at the Casa Sassi during his visit to the Holy City were such assemblages of excavated classical sculpture and architectural ornaments were to be seen at the residences of quite a few learned collectors with antiquarian interests. Note the lantern on a cord and the pot-plants on the parapet. This drawing was the subject of an engraving by Dirks Volkertsz Coornhaert published in 1553.

Martin van Heemskerck, *The courtyard at the Casa Sassi*, drawing
Kupferstichkabinett, Berlin (2783)

318

319

stairs].[11] A century later Torquato Tasso describes how he had to climb the stairs to the *studio* of a collector in Rome, and how he collapsed exhausted onto a chair when he reached the top. Fortunately the collection was so impressive that he felt it all well worth the effort.[12]

The architect Filarete*, writing in about 1460, describes Piero de' Medici's elaborately decorated closet in the family's *palazzo* in the Via Larga (Pl. 334). This *studietto*, he tells us, was also decorated with the very finest books and other objects of worth [*hornato di degnissimi libri et altre cose degnie*].[13] This room was truly what later would be called – in Germany, and now everywhere – a *Wunderkammer*. Increasingly, the decoration of *studii* claimed the attention of their owners and no one in her day took more trouble in this direction than Isabella d'Este who, in 1504, could write to her brother, Cardinal Ippolito, that she had indeed taken *grande cura in recogliere cose antique per honorare el mio studio* [great care in collecting antiquities to grace my study].[14] Having classical antiquities – marble busts, vases, gems, spear-heads, coins and fragments of sculpture – in one's *studio* became almost obligatory, so that eventually many of these small rooms were filled with relics, mostly placed alongside fine examples of modern craftsmanship – bronze statuettes (often inspired by classical originals), caskets, glass vessels, maiolica and even sometimes Oriental porcelain – to the extent that it soon became necessary to organize all these objects in some coherent manner. In certain cases, the collections were of such scale and significance that they could be organized by classes of object and it was then only a few short steps before one could call the room and its collections a 'museum', a seat of the Muses.[15]

It was during the second quarter of the sixteenth century that collections of curiosities, rarities and antiquities first began to be set out in regular arrangements in the small, or fairly small, rooms in which they were housed. When the erudite Bolognese scientist, Ulisse Aldrovandi, was in Rome in 1549/50 on Inquisition business, he visited the collections of several cardinals including that of Federico Cesi at his *palazzo* in the Borgo near St Peter's. This had walnut panelling that included a portrait of the Emperor apparently executed in *lavoro di intarsio*. There were ten busts of Roman emperors set on columns standing out in front of the panelling while a bust of Caesar stood in a niche. He also saw the *camerino, che serve per studio* [the small room which serves as a *studio*] of the late Cardinal Giovanni Gaddi in which were kept his *cose più elette, ma piu picciole* [the smallest of his most select things]. Once again busts of emperors were arranged all round 'at proper intervals' [*intorno con i suoi intervalli*].[16]

Strangers with introductions from friends of the owner, or some other proper form of credential, could usually visit such collections. Already by 1552, Anton Francesco Doni was describing important Venetian collections, including the *scrittoio d'anticaglie* [antiquities] of Gabriel Vendramin which was one of the glories of Venice.[17] Writing of a collection (housed in a *studio*) in the Veneto, a writer in 1590 could say that 'there is no one who passes nearby in the region who does not want to visit it, as something marvellous and singular'.[18] The Venetian, Francesco Sanso-

vino, who wrote so informatively about his native city (1581), actually provided a list of *case aperte*, houses open to the public, many of which had *scrittoi* that one could inspect, while Scamozzi*, in his treatise on architecture of 1615, mentions a friend's collection of sculpture that 'he proudly shows to all the most important people in Venice'.[19] As an antiquarian wrote to Cardinal Alessandro Farnese in 1566, an *antiquario* or *studiolo* 'will give pleasure to yourself regularly and to others on occasion'.[20]

It should be added that a person's *studio* might be established in one corner of the owner's bedchamber (Pl. 318) rather than in a separate room. Many scenes of the Annunciation painted during the second half of the fifteenth century show Mary reading at a desk-unit set up in her bedroom when she is interrupted by the Angel (Pls 131, 303, 379). Several descriptions in inventories seem to refer to such an arrangement[21] and Pietro Bembo, whose collection of antiquities was thought to be second to none in the 1530s, seems to have housed them in a *camera dov'e lo studio* [a bedchamber in which is the *studio*].[22] Was Bembo's arrangement similar to that shown in Pl. 318 which depicts a clerk seated among his treasures with a bed in the background? Or does the word *camera* here literally mean 'chamber' – a space in which this collection was housed?

The distinguished architect Francesco di Giorgio,* writing his treatise in about 1480, wanted the two main bedchambers in a fine house to be furnished *con destri, studi e camerini, nelle streme parti d'esse* [in the innermost parts of it],[23] while at the very back should be a spiral staircase – for service or the occasional quick get-away. A *destro* is what we would now call a lavatory, a WC or loo (the last word being a corruption of the French *lieu*, the place). All our words are euphemisms and *destro* is no exception; it means a convenience. Italians also spoke of *necessari* and in one inventory this little closet is described as the *retro camerotto in quo est privatum* [the small back-room in which stands the privy] (Guinigi Invt., Lucca, 1430).

Destri were tucked away in odd corners, often under the spiral stairs at the back of apartments (where it was easier to contrive effective ventilation). However, grand people tended to have close-stools which they at first placed actually in their bedchambers. Later, in the better sort of houses, these potentially rather smelly pieces of household equipment were placed in one of the small rooms near the bedroom, as such *camerini* began to proliferate (p. 298).

It is often thought that close-stools were placed in a *guardaroba* (probably because the French later referred to a lavatory as a *garderobe*) but there is no evidence that this was usual in Renaissance Italy. In fact a *guardaroba* was apparently exactly what the name implies – a room where belongings were stored. One finds clothes there, furnishings, and objects of all kinds. Cardinal Soderini had four clothes-presses in his *guardaroba* in 1523, for example[24]. At Urbino, in the 1580s, clothes, armour, weapons, saddlery, linen and jewellery were stored there, all in the custody of a man called *il guardaroba* because he did in fact guard them, signing for them regularly to certify that the things were in his care (Urbino Invt., 1582). A manual of 1625 recommends that this room

320 An astronomer's *studio*, 1514

With built-in seat, desk and book-cupboard all neatly tailored to his requirements, a rotating lectern within easy reach (with a lighting-arm above; see Pl. 295), this scholar has good reason to look contented as his is an extremely comfortable and convenient room for intellectual activity.

Title-page of a Florentine edition of Bernardo de Granollach's *Lunare cioe la ragione della luna*, a 15th-century work of a scholar living in Barcelona published in numerous editions in Italy 1514
Houghton Library, Harvard University, Cambridge, Massachusetts

321 Sixteenth-century shop-front

Many Italian *palazzi* had shops on the ground floor, facing onto the street. The brick and plaster counter is covered with a cloth bearing the merchant's mark. A hinged extension to the counter-top closes off the entrance to the shop itself. Stairs rise to the mezzanine above where there was no doubt an office and storage space. The front of the shop was entirely closed at night by a huge top-hinged shutter that swung down and could be locked. During the day it provided protection against sun and rain for the shoppers. Note the suspended oil-lamp in a glass vessel, and the arms of the city of Venice on the back wall.

From a book on exchange-rates, Venice, 1558 (first printed in 1538)
Houghton Library, Harvard University, Cambridge, Massachusetts

320

321

322 Section of the Palazzo Spinola, Genoa, late 1550s

Showing location of mezzanine rooms tucked in where small main rooms with low ceilings permit. By Bernardino Cantone, assistant of Alessi.

A *Portico* [entrance hall]
B *Sala*
C *Camera*
D Mezzanines, 'for servants'
E Mezzanines
F Cellars
G Water cistern

Based on a plan from Rubens' *Palazzi di Genova*

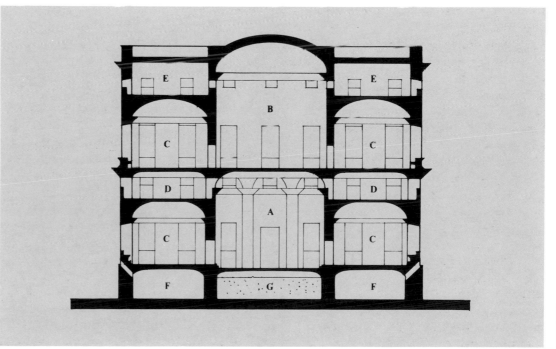

322

299

should be upstairs, out of the way, where security was greater and whence the noise of the clothes and hangings being beaten (to get the dust out) could not be heard in the 'polite' rooms below. Ideally the staircase up to it should be wide so that bulky goods could easily be carried up there but there should also be a small, secret staircase up to this important room.[25]

Some important people found it necessary to have private bedchambers near their more official ones (p. 288), and these small rooms may perhaps be masquerading under the title of *camerino*, in inventories and on plans of houses.

If, say, on the *piano nobile* of a grand house the *sala* has a high ceiling and this ceiling-height thus determines that of all the other rooms on that floor, then any small room will of course have a ceiling of a height that is much too tall in proportion to the room's size in plan. In such circumstances it was not uncommon to install a lower ceiling to suit the proportions. Virtue could be rescued from this necessity by introducing a floor on top of this inserted ceiling, thereby creating a mezzanine room [*mezzanino, mezzado, meza, mediano*, in Italian; Pl. 322]. Sometimes a whole horizontal sequence of such rooms was contrived, with small windows set in the façade as part of a considered design. A mezzanine was also sometimes called a *stanza di sopra*, because it was above another room and could often only be reached from that room;[26] it could also be called a *soffito*, which actually means a ceiling, but such a room is of course set above the ceiling of the room below.

Sometimes a staircase also led upwards from a *mezzanino* (e.g. up to the *piano nobile*) and was also carried on down to street-level. In a comedy called *La Venexiana*, a young woman receives her lover *nel mezzanino*, having descended from the main floor while he had climbed the stairs from the canal entrance.[27] Describing the plan of a villa, Serlio* writes of a *camerino* that it was *ammezzato* and that in order to reach the *mezato si montera per la limica* [one mounts via the spiral stairs].[28]

Small staircases, often spiralling, in the innermost parts of a building were an important means of servicing bedchambers and other rooms from the back, the main stairs being very much at the front, as far as visitors were concerned. Backstairs also provided a means of escape in case of trouble, or a means of going out or bringing people in discreetly, without their being seen by anyone – except of course the personal staff from whom secrets could rarely be hidden.

The Apartment

Devising the apartment was the most important contribution made by the Renaissance to the civilizing of life indoors. It was among Italians that the concept was first realized, in the third quarter of the fifteenth century. It took firm root in Italy and France during the sixteenth century but it was left to the French to develop the idea fully, during the seventeenth and eighteenth centuries, doing so with numerous subtle permutations.

The apartment was a group of rooms closely associated with a single person.[1] In its pure form the rooms were arranged in a linear sequence like beads on a necklace. The rooms of the 'necklace' could be laid out straight (Pl. 329) or could encompass a right-angled bend (Pl. 326); in some highly sophisticated examples the line doubled back on itself to form a 'U' (Pl. 330). The sequence proceeded from the more public parts of the house through to rooms that became increasingly private the deeper one penetrated. At the end was a secret exit. The rooms at the front, the public end, were larger than the innermost, the decrease in size usually being progressive along the line. A series of obvious entrances led from one room to the next and, while there might also be doors at the side, these were not supposed to be evident to a visitor.

The general arrangement is made clear in Pls 323–4, although the names and function of the rooms, and their order, could vary to some extent from one apartment to another. In every case, however, a bedchamber formed the heart of an apartment, with the more or less public rooms strung out in front of it (to continue the necklace analogy) and with the private rooms behind.

An apartment provided privacy, which is an important part of comfort indoors. It protected the occupant of the bedchamber against vexatious intrusion from the outside world. Because visitors entering from the public end were channelled within the tunnel-like form that an apartment constituted, it was easy to control access to an appropriate degree for those people the occupant wished to welcome into his rooms. In this and other ways it provided a convenient framework within which social life and ceremony could function in a regulated manner.

The standing of a visitor in the eyes of the occupant of an apartment could be gauged by how far the visitor was allowed to penetrate, close friends or people the occupant wanted to honour being permitted to come in further than others. Very intimate friends might be allowed to accompany the occupant right into one of the innermost rooms. Moreover, the occupant could bestow exceptional honour on a visitor by going out to one of the forward rooms to greet him and then bringing him back into one of the more private inner rooms. Delicate nuances of rank and honour could be signalled by such means to the on-looking world, and in the houses of the great such niceties have never been entirely absent.[2] But it was reserved for the French in the seventeenth century to develop particularly refined procedures of this kind although one gets the impression that popes and cardinals in sixteenth-century Rome did not lag far behind in this respect.[3] Nor were such concerns unknown at the princely courts of Italy, even though attitudes to these matters could be fairly relaxed at some of them, and we can be reasonably sure that behaviour based on similar notions was played out in important buildings all over Italy throughout the period. However, when the principal occupant of a great house had his personal rooms organized as an apartment – in the strict sense defined above – it was possible to manage such things in an especially satisfactory manner.

The desire for privacy was nothing new among the great (or even among lesser mortals, for that matter) at the beginning of the quattrocento, and most of those who could afford this luxury had secured it in some measure by then. Many had private dining-rooms, as we have seen, some were acquiring an *anticamera* next to their bedchamber and a few even owned a *studio*. Furthermore not a few had villas in the country where they could expect to find peace, away from the cares of the city.

The notion that greater privacy and safety could be achieved the deeper into a great house one retreated, was firmly established by the middle of the fifteenth century. Writing at that time, Alberti* envisaged the entire building organized on a linear sequence progressing from public to private areas (Pl. 325). Out in front near the main entrance lay the kitchen and other offices. At the centre lay the master's lodging and, at the back, the women's quarters. There is no mistaking the seclusion of the latter which 'ought to be sacred like Places dedicated to Religion and Chastity', where only men who are 'the nearest kindred' may set foot.[4] Moreover he insisted that he was 'entirely for having concealed Passages and hidden apartments'[5] and we have already noted how he implies there was a progression into privacy when he speaks of dining-rooms coming 'after' the courtyard, while 'further inside' are the bedchambers 'and finally' the closets [*Dopo ... sono le sale, e più adentro le Camere, e finalmente i Cabinetti*].[6]

Francesco di Giorgio,* writing around 1480, likewise hints at progression into privacy, speaking of bedchambers being associated with various small rooms that lie in 'the innermost parts' [*con destri, studi e camerini in nelle streme parti*].[7] He too urged the builder to instal *lumache o altri segrete scale* [spiral or other secret staircases] so that the owner could leave the building without being seen, which he could only have done if this private exit were somewhere well away from the front entrance. Although he was a highly practical man, one of the great engineers of all time, the house-plans he published[8] do not seem to offer the conveniences he describes to any great extent. He was at that stage greatly preoccupied with imposing symmetry and regularity on his idealized ground-plans. But in practice, he certainly knew how to contrive these comforts and will have done so for discerning clients on many occasions – and in many parts of Italy, one may presume, for he worked in most of the important cities during his very active career.

The treatise-writers were outlining principles to guide those about to put up new buildings or planning to alter existing edifices. Do the surviving buildings tell us more about the early development of the apartment as a concept?

What is certainly a very early example of a fully developed apartment, with all the required features mentioned above, is still to be seen today at the Palazzo Venezia, in the very centre of Rome (Pl. 326). It may even be the first true apartment anywhere, as it was created for papal use and popes could usually command the best brains among architects to carry out their building projects. At any rate, this vast apartment was conceived by Francesco del Borgo who must be counted among the most brilliant architects of his day, if only for what he did at the Palazzo Venezia in the mid-1460s.[9] Although the scale is enormous, because the building had to accommodate papal ceremonial as well as a pope's domestic requirements, the pattern is here already fully established and without doubt provided an example that others could follow. At this stage it is not easy to plot the spreading influence of this great Roman example but a not very well known early example of an apartment (now much altered) survives at the Villa Imperiale at Pesaro which was built for Alessandro Sforza between 1469 and 1472 (Pl. 327).[10] A few other examples survive from this early period but the concept was by no means widely adopted until well into the next century (Pls 328–31). The great apartment at the Palazzo Venezia should be seen as a precursor of all those Baroque apartments in great houses all over Europe with which many readers will be familiar.

A few years before the Palazzo Venezia apartment was created, an impressive suite of rooms was built in the Palace at Urbino which has most of the hallmarks of a true apartment although it does not terminate with a backstairs as a fully developed apartment should (Pl. 332).[11] This proto-apartment was built in the late 1450s and completed for the wedding in February 1460 of Federigo da Montefeltro, the future Duke of Urbino. Today called the 'Apartment of Iole', it is apparently not known who was the architect at Urbino during this early phase in the history of this important and fascinating building but one may suspect the influence of Alberti* who certainly knew Federigo and advised him on questions to do with architecture.[12] This suite, incidentally, is far more rationally planned than the more famous 'Appartamento del Duca' that was conceived by Francesco di Giorgio* or by Luciano Laurano between 1465 and 1472.[13] The site of this later apartment was admittedly awkward and cramped but, whatever the reason, one has to say that, in terms of the history of distribution, the arrangement of this suite is retrogressive. There is no clear sequence of rooms, and the architecture did not automatically channel visitors, so it must have been far less easy to control access to this later apartment than to the earlier one.[14]

Often cited as a brilliant example of planning is the Palazzo Medici in Florence, the building of which started in 1444 to the designs of Michelozzo (Pl. 334).[15] There is a sense of linear organization in the main apartment, with large rooms at the front and smaller ones at the back, but no attempt was made to channel visitors through the principal rooms; indeed there was a major corridor running alongside so that visitors could (at least, in theory) enter these rooms from the side – an arrangement that one would have thought could not ensure total peace of mind or privacy for the occupant of this suite of rooms.[16] Maybe in republican Florence it was not at this stage thought proper to channel one's fellow-citizens, or indeed other visitors, in too overt a manner although the wish to do so

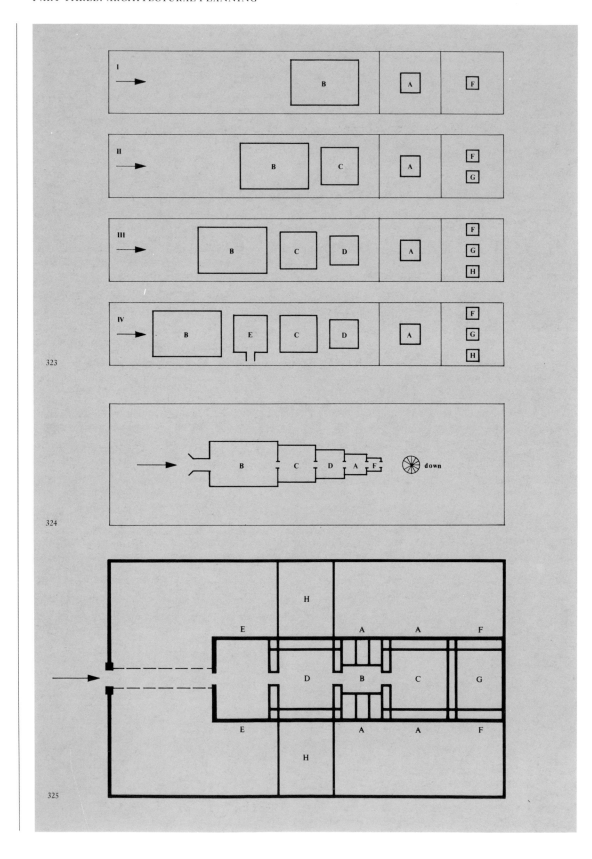

323 Room sequence development

→ Visitors' direction of approach from front entrance.

A   Bedchamber [*camera*]; owner's bedroom
B   Main hall [*sala*]; dining and reception
C   Private dining-parlour [*salletta/salotto*]: for owner's greater privacy
D   Antechamber [*anticamera*]; associated with the bedchamber
E   Audience chamber with private access/exit
F   Closet [*studio*]
G&H Other small rooms associated with the bedchamber

324 The principle of the apartment

Controlled linear approach of visitors into areas of increasing privacy.

A Bedchamber [*camera*]; owner's bedroom
B Main hall [*sala*]; dining and reception
C Private dining-parlour [*saletta/salotto*]; for owner's greater privacy
D Antechamber [*anticamera*]; associated with the bedchamber
F Closet [*studio*]

Service stairs at back also serve as a private route for owner – and escape, if need be.

325 The principle applied to an entire building

Based on a French interpretation of 1553 of Alberti's mid-fifteenth-century text describing an ideal scheme where the entire building is geared to providing increasing privacy, the deeper one penetrates from the entrance (left).

A The owner's residential quarters with courtyard (C)
B Main hall for dining and reception
C Owner's private courtyard and garden with surrounding *loggia* offering view also over main garden areas outside
D Main courtyard with *loggia* around it
E Service areas including kitchen
F Ladies' quarters with courtyard (G)
G Private courtyard and garden for the ladies
H Outbuildings amid gardens, vineyard and paddocks

326 Palazzo Venezia, Rome; *piano nobile* mid-1460s

The fully-developed apartment in a papal residence.

A   Pope's bedchamber and private audience chamber (*Sala del Papagallo*)

B   Pope's antechamber; assembly room for cardinals (*Sala dei Paramenti*)

C–E Chief reception rooms

C   Innermost chief reception room (*Sala del Mappamundo*)

D   Second *sala*; used for consistories, etc.

E   Main *sala*

F   Main staircase, from entrance

G   *Loggia*

H   Service corridor links all reception rooms to stairs (L) down to kitchen

J   Entrance from street on ground floor leads to stairs (K) up to Pope's audience chamber (A)

K   Stairs up from kitchen and entrance J

L   Guard-chamber controlling access to Pope's rooms and service corridor

M   Pope's private bedchamber

N   Pope's closet and a second small room?

P   Pope's other private rooms including strong-room

M–P This area lies within thick walls supporting a tower which thus both materially and symbolically defines its special status

Q   Back stairs and access to private roof-garden

Based on various plans, chiefly those published by Frommel

327 The first Villa Imperiale, Pesaro; *piano nobile*, 1469–72

Built for Alessandro Sforza, Lord of Pesaro (d. 1473).

A   Owner's bedchamber?

B   Antechamber?

C   *Sala*; once had two fireplaces, so for use in winter

D1 & Possibly once a single large room? If so, it

D2   would have served as the principal *sala*

F   Owner's closet?

G   Back stairs

J   Called a *salottum*; probably private dining-room

K   Originally a loggia facing south? There was a loggia immediately below, facing onto the courtyard.

Based on Eiche, with some conjecture

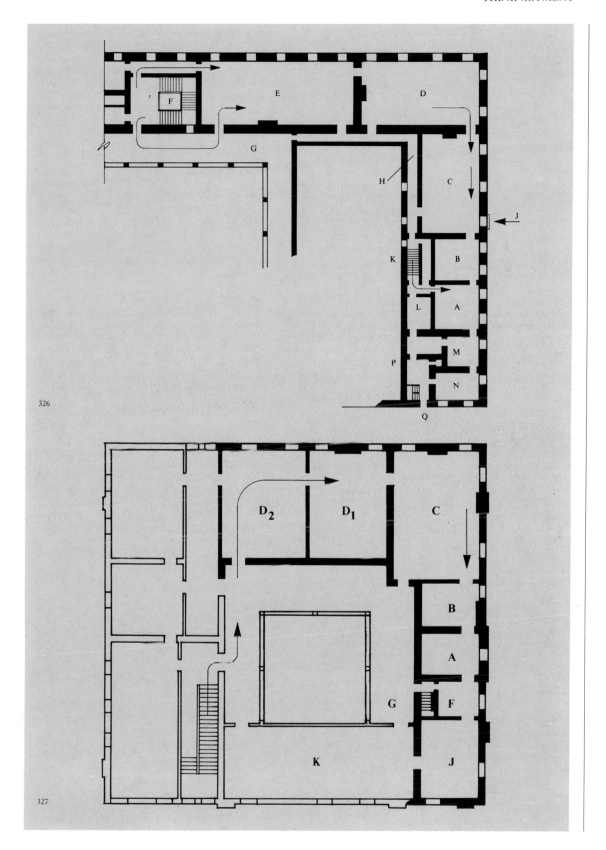

326

327

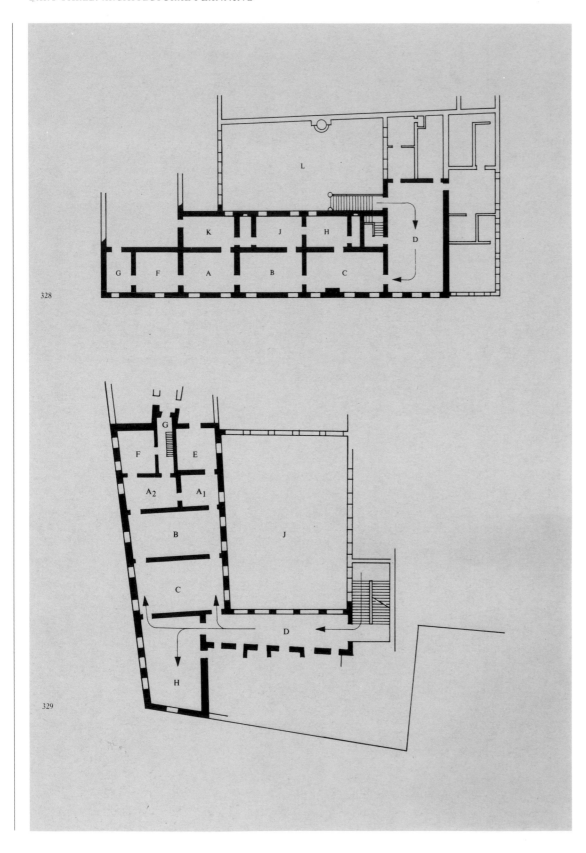

328

329

328 Palazzo dei Penitenzieri, Rome; *piano nobile*, about 1478

Built for Cardinal Domenico della Rovere.

A   Owner's bedchamber
B   Antechamber
C   Private dining-room (called *salotto* on 1563 plan)
D   *Sala*
F   *Postcamera*? or private bedchamber?
G   Closet
H   Chapel
J & K   Associated rooms
L   Courtyard

Based on 1563 plan reproduced by Frommel

329 Palazzo Altemps, Rome; *piano nobile*, late 1470s

Built for Count Girolamo Riario, nephew of Pope Sixtus IV. Later acquired by Cardinal Altemps.

A1   Bedchambers of owner and his wife (Catarina
A2   Sforza) linked in the Albertian manner
B   Joint antechamber
C   *Sala* (see Pl. 101)
D   Open *loggia*; approach from main staircase
E   The owner's closet
F   His wife's closet
G   Back stairs
H   Second *sala*? with frescoed columns in perspective as advocated by Alberti
J   Courtyard

Based on plans in a monograph on the building

330 Palazzo Strozzi, Florence;
piano nobile, 1489–90

Architects Benedetto da Maiano, followed by Cronaca.
Showing two symmetrical apartments.

A Bedchamber; position of bed is shown
B Antechamber; that on right later made into two
   rooms
C *Sala*, one for each apartment
D *Guardaroba*? with back stairs
E Closet?
F Staircase up from courtyard, one to each
   apartment
G Open *loggia*; access to *sala* from staircase, no direct
   entry to bedchamber
H Courtyard

Based on various plans

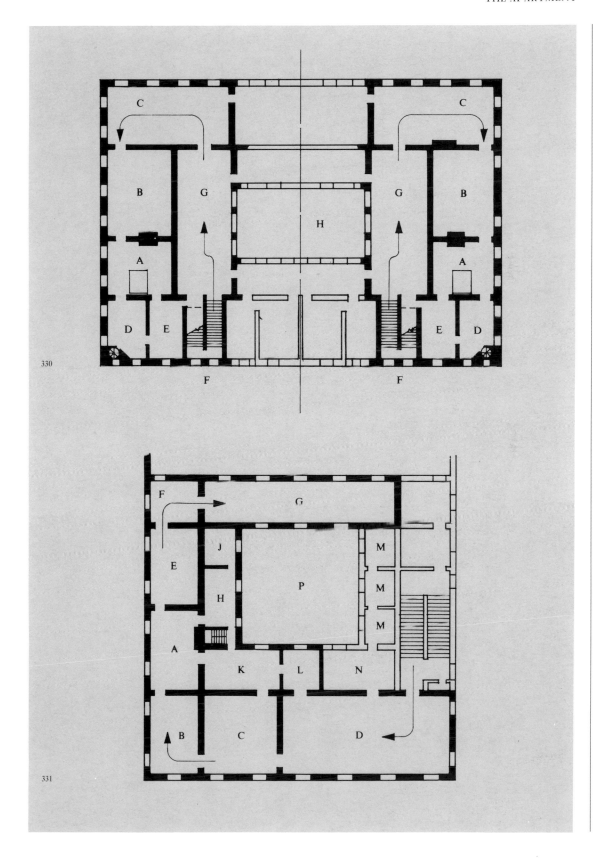

331 Palazzo Castellesi, Rome;
piano nobile, 1504–13

Architect probably Bramante. Built for Cardinal Adriano Castellesi (created Bishop of Hereford by the King of England). Showing an innermost private suite alongside main apartment. Now called Palazzo Torlonia.

A The Cardinal's main bedchamber
B Antechamber
C Private dining parlour, called *salotto* on *c.* 1590
   plan
D *Sala*
E Room associated with main bedchamber;
   postcamera?
F Closet; more public than J
G *Galeria*, so called in *c.* 1590; was this formerly an
   open *loggia* overlooking the garden at the back?
H Private bedchamber of the Cardinal
J Private closet
K Called a *camera* in *c.* 1590; perhaps originally a
   second antechamber
L Chapel
M Separate apartment
N *Saletta* associated with M in *c.* 1590
P Courtyard

Based on plan of *c.* 1590 published by Frommel

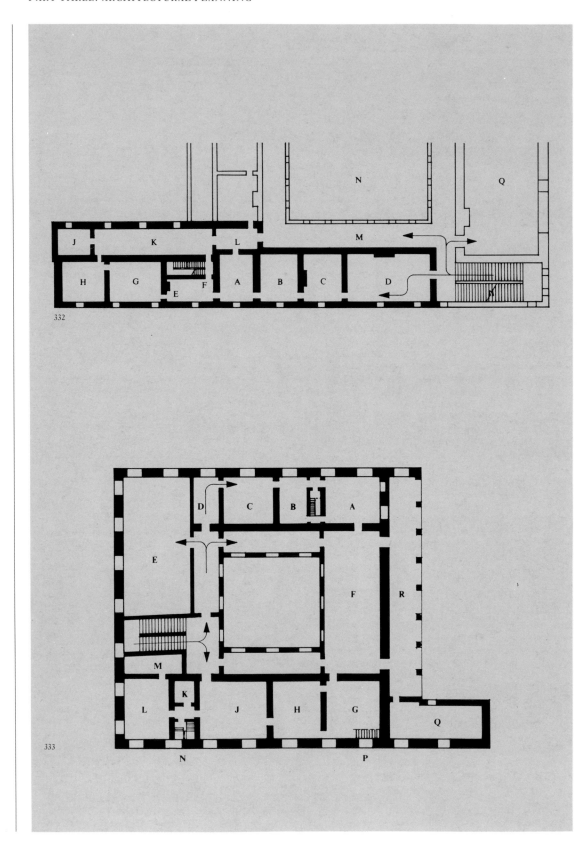

332

333

332 The Iole Apartment, Palazzo Montefeltro, Urbino

Probably achieved by 1460 when Battista Sforza came to marry Federigo da Montefeltro, the future Duke. Likely to have been planned with Alberti's aid.

A Federigo da Montefeltro's bedchamber
B Antechamber ⎫
C Audience chamber ⎬ (or *vice versa*)
D *Sala*
E Closet? called *camerino*
F Secondary stairs in the middle rather than at the back
G Battista Sforza's antechamber?
H Her bedchamber
J Her closet; was there a further staircase nearby? It seems not
K Gallery or connecting passageway
L Guard-chamber controlling access to private areas?
M Open *loggia* round courtyard
N Courtyard
Q The main *sala* for important feasts

Based on plans published by Polichetti and others

333 Palazzo Piccolomini, Pienza; *piano nobile*, 1458–62

Architect Bernardo Rossellino working closely with his patron, Pope Pius II. Encompasses summer and winter apartments but not with strict symmetry.

A–E The Pope's summer apartment facing east
A His bedchamber (the niche for a close-stool may possibly be original)
B His antechamber?
C Private dining parlour?
D Chapel
E *Sala* for summer use (*aestivum coenaculum*)
F Principal *sala* with view over courtyard, and opening into a loggia (R) with splendid view.
G–J The Pope's winter apartment? Faces west.
G His bedchamber? Like A, said to be particularly richly decorated
H Antechamber?
J *Sala* (*aula*). Smaller than E; easier to heat
K Small room, perhaps for private secretary
L Pope's study? Has even light from the north May have contained a day-bed.
M Secret strong-room (*conclave*).
N Stairs
P Back stairs
Q Kitchen block (kitchen for each of three floors)
R *Loggia*

Based on various plans: with some conjecture

334 Palazzo Medici (Via Larga), Florence

Begun in 1444 to designs by Michelozzo for Cosimo de' Medici. A proto-apartment.

A *Camera grande*
B *Sala*; subsequently two rooms
C *Anticamera* behind the bedchamber
D Private study (*scrittoio*)
E Wide passage leading from head of staircase direct to the chapel (F) allows access to bedchamber from the side
F Chapel that could serve as audience chamber
G Back stairs; precise conformation unclear
H Courtyard

Based on 1650 plan published by Bulst

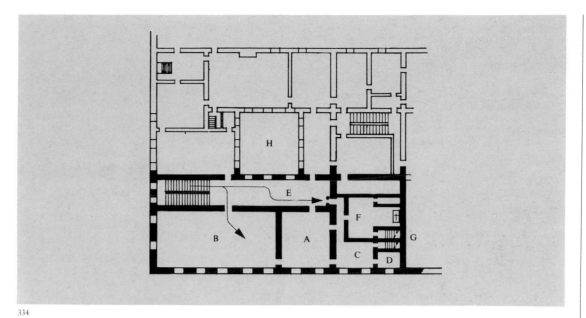

334

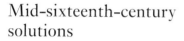

Mid-sixteenth-century solutions

Plates 335–41 are based on plans from Serlio's *Treatise on Architecture*, Vol. VII, which was published posthumously in 1575 but presumably reflects Italian practice in the mid-16th century.

335 A town house

Plan for a town house on an irregular site showing a skilfully planned apartment on the ground floor. A similar apartment was to be on the first floor, along with a *sala*.

A *Camera*
B *Dietro camera*
C *Camerino*
D Space for close-stool
E Back stairs
F Private courtyard
G Garden
H Main courtyard
K–J Subsidiary apartments
M *Saletta*, a dining-parlour presumably for use by the family, but its forward position suggests it may have been for the senior staff

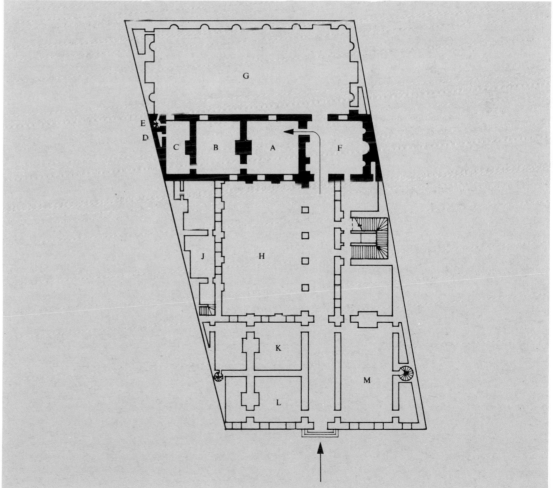

335

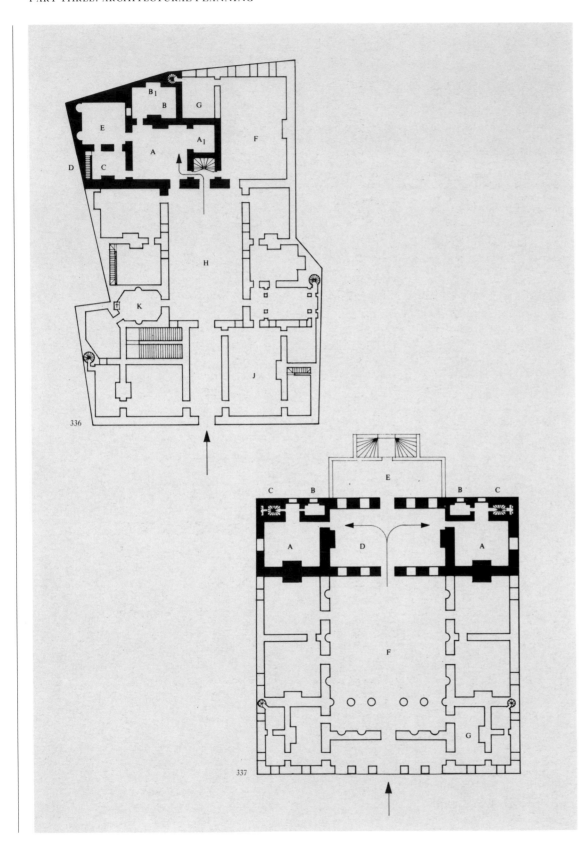

336 Another irregular site

This shows rooms cleverly distributed and one important apartment; the ground floor.

A *Camera* with bed-alcove (A1)
B *Dietro camera* with niche (B1) for a *lettuccio*
C *Camaretta* (closet)
D Back stairs
E *Cortiletto* (small private courtyard)
F *Sala*; there is no *sala* on the first floor, we are told
G *Camera* associated with *sala*
H Courtyard
J *Saletta*; its position suggests this was a dining-room for senior staff
K Chapel

337 Twin apartments

Symmetrically disposed twin apartments on the ground floor of a villa in the countryside.

A Bedchamber
B *Camerino*
C Back stairs with *necessarii* (two seats each)
D *Sala* with two fireplaces
E Terrace overlooking garden
F Courtyard
G *Saletta*; possibly may have served as a private dining parlour

338 Four identical apartments

Ground-plan of a villa with four identical apartments symmetrically disposed around a central octagonal *sala*. Such intellectual symmetry was easily achieved only in the unencumbered space of the countryside.

A Bedchamber
B *Dietro camera* (antechamber behind the *camera*)
C Closet reached via foot of spiral staircase off which was also a cabinet for the close-stool
D Central *sala*

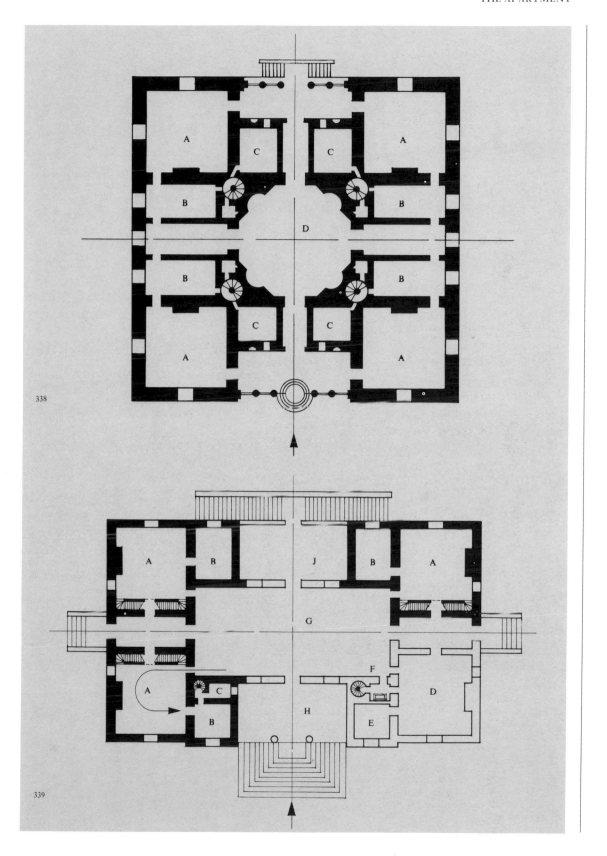

339 Almost symmetrical ground-plan

Ground-plan of a villa that is almost symmetrical but actually comprising three apartments and a dining-room.

A Bedchamber
B Antechamber or closet (*camerino*)
C Stairs (and space for close-stool?)
D *Saletta* or private dining-room
E Service room associated with D
F *Lavabo* for rinsing glasses, etc. and stairs down to kitchen
G *Sala*
H Covered entrance *loggia*
J Open *loggia* that can be covered with an awning in the summer heat

Note staircases to turrets on the roof.

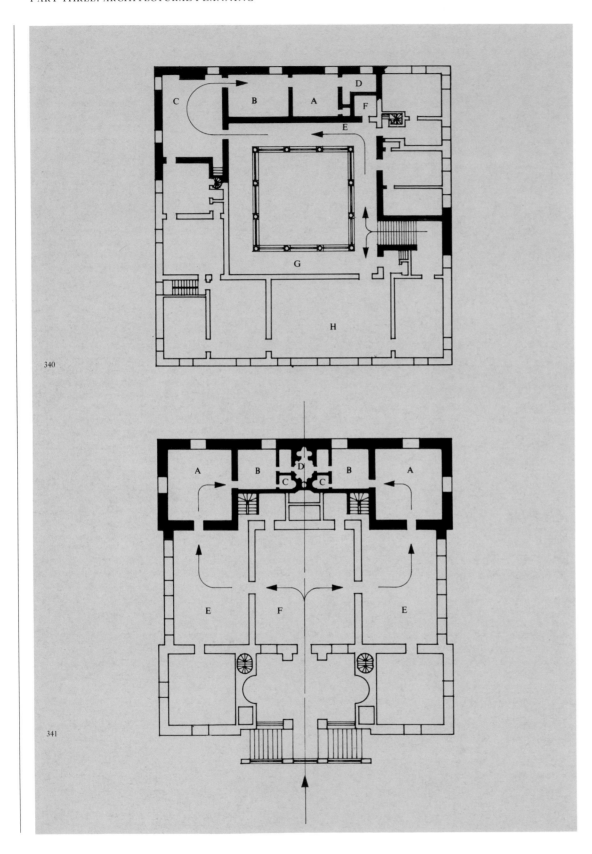

340 Palazzo Doria-Spinola, Genoa; *piano nobile*, about 1540

Architect Giovanni Battista Castello, for Antonio Doria. Advanced planning in Genoa just before Alessi arrived from Rome bringing fresh notions.

A Bedchamber?
B Antechamber?
C Private dining-room?
D Closet
E Space for close-stool
F Chapel
G Open *loggia* provides access from staircase which is awkwardly placed
H *Sala*

Based on a plan from Rubens' *Palazzi di Genova*

341 Villa Grimaldi, Genoa; ground floor, completed 1568

Architect Galeazzo Alessi, built for Battista Grimaldi on an ancient fortress and known therefore as La Fortezza. Twin apartments share a central bathing-complex.

A Bedchamber
B *Recamera* [antechamber behind, i.e. *retrocamera*]
C Close-stool house?
D Bathing-complex; probably with central plunge bath, *sauna* [*stufa*] and two rest-rooms
E *Salotto* for dining and reception
F *Portico*, i.e. central hall

Based on a plan from Rubens' *Palazzi di Genova* (Rubens stayed in this house in 1606)

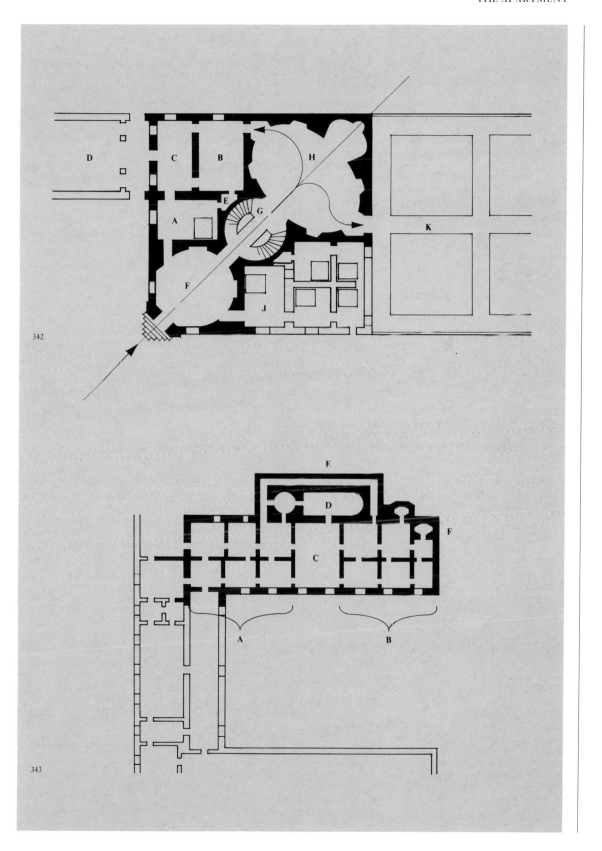

342 Design for a villa, 1570s

By the Florentine architect, Giovanvittorio Soderini, probably for his own use. A highly original scheme on a diagonal axis looking forward to Baroque forms.

A Main bedchamber, the bed shown
B Antechamber?
C *Salotto*?
D Terrace?
E Space for close-stool
F Entrance vestibule
G Staircase with paired flights
H *Salone*? with fountain in niche
J Five subsidiary bedchambers (for the family?); note the beds
K Garden

343 Palazzo Pitti, Florence; first floor, late 1590s

This shows the pair of apartments of the Archduke Ferdinand and his wife, Christina of Lorraine, joined by a private passageway running behind the chapel.

A The Archduke's apartment
B His wife's apartment
C Central *sala*
D Chapel
E Private passageway connecting the two apartments
F The Archduchess's bathroom

Based on a plan published by Laura Giusti

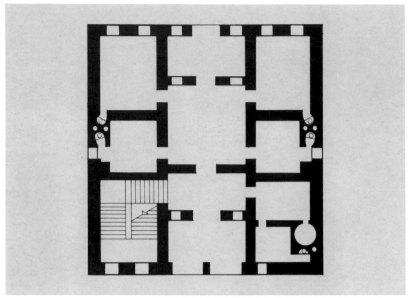

344

344 Project for a house in Florence

By Antonio da Sangallo the Younger (d. 1546), for Angelo da Castro showing clusters of lavatories apparently with a flushing system (relying on rainwater?) and ventilation pipes.

Based on a drawing in the Uffizi

cannot, even there, have been entirely absent. Presumably because there was no sense of progression *through* the rooms, there was no reason to have rooms interposed 'out front', at the Palazzo Medici, so the *camera* comes immediately after the *sala*; there is no *salotto* acting as an initial buffer against the world outside and the *anticamera*, which in fully developed apartments came to be placed in front of the *camera* to increase the number of buffers, as it were, remains behind the *camera* in the then still traditional manner. The interposing of rooms between the *sala* and the *camera*, set in a linear sequence, was to be a characteristic of the true apartment; it was not present at the Palazzo Medici.

The Palazzo Piccolomini in Pienza, built for Pius II between 1459 and 1462 by another Florentine architect, Bernardo Rossellino, is also often cited as a clever example of planning – which indeed it was – but there are no small rooms at the back of the two papal apartments (for winter and for summer use) and it seems these suites should once again be seen as proto-apartments (Pl. 333).[17] As this is essentially a country residence, there was perhaps no pressing need to introduce very formal measures for controlling access. Besides, these were early days; the Palazzo Venezia apartment had not yet taken shape. Even the most advanced architects were still feeling their way, in the years around 1460, towards creating an apartment in the true sense of the word.

While the idea of an apartment had been fully realized by 1470 and became well understood in advanced circles in the next few decades, no special term was used to describe such a phenomenon. The word *appartamento* was first used in print, it seems, in Bartoli's 1550 translation into Italian of Alberti's* treatise which had been written in Latin about a century earlier. However, in most of the places where he is speaking of apartments, Bartoli calls them *luoghi* [places] or *stanze* [rooms], and this was apparently the normal practice until the middle of the sixteenth

century. Only once does Bartoli use the new word when he speaks of *l'ultimo appartamento* [the last or ultimate] in a princely house being that where the husband's and the wife's two suites are conjoined to form a matrimonial apartment.[18] As we have shown, it was normal for husbands and wives to have separate apartments or groups of personal rooms, but the more usual solution was to have a linking passage between the two areas rather than an additional joint 'apartment' – or so it seems.

Serlio* mentions *appartamenti* several times in his Book VII which was not published until 1575, twenty-one years after his death (1554). It has been suggested that his plates, which in this volume include many ground-plans, may have been altered posthumously by his editor but, if so, they were presumably only changed in small details (Pls 335–9). The same is probably true of the text although this would be easy to change. However, if we assume that very little needed changing, then what was published must have taken shape in the 1540s which would agree with the occurrence of the new word. In fact Serlio, if it was he, used the term both in its strict sense and more loosely to mean 'rooms'. It has been suggested that the term apartments at first was only applied to paired suites of rooms that were symmetrical.[19] This does not seem to be borne out by Serlio's published plans[20] and was certainly not true of seventeenth-century building. But many apartments were symmetrical as this was a neat way of providing equally significant space for a wife and for her husband, reflecting their equal status (p. 288). It had nothing to do with the structural problem of supporting the roof, as Palladio* at one point claimed;[21] but it happened to suit Renaissance architects who regarded symmetry in their ground-plans as being highly desirable (p. 319 and Pls 330, 337, 339).

Scamozzi*, whose book was published in 1615, sums up the, by then, widely accepted perception of how an apartment worked when he wrote that one should 'lett the principall parts be Great and little Salaes & the great roomes, next the middle ones and then the least. To the end that those who go onely to accompanie the owner, may remaine in the first places, his intimate friends into the second, but those who have businesse to treate with him, must goe into the innermost of all: and lett this order be observed not onely in the Palaces of principall Lords, but also according to proportion in well governed houses of private Gentlemen.'[22] By his time, Scamozzi is saying, one could expect to see the apartment system applied in all houses of consequence in Italy.

Other Rooms, Other Levels

The rooms we have discussed so far in Part Three – the *sala*, the *salotto* or *saletta*, and the rooms making up the main apartments – have all lain on the *piano nobile* which means they were on the first floor, at any rate in buildings of any great size. Only in small houses, notably villas, might the *piano nobile* be on the ground floor.

Among the rooms on the *piano nobile* there might be a private chapel or oratory. Only persons of high standing and much influence could have a chapel, as it apparently required special papal dispensation to do so: otherwise people were expected to take the sacrament in a church. Usually chapels were elaborately decorated and some great people saw no harm in using the room as an audience chamber, on occasion. After all, the visitor might be dazzled by the decorative effects, and more than a usual amount of Divine Blessing might attend the discussions and decisions taken in such surroundings. Considerations of this kind must have governed the location of the chapel in the Palazzo Medici which is situated at the end of a wide corridor leading from the head of the main staircase (*andito di chapo di schala che va alla chappella*),[1] an arrangement clearly intended to lead visitors to the sumptuous little room (with its Gozzoli frescoes, that we can still see today) and to impress them in doing so; this was not simply a room for private devotions (Pl. 334). Nicholas v's delightful little chapel in the Vatican, decorated with frescoes by Fra Angelico, served a similar dual purpose, as may have the chapel shown on the plan given in Pl. 331.

Corridors, incidentally, were not a common feature of fifteenth-century Italian *palazzi*. Normally one had to pass through a room to reach the room beyond, or one could in many cases use the *loggia* that ran round the well of the courtyard, providing an open-air connecting passageway to most parts of the building at that level. Moreover, once the fully-fledged apartment had been devised, where the intention was to channel visitors *through* a sequence of rooms, a true corridor would have nullified such an arrangement, although there often was a more or less secret passage alongside an apartment whereby the servants could enter the rooms from the side (Pl. 326). If gentlefolk used such passages, it was on occasions when they did not want to be seen.

Related to the open *loggia* around the courtyard was the *galleria*. The *loggia* at the Villa Farnesina in Rome where Raphael's *Galatea* is still to be seen was called a *galleria* in 1523.[2] The term seems to have been introduced from France where the concept of a long enclosed room for exercise, recreation and display of sumptuous decoration was first evolved.[3] The earliest use of the term in the Italian inventories studied in

345 The womens' *loggia*

Two girls look down from a first-floor loggia, which presumably forms part of secluded quarters set aside for the women of the family. Below, the three principal figures converse, seated on chests. There is a lantern above, one of the courtiers holds a tall candle, and the spigot of a small candle-holder has been set into a hole bored in the column. (See diagram 20, page 361).

From *Guiron Le Courtois*, 1370s
Bibliothèque Nationale, Paris (5234/34)

345

346

347

346 Dining in a covered *loggia*

In this open-air space on the *piano nobile* a long table covered with a fine Turkish carpet has been set up for dining. A tumbler has fallen down into the courtyard (or street?) and miraculously remains intact.

Girolamo del Santo, *Miracle of the Tumbler*, Scuola del Santo, Padua, *c.* 1510
Photograph: Alinari Archives

347 Room next to the kitchen; 1570

With figures drawn badly out of scale (note the door-handles well above head height) and an oil-lamp suspended from the ceiling shown much too large, this scene is nevertheless instructive. On the left is a well, while a sink with piped water is visible beyond. On the right is a heavy 'controlled' pestle and a small brick cooking stove. At the large table, *pasta* is being prepared and a man on the left is making 'white pudding'. The paintbrush in the bottom right corner is 'for gilding pastry'. The shelf high on the left has hooks underneath which are labelled *rastelli* (see p. 240).

From Bartolomeo Scappi, *Opera*, Venice, 1570
Metropolitan Museum of Art, New York, Elisha Whittelsey Collection, Elisha Whittelsey Fund, 1952 (52.595.2[2])

connection with the present work occurs in one from Piedmont of 1512, that of the Montebello family's castle at Frossasco (Frossasco Invt.), where we find a *sub gallaria apud hostium sale* which must have been in the nature of a corridor leading to the *sala*.[4] Piedmont was of course more closely linked to France than any other Italian province. François I's famous gallery at Fontainebleau, a creation of the 1530s, was to inspire quite a few Italian grandees, special attention having been drawn to it among Italians because notable Italian artists had been involved in its decoration. An early example of this influence was the gallery at the Palazzo Spada in Rome, designed by Il Baronino in 1548–9, while a decade later a *galeria* for the display of portraits of the Este family was established in the castle at Ferrara.[5] A particularly famous example is the gallery at the Palazzo Farnese of about 1575. It was while walking in an Italian gallery in the 1590s, incidentally, that Fynes Moryson noted how he and an Italian companion saw 'two English gentlemen entring their chamber [and] shutt the door close after them' whereupon his companion enquired 'if the younger were not a woman in mans apparell', giving 'the shutting of their dore for the reason of his suspition'. Italians thought it very bad manners to 'shutt their doores by day lest they should seeme to doe or have any thinge they would be loath should be seene',[6] Moryson said.

Scamozzi* tells us that, by the end of the period, galleries were 'much used in Rome & Genoa, and other Cities of Italie' in the houses of 'Lords and great persons'.[7] Speaking particularly of Venice, he goes on to say that 'since a certaine time [or, as we might say, 'for some while, now'] many Senators & Nobles & vertuous persons ... have gathered together diverse antiquities of Marbles, Bronzes, Medalls, & rich carved things, as Likewise Pictures made by the most skillfull masters, & the notedest workemen of these our dayes' and housed these assemblages in galleries. He then mentions the celebrated collection of Giovanni Grimani, Patriarch of Aquilea, 'of glorious memorie', for whose collection Scamozzi had recently (i.e. prior to 1615) created 'a Studio or Gallerie' in which the objects were displayed 'in verie good order', which implies that they were disposed according to a regular and carefully considered scheme. It is noteworthy that he calls it a 'studio *or* gallery', as if there were no great distinction. We have already said something about the *studio* (p. 296) which could simply be a study but in many cases had become a repository for curiosities and valued 'treasures' that were often arranged according to formal principles.[8] If the collection were large, the room needed to house it could no longer be called a *studio*, and it only had to be rather long in its proportions readily to qualify for the name of *galleria*. In some cases a gallery of antiquities would have a *studio* attached; in which case the latter might serve more as an office or study-room for the collector or his curator. At the Palazzo Farnese in Rome a *studiolo* was created next to a library. Fulvio Orsini, learned antiquarian and humanist, was Cardinal Alessandro Farnese's curator of antiquities, and he devoted much attention in the 1570s to the arrangement of the works of art on display there. The library and its little adjacent gallery were open to serious students, to the extent that this amenity was regarded as a *schola publica*.[9]

If we now descend the main staircase from the *piano nobile* we should find ourselves in some form of vestibule (a 'front hall' as we might call it today) with the main entrance beyond. As vestibules are 'like Places of publick Reception', as Alberti reminds us, they ought to be in the centre 'like Squares and other open Places in Cities'.[10] Although these spaces were scarcely less public than the street or square outside, there was a front door or gate through which a visitor had to pass in order to enter the building and this was controlled by a porter 'that nobody may come in, nor anything be carried out, without [his] Knowledge'. It was also here that arms were kept, ready to defend the entrance if necessary. In a large establishment there might be a guard, a troop of men, fulfilling this purpose, as there was at the palace in Urbino.[11] However, as we are primarily concerned with domestic arrangements, we will pass quickly through these central entrance areas, noting merely that they were made as handsome as possible so as to impress the visitor. The same may be said of the courtyard around which were disposed most houses of any size erected in Italian cities during the Renaissance.

In the majority of city *palazzi* there were shops on the ground floor. Only in very grand residences indeed was this not the case. When the Palazzo Strozzi in Florence was built (begun in 1489) the family felt that shops would have marred the building's beauty.[12] One could not normally enter the house through such a shop but there was often a mezzanine floor inside the shop with its own individual staircase (Pl. 321). There would also be storage areas on the ground floor and in cellars below. Even very great merchants, with splendid town-houses, tended to keep their merchandise on their own premises. In the fifteenth century they did not go off to distant offices, no one commuted. Business was largely done on one's own doorstep or actually indoors. It was not until well into the sixteenth century that it became common for palaces to be purely residential, with all signs of commerce removed to other premises.

On the ground floor also lay the summer apartment of the owner, if he had one (p. 288), and usually also the kitchen. The latter had often been at the top of the house, in mediaeval times, when most houses were made of timber. If such an upstairs kitchen caught fire, the conflagration was less likely to engulf the building; but it cannot have been easy carrying everything needed for food-making up several flights of stairs. It must have restricted the amount of water used, water being heavy and awkward to carry in substantial amounts. Certainly to have piped water must have been out of the question in upstairs kitchens and when this became a common requirement, kitchens came to lie on the ground floor or even

below ground level, and there would be a water source in the room or close by (Pl. 347). Once the whole building was made of stone or brick, the danger of fire was anyway considerably reduced.

In large establishments there was sometimes more than one kitchen and we noted how Pius II at Pienza had a 'kitchen wing' separated from the house proper by an interior wall in order to keep out the smell of food. It was tower-like and contained a kitchen at each level (Pl. 333).

Latrines for the staff were often located somewhere on the ground floor, preferably where vents could effectively draw away the evil stench associated with such places. A sluicing system using rainwater was sometimes installed.[13] The rather more private arrangements of this nature, made in the main apartments, have already been discussed (pp. 245-9).

Bathrooms had usually to be situated on the ground floor or in the basement as they were normally vaulted with heavy masonry, timber ceilings being impractical in damp and steamy conditions.[14] Moreover, the water-source mostly entered the house at ground-level; obviously it was not easy to get water lifted up to higher floors. Apparently a water-lift was installed in the Castel Sant'Angelo in Rome to service the papal bath upstairs[15] but such apparatus cannot have been common. At the Palazzo Medici the bathroom was next to the kitchen where there would have been a source of water and a means of heating it.[16] This arrangement meant that the runs of piping were kept quite short.

We are here speaking of rooms in which baths are installed as a permanent fixture, what one historian of these matters has called a *stanza-stufa*.[17] One could of course also take a bath in one's bedchamber (Pl. 277); the servants had to carry in the wooden tub, and a tent-like pavilion might be erected over it.[18] People of refinement had the tub lined with a special linen cloth so that delicate skin did not come in direct contact with the clammy sides of the bath.[19] In some cases a stool was placed in the tub for the bather to sit on. Once everything was in place the vessel had to be filled. Afterwards it had to be emptied and all the paraphernalia removed. One of the stories in the *Decameron* speaks of four slaves being required to assist a lady with her bathing.[20] The *calderonum unum rami cum sua tromba pro balneo* [brass cauldron with its funnel, for the bath] which were in a kitchen in Genoa in 1456 must have been for bathing in a chamber or there would have been no need for a funnel (to fill the tub). Fixed baths had piped water with taps (Pl. 350).[21]

A bath-tub was called a *bagno* but so was the room in which a bath-tub was fixed or built-up permanently. A more ambitious arrangement was to have what the English sometimes called a 'sweating closet' next to the bathroom proper.[22] Sweating could be brought on by filling the room with dry hot air or with steam, the latter being what we today call a *sauna* (a Finnish word, the *sau* being correctly pronounced like the word for a female pig, rather than the name of a woodworking-tool with teeth). Such a closet was called a *stufa* in Italian although the word was also used to describe the stove (same word)[23] that was necessary for providing the heat, both *bagno* and *stufa* often being used indiscriminately to mean any kind of bathroom – or so it seems.

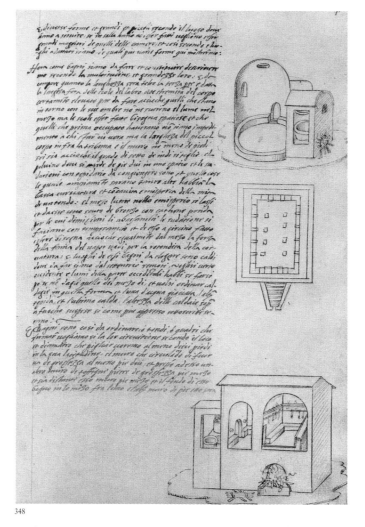

348

348 Bathrooms in 1480 or thereabouts

The upper sketch shows a *bagno* with a furnace under a cauldron heating water. A source of cold water must also have been present. The bottom sketch shows a bathing complex with a *frigidarium* on the left, and a *sauna (stufa)* on the right. The latter has hollow walls and the central sketch shows a plan of the floor which is built on small columns so the heat travels under the floor and up into the wall. Note the seats, and towels hanging on pegs.

From an early 16th-century copy of Francesco di Giorgio's *Treatise on Architecture*, written about 1480; the sketches in the earliest versions differ little from those in the handful of copies that survive
Courtesy of the Trustees of Sir John Soane's Museum, London (photograph: Ole Woldbye)

349

349 A bathroom in about 1530

The bath itself is of marble; a linen cloth lines it to prevent the bather's skin from coming in direct contact with the stone. In the corner is a tiled stove for heating the room. On the right is what appears to be a sunken plunge bath, and beyond is a bedchamber where one can relax after bathing.

Engraving after Francesco Salviati, *Psyche served in her bath*
British Museum, London

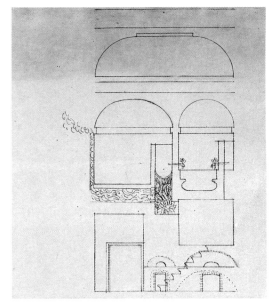

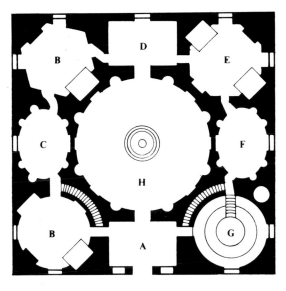

350

352

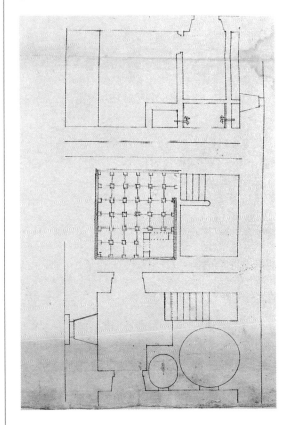

351

350 An elaborate bathing-complex

Apparently by a French sixteenth-century draughts-man, one of a collection of drawings (here split into two for clarity) most of which concern modern or antique Roman architecture. The section at the top shows the bath with hot and cold taps. The former comes from a cauldron that is heated from below (the fire being serviced from a small room directly below the bath) and would have given off steam that would fill the *sauna* on the left. The latter room has under-floor heating and hollow walls. Three levels are shown in the plan below; the actual bathrooms, the underfloor construction, and the basement with two curious igloo-like structures which may be for the storage of wood. Dating perhaps from the 1560s.

Unknown artist. *Same source as Pl. 265*
Metropolitan Museum of Art, New York, Gift of Janos Scholz and Mrs Anne Bigelow Scholz in memory of Flying Officer Walter Bigelow Rosen, 1949 (49.92.66)

351 A separate bathing-pavilion

Illustrated in the French edition of the *Hypnerotoma-chia*, published in 1546. A bath with concentric staging or steps very like this was drawn in Serlio's unpub-lished (until recently) Volume VI which was written while he was in France (see Pl. 352). The cultural links between Italy and France were especially strong at this stage.

From Francesco Colonna, *Hypnerotomachie de Polifili*, Paris, 1546
Courtesy of the Trustees of Sir John Soane's Museum, London

352 Design by Serlio for a bathing pavilion, 1541–7

Intended for Fontainebleau. Probably for the *Grotte des Pins*

A Vestibule
B Bedchamber, with bed shown in niche
C *Camerino*
D *Guardaroba* (for towels, bed-linen, etc.)
E Twin bedchamber 'for undressing'
F *Sauna* [*Stufa col forno di sotto*, i.e. underfloor heating]
G Plunge bath with steps down. Hot water coming from built-in cistern

Based on a plan from a drawing in the Avery Library not published until recently

Bathrooms were by no means uncommon in houses of consequence from the late Middle Ages onwards. Boccaccio mentions rooms of this type at least twice in the *Decameron*.[24] There is evidence of bathrooms being installed in houses in Florence, Prato, Pistoia and San Gimignano in the late 1420s.[25] There was one in Niccolò da Uzzano's residence in Florence in 1424 (Uzzano Invt.) which was called a *stufa* and lay on the ground floor next to the owner's summer bedchamber [*camera terrena che si dice la chamera di Nicholo*]. We also know of a *stufa* in the house of a successful lawyer living in Padua in 1460, a comfortable but in no way sumptuous establishment (Alvarotti Invt., 1460). There was a *stufa* in the house of Francesco Gonzaga in Rome in 1479.[26] Francesco di Giorgio* had a good deal to say on the subject of baths in his treatise on architecture of about 1480 and included several illustrations (Pl. 348). From him we get an insight into the know-how of late fifteenth-century hydraulic engineers which was evidently considerable, as has also been borne out by the investigations carried out not long ago at the Palazzo in Urbino.[27] These specialists (*stufaiuoli*) were among the élite, as craftsmen; some were potters capable of making jointed piping and special tiles for stoves and hollow walls, others were metalworkers who dealt with taps, tubes, boilers and vessels of all sizes, and yet others were glassworkers who could manage most of these things.[28]

Giuliano della Rovere, Bishop of Ostia, and later pope (as Julius II) caused an elegant oval bathroom to be created at his palace at Ostia in the mid-1480s.[29] He later had a *stufa* installed at the papal Castel Sant'Angelo in 1504 but it seems to have been remodelled to its existing shape in 1514 by Antonio da Sangallo.[30] At this stage, it was clearly becoming something of a status symbol to have a bathroom (with sweating-closet attached, in many cases). There was one at the Palazzo della Cancelleria (1514), one in Cardinal Bibbiena's apartment at the Vatican (designed no later than 1515 and still surviving); Raphael was to have one in his own house. His was to be next to his bedchamber which was much more practical than having it in the basement, far from where one slept. Duke Ercole I d'Este had managed to achieve such a juxtaposition in the Palazzo at Ferrara already in 1485.[31] Giuliano da Maiano installed hot and cold baths at Poggio Reale, Alfonso II's spectacular villa outside Naples, at the end of the century.[32] At Ferrara they were installing two new bathrooms in the ducal apartments in 1507.[33] By 1520 or so, there were bathrooms in most great or elegantly appointed houses, and in 1553 a physician, Bianchello Menghi, wrote a treatise on bath-cures with the title *De stuphis*.

In a really comfortable bath-apartment, if we may call it that, there had also to be a small bedchamber close by. Francis Bacon, writing early in the seventeenth century, explained that one should 'anoint the body with oyle and salves' before taking a bath and then sit in it for two hours. After bathing one was supposed to wrap oneself in a cloth steeped in 'mastiche, myrrh, pomander and saffron, for staying the perspiration' and lie for twenty-four hours until the body once again had 'growne solid and hard'.[34] This, at any rate, was what was recommended in England but perhaps Italian practice was different. However, there is some evidence

that bedchambers were sometimes placed next to bathrooms in Italian houses of the better sort, which suggests that a period of rest was thought necessary in Italy too (Pl. 349). Next to the bath at the palace at Urbino lies a small cubicle which would just be large enough for a day-bed; there is a fireplace which suggests someone intended to stay there for some while. The room is located deep inside the building but apparently connects with the Duke's apartment on the main floor. The suite was probably created around 1480 by which time Francesco di Giorgio was chief architect at Urbino; he was particularly interested in hydraulic technology.[35] A century earlier it was recorded that among the furnishings associated with a bathroom at Pistoia was a *strama*; this one may suppose was some sort of mattress (*stramazzo*) or couch.[36] Mention is made in the *Decameron* (i.e. a generation earlier still) of a mattress lying on a bed [*maternasso ... sopra una lettiera*] in *una camera del bagno* which could well refer to an adjacent room rather than the actual bathroom. Moving on, we find Princess Anna d'Este taking over the apartment of her deceased mother-in-law in 1494 and installing a bed for her husband's use 'when he took a bath'; it seems to have folded away into a large cupboard [*uno armaro grande lungo piede 12 ... lui ge fece una testiera in forma de una letiera per il Illustro don alfonso ge va a dormire quando lui va in bagno*].[37] In one of his designs Serlio* shows us a very splendid bathing pavilion 'in the French style' where there were to be twin bedchambers, each with a bed in a niche and a fireplace (Pl. 352). One was supposed to undress in another room which had two beds in it. Next door was the *sauna* [*stufa col forno di sotto*, i.e. with under-floor heating] and beyond that the circular *bagno* with separate boiler. This design of Serlio's was not published until the present century but it probably reflects what wealthy people were requiring of a bathroom-suite by the middle of the sixteenth century. Galeazzo Alessi was certainly providing Genoese noblemen with elaborate schemes not unlike Serlio's by the 1560s (Pl. 341).

Although scenes of bathrooms or public bath-houses usually show the bathers wearing no clothes, many people wore a bath-gown for reasons of modesty. The learned doctor Bartolo Tura, who knew all about the curative properties of medicinal baths, wore a *camiciotto da bagno* [a bath shirt] when he used his own bathroom.[38] Pope Clement V had a similar garment made of very fine cloth *da Alamannia*. It is possible that this was of wool made in Germany but it was more probably of fine linen from the Low Countries.[39] Although it is not entirely relevant to our theme, it is said that Pope Adrian VI wanted to demolish Michelangelo's frescoes in the Sistine Chapel because they resembled a bath filled with naked people [*stufa d'ignudi*]. He was of course thinking of public baths which were large establishments used by ordinary people, notorious seats of licentiousness and contagion.[40] Licentiousness was of course by no means always absent from private bathrooms either (one has only to think of the erotic frescoes painted on the walls of Cardinal Bibbiena's *stufa* in the Vatican), but the character of these elegant small rooms was very different from that of the great public stews (Pl. 349).

In an excellent thesis-dissertation on Renaissance baths by Nancy Elizabeth Edwards[41] she explains how fresh impetus to the building of baths was given when interest in medicinal thermal bathing increased in the early fifteenth century. The dedication of Michele Savonarola's treatise *De Balneis* of 1448/9 to Duke Borso d'Este reflects the importance of this movement. Edwards suggests that bathing for pleasure of even the mildest kind was banned by Counter-Reformation thinkers, and supposes that the building of elegant bathrooms therefore went out of fashion towards the end of the sixteenth century. A letter of 1625 is cited in which it is stated that 'The use of baths has almost completely ceased, although in a few palaces they can still be seen'.[42] The central idea of this thesis is that 'an awareness of bathing as an integral and important part of daily life in the ancient world undoubtedly encouraged the construction of domestic baths in the Renaissance' and that this special interest waned in the late sixteenth century. Bathrooms were certainly created in important Italian houses thereafter, but primarily for reasons of health and hygiene; imitating the Ancients was no longer of any great concern to the builders of such rooms. But they did not cease to be built.

Montaigne saw a shower-bath in Rome, in 1581. He explained that it was called a *doccia* and that one received hot water through pipes onto various parts of the body, especially on the head.[43] He does not seem to have tried taking a shower.

Symmetry

The writers of treatises on architecture were insistent that symmetry should govern the design of a building wherever possible. It should be applied to the disposition of the features on the front façade and to the distribution of rooms on the ground-plan, to speak only of two of the main fields affected by this dictum. As we are not here concerned with the outsides of buildings, we need merely note that symmetry tended to ensure that a façade presented a harmonious aspect to the world, which was indeed pure gain at a time when the aim was to replace the seemingly haphazard manner of medieval building with one that spoke clearly of order and measured calm. Unswerving application of symmetry to the ground-plan, on the other hand, did not necessarily bring similar undoubted advantages and it is curious that the treatise-writers should have been quite so dogmatic about this particular matter. Palladio,* for example, tells his readers that 'rooms ought to be distributed on each side of the entry and hall; and it is to be observed that those on the right correspond with those on the left',[1] while Francesco di Giorgio,* almost a century before, had spoken of rooms being *tutti dupricati e conferenti* [completely duplicated and corresponding], *E quello che è a una parte, dall-altra ordenato sia* [and that which is on one hand is present on the other]. He does, however, add a let-out clause about opportunity needing to be present, and this was not always the case, naturally enough.[2]

One has of course to remember that these treatises were essentially guides through difficult territory. The rules laid down in them were an attempt to codify a mass of information, to provide patterns and suggest ways of proceeding but only the timid and the unimaginative were expected to adhere strictly at all times to these precepts. If you really thought you had a better idea, there were plenty of people around who would be willing to give it a try, in those times of boundless enterprise.

Symmetry on the front elevation usually meant that the main entrance came to be in the centre, as a bold focal point of the façade, and this in turn tended to determine the position of the vestibule inside,[3] and of the passageway through to the central courtyard (if it were a city building) or to the back of the house and garden (if it were a free-standing house in the country). None of this presented much difficulty but serious problems came once it was felt desirable to apply symmetry, or rather axiality (which is of course an essential ingredient of symmetry), to the location of the main staircase which usually had to be located somewhere near the vestibule. This was a matter that greatly exercised the minds of Italian architects in the sixteenth century. Various solutions were arrived at and making a staircase rise nobly and harmoniously to the *piano nobile* added enormously to the dignity of those great *palazzi* in which such a feature was present.[4] It also made sense to try and place centrally the great *sala* on the *piano nobile* so that its large windows could coincide with the central bays of the façade.[5]

However, once these things had been achieved – and they were no mean achievements, be it noted – there was really no great virtue, from the practical point of view or in terms of comfort, in making all the rooms on one side of the building's central axis correspond mirror-wise exactly with the rooms on the other side. One could not normally see the counterpart room opposite when standing in its notional pair, and most people would not even be aware that a counterpart existed over on the other side of the house. The architect of course knew and so presumably did his client. Visitors of an intellectual cast of mind will have suspected its presence, knowing, as did the architect and his client, that Vitruvius had recommended that this was how buildings should be planned, this was how the rooms should be distributed, and that, moreover, all those modern writers who had sought to up-date and adjust Vitruvius' statements – Alberti,* Filarete,* Francesco di Giorgio,* Serlio,* Palladio* and the rest – had all said the same thing. This was powerful stuff and it was clearly a source of profound satisfaction to people thinking along these lines to feel that the building, in this respect (and no doubt in many others as well), was conceived within the great tradition that reached back to classical Antiquity. Of course the idea was to some extent romantic but it also satisfied an austere demand springing from an intellectual refinement that was surprisingly widespread. Nevertheless architecture has also to be practical. However beautiful, however splendid, however elegant, it has also to work, and it is inconceivable that a robust architect like Francesco di Giorgio, brilliant fortifications engineer, expert in advanced hydraulics, a real 'Renaissance Man', who put forward in his treatise plans that were rigidly symmetrical, could have allowed himself to be hemmed in by such constrictive theorizing. In real life he must constantly have adapted the ideal; had he not done so, one cannot believe that he could have numbered so many of the great men of his time among his patrons (p. 339).[6]

Symmetry in the ground-plan was of advantage in one important circumstance – when a married couple had to have two apartments of equal size (p. 288). Then it provided a very neat solution (Pls 337, 343).

The planning of a Renaissance house of consequence was usually based on a rectilinear system with the interior walls set parallel to, or at right angles to, the façade. For this reason it was of course only possible to achieve complete symmetry on a rectangular site, or at least on one of regular shape. Faced with an irregular site, as often occurred in a city where existing buildings for the most part had to be left standing, complete symmetry was unattainable and the best an architect could do was to straighten up the site by dividing it with interior walls running straight back from the front façade (i.e. at right-angles to it). Symmetry

could then be suggested and regularity achieved, at any rate within the parallel walls (Pls 335, 336).

It was because city sites were so often irregular and hemmed in by neighbouring buildings and streets that architects of the period greatly preferred to build in the countryside where there were usually no restrictions of this kind.[7] On a regular site exactly suited to requirements, one could much more readily indulge in 'ideal planning'. The villa or small country house therefore lent itself particularly well to such experimenting and this was why some of the most exciting architectural schemes of the time were developed in these occasional residences out in the country. It should be added that as the life lived in such houses tended also to be more relaxed than that possible in the city, far less formal solutions were acceptable, and it was therefore in these buildings that formulae were first put forward – in the late fifteenth and the sixteenth centuries – that were to have far-reaching influence on architecture right into the nineteenth century and down to our own times, in the field of what one may perhaps call 'non-palatial building', which is of course the class of building in which most of us prefer to live today.

As in other periods, Renaissance rooms were mostly rectangular but occasionally the corners were cut off to form an octagon (with quite useful spaces in the cut-off corners). Very rarely were rooms circular, in residential buildings, and it was not until the second half of the sixteenth century that experiments were made with oval rooms and with axes set diagonally – schemes that were forerunners of Baroque conformations (Pl. 342).

When a suite of rooms was organized in a straight line it was quickly appreciated how impressive the effect could be if the connecting doorways were aligned in an *enfilade*. One can see splendid examples of this at the Palazzo Venezia and in the Palace at Urbino where in both instances superb marble door-cases enframe the doorway (Pls 326, 332). It will be noticed that these are all offset towards the window side. This allows greater freedom in arranging the furnishings – greater, that is, than if the doorways had been placed centrally in their walls. Symmetry was thus sacrificed to a practical consideration and to the gaining of an imposing view, through the aligned doorways, of the sequence of rooms beyond.

The idea of having counter-balancing blind doorways to produce an effect of symmetry in a wall, with the real doorway to one side being balanced by an imitation doorway (feint and not pierced) to the other side, does not seem to have been introduced much before the end of the sixteenth century. Such a *porta finta* is to be seen in Pl. 299.

Francesco del Cossa, *Annunciation*, before 1472
Gemäldegalerie, Dresden. See Plate 1.

Part Four:

CREATING THE
INTERIOR

Costs

The cost of building a *palazzo* or a smart villa in the country, and then of furnishing it, was of course enormous but it is difficult to assess today the magnitude of the sums involved, in modern terms.[1] To try and establish modern equivalents of sums expressed in ducats, florins or *lire* is virtually meaningless because our own money loses its value so rapidly. A more revealing measure of value can be gained from comparing the costs of various goods and services. But here, too, it is not easy to provide a yardstick that remains sufficiently accurate to be applicable over a period of two hundred years. What follows is therefore offered simply as a very general guide.

The Florentine *fiorini* and the Venetian *ducati* were accepted as of equal value subject to the coins being weighed and assayed, which was an essential part of all banking transactions at the time. There were also *scudi*, *genovini* (in Genoa) and Milanese *ducati* but all the various currencies were converted into *lire* for inter-state accounting purposes and this fact has made it possible for one modern scholar to draw up a rough comparative table of income for different social groups in Florence, Milan and Venice in the fifteenth and early sixteenth centuries.[2] A great Venetian merchant could have an income of about 77,000 *lire* per annum in 1500. The Doge received a salary of 21,000. A well-known professor got 2,500 and a master shipwright (*c.*1550) got 900. A Milanese soldier in about 1520 had 250 and a Florentine domestic servant in 1400 got 40. The important merchant, Francesco di Marco Datini, based in Prato but with branch offices in Barcelona, Avignon, Genoa and Pisa, would pay each of his four Tuscan maids 10 florins p.a. (his French maid, however, got 12) although they got their board and lodging free. A Tartar slave cost him 49 florins while a slave-girl of 10 or 12, bought in Venice, cost him 50 ducats in 1394 (plus 5 in value-added tax) and 3 for her journey to Florence where Datini was by then established. He paid 22 florins for a good riding horse in 1402 but a Spanish mule from Valencia cost him 122 florins. Goods that had to be imported were always more costly than those produced locally, as one might expect.[3]

If we now switch our attention to the annual incomes of cardinals in

353

353 Dining in the field

Top people travelled a great deal, generally speaking (see p. 324). It was not normally necessary to erect a tent and sleep in the open; they would usually stay with friends or other people who thought it a good idea to put them up. If they had to rough it and stay at an inn, they had with them everything that might be required including their personal camp-bed. A scene like the above was more likely to be enacted during a lull in some military activity – a tournament or a parade – or during a hunt. We see here a *padiglione* (with the usual central tent-pole to keep it up) and a trestle-table; both are items that can be dismantled and carried on a cart to the next resting-place.

From a Lombard manuscript, *Story of Lancelot*, 1370
Bibliothèque Nationale, Paris (MS.fr.343, 31v)

Rome in 1500 we find Ascanio Sforza topping the list with 30,000 gold ducats and the future pope Julius II (della Rovere) with 20,000. Ippolito d'Este, who has figured in our story already, had 14,000 and Cardinal Carafa 10,000. At the bottom of the scale were cardinals with only 2–3,000 p.a.[4] An ordinary priest or a schoolmaster would be getting 25–30 ducats p.a., let it be noted by way of comparison, but a cardinal had many obligations and it was probably difficult for such a prelate to live on much less than 4,000 (they might ask for a subsidy from the papal coffers if their income fell below 6,000).[5] A cardinal's household might number 150 persons although the less wealthy might have between 40 and 80 to support. The papal household numbered some 700. Francesco Priscianese, who wrote a book on the management of a great man's house in Rome (published in 1542), and was himself on a cardinal's staff, reckoned that it cost 6,500 *scudi* to run a household of 100 persons, of which 4,000 was spent on food and the rest on salaries and the stables.[6]

Wealthy cardinals had their own residences but their poorer brethren might rent a palace, one of moderate size costing 200–400 ducats p.a. In the early part of the sixteenth century one could apparently buy a palace for 5,000–6,000 ducats but the Palazzo Farnese, at the time by far the most expensive private building of all, had cost 243,000 ducats by 1549.[7] One of the previous most expensive buildings was that elegant extension of the Vatican, Villa Belvedere, built as a place for recreation by Innocent VIII in the 1480s, which cost 60,000 ducats.[8]

All this puts into perspective the magnificence of Alfonso of Aragon, King of Naples (1443–58; Naples was the only kingdom in Renaissance Italy), when he spent 150,000 ducats on the wedding celebrations of his niece.[9] When Bernardo, son of the canny Florentine patrician Giovanni Rucellai, married Cosimo de' Medici's daughter in 1466, the wedding expenses came to 6,638 florins.[10] The bride's dowry amounted to 2,500 florins in cash and sumptuous goods valued at 1,200; this did not include many other wedding presents of great value that were not counted in with the actual dowry.

The finding of sufficient money to pay a daughter's dowry was a vexing problem for many a father. The dowry was after all the man's own assessment of his standing in the world at that point. If his was a proud family, this had to show in the size of the dowry. Attempts were made by various governments to set limits on the size of dowries, but without much success, and dowries in general grew larger throughout the period.[11] A rich Roman nobleman, Domenico Massimi, provided dowries for his daughters in 1511, 1512 and 1523; these were set respectively at 1,500, 1,800 and 3,500 florins.[12]

The cost to the bridegroom of furnishing, or refurnishing, the principal rooms of a grand house (and particularly the bedchamber) prior to a marriage would often more than offset the cash value of a bride's dowry, and he would be expected to give the bride fine clothes and jewellery as well.[13] He had also to pay for the bride's procession through the streets to her new home (Pl. 377) and subsequent celebrations.

The sumptuously decorated bedchamber was going to be seen by the wedding guests (Pl. 374) and again when, if Fortune smiled benignly on the couple, the wife was in due course lying-in and receiving the congratulations of family and friends on the birth of a child (Pls 165, 284). The oft-quoted description of a visit to the lying-in of a high-born Venetian lady, a member of the Dolfin family, in 1494, is still the most telling.[14] The room was some twenty-two feet in length but its decoration was said to have cost 2,000 ducats or more. The ceiling was blue and gold and the chimneypiece of Carrara marble was of particular splendour (p. 23). The bed alone had cost 500 ducats; it had beautiful ornaments and so much gold that the visitor could not believe his eyes. The young mother was obviously sitting up in bed, welcoming her friends and other well-wishers, and propped up by no less than six splendid pillows – itself a measure of a person's standing (not least in their own estimation, be it added). But the visitor was even more struck by the twenty-five young Venetian women who were already in the room when he called. Like the young mother, they too were loaded with jewels 'to the value of 100,000', although what surprised him most was the depth of their décolletage. 'You will scarcely believe it … four, even six inches down from their shoulders', he added. He seems not to have realized that this was the current fashion in Venice.

The visitor was from Milan where reticence in degrees of opulence was not exactly prevalent in high society at that time. When Lodovico Sforza's wife gave birth to a child in 1493, a suite of rooms had been done up specially for the event. One had had a *padiglione* the borders to the front opening of which had alone cost 3,000 ducats (Milanese?) to decorate – presumably with embroidery. Another bed of velvet richly embroidered with gold cost 8,000. The child's grandfather, the Duke of Ferrara, had sent over a special present for the baby boy – a couple of diamonds worth 18,000 ducats.[15]

These are examples of exceptional expenditure but the bed of a rich Florentine patrician or the pair of chests that he bought for his wedding might easily cost what a skilled worker earned in a whole year.[16]

An architect, faced with building a large house for a client, is even today tempted to give an estimate of the cost that is on the low side, knowing full well that the final sum will very likely be much higher. It says much for the magnanimity of Pope Pius II, and the interest he must have had in building, that he actually praised his architect (Bernardo Rossellino) for having given him a low estimate for building a palace and a church at his country seat, Pienza, in the early 1460s.[17] This saved the Pope from cancelling the project, or trimming it, and resulted in the creation of one of the most advanced residences of its day and a highly satisfactory church. 'You did well, Bernardo [Rossellino], in lying to us about the expense involved in the work. If you had told the truth, you could never have induced us to spend so much money and neither this splendid palace nor this church, the finest in all Italy, would now be standing.'[18]

Fashion and the Spread of Ideas

It may be thought that Italians of the Renaissance period had their thoughts on higher things and were not affected by fashion. This was by no means the case. Virtually everyone is, and has always been, influenced by fashion and one has to be quite exceptionally poor or ascetic not to be touched by it at all. Among the élite, 'Fashion is in ceaseless pursuit of things that are about to look familiar and in uneasy flight from things that have just become a bore', as the witty 'Feminine Fashions' correspondent of the *New Yorker* wrote in 1970.[1] The pursuit is rather less hectic, lower down the social scale, but it affects the less affluent none the less.

Fashion is a lens through which society perceives itself. In the past, fashion was essentially a question of appearances, of images and the surfaces of things. Changes in fashion were brought about, obviously, by someone having a fresh idea but ideas themselves were not formerly subject to fashionable change; that is a more recent development, fostered largely by journalistic enterprise. Be that as it may, it is the visual aspect of fashion that concerns us here.

During the Renaissance there were of course no fashion magazines or newspaper reports on the latest modes, so the pressure to change the fashions was much less strong, less urgent, than it is today. But it was present; it just developed more slowly. There was definitely a difference between the tastes of parents and that of their children, for instance. 'Since the introduction of new habits [i.e. clothes], the old have an uncouth sort of appearance', a character in Castiglione's *The Courtier* explains.[2] It was of course in clothes that fashion expressed itself most obviously but similar sentiments lay behind the seeming ingratitude of Jacopo Niccolini, a young Florentine patrician who got married to Giovanna Portinari under the auspices 'of Lorenzo de' Medici himself' in 1473. Jacopo's father had bought his son a bedstead with chests, a *lettuccio* and a hat-rack 'all veneered and very beautiful' but the son was displeased with this furnishing suite which he evidently thought was old-fashioned, and he sold it, buying with the proceeds a pair of great chests.[3] These were no doubt in the newest fashion. It was probably for the same reason that Marco Parenti, marrying Catarina Strozzi in 1448, had his bed refurbished, fitted with a cornice (presumably of a more modern form) and, it seems, with pilasters.[4] The same bed was apparently done over again twenty-one years later.[5] If one could not adapt or otherwise disguise the age of an ancient piece of fine furniture, it was tempting to place it in the kitchen or in some other humble room. The two painted chests [*forcieri*] in a kitchen in Faenza in 1566 were probably once-handsome items that had been relegated to the back regions.[6]

Novelty of course plays an important role in the constant evolution of fashion but it has always been the problem for discriminating people, those who aspire to be pace-makers in this field, to determine precisely how far along the path of novelty it is safe to adventure without appearing ridiculous to their peers. Again, this manifests itself primarily in clothes, but affects architecture and decoration as well, although in other fields like this changes are made less frequently. Sebastiano Serlio, in his important treatise on architecture, was of course fully aware of this phenomenon, as is shown by a comment he made about a design for a doorway he illustrates. It was couched in the Doric style but he had felt it necessary to break up, nay, 'to ruin' what would otherwise have been a well-mannered composition [*rompere e guastare la bella forma*], in order to meet the new demand for un-mannered (Mannerist, if you will) patterns from 'crazy people, in search of novelty' [*huomini bizzarri, che cercano novità*].[7]

Reading the sumptuary laws of the period gives us a good idea of what people thought desirable both to wear or in the furnishing and decoration of their houses, at any given time.[8] These regulations were constantly being revised and reissued – probably, in the first place, because many people ignored them fairly soon after the publication of each successive law, but also presumably because the emphasis of excessive expenditure (for that is what these laws were trying to control)[9] switched from one class of object to another, in answer to the movements of fashion. Take, for example, the *restello*. As we have shown (p. 239), this class of furniture – a glamorously framed dressing-mirror – for a while became the smartest furnishing item in the houses of rich Venetians, the finest specimens being extremely costly. *Restelli* of the richer kind were in consequence banned; people were forbidden to have one made or to put one up on their wall, for a few decades around 1500. Thereafter, it disappears from the lists of prohibited items.

New fashions probably spread far more rapidly than is generally supposed. In theory they could be transmitted as speedily as the fastest messenger could gallop from one city to another – in a matter of days – but other people of course moved more slowly.[10] A fine lady, travelling from Milan to Ferrara to see a friend at the Este court, and bringing with her a trunk-load of garments including some gowns in a new French style, would be seen by everyone who cared about such things in Ferrara within a matter of a few weeks. Members of the lady's retinue might in turn see and carefully note the way the bed-curtains were rigged up in the bedchambers of a new wing in the Este palace. Perhaps a man who knew how to fix such curtains would be seduced away from the court and taken back with the visitors to Milan where he proceeded to make beds just like those in Ferrara. These things could be achieved in a matter of months, if the will were there. Designers and architects, with the latest know-how, likewise travelled and might bring with them books of sketches of the sort of thing they had seen on their visits to 'foreign parts' of Italy and which they could reproduce or improve upon if required (Pls 264, 368).

Knowledge of stylistic novelties could be transmitted from one centre in Italy to another by the travelling classes – which, to a large extent, meant the cultural élite, many of whom were interested in matters that are governed by fashion. In fact, fashions spread with great speed among top people, geographically; what took time, sometimes many decades, was for the same fashions to percolate downwards through the social strata, and they percolated at different rates in different places. These questions are, however, not central to our theme. Suffice it to say that, in matters that relate to fashion, ideas could spread rapidly amongst the élite.

354 Illustrations in books

A detail from the famous Bible executed in Florence in 1488 for Matthias Corvinus, King of Hungary, for his important library in Buda. The commission was important and the finished work attracted much attention. It will have helped spread the new style, coming up in the 1480s among serious artists and architects, in which carefully observed Antique ornament played a dominant role. Decorated manuscripts must have been an important vehicle for the transmission of ornamental styles among people of culture, before the introduction of printing.

Monte di Giovanni, from Didymus Alexandrinus *De Spiritu sancto*, 1488
Pierpont Morgan Library, New York (MS.496, f.32)

354

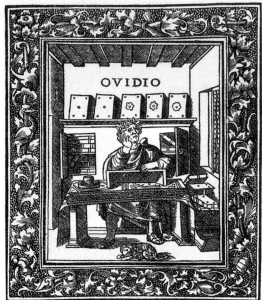

355

355 A comfortable ideal

A title-page of 1522 for a Roman edition of Ovid's *Metamorphoses* showing the poet, crowned with laurels, sitting in his study composing a poem. This illustration of a learned man enjoying the comfort of his own very private small room – and many similar illustrations were produced in other works of the period – appeared in a book which will have been printed in editions of some hundreds of copies (at least) and cannot have failed to convey to those who saw the book some notion of the amenities one might likewise enjoy if one introduced arrangements at home along similar lines.

Title-page from Ovid, *Metamorphoses*, 1522
Victoria and Albert Museum, London

356 Engraved ornament

Three from a set of twelve engravings for *candelabra* patterns now attributed to Giovanni Pietro da Birago who executed them between 1505 and 1515. Such prints were immensely influential and of course helped artists of all kinds to compose fashionable ornament for commissions on which they were engaged.

Pietro da Birago, Candelabrum designs, 1505–15
Metropolitan Museum of Art, New York, Harris Brisbane Dick Fund, 1923 (23.39.7)

357 The print as potent inspiration

A superb engraving thought to be after a drawing by Perino del Vaga and anyway dated 1532. Part of a set which, like the designs in the previous plate, must have constituted a powerful source of inspiration for artists wishing to produce grotesque patterns. The inscription explains that the designs were made for artisans and had been taken from paintings in 'grottoes' in Rome.

Attributed to the Master of the Die, panel ornament design
Metropolitan Museum of Art, New York, Harris Brisbane Dick Fund, 1953 (53.600.62)

There was of course at that time no means of disseminating information about new fashions in any regular way. That had to wait until the arrival of fashion journals on the scene in the late eighteenth century. But the development of printing with engraved wood-blocks or copper plates speeded up the process considerably, for then it became possible to transmit images of new patterns to any part of Italy or, indeed, of Europe. In a little-known Elizabethan play called *Cynthia's Revels*, there is a scene in which a young woman shows her girlfriend how she has just changed her hair-style, imitating the coiffure shown in an Italian print the two of them had been looking at the evening before.[11]

The first pictorial engravings of consequence were those of Pollaiuolo in Florence and Mantegna in Mantua, produced in the 1460s.[12] These were renderings, in the form of prints, of paintings by the two artists. They were the forerunners of one of the principal classes of printed image – the reproduction of modern pictures – that was developed into an important source of pictorial inspiration for artists of all kinds, most notably by Marcantonio Raimondi who was working in close connection with Raphael's studio in Rome in the 1520s.[13] This essentially scenic genre was rather different from the class of print which conveyed information about ornament and elements of decoration: this class was of far greater significance for the history of the decorated interior, as virtually every type of furnishing object discussed in this book – not to speak of the ceilings, floors, friezes and doors of rooms – could bear decoration that was based on a sheet of printed ornament (Pls 43, 357, 358), ornament that might be painted, carved, incised, inlaid, or worked with a needle.

Prints showing ornament that was useful as a source of inspiration for artisans and decorative artists began to be published in the late fifteenth century. Some of the earliest seem to be a group of designs for the tops of boxes associated with the toilette.[14] Series of patterns for the so-called *candelabra* ornament were being published in some quantity before the end of the century, it would seem (Pl. 356). The names of Nicoletto da Modena,[15] Antonio da Brescia, Zoan Andrea and Girolamo Mocetto are linked with this early phase of the ornamental print but this class of engraving did not begin to flourish truly before the 1540s. *Candelabra* patterns, and their relations, the *grottesche*, were popular during the first half of the century (Pls 43, 357). One of the most prolific engravers during this period was Agostino Veneziano, a pupil of Raimondi's, who worked in Rome and produced prints of grotesque ornament (one dated 1521), of antique vases (1530–31) and of strictly architectural ornament (e.g. 1528). Of even greater importance was Enea Vico who also produced a suite of grotesques (1541; *Picturae quas grotteschas vulgo vocant*). Pl. 308 shows one of his designs for a candlestick; this designer in fact had a powerful influence on goldsmiths. He was an expert on numismatics, publishing in Venice a series of *Le imagini . . . degli imperatori* with portraits of Roman emperors (1546) and, in 1557, a series *. . . delle donne auguste* which showed medals bearing the portraits of the emperors' wives, each set in a framework of great originality that formed a potent source of inspiration for other designers (Pl. 358).

Prints were sold at special shops and were not cheap. In Rome, the most famous print-seller was Antonio Salamanca whose heyday was in the 1540s. In 1553 he was joined by Antoine Lafrery who later took over the business. A list of the wares he had for sale in 1572 includes a series on the costumes of Roman women, another on the cornices, capitals and bases of columns based on antique fragments *quali giornalmente si trovano a Roma* [of the sort which are found in Rome every day]; another devoted to

356

Il poeta el pittor Vanno di pare
Et tira il lor ardire tutto ad un segno
Si come espresso in queste carte appare
Fregiare dopre e dartificio degno

Di questo Roma ci puo essempio dar
Roma ricetto dogni chiaro ingegno
Da le cui grotte oue mai non saggio
Hortania luce asi bella arte torna

357

compartimenti or shaped panels of the kind found on ceilings; one of trophies of arms based on designs by Polidoro da Caravaggio; a book of masks, one of friezes and foliage, and one of vases and candlesticks.[16] This gives us some idea of what was available – and in demand.

Some of these prints were sold sewn together as books and sometimes several such series were assembled and encompassed in a larger volume. Rather different were printed books in which engraved illustrations were included. A somewhat incidental source of inspiration with regard to ornament was the *Hypnerotomachia Poliphili* of 1499 which is illustrated with exquisite woodcuts, some of which relate to architecture and others to the applied arts (Pls 144, 215). Although a rich fantasy informs the pictures, only a few are absolutely implausible and one should probably read them for the most part as no more than fairly extreme expressions of luxurious late-quattrocento taste in Venice.[17] Sebastiano Serlio, a Bolognese architect who had spent some years in Rome and had then moved to Venice, was clearly impressed by the quality and usefulness of Venetian engravings in books. He was the first writer on architecture to bring out a liberally illustrated book, and very helpful these were, too. Indeed, much of the text is really a series of commentaries on the plates. Several examples are reproduced here (Pls 60, 336, 363). Another class of illustrated book that served a specialist public was the manual devoted to

needlework which provided, chiefly for skilled amateur needlewomen, patterns alongside hints on how to execute them. A large number of these was produced, some in several editions, so there was clearly a great demand for them. Designs for metalwork were readily consumed by craftsmen working in that field. On the other hand maiolica makers only found prints helpful if they provided inspiration for painted scenes or if they were seeking to copy the shapes of metalwork vessels that had been thus illustrated. Italian furniture-makers seem not to have had any prints produced for their benefit, in the Renaissance period, which is a little

358

359

The print-maker Enea Vico was an antiquarian and a numismatist; indeed, he became adviser on numismatic matters and collecting to Alfonso II d'Este at Ferrara in 1563. Some years before he published a work with sixty-three plates entitled *Imagini delle donne auguste* which reproduced the portraits of the wives of the Caesars as seen on classical coins. He surrounded these representations with elaborate compositions of his own time that must have been a fruitful source of inspiration for his contemporaries, seeking elegant designs in a modern Venetian idiom.

Enea Vico, *Antonia*, from *Portraits of Roman Empresses*, c. 1555
Metropolitan Museum of Art, New York, 1941 (41.67)

359 With wider application

Frontispiece of a pattern-book with friezes of leaf-ornament in the Antique style useful to artists of all kinds. Dedicated to Giovanni Grimani, Patriarch of Aquileia, and member of an illustrious Venetian family. Mutiano was an armourer from Brescia. From the dedication it is clear that he had read Vasari's *Lives*.

From Giovanni Battista Mutiano, *Il primo libro di fogliami antiqui*, Venice, 1571
Houghton Library, Harvard University, Cambridge, Massachusetts

surprising when one thinks of the relatively large output of printed furniture-designs published in France, the Netherlands and Germany during the sixteenth century.[18] Nothing parallel occurred in Italy.

While all this interchanging of ideas spread information about new fashions rapidly from one city to another, among the élite, so that there was in a sense an 'élite style' that was acceptable to top people all over Italy at any given time, these same people were perfectly aware that there were also regional styles and preferences which governed the appearance of many classes of object. We have seen how, in the 1480s, there was a type of bed which was described as being *alla Veneziana*, presumably because this variant of the standard *lettiera* was particularly favoured in Venice (p. 114). There were chests in the Ferrara style, chairs of the Pistoia type, and others which could be recognized as being Genoese for some reason (pp. 174, 188, 200). We could cite numerous such examples. Sometimes these appellations spring from a local preference among the customers, at other times they stem from a strong craft background that was conservative and kept to old ways and well-tried formulae.

People were equally aware that styles were different in regions outside Italy. We see this amusingly exemplified in a late fifteenth-century description of a Milanese gentleman's clothes. He wore *Uno capello negro ala todesca. Uno zipone ala taliana. Uno vestito de meschio scuro curto a meza braghetta de pelle, facto a la Borgogna. Uno tabarone de panno de londra facto ala borgogna longo fin in terra. Uno stoccho lombardo asai et asai longho. Uno cento ala cathalana com una taschetta*. The various garments were in the styles favoured in Germany, Italy, Burgundy, Lombardy and Catalonia, and in one case the cloth came from London.[19] Moreover, even

if this description is meant to be funny and an exaggeration, the élite would evidently understand what was meant by these various labels.

Whether you condone or condemn fashion, it is a phenomenon that is inextricably entwined with aspects of human nature. To ignore it is virtually impossible; and because helping to create, or keeping up with, fashion requires a deep purse, it follows that doing so is a demonstration of power, however politely this is disguised. Inevitably, therefore, fashion provides a playground for 'the ruling classes' where delightful games may be played but where the serious business of supporting the established centres of power is at the same time being prosecuted in a more or less covert manner. The ruling classes in Renaissance Italy were not only in many cases linked by ties of marriage, friendship or common interests, but also by their common concern with matters affected by fashion. It is for this reason that the claim is made here that top people in Italy at the time were generally quick to pick up information about new fashions in all the fields that were of concern to them, and that this process was not affected by geographical distance or political boundaries to any great extent. This process transcended regional preferences.

The truly creative designer or craftsman was immensely stimulated by the demand among rich patrons for something a little different from the fashionable norm. Although those who had to draw up sumptuary regulations mostly believed that keeping up with fashion was a wasteful exercise in terms of money and energy, fashion applied at the sharp end of creativity was also responsible for the production by Italian artists of works of great beauty that were a source of delight when they were new and which, where they survive, still give us enormous pleasure today.

Patrons and Clients

Something needs to be said about the men who commissioned buildings or new apartments and their relationship with those who carried out the work for them – with particular reference, naturally, to the creation of interior spaces, their decoration and furnishing.

It is convenient to make a distinction between patrons, who would take architects, artists and artisans onto their payroll on a long-term basis, and clients whose relationship with these 'creators' was a temporary one arising from the commissioning of a single work. Florence and Venice were the chief centres of clientage; patronage was dominant elsewhere in Italy but most particularly at the princely courts in the north of the country.

Princes liked to take such people into permanent service. There were definite advantages in this arrangement for the artist (let us here use this term to cover all three classes of 'creator'); he enjoyed relative job-security, he received free lodging, board and heat,[1] and his position as artist to a court – by ducal appointment, as it were – carried a certain amount of prestige.[2] But he was not his own man; he had to accept whatever tasks were given him by the prince, he was not allowed to work for others without special permission, and he could not travel without a permit to do so.[3] The tied artist could very easily find himself acting as a sort of odd-job man.[4] On the other hand, the freelance artist, who would operate in, or from, a shop in the city, was regarded as a tradesman and therefore of somewhat lower status than his courtly counterpart – but he *did* enjoy freedom of action, in that he could evade a client's demands that were unwelcome, he could chose which commissions to accept – that is, if he were any good at his job; unsuccessful practitioners could not afford this luxury.

Patrons sometimes found it necessary to be firm with the artists in their pay. 'We are not amused', wrote the Duke of Mantua to Giulio Romano who was in charge of a team of painters decorating part of the Palazzo Tè in the 1530s, 'that you should again have missed so many dates by which you had undertaken to finish; if you do not wish to do this, we will provide other painters who *will* finish.'[5] Faced with this threat, Giulio Romano grovelled. It was this kind of thing that made Michelangelo exclaim that, 'I cannot live under pressures from patrons, let alone paint',[6] while Leonardo excused long delays in completing a task for the Duke of Milan by suggesting that 'Men of genius sometimes accomplish much when they work the least; for they are thinking out *inventioni*'.[7] It sometimes seemed more desirable to have a reliable artist on one's payroll than a wayward genius. When the Duke of Ferrara wanted to fill the important musical post of *maestro di capella* he sent his agent to look at two Flemings with an international reputation, Josquin des Prés and Heinrich Isaak.[8] The agent wrote home to say that 'It is true that Josquin composes better, but he does it when he feels like it, not when he is asked to'. Isaak, on the other hand, 'is a man . . . who can be managed as one wants', and it was he who got the job.

High-born patrons could feel quite fatherly towards those who worked for them. In the early fifteenth century, at any rate, this was evidently the case with the Marchioness Parisina at Ferrara where a small team of artists was evidently working to her personal instructions, and she addressed orders to them in fond terms. *Carissimi nostri* is how she writes to her chief embroiderer in 1424, for instance, referring to him as *nostro mag[istro] da coltre* [our master of quilting].[9] Later generations of princely patrons seem to have dealt with such skilled artisans through a court official who wrote out requisitions, and the personal contact appears to have been lost. But many princes – and princesses – took an enormous interest in what was being created for them and we can be sure that they often saw, and spoke to, such artists even if they rarely committed their thoughts and instructions to paper. An example of this is a letter written by Duke Ercole II d'Este on the death of Giulio Romano in 1546. *La morte di questo raro homo* [the death of this exceptional man], he writes, has robbed me of the desire to build and to enjoy silver plate, paintings and so on, because I find I have lost the urge to do this sort of thing without the talent for design possessed by this fine genius [*senza il desegno di quel bello ingegnio*]. He ended by saying that he felt like burying with Giulio all his aspirations in the field in which they had worked together.[10]

Nevertheless, patrons did not always treat those who served them with great consideration, especially in the matter of payment. Leonello d'Este received a rather pathetic letter from his top worker in wood (a man we would now call a cabinetmaker), Arduino da Baiso, saying that he was just off to Belriguardo to assemble the wonderful *studio* with his superb woodwork that he had made for the prince, but that he needed money and provisions for his family who were remaining in Ferrara. He pointed out most respectfully that he had not been paid for another big job that he had carried out in the Duomo but could he please have a barrel of corn and six of wine, as well as twenty *lire* on account.[11]

Many patrons and clients were possessed of good judgement in artistic matters and some had considerable expertise, most notably in the field of architecture which was the first of the Fine Arts to become a respectable subject in which a gentleman might take a serious interest. Cosimo de' Medici (d.1464), the chief private builder in Florence in the mid-fifteenth century, took a very keen interest in the many buildings he erected and was consulted on architectural matters by his contemporaries. He is known to have made pertinent critical observations on a design in the form of a model that was submitted to him. So well versed in architectural theory was his grandson, the famous Lorenzo the Magnificent, that he actually submitted a design of his own to a competition for the façade of the cathedral in Florence, in 1491. When the Duke of Calabria and the King of Naples wanted to build themselves new residences, they asked Lorenzo for help in the selection of a suitable architect. It is believed that Federigo da Montefeltro was scarcely less responsible than his architects for the design of his great palace at Urbino,[12] and several 'princes' took the trouble to obtain drawings of the building – including the Duke of Mantua and Lorenzo de' Medici. Isabella d'Este took an active part in the creation of her own private apartments, paying much attention to the

360

360 The Pope as patron

One of the greatest patrons of the Arts during the Renaissance was Julius II, pope from 1503 to 1513, who is here shown kneeling at prayer in front of a stool supporting a massive cushion. He was responsible for the large-scale reshaping of much of Rome (one of the new streets was the Via Giulia, named after him), greatly extending the Vatican, expanding its library, starting the papal collection of antiquities, engaging Bramante to work on the new St Peter's, commissioning Michelangelo to execute the famous ceiling of the Sistine Chapel, and using Raphael to create brilliant schemes of decoration and architecture, often of a relatively playful nature that pointed the way to the future; few people have had such a powerful influence on European culture as this enlightened and learned man.

Copy after Raphael, sketch for detail of *The Mass of Bolsena* in the Stanza d'Eliodoro, Vatican
Teyler Museum, Haarlem

---

details of the decoration – and what a demanding taskmistress she was. Later she advised her brother, over at Ferrara, on how to decorate his *studio*.

Popes, determined to create in Rome a city worthy of being Christendom's capital, often took an informed and enthusiastic interest in building magnificently and in contriving domestic quarters of great comfort. Martin V started to rebuild the city in the 1420s, no doubt inspired by having spent two years in Florence when men like Ghiberti, Brunelleschi and Masaccio were at the height of their powers. His successor Eugenius IV was a cultivated Venetian who started building the Vatican; he invited the Florentine architect Bernardo Rossellino to build his chapel and had Fra Angelico decorate it. He also called Donatello to Rome to embellish part of the Lateran. Nicholas V was praised for his building work by Pius II who was himself deeply interested in architecture. Nicholas built a very modern apartment for himself in the Vatican in the early 1450s. Pius' main achievement in this field was the building of a papal residence and church at Pienza (p. 312). Paul II was important in our story as the builder of the Palazzo Venezia which, like the Pienza residence, marked a new advance in planning and elegant decoration (see p. 301 and Pl. 326). Under Sixtus IV, there was a great upsurge in building, cardinals vying with each other to put up ever grander palaces

while the pope himself built the splendid Vatican Library and the Sistine Chapel. He was followed by Innocent VIII who, in the 1480s, built the Villa Belvedere at the Vatican which set a new high standard for elegance and relaxed comfort in buildings of this kind. Julius II was perhaps the most enlightened of all papal patrons of the arts; Bramante and Raphael worked for him and it was he who started building the new St Peter's (Pl. 360). One could continue in this vein, but the main point is to stress the importance of the papacy in initiating buildings of significance during the period, and to note that there was a virtually unbroken sequence of popes who were well informed in architectural matters.

Apart from cardinals (in Rome) and the nobility (in most cities), one interesting group of builders was the bankers. Such men were used to taking risks with large sums of money and in consequence were often the most adventurous builders. Many of the great quattrocento palaces of Florence were built by bankers (they were of course also members of a ruling and essentially mercantile oligarchy), and bankers loomed large among the builders of grand houses in Rome during the second half of the sixteenth century. The most famous example of a banker-builder is Agostino Chigi, however, whose villa of 1509 on the banks of the Tiber (known to us as the Farnesina) is still one of the most charming of all Renaissance buildings and must have been the setting for delightful

361 A cardinal with refined tastes

Whoever he was, this cardinal would seem to have been a patron of the Arts. He is seated at a cunningly designed writing-desk which is circular in plan and could perhaps rotate. It is decorated with delicate ornament. All the items on the desk and shelf behind him are elegant and refined.

Attributed to Lorenzo Costa (1460–1535) who worked at Ferrara
Minneapolis Institute of Arts, Minnesota, John R. Van Derlip and
William Hood Dunwoody Funds

361

entertainments that pleased all the senses in the most voluptuous manner. Designed by Peruzzi, it was largely decorated by him but with important features carried out by Giulio Romano and Raphael, no less. Top-flight craftsmen of all kinds were undoubtedly engaged to make this relatively small building one of the most elegant to be seen anywhere in its day, one that has stood as a model for other *maisons de plaisance* ever since.[13]

It was for cultivated and wealthy men like those already mentioned that the writers of architectural treatises composed their works (pp. 338–40) which, in the fifteenth century, could be consulted by acquiring or borrowing a manuscript copy. Printed editions began to appear towards the end of the century, while those published in the next century were all printed, from the start, and therefore reached a much wider public. Less

wealthy men, desirous of building houses for themselves, might now readily obtain such manuals and could in consequence be as well informed as their richer contemporaries.[14] There were quite a few gentlemen-architects who were very well versed in the mysteries of this art, two of the most notable being Gian Giorgio Trissino (1478–1550), a poet who built a house for himself at Cricoli (near Vicenza) and was the mentor of Palladio, and Alvise Cornaro who wrote several intelligent essays on architectural theory and built, with the help of Giovanni Falconetto, the so-called Odeo Cornaro at Padua, which stylish building is embellished with exquisite stucco decoration.

Artists for the most part lacked a classical education, so when they were faced with having to devise a scheme of decoration involving mythological

362

Donato Acciaiuoli in his study, a room which he will certainly have had created specially for his private and personal use. It is beautifully decorated in a rich but sober manner and all the built-in furniture has been designed to satisfy his own individual requirements. Member of one of the principal families in Florence, Donato was a diplomat, scholar and man of letters who translated into Latin a history of his native city, of which this is a page with miniatures.

Master of the Hamilton Serafonte, *Donato Acciaiuli in his Study,*
c. 1480
Biblioteca Nazionale, Florence (b.p.53, C.IIR)

or historical subjects, they tended to need advice on how to get the details right. The patrons and clients might well be better informed but they, too, often needed guidance in these matters – if only so as not to appear ridiculous for having permitted an artist to provide the wrong attribute for some mythological character or some similar solecism. A cultivated middle-man was required and such people were often found among the learned humanists, many of whom were probably quite pleased to be consulted.[15] Although there had been intellectuals who were prepared to give advice like this in the fifteenth century, it became a more common practice in the sixteenth century. Three superstars among the iconographic programmers of the later decades of that century were Annibal Caro, Fulvio Orsini and Pirro Ligorio.[16] When Pope Julius III built his Villa Giulia in the 1550s just outside Rome's Porta del Popolo, Caro was involved in giving advice on the decoration of a grotto overlooking the nymphaeum, which still survives.[17] The villa was decorated at enormous expense but the pope spent much time there, and even today, stripped bare and bereft of most of its magic, the place has great charm. But, already in the next decade, the contents were being removed. Pope Pius V,

the severe upholder of Counter-Reformationist doctrine, consulted Fulvio Orsini about the suitability of the decorations at the various villas around Rome, in the light of reformist thinking. The learned archaeologist doubted whether it was actually necessary to bury *all* the nude statues, as someone had suggested [*Io dubito che bisogni sotterrare tutte le statue ignude*] but some were certainly outrageous, like the hermaphrodite with a satyr in the chapel at one villa, not to speak of the male herms to be seen at others. Indeed, there were altogether too many 'veneries and other lascivities' [*tante veneri et altre lascivie*] and these ought to be removed.[18] The third expert adviser, Pirro Ligorio, was an erudite antiquarian (he excavated Hadrian's Villa at Tivoli) and a brilliant architect. Apart from building the small *casina* in the grounds of the Vatican for Pius IV, which is still to be seen, he created the Villa d'Este in Rome for the Cardinal of Ferrara where he maintained the old Este tradition of building a comfortable country residence, of no especial grandeur, which was then set in gardens of unbelievable loveliness. The Este *delizie* lying near Ferrara were the inspiration for Cardinal Ippolito's famous villa at Tivoli where the gardens still astonish us. Ligorio filled the place with statues, many of them found in the ruins of Hadrian's villa which lay not far away.[19]

Artistic advisers such as these three played an important role in the creation of important buildings erected during the Renaissance and their influence should not be underestimated.

Architects and Other Designers

A revised conception of architecture in which consonance and a harmonious relationship of its components were the essential ingredients evolved in Italy during the fifteenth century and produced a new architectural style. To erect a building couched in this new, unified style required a high degree of co-ordination and, in consequence, a need for someone who could exercise overall control of the project. This need led in turn to the emergence of the architect as a dominant figure in any building enterprise of importance, one who in the first place designed the entire building (both the outside and the interior), and then saw to its erection by tradesman of various kinds whom he must always control.

The architect was a man set apart, therefore, from even the most skilled artisans because of his 'ingeniousness', those special qualities which suited him for the task of being both overall designer and co-ordinator. He had not risen from the ranks of the building trades, as had the master-masons who had commonly controlled building enterprises before. We see an early reflection of this new development in a letter of 1428, written from Bologna by the famous sculptor, Jacopo della Quercia, to a nobleman in his native city of Siena where they were looking for someone to take charge of an important building project. The sculptor recommends one Giovanni da Siena (i.e. another fellow-countryman) who was at that moment planning 'the large and strong castle' at Ferrara for the Marquis (Niccolò III d'Este). He was being paid the handsome salary of 300 ducats a year, with expenses, Jacopo said, but he was not sure how much Giovanni would ask if he were to return from Ferrara and undertake the job in Siena. He stressed, in this connection, that the man 'is not a master with a trowel in his hand, but a planner and deviser' [chonponitor e giengiero, i.e. compositore and ingegnere].[1]

It will have been noted that Giovanni da Siena was working in Ferrara as a fortifications engineer. Many, perhaps most, quattrocento architects spent much of their time engaged on military works[2] which were a good training-ground for learning to build robustly.[3] Castle walls, bastions and gate-houses had to be able to withstand bombardment by artillery which was speedily becoming increasingly effective; this was literally a matter of life and death to military men, and fortifications engineers (or military architects, if you prefer) tended to consort with the great captains and commanders, who undoubtedly valued their specialist skills. Indeed, this branch of architectural practice was the first to acquire independent recognition among the élite. These same military employers would turn very naturally to the architects whom they had learned to trust when building castles, if one of them, or their relatives and friends, subsequently wanted to put up other kinds of buildings – a palace or a villa, for instance, many of which did often actually have a castle-like character, in the first half of the century.[4] What mattered in selecting someone to assist one in building a new residence was that the man should be able to draw, was an ingenious designer, and knew how to make a sturdy edifice that was well fitted for its purpose.

Architects might sometimes be the sons of architects but most came from other artistic fields. For instance, a number had been trained as goldsmiths, a trade in which expensive materials were formed into eye-catching articles, made for discriminating clients who tended to be fairly sure of what they wanted. Goldsmiths needed to be able to draw and often had to make models prior to carrying out a particularly elaborate piece of work. Moreover, some of their creations (reliquaries and shrines, for example) were often of architectural form. Michelozzo, the brilliant architect who designed the Palazzo Medici in the 1440s, was a goldsmith by training. From a rather different background were workers in wood who often had to create large schemes that were couched in an architectural language (e.g. panelling, choirstalls, and the furnishing of sacristies). Many of them were therefore perfectly familiar with the art of large-scale design that formed an integrated whole. It was a Florentine *maestro di legname* [master-joiner], Giovannino de' Dolci, who had come to Rome to work for Pope Nicholas V, who was later to build the Sistine Chapel.[5] Antonio da Sangallo, who became architect of St Peter's after the death of Raphael and started the great Palazzo Farnese (begun in 1516 but not completed for many decades), had been a joiner before going to work under Bramante, Raphael's predecessor at St Peter's.[6] It was, curiously enough, only towards the end of the fifteenth century that painters became involved with architectural design (as opposed to decoration; see below), although they often depicted buildings in townscapes in their pictures, sometimes bringing considerable imagination to the task. Many sixteenth-century architects *were* also painters, on the other hand: one has only to think of Raphael, Vasari, Giulio Romano, Michelangelo, Peruzzi, Buontalenti, Leonardo and Vignola – to mention only the most outstanding.[7]

The fact that the building trades in Italy were not well organized in powerful guilds (as they were in France, for example), made it easier for a would-be architect to establish himself in the professional role that was being outlined for him during the Renaissance period. What set architects even further apart from the artisans they were supposed to supervise, however, was the need to understand something of classical architectural theory; this require a degree of education that was not normally possessed by builders. This fact did, on the other hand, bring architects closer to the patrons and clients they served – through the experience they shared as cultivated individuals and their common interest in the building projects upon which they were jointly engaged. This in turn must have increased the chances of their getting the building right, not just as pure architecture (in a sculptural sense) but as a place in which the patron/client and his family were to live their lives. The various treatises written by Italian Renaissance architects, which we shall discuss in a moment, were primarily directed at patrons and clients in order that, through a better understanding of the principles that governed the art of building, of the possibilities on offer, and of the problems that might be involved, this dialogue should be even more fruitful. Of course not all architects enjoyed a close relationship with their employer, nor were they always treated with all that much respect. Even an architect like Filarete,

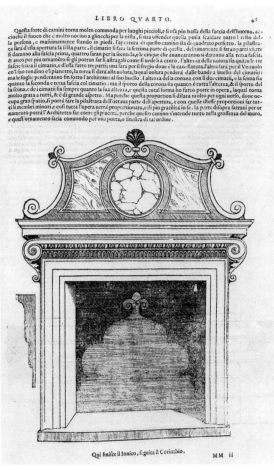

363

363 The influence of the architectural treatise

A 'spread' from the first volume on architecture published by Sebastiano Serlio, his Volume IV which came out in 1537. Other volumes were published later. His was the most useful of all the printed manuals on architectural matters that appeared in the sixteenth century. It was issued in numerous editions in Italy and was translated into several languages; it was still relied upon as a source of helpful information until well into the seventeenth century. Here he shows a chimneypiece couched in the Ionic order and explains that a feature of this kind is best suited to small rooms. He has a lot to say about the proportions of the various parts and ends by saying that the superstructure, which is purely decorative because the hearth and flue are encompassed entirely within the thickness of the wall, may also be used as an overdoor or for a window (he presumably meant as a dormer). A painting of 1510–19 shows an almost identical fire-back, which is a reminder that the designs reproduced in such manuals were not necessarily of an exceptionally advanced taste.

From Serlio, *Treatise on Architecture*, Volume IV, 1537
Courtesy of the Trustees of Sir John Soane's Museum

---

who seems to have got on quite well with his patron, the powerful Francesco Sforza, Duke of Milan, must often have felt put upon; for, in his own treatise (see below) he describes the architect as a courtier who not only puts up buildings but is likely also to be called upon to devise entertainments of all kinds and to provide designs for fresco-cycles, monumental sculpture, and much else. Leonardo da Vinci, whom we think of as a giant among artists, a scientist and designer, served the Sforza court in much the same capacity, half a century later.[8]

The social position of the architect in Renaissance Italy, then, was by no means clearly defined. Much depended on his ability and on how far he could exploit the circumstances in which he found himself. He might attain great heights, like Raphael who is said to have lived like a prince, or he may have slotted in rather lower down the scale. If we can trust Vasari, this was where Antonio da Sangallo belonged although the latter's wife liked to live 'rather in the manner of a splendid lady than an architect's wife'.[9] But Vasari rather looked down upon Sangallo because he had been trained as a worker in wood and was not therefore, in Vasari's estimation, a gentleman. It is in fact not clear how even a successful architect was able to live like a professional man, because architects do not seem to have been

paid much for their designs, so it would seem that they had to rely more on the fees they received as consultants and overseers. Raphael's princely life-style was probably made possible more from what he earned as a painter than from his activities as an architect, and one should probably admire Sangallo's wife for putting on rather a brave show in circumstances that were perhaps not all that easy. It has, however, been suggested that architects were paid in some manner that did not appear in the building accounts – by a benefice or through some private account.[10]

As the architect's professional know-how became increasingly complicated and abstruse, it was important that he was able to convey his intentions clearly to those who had to carry them out. The two principal ways of doing this was by building a model or by drawing designs on paper; both might be referred to as a *disegno*, a design. If someone wanted to distinguish a design on paper from other renderings, one might call it *un disegno in foglio*.[11] Models were easy to understand but they were awkward to manage, easily damaged, and expensive. And even a model will have been based on a drawing. But drawings had to be intelligible and had to provide precise information. The problem of devising a system that satisfied these criteria took a while to solve and one of the great contributions made by architects of the High Renaissance was the development of the orthogonal method which comprises a plan coupled with elevations of front and sides, all drawn to scale and therefore relating to each other. This formula is still used today; it was an Italian invention that crystallized in the early decades of the sixteenth century. A refinement was to show one or more sections through the main parts of the building and this of course was of particular importance in connection with the appearance of interiors. Details of the interior architecture were often first proposed on such sectional drawings, detail drawings of the individual elements then being provided where necessary.

The celebrated architect Francesco di Giorgio seems to have played an important role in making representational drawings essential to the architectural process. He certainly included drawings of many kinds (including numerous plans and a few elevations) in his own treatises of the 1470s and 1480s, believing that the writings of earlier authorities had been difficult to understand 'through lack of drawings'.[12] It was, however, left to Raphael's generation to work out an acceptable method for communicating ideas effectively through drawings.

The necessity of knowing how to draw in the new way and, indeed, of mastering the many other skills required of a good architect, soon made it plain that some form of training was required for those who wished to follow this still relatively new profession.

Most architects were trained through being apprenticed to others who were already established in the business but a few attempts were made to set up schools where groups of students could receive instruction. Leonardo and Boltraffio did something of the sort in Milan; Bandinelli did the same in Rome (in the Belvedere); and, in Florence, Cosimo de' Medici placed part of his collection of Antique sculpture on show in the garden at San Marco, and organized a kind of simple academy where young people could be trained. In 1561, however, something more formal was vouchsafed by the newly established Accademia Fiorentina, the brainchild of Vasari, of which Cosimo was patron. Fifteen years later, the Accademia di San Luca was founded in Rome.[13] All these institutions seem to have been set up to assist artists in general, however; there was no specialized training for architects during the period, except on the job.

Two treatises, those of Alberti and Filarete (see below), had appeared before that of Francesco di Giorgio. These mid-fifteenth-century authors had been concerned less with practical matters than with seeking to convince their readers that expenditure on building, and especially on private building, was a moral activity in which it was both enjoyable and rewarding to indulge (p. 11). They were also propagandists for classical architecture which they regarded as superior to Gothic.

It is easy to forget that, in the early fifteenth century, the Gothic style was that which had long been associated with Christianity whereas the

364 The architect-designer attending to detail

Sketches by Giulio Romano for a table-service, presumably for use at the Gonzaga court at Mantua.

Christ Church, Oxford (Nos 440, 442, 445 and 446), second quarter 15th century

364

365

366

classical style was of pagan origin and, even if the Greeks and the Romans had been admirable people in so many ways, its adoption for modern use could all too easily be seen by contemporaries as a rejection of Christianity. In order to introduce classicism into modern building, it was first necessary somehow to convince the generality of people that this style possessed equal or even greater moral conviction than Gothic. This was achieved in various ways but an important argument that made classicism more appealing was based on the proposition that Gothic was a German style and therefore foreign to Italy. Not only was there some truth in this but, at a time when the Holy Roman Empire (based for centuries on German soil) was trying to re-assert its control over much of northern Italy, and a succession of emperors at the head of largely German armies were making occasional forays far down into the Italian peninsula, the population of states that did not welcome such manifestations of imperial ambitions became much more ready to abandon a style that carried echoes of Germanic domination, and to take up instead the style of a time when Italy itself had been the centre of an empire far greater than the one which still claimed to be not only holy but also Roman, neither of which seemed any longer self-evident. Nevertheless, even in the second half of the fifteenth century, the Gothic style continued to enjoy 'an absolutely higher religious status than classical forms' and was even then being used in certain religious buildings.[14] During the same period, on the other hand, classicism triumphed as a style suitable for secular building, which is what interests us here. It now no longer needed an apology.[15]

In Renaissance Italy there was no shortage of antique models of classical architecture, albeit that most of them had long since been reduced to ruins. The ruins of ancient Rome itself stretched seemingly endlessly out beyond the confines of the comparatively small Renaissance city, and must have looked even more impressive then than they do now.[16] Alberti's treatise, available from the 1450s in manuscript form and in a printed edition in 1486, helped to establish Greek and Roman architecture as a canon of excellence, and soon many architects and antiquaries were busy among the ruins, systematically measuring and recording details, so that a corpus of more or less accurate drawings was gradually amassed[17] and it became possible to piece together the language of architecture, ready for application to modern needs.

Although, in material terms, Renaissance architects had all the information they could desire lying just by their doorsteps, it was another thing to discover the underlying principles. For this they turned to the treatise of Vitruvius, a Roman architect of the first century BC who had served under Caesar in Spain as a military engineer, and was for a time responsible for maintaining Rome's water-supply which will have involved repairing and building aqueducts, among other things.

Only one of Vitruvius' buildings is known to survive and no one after him seems to have paid much attention to his teachings in classical times. He also lived too early to be able to tell us much about the great technical achievements of later Roman architecture. And yet the treatise of this 'pedantic little engineer', as H. S. Goodhart Rendel so dismissively called

365, 366 Unified room-decoration, 1530s

Two designs by Giulio Romano which may well be for the same scheme of decoration. One is for a day-bed (*fulcra*, it says) and the other is for mural decoration – either a tapestry or a painted scheme. The two designs seem to be stylistically related and have much the same density. Moreover, both include vines growing on trelliswork. Giulio Romano decorated two or three rooms with motifs of this kind in Federigo Gonzaga's private apartment at the Palazzo Tè, outside Mantua, in 1532, and one can still see a charming ceiling showing a *pergola* with vines in the Camerino delle Stagioni in the city's main castle, a room which formed part of an apartment made to receive Federico's wife, Maria Paleologa, whom he married in 1531. Maybe these designs were associated with one of those schemes although it must be said that there is no direct evidence that this was the case.

Giulio Romano, bed design, drawing
Strahov Library, Prague

Giulio Romano, putti mural design of playing boys
Victoria and Albert Museum, London

367 Unity through upholstery in 1595

A unified effect has here been achieved by using the same material for the curtain and the table-carpet. If there were other textile components of the room's decorative ensemble (chair-covers, perhaps, or a day-bed), they might well have been made of the same material – by this date when such unified schemes were becoming commonplace. Note the fine lace borders of cuffs and collars.

Federigo Barocci, *Portrait of the Duchess of Urbino*
Museo Filangeri, Naples (Photograph: Alinari Archives)

367

337

him, acquired 'almost scriptural authority' during the Renaissance period[18] and has retained this position for neo-classical architects ever since.

Because he referred to a relationship between architecture and the fields of ethics and rhetoric, a notion that appealed to Italian Renaissance humanists as they were already familiar with the ancient writings on these two subjects, Vitruvius' work received the approbation of scholars.[19] As his subject was the architecture of ancient Rome, moreover, and his was the only literary work of importance on the subject which had come through the 'Dark Ages', his book was widely welcomed among the élite in Renaissance Italy. That it was ill written (according to Alberti), and in many places unintelligible, mattered little; Vitruvius provided a direct link with the classical past and offered a great deal of information, set out in an orderly manner, of the sort that his Renaissance followers wanted to know. The work therefore became enormously popular.[20]

The first printed edition of Vitruvius was published in Rome in 1486. Before that, it had only been known through manuscript copies[21] of very ancient manuscripts that were probably themselves copies of the original classical text. An illustrated edition appeared in Venice in 1511, edited by the erudite Fra Giocondo. The work was next translated into Italian by Cesare Cesarino, an architect who seems to have been a pupil of Bramante in Milan (before the master moved to Rome); this was published at Como in 1521 and contains some highly imaginative illustrations and a lively commentary which throws much light on contemporary practice.[22] But it was left to the learned antiquary Daniele Barbaro to make a translation that overshadowed all previous attempts (there were others, not mentioned here) and has been accepted as the authoritative edition until very recent times although it was actually more of a paraphrase of the Vitruvian text.[23] Barbaro was a member of the 'Vitruvian Academy', founded in 1540, a group of scholars who spent much time trying to interpret Vitruvius' meaning. One result of their deliberations was that many of them built bathrooms for themselves on Vitruvian principles.[24]

Almost all the architectural treatises written in Italy between 1450 and the early years of the seventeenth century were based on Vitruvius' work and however much these later authorities may have wanted to clarify, re-interpret or correct what Vitruvius had said, the ghost of Julius Caesar's engineer is never entirely absent from their texts.[25] In briefly surveying the most important of these Renaissance treatises, their relevance to the history of interior design is here once again of chief concern.

We have mentioned Alberti many times already. Member of an exiled Florentine patrician family, he was born in Genoa in 1402 and educated at the universities of Padua and Bologna. His career was mostly spent in the papal service and, in pursuing this, he travelled widely, meeting people of influence wherever he went. He was secretary to Eugenius IV when the papacy for a while moved to Florence, and later served in Rome under Nicholas V to whom he presented an early copy of his treatise in 1452.

It was written in Latin (and was of course at first only available in the form of manuscript copies) with an essentially humanist readership in mind. Although Alberti provides information on a number of practical matters, his is primarily a theoretical work directed at other intellectuals. Thus, while he makes sound points about selecting timber or on how to ensure foundations are well laid, and has interesting views on painted wall-decoration, his real interest lies in expounding general principles, notably in the field of planning houses, which he expresses with insight and clarity. He had a well-developed sense of how comfort and privacy could best be achieved, and the pattern of life indoors that he formulates is likely to have done much to further the evolution of the apartment, that systematized sequence of rooms designed for occupation by a single important person (pp. 300–312).

However, Alberti's work cannot have been all that widely read during his lifetime (he died in 1472; the first printed edition came out in 1486).[26] Yet the early evolution of the apartment seems to have coincided with the later years of his life. Whatever influence he may have had must at any rate have been directed less through his book than through the advice he gave personally to those who consulted him – people who, of course, knew that he was a considerable expert on architectural matters and had even written a book on the subject. If this reasoning is correct, then Alberti's contribution to the art of the distribution of rooms (p. 284) is likely to have been of paramount importance to the history of civilized living indoors. When writing about planning, he himself commented that the aim should be to arrange matters 'for the greatest convenience of the Inhabitants'.[27]

The second architect to write a treatise during the period was Filarete.[28] Born in Florence in 1400, his treatise was written in the early 1460s. At that point it was not obvious how one should organize the material in such a treatise and we ought not to be too censorious of Filarete's unstructured offering which is largely anecdotal.[29] For all its rambling character, it contains interesting information (p. 244) but cannot have been of much help to would-be builders in its day. It is written in Italian, not in Latin, a fact which in itself suggests Filarete instinctively adopted an approach to his profession that was non-intellectual. But he was undoubtedly good at his job or he would not have enjoyed the patronage of Francesco Sforza, one of the most powerful men in mid-fifteenth-century Italy. Filarete was at first engaged as a fortifications engineer on the castle at Milan, the main seat of the Sforza court, where he had to deal with drawbridges and the like. But he no doubt soon became involved in fitting out the interior of the castle, judging by the content of his treatise which deals with matters like dining arrangements, fireplaces, washing facilities and flushing drains. He clearly proved himself a capable architect who could be entrusted with work on buildings of widely differing kinds, for he was put in charge of building the Milan Cathedral, erected a major hospital, and built the Milan branch of the Medici Bank (he dedicated his treatise to Piero de' Medici in 1464). Filarete's treatise should be seen more as a contribution to courtly literature and as an autobiography, rather than as a manual for builders.

The third treatise-writer that concerns us is Francesco di Giorgio[30] whose name has been mentioned many times in the present work because his contribution is to be reckoned the most important of all, after that of

Serlio – when it comes to matters affecting the interior. He was Sienese, born in 1439. He was a brilliant fortifications engineer and much of his treatise deals with this subject. He was also well versed in hydraulics, and the complicated plumbing system to be seen at Urbino undoubtedly owes much to his intervention (Pl. 348). Like Filarete, Francesco di Giorgio wrote in Italian[31] but, although an eminently practical man, he organized his book in an admirably clear manner, and makes intelligent and helpful comments throughout. His advice on planning is extremely useful although one does not get this impression from the ground-plans he includes among his illustrations, for these are all for strictly symmetrical schemes of an ideal character that do not seem to square up to the practicalities of real life (p. 318). An early version of his treatise was ready in the late 1470s but he recast it and revised it considerably in the mid-1480s, probably after the printed editions of Alberti and Vitruvius had come out, and had perhaps shown him where his own essays could be improved.[32]

Then there is quite a long gap before a fresh attempt to produce an architectural treatise was made.[33] The new treatise was that of Sebastiano Serlio, a Bolognese architect (born in 1475) who had worked under Peruzzi in Rome but who moved to Venice after the Sack of Rome in 1527. Serlio had planned to bring out his treatise in seven volumes but only five of them had been published by the time of his death in 1554 (Vol. IV, which appeared in 1537, Vol. II of 1540, Vols. I and II of 1545, and Vol. V of 1547).[34] An additional volume, not projected from the outset, came out in 1551 and Volume VII was published posthumously in 1575. The sixth volume came out only in this century (1966 and 1978). Each book is profusely illustrated with woodcuts which greatly enhance the work's usefulness. In many parts of his work, the text is essentially a commentary on the adjacent illustration.

Serlio is not concerned with technical matters but was a highly practical man who thought hard about bringing comfort, privacy and convenience to domestic buildings, and whose ground-plans show a sophisticated grasp of the problems involved and how they might be solved (Pls 335, 336). He never allows himself to be hemmed in by the fashionable demand for symmetry so that, even when a plan appears to be symmetrical, he often adjusts to cater for the requirements of real life (Pl. 339).

He is also interested in the decorative components of interior architecture and provides many illustrations of chimneypieces, doors, ceilings and window treatments (Pls 14, 60, 363).

Serlio's work was much in demand, because it was so useful and comprehensive. New Italian editions continued to appear throughout the century, a 'complete works' being brought out in the 1580s. It was also translated into several foreign languages. If you wanted to build yourself a handsome house, during the second half of the sixteenth century, it was prudent to get hold of a copy of Serlio's works for he told you what you needed to know in order to make the building truly convenient to live in and to ensure that it was decorated in style. As Sir John Summerson has said, Serlio was 'by far the greatest architectural writer of the sixteenth century'.[35]

If, in choosing Serlio as your architect, you were ensuring that your house would be comfortable and convenient, in selecting Palladio for the task you were likely to achieve immortality – but not necessarily convenience. Palladio was a master of proportion and it is delightful to spend time in a room created by him because his rooms are conceived as pure architecture, in spatial terms. But he was not particularly concerned with what you made of each room. Apart from the *sala* and the entrance hall (as always, the only two large spaces in a house), Palladio gives us no indication of how any of the other rooms should be used (were they bedchambers, antechambers, or closets?); they should be used for whatever purpose one chose and one could furnish them as one pleased.[36] The rooms might vary in size but that was all. And even if Palladio had wished to provide accommodation that more closely matched his client's pattern of life, flexibility was further restricted by the rigid corset of symmetry that he insisted on imposing on his ground-plans. Behind all this lay the antithesis of much of the thinking which had gone into working out the apartment system during the previous one hundred and twenty years (Palladio's treatise was published in 1570). His arrangements do not impose a direction on visitors so that they are forced to pass through several rooms to reach the innermost and most private spaces (p. 300). Palladio allows people to float unimpeded about the house, uncontrolled – or, at least, not controlled by the architecture. This at any rate is what one must infer from his published plans and the houses one can visit. In practice, things may have been different but Palladio himself does not seem to have helped his clients all that much, in this respect.

Architects, and those who study ancient architecture, greatly admire such 'spatial architecture' (which is why it is suggested above that, by engaging Palladio as your architect, you would gain immortality) but that must be because many architects tend to place spatial considerations above those of human comfort and well-being. At any rate Palladio is today so much more famous than Serlio although, from our present point of view, the latter should be rated at least as highly. Andrea Palladio was no doubt more of an intellectual than Serlio; his treatise, which was published in 1570, was a synthesis of Vitruvius' and Alberti's treatises with his own theories, producing an architectural system that had a marked consonance with late sixteenth-century thinking among the élite and was to have enormous influence in the seventeenth and eighteenth centuries.

We will pass over various minor figures who also wrote essays on architectural matters, and will ignore Vignola whose treatise of 1562 was primarily concerned with the classical orders.[37] Vignola (Giacomo Barozzi da Vignola, was his full name) was actually a very clever architect and was responsible for some charming interiors, but that is not what he wrote about.

We can therefore turn to the last of the great Renaissance architect-writers, Vincenzo Scamozzi, who was born at Vicenza in 1552 but worked mostly in Venice where his treatise was published in 1615. It is a compendium of useful and interesting information organized fairly logically, with handsome illustrations (Pl. 19). He has a great deal to say

368

368 A craftsman's pattern-book

Design for an *ottangolo*, with alternative proposals for the legs – which are especially sturdy as the top was evidently to be of inlaid marble. This drawing is in a book of designs for furniture that a competent joiner, in this case perhaps a Florentine, might have shown to intending customers so they could select the kind of thing they required.

Unknown artist, Design for a table, mid-16th century
Metropolitan Museum of Art, New York, Rogers Fund, 1966 (66.621.2r)

369 Sketch of upholstery

Although not intended for house furnishing, these paired seats for a very splendid coach are upholstered in the same way as would be armchairs in a well-appointed room of the 1590s. The seats are padded to form a flattened dome with wide embroidered borders. The wooden members are close-covered, the material being held in position by rows of gilded nails. The finials will also have been gilded. The sketches were evidently prepared so that the quantity of the costly material that the work would require could be calculated by the Medici Wardrobe staff. (See Pl. 139)

Unknown artist, upholstery
Archivio di Stato, Florence (Guardaroba 143)

about matters that affect the appearance of rooms and about planning. Scamozzi's work rounds off the sequence of Renaissance treatises on architecture.[38]

The treatises we have mentioned were written by architects (or a consultant, in the case of Alberti) who were eminent by any reckoning, but there were of course other brilliant practitioners in the field who were no less celebrated in their day. Yet, because they did not write a treatise, they are much less well remembered, now. The names of Bernardo Rossellino, Biagio Rossetti, Michele Sanmicheli, Galeazzo Alessi, Pirro Ligorio or Bernardo Buontalenti are hardly familiar, even to the average student of Renaissance art, although one must count them all as being the peers of the treatise-writers (again, with the exception of Alberti who simply is different from them all). Moreover, the name of Francesco del Borgo, who was responsible for one of the most important and innovative buildings erected during the Renaissance (the Palazzo Venezia; p. 301 and Pl. 326), had been all but forgotten until a few years ago. It would have been marvellously exciting if we could have had a treatise from his hand.

Architects are of course in the first place designers of buildings but we have seen how the treatise-writers mostly included among their illustrations the odd design for important ornamental features of rooms – notably chimneypieces and ceilings (Pls 18, 363). If an architect wished to ensure that a room was decorated in a uniform manner, it was necessary for him to design, or control the design of, all the elements that made up the room; not simply the fixtures but all the more important movable items as well. Very few Renaissance architects were in a position to exercise such overall control but we see, already in the later decades of the fifteenth century, early manifestations of this desire to unify schemes of decoration. Benedetto and Giuliano da Maiano, for example, who were architects but also directors of the principal workshop in Florence producing high-class woodwork, could make superb day beds [*lettucci*; p. 149] as well as other fine woodwork (p. 94). They provided a pair of chests, a bed, a *lettuccio* and a cupboard for Piero Capponi's bedchamber when he got married in 1466 and it could well be that he had the walls panelled as well.[39] The terracotta relief by Benedetto shown in Pl. 37 indicates how a room by their firm must have looked. No mention is made of how Capponi's furnishings were decorated but they were almost certainly embellished with *lavoro di intarsio*.[40] Furnishing-suites for bedchambers, presumably decorated *en suite*, are mentioned not infrequently in documents of the time, usually comprising a bed, *lettuccio* and *cappellinaio* [hat-rack] but other elements could evidently be added, as the Capponi purchase shows.

We get a hint that a similar kind of unity was present in a house in

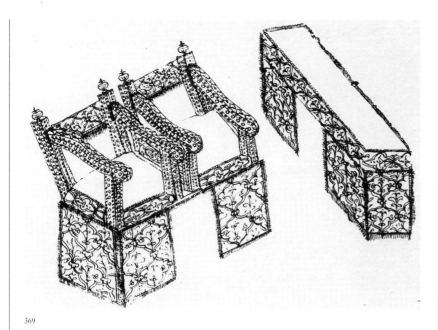

369

Genoa in 1451 (Italiano Invt.) where, in a bedchamber, were to be seen a bed, benches and coffers there were each described as being *tallia quallia*, which would seem to mean 'of the same kind'; in another room were to be found two benches decorated with *tarsie*, two coffers *tallia quallia*, a box for writings and a lady's *cassetta 'tallis quallis'*. This presumably implies that they were all decorated with inlay but were they also designed *en suite*, was there a sense of unity in their ornament?[41]

A sense of unity could also be contrived by kitting out a room with textile furnishings of unified character. A Milanese inventory of 1487 (Borromeo Invt.) may reflect something of the sort where there is listed 'a bedchamber of tapestry 141 *braccia* long' (i.e. a room's worth of wall-hanging) with two *spaliere* [narrow wall-hangings, probably behind a bench], two bench-covers [*banchali*] and two cushions, all of tapestry [*de razo*]. The tapestry components may not all have been of the same design, but the way the list is written suggests that they could have been.

We have suggested that there may have been a number of unified schemes of decoration to be seen in Italian houses before 1500 but they cannot have been all that common or there would surely have been more evidence. In fact, it is not really before the third quarter of the sixteenth century that documentary evidence begins to betray their presence for sure. One begins to find sets of wall-hangings with portières *en suite* (e.g. at the Palazzo Vecchio in Florence, where one rich *paramento* had two *portiere* that were *en suite*; Medici Invt., 1553) and soon the wall-hangings in some rooms are matching the bed-hangings and items like a table-cover (e.g. Pitti Invt., Florence, 1577). By this stage the upholstery of a fine room had usually become the most dominant of its features and it was no difficult matter to arrange that the components were made in matching sets. We can see an example in Pl. 367. By the end of the century this was the normal practice (see the Medici Invt., Rome, 1598).

Giulio Romano, a painter who had worked under Raphael on major schemes of decoration in Rome, moved to Mantua in 1524 where he soon proved that he was a very able and inventive draughtsman. He could design anything from a complex building like the Palazzo Tè to a salt-cellar for the Duke's dining-table, from a bed to a wine-glass (Pls 281, 364, 365). By this means he kept a host of artists and artisans engaged. As someone at the time wrote of Giulio's inexhaustible talent, *tutti vivano del suo pane* [literally 'everyone lives off his bread', i.e. 'they are all dependent on him'].[42] Through being responsible for the design of virtually every decorative feature and artefact produced for the Ducal court at that time, Giulio could excise control, if he wished, and made sure that all the elements of a room, or some decorative ensemble, were in the same style.

At Mantua Giulio Romano (d.1546) was certainly carrying out all the duties of an architect while at the same time controlling the design of whatever else was needed to complete whole schemes of decoration.[43] This may not have been a carefully considered policy, systematically applied. It is more likely to have arisen through Giulio's own strength of character and a single-minded wish to have his way. Whatever the case, Giulio Romano does seem to be the first person who exercised this kind of centralized artistic control. Maybe Raphael and Peruzzi, both papal architects, had been trying to do something of the same sort in Rome, supervising the many schemes for building and decoration of which they were in charge. Perino del Vaga, with a background almost identical to that of Giulio, was certainly capable of designing ornaments of every kind (Pls 20, 61). But Giulio's activities are well documented and supported by a wealth of superb drawings demonstrating the breadth of his intervention and his skill as a designer. In this respect he foreshadows the role played by Charles Le Brun (1619–90) who coordinated the interior design and decoration of Louis XIV's palaces during the second half of the seventeenth century. Stages in this development were marked by the careers of Giorgio Vasari (1511–74) and Bernardo Buontalenti (1531–1608), architects who both filled a somewhat similar central role in the service of the Medici grand-ducal court at Florence. Galeazzo Alessi (1512–72) seems likewise to have paid attention to the smallest details of design, in the buildings he was erecting in Genoa in the 1560s, and he was certainly able himself to design ornaments of various kinds.[44]

Such architects were placed, or placed themselves, at the head of a more or less structured hierarchy of designers. They would work out general concepts and would tend to design principal features themselves but would farm out a great deal of less important work to assistants. They might also design a few one-off commissions themselves, like the inlaid table for which Vignola is said to have provided the design (p. 282). Elsewhere we have raised the question of who designed grand posted beds which, almost from the outset, took on an architectural character (p. 148). Did Peruzzi have anything to do with the design of the superb bed shown in Sodoma's famous painting on the wall of a bedchamber in the Farnesina (Pl. 148)? Did Bartolomeo Neroni (1500–71), a pupil of Peruzzi's who married Sodoma's daughter, and who depicted a fine bed in a painting (Pl. 137), design beds himself? The architect G. B. Montano certainly designed posts and testers for beds, as Pl. 150 shows. Indeed, a class of what should perhaps be called architect-designed furniture begins to take shape in the sixteenth century. It includes fine beds, ornamental cabinets, thrones and some tables – each individual conception being an item of particular importance deserving such special attention (Pls 365, 265, 198); we are not speaking of everyday furnishings.

There were many excellent designers who did not act as architects, of course, but some of them nevertheless exercised a centralized control of sorts over schemes of decoration in buildings of importance. This was particularly the case at Ferrara where several important painters filled such a role at court for a century or more. They have already been mentioned when we were considering painted decoration on woodwork (p. 97) but they did not confine their activities to decorating chests or doors in glamorous apartments. Jacopo Sagramoro, who led a team of decorators, would at one moment have to paint playing-cards, then provide designs for an important inlaid table and next make drawings for tapestries that were to be sent to Flanders for weaving.[45] Sagramoro was active between 1419 and 1456 or so. He clearly played an important role in the field of artistic creativity in Ferrara, a good deal of it affecting important interiors. Somewhat later, the artist, Cosmè Tura (1429–95), occupied a similar post at the Este court. He is of course well known to us as a painter but designed articles in wide variety – embroidery, silver plate and horse-trappings for instance, and he decorated the state barge and painted coats of arms, clock-dials and terracotta reliefs. He, too, had to provide designs for tapestries that were to be woven in Flanders.[46] In this appointment, which clearly required versatility and energy, he was followed by Ercole de' Roberti. We know, however, that the latter had to work to the instructions of the court architect, Biagio Rossetti.[47] Presumably Ercole de' Roberti likewise supervised a shoal of lesser painters and decorators; he could hardly have executed by himself the ducal coats of arms on seventy-six shields of cardboard, required for decorating the *sala* at Ferrara Castle in connection with a theatrical performance for which he had to provide stage-furnishings as well.[48] The no less famous painter, Dosso Dossi, occupied a post in the 1530s similar to that earlier filled by Ercole de' Roberti. Dossi not only painted excellent pictures (Pl. 197) but was responsible for gilding a coach, composing patterns for decorating maiolica, painting window-frames, and designing silk brocades.[49] There is no direct evidence that the control exercised over the teams of artists that these painters headed resulted in the creation of unified schemes of decoration but it is likely that this was in fact what often happened, especially within the confines of a court establishment like that prevailing at Ferrara.

Away from the princely courts, in the republics or wherever artists tended to work individually or in small businesses on commissions given by private clients, it was far less easy to control or coordinate decorative schemes unless they were executed by a single firm like that of Benedetto and Giuliano da Maiano, already mentioned (p. 94). In this connection it is interesting to study a list made by Giovanni Rucellai in 1466 in which he notes down the 'items of sculpture, painting, and inlay of various kinds

which we have in our house, from the hand of the best masters . . .'.[50] The list runs as follows:

Maestro Domenicho da Vinegia, pittore [i.e. Domenico Veneziano, painter]
frate Filippo de l'ordine . . . pittore [i.e. Fra Filippo Lippi, painter]
Giuliano da Maiano, legnaiuolo, maestro di tarsi e commesso [woodwork, master of inlay, both simple and intricate]
Antonio d'Iacopo del Polaiuolo, maestro di disegno [i.e. Antonio Pollaiuolo, master of drawing/design]
Maso Finighuerra, orafo, maestro di disegno [i.e. Tommaso Finiguerra, goldsmith and master of drawing/design]
Andrea del Verochio, schultor e pittore [i.e. Verocchio was both sculptor and painter]
Vettorio di Lorenzo Bartolucci, intaglatore [carver, either in wood or stone]
Andreino dal Chastagno . . . pittore [i.e. Andrea del Castagno, painter]
Paolo Ucello, pittore [the famous painter]
Disidero da Settignano   maestri de scharpello [literally masters
Giovanni di Bertino   of the chisel, i.e. carvers]

It will have been noticed that two of these mostly famous masters are described as 'masters of drawing or of design'. Finiguerra was a goldsmith, a trade that required careful preliminary design and often involved finishing by engraving. Both trained the artist in designing so that he was able to provide designs for others as well. Pollaiuolo was in fact also a goldsmith. However, while many fifteenth-century goldsmiths became professional designers for art-objects, in the next century it was mainly painters who turned to design, as we have already seen. Thus Andrea Schiavone, the painter, who seems to have first worked for Parmigianino before moving to Venice in about 1541, took to designing and even published a set of twenty engraved designs for picture-frames.[51] The prolific decorative painter Taddeo Zuccaro designed stuccowork and other forms of room-decoration but was in 1560 summoned to Urbino to design an important maiolica service which was executed at Castel Durante. Lelio Orsi (1511–87), again trained as a painter, is known to have designed furniture, silver vessels, jewellery and an important cradle. He received commissions from both the Houses of Gonzaga and of Este. An example of his work as a decorative painter is reproduced in Pl. 299.

Most interiors of importance were the result of combined creativity by a handful of masters of various trades, each fully conversant with the decorative language of their time. During the period very few architects were sufficiently powerful or sufficiently determined to achieve a completely integrated scheme of decoration. This could most easily be accomplished under court patronage (which, for our purposes, includes the papacy). Elsewhere, the best a coordinating architect could hope for was to have his building decorated by artisans who had worked with him before, who would be in sympathy with his style and aspirations, and would want to complement his creation with work of their own. Palladio usually describes the decoration of his buildings, briefly but mostly in eulogistic terms mentioning the name of the artist concerned. In the case of the Villa Maser, however, he makes no comment. Presumably he was not consulted before Veronese was engaged to paint on the walls the charming scenes that delight us all today. To us they seem to complement the rooms perfectly (even if they make one wonder where the furniture was to go) but Palladio may have thought otherwise.[52] It was of course profoundly irritating if one felt, as the controlling architect, that the painter (or the upholsterer, later on) had gone and spoiled one's carefully worked-out effects.

The idea that a room ought to present a unified appearance in its decoration, took shape during the Renaissance period and it is likely that Italians were ahead of the rest of Europe in shaping what was to become the dominant theme of European interior decoration during the seventeenth century, retaining that position until very nearly the end of the last century. Seeking to plot the shaping of this tradition is an interesting exercise to which justice can certainly not be done here (what has been said above should merely be seen as a series of notes paving the way for such a study) but, when we approach the subject, we need to bear in mind that it was not self-evident before 1500, even to intelligent people, that a unified décor was desirable. A few designers and their clients may have begun to realize that unity in terms of style and colour was pleasing, but the tradition did not exist. It had to be invented.

The *Maestro di Casa* and his Staff

In the *Decameron**, Boccaccio often mentions a functionary called *un siniscalco* who clearly exercised considerable power over domestic arrangements. The young ladies and gentlemen who are telling each other the famous stories are also continually instructing this man to rig up some comfortable pavilion in the park, to set up dining-tables, to bring in wines and sweetmeats and so forth. On one occasion the story-teller commences after 'everything had been organized by the extremely tactful seneschal' [*essendo ogni cosa dal discretissimo siniscalco apparecchiata*].[1] In the introduction Boccaccio has a chief character explain that *lo mio siniscalco* has *la cura e la sollecitudine di tutta la nostra famiglia commetto, e ciò che al servigio della sala appartiene*[2] – he is responsible for the welfare of the entire household and is in charge of the staff; his particular charge is that of supervising arrangements in the *sala*, the main room of reception and dining. By extension, he will also have had charge of a private dining-room, if such existed in the house, and of arrangements for taking meals *al fresco* – which is something the young gentlefolk of *The Decameron* were always doing.

From what has been said, it will be seen that the seneschal was a man of importance in the mid-fourteenth century, but the post seems to have become demoted by the sixteenth century when he is called a *scalco* and at least one officer – usually a *maestro di casa* or *maiordomo* – was placed over him. When Alfonso V of Aragon made himself King of Naples, ruling that extensive kingdom between 1442 and 1458, he introduced an Aragonese pattern of household organization. The senior official at the court in Aragon had been the *mayordomen* although at Naples he was apparently called a seneschal.[3] On the other hand, at the small Sforza court at Pesaro, in the middle of the fifteenth century, the household was overseen by a *maggiordomo* or *maestro di casa* who was so important that he was provided with a private office in the palace *in honorato loco, dove el discorso de tuto sia facillissimo* [in a respectable place where the discussion of all matters is greatly facilitated].[4] There, the *siniscalco* was in a subordinate position, with responsibility only for matters concerned with the lord's table and *sala*. At the Urbino court, in the early years of the sixteenth century, the *maestro di casa* was placed *sopra tucto* [above all the staff] and likewise acted on the lord's behalf, while the *scalcho de signore* again supervised the lord's table and ensured that his master was properly honoured when dining. This officer was supposed to have *intellecto, practica*, and to be *apparente, eloquente et di bona maniera*.[5] By the 1540s, the *scalco* had lost ground, at least in Rome,[6] although in Ferrara and Urbino, he seems to have remained in charge until much later, because the *scalco* of Lucrezia d'Este, Duchess of Urbino, in 1584 published a manual on the responsibilities of his post under the title, *Dello scalco*.[7] A *scalco* has to have eyes in the back of his head, he insisted [*Di molti occhi ha mestieri lo Scalco* . . .]. No mention is made of any superior officer.

This senior functionary, whether called *siniscalco* or *maestro di casa*, carried out the lord's instructions and naturally, in doing so, gave many

370

370 Versatility was required of servants in a great household

A luncheon-party is taking place in a small 'banqueting house' set on an artificial mound (or a natural hillock) that provides an overall view of the formal garden and the wild country beyond. In the sixteenth century it was customary to extend the architecture of the house into the garden with covered walks or avenues linking the main building to small 'rooms' or pavilions skilfully contrived with verdure or, in some cases, with actual masonry.

From MS *Voyages and Adventures of Carlo Maggi*, 1571
Bibliothèque Nationale, Paris (Ad.134 Res.)

371 Upholding the master's honour

Behind the great *credenza* stands a senior officer of the household, keeping a watchful eye on the servants who attend the diners. He is probably a *siniscalco* or *scalco*, who supervised all arrangements in the dining-hall, making sure that the food was served with dignity, and that everything proceeded smoothly. This meal is probably taking place in a *loggia* that may be open to the street so that the populace can see the magnificence of the family's life-style.

Apollonio di Giovanni, from the *Aneid*, 1450s
Biblioteca Riccardiana, Florence (MS.492.75r)

orders to the staff on the lord's behalf. He saw to all arrangements that needed to be made in the building and this will have included much that affected the appearance of rooms although many of the details will have been left to others. He must have given the orders when it was decided that the family should move down into the cooler ground-floor rooms in summer, or will have ensured that the winter hangings were replaced by those used in summer when the time came, in rooms where two sets had been provided. He would have given instructions regarding ceremonial functions and court festivities, and he will have told the appropriate subordinates to make the requisite arrangements when the family had to make a journey or decided to move out to stay for a while at their villa in the country.[8] On him depended the smooth running of the entire household.

While the *scalco*'s duties, in the later stages, seem to have been confined to supervising dining-arrangements in the dining-hall [*sala*] and private dining-room [*saletta*], another officer of about the same rank was responsible for the lord's bedchamber – which, as we have seen, was his chief personal room where he might spend much time and to which only the favoured were admitted (p. 285). Controlling access and keeping this room in a proper state was the task of a *camarlengus* at the Aragonese court at Naples in the mid-fifteenth century (in Aragon he was called a *camarlench*; our *chamberlain* derives from the same stem).[9] At Urbino, a

century later, the equivalent officer was called a *cameriero magiore*.[10] His job was not only to maintain the lord's bedchamber in good order but to help the lord rise in the morning and go to bed at night. Since he was such a very personal servant of the lord, this officer did not come totally under the control of the *maestro di casa*. This must have been a recipe for much friction but, outside the lord's *camera* and *anticamera*, the *cameriero magiore* had no jurisdiction.

Assisting the *camerlengus* or *cameriero magiore* were several *camerieri* (*camerari* at Naples, under Alfonso) who were also officers of some standing. One of them, for example, was thought sufficiently reliable to be sent from Naples to Flanders to bring back a consignment of tapestries and paintings for Alfonso's rooms.[11] According to Francesco Priscianese, writing in the 1540s on these matters, a *cameriere* should be *nobile, gentile e onorevole, e giovanne di bello aspetto e d'onesta e grate presenza*, which needs no translation. The *cameriere*'s duties were to keep and maintain the lord's *camera* [his bedchamber], his bed, and the rooms associated with the bedchamber (in fact, the lord's apartment) in a clean and tidy state, with the utmost care [*con somma cura, pulitezza e nettezza tenuti e conservati*].[12]

In performing this task the *camerieri* were supported by a host of humbler servants, and also by the staff of the wardrobe [*guardaroba*] which was presided over by a *maestro di guardaroba* (sometimes himself simply called 'the *guardaroba*'). At Naples, under Alfonso, this officer was

371

Arrangements for feeding the assembled cardinals when they had to choose a new pope in secret conclave. The guards control access (left) and egress (below). The servants entering are led by a senior officer of the household carrying a mace (hence his title, *Mazziero*). The file of servants departing are led by another officer with a mace. The rotating cylinders whereby messages, food and other necessities could be conveyed to the sequestered cardinals from the outside world are built into the wall at the back.

From Bartolomeo Scappi, *Opera*, 1570
Metropolitan Museum of Art, New York, Elisha Whittelsey Collection, Elisha Whittelsey Fund, 1952 [52.595.2(20)]

372

a *sub-camerarius*. He looked after the King's clothes (and presumably also his bed-clothes and hangings) which were kept in a *guardaroba*. The *maestro di guardaroba* and his staff were supposed to ensure, with *una estrema diligenza e cura, che le robe siano ben custodite e guardate e riposte con ordine e acconciamente ne' luoghi loro senza alcuna confusione*' [with the utmost diligence and care, that the items on charge to him are well looked after and protected, and are kept in proper order in their appointed places without any untidiness].[13] The *guardaroba* staff would of course repair anything that had got damaged and would be the obvious people to put up or take down hangings and fix up beds, etc. Whether they could manage the stuffing and padding of seat-furniture, is another matter: but they would have known where to turn to get this done – to saddlemakers or coachmakers, perhaps, or those who made travelling-coffers (pp. 184, 188).

This raises the question of upholstery in general. Who produced upholstery – by which we mean the complete textile embellishment of a room, that, by the 1570s at least, and perhaps before that, was often made up as a matching set of components? We know that it was cared for by the *guardaroba* staff but who actually made it? Did they?[14] Or were there specialist firms who undertook such work? Such firms were certainly operating in the seventeenth century but did they exist in the sixteenth? We seem to have no information on this matter so far, mainly probably because no one has been looking out for it. All we can say at present is that

Florio*, writing in 1611, could tell us that a *tapezziero* was 'an Upholster', so the concept was evidently understood some years before that. The Duke of Ferrara had a *tapeciero* on his staff who, in 1582 fitted up a cupboard to hold the music-books of the ducal orchestra. The shelving was neatly finished and apparently lined.[15] This was precisely the sort of work that later upholsterers would carry out, being ready to provide furnishings of all kinds, especially if textiles were involved.

Lists of officers and their staffs attending a princely court, like that at Ferrara, are long and it would be tedious and irrelevant to our purpose, to enumerate them here.[16] However, a few may be mentioned, as they are curious. Alfonso of Aragon's household, for instance, included astrologers, an apothecary, a seamstress, secretaries, a physician, a surgeon, a barber, and some people called *juglars* who played fanfares and danced at public feasts.[17] At Pesaro, the lord's children had a humanist tutor; there was also a librarian who had instructions to shelve books according to an orderly system and was expected to use his judgement as to who should be permitted to look at books and for how long;[18] and there was a Milanese *ballerino* who had recently (shortly before 1466?) been in Naples instructing the young princess Eleonora d'Aragon in how to dance in the Lombard manner [*alo ballare lombardi*]. At Urbino, a century later, there were no fewer than five 'readers at table' who presumably read uplifting texts aloud to the Duke when he was dining in private. There were also three cantors who sang in the ducal chapel, a master tapestry-weaver, three architects, tutors (in grammar, philosophy, logic and astrology), and a keeper each for a leopard and a panther.[19] In addition to these, and the many others who seem less colourful, the respective lords' wives each had a personal staff of their own, together with ladies-in-waiting and *their* attendants.

The ordinary daily routine of the household staff was unremarkable and no one therefore bothered to record it. Just occasionally we catch a glimpse of it *en passant*, as some anecdote is told that is otherwise irrelevant. It is only special occasions that are described and then the intention has usually been to show how magnificent were the arrangements. Indeed, we are left in no doubt that they were stunning events and must have required an enormous amount of careful preparation by a skilled staff that was cleverly managed. One gets some idea of what was involved in organizing these occasions – great feasts, receptions, balls, marriage ceremonies, and jolly picnics for grand people – from glancing through some of the manuals that were written by men who had occupied positions of responsibility in great households.[20] The arrangements were incredibly complicated because, in the first place, a large number of people had to be catered for and, secondly, because the aim was so often to go one better than a rival host had managed on the last occasion of a similar kind. Most of these manuals are boastful and full of practical details. Rather different, and much more entertaining, are the memoirs of Johan Burchard, who became master of ceremonies to Pope Alexander VI in 1481.[21] His chronicle reveals that, quite often, his well-laid plans went wrong – usually due to the cussedness of some cardinal – and he was forced to use much ingenuity in patching things up as best he could, as the day proceeded.

The weather could also occasionally mar a splendid occasion. When Lorenzo de' Medici got married in 1469, the proceedings began on a Friday and lasted through the following Tuesday, with much feasting between the various ceremonial incidents. On the Monday it rained, 'just when the feast was at its highest ... It enveloped everything and wet the beautiful dresses, for the rain was so sudden and so heavy ...'. However, quattrocento Florentine weather-forecasting was so accurate that the guests had been able to take steps to minimize the effect of the anticipated downpour. 'The youths and women had not put on the finest clothes which they had reserved for that day', on which was to take place the principal ceremony of the wedding. Instead, they turned up in their second-best but, not wanting to have spent their money in vain (and the sums involved will have been very considerable), they instead donned their finest garments on the Tuesday, so that, when the bride entered S. Lorenzo to hear the mass 'all the youths and maidens who attended her at the wedding, everyone was in their finest clothes'.[22] A banquet was held afterwards and the writer of the letter reporting all this added that 'I warrant you that there were about fifty maidens and young girls and as many or more youths, so richly dressed that I do not think that anywhere among so many people could such a splendid and fine spectacle be seen.'

At this stage of the family's history, the Medici were trying not to be too ostentatious (only one roast was served at this banquet, for example);

others were less reticent. A fifteenth-century notebook connected with arrangements in the court kitchens at Ferrara informs us that, if you want greater magnificence at a dinner-party, your roast peacock should be covered with gold-leaf [*per più magnificentia, quando el pavone e cocto, se può adornare con foglie d'oro batuto*].[23] In the same volume we are also told that, at one court feast, the marzipan confectionery was gilded with no fewer than 27,600 sheets of gold leaf. That was conspicuous expenditure, *par excellence*.

Whether on this occasion the confectionery was cut (perhaps fancily shaped) from rolled sheets of marzipan or was modelled in three dimensions, is not clear, but modelled figures executed in sugar-paste were striking ornaments for dining-tables in the sixteenth century and later, excellent sculptors often being engaged to fashion these embellishments.[24] Early manifestations of this were the table ornaments to be seen when Beatrice, the Duchess of Milan, was entertained in the Ducal Palace by the Venetian Senate in 1493, at which brilliantly illuminated collation, to the sound of trumpets, the company was treated to a *bellisimo spectaculo* in which no fewer than three hundred *diverse cose tute lavorate de zucharo dorate* [objects of various kinds made entirely of gilt sugar-paste] played a central part.[25]

A century later, these *diverse cose* had become enormously elaborate and were sometimes of real aesthetic merit. We have only to glance through Vincenzo Cervio's manual on carving at table, in which he describes in great detail a number of stupendous feasts given in the last three decades of the sixteenth century (his book appeared in 1593), to appreciate this. 'Five statues of nudes of gilded marzipan nearly two feet high', 'A Hercules and his mace of *pasta reale*', 'A galley and a sailing ship of paste, complete with oars and sails, filled with sweetmeats', 'A large eagle entirely of paste, with a crown on its head, which is standing up', 'Castles of paste with pennants on top, with fireworks all round like bombards', 'In the centre of the table a column over four feet high made of sugarpaste ... with a gilt capital and a crown on top ... and two figures of slaves at the base ...', 'A gilded statuette in front of each diner nine inches high, each holding a bunch of flowers, delightfully scented'.[26] These examples are picked almost at random from Cervio's lists and only concern this particular class of table-ornament. Decorative dishes of every kind, of extreme elaboration, are also listed, as are the several fine damask table-cloths that were removed at successive stages during these stupendous meals, and the fine arrays of ornaments on the *credenze*. A crazy example of how complicated matters had become by Cervio's time is provided by his treatment of a roasted peacock. At Ferrara in the fifteenth century, it will be remembered, it was considered fairly extreme to gild the roasted fowl all over. Cervio, however, first had it roasted and thereafter replaced all its feathers.[27] He does not explain how he carved the bird afterwards; perhaps it was just a *tour de force* of cookery, for show.

Cervio was clearly trying to impress his readers but paradoxically manages to make the whole business sound tedious. Everything, by this time, had become too complicated and thus, of necessity, too well regulated.[28] Great feasts were now undoubtedly of overwhelming magnificence, but had they not also become rather a bore? It is as if the organizers of these occasions had decided that only startling arrangements would make any impression on the participants who, they must have felt, were world-weary, cynical and possessed of jaded palates. Is it too fanciful to believe that things had been different in the quattrocento, that in those far-off days such events had been more light-hearted, less regimented, more fun? All we can say with certainty is that grand people in the late sixteenth century greatly prized the reverse of the medal, the moments of relaxation between episodes of formality and ceremonial, often enjoyed with just a few friends in private and intimate rooms, or in the garden – or, perhaps, if time allowed, in the family villa out in the countryside.

Whatever the case, the periods of relaxation, just like the great ceremonial occasions, were made possible by an attentive and obliging staff. For the smooth operation of an important household, it was vital that the key posts were filled by skilful managers possessed of tact and much imagination, and that these senior officers were supported by a well-trained staff. Without such an establishment, all would have been chaos.

Women's Influence

L'histoire des moeurs est surtout celle de la femme, wrote the great French historian, Jules Michelet (1798–1874). For our purposes this may be translated, 'The history of good manners is essentially the history of women.' Domenico Bruni, who wrote a small book on women's qualities in the mid-sixteenth century, explained that women were 'by nature given to cleanliness, elegance, refined manners, chastity and piety', and that, 'without their beneficent influence, human beings would be indistinguishable from wild beasts.'[1]

In polite society in Renaissance Italy, men by and large strove to please women. This was not simply a hangover from an age when chivalrous love had been the fashion.[2] The arts of the courtier, emulated all over Italy, even in the republics,[3] were directed primarily at giving pleasure to women.[4] Of course men not only found this in itself enjoyable and entertaining; it could also be rewarding since women tended to exercise, as they have always done, power within the domestic setting and, from that stronghold, often far beyond. It is not that matters are all that different today but that Italians at the time seem to have given a lot of thought to this question.

The law did certainly not favour women but quite a few upper-class women were well educated and as a result possessed an intelligence that was well stretched and developed, enabling them the better to take advantage of situations in which their wishes could be fulfilled.[5]

In private houses, a man's wife ran the household while he went about his business.[6] Often, she was responsible for a wide range of activities (pp. 252–60) but the grander her husband, the more her domestic obligations were delegated to members of a staff presided over by a steward or some similar official (p. 343). In courtly circles, the prince's consort enjoyed a status virtually equal to his own and could issue instructions concerning the running of the household (and, certainly, concerning her own private staff and attendants) and would usually commission work on her own authority that affected the domestic setting – new furnishings, articles for her personal use (often of an eye-catching nature), and fine clothes. (It is worth mentioning a grand lady's clothes because they, along with the jewellery she was wearing, would usually be the most expensive and striking items in any room she occupied.)

Quattrocento women got married young, often to husbands who were a good bit older.[7] In the natural order of things, therefore, many wives were left as widows in early middle age, and thus as *de facto* heads of a household, often with not inconsiderable financial means.[8] They had of course to see to the education and general upbringing of their children and they still had to run their households, but they could now do all this in a manner that suited themselves. Many could now find time to enjoy themselves, to pursue cultural activities (music-making, attending sermons, reading, and dressing elegantly), and to make what they would of the fact that much of the ardour expressed by amorous men was in those days directed at the mature woman rather than at young girls.[9]

In the sixteenth century women tended to marry later, in polite society, but marriages continued to be arranged for them by their families. By and large, virtuous women stayed at home, venturing out only to go to church or to visit friends (they would normally be accompanied when going anywhere).[10] They only went on parade, dressed in their most gorgeous finery, to dazzle at some formal reception or other great occasion.[11]

To what extent all that has been said so far on this question affected the way the rooms of respectable women were organized and decorated, and how much say they had in the matter, is difficult to assess because the ways of women are subtle and often unrecorded, but it is unlikely that their influence was small, and it is likely to have been particularly strong in the matter of introducing measures affecting comfort indoors.

When a man got married, whether he were a prince surrounded by a court, a patrician in a great republic, or a merchant in a city-state, he usually made special arrangements to receive his bride into his place of residence. These might include building a new wing for her occupation, or doing over an existing apartment to bring it up to modern standards (p. 11).[12] Once ensconced, the bride might make further changes. What was done would of course be noted by other members of the bride's entourage, and by visitors, some of whom might proceed to modify their own habitations in a similar way.

Young women were carefully protected and were often confined within specially secluded private apartments. This, too, affected the planning of houses (see Part Three). While strange men (i.e. not of the family) never entered these 'sacred' areas, they might penetrate into the more public spaces of the house and there they might contrive to chat to the daughters of the house. Measures had sometimes to be taken to prevent this.[13] Importunate youths who did not enjoy the entrée to the house might try to penetrate through a window. Measures like that shown in Pl. 29 put a stop to this sort of thing but the presence in cities of a great many young, unmarried men resulted in much unruly behaviour and great erotic tension.

Important occasions in an Italian Renaissance woman's life were her marriage (which consisted of two or three formal events), the presentation of her new-born children while lying-in after their birth, the children's christening, and the wedding of her children, if she lived that long.

Once the respective parents had decided that their children should wed, a marriage contract was drawn up by a notary, recording what had

373 Women at court

This painting by Girolamo da Cremona, a follower of Mantegna, shows the kind of life led by some of the younger members of a princely court like that at Mantua, possibly at one of the Gonzaga villas outside the city. The young women – perhaps the companions of one of the chief ladies at the court – tended to be good-looking, lively, well-mannered and intelligent. The woman playing chess undoubtedly possesses the first and last of these qualities, even if it looks as if she is about to lose the game. She sits behind a trestle table covered with a green velvet table-carpet. The other player sits on a seat somewhat like that shown in Plate 186. The painter was active between 1467 and 1473.

Girolamo da Cremona (fl. 1467–73), The Chess Players
Metropolitan Museum of Art, New York, Bequest of Maitland F.
Griggs, 1943, Maitland F. Griggs Collection (43.98.8)

373

374

374 Bedding the bride

A husband chases his wife's girl-friends out of the bridal chamber after the wedding. The somewhat shy wife lies in a bed that is probably new, acquired recently as the focal point of a bridal suite done up in the modern taste. A tabernacle-shrine hangs prominently on the wall.

From *Questo sie la nobilissima hi[s]toria di Maria per Ravenna*, Venice, *c.* 1540?, woodcut, probably late 15th century
British Library, London

375 Household tasks

Women in the domestic setting. Two young women embroider (note the work-box and scissors) while the family's old nurse spins. The baby is learning to walk. The bed has a heavy wooden tester suspended from the ceiling and two pillows are displayed.

Luca Bertelli (whereabouts unknown), Venice, mid-16th century

376 Helping the silk industry

This was hardly a cottage industry but nevertheless a strange activity for a fairly well-to-do household. The women here are hatching the eggs of silkworms by putting them into their bodices (in bags) where they will be kept warm and will eventually turn into caterpillars that will spin the precious thread. Note the frieze with panelling below, the posted bed *a tribuna*, the rush-seated chairs. The aged mother(?) wears spectacles. This probably shows a Florentine interior; the engraved version is dedicated to a Florentine nobleman.

Jan van der Straat (Giovanni Stradano), *Preparing the Eggs of Silkworms*, third quarter of 16th century
By gracious permission of Her Majesty the Queen, Royal Library, Windsor Castle

375

376

been agreed between the two parties with regard to the size of the dowry and matters of that kind.[14] Later (sometimes months, and even years, later) rings were given or exchanged and the couple were then officially wed – after which a banquet was usually held in their honour. None of these ceremonies need take place in a church although the couple sometimes went to church to receive a blessing. The Church asserted control of marriages in Italy only during the course of the sixteenth century, by which time the sequential ceremonial just described had been much simplified. The final event, in any case, was the consummation which was also a ceremonial occasion (Pl. 374).[15] Later, the bride paraded through the streets to her husband's house where she was to live, many of her wedding presents being carried in procession with her. This widely signified to the community that a wedding had taken place (Pl 377).

Women kept to their beds for about twenty days after the birth of a child and, on about the eighth day, the young mother would receive her family and friends while lying on her bed, and would show them the new child.[16] This is the event depicted so frequently by Italian Renaissance painters under the misleading title *Birth of the Virgin* (or of *St John the Baptist*); the birth had in fact taken place some days before. As the bedchamber, which was the setting for this important family event, was to be seen by many visitors on this occasion, parents felt it important to have the room looking as splendid as possible and much trouble and expense was devoted to bringing this about. The results could be impressive (p. 323). It was in association with this occasion that special 'birth-trays' were made, as were also ceremonial cradles like those shown in Pls 3 and 284.

Women servants helped to make the household function but one gets the impression that there were proportionately fewer of them than their male counterparts. Many of the task performed in Victorian times (and later) by female servants were previously undertaken by men but there were several traditionally 'female' activities – lady's maid, wet-nurse, and so forth. Servants were not well paid but got their board and lodging free.[17] In many households, a slave or two might be attached to the workforce. Again, these were of both sexes and were by no means all black.[18] They smoothed the family's path in various ways[19] and were usually freed after long service.

If a slave-girl, or any other woman, had a child by the master or a son of the house, it was not uncommon for such natural children to be accepted into the household without demur. This is not the place to discuss morals. Suffice it to say that they were rather different from those which in the main prevail today. Great men had mistresses and these were tolerated by all and sundry, including the men's wives (at least, in public). Wives were encouraged not to be too censorious about their husbands' peccadilloes. Married men disliked being cuckolded but few people attached much blame to the wife if he were. Married women had to be guarded, or you never knew what might happen.[20] Of course there were plenty of virtuous women in Renaissance Italy but virtue mattered primarily in so far as the legitimacy of children and the family's inheritance were concerned, not so much for its own sake.

Attitudes to matters such as these inevitably coloured the way houses were used and organized – not overtly, and perhaps perceived only subconsciously, but leading nevertheless to practical adjustment.

One class of woman who must have influenced the history of interior decoration and the pattern of life indoors considerably were the courtesans – or, rather, the most successful members of their profession. Before attempting to justify this claim, however, something must be said about the position these young women occupied in Italian Renaissance society.

There have been prostitutes at all times but the great age of the *cortigiana* in Italy lasted from about 1480 until the middle of the sixteenth century, although there were still many notably successful members of the profession active after that. Prostitutes were normally called *meretrice* or *puttane* but, well into the sixteenth century, the name *cortigiana* was coined to describe the aristocrats of the business. A writer in 1561 explained that there were two sorts of *puttana*, those *di bordello* (i.e. belonging to a brothel) and the *cortigiane*, the basic difference being that the latter, as Pasquino so pointedly put it, sold her fruit more expensively (*le cortesane ... più caro vendon lor frutto*).[21] In Venice a tariff was published showing the fees charged by each of the ladies and it is evident from this that the top *cortigiane* could earn a great deal of money during their relatively short working lives (fifteen years was considered a good run). What is more, there seems to have been a scale of fees for the various favours provided.[22] However, it was not merely her 'fruit' which the high-class courtesan was prepared to offer; the other delights she could provide were of far greater importance – at least, for much of the time.

It almost goes without saying that most of these young women were exceptionally good-looking and, when this was not quite the case, they were adept at improving on Nature.[23] However, what mattered at least as much was that they should be charming and entertaining – in fact, that it should be a delight to be in their company. Many of them were well educated and several were apparently accomplished musicians.[24] In a book entitled the *Puttana errante* of 1584, it was explained that, to be successful, a *cortigiana* should be good-looking, have a trim figure, be lively and cheerful with everyone, and should be able to talk seriously about a wide range of subjects.[25] One contemporary student of these matters explained that they lay great store in giving pleasure, which was of course their business, but that 'the royal way in which they treat you, their graceful manners, their courtesy and the luxury with which they surround you ... make you feel another being, a great lord, and while you are with them you do not envy even the inhabitants of Paradise'.[26]

The writer of this comment was himself no 'great lord' but many of the men who patronized the high-class courtesans were from the highest echelons of society, and to consort with these evidently delightful young women carried with it little or no social stigma. Men of standing in every field were to be seen in the company of the top *cortigiane*, and even princes of the Church for the most part felt in no way inhibited from indulging in these pleasures.[27] Much of the time, of course, it was not easy to tell a *cortigiana* of the superior sort from a respectable lady (reporting back to

377

377 Presents for the bride

This probably shows a man bringing wedding presents
to the house of his future bride. Apart from the fine
white palfrey, with its splendid accoutrements, and the
haughty maid-servant bearing a bundle of fine cloth or
a robe on her head, a porter is carrying a heavy painted
and gilded chest. By the time this picture was painted,
the 1470s, it was the husband, rather than the bride's
family, who took it upon himself to provide the
expensive marriage chests (they usually came in pairs).

Attributed to the Fucecchio Master, *Wedding Scene* (detail)
Courtesy of Sotheby's Inc., New York

Mantua in 1512, the young marquis Federico Gonzaga's secretary explained to the boy's mother, Isabella d'Este, that it really was difficult to *conoser una dona da bene da una cortesana*),[28] and when Tullia d'Aragona, one of the most highly respected and learned courtesans of all time, visited Ferrara, a local poet noted how no member of the elegant Este court gave any sign of disapproval.[29] These often honoured, and certainly much praised, women could usually count on the protection of some prince, of a cardinal or two, or bankers and of writers (the last were important to have on one's side; they could very easily blacken a girl's reputation).[30]

The high fees these women could command, together with the lavish presents delighted admirers showered upon them, made it possible for the great *cortigiane* to set themselves up in considerable splendour and many are the descriptions of their dress, their numerous servants, their lavish dinners and other entertainments – and of the magnificence of the houses in which they lived. After a visit to Rome in 1506, Matteo Bandello devoted one of his many *novelle* to Imperia, the most illustrious *cortigiana* of her day and mistress for many years of the rich banker Agostino Chigi.[31] Bandello describes her sumptuous rooms, one hung with velvet and another with cloth of gold embroidered and draped in rich folds, while the floor was scattered with carpets. The deep cornice above was painted blue with gilded details and on the ledge stood vases of serpentine, porphyry and other expensive materials. Everything was of the greatest possible opulence.[32] Imperia died rich and was buried in a tomb in S. Gregorio on the Coelian hill in 1522.

At about the same period Pietro Fortini wrote a *novella* about a young Sienese gentleman (perhaps the story was autobiographical) who was unexpectedly taken into the house of another of the *prima donne* of the Roman *demi-monde* and is then charmingly entertained. He must have been an engaging young man because the *cortigiana* charged him nothing for staying the whole night. He says that the house had a wide staircase (by no means a standard feature at that date) and the main room looked out over the Tiber towards the Vatican. The room was hung with gilt leather and the ravishing young woman, who was about eighteen, was waiting to welcome him, seated in a luxurious chair. After having enjoyed a splendid supper they retired to her bedchamber which was hung with silk. The bed-hangings were superb, he says, and the sheets were as white and 'fine as the membrane of an egg'.[33]

Scipio Ammirato, who wrote a dialogue under the title *Il Maremonte* in the later decades of the sixteenth century, makes one character say, 'I believe you have heard of La Panta and of Angela, both very famous prostitutes, the former in Rome and the latter in Naples, and of the respect and reverence and the courtesies that are paid them by every fine gentleman, and with what magnificence and grandeur they are surrounded in their houses.'[34] La Saltarella, a young woman of Rome who apparently enjoyed the patronage of several cardinals in the years around 1540, is known to have had a bedchamber hung with blue silk damask, very richly fringed [*di Domasco turchino con frange ricchissime*] in which stood *una cuccia della piu belle che habbi mai più vedute* [one of the finest posted beds that has ever been seen].[35] But perhaps the best description of

a courtesan's house is the poem entitled *Il vanto della Cortigiana Ferrarese* [The Boast of the Courtesan from Ferrara].[36] The subject of these verses was almost certainly the widely famed Beatrice di Ferrara who became one of the top *cortigiane* in Rome during the 1520s. The poet makes her say how proud she is of her looks, her fine clothes, her table and the *credenza* loaded with vessels of silver. She speaks of her pictures, wall-hangings including tapestries, and the huge amount of linen all 'whiter and more delicate than snow [*più che candida neve delicati*] which stupefies everyone who sees it, all scented with fine perfume', that grand gentlemen have given her. She tells of the parties she has thrown and the splendid food she has served. She describes her bed, with its counterpane so richly decorated that no pope has ever had anything like it. And finally she speaks proudly of her golden carriage which was carved and painted with blue and white arabesques, and was pulled by six white horses. The full text merits attention because it sums up so neatly the aspirations of a fashion-conscious woman of the period.

A foreigner's amazement at the voluptuous surroundings in which the great Italian courtesans lived is shown rather charmingly by Thomas Coryat's description in his *Crudities** (1611) arising from his visit to Venice in 1608. He writes of the 'infinite . . . allurements of these amorous Calypsoes', their beauty and 'pleasing dalliances', and 'the variety of the delicious objects they minister to their lovers', and how 'they want nothing tending to delight'. But it was their houses which astonished him most, 'For when you come into one of their Palaces (as indeed some few of the principallest of them live in very magnificent portly buildings fit for the entertainment of a great Prince) you seem to enter into the Paradise of Venus. For their fairest rooms are most glorious and glittering to behold'.[37]

None of these descriptions speak of new fashions or novelty as such but references are sometimes made to some possession being finer than that of anyone else. Beatrice of Ferrara's coverlet was finer than any pope's, as we have seen; another courtesan had a little white cat (*el pi umele bestioleto che mai avè visto*; the most gentle little creature you have ever seen) as well as a parakeet and a pheasant so that her menagerie was 'better than that of any other courtesan' at the time, or so someone claimed [*che vu siè cusi ben servia de animali, quanto altra cortesana che viva*].[38] We can anyway be fairly sure that the top courtesans vied with each other in surrounding themselves with ever greater opulence and with ever more enchanting effects. To this extent, at least, they must often have been willing to try novel forms of furnishing and decoration – and one thing a courtesan is rather unlikely to be is conservative in her tastes. What is more, not a few of her patrons were men used to taking risks – bankers, military commanders, powerful cardinals, great men of business – who no doubt would tend to see that their particular favourite was housed in a manner that reflected well on themselves – on their generosity, on their good taste, on their ability to secure the best that was going at the time. If it was a new bedchamber the young woman wanted, it had to be beautiful, evidently costly, and not like that of everyone else. Such requirements must have done much to encourage novelty, and some of the best designers, artists and craftsmen would in that case have had to rack their brains in order to meet such exacting demands.

If these assumptions are correct, then it is not unreasonable to claim that it was in the rooms of the great courtesans that many new fashions in interior decoration were forged. At that period, this was not part of a carefully nurtured process, as it was to become in the seventeenth century; there was as yet no feeling that new fashions had to be introduced each season, for instance. But it is likely to have been in these houses, where convention could to a large extent be flouted and experiment was not likely to be discouraged, that many new ideas in the field of decoration and furnishing were first to be seen.

It would be satisfying to be able to produce evidence to support this assertion but none seems to be readily available. However, inference can perhaps be drawn from later history. Great men in the seventeenth and eighteenth centuries set up their mistresses in delightful houses that often had a profound influence on the subsequent development of comfort indoors and on fashions in decoration. Much the same may be said of the great *demi-mondaines* of the nineteenth century.[39] Indeed, one should always keep an eye on the arrangements adopted by the *demi-monde* when studying fashion in this field. Is it not likely, therefore, that the sixteenth century, at any rate, and perhaps also the latter part of the fifteenth, saw early manifestations of this phenomenon which was to become so evident in the future?

Whether the effects were novel or not, visitors to these houses thought them wonderful – there is plenty of evidence for that. No doubt the multiplicity of delights on offer, and the atmosphere of ease, lent everything a particular aura of glamour which would have been enhanced for many of the clients because these enchanting features were not associated with the tiresome cares and responsibilities that so often attended the more familiar comforts of domesticity or of life at court. To many visitors, therefore, this must have seemed the perfect way to live and a few at least must have endeavoured to copy some of the more respectable features of the courtesans' arrangements, in their own villas and *palazzi*. And it was not only Italians who must have been thus influenced. As Coryat said of Venetian courtesans, 'the fame of them hath drawen many to Venice from the remotest parts of Christendome, to contemplate their beauties'.[40] Indeed, as far as Venice was concerned, the *cortigiane* were an important tourist attraction, which explains why the government tended to be rather half-hearted about curbing their activities with sumptuary laws and other regulations – after all, these women were a notable source of revenue through the taxes they paid and the trade that foreign visitors generated.[41] One way or another, therefore, it seems probable that the *cortigiane* played their part in the spread of new fashions in decoration and furnishing, at least during the sixteenth century and perhaps even before that.

The descriptions of the top courtesans' apartments are far too general, however, to reveal how their rooms differed from those in splendid palaces and grand villas. All they really tell us is that they were surprisingly sumptuous, and tended to be stylish and enchanting.

Inventories are of no help because courtesans mostly died in relative poverty, so inventories taken after their death tell us nothing about their possessions when they were at the height of their fame and are therefore useless for purposes of comparison. Contemporary pictures of rooms would be helpful if we could decide which were the rooms of courtesans and which were those of highly respectable ladies, but as Federico Gonzaga and his companions were unable, in their own day, to tell the difference between respectable Roman matrons and Roman courtesans (p. 354), there is not much hope that, at this distance in time, we can distinguish a courtesan's room from that of a contemporary matron.[42] And yet, perhaps there are clues.

One possible clue may lie in the character of the beds that are to be seen in illustrations dating from the sixteenth century (and just possibly from the end of the fifteenth) showing scenes from the Bible and classical mythology which involve a woman and in which there is an erotic element that allowed the artist to place the scene in a bedchamber. Favourite subjects in this genre were Venus when associated with Mars or Vulcan, Cleopatra when expiring after clasping the asp to her bosom, Joseph trying to elude the embraces of Potiphar's wife, Danaë being seduced by Jupiter in the form of a shower of gold coins, and poor Lucretia being assaulted by Tarquin.[43]

The beds in these scenes are usually elaborate, both in the form of their hangings and in the woodwork of the bed itself. It seems as if those who were to view these erotic scenes expected to see them enacted in the presence of this class of bed (Pls 7, 217, 378). Could it be that this type of bed was especially favoured by courtesans and that therefore it was not inappropriate to show, in beds of the same sort, those ladies of the myths and Bible stories whose virtue was supposedly of a rather easy kind? All we can say is that beds of a similar type, and clearly derived from these sixteenth-century models, came to be known in France during the seventeenth century as *lits à la romaine*.[44] Whether this term stems from the fact that they had been developed from sixteenth-century Roman beds, or whether the form was all along recognized as being based on classical Roman prototypes, is not at present known. It is however relevant that, in the seventeenth century, such beds seem to have been considered more suitable for royal mistresses than for queens, and that those who considered themselves pillars of society favoured beds of a more sober conformation – which meant 'four-posters' where the hangings and tester formed a box-like cubicle around and above the bed. The *lit à la romaine*, and its sixteenth-century Italian predecessors, did not have posts but invariably had a conical canopy or *padiglione* suspended above it (p. 121). The curtains of such beds had to be very full in order to enclose the whole bed, hanging as they did from the bowl or cone overhead. These ample curtains had to be pulled back out of the way when the occupant of the bed was not actually asleep, and a tumbling effect of bunched-up drapery could be contrived that looked opulent and voluptuous (Pl. 171).

It would be going too far to say that no courtesan ever occupied a four-post bed, or that virtuous citizens never slept in a *lit à la romaine* (Pl. 172),

378

378 Bedchamber of a prominent courtesan?

Giulio Romano, the brilliant designer and decorator who had first worked under Raphael in Rome and then moved on to work for the Gonzagas in Mantua, is also famous for his erotic pictures of which this is a mild example. The great elegance of the furnishings, and the precision with which they are shown, suggests that he has based this scene on the kind of setting in which one of the famous Roman courtesans welcomed their clients. The decorative detailing of the day-bed hardly suggests that this room was to be found in a normal domestic setting.

Giulio Romano, *Two Lovers*
Hermitage, Leningrad

379 The perfect lady

Many illustrations of the Annunciation are included in this book, not because this episode was central to the cult of the Virgin Mary that had such a strong hold on popular imagination in Renaissance Italy, but because Mary is usually shown in a glamorous domestic setting which tells us much about contemporary taste. It also depicts an ideal of female excellence. The quattrocento Mary was fair of face, knew how to dress chastely but with elegance, could read and was therefore evidently intelligent, and was of a happy disposition that made her able to welcome the Angel's astonishing news with a gentle and serious smile (cinquecento Virgins often display much less equanimity in that circumstance). Of course it took money to dress well and live with luxurious furnishings (it has always done so) but it was generally believed that the most prized female virtues could best be sustained within a framework of security, comfort and ease. Few could attain this state but that, in a sense, was why the ideal seemed so attractive.

Filippo Lippi, *Annunciation*, 1450s
Palazzo Doria Pamphilij, Rome (photograph: Scala)

379

but it may well be that the latter form of bed was associated in the public consciousness with a rather racy way of life, in the sixteenth as well as the seventeenth century. It was a stylish piece of furniture from which were developed the elegant day-beds of the late seventeenth century and the many variations of informal bed and couch of the eighteenth. These later manifestations were supreme expressions of comfort and it is surely not far-fetched to suggest that, in the field of material comfort, it was in the houses of leading courtesans that the way ahead was often first unwittingly indicated.

Whatever the case may be, however, it is true to say that in the whole field of social history, a discipline that touches upon the subject of the present study at so many points, one should follow the advice of the French detective – *cherchez la femme*. Her role has not always been central in an obvious way but it is unwise to take for granted that her contribution has been insignificant.

6545LBS19885P

DIAGRAMS

1. The box-like hangings are suspended from a hook in the ceiling. See Pls 89 and 12.

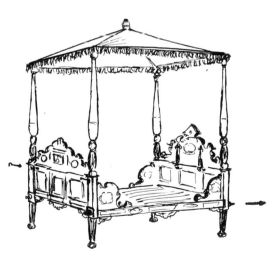

2. Related to early posted beds. A German field bed of about 1580. Bolts secure the main frame. Hooks hold head- and foot-boards upright. Posts dismantle in sections. See Pls. 140–60.

3. Bed with a half-tester. This only covers the head-end of the bed. See Pl. 178

4. Interpretation of the confusing illustration in Pl. 158 of a heavily carved posted bed. It may not have had a domed tester but such a massive structure must have been capped by a substantial feature.

5. One cannot be sure that such a day-bed as seen in Pl. 167 existed, but it has so many plausible features that one may conclude it did – as a 'seat of audience' or '*lit de justice*'. The two small sketches show how the front curtains were knotted and turned inside themselves, out of the way.

6. The box-bench in Pl. 186 would have looked like this.

7. This handsome bench, one of a pair, stands in the Carmine church in Florence. It is probably what was sometimes called a *ciscranna*. The back can face either way; it swings up and over. See p. 173

8. The back of the stool in Pl. 183 would have looked something like this. The dished depression in the seat-top was a common feature.

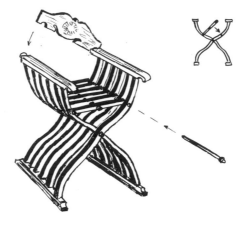

9. The scissor-action of a folding-chair hinges on the lower central pin. The seat requires three pins. That on the lower left forms a hinge (see diagram). The central pin holds seat members together. The pin on the right locks the seat in position or can be removed, allowing the chair to fold. The back-rest locks the arms in the open position. See Pl. 196

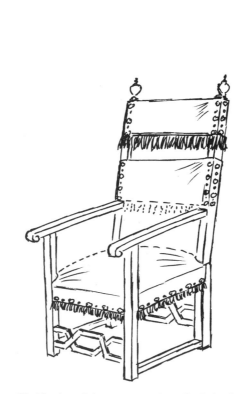

10. Clarification of the representation of a chair of state as seen in Pl. 209. Bergamo, about 1590.

11. The Procurator of St Marks' enthroned. See Pl. 211.

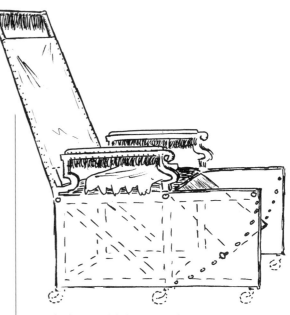

12. Andrea Doria's invalid chair. Attempted reconstruction based on the portrait reproduced in Pl. 214. The whole base is conjectural.

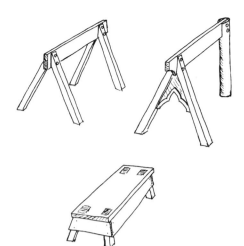

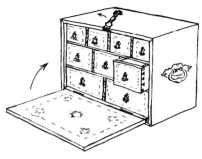

13. *Left*: a standard form of trestle for humble use. *Centre*: a tripod trestle [*trespiede*] for use with a dining-table; the single leg was placed on the side where the diners sat. *Right*: conjectural sketch of a sturdily-built trestle suitable for supporting a bed (see p. 111).

16. The portable chest or coffer of around 1500, as seen in Pl. 229, could be mounted in pairs on a pack-animal.

19. The Spanish style *escritorio*, with its hinged falling front forming a writing-leaf that locks with a hasp when closed. Can be carried. See Pl. 265

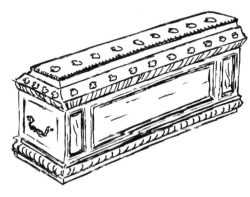

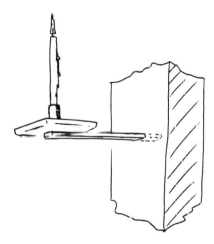

14. Design for a table with fixed supports suitable for heavy stone slabs but also used for wooden tops once the form became widely fashionable. After a design by Perino del Vaga (Uffizi, Florence; No. 1605 E).

17. Attempt to interpret the representation of two chests in the background of Pl. 223. Apart from being badly drawn, the chests were covered with fine veils of linen with fringed ends.

20. Candleholder with spigot for inserting in a hole in masonry or stone column, as seen in Pl. 345.

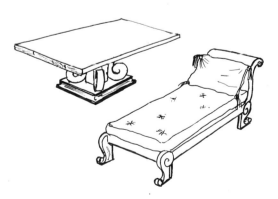

15. A table supported by four dolphins on a base. See Pl. 223.

18. Writing-desk with overhang. The construction is carefully observed in the painting shown in Pl. 255 but there are nevertheless puzzles for the would-be interpreter.

21. The low table and three reclining couches shown in Pl. 315 would have looked like this. Even if imaginary, the idea was real enough.

22. The day-bed and *lettuccio* to be seen in the
complicated representation in Pl. 7 looked
something like this.

INVENTORIES

Abbreviated titles of inventories from which quotations have been taken, arranged chronologically. The facts embodied in these abbreviated titles are sometimes given in a different order in the text but the sense will always be clear. A concordance, with the abbreviated titles in alphabetical order, follows this list.

Monte Invt., Bologna, 1290 Ludovico Frati, *La Vita Privata di Bologna dal secolo XIII al XVII*, Bologna, 1900, p.227 et seq., Invt. of the possessions of Giovanni de Monte; made in connection with a family lawsuit, 16 Feb. 1290.

Parisi Invt., Bologna, 1313 Ludovico Frati, *loc. cit.* under Monte Invt., 1290. Invt. relative to a lawsuit between members of the Parisi family.

Papal Invts., 1314–53 Hermann Hoberg, *Die Inventare des Päpstlichen Schatzes in Avignon, 1314–76*, Rome, 1941.

Belvisi Invt., Bologna, 1335 Ludovico Frati, *loc. cit.*, under Monte Invt., 1290. Invt. of the belongings of Jacopo Belvisi, Doctor of Law.

Malavolti Invt., Siena, 1350 Curzio Mazzi, 'Il Vescovo dei Malvolti e l'Ospizio di Santa Marta in Siena.' Reale Accademia dei Rozzi, *Bollettino senese di storia patria*, XIX, 1912, pp.201–48. 5 Dec. 1350; invt of furnishings, silver and books of Bishop of Siena.

Acciaiuoli Invt., Florence, 1363 Curzio Mazzi, 'Argenti degli Acciaiuoli', *Nozze Bacci-del Lungo*, Siena, 1895. Schiaparelli* says this is dated 1388.

Charles V Invt., France, 1379–80 J. Labarte, *Inventaire du mobilier de Charles V, roi de France. Collection des documents inédits de l'histoire de France*. Paris, 1879. This French king ordered an invt. of his possessions to be made at the beginning of 1379 which was incomplete at his death in 1380. He took a close personal interest in its compilation.

Amato Invt., Naples, 1399–1400 Soc. Siciliana per la Storia Patria. *Archivio Storico Siciliano*, 2nd series, XXI, Palermo 1896.

La Grua Invt., Sicily, 1403 Salvatore Salamone-Marino, *Le Pompe nuziali e il corredo della donne siciliane ne' secoli XIV, XV, e XVI*. Palermo 1876, printed in *Nuove Effemeri Siciliane*, Palermo 1876. Invt. of wedding presents of Ilaria La Grua, noblewoman, who married Giliberto Talamanca.

Aleardi Invt., Verona, 1408 Carlo Cipolla, 'Libri e Mobili di Casa Aleardi', *Archivio Veneto*, 1882. Invt. of the belongings of Ireco Gaspare Aleardi, nobleman and member of the ruling Council of Fifty which had been established after the Venetian domination of Verona in 1405. He died n 1407.

Zambecari Invt., Bologna, 1412 Ludovico Frati, *loc. cit.*, under Monte Invt., 1290. Possessions of Niccolo de Zambeccari.

Monticoli Invt., Udine, 1413 Pio Paschini, 'La casa ed i libri di un giurisperito udinese'. *Memorie Storiche Forogliuliesi*, XXXII, Udine, 1936, pp. 121–149. Invt. of Andrea de' Monticoli, a prominent jurist in Udine, whose family had come from Verona.

Trivulzio Invt., Milan, 1420 Same source as Trivulzio Invt., 1465.

Uzzano Invt., Florence, 1424 Walter Bombe, *Nachlass-Inventare des Angelo da Uzzano und des Lodovico di Gino Capponi*, Beiträge zur Kultur und Universal-geschichte, Leipzig and Berlin, 1928. Invt. of household goods of Niccolo da Uzzano, whose house in the Via dei Bardi was designed by Lorenzo de Bicci.

Guinigi Invt., Lucca, 1430 Salvatore Bongi, *Di Paolo Guinigi e delle sue richezze*, Lucca, 1871. Invt. of the tyrant of Lucca.

Este Invt., Ferrara, 1436 Giulio Bertoni and Emilio P. Vinci, *Il Castello di Ferrara al tempi di Niccolo III. Inventario della suppelletile del Castello, 1436*, Bologna, 1906. This should be studied in conjunction with Giuseppe Pardi, *La Suppellettile dei Palazzi Estensi in Ferrara nel 1436*. Ferrara, 1908, an analysis and commentary on Bertoni and Vicini's publication. Where page refs. are given, they are to Pardi's work.

Barzizza Invt., Padua, 1445 Roberto Cessi, 'Cristoforo Barzizza, Medico del secolo XV', *Bollettino della Civica Biblioteca di Bergamo*, Anno III, no 1, 1909, pp. 1–13. Invt. of Doctor of Medicine and humanist, nephew of scholar and grammarian Gasparino Barzizza

Pucci Invt., Florence, 1449 Carlo Merkel, 'I beni della famiglia di Puccio Pucci.' *Miscellanea Nuziale Rossi-Theiss*, Pavia, 1897.

Eustachi Invt., Pavia, 1449 L. Rossi, 'Gli Eustachi di Pavia', *Bollettino della Societa Pavese*, XV, 1915, p. 155.

Fece Invt., Siena, 1450 Curzio Mazzi, 'Libri e masserizie di Giovanni di Pietro di Fece (Fecini) nel 1450 in Siena', Reale Accademia dei Rozzi, *Bollettino senese di storia patria*, XVII, 150, 1911, pp. 150–172.

Italiano Invt., Genoa, 1451 Emilio Pandiani, *La Vita Privata Genovese*, Genoa, 1915. Documenti. Invt. of Tomaso Italiano.

Ricobono Invt., Genoa, 1451 Emilio Pandiani, *loc. cit.*, under Italiano Invt., 1451. Invt. of 23 April 1451.

Venturini Invt., Venice, 1454 P. Molmenti, *La Storia di Venezia nella vita privata*, 1880, Vol. I Turin, p. 205.

Pinelli Invt., Genoa, 1456 Emilio Pandiani, *loc. cit.*, under Italiano Invt., 1451. Invt. of Almone Pinelli.

Medici Invt., Florence, 1456 Eugene Müntz, *Les Collections des Medici au XVe siècle*, Paris and London, 1888. Invt. of Piero dei Medici, son of Cosimo. Includes his residences in Florence and his villas at Careggi and Cafaggiolo.

Negri Invt., Genoa, 1456 Emilio Pandiani, *loc. cit.*, under

Italiano Invt. 1451. Invt. of Luchina, widow of Giacomo di Negri.

Vivaldi Invt., Genoa, 1456 Emilio Pandiani, *loc. cit.*, under Italiano Invt. 1451. Invt. of Benedetto de Vivaldi.

Lomellini Invt., Genoa, 1458 Emilio Pandiani, *loc. cit.*, under Italiano Invt. 1451. Postmortem invt. of Brigida, widow of Giuliano Lomellini.

Spinola Invt., Genoa, 1459 Emilio Pandiani, *loc. cit.*, under Italiano Invt. 1451. Invt. of Niccolo Antonio Spinola.

Alvarotti Invt., Padua, 1460 Mirella Blason Berton, 'Una famiglia di Giuristi Padovani', *Bollettino di Museo Civico, Padua*, LIII, 1964.

Busarini Invt., Genoa, 1461 Emilio Pandiani, *loc. cit.*, under Italiano Invt. 1451. Invt. of Leonardo Busarini.

Vario Invt., Genoa, 1462 Emilio Pandiani, *loc. cit.*, under Italiano Invt. 1451. Invt. of Lazarino Vario de Albignana.

Trivulzio Invt., Milan, 1465 Emilio Motta, *Nozze Principesche nel quattrocento. Corredi, inventari e descrizioni. Nozze Trivulzio-Cavazzi della Somaglia*, Milan, 1894. Dowry of Ippolita Sforza, who married Alfonso of Aragon in 1465.

Rucellai Invt., Florence, 1466 Alessandro Perosa and others, 'Giovanni Rucellai ed il suo Zibaldone', *Studies of the Warburg and Courtauld Institutes*. vol. 24, London, 1960. Wedding gifts of Nannia de' Medici who married Bernardo Rucellai. See also G. Marcotti, 'Un mercante Fiorentino e la sua famiglia nel secolo XV', *Nozze Nardi-Arnaldi*, Florence, 1881, with commentary. Gives different readings and interpretations.

Trivulzio Invt., Milan, 1469 Emilio Motta, *loc. cit.*, under Trivulzio Invt. 1465, above. List of presents given by Galeazzo Maria Sforza to his wife Bona di Savoia in 1468.

Manfredi Invt., Faenza, 1469 Evelina Ciuffolotti, *Faenza nella vita privata*, Bagnacavallo, 1922. Invt. of possessions deposited by Astorgio III Manfredi, lord of Faenza, during period of political unrest.

Artegna Invt., Aquilea, 1473 Mario D'Angelo, *Notizie inedite su Guarnerio D'Artegna da un antico regesto*, San Daniele Del Friuli, 1970. Invt. of Guarnerio d'Artegna.

Pico Invt., Modena, 1474 Alfonzo Morselli, 'Il corredo nuziale di Caterina Pico', *Deputazione di Storia Patria per le Antiche Provincie Modenesi*, Modena, 1956. Trousseau of the daughter of the Lord of Mirandola, near Modena.

Gregorio Invt., Sicily, 1475 Salvatore Salamone-Marino, *Le pompe nuziali e il corredo delle donne siciliane ne' secoli XIV, XV e XVI*. Palermo 1876. *Nuove Effemeri Siciliane*, Palermo 1876. List of wedding presents of Angela di Gregorio.

Tura Invt., Siena, 1483 Curzio Mazzi, *La Casa di Maestro Bartolo di Tura*, Siena, 1900. Invt. of famous doctor, who had treated Pope Pius II, and had married into the latter's family, the Piccolomini. Rich and well-informed commentary.

Fiesso Invt., Ferrara, 1484 Adriano Franceschini, *Inventari inediti di biblioteche ferrarese del secolo XV*, Ferrara, 1982, p. 130. Invt. of the bibliophile Francesco de Fiesso.

Borromeo Invt., Milan, 1487 Alessandro Giulini, 'Nozze Borromeo nel Quattrocento.' Società Storico Lombarda, *Archivio Storico Lombarda*, Milan, 45, XIII, 1910, pp. 261–84. Invt. of wedding gifts of Maddalena of Brandenburg on her marriage to Count Gilberto Borromeo.

Ponzone Invt., Genoa, 1488 Emilio Pandiani, *loc. cit.*, under Trivulzio Invt., Milan, 1465. Postmortem Invt. of Giacomo Ponzone.

Valle Invt., Genoa, 1488 Emilio Pandiani, *loc. cit.*, under Trivulzio Invt., Milan, 1465. Invt. of Battista Valle.

Gonzaga Invt., Mantua, 1488 L. A. Gandini, 'Il Corredo di Elizabetta Gonzaga Montefeltro', A. Luzio and G. Renier, *Mantova e Urbino. Isabella d'Este ed Elizabetta Gonzaga nelle relazioni familiari e nelle vicende politiche*, Turin, 1893, pp. 293–306. Elisabetta Gonzaga married Guidobaldo Montefeltro at Urbino in 1488.

Franceschino Invt., Cesena, 1489 Antonio Domeniconi, 'Un inventario relativo a un custode della Biblioteca Malatestiana: Frate Franceschinò da Cesena (1489).' *Studi Romagnoli*, XVI, 1965, pp. 179–81.

Medici Invt., Florence, 1492 *Mobili e Robe esistenti alla morte de magnifico Lorenzo nelle sale terrene del Palazzo, oggi sede del Museo Mediceo*, Florence, 1930. A transcript of 1512 in the Archivio di Stato, Florence (*Mediceo Avanti il Principato*, Filza CLXV). Lists contents of ground-floor rooms at the town residence in what was then called the Via Larga, now re-named the Via Cavour. This material together with inventories of the Medici villas at Careggi and Poggio a Caiano, are included in a typescript in the Warburg Institute, London.

Careggi Invt., Tuscany, 1492 Guido Biagi, *Nozze Olschki-Rosenthal*, Florence, 1912. Invt. of the Medici villa at Careggi, included in the typescript in the Warburg Institute, mentioned above.

Poggio Invt., Tuscany, 1492 Inventory lists the contents of the Medici villa at Poggio a Caiano. Included in the typescript in the Warburg Institute, mentioned above.

Sforza Sisters Invt., Milan, 1493 Eugene Van Overloop, *L'inventaire Sforza, 1493*, Gembloux, 1934. The trousseaux of two sisters, Angela and Ippolita Sforza, daughters of Count Carlo Sforza. Angela married Ercole d'Este, and Ippolita married Alexandro Bentivoglio. This invt. of 12 Sept. 1493 was prepared when their mutual possessions had to be divided.

Sforza Invt., Milan, 1493 F. Calvi, 'Il corredo nuziale di Bianca Maria Sforza Visconti', *Archivio Storico Lombardo*, March 1875, pp. 51–76. Trousseau of Bianca Maria Sforza at her marriage to the Emperor Maximilian.

Della Rovere Invt., Bologna 1493 Ludovico Frati, 'L'Inventario di Bartolomeo della Rovere', *Atti della Deputazione Ferrarese di Storia Patria*, Ferrara, 1906. The inventory of Bartolomeo della Rovere, Bishop of Ferrara, nephew of Pope Sixtus IV and brother of Julius II.

Gaddi Invt., Florence, 1496 Carlo Bologna, *Per Nozze Bumiller-Stiller*, Florence, 1883. The inventory of Francesco di Angelo Gaddi.

Savoy Invt., 1497–8 Pietro Vayra, 'Inventario dei Castelli di Ciamberi [Chambery], di Torino e di Ponte d'Ain, 1497–8', *Le Lettere e le Arti alla Corte di Savoia nel secolo XV*, Turin, 1888. Invts of three widely separated castles in the Franco-Italian state of Savoy.

Castello Invt., Tuscany, 1498 John Shearman, 'The Collections of the Younger Branch of the Medici', *The Burlington Magazine*, January 1975. With an extremely informative essay. Invt. of Medici villa at Castello.

Cafaggiolo Invt., Tuscany, 1498 John Shearman, *loc. cit.*, under Castello Invt., 1498 Invt. of the Medici villa at Cafaggiolo.

Il Trebbio Invt., Tuscany, 1498 John Shearman, *loc. cit.* under Castello Invt., 1498. Invt. of the Medici villa, Il Trebbio, near Florence.

Fiesole Invt., Tuscany, 1498 John Shearman, *loc. cit.*, under Castello Invt., 1498, above. Invt. of the Medici house, not the villa, at Fiesole.

Da Maiano Invt., Florence, 1498 L. Candali, *Giuliano e Benedetto da Maiano*, San Casciano Val di Pesa, 1926.

Rinuccini Invt., Florence, 1499 V. R. Giustiniani, *Alamanno Rinuccini*, Cologne and Graz, 1965, p. 42. The will and inventory of A. R. (1426–99), a famous Florentine official and writer.

Borgia Invt., Ferrara, 1503 L. Beltrami, *La Guaderoba di Lucrezia Borgia, Dall'Archivio di Stato di Modena*, Milan, 1903. Her invt. divided into four categories includes items brought by her from Rome as well as those given to her by Alfonso d'Este, and so recording the state of her Guardaroba before she became Duchess of Ferrara.

Sanuti Invt., Bologna, 1505 L. Frati, *La Vita Privata di Bologna*, Bologna, 1900, pp. 21–4. From an invt. of the contents of the Palazzo Sanuti, one of the most splendid houses in Bologna at the time.

Frossasco Invt., Piedmont, 1512 Piero Giacoas, *Un Inventario di un Castello Piemontese . . .*, Turin, 1890. Seat of the Montebello family (sometimes shortened to Mombel).

Badoer Invt., Venice, 1521 P. G. Molmenti, *La Storia di Venezia nella vita privata dalle origini alla caduta della republica*, Turin, 1880, Documenti, IX, pp. 607–9. Invt. of Agostino Badoer.

Di Challant Invt., Turin, 1522 Luigi Vaccarone, *Bianca Maria di Challant e il suo corredo*, Turin, 1898.

Farnesina Invt., Rome, 1526 C. L. Frommel, *Die Farnesina und Peruzzi's Achitektonisches Frühwerk*, Berlin, 1961, appendix II, pp. 171–98.

Trivulzio Invt., Milan, 1529 Emilio Motta, *loc. cit.*, under Trivulzio Invt., 1465.

Medici Invt., Florence, 1531 Luigi Cibrario, 'Lezione Storico-Filologica sopra alcuni vocaboli usati nei piu antichi registri della Guardaroba Medicea', *Archivio Storico Italiano*, III, 1867, p. 158 et seq.

Fieschi Invt., Genoa, 1532 Antonio Manno, *Arredi et Armi di Sinibaldo Fieschi, da un inventario del 1532*, Genoa, 1876, with glossary.

Capponi Invt., Florence, 1534 Walter Bombe, '*Nachlass-Inventare des Angelo da Uzzano und des Lodovico di Gino Capponi*', section on 'Das Florentinisches Wohnhaus des Lodovico Capponi in Via dei Bardi 28.' *Beiträge zur Kultur- und Universal-geschichte*, ed. Walter Goetz, Leipzig and Berlin, 1928.

Marcello Invt. From Molmenti*, see Badoer Invt., 1521.

Medici Invt., Florence, 1553 Cosimo Conti, *La prima reggia di Cosimo I de' Medici nel Palazzo gia della Signoria di Firenze*, Florence, 1893.

Odoni Invt., Venice, 1555 Inventar des Nachlasses des Alvise Odoni, aus dem Nachlass Gustav Ludwigs. *Kunsthistorisches Institut, Florenz, Italienische Forschungen IV–V*, Berlin, 1911, pp. 56–74. Invt. of Andrea Odoni (or Udoni?), famous collector whose portrait was painted by Lorenzo Lotto, and whose collection was described by Marc Antonio Michiel in his notes on collecting in the Veneto.

Requesens Invt., Palermo, 1561 S. Salamone Marino, 'Inventario di Don Berlinghieri Requesens', *Archivio Storico Siciliano*, XXI, 1896, pp. 374–396. Invt. of the Captain-General of the Sicilian galley-fleet, who was captured by the Turks and died in captivity in Constantinople in 1560.

Doria Invt., Genoa, 1561 E. Pandiani, 'Arredi ed Argenti di Andrea Doria', *Atta Società Liguria Storia Patria*, LIII, 1926. Invt. of the powerful Prince Doria of Genoa.

Pitti Invt., Florence, 1577 Marilena Mosco, 'Una Descrittione dell'apparato della stanze del Palazzo de' Pitti in Fiorenza edita a Venezia nel 1577', *Antichita Viva*, XIX, 2, 1980, pp. 5–20. A description of the appearance of rooms in the Pitti Palace in the time of the Grand Duke Francesco de' Medici in 1576, as given in a report made to the Venetian Senate. Taken from a printed book of the same title, printed in Venice in 1577.

Caro Invt., 1578 Aulo Greco, *Annibal Caro*, Rome, 1950. This famous scholar died in 1556 but this inventory of his study and adjacent rooms was not taken until 22 years later.

Pasqualigo Invt., Venice, 1579 Archivio di Stato, Venice, Cancelleria Inferiore, Miscellanea notai diversi, busta 42. Notary C. Ziliol, 9 March 1589. Invt. of Andrea Pasqualigo, member of patrician family, a poet, writer and collector. Communicated by Dora Thornton.

Urbino Invt., 1582 F. Sangiorgi, *Documenti urbinati, inventori del Palazzo Duccale (1582–1631)*. Urbino, 1974.

Vitelli Invt., Perugia, 1582 G. Magherini-Graziani, *Per le Nozze Nuti-Scalvanti*, Perugia, 1912, pp. 67–73. Invt. of Faustina and Vicenzo Vitelli.

Gonzaga Invt., Mantua, 1582 *Il Corredo Nuziale di Anna Caterina Gonzaga, Principessa di Mantova e di Monferrato*, Mantua, 1876. From the Gonzaga Archives.

Correr Invt., Venice, 1584 From Molmenti*, see Badoer Invt., 1521. The invt. of Lorenzo Correr, patrician and official.

Zarlino invt., Venice, 1589 Archivio di Stato, Venice, Cancelleria Inferiore, busta 43, 20 February 1589, notary N. Doglione. Communicated by Dora Thornton. Invt. of a chapel Master of Saint Mark's; well-known author of books on musical theory, and friend of Tintoretto whose daughter he taught.

Moncada Invt., Sicily, 1598 See La Grua Invt., 1403 (From the same source).

Medici Invt., Paris, 1589 Edmond Bonnaffé, *Inventaire des meubles de Catherine de Medicis en 1589. Mobilier, Tableaux, Objets d'Art, Manuscrits*, Paris, 1874. Invt. of L'Hôtel de la Reine, July 1589.

Pollani Invt., Venice, 1590 P. G. Molmenti, *La Storia di Venezia nella vita privata dalle origini alla caduta della repubblica*, Turin, 1880, pp. 622–29. Invt. of Hieronimo Pollano.

Ram Invt. Venice, 1592 From the same source as the Odoni Invt., Venice, 1555.

Villa Medici Invt., Rome, 1598   Glenn M. Andres, *The Villa Medici in Rome*, New York, 1976. Quotations from this D. Phil. dissertation of 1970 made by kind permission of the author.

Urbino Invt., 1599   See Urbino Invt., 1582; same source.

Villa Medici Invt., Rome, 1616   Mazzino Fossi, 'Documenti per la storia di Villa Medici e di Palazzo Firenze a Roma', *Antichita Viva*, 1976, no. 3, pp. 37–45.

CONCORDANCE

Arranged in alphabetical order.

Acciaiuoli Invt., Florence, 1363
Aleardi Invt., Verona, 1408
Alvarotti Invt., Padua, 1460
Amato Invt., Naples, 1399–1400
Artegna Invt., Aquilea, 1473
Badoer Invt., Venice, 1521
Barzizza Invt., Padua, 1445
Belvisi Invt., Bologna, 1335
Borgia Invt., Ferrara, 1503
Borromeo Invt., Milan, 1487
Busarini Invt., Genoa, 1461
Cafaggiolo Invt., Tuscany, 1498
Capponi Invt., Florence, 1534
Careggi Invt., Tuscany, 1492
Caro Invt., 1578
Castello Invt., Tuscany, 1498
Charles V Invt., France, 1379–80
Correr Invt., Venice, 1584
Da Maiano Invt., Florence, 1498
Della Rovere Invt., Bologna, 1493
Di Challant Invt., Turin, 1522
Doria Invt., Genoa, 1561
Este Invt., Ferrara, 1436
Eustachi Invt., Pavia, 1449
Farnesina Invt., Rome, 1526
Fece Invt., Siena, 1450
Fieschi Invt., Genoa, 1532
Fiesole Invt., Tuscany, 1498
Fiesso Invt., Ferrara, 1484
Franceschino Invt., Cesena, 1489
Frossasco Invt., Piedmont, 1512
Gaddi Invt., Florence, 1496
Gonzaga Invt., Mantua, 1488
Gonzaga Invt., Mantua, 1582
Gregorio Invt., Sicily, 1475
Guinigi Invt., Lucca, 1430
Il Trebbio Invt., Tuscany, 1498
Italiano Invt., Genoa, 1451
La Grua Invt., Sicily, 1403
Lomellini Invt., Genoa, 1458
Malavolti Invt., Siena, 1350
Manfredi Invt., Faenza, 1469

Marcello Invt. (See Badoer Invt., 1521)
Medici Invt., Florence, 1456
Medici Invt., Florence, 1492
Medici Invt., Florence, 1531
Medici Invt., Florence, 1553
Medici Invt., Paris, 1589
Moncada Invt., Sicily, 1598
Monte Invt., Bologna, 1290
Monticoli Invt., Udine, 1413
Negri Invt., Genoa, 1456
Odoni Invt., Venice, 1555
Papal Invts., 1314–53
Parisi Invt., Bologna, 1313
Pasqualigo Invt., Venice, 1579
Pico Invt., Modena, 1474
Pinelli Invt., Genoa, 1456
Pitti Invt., Florence, 1577
Poggio Invt., Tuscany, 1492
Pollani Invt., Venice, 1590
Ponzone Invt., Genoa, 1488
Pucci Invt., Florence, 1449
Ram Invt., Venice, 1592
Requesens Invt., Palermo, 1561
Ricobono Invt., Genoa, 1451
Rinuccini Invt., Florence, 1499
Rucellai Invt., Florence, 1466
Saniti Invt., Bologna, 1505
Savoy Invt., 1497–8
Sforza Invt., Milan, 1493
Sforza Sisters Invt., Milan, 1493
Spinola Invt., Genoa, 1459
Trivulzio Invt., Milan, 1420
Trivulzio Invt., Milan, 1465
Trivulzio Invt., Milan, 1469
Trivulzio Invt., Milan, 1529
Tura Invt., Siena, 1483
Urbino Invt., 1582
Urbino Invt., 1599
Uzzano Invt., Florence, 1424
Valle Invt., Genoa, 1488
Vario Invt., Genoa, 1462
Venturini Invt., Venice, 1454
Villa Medici Invt., Rome, 1598
Villa Medici Invt., Rome, 1616
Vitelli Invt., Perugia, 1582
Vivaldi Invt., Genoa, 1456
Zambecari Invt., Bologna, 1412
Zarlino Invt., Venice, 1589

ABBREVIATED TITLES

Abbreviated titles of much-cited publications and theses.

Alberti   Leon Battista Alberti, *De re aedificatoria*, treatise on architecture completed 1452, probably amplified until time of his death in 1472; first printed 1485. Quotations in Italian here taken from first printed Italian edition by Cosimo Bartoli, Florence, 1550; English quotations are from Giacomo Leoni's edition, London, 1726.

Belgrano*   L. T. Belgrano, *Della vita privata dei Genovese*, Genoa, 1875; edition of 1970, Rome, consulted.

Beltrami*   L. Beltrami, *La Vita nel Castello di Milano al Tempo degli Sforza*, Milan, 1900.

Bistort*   G. Bistort, *Il Magistrato alle pompe nella Republica di Venezia . . .*, Bologna, 1912.

Burckhardt, *Architecture**   Jacob Burckhardt, *The Architecture of the Italian Renaissance*, English edition by Peter Murray, London, 1985, original in German was written in 1860s.

Burckhardt, *Civilisation**   Jacob Burckhardt, *The Civilisation of the Renaissance in Italy*, first edn 1860, Basel. 1945 edn by L. Goldscheider consulted here.

Castiglione, *Courtier**   Baldassare Castiglione, *Il Cortegiano*, redrafted from 1508, published 1528, in Venice. A dual edition with an English text opposite the original Italian was published in 1727 and has been consulted here.

Coffin*   David R. Coffin, *The Villa in the Life of Renaissance Rome*, Princeton, 1979

Coryat*   *Crudities*, London, 1611. Glasgow edition of 1905 consulted.

Delumeau*   Jean Delumeau, *La Vie économique et sociale de Rome dans la seconde moitié du XVIe siècle*, Paris, 1957-9.

Decameron*   Giovanni Boccaccio, *Decameron*, written about 1350. Edition consulted, Mario Marti, Milan, 1950.

Dora Thornton, Thesis*   Ph. D. Thesis. The Study Room in Renaissance Italy, with particular reference to Venice circa 1560–1620, Warburg Institute, University of London, April 1990. Copy in Warburg Institute.

Eames*   Penelope Eames, 'Furniture in England, France and the Netherlands from the Twelfth to the Fifteenth Century.' *Furniture History*, Vol. XIII, 1977.

Filarete*   Antonio (or Pietro?) Averlino, called Filarete. Treatise on architecture written in early 1460s, ed. A. M. Finoli and L. Grassi, Milan, 1972.

Florio*   *Queen Anna's New World of Words or Dictionarie of the Italian and English tongues . . . by Giovanni Florio, Reader of the Italian unto the Soveraigne* [Queen Anne, wife of James I], London , 1611.

Francesco di Giorgio*   Correctly called Francesco di Giorgio Martini. Treatise on architecture, drafted in late 1470s but recast and revised in mid-1480s. No complete edition published until 1841. See edition by C. Maltese and De Grassi, Milan, 1967.

Frati*   Lodovico Frati, *La Vita Privata di Bologna dal Secolo XIII al XVI*, Bologna, 1900.

Frommel*   Christoph Luitpold Frommel, *Der Römische Palastbau der Hochrenaissance*, Tübingen, 1973. A revised edition is in preparation.

Fynes Moryson*   *Shakespeare's Europe, . . . Being unpublished chapters of Fynes Moryson's Itinerary (1617)*, edited by Charles Hughes, New York, 1903; reissued 1967. Moryson visited Italy in the 1590s.

Gage*   John Gage, *Life in Italy at the time of the Medici*, London, 1968; edited by Peter Quennell.

Gay*   V. Gay, *Glossaire archéologique du Moyen Age et de la Renaissance*, Paris, 1882–1920.

Giulio Romano exhib. cat*   Catalogue of the *Giulio Romano* exhibition, held in Mantua, 1990, edited by Sergio Polano.

Goldthwaite, *Building**   Richard A. Goldthwaite, *The Building of Renaissance Florence*, Baltimore and London, 1980.

Guidotti*   Gabriella Cantini Guidotti, 'I Tessili: nome, problemi e metodi', Centro di elaborazione automatica di dati e documenti storico artistico, *Bolletino d'informazione*, IV, Pisa, 1983.

Gundersheimer*   Werner Gundersheimer, *Art and Life at the Court of Ercole d'Este*, Geneva, 1972.

Havard*   Henry Havard, *Dictionaire de l'ameublement . . .*, Paris 1887-90.

Hypnerotomachia*   Francesco Colonna, *La Hypnerotomachia di Polifilo*, Venice, 1499; a second edn appeared in 1545 and a French edition the year after.

Jervis, *Printed Designs**   Simon Jervis, *Printed Furniture Designs before 1650*, London, 1974. Obtainable from The Furniture History Society.

Jervis, *Design Dictionary**   Simon Jervis, *The Penguin Dictionary of Design and Designers*, London 1984.

Liebenwein*   W. Liebenwein, *Studio, die Entstehung eines Raumtyps und seine Entwicklung bis um 1600*, Berlin, 1977.

Lydecker, *Ceti**   J. K. Lydecker, 'Il patriziato fiorentino e la committenza artistica per la casa', *I ceti dirigenti nella Toscana del Quattrocento*, Impruneta, 1987.

Lydecker, Thesis*   J. K. Lydecker, *The Domestic Setting of the arts in Renaissance Florence*, Johns Hopkins University, Baltimore, Maryland, 1987. Doctoral thesis.

Malaguzzi Valeri*   Francesco Malaguzzi Valeri, *La Corte di Lodovico il Moro*

Manni   *Mobili di Lodovico in Emilia*, Modena, 1986.

Molmenti*   P. G. Molmenti, *L'arte Veneziana nella vita privata . . .*, Turin, 1880; English and French editions 1882. Revised edition 1905-8; also in English. All these editions consulted at various times.

Montaigne*   Donald M. Frame, *Montaigne's Travel Journal*, San Francisco, 1983; Montaigne visited Italy in 1580.

Onians*   John Onians, *The Bearers of Meaning. The Classical Orders of Antiquity, the Middle Ages and the Renaissance*, Princeton University Press, 1988.

Palladio*   Andrea Palladio, treatise on architecture, *I Quattro Libri dell' Architettura*, Venice, 1570. Many later editions.

Pandiani*   Emilio Pandiani, *Vita Privata Genovese nel Rinascimento*, Genoa, 1915.

Pardi*   Giuseppe Pardi, *La Suppellettile dei Palazzi Estensi in Ferrara nel 1436*, Ferrara, 1908. A detailed commentary of the *Este Invts, Ferrara, 1436*, published by Bertoni and Vinci (see list of inventories on p. 363).

Polichetti*   Maria Luisa Polichetti, *Il Palazzo di Federigo da Montefeltro* (Urbino), catalogue of an exhibition held at Urbino in 1985.

Pius II Commentaries*   *The Secret Memoirs of a Renaissance Pope. The Commentaries of Aeneas Sylvus Piccolomini, Pius II*, edited by Florence Gragg and Leona Gabel, New York, 1959.

Priscianese*   Francesco Priscianese, *Del governo delle corte d'un signore in Roma*, first published in 1542; edition of 1883, Citta di Castello, consulted.

Ryder*   Alan Ryder, *The Kingdom of Naples under Alfonso the Magnanimous*, Oxford, 1976.

Sabba da Castiglione*   Fra Sabba da Castiglione, *Ricordi*, Venice, 1554.

Scamozzi*   Vincenzo Scamozzi, treatise on architecture, *L' Idea dell'architettura universale*, Venice, 1615.

Schiaparelli*   Attilio Schiaparelli, *La Casa Fiorentina e i suoi Arredi nei secoli XIV e XV*, Florence, 1908. Only the first volume of this important and useful book was published; no trace has been found of the text for Vol. II. A photographic reprint of Vol. I with notes and a commentary, appeared in 1983, edited by M. Sfameli and L. Pagnotta.

Schubring*   Paul Schubring, *Cassoni. Truhen und Truhenbilder der italienischen Frührenaissance*, Leipzig, 1915.

Serlio*   Sebastiano Serlio, treatise on architecture. Intended to be in seven volumes but not published in numerical sequence (Vol. IV, 1537; Vol. III, 1540; Vols. I and II, 1545; Vol. V, 1547, Vol. VII, 1575) and an additional volume in 1551, with Vol. VI only appearing in this century.

Thornton, *17th Cent. Int. Dec.**   Peter Thornton, *Seventeenth-Century Interior Decoration in England, France and Holland*, New Haven and London, 1978.

Thornton – Di Castro*   Peter Thornton and Daniela di Castro, 'Some late sixteenth-century Medici Furniture', *Furniture History*, Vol. XX, London, 1984.

Vasari*   Giorgio Vasari, *Le Vite de più eccellenti Architetti, Pittori et Scultori Italiani . . .*, Florence, 1550; edited by G. Milanesi, 1878-85.

Verga*   Ettore Verga, 'Le leggi suntuarie milanesi', *Archivio Storico Lombardo*, IX, XXV, Milan, 1898.

NOTES

* Denotes abbreviated titles. See p. 366.

1 Readers may notice that when I come to matters that do not particularly interest me (or about which I am rather ignorant, which comes to the same thing), I say very little; I mention these matters in the appropriate places merely so that my coverage of the field should be fairly comprehensive.

2 Curzio Mazzi was *sottobibliotecario* at the Laurentian Library in Florence in the 1890s, when he was doing his best work.

3 *The Furnishings and Decoration of Ham House* (with Maurice Tomlin), The Furniture History Society, London, 1980, and as Vol. XVI of its *Journal*. Also *Seventeenth-Century Interior Decoration in England, France and Holland*, New Haven and London, 1978.

4 Although the present study was first actively prosecuted in 1980, I broke off the work for about three years in order to publish a book entitled *Authentic Decor, The fashionable interior, 1620–1920*, London, 1984.

5 The last serious attempt was that made by Frida Schottmüller (*Wohnungskultur und Möbel der Italienischen Renaissance*, Stuttgart, 1928; also published in Italian). I am extremely grateful to Kent Lydecker for sending me a copy of this thesis, from which I have quoted a number of passages.

6 Professor Waddy has kindly sent me a copy of her book which is clearly of the greatest interest. Unfortunately it reached me only a few days before my own work had to be handed in. Her book is entitled *Seventeenth-Century Roman Palaces. Use and the art of the plan*. The Architectural History Foundation, New York, and the Massachusetts Institute of Technology, 1990.

7 Particularly confusing can be the transposing of letters which occurs frequently in Italian inventories, e.g. *vreto* for *vetro* [glass], *catreda* or *catedra* [a great chair]. The distortions can be even greater, e.g. *grillanda* for *guirlanda* [a garland], *primacci* for *piumacci* [a feather-bed], *lecteria* for *lettiera* [a form of bed], and *nenzuoli* or *nurzoli* for *lenzuoli* [sheets].

Introduction pp.11–18

1 Richard A. Goldthwaite, 'The Economy of Renaissance Italy. The Preconditions for Luxury Consumption', *I Tatti Studies. Essays in the Renaissance*, Vol. II, 1987, p. 19. This paper was originally given at a symposium in 1984.

2 *Ibid.*, p. 32.

3 Goldthwaite*, p. 77. The jealousy of less succesful fellow citizens all too readily followed upon the footsteps of official disapproval, 'Spending a lot and making a big impression are in themselves too dangerous', a 14th-century Florentine merchant had written.

4 Stefano Porcari, in a speech in 1427. See Gage*, p. 56.

5 *Ibid.*, p. 62.

6 Goldthwaite*, *op. cit.*, p. 89.

7 'Since all agree that we should endeavour to leave a reputation behind us ... we erect great structures that our posterity may suppose us to have been great persons', wrote Alberti (Goldthwaite, *op. cit.*, p. 83: see also the same author's 'Private Wealth and the Family', *Private Wealth in Renaissance Florence*, Princeton University Press, 1968, p. 258).

8 Frommel*, p. 4, 'In order that posterity should retain the memory of Bartolommeo Ferratini, he erected this house with the fruits of his earnings'.

9 Gage*, p. 55. 'Easily one-third to one-half of the owner's estate could be tied up in his palace' (Goldthwaite, *op. cit.*, p. 102). The Rucellai mansion in Florence, under construction between 1446 and 1451, was based on a design by Alberti executed under Bernardo Rossellino's direction.

10 In about 1470 a Florentine listed about thirty such palaces that had been built in his own day. Rather over half a century later, another historian added thirty-five to the earlier list and mentioned a further twenty built since. Anyone who wanted to list all the buildings of significance 'would have too much to do', he added (Goldthwaite*, p. 15). While building activity was particularly vigorous in Florence, especially during the 15th century, it was unmistakably evident in other major cities. In the 16th century the lead in this respect was taken by Rome and Genoa. See Delumeau*, especially pp. 263–79 and p. 358.

11 See Luisa Giordano, 'Interventi quattrocenteschi a Piacenza', *La maison de ville de la Renaissance*, papers of a conference held at the Centre d'études supérieures de la Renaissance at Tours in 1977, p. 65.

12 Two-thirds of the territory circumscribed by the walls of the ancient city (those erected by Marcus Aurelius) was open country over which wolves roamed. Goats clambered on the Tarpeian Rock alongside the Capitol while cows grazed in the Forum – still, until the last century, known as the Campo Vaccino, the cow-pasture.

13 See Delumeau*, *op. cit.*, *passim*.

14 '*Parva sed apta mihi sed nulli obnoxia sed non Sordida parta meo tamen aere domus*' [Small, but suited to my needs, freehold, not mean, the fruit of my own earnings]; see J. Addington Symonds, *Italian Literature*, London, 1880–81, p. 262.

15 Giovanni della Casa, whose *Il Galateo* (published in 1558 and constantly reprinted) was the most influential of all Italian 16th-century handbooks on behaviour, insisted that 'Everyone should dress well, according to his age and his position in society. If he does not, it will be taken as a mark of contempt for other people'. See Gage*, Chap. 13.

16 In the 1540s, a wealthy Paduan lawyer, sensitive about the image he might project through erecting in his garden an exceptionally handsome loggia, sought to deflect criticism by inscribing a tablet set into the façade: *Id facere laus est quod decet non quod licet* [It is praiseworthy to do what is appropriate, not what licence permits]. The implication is that a rich man can do almost anything but he will gain credit only if he restrains himself and does that which is morally appropriate. See John Onians, *Bearers of Meaning. The Classical Orders of Antiquity, the Middle Ages and the Renaissance*, Princeton University Press, 1988, p. 319.

17 Burckhardt, *Architecture*, p. 4; the original work in German was being written in the 1860s. Over the entrance to the 15th-century Palazzo Castani in Milan is written *Elegantiae publicae et commoditati privatae* [For the city's (greater) elegance and the family's comfort; see Frommel*, p. 4.

18 Arturo Graf, 'Una Cortigiana fra Mille. Veronica Franco', *Attraverso il Cinquecento*, Turin, 1888, pp. 329–32. The visit she paid was to the villa of Count Marc' Antonio della Torre in Fumane, near Verona, which was the seat of such delight that her poem in its praise ran to no less than 565 verses! She particularly draws attention to the *commodita di dentro e gli agi*, which *son cosi molli che gli altrui diletti al par di questi sembrano disagi* [the ease and comforts of the interior are so luxurious that the delights of others by comparison seem like discomforts]. She particularly mentions the rich textiles with which these accommodating effects were achieved.

19 Such statements were commonplace during the period and were based on classical quotations (notably Horace's *Odes*). See Brian Vickers, 'Leisure and idleness in the Renaissance; the ambivalence of otium', *Renaissance Studies*, IV, pp. 1–37 and 107–54.

20 Alberti*, V, 14. 'In urban building there are restrictions such as party walls, dripping-gutters, public grounds, rights of way, and so on, to prevent one's achieving a satisfactory result'. There was no need for buildings in the country to be tall; there is plenty of space. So villas tended to be low with the *piano nobile* at ground level; on a platform, perhaps, but not on the first floor.

21 See Goldthwaite, 'The Economy . . .', *op. cit.*, p. 26.

22 Wives would not be all that keen to leave their comfortable houses in town and move out into a primitive cabin in the countryside, so the villa had to be fitted up with most of the 'mod. cons.' that were present in the town residence.

23 This is true of the great villas around Florence, Rome and Genoa but not so much of those lying in the Veneto where many did indeed have farms attached and stood on estates of some magnitude. Much has been written about Italian villas. An excellent summary is to be found in James Ackerman. *The Villa*, London, 1990. See also the

Bollettino of the Centro Internazionale di Studi d'Architettura Andrea Palladio, Vicenza, Vol. XI, containing the papers of a conference devoted to Italian villas, held in 1969. Also the long essay in Vol. 11 of the Einaudi series on *Arte italiana*.

24 Burckhardt, *Civilisation**, p. 243. The whole of Part V of this seminal work, on 'Society and Festivals', still makes good reading as a background to our concerns here.

25 Whereas the bulky household furnishings of the seigneurial classes had in the main been designed so that they could be easily packed onto a cart, for moving on to the next resting-place, the more static way of life that became established in most parts of Italy during the first half of the 15th century made it possible to have furniture that was larger but also more delicate. For those who still had to make journeys – those among them who cared greatly for their comforts – new and much lighter forms of travelling-furniture were devised, some of which was in turn influential on later furniture design, when people grew tired of massive pieces.

26 See Richard Goldthwaite. 'The Empire of Things: Consumer Demand in Renaissance Italy', essay no. 9 in *Patronage, Art, and Society in Renaissance Italy*, eds. F. W. Kent and Patricia Simons, with J. C. Eade, Oxford and Canberra, 1987, espec. p. 170.

27 Goldthwaite, 'The Economy . . .', *op. cit.*, pp. 15 and 16. See also Goldthwaite, 'Empire of Things' *op. cit.*, p. 168–75.

28 *Giulio Romano*, exhib. cat., Mantua, 1990, ed. Sergio Polano, p. 387.

29 Benedetto Varchi, writing in about 1530 about palatial Florentine buildings, maintained that what a writer in about 1470 had called *palazzi* would now be regarded merely as large, comfortable houses [*grandi ed agiati casoni, che palazzi*; see Frommel*, p. 1: his introduction provides much additional information on the questions raised here].

30 'I am now in Rome but I cannot recognise the place. Everything appears new; the houses, the streets, the fountains, the acqueducts, the obelisques, and many other marvels – all done under Sixtus V'; see Delumeau*, p. 358.

31 A neat example of the degree to which scholars can rely on the accuracy in the depiction of details in Renaissance pictures is provided by a Ph.D. thesis submitted in Munich in 1977 by Elfriede Schiel. She reproduces paintings showing maiolica in use (*Fayencen in der Malerei des Mittelalters* is her title) and then illustrates surviving specimens which are identical or, at least, very similar indeed. The paintings show the pottery with quite remarkable verisimilitude. Schiaparelli*, p. XI, believed that pictorial evidence was at least as important as that provided by documents. When Ludwig* (p. 172) wrote that it was almost impossible to form an idea of the furniture used in quattrocento Florence through looking at paintings, he had 'fallen into a great exaggeration', Schiaparelli insists, and goes on to explain how one should view these pictures, what allowances one may need to make. Lydecker*, in his Thesis, pp. 9–25, agrees more with Ludwig. Dora Thornton*, in her Thesis, reminds us that those who drew up inventories varied considerably in literacy, education and culture (introduction to appendices, pp. 316–28). See also pp. 332–36 on pictures as sources: she agrees with Schiaparelli.

32 It is at present fashionable to seek symbolic meaning in every item represented in such paintings. Before plunging into these murky iconographic waters, it is probably not a bad idea first to try and read the picture literally – at least in so far as the details are concerned – and to bear in mind Freud's comment on the matter, namely that 'sometimes a cigar is just a cigar'.

33 Silver and gold plate, for instance, were often omitted from household inventories; so, sometimes, was linen (which was commonly listed separately even if included). Personal belongings were often left unrecorded. There were many reasons for such omissions. Unfortunately, modern scholars, when reproducing an inventory, have often tended to leave out items that did not interest them. Particularly guilty of this have been those studying paintings. The editing-out of 'boring' material can produce a very distorted image of a house's contents. If an inventory is reproduced complete, one can often learn much about the planning of the house and what was considered important, about out-of-date items and, conversely, what was deemed fashionable at the time.

34 *Cymbeline*, Act II, scene II; written in about 1605. I am indebted to Fiona Czerniewska of The Warburg Institute for drawing my attention to this charming passage.

35 One bed does survive in Santa Maria delle Grazie at Pistoia but it is damaged and incomplete. Dated 1337 in a painted inscription, I would prefer to believe that it dates from the early quattrocento but I have not seen it and cannot express a view. See Schiaparelli*, II, Fig. 152b.

36 Cosimo Conti, *La Prima Reggia de Cosimo I de' Medici nel Palazzo gia della Signoria di Firenze*, Florence, 1893, p. 45.

37 Francesco di Giorgio*, p. 258; plan of a house (Tav. 29) described as *pianta di degna casa*.

38 As is really still the case in Britain today.

39 In Venice only the Doge lived in a *palazzo*. This dignity was later bestowed on the house of any family that numbered a Doge among its forebears. That very sumptuous houses were called *case* in Venice is borne out by the name Ca' d'Oro carried by one of the finest 15th-century *palazzi* in that city. *Case di statio* was apparently the legal term used to describe a residence of substance.

40 Andrew Wallace-Hadrill, 'The Social Structure of the Roman house', *Papers of the British School at Rome*, Vol. LVI, 1988, p. 58. I would like to thank Professor Michael McCarthy for calling my attention to this interesting paper.

41 The Duke of Urbino, for instance, believed that Florentine architects were particularly talented and based his famous palace on a Florentine pattern. The Marquis of Mantua in turn commissioned drawings of the palace at Urbino, 'desiring to make this house of ours [i.e. his own palace] on the pattern of what has been done there, and which we hear is wonderful'. Polichetti*, p. 55; and S. Bertelli, F. Cardini and E. G. Zarzi, *Italian Renaissance Courts*, London, 1986, p. 35 (orig. Italian edition, 1985).

42 Other cases in point are Francesco Guicciardini's *History of Italy* (1561) and Leandro Alberti's *Descrizione di tutta l'Italia* (1577). One Carlo Sigonio of Modena published a book *De Regno Italia* in 1574 in which he envisaged a united Italy but the political will for this was not to be sufficiently strong for another three hundred years.

43 In a despatch of 29 January from a member of her staff reporting to her husband, Gianfrancesco Gonzaga, Marquis of Mantua. The room had been adorned with the Gonzaga arms and the frieze painted with ornament based on a classical model which was likewise *el piu bello che sia in questa terra*. See Alessandro Luzio, 'Isabella d'Este . . . e il suo viaggio a Roma . . .' *Archivio storico lombardo*, Milan, Serie 4, VI, 1906, p. 482.

44 Onians, *op. cit.*, p. 299. Writing to a friend in 1546, Aretino said that 'I like to think that your regal mansion in Naples is modelled on the great spirit which fills your breast; and the statues which adorn that beautiful palace represent the generosity which gives sustenance to your heart. Whence you are truly more a splendid aristocrat than a wealthy merchant'.

Part One: The Architectural Shell and Its Embellishment
The Chimneypiece
Design pp. 20–23

1 An old Tuscan saying has it that *Una bella porta rifà una brutta facciata, un bel naso fa un bell'uomo, e un bel cammino fa una bella stanza* [taken literally, this means that a beautiful doorway puts right an ugly façade, a beautiful nose makes a handsome man, and a fine chimneypiece makes a splendid room] (*Tuscan Proverbs*, ed. G. Giusti, Livorno, 1971).

2 By 1400 it is unlikely that rooms of any importance were being built in Italy with a hearth [*focolaro*] out in the centre of the floor, from which the smoke eventually found its way up to a hole in the roof. The then modern form of fireplace was placed against the outside wall of the house. Where the walls were thick (e.g. on the lower floors), the flue could run up in the thickness of the wall towards the chimney on the roof. With thinner walls the flue had to be built outside the wall, encased in masonry that rested at its base on a bracket of some kind. This arrangement had one real advantage, namely that it was easy to clean the chimney from outside, a trap for the purpose usually being provided. Later, fireplaces were moved to the inside walls so that flues embedded in them could run up to chimneys placed higher up the slope of the roof (i.e. closer to the ridge) where there would be fewer eddies and other factors that could affect the drawing properties of the chimney. It seem that the mural chimneypiece was called a *camino francescho* [i.e. French] in the 14th century, when it was still a new form (Schiaparelli*, pp. 96–7). Scamozzi, in his treatise of 1615 (see Pl. 21) tells us that a hood projecting far into the room (i.e. with little or no recessing) was called *alla francese* (Bk. II, Chap. XXXV) but, by his time, this was only one of several forms of mural chimneypiece.

3 Scamozzi, *loc. cit.*, says the supports may take the form of *Colonne, Pilastri, Statue, Termini*.

4 Molmenti*, p. 247. Father Pietro Casola, a Milanese priest on his way to Jerusalem in 1494, stopped in Venice and was taken to see this event. He was so struck by the sumptuousness of the room that, as he put it, even the Queen of France is not surrounded by such splendour (P. Casola, *Il Viaggio a Jerusalemme*, Milan, 1855).

Fire-irons, ornaments and other equipment pp. 23–6

1 Schiaparelli*, p. 109.

2 Alvise Cornaro, *Trattato*, 2nd version, Padua, between

1547 and 1550; ed. C. Semenzato, Edizioni il Polifilo, 1985, p. 97.

3 Schiaparelli*, p. 109, e.g. *ii sportelli d'albero al chammino* (1499).

4 Serlio*, VII, p. 72.

5 Manni*, p. 78.

6 *Alari* was the common Florentine term. *Capafuochi* was used further south (e.g. Siena and Rome). *Brandinalli* was the northern term (e.g. Verona and Genoa). *Cavedoni* was used in Venice and Ferrara. No doubt there was a good deal of terminological cross-fertilization but there do seem to have been regional preferences.

7 A Florentine pair had scrolls that could be described in 1418 as *a collo di gru* like a crane's neck; see Schiaparelli*, p. 111].

8 For an Este fireplace in 1504 was ordered a pair of fire-dogs with pommels of brass [*pomi di otone*, Manni*, p. 113], and Cosimo de' Medici at the Palazzo Vecchio in 1553 (Medici Invt.) had a pair with *palle d'ottone*. Another pair of brass fire-dogs elsewhere in that palace was given a black finish [*vernicati di nero*].

9 A large pair of *capafuochi* with masks holding chains in their mouths [*con due visi che hanno in bocha catene*] was to be seen in the Tura mansion in Siena in 1483 (Tura Invt.) Star or flower-shaped finials were also used.

10 Bistort*, p. 396. The nature of damascening is described here on p. 103.

11 Schiaparelli*, p. 112; fire-dogs, shovel and fork all *coll'arme di chasa*.

12 *Ibid*.

13 *Ibid*.

14 Today called *mantici*, which is the term that a pair of bellows has enjoyed in Italy for many centuries,; it would appear that in 1390 they were described in the singular as a *mantachuzo da fuocho* (Schiaparelli*, p. 113).

Other sources of heat pp. 26–7

1 It was actually called the *Sala bianca grande dai due camini* (Pardi*, p. 21). On the term *caminata*, see Schiaparelli*, p. 89 and Pandiani*, p. 70.

2 Petrarch's *studio* was *sine camino*, it appears, and his example was probably followed by other persons of a studious turn of mind (see Liebenwein*, *Studiolo*, Berlin, 1977, p. 48).

3 A particularly handsome bedwarmer must have been that provided in 1550 for the Duke of Ferrara. It was of brass *con uno arabesco nel coperchio straforata* [an arabesque in the pierced cover, i.e. the piercing formed an arabesque pattern], and had an iron handle of wrought work, silvered and partly gilt [*ferro lavorato … che e inargentato et in parte dorato*; Manni*, p. 129].

4 Florio*, explains that a *scaldapie* was 'a pot to keepe cinders in that women use to set under their feet'. Cosimo de' Medici had special walnut *cassette* to hold the braziers that would warm the feet (Medici Invt., 1553) and Annibale Caro kept three such heaters in a box in his study (Caro Invt., 1578). He called them *stuffette* [little stoves].

5 Malaguzzi Valeri*, p. 332.

6 Alberti*, IV.

7 Manni*, p. 78, suggests the stove may have heated a water-system like modern central-heating.

8 Manni*, p. 117.

Windows
Glass pp. 27–8

1 Pius II, *Commentaries**, p. 285.

2 See Eve Borsook, 'A Florentine *Scrittoio* for Diomede Carafa', *Art, the Ape of Nature. Studies in honor of H. W. Janson*, eds Moshe Barasch and Lucy Freeman Sandler, New York and Englewood Cliffs, New Jersey, 1981, p. 92.

3 Frati*, p. 234.

4 Belgrano*, p. 50.

5 Schiaparelli*, p. 125.

6 They were called *rulli* or *rui* in Venice.

7 The 1391 reference quoted above mentioned white and red glass, for instance.

8 The 1335 inventory quoted by Frati (*loc. cit.*) seems to show that the glass windows had additional window-frames with brass wire across, to protect the glass [*et duas fenestras de fillo rami pro custodia dictarum fenestrarum*].

9 Manni*, p. 20 and Schiaparelli*, p. 125

10 Vasari*, I, p. 205

11 Gundersheimer* p. 71.

12 *Pincta de gente illustre che ucellano con dame a falconi, aghironi, a quagloni* [sic., they were chasing herons and quails].

13 Gundersheimer*, p. 72. The passage is given in English in his *The Style of a Renaissance Despotism*, Princeton, 1973.

14 Giovanni Sabadino degli Arienti was a learned humanist, secretary to Andrea Bentivoglio, a leading Bolognese patrician, who would not have been overawed by glazed windows of the ordinary kind.

15 Cennino Cennini, writing his thesis on painting in the 1390s, claimed that *Vero e che questa tall arte poco si pratica per l'arte nostra* (Francesco Negri Arnoldi, 'Technica e scienza', Einaudi series, *Arte Italiana*, IV, p. 153).

16 Manni*, p. 155.

17 Medici Invt. 1553, p. 53; *Vasari**, under 'Salviati'.

Shutters and *impannate* pp. 28–9

1 Montaigne*, p. 65. Although he was writing about his journey in 1580, what he said would have applied to Italian shutters throughout the period.

2 Castiglione*, p. 45.

3 See Patricia Waddy, *Seventeenth-century Roman Palaces*, New York, 1990, p. 23.

4 Schiaparelli*, p. 119, cites a bill of 1384 for the costs *in fare la finestra della chamera, in panno, in bollette, in trementina, nel legname …* [of making the window for the chamber, to cloth, to nails, to turpentine, to wooden frame].

5 A Florentine inventory of 1417 refers to one painted with an Annunciation [*una finestra impannata … picta cum inuntiata*] Schiaparelli*, p. 120.

6 A long hook of iron or a wooden strut could be used to hold them open. Some top-hinged *impannate* had cords threaded through the top of the frame and reaching down in front to the lower edge of the hinged section, by means of which it could be lifted up and held open, operated from inside.

7 *Telarj tre da fenestre panadj* [three frames for windows *impannati*] were in the great *sala* at the Este Castle of Ferrara in 1436 (Este Invt.). In the Medici inventory of 1553 (Medici Invt.) we also find the wooden frame for

such equipment in store [e.g. two *telai da fenestre impannate*].

8 *Portrait of an astrologer* by Prospero Fontana (1512–97), Palazzo Spada, Rome, No. 63.

Other optional window features p. 29

1 In 1531 the well-known painter Dosso Dossi was paid for having varnished doors and windows [*per invernizare ussi e finestra*] in the castle at Ferrara (Manni*, p. 118).

2 *Per dorare le fenestre del studio adorato de Sua Ecc. ia in Castel* (Manni*, p. 146). As the entire room was *adorato* [gilded], it is perhaps not so strange that the window-frames were treated *en suite*.

3 In the Guinigi inventory (Guinigi Invt. Lucca, 1436) a cassone is identified because it was near the *finestras graticolatas* [with gratings or grilles]. A *finestra di ferro da metterre in mura* [of iron to fix in the wall] was in store in the Uzzano house in Florence in 1424 (Uzzano Invt.).

4 The only reference to a window-curtain noted in the inventories surveyed here occurs in an inventory from the end of the period. *Tre coltrine [cortine] d'ormesin de finestra* [made of the lightweight silk, *ormesino*; Correr Invt., 1584] The *cortina di taffeta tur[chi]no p[er] la finestra che guarda in sala con sua ferro* [of blue taffeta for the window which looks into the *sala*, with its iron rod] to be seen in the Villa Medici in Rome in 1598 (Medici Invt.) afforded privacy for the Cardinal when looking down into the hall from his apartment. It was a screened interior window.

5 Pandiani*, p. 396.

Doors pp. 30–33

1 Rab Hatfield. 'Some Unknown Descriptions of the Medici Palace in 1459', *The Art Bulletin*, 52, 1970, p. 248.

2 Pietro Cataneo, *I quattro primi libri de architettura*, Venice 1554, ed. E. Bassi, *Edizioni di Polifili*, Milan, 1985, p. 340.

3 The French term is used here, it being current in English usage while no proper English term exists. The Italians adopted the word *portiera* in the late 16th century but the normal term before had been *usciale*, as we shall see.

4 In the same inventory, one item was *dui ferri de tenere portali* [two irons to hold *portières* [i.e. rods].

5 With this silk damask hanging was *Un ferro da portiera*. Elsewhere in the same Roman inventory we find *Un ferro torto da portiera*, the twist in the rod perhaps being a device for clearning the hanging out of the way when the door was opened.

6 A Tuscan glassmaker had an *usciale di stuoia* in 1546, for example Gabriella Cantini Guidotti, 'Tre Inventari de Bichierai Toscani …', *Quaderno 2*, Accademia della Crusca, Florence, 1983, p. 113.

7 Ryder*

8 From the English 'translation' by Sir Robert Dallington of 1592, p. 45 (see p. 49 in the original Italian). Dallington's rendering is lively but very imprecise and cannot always be relied on to give a true sense of what the Italian said.

9 Manni*, p. 106, quoting some letters to Isabella d'Este transcribed by Dr Charles Hope, reporting on matters at Ferrara.

Walls
Woodwork pp. 33–5

1 So called in a description of 1493 when the room was being used as the nursery for the first-born of Ludovico il Moro and his wife, Beatrice d'Este (Malaguzzi Valeri*, p. 330).

2 Five years later Leonardo da Vinci decorated another room in the same castle with a ceiling simulating trees seen from below, their trunks rising up the walls. He has incorporated some actual boughs in order to increase the verisimilitude. The room survives, its original state still discernible if sadly mutilated. It is called the *Sala de Asse* because it formerly had some form of wooden revetment (see the guidebook to *I Musei del Castello Sforzesco*, Milan, 1982, Federico Garolla Editore).

3 Pius II Commentaries, Book IX.

4 I believe an important room in the papal apartment of the Palazzo Venezia in Rome was panelled with pine in 1466–7.

Painted decoration pp. 35–44

1 Charles Dickens, *Pictures from Italy*, New York, 1974, p. 36.

2 A chest decorated with this same pattern is to be seen in the Naepolitan miniature reproduced in Pl. 224.

3 Beltrami*, p. 242 (Ch. VIII deals with the work carried out under Galeazzo Maria Sforza).

4 See Amando Schiavo, *Il Palazzo della Cancelleria*, Rome, 1983, Pl. XXI. The room is known as the *Saletta del Peruzzi*.

5 Alberti*, Ch. IX.

6 Andrew Wallace-Hadrill, 'The social structure of the Roman house', *Papers of the British School at Rome*, Vol. LVI, 1988.

7 Well illustrated in Marita Horster, *Andrea Castagno ...*, Oxford, 1980, figs. 105–6.

8 See Frommel*, fig. 63c.

9 See Ezia Gavazza, *La grande Decorazione a Genova*, I, Genoa, 1974, Pl. 19. The owner of the Peschiere had been a friend of Agostino Chigi, who built the Farnesina, in Rome.

10 A small room in the castle at Torrechiara, near Parma (the *Sale del Pergolata*), is so decorated and apparently dates from the 16th century. Giulio Romano's frescoed room at the Palazzo Tè (early 1530s), showing columned masonry tumbling down on a group of giants is an amusing if rather violent expression of the ruin-theme coupled with the depiction of columns advocated by Alberti; it is also, of course, a joke which makes fun of this genre of painting.

11 The Italians spell it thus. In England we would speak of a candelabrum, using the Latin term in the singular.

12 The term had been coined by 1502 (see *Jervis, Design Dict.*, 'Grotesque', an article which neatly sums up the development of this idiom).

13 Notably by Cristina Acidini Luchinat, article on *La grottesca*, in the Einaudi *Arte Italiana* series, Vol. 11, pp. 161–200 with illustrations.

14 *Giulio Romano* Cat.*, p. 317. Executed 1526–8.

15 *Hypnerotomachia*, p. 50.

16 Polichetti, *Urbino*, pp. 216 and 382. Sometimes a painted room was called the *camera dipinta*.

17 Castello Invt., see Shearman's excellent introduction.

Wall-hangings pp. 44–53

1 Niccolò III, Lord of Ferrara, had hangings on the wall of his bedchamber which were so valuable that they were usually removed and kept in the *guardaroba* (the store-room for valuable furnishings) and a set of less costly curtains were put up for ordinary occasions (see Pardi*, p. 110; he refers to the Este inventories of 1436). Another instance of good conservation practice in connection with valuable hangings is considered on p. 161.

2 Hangings are quite often simulated in fresco on Renaissance walls, sometimes stretched flat like wallpaper but sometimes draped or at least with a certain fullness. Often these simulations date from the 19th century when people were more aware than we generally are today of the fact that such walls had formerly been clad with hangings, and as a result often felt the urge to make good the lack. A notable example of 'soft' hangings, simulated in fresco-painting, are those depicted below Raphael's famous picture of Galatea in the Farnesina. These were not present in Raphael's day but may represent what was previously there in reality.

3 Decameron*, Bk. VIII, IX. Another reference to *capolletti* in the *Decameron* (VII, Intro.) has them rigged up out of doors forming enclosures round some beds.

4 When Magdalena of Brandenburg came to Milan to marry Count Gilberto Borromeo in 1487, she was richly equipped, as was usual with such high-born brides. In her trousseau was a set of tapestry-woven seat-furnishings comprising a bench-cover, two cushions, and the accompanying long *spalliera* (Borromeo Invt.)

5 The term was also applied to wall-panelling, which tended to run 'horizontally' round a room (i.e. it rarely covered the full height of the wall). The horizontal strip of material forming a back-rest on many 16th-century chairs was also commonly called a *spalliera*.

6 Pitti Palace Invt., 1577

7 G. Gnoli, *La Roma di Leone X*, Rome, 1938, p. 200.

8 Alberti* (X, 16) had noted that 'if you cover a wall with Hangings made of wooll it will make the room warmer, and if they are of flax [i.e. linen], colder.' Scammozzi made a similar observation.

9 Medici Invt., Florence, 1492.

10 Tapestry is woven on a loom and each patch of colour is built up separately by a laborious localized hand-weaving process. When making a large hanging, several weavers might be working side by side. The basic material is wool but shiny passages (highlights, representations of metalwork, etc.) may be executed in silk. In especially expensive grades, gold or silver thread might be included in the make-up as well. Tapestries woven entirely of silk were produced in the East but need not concern us here. The important point is not to confuse tapestries with embroideries; the two techniques, tapestry-weaving and needlework, are entirely different. Experiments have shown that it takes a tapestry-weaver about 250 hours to produce one square metre (I. Goecke, 'Technique and Costs', *CIBA Review*, 1973, III).

11 Schiaparelli* discusses this question at some length (pp. 207–12).

12 Schiaparelli*, p. 209.

13 An old photograph of this fresco seems to show a velvet pattern on the wall-hanging. Whether that was a vestige of the original or the figment of a restorer's imagination is not known to me. That portière and hanging were *en suite* is more likely.

14 e.g. *una spalera d'herbaria con l'arma Triulza in mezo* (Trivulzio Invt., Milan, 1529) and *pezzi dodeci a divisa d'oria inramati de verdura* (Doria Invt., Genoa, 1561) were both verdure tapestries with the arms, respectively, of Trivulzio and Doria.

15 M. Baxandall, 'A Dialogue from the Court of Leonello d'Este', *Journal of the Warburg and Courtauld Institutes*, London, 1963, p. 316.

16 The Raphael Cartoons are on display in the Victoria and Albert Museum in London. The Museum has published short monographs on them at various times and an extensive literature on them exists. An excellent general survey of the history of tapestries, in so far as this concerns Italy, will be found in the Einaudi series of volumes on *Arte italiana* (Mercedes Viale Ferrero, 'Arrazzo e pittura'); this deals in general terms with Raphael's designs and their influence.

17 See particularly Candace Adelson, 'The decoration of Palazzo Vecchio in tapestry ...', a paper published after the Conference *Giorgio Vasari. Tra decorazione ambientale e storiografia artistica* (Arezzo 1981) published by Leo S. Olschki Editore, 1985. This contains a notable bibliography.

18 In the 18th century it was a common practice to fit tapestries flat against the wall and to frame them with a moulding that formed part of the panelling. The practice was introduced in the 17th century but it would not be a surprise to learn that it had its origins in 16th-century Italy.

19 See Ferrero, *op. cit.*, Schiaparelli*, *loc. cit.*, etc.

20 Manni*, p. 68.

21 Some members of the Corradi family of painters apparently supplied the Gonzagas with designs for tapestry from at least as early as 1427 but it is unlikely that these designs were executed locally or that, if they were, it must have concerned quite small items (see R. Lightbown, *Mantegna*, Oxford, 1986, p. 133).

22 Piero Boccardo, 'Fonti d'archivio per una storia degli arazzi a Genova', *Studi di storia della arti*, Genoa, 5, 1983–5.

23 *Ibid*.

24 Designs for a border attributed to Salviati are in the Louvre (Cat. of Italian drawings, 'Vasari et son temps'. Paris, 1972, 131 & 132).

25 Ferrero, *op. cit.*, p. 138, f.n.

26 *Ibid.*, p. 136, f.n.

27 G. M. Urbani di Ghelthof, *Degli Arazzi in Venezia*, Venice, 1878.

28 Ferrero, *op. cit.*, p. 124.

29 Lightbown, *op. cit.*, p. 488. A cock and a hen were to be portrayed. The peacock is probably that to be seen on the tapestry now in Chicago (Pl. 51).

30 Manni*, p. 64.

31 Manni*, p. 122.

32 Ferrero, *op. cit.*, p. 128.

33 Boccardo, *op. cit.*, p. 121.

34 Adelson, *op. cit.*, pp. 156–64. This is an important passage on the way tapestry was displayed and used.

35 Cosimo Conti, *Richerche storiche sull'arte degli arazzi in Firenze*, Florence, 1875, p. 67.

36 Bistort*, p. 356.

37 Bistort*, p. 396

38 e.g. In the Medici Invt., 1553 we find a *paramento* for a room of cloth of silver alternating with turquoise damask, which had *passamani di seta verde et d'oro fra l'un tela et l'altro* [trimmings of green silk and gold thread between one width and the next]. Another set had gold and red lace *su le costure* [on the seams].

39 e.g. one of the rooms at the Pitti Palace in 1576 (Pitt Invt.) had hangings of gold damask [*Damasco d'oro*] with a border [*fregio*] at the top and between each width of a rich green silk material [*broccato riccio in seta verde*].

40 e.g. *Una spaliera rossa vecchia a colonne* (Ram Invt., Venice, 1592).

41 *Una tela dipinta* was the term commonly used in 15th-century inventories to describe a painting executed on canvas – before people began to mention the name of the artist.

42 The leather panels were *facto in Spagna e lavorati con hopere d'orpelle alla brochato* [decorated with brocade patterns worked in imitation gold; Florio* tells us that *orpello* was 'Base painter's gold' while *orpellato* meant 'shining like gold'] (Fiesole Invt., Florence, 1498).

43 The Botticelli was simply described as a painting on wood on which are depicted nine figures of women as well as men [*nel quale e depinto nove figure de donne ch'omini*].

44 Sabba da Castiglione*, p. 52.

45 Letter quoted in connection with the Villa Medici Invt., 1598.

47 *Boida pro caminata* (Negro Invt., Genoa, 1456).

46 Gabriella Cantini Guidotti, 'Tre inventari di bicchierai toscani ...', *Quaderno 2*, Accademia della Crusca, Florence, 1988, p. 121.

48 Sabba da Castiglione,*, p. 53.

Ceilings pp. 53–60

1 Schiaparelli*, pp. 19–22; see also pp. 137–40.

2 This helped to keep ground-floor rooms cool in the summer heat. In many grand houses the family moved down from the *piano nobile* on the first floor in summer and occupied rooms on the ground floor for this reason (see p. 315).

3 See W. Terni de Gregory, *Pittura Artigiana Lombarda del Rinascimento*, Milan, 1981, where many paintings of this kind are illustrated.

4 Manni*, p. 65. Gerardo Costa was paid for the *depintura de chaselle trentaquatro de boni colori cum Arme et devise duchali cum li campi da lado a le chaselle fate in forma de marmorj per lo pezolo novo de la via Coperta nova* [34 *caselle* painted with fine colours with the ducal arms and devices with the area at the sides of the *caselle* made to look like marble ...].

5 One of the earliest was that in the *sala* of the Palazzo Medici of about 1450. It was remarked upon at the time as being exceptional. Filarete*, writing around 1460, called it a *cosa stupenda*; and a description in verse of 1459, after mentioning the marvellous carving and blue and gold decoration, adds that 'to tell of it not just my tongue, but that of a man divine would fall short before it were halfway imagined' (Rab Hatfield, 'Some Unknown Descriptions of the Medici Palace in 1459', *The Art Bulletin*, 52, 1970). Part of this ceiling survives.

6 Two famous and accessible examples are to be seen in Federigo da Montefeltro's *studiolo* at Urbino of about 1476 and in the Palazzo Vecchio in Florence (by del Tasso) of roughly the same date. A slightly later example is in the Palazzo dei Penitenzieri in Rome.

7 The Palazzo Medici ceiling was blue and gold, as both the contemporary descriptions that have come down to use noted (see n. 5, above). Serlio*, Bk. IV, actually writes that if you want to add colour to a wooden ceiling, you should choose blue for the panels because it then comes to look as if you can see the sky between the wooden framework. He warned, however, that if you had rosettes at the centres of the panels, they would look ridiculous hanging, as it were, in mid-air. On the other hand, if you painted some leaves around the rosettes they would look quite acceptable, he assured his readers. We saw how an Este court painter decorated a ceiling with 34 *caselle* with coats of arms and marbling in fine colours (see n. 4, above). I should like to thank Dr Arthur Haase for sending me some extremely helpful notes on Italian Renaissance ceilings about which he was writing a thesis in 1987.

8 Scamozzi* writes of the *corrispondenza et armonia* that should be present in the relationship between the walls and the ceiling.

9 e.g. Franzsepp Wurtenberger, 'Die Manieristische Deckenmalerei in Mittelitalien', *Römisches Jahrbuch für Kunstgeschichte*, IV, 1940; J. Schulz, *Venetian Painted Ceilings of the Renaissance*, Berkeley (Calif.), 1968; Wolfgang Wolters, *Plastische Deckendekorationen des Cinquecento in Venedig und im Veneto*, Berlin, 1968.

10 See Sabine Eiche, 'The Villa Imperiale of Alessandro Sforza at Pesaro', *Mitteilungen des Kunsthistorischen Institutes in Florenz*, XXIX, 1985, Vol. 2/3, fig. 26.

11 *Ibid.*, fig. 29. Shown in colour by Giuseppe Marchini, *La Villa Imperiale di Pesaro*, Pesaro, n.d. (*c.*1980), Pl. XVII. The acorns allude to the della Rovere family who then owned the Villa (*rovere* = oak tree).

12 Marchini, *op. cit.*, Pl. XVIII.

13 See Sabine Eiche and Massimo Frenquellucci and Maristella Casciato, *La Corte di Pesaro ...*, Modena, n.d., (*c.*1985), p. 47. Arthur Haase (see n. 7, above) also suggested that much three-dimensional ornament on ceilings might be executed in *papier mâché* as well as in stucco. Burkhardt, *Architecture** mentions *carta pesta* in connection with ceilings.

14 '*Le volte piene di pitture riescono tetre anche di giorno, e la notte non sono mai illuminabili per quanti gran lumi vi si mettono*' [Ceilings covered with paintings seem sombre even in daytime, and at night cannot be illuminated at all, however much light is introduced]; Francesco Milizia, *Principi di Architettura Civile*, Bassano, 1785.

15 The Library of Sixtus IV at the Vatican has such a ceiling (*c.*1470).

16 Beltrami*, p. 23.

17 A similar ceiling, painted to resemble an outdoor space covered by a painted *tenda* stretched over it as a temporary velarium, is to be seen at the Castle of San Secondo, not far from Parma. It probably dates from the 1540s.

Floors
Surfaces pp. 60–64

1 Francesco di Giorgio*, writing in about 1480, stated that in recent years bricks were one *piede* long and one half wide. Writing from what was evidently personal experience, he insisted that bricks should be four times as long as they were thick and that their width should be half their length. This way one could hope to achieve regular building (p. 315).

2 C. Lupi, 'La Casa Pisana nel Medio evo', *Archivio Storico Italiano*, V, XXVII (1901), pp. 264–314.

3 Giovanni Antonio Rusconi shows the various patterns commonly used, in his *Della Architettura ...* (Venice, 1590), pp. 98 & 99.

4 Pius II *Commentaries**, IX, p. 284.

5 Eve Borsook, 'A Florentine Scrittoio for Diomede Carafa', *Art the Ape of Nature. Studies in honor of H. W. Janson*, eds. Mosche Barasch and Lucy Freeman Sandler, New York and Englewood Cliffs (N.J.), 1981, p. 93.

6 Borsook, *loc. cit.* See also Schiaparelli*, p. 136. Giuliano da Maiano had to procure 20,000 tiles from Florence; Schiaparelli assumed that the order concerned maiolica tiles as their cost was exceptionally high. As this work was about to go to press, my attention was drawn to F. Quinter, *Maiolica nell' architettura del Rinascimento italiano*, Florence, 1990?, which I have not seen.

7 Filarete* (p. 318) tells us about the Ospedale Maggiore in Milan which he built in the mid-15th century and how the marble floors were of white, red, black 'and other colours', worked in the mosaic technique by one Marino, the son of the mosaic-artist Angelo da Murano who have been famous in Venice earlier in the century.

8 G. Vasari, 'Introduzione all' Architettura',1568, included in Vol. I of the *Lives*, p. 159.

9 Francesco di Giorgio* (p. 354) recommends mixing in crushed antique vases when making *terrazzo* [*vasi pesti antiqui*].

10 Rusconi, *op. cit.*

11 Palladius' book was translated by Francesco Sansovino, the well-known historian of Venice. Presumably he made a straightforward translation but it must always have been tempting to include information that was based on modern experience. One needs to check the original Latin to be sure of precisely what an ancient author said, and what therefore must have been added later.

12 Manni*, p. 76. There were 65 squares alternating to form a chequered effect, it would seem.

13 I am greatly indebted to Dr Arthur Haase for mentioning to me this description and for various other comments on floors in Renaissance Rome.

Floor-coverings pp. 64–6

1 Bistort*, p. 386, considers the term *carpeta* as used in 16th-century Venice. The word was also applied to an item of costume, which can cause confusion among scanners of inventories.

2 *Ibid.*

3 Pandiani* (p. 100) believed there was a distinction made between *tapeta* and *tapeto*, in Genoese documents of the Renaissance period, but this seems improbable. The former were spread on the floor, he claimed, the latter lay on tables.

4 Odoni Invt., Venice, 1555. There were six *tapeti* in store *et uno da tavola* [plus one for a table, which would seem to imply that the others went on the floor].

5 Schiaparelli* (p. 224), citing a Florentine inventory of 1431 and another of 1492 (the latter is our Medici Invt. of that date), where the carpet was so small that it was described as a *tappetello*.

6 Schiaparelli*, p. 224. These *tappeti da letto* may have been 'Irish ruggs' (see p. 000)

7 Schiaparelli*, p. 226.

8 e.g. *un tapedo gialdo da seda* [of yellow silk; Trivulzio Invt., 1529] and *Tapeydi doi de damasco* [two, of damask that was almost certainly of silk; Fieschi Invt., Genoa, 1532].

9 Schiaparelli*, p. 224.

10 *Tapedi de diverse sorte turcheschi no. dodese, et uno grando da tavola vecchi* [twelve ... of various kinds and one large table-carpet, all old; again the implication is that the twelve were for the floor Marcello Invt., Venice, 1534]; see also Correr Invt., Venice, 1584.

11 e.g. Badoer Invt., 1521 and Correr Invt., 1584, both Venetian. The French were using the term *mosquets* by the late 16th century to describe what were probably prayer-rugs; in England the term *musketta carpetts* was some-times used (see Thornton, *17th cent. Int. Dec.*, p. 109 and f.n.18). It should be borne in mind that a *moschetto* was a form of canopy originally made of net to keep flies [*mosci*] away from the occupant of a bed (see p. 124).

12 An excellent summary of our knowledge concerning Near Eastern carpets that matches our present purpose is provided by the catalogue of the Arts Council Exhibition *The Eastern Carpet in the Western World*, held at the Hayward Gallery, London, in 1983. The masterly catalogue entries are by my former colleague, Donald King.

13 In more recent centuries people in England spoke of 'Smyrna carpets', these being carpets from the Anatolian hinterland that were exported through Smyrna. The same concept applied to Chios where a Genoese notary and chronicler transacted a piece of private business, buying fifty carpets and having them shipped direct to England in exchange for English cloth (E. Pandiani, 'Vita Privata di Antonio Gallo', *Archivio Muratoriano*, 14, 1914, pp. 144–60; (Gallo was active in the last decades of the 15th century and is famous for his narrative of the journey and discoveries of Christopher Columbus.) The learned collector, Fra Sabba da Castiglione, describing various ways of decorating a room, writes of *tapeti & moschetti turcheschi & soriani* [carpets and prayer-rugs from Turkey and Syria; *Ricordi*, Venice, 1554, no. CIX].

14 Some of the big so-called 'dragon carpets' (Pl. 72) were produced before the Ottoman Turks had captured Constantinople. Their colouring is reminiscent of 'modern' Caucasian carpets and it may be they were produced somewhere east of Anatolia, being shipped through ports like Trebizond (which was a Genoese outpost) on the Black Sea.

15 Spanish carpets of the 15th century are woven with a knot that is slightly different from the Turkish knot but this makes little difference to the appearance of the surface. In the 16th century, one Spanish centre adopted the Turkish knot.

16 Lina Montalto, *La Corte di Alfonso I di Aragona*, Naples, 1922, p. 125.

17 Manni*, p. 88.

18 G. Pazzi, *Le Delizie Estense e Ariosto*, Pescara, 1933, p. 73.

19 e.g. *Tapeyda grande pelosa da mettere in terra*; Fieschi Invt., Genoa, 1534 and *tapeta una piloza misera ... in a bedchamber in the Spinola mansion in Genoa (Spinola Invt., 1459).

20 By the late 16th century imitations of Anatolian carpets, woven with a knotted pile, were being made in Europe, north of the Alps, but in small quantities which cannot have had any effect beyond the immediate locality of their production.

21 According to one traveller's account, the Shah had his pet cheetahs lying on such a carpet by his throne.

22 Boccaccio makes his young people sit on carpets spread on the ground, in one of his stories, having ordered the *siniscalco* to *fatti in su l'erba tappeti distendere e vicini al lago a seder postisi* [go and place carpets on the grass by the lake where one can sit] (Decameron*, VII, Intro.).

23 The regulations of 1410 concerned *tapisserie sarrasinoise appelée a lemarche*. Whether *à le marche* referred to the loom employed or to the way the material was used (i.e. on the floor) is not clear and the whole question is so complicated that we can do no more than refer the reader to E. Soil, 'Les Tapisseries de Tournai ...', *Mémoires de la Société Historique et Litteraire de Tournai*, Vol. 22, Tournai, 1891. Tournai was to become an important centre for the weaving of woollen velvet including qualities for use on the floor (see p. 77).

24 Tura Invt., Siena, 1483

25 See also p. 53.

26 Lydecker, Thesis*, p. 195; Martelli Invt., 1510.

Part Two: Furnishings
Materials and Techniques p. 68

1 I have no doubt that a truly helpful glossary of Renaissance textile terms will eventually become available. Attempts are currently being made at the archival end with the aid of a computer but it is to be hoped that people familiar with actual historic textiles are engaged in the project. My own qualifications for making pronouncements on this subject are that I spent some eight years in the Department of Textiles at the Victoria and Albert Museum in London (1954–62) and subsequently, when in the Department of Furniture and Woodwork (until 1984), kept an eye open for information on Renaissance textiles. I know enough about the subject to recognize that this contribution is in no way definitive but I hope it will be seen as better than nothing – for the time being. One of the first swallows of the summer that must eventually come has been drawn to my attention as this work was in preparation. It is Donald and Monique King, 'Silk weaves of Lucca in 1376', Festschrift in honour of Agnes Geijer, Museum of National Antiquities, Stockholm, *Studies*, 8, 1988. This has even more recently been followed by Lisa Monnas, 'Silks purchased for the Great Wardrobe of the Kings of England, 1325–1462', *Textile History*, Vol. 20, No. 2, 1989 (Studies in honour of Donald King).

Textiles p. 69

1 While *tela* meant a cloth, *telo* was a width of material. Sheets were commonly described as being of two or three *teli* which was therefore an indication of their width.

2 *Drappo* could also mean a towel or napkin in some regions, e.g. there were some *drapi ... de tela sotile ... de bamboxo* in an Este residence in 1436 (Este Invt.), which must have been towels of fine cotton cloth.

Silks pp. 69–72

1 Bistort*, pp. 357–8.

2 'Changeable taffeta', as it was called in England, had the warps of a different colour to the wefts.

3 Florio* calls it a 'taffeta-sarcenet'. In English and French it was called *cendal*.

4 The French sometimes called this *cendal tiercelin* (e.g. in the Charles V Invt., 1380, p. 344).

5 The Florentine silk-weavers' regulations of 1512 refer to *tabi e trezanelli che hanno marezzo* [which have a watered effect]; this should probably be read as 'those which are watered'. Gay* found a reference of 1380 to *zatabis azurées, tres fin, bien ondoyant* [blue *tabi*, very fine, well waved, i.e. watered]. *Zatabi* was the original Near Eastern term for this material; indeed Gay gives a reference to *zatabis ynde ondoyant* [with waves, from India, i.e. the East]. A Venetian silk-merchant in 1537 had rolls of *tabi* in stock, some being *manganado* [pressed or mangled] while others were *sensa mangano* (Molmenti*, p. 632).

6 Guidotti*.

7 See Leonardo Fioravanti, *Dello Specchio di Scientia Universale*, Venice, 1564, p. 24. The process of 'lustrating' silk is explained at length in Savary des Bruslons, *Dictionnaire de Commerce*, Paris, 1723, under 'Taffetas'.

8 Lina Montalto, *La Corte di Alfonso I di Aragona*, Naples, 1922.

9 Florio* also gives 'Broccami' as 'all manner of cloth of gold'.

10 Gay* cites a reference to *un baudequin de Lucques vermeil ouvré à oyseaux d'or ... et chiens blues* [worked with birds in gold and with blue hounds] acquired in 1416. See also D. and M. King, *op cit*.

11 Montalto, *op. cit.*; *broccato di damasco* or *su damasco*, or *brocat di domasqui* (1450).

12 Gay*, p. 352; Ram Invt. It should here be noted that Florio*, in 1611, claims that *Brocatello* was 'a thin tinsell of gold' which suggests a much less robust material. His information may have been incorrect or out of date; a brocatelle may well have had a different character in earlier times. This is a good example of how confusing this question of ancient textile nomenclature can be.

13 See D. and M. King, *op. cit*. Items made of *camoca* are listed among silk materials in the Charles V Invt., 1380.

14 When the silk-weavers of Genoa received new statues in 1432, reference was made to *camocato* so it must then have been of importance. The term still occurs a century later, in the Fieschi Invt., Genoa, 1532.

15 Lomellini Invt., Genoa, 1459.

16 L. Montalto, *La Corte di Alfonso I di Aragona*, Naples, 1922.

17 A merchant from Lucca, based at Bruges, sold *velueau sur velueau* [velvet on velvet] at the high cost of 110 *écus d'or* the piece, in 1416 (Francisque Michel, *Recherches sur le Commerce, la Fabrication et l'Usage des Etoffes de soie, d'or et d'argent ...*, Paris, II, p. 199). A piece was a length of cloth, standard for each class at each centre of production but varying considerably from one centre to the next. The average length probably lay between twenty and thirty yards, for a piece of velvet. In the Aragonese Court Treasury in 1453 velvets were listed under the headings *de*

hun pel [of one pile], *de dos pel* and *de tres pel*, the last being exceptionally rich and complicated to weave; it has left its name in modern Spanish, for velvet is still called *tercio pelo*, although today a single height of pile is considered quite luxurious enough (L. Montalto, *op. cit.*).

18 e.g. *zetani vellutati alti et bassi broccati* (1463; see C. Merkel, 'Tre corredi milanese …' *Bollettino dell'Istituto Storico Italiano*, 13, 1893, pp. 97–184), and *domasco vellutato* (1587, Gay*).

19 Vitelli Invt.

20 The very best velvets from Genoa were actually woven in the outlying village of Zoagli (Pandiani*, p. 48).

21 In French inventories *velours alexandram* (1386) and *alixandrin* (1370) are met with quite frequently (see Gay*).

22 See an excellent article by Lisa Monnas, 'The Artists and the Weavers; the design of woven silks in Italy 1350–1550', *Apollo*, June, 1987.

23 *Coryat**, p. 399.

24 A. Luzio, *Pietro Aretino nei suoi primi anni a Venezia …*, Turin, 1888, p. 39.

Linen, cotton and hempen materials pp. 73–5

1 The English terms of the time were 'raynes' and 'cambric', the latter certainly remaining until recent times synonymous with fine linen. There are so many references in Italian inventories to these expensive materials; let it therefore suffice to cite the Sforza Invt., Milan, 1493, which has whole sections with headings like *Drapi cambraie* and *Drapamenta tele Rheni*. In Italy this class of material was also called *lino di Flandra* and *di Borghogna* [from Flanders, from Burgundy]. On this whole subject, the reader should consult Marguerite Prinet, *Le Damas de Lin Histoire du XVI au XIX siècle*, Berne, 1982; this includes a good bibliography – see particularly the work of Van Ysselsteyn and of C. A. Burgers.

2 Linen *alla parigina* seems only to be found among table-linen, not among bedclothing; the same applied to diaper, which does rather suggest a connection. The coarse linen (or 'flaxen') material known as *gréze* could also be *alla parexina* which furthermore suggests the term concerns a pattern rather than a quality (see the Sforza Sisters' Invt., Milan, 1493, p. 45); Prinet (*op. cit.*, p. 45) draws attention to the fact that the Parisian weavers' statutes of 1281 refer to *la lozenge* although precisely how this should be interpreted is not certain; if a pattern is being referred to, this might seem to confirm our suggestion.

3 Guinigi Invt., Lucca, 1430. Prinet (*op. cit.*, p. 38) claims that the earliest French reference to linen *à l'ouvrage de Damas* [worked in the Damascus fashion] dates from 1416; as it was described as being torn, it is unlikely to have been quite new at that point.

4 See Prinet, *op. cit.*, p. 46, where she shows that *ouvrage de Venise* was either identical, or very similar, to *ouvrage de Damas*.

5 In the Guinigi Invt., 1430, for instance, we find *tovallie nuove nostrale listate* [i.e. with borders], some with borders described as Sienese [*alla senese, listata*], some *a draghi* [with dragons], and some *a buchi alla fiorentina* [holes or openwork in the Florentine style]. Where the term *alla perugina* occurs in an inventory (e.g. in one of 1574 for Vasari's house in Florence), one can never be quite sure

that the transcriber did not actually misread *alla parigina* (i.e. Paris instead of Perugia).

6 It must have been smooth and quite fine because a bed in the Medici villa at Careggi in 1456 had a pair of curtains of *bocchaccino biancho dipinte* [white, painted]. They are listed among some very fine furnishings.

7 See Thornton-Di Castro*, p. 6; the hangings were red.

8 Fieschi Invt., Genoa, 1532, *una coperta de dimito cremisile* [i.e. a coverlet of crimson dimity].

9 Pandiani*, p. 49, *bambaxina cum pilo* and *sine pilo* [with, and without pile].

10 Florio* gives '*Trippa* … a kind of tripe velvet as our fustion of Naples'. Most *trippes* had a worsted pile and were woven at Tournai, Lille and Douai during the 16th century. Already in their statutes of 1380, however, the makers of *draps velus* at Tournai had received regulations governing the amount of cotton they could mix with linen in the pile of their weaves. A 16th-century Tournai *trippe* could be of several colours and have a pattern, probably regular and repeating like those on linen damasks. See E. Soil, 'Tapisseries de Tournai', *Mémoires de la Société Historique et Littéraire de Tournai*, Vol. 22, 1891, pp. 181–3.

11 Thornton-Di Castro*, p. 3.

12 The most authoritative essay on this subject will be found in Santina M. Levey, *Lace …*, London, 1983. Excellent photographs of lace may also be found in Margaret Simeon, *The History of Lace*, London 1979.

13 Dr Bartolo di Tura of Siena owned many items described as being decorated with *reticella* (Tura Invt., 1483) including a fine pair of sheets *con ritcelle in mezo* [with *reticella* panels in the middle]. Moreover, a number of items had edgings of *reticella* [*con verghe facte ad reticelle*]. Some pieces were described as *facte a la moderna* while others were called *antique* but precisely what this meant is not clear. It is probable that it had more to do with the pattern than the technique.

14 Giovanni Andrea Vavassori, *Flor di gli essempli …, nella quale vi troverrai varie sorti di frisi con li quali si potra ornar ciaschna donna, & ogni letti con ponti tagliati … & ogni altra sorte di ponti*, undated (c.1545).

15 See Levey, *op. cit.*, opening chapter.

16 The distinction between needlepoint lace and bobbin lace is explained by Levey, *op. cit.*, and others. Onto the bobbins of 'bone lace' is wound linen thread. Operated in pairs, with the loose ends anchored firmly, the threads are crossed around an arrangement of pins set in a pattern, which eventually builds up an openwork design. Needle-point laces are built up entirely with a needle but, for the layman, the difference is not always easy to discern.

Woollen materials pp. 75–7

1 *Bigello* is a shade of grey.

2 Bed-hangings of *scotto* were round the bed of a young Venetian in 1584, as my daughter Dora discovered when looking for something entirely different in the Venice Archives. In the Badoer Invt., Venice, 1521 are several references to bed-hangings of *botana* including a *moschetto* (i.e. *padiglione*), and a red and yellow striped coverlet. Florio* tells us the material was 'a kind of flanell stuffe'.

3 My old colleague Donald King very kindly told me of this, the earliest reference he had found to the *moirage* of woollen materials.

4 Pandiani*, p. 44.

5 Gay* cites several references to camlets of silk, e.g. from 1467, 1541 and 1578. The silk may of course have been mixed with the normal worsted yarn.

6 Bistort*, p. 431, citing the Venetian sumptuary regulation of 1644 under which it was permitted only to have silken wall-hangings in the two best rooms; elsewhere they should be of camlet or similar woollen stuffs.

7 This camlet was made up into a quilt and used in association with the bath at the Lomellini house in Genoa (Spinola Invt., 1459), probably on a bed in a neighbouring chamber.

8 Cecchetti, *La vita dei Veneziani nel 1300*, Venice, 1885 [reprinted Bologna, 1980], p. 14 where this and other woollen stuffs are mentioned together.

9 *Decameron**, v, 4.

10 Among the splendid furnishings of Clement v's bedchamber at Avignon were four *sargie*, two red [*rubeas*] and two striped [*virgatas*]; all, however, were described as being in a poor state [*viles*] (Papal Invts., Avignon, 1314 and 1316). A *sargia scaccata* [checked or perhaps tartanned] was on one of the Uzzano beds in 1424.

11 This whole question was opened up by Eugéne Soil, 'Les Tapisseries de Tournai', *Mémoires de la Société Historique et Litteraire de Tournai*, Vol. 22, 1891. A more recent summarizing of the evidence, with some new facts, is to be found in Marguerite Prinet, *Le Damas de Lin …*, Fribourg, 1982, pp. 48–56. See also Peter Thornton, 'Tapisseries de Bergame', *Pantheon*, March 1960, especially n. 8.

12 Soil, *op. cit.*, p. 162, also 355 *et seq.*

13 *Ibid*, p. 391.

14 Thornton, *loc. cit.*

15 *Ibid*, and Soil, *loc. cit.*, p. 181.

16 Prinet, *op. cit.*, p. 49.

17 Soil, *op. cit.*, p. 27.

18 Soil, *op. cit.*, p. 34.

19 *Ibid*, p. 29. It must here be admitted that the weaver concerned called himself a *tapissier* but the distinction between this trade and that of *hautelisseur* was probably not absolutely clear-cut at this stage.

20 *Decameron**, III, Intro.

21 The spelling varied. In Naples they were sometimes called *chalone* which is still fairly close to 'Châlons'. In Venice they were commonly *zaloni* and in Genoa *claroni*. The English word derived from the same source was 'shalloon', a term still used in the 19th century but by then to describe quite a humble material. See also p. 164.

22 A tarif of import duties payable at the gates of Florence in 1402 lists together *celoni o sargie oltremarine* [from across the sea, which probably here just meant 'from abroad']; see Schiaparelli*, p. 227.

23 Verga*, p. 56.

24 *Unus zalonus … super dicta leteria* (Aleardi Invt., Verona, 1408); and *1 celoni da lecto* (Di Challant Invt., 1522).

25 Schiaparelli*, p. 201.

26 Este Invt., 1436, p 445, *Cosse due da telaro da fare zalauni* (two sets of equipment for making *celoni*).

27 I am grateful once again to Donald King for this information (see n. 3 above).

28 Lindsay Boynton and Peter Thornton, 'The Hardwick Hall Inventories of 1601', *Furniture History*, 1971.

29 See Thornton, *17th cent. Int. Dec.**, p. 112 and f.n. Florio* gives '*Moccaiaro*, Mokado stuffe'.

30 Guidotti*., pp. 79–80.

31 Florio*, 'Trippa, a kind of velvet tripe . . .'.

32 From the Tournai records – trippes e haulteliche (1441), pièces de haulteliche . . . appelées trippes (1542) and trippes de velus (1492). See Soil, op. cit., pp. 183 and 217.

33 A Tournai hautelisseur was weaving trippes de plusieurs couleurs [of several colours, i.e. in each piece] (Soil, op. cit., p. 181. What must be either a trippe or a moucade is illustrated in colour in Thornton, 17th Cent. Int. Dec.*, Pl. VIII.

34 Guidotti*, loc. cit.

35 An incomplete reference in my notes has not so far enabled me to trace the source of this piece of information.

36 Farnesina Invt., 1526; the 1525 list was published with it.

37 'Mantelles de Hiberniae' were exported to England and the Continent from south-eastern Ireland. A papal agent in Ireland was making some arrangements concerning the trade with Italy in 1462. (Ada K. Longfield, Anglo-Irish Trade in the Sixteenth Century, London, 1929; see also Mairead Donleavey, Dress in Ireland, London, 1989).

38 One such cloth was so beautiful that non se po vedere, per la soa bonta (Pardi*).

39 A savastina una piloxa (with a pile) was in the Vivaldi mansion at Genoa, 1456 (Vivaldi Invt.) This may of course be a mis-reading of Schiavina.

40 In the Medici Invt., 1492, the fact that a carpet has a pile surface is sometimes mentioned [tappeto col pelo]. In one instance, however, a tappeto . . . alla moresca is described as being raso [with a flat or plain surface]. This would seem to imply a kilim weave (see p. 65) I am indebted to Candace Adelson for pointing this out to me.

Needlework pp. 77–84

1 Este Invt., Ferrara, 1436, p. 169 (note in the Glossary under Aparamenti); also Manni*, p. 64.

2 Manni*, pp. 55–56.

3 G. Pazzi, Le 'Delizie Estensi' e l'Ariosto, Pescara, 1933, p. 73.

4 Girolamo Adda, 'Le Lit de Castellazzo', Gazette des Beaux Arts, Aug. 1870, p. 107.

5 Enciclopedia Italiana, Treccani, Milan, 1936–44, Ricamo.

6 Anton Francesco Doni, I Marmi, Venice, 1552, p. 138.

7 Likewise evidently directed at women were Mateo Pagano, Il spechio di pensieri delle belle et virtuose donne, Venice, 1544, and Isabetta Catanea Parasole, Pretiosa gemma delle virtuose donne, Rome, 1598.

8 An instructive and entertaining introduction to engraved ornament, including needlework pattern-books, during the Renaissance period is Janet S. Byrne's Renaissance Ornament Prints and Drawings, New York, 1981, in which patterns from the three books mentioned in our main text are reproduced and discussed. All the items on which she comments are in the Print Room of the Metropolitan Museum. See also Margaret Harrington Daniels, 'Early books for lace and embroidery', Bulletin of the Needle and Bobbin Club, 17, New York, 1933.

9 See Adda, op. cit., pp. 109 and 114.

10 Jervis, Design Dict.*, 'Ligozzi'.

11 Adda, op. cit., pp. 106 and 107. Doria also brought in four Milanese embroiderers to work for him in Genoa (Enciclopedia Italiana, op. cit., Ricamo).

12 Pellegrin's work was re-issued, with an introduction and notes by Gaston Migeon, in Paris in 1908.

13 See Migeon's introduction (see previous note), p. 5; also Adda, op. cit., p. 108.

14 Indeed opera fiorentina was so renowned a class of needlework that the term appears in many cathedral inventories of the 14th century. The famous Jean, Duc de Berry, ordered a cope from Florence in 1387 which was to cost him an astronomical sum (Enciclopedia Italiana, op. cit., Ricamo).

15 Leopold Ettlinger, Antonio and Paolo Pollaiuolo, London 1978, figs. 61–4.

16 Adda, op. cit., p. 116.

17 Ibid., p. 106. Francesco Bacchiacca later also designed tapestries.

18 Ibid., p. 114. The poem was published by the famous house of Aldo Manuzio in Venice in 1505 with the title Joannis Aurelii Augurelli Jambici.

19 Manni*, p. 9.

20 Lina Montalto, La corte di Alfonso I di Aragona, Naples, 1922, p. 125. Other officials were a goldsmith, a painter, a carver [trepador, i.e. intagliatore], and a maker of carpets.

21 Bistort*, p. 369.

22 Adda, op. cit., p. 109.

23 One of the most exquisite specimens of opus anglicanum is at Pienza. It must have been more than a century old when Pius II gave it to the cathedral in that small city which he re-created in the mid-15th century.

Leather
Gilt leather pp. 85–6

1 See Waterer, Spanish Leather, London, 1971. An ambiguous reference of 1454 to a designer (Gerardo Costa) having painted designs for corami with the arms of Borso d'Este at Ferrara suggests that hangings of leather were being used there by the mid-15th century but there is no reference to gilding and we cannot be sure (see Manni*, p. 62).

2 Waterer, op. cit., pp. 22–7, claimed that early Islamic gilt leather made in North Africa was of goatskin whereas medieval Spanish gilt leather was mostly made of the pelts of 'hair-sheep' (which some people might call mountain-goats). Fitz Scholten, Goud Leer, Swolle, 1989, a book primarily devoted to Dutch gilt leather, insists that the skins were always of calf (p. 13).

3 Waterer, op. cit., passim. Leonardo Fioravanti, Dello Specchio di Scientia Universale, Venice, 1564, speaks of the printing of a design which was intagliata in legno [carved in wood]. Waterer took this to mean that the patterns were printed in ink, or some other pigment, on the flat surface which remained flat. However, Simon Jervis (Newsletter of the Furniture History Society, London, Feb. 1989) quotes Thomas Platter, the Swiss traveller, visiting Barcelona in 1599 and there seeing gilt leather 'pressed' with beautiful designs. Jervis suggests this meant they were embossed, using deeply cut moulds and much pressure – a technique widely used in the second half of the 17th century which produced a repoussé effect. Nevertheless, leathers bearing patterns that one would associate with the Renaissance period are stamped, not embossed. Perhaps the new technique was developed in Spain at the very end of the 16th century. The point is an academic one with which someone else can be left to struggle.

4 Fioravanti, op. cit.

5 F. Cognasso, L'Italia in Rinascimento, II, 'Societa e Costume'. Turin, 1965; Molmenti*, p. 238. See also Anna Contadini, 'Cuoridoro': tecnica e decorazione di cuoi dorati Veneziani . . .', Venezia e l'oriente Vicino, ed. E. J. Grube, Venice, 1989.

6 Franco Brunello, Arte e Mestieri a Venezia . . ., Vicenza, 1981, p. 165.

7 A. Luzio and R. Renier, 'Il Lusso . . . di Isabella d'Este', Nuova Antologia, LXIII, LXIV and LXV, Rome, 1896, p. 86.

8 Belgrano*, p. 77.

9 Manni*, p. 210.

10 Information kindly communicated in a letter from Dr Graziano Manni to the author.

11 Thomas Coryate, Coryat's Crudities, 1611.

12 Belgrano*, p. 77. Lydecker, Thesis*, p. 193, quotes a bill of 1581 from a Giuseppo di Niccolao Cresi da Empoli, maestro di guoi dorati, for 154 skins of blue and gold 'gilt leather'. Presumably Cresi was working in Florence, not in Empoli.

13 Isabella d'Este commented in 1516 that Spanish gilt leather was better than Italian (Luzio and Renier, loc. cit.).

14 See n. 3, above.

15 Essay on the painter Camillo Mantovano in Kunsthistorisches Forschungen, Kunsthistorisches Institut, Florence, IV (Berlin, 1911), p. 107.

16 Scholten, op. cit., makes no claim for gilt leather being produced in the northern Netherlands prior to 1600 but one supposes it was made in the southern provinces before that.

17 Havard*, Cuir.

Other types of leather pp. 86–9

1 This material was in use right through the period, e.g. eleven silver spoons were contained in una vagina coraminis cocti [a sheath of cuir bouilli] in the Aleardi mansion in Verona in 1408 (Aleardi Invt.). This process involved softening the leather in a tepid mixture of resin and wax so it could be moulded on clay forms. Once it had set hard, it could be decorated with incisions, carving and stamping.

2 See previous note; also the Pico Invt., Modena, 1474 has two silver-handed knives cum la guayna de coro verde [with its sheath/case of green leather] which was probably of this material.

3 John W. Waterer, Spanish Leather, London, 1971, Pls. 80a–c, pp. 86–7. Two French royal chairs in 1399 had covers of cordouen vermeil, escorchie with the arms of the king and queen.

Woodwork
Timbers pp. 89–92

1 A chest in the Requesens house in Palermo in 1561 was of nuchi muscata which presumably meant a flecked piece of walnut [moscata being analogous to the French moucheté, with flies all over]. The fact that Florio* gives nuchi muscata as nutmeg must be irrelevant as one could not make a chest of that, so it must have had a second meaning, as is here suggested.

2 It is usually thought that this wood came from the familiar tall, dark cypress tree but it may well be that other trees of the genus Cupressus yielded timber suitable for such

chests. However, it was sometimes called *legno di Candia* after the port on the island of Crete whence some of it came. It is indeed suggested by Oliver Rackham, an historical ecologist, in a letter to me, that these chests were made in Crete. An authority in 1555 apparently wrote of *des caisses de Cypres moult large faictes en la ville de Candie*.

3 See Schiaparelli*, p. 250. See Maddalena Trionfi Honorati, 'A proposito del 'Lettucio', *Antichità Viva*, XX, 3, 1981, f.n.36.

4 Francesco Sansovino, *Venetia*, Venice, 1581, p. 134. This information was kindly communicated by Dora Thornton.

5 A. Luzio and R. Renier, 'Il lusso di Isabella d'Este, marchesa di Mantova', *Nuova Antologia*, anno XXXI, Series LXIII, LXIV, LXV, Rome, 1896.

6 Manni*, pp. 102 and 112.

7 Edward Hutton, *Pietro Aretino . . .*, London 1922, p. 134.

8 Coffin*, p. 172.

9 H. Kreisel, *Die Kunst des deutschen Möbels*, I, Munich, 1968, p. 103.

10 S. Jervis and R. Baarsen, 'An ebony and ivory cabinet', *Victoria and Albert Museum Album*, IV, London, 1985.

11 Kreisel, *op. cit.*, p. 105.

Techniques pp. 92–6

1 Lorenzo de' Medici (Medici Invt., 1492) had a *lettuccio* of cypresswood panelled with walnut [*d'archipresso . . . quadrata di noce*] in his town house in Florence, for example.

2 Manni*, p. 73.

3 Schiaparelli*, p. 239, cites an inventory of 1459 which gives *uno cassone con regholi di noce* [a chest with mouldings of walnut], while the Acciaiuoli Invt.*, Florence, 1388 has *i casse pancha anticha con bullete e regholi* [an old bench-chest with nails and mouldings].

4 English furniture historians have for long been using the term *intarsia* when speaking of early inlaid wood executed in Renaissance Italy. This term is not used by Italians and, I believe I am right in saying, never has been. They speak of *lavoro di intarsio* or of *tarsia* (plur. *tarsie*). If an item is inlaid, they say it is *intarsiato*. So *intarsio* is a technique by means of which *tarsie* are made; objects that are embellished by this process are *intarsiato*.

5 Fritz Hellwag, *Die Geschichte des deutschen Tischlerhandwerks*, Berlin, 1924, pp. 302 and 454.

6 It was such a widespread technique that it cannot have been confined to workshops in Carthusian monasteries – or to monasteries generally. On the other hand, a surprising number of monks became celebrated experts in the fully-developed *lavoro di intarsio* during the second half of the 15th century. Many travelled and set up workshops wherever needed; few were confined to monasteries during their active life.

7 Manni*, p. 17.

8 Manni*, p. 25.

9 Manni*, p. 76; *fata a tarsie da una la* [lato] *ermelini, da laltro la già duo Simia*.

10 An interesting essay on this question is Maddalena Trionfi Honorati's 'Prospettive architettoniche a tarsia: le porte del Palazzo Ducale di Urbino', *Notizie da Palazzo Albani*, Rivista semestrale di Storia dell'Arte, Università degli Studi di Urbino, XII No. 1–2, 1983, in which

material from elsewhere is also discussed.

11 *Ibid.*, also Manni*, *passim*, but especially pp. 33–8. The Lendinara brothers' proper surname was Canozi.

12 Manni*, p. 98.

13 Manni*, p. 119.

14 See *Schiaparelli**, pp. 247–54, and Vol. II, the commentary of 1983. Giovanni Rucellai called Giuliano '*legnaiuolo maestro di tarsie e comessi*' – woodworker, master of inlay and of composed inlaid pictures (*commesso* implies that many pieces have been assembled); 'Giovanni Rucellai ed il suo Zibaldone', ed. A. Perosa, *Journal of the Warburg and Courtauld Institutes*, Vol. 24.

15 *Ibid.*

16 The names of important woodworkers active in Venice during the period are mentioned by Franco Brunello, *Arti e Mestieri a Venezia . . .*, Vicenza, 1981.

17 Vasari*, II, p. 459. The *Remesseri* who executed such work are discussed on p. 000.

18 Manni*, p. 78, *un scremaio de nogara Intaiado . . . come doe balle de sopra li cantonali elquale fo fato per madona Ixabela* [a screen of walnut carved . . . with two balls topping the sidepieces which has been made for Madonna Isabella]; Stefano di Bona Dona was paid 631 *lire* for this.

19 I believe Graziano Manni deserves the credit for pointing this out. See Manni*, p. 39. Malaguzzi Valeri* (p. 83) speaks of *cassettine* made with reliefs executed in *pasta di riso* [rice paste] and thought such things came to Milan from Tuscany.

20 Manni*, p. 68. In this particular case some of the *pastiglia* was scented with ambergris [*ambracha*].

21 It would appear that *Mo. Johannes Karolus di Britanya* was primarily an engineer in the service of Nicolò III (d. 1441) and was familiar with artillery (hence *Mo. Giovan Carlo dalle bombarde*). He therefore had his lodgings in the castle at Ferrara – where he had the necessary equipment for producing scents when not minding his master's ordnance. See Manni*, p. 40.

22 Manni*, pp. 39 and 40.

23 Manni*, p. 80.

24 It did not become necessary to introduce regulations governing the turners' activities in Germany until well into the 16th century, first in Cologne in 1536 (Hellwag, *op. cit.*, p. 66).

25 Manni*, p. 48.

26 Alfonso also made *vasi bellissimi di terra* [very beautiful vases of earthenware], and was a founder in bronze (Paolo Giovio, *La vita di Alfonso d'Este*, Florence, 1553, p. 15; also Manni*, p. 100).

27 See Hellwag, *op. cit.*, p. 455. L. Fioraventi, *Dello Specchio di Scientia Universale*, Venice, 1564, insists that a woodworker should 'know how to straighten with fire' [*saperlo dirizzare col fuoco*].

Finishes pp. 97–101

1 Schubring*, p. 17, or *Vasari**, II, p. 148. In 1498 a pupil of Mantegna named Bernardino Bolasco painted the showy part of an important bed in Genoa (Belgrano*, p. 82) and we give other examples on pp. 100, 157 and 195.

2 *Ibid.*, p. 88.

3 E. Callmann, *Apollonio di Giovanni*, Oxford, 1974.

4 Graziano Manni, (*Mobili in Emilia*, Modena, 1986), has broken much fresh ground for the furniture historian with

his numerous quotations from the Este Archives.

5 Manni*, p. 20; *a M[aestr]o Jacopo de Sagramoro et compagni depintori per depinzere dui forcieri vechii . . . per bisugni de Madona Margerita . . .* (note the inclusion of his 'companion painters', or assistants, in this account).

6 Manni*, pp. 41–2.

7 Manni*, p. 66.

8 Manni*, pp. 19–33.

9 Manni*, p. 54.

10 Manni*, p. 88.

11 Manni*, pp. 119–20; Gabriele da Carpi, who seems to have had a workshop that could execute both the woodwork, and the painting and gilding, was paid for having *fatto uno letiera per la principesa* and for having *dorato quatro colonele de la letiera . . . con quatro vaxiti* [vase-finials] *et datoli dazuro. . . .*

12 Manni*, p. 122. Because musical instruments are often dated (sometimes a provenance is also given) they form a helpful class of material when it comes to dating ornament and techniques. Italian keyboard instruments of the 16th century are particularly interesting in this respect. See P. Thornton, *Musical Instruments as Works of Art*, London, 1968; revised ed. 1982.

13 Manni*, p. 120.

14 Manni*, pp. 197–219 with colour illustrations: see also Elio Durante and Anna Martellotti, *L'arpa di Laura*, Florence, 1982, with a note on its decoration by Maddalena Trionfi Honorati (this study formed part of the series *Archivum Musicum*, Collana di Studi C., Studio per edizioni scelte, Florence). Laura Peperara's skill on the harp was described by Count Annibale Romei in 1584 (when the present harp was still being decorated); she accompanied her songs on the harp, *ella cante cosa soavemente, che al suono di quella dolce armonia parea che l'anima rapita se m'uscisse volando del cuore a chiunque l'udia* [she sang so sweetly in this manner that at the sound of this delightful harmony it seemed as if the soul thus stolen flew up from the heart of everyone who heard it] (Durante, p. 26). The ladies were instructed by the *maestro di capella* at the Ferrarese Court, Ippolito Fiorino, and the famous organist Luzzasco Luzzaschi. It has sadly to be added that the beautiful Anna Guarini was eventually murdered by her husband with the aid of an accomplice; the fact that this required the use of axes as well as razors caused something of a sensation at the time.

15 Manni*, p. 202. Fine colour illustrations of the harp are included in this work.

16 Thornton, *Musical Instruments . . ., op. cit.*

17 Manni*, p. 160.

18 *Ibid.*, p. 206.

19 *Ibid.*, p. 204.

20 Winifred Terni de Gregory, *Pittura artigiana Lombarda del Rinascimento*, Milan, 1981.

21 Baldasarre d'Este and Antonio Orsini of Venice, both described as *depintori*, worked under Cosmè Tura on decorating the chapel at Belriguardo (Manni*, p. 48).

22 Terni de Gregory, *op. cit.*, p. 20.

23 Schiaparelli*, p. 265. *Lavoro di silio* was executed with the single type of wood (i.e. silio = spindlewood) and not with a mixture of woods. See pp. 000, f.n. 00.

24 Bistort*, p. 241.

25 See Calmann, *op. cit.*, who shows how the gilding and carving of a painted chest cost more than the painting, and that one gilder attached to a painter's workshop expected

to earn and take home half the firm's profits. A circular picture with a heavy gilded frame designed to hang on a wall as a work of art (a *tondo*) and produced in a Florentine workshop in 1510 cost $19\frac{1}{2}$ florins; the painting cost $7\frac{1}{2}$, the gilded frame with painted details cost 12 (Lydecker, Thesis*, p. 138).

26 Coarsely woven material with an open weave was usually pasted onto the wooden ground first, to provide a key for the gesso.

Craftsmen p. 101

1 Information on these matters is sparse but see the catalogue of the exhibition *Civiltà del Legno*, held at the Palazzo Bianco, Genoa, 1985; also F. Brunello, *Arti e Mestieri a Venezia* ..., Vicenza, 1981.

2 *Civiltà del Legno, op. cit.* It was noted that *caselle* were pigeon-holes but that most early drawers, especially small ones, were housed in spaces just like pigeon-holes, so drawers came also to be called *caselle* – and sometimes also *cassette*, which meant small boxes as well as casquets. At any rate, the *caselleri* must have been the forerunners of the craftsmen later called cabinetmakers.

3 This is exemplified well by the collection of lutes in the Victoria and Albert Museum, which includes instruments by Laux Maler of Bologna (early 16th century), by Max Unverdorben of Venice who was probably his pupil, Wendelin Tieffenbrucker of Padua, Matteo Buechenberg of Rome, and Andrea Taus of Siena – the last three being active in the early 17th century (see P. Thornton, *Musical Instruments as Works of Art*, Victoria and Albert Museum, London, 1968 and 1982; also Anthony Baines, *Catalogue of Non-Keyboard Instruments*, Victoria and Albert Museum, London, 1968)

4 Manni*, p. 28; see also p. 94.

5 S. Jervis and R. Baarsen, 'An Ebony and Ivory Cabinet', *Victoria and Albert Museum Album*, IV, 1985.

Metalwork pp. 102–5

1 Listed under the heading *Argenti* [silver plate]. The previous item concerned three basins, with the Bishop's arms in the centre, that were presumably *en suite* with the respective ewers (Della Rovere Invt., 1494).

2 A. Luzio, *Mantova e Urbino*, 1893, pp. 230–31.

3 *basile quatro de bronzo, cum li bronzini* (Pico Invt., Modena, 1474). A *bronzino* of silver is listed in the same document.

4 In the *saleta de le done* [the parlour of the ladies-in-waiting] at the Fieschi mansion in Genoa in 1532 (Fieschi Invt.) was *Uno stagnono col suo bacille de ramo sotto* [a ewer with its basin of brass under it, i.e. standing in it]. In the family's country residence there was, among the silverware, *Una stagnara* of silver-gilt with relief ornament with the arms of the Governor of Corsica on it. The next item is a silver basin which may have accompanied it. There was not necessarily any difference between a *stagnono* and a *stagnara* as the two inventories may well have been compiled by different people.

5 Ram Invt., Venice, 1592.

6 Dora Thornton, Thesis*, 'Sculpture in inexpensive materials', pp. 165–71.

7 e.g. *Doi refrescadori uno di latone* ... [two wine-coolers,

one of latten] (Ram Invt., Venice, 1592) and another wine-cooler of over a century earlier [*refreidorium unum latoni*] (Lomellini Invt., Genoa, 1459).

8 A payment was made in 1504 by the Ferrara 'Office of Works' [*Munizioni e Fabbriche*] for some firedogs with brass ball-finials [*cavedoni* with *pomi de otone*] (Manni*, p. 113). Some fire-dogs with ball-finials of rather later date are visible in Pl. 000.

9 e.g. *Una spera in astrologia d'ottone* [an astrological sphere, i.e. an armilliary sphere of the heavens, of brass]. Astrology was of course a science closely related to astronomy; an astronomer of the period might often be required to tell the fortune of a new-born child on the basis of the astrological circumstances pertaining at the moment of birth.

10 The second wine-cooler mentioned in the entry in the Ram inventory quoted above (n. 6) was *alla damaschina*. Listed under *Octoni* [brassware] in the Gaddi house in Florence in 1496 (Gaddi Invt.) was *Uno bacino grande alla domaschina*; it is the first item in the list. A number of items, including basins, a holy-water stoup, an inkwell and a pen-case, all *alla damaschina*, are listed in the Venetian Badoer Invt., 1512.

11 Vasari*, I, p. 211.

12 Bistort*, p. 397. It seems that the Venetian authorities were particularly concerned with elaborate fire-dogs. *Siano del tutto prohibiti li cavedoni et suoi fornimenti da fuogo dorati, o di lavoro alla damaschina o di bronze* [Totally forbidden are fire-dogs and fire-irons that are gilded or of damascene work or of bronze].

Ceramics pp. 105–11

1 One can presumably discount the notion that these things were of no great value and so were not worth listing, but in some cases the fact that a common household object was of pottery may not have been necessary to record since everyone would know that that was generally the case.

2 Some *scodelle di terra* were in the kitchen in the Uzzano house in Florence in 1424 (Uzzano Invt.) A *scodella* was a deep dish, a porringer. A helpful essay on the terminology applied to household vessels may be found in Cipriano Piccolpasso, *The Three Books of the Potter's Art, A facsimile*, London, 1980; translated and introduced by Ronald Lightbown. This commentator discusses terms like *bronzo*, *bacile*, *piatto*, *tondo*, *piatello*, *saliera*, *fiole*, *tazzone*, *boccale*, *scudellino*, *crottoletta*, *piadena* and *ongarescha*.

3 There are several general histories of ceramics but, for our present purposes, *World Ceramics*, skilfully edited by Robert Charleston and with articles by many other renowned authorities (Paul Hamlyn, London, 1968), remains an excellent illustrated introduction. Illustrations of Italian *sgraffio* wares will be found on pp. 117–19 and col. pl. 26; the term, incidentally, was coined in the last century. It is today called incised slipware. Another general survey, bringing together much information that has recently come to light, is the catalogue of the exhibition of *Ceramic Art of the Italian Renaissance*, ed. Timothy Wilson, held at the British Museum in 1987. Wilson also edited *Italian Renaissance Pottery*, papers for a colloquium held at the British Museum at that time, now published in 1991 and full of fresh information. A succinct but unillustrated survey forms part of Richard A.

Goldthwaite's paper, 'The Economic and Social World of Italian Renaissance Maiolica', *Renaissance Quarterly*, XLII, No. 1, 1989.

4 *World Ceramics, op. cit.*, pp. 139–45 and pl. 37.

5 *Scudellas de maiolica duodecim* (Monticoli Invt., 1413); and listed in the De Fece Invt., 1459 were more *scudelle*, some *piatelli* and *piatelletti*, and a *conca* with its lid – all *di maiolica*.

6 Pinelli Invt., Genoa, 1456 and Ponzone Invt., Genoa, 1488, both from Genoa, [*stagnarie tres terre de Valentia*, i.e. three ewers of Valentia earthenware].

7 See exhib. cat. of *Le Arti Decorative del quattrocento in Sicilia* Messina, 1981–2, p. 92. Before the Malaga industry transferred to Valencia which started about 1380, some lustreware potters had set up at Murcia. The Murcians subsequently also moved to Valencia and several as a result were known as 'di Murci'. One Juan di Murci was a celebrated Valencian lustreware potter (d.1458) who amongst other things provided a large number of tiles for Alfonso V's Castello Nuovo at Naples in the 1440's. (See Timothy Husband, 'Valencian Lustreware of the 15th Century'. *Metropolitan Museum Bulletin*. 1970.)

8 *World Ceramics, op. cit.*, p. 155.

9 None of these wares was of course decorated with a lustre finish which requires much sophistication on the potter's part – and a second firing. The range of colours available to the early Italian potters was very small.

10 See M. Spallanzani, 'Maioliche di Urbino nel collezioni di Cosimo I, del Cardinale Ferdinando e di Francesco I de Medici', *Faenza*, 1979, p. 117. The term was often expanded to *terra da Urbino*, with further elaboration like *dipinto* or *lavorato a grotesche*.

11 Some Italian potters actually called themselves *maiolicari*. Other names were *boccalari*, *vasai* and *orciolaii*.

12 A large dish painted with a shield bearing the well-known Roman cipher *S.P.Q.R.* was in the Sienese Bartolo di Tura's Inventory of 1483 where it was described as *uno piatello grande, di terra*. It was almost certainly of maiolica and is likely to have come from Viterbo, just north of Rome. A basin of what may have been early Savona *maiolica* is listed in the Genoese Lomellini Invt., 1459 [*Concheta una terre Saone*]. A service of maiolica was provided by a potter at Montelupo for the use of Clarice Strozzi in 1517 [*uno fornimento de terra*]; several pieces of maiolica bearing the Strozzi arms survive as do wasters actually of this service found at Montelupo (see M. Spallanzani, 'Un fornimento di Maioliche di Montelupo per Clarice Strozzi de' Medici', *Faenza*, 1984. *Lavoro da Montelupo* occurs in a document of 1429 quoted by the same authority ('Una bottega da Scodellai ...', *Faenza*, 1978).

13 Coats of arms are also to be found on much incised slipware of the grander sort, which dates from much the same phase, i.e. twenty years either side of 1500.

14 Pius II *Commentaries**, pp. 102 and 108.

15 Letter of 15 November, 1524; see Mariarosa Palvarini Gobio Casali, *La Ceramica a Mantova*, Ferrara, 1987, pp. 182–211. I am much indebted to John Mallet for drawing my attention to this point.

16 G. Cora, *Storia della maiolica di Firenze e del Contada*, Florence, 1973.

17 I am much indebted to Dora Thornton for this quotation. Barpo was a native of Belluno.

18 Goldthwaite, *op. cit.* (see n. 3 above), p. 27.

19 e.g. in the Odoni Invt., 1555 of Venice, and in the Vitelli Invt., 1582 of Perugia (*una bacinella di Terra bianca*), and it is to be noted that this last item was in the Vitelli's villa known as *Schifanoia* – not to be confused with the more famous palace of that name at Ferrara.

20 British Museum catalogue, *op. cit.*, p. 148.

21 Manni*, p. 183.

22 *Ibid.*, p. 115.

23 See John Gere, 'Taddeo Zuccaro as a Designer of Maiolica', *The Burlington Magazine*, 1963, pp. 306–9; and T. Clifford and J. V. G. Mallet, 'Battista Franco as a designer of Maiolica', *The Burlington Magazine*, 1976, pp. 387–410.

24 Spallanzani, 'Maioliche di Urbino...', *op. cit.*, see n. 12.

25 Manni*, p. 22.

26 e.g. Cora, *op. cit.*, Pls. 299c–300c; also A. Marquand, *Andrea della Robbia*, Princeton, London and Oxford, 1922.

27 *World Ceramics*, *op. cit.*, figs. 418 and 419.

28 Walls faced with gilded terracotta tiles of the 1450s may be seen at the castle of Torrechiara, south of Parma, and in the Capella Ducale at the Castello Sforzesco in Milan which are believed to date from the 1480s. For more on tiles used in architecture, see p. 60.

29 The thirty pieces of *Magioliche da Costantinopli* in a Venetian collection in 1587 were presumably Isnik wares (information kindly given by Dora Thornton).

30 See M. Spallanzani, *Ceramiche orientali a Firenze nel Rinascimento*, Florence, 1978; and R. W. Lightbown, 'Oriental Art and the Orient in late Renaissance and Baroque Italy', *Journal of the Warburg and Courtauld Institutes*, XXXIII, 1969, pp. 229–31.

31 M. Spallanzani, 'Le porcellane cinesi nella guardaroba del Cardinale Ferinando de' Medici', *Faenza*, 1979. Alvise Odoni owned some celadon too (Odoni Invt., 1555).

32. Some specimens bear dates in the 1580s. One piece is marked *Prova* [test, or test-piece] which reveals the experimental nature of this ware (see *World Ceramics, op. cit.*, p. 212). Molmenti*, p. 318, cites a letter of 1470 from *maestro Antonio archimista* who had a pottery in the San Simeone area of Venice where he claimed to be able to produce *porcelane trasparenti et vaghissime, che pareno venuti da barbaria et forse megliori* [very beautiful transparent porcelain that looks as if it came from Barbary but is perhaps even better]; he was clearly exaggerating or we would surely have heard more of his enterprise.

33 G. Pazzi, *Le 'Delizie Estensi' e l'Ariosto*, Pescara, 1933.

Beds, Canopies and the *Lettuccio*
The basic structure and simple beds pp. 111–13

1 Examples of *letto* meaning 'mattress' are found, for instance, in the Venetian Badoer Invt., 1521 where reference is made to four *lette dilana cipriota* [four beds of Cypriot wool, i.e. these mattresses were filled with such wool], and in the Tura Invt., 1483 of Siena, where we see *uno letto di penna* [feathers] along with *due capezali di penna* [two bolsters also filled with feathers]. In the Milanese Sforza Invt., 1493 the weight of feathers in each *letto* is specified. There is no need to cite references to *letto* being used to describe a bedstead as the concept is still current.

2 *Arlotti* were the supports of *banche* which are cut from planks; we should speak of 'forms' rather than benches. Later on a *letto di panchetti* was usually to be found only in servants' rooms.

3 Montaigne*, p. 124.

4 e.g. *Un ... per di cavaletti indorade da bancho da letto* [a pair of gilt trestles for a bed-base]. (Marcello Invt., Venice 1534).

5 Matteo Boiardo, *Orlando Inammorato*, 1483, Canto 1, 14.

6 See Havard* 'Couche'; also Eames, Med. Furn.*, pp. 85–93.

7 *Havard**, 'Couche'.

8 *La chariolle dessoubz le lit du roy* [i.e. beneath the King's bed] occurs in the *Comptes du Roi René* for the year 1449 (V. Gay, *Glossaire archéologique du Moyen Age et de la Renaissance*, Paris, 1882–1928)

9 Tura Invt., Siena, 1483, f.n. p. 110.

10 Sforza Invt., Milan, 1493, f.n. p. 16, quoted by the editor.

11 *Due letti salvatichi* were in bedchambers of the *famigli* [members of the household staff] in 1496 in the Florentine mansion of the Gaddi family (Gaddi Invt.)

12 Pandiani*, *passim*.

13 e.g. a *lettiera ... col trespolo e canario* in a main room in the Uzzano mansion in Florence (Uzzano Invt., 1424) with several more in other rooms, always associated with a mattress [*saccone*]. At the Medici villa at Poggia a Caiano in 1492 (Poggio Invt.) no less than sixteen beds of varying qualities were *tutte con trespolo et channaio* [i.e. all with these features] and at Carreggi (Carreggi Invt.) Lorenzo de' Medici's own bed had *trespolo[,] channaio et sachone confitto* [i.e. made up with these components]. At Bartolo di Tura's villa at Camollia, outside Siena, his bed was similarly equipped (Tura Invt., 1483). It must be said, however, that in the Uzzano inventory, one *lettiera bassa* is given as having *trespoli* [i.e. plural] *et canario*, which could be due to an error or because this low *lettiera* for some reason required more than one trestle; another bed in the same list had a *trespolo* and *saccone* when no *canario* is mentioned, which suggests the clerk may not have been very thorough.

14 V. R. Giustiniani, *Alamanno Rinuccini, 1426–1499*, Cologne and Graz, 1965.

The *lettiera* pp. 113–20

1 See Pandiani*, pp. 42 and 43; also p. 48 here.

2 Florio*, tells us that *Bancali* [were] all manner of benches and forms' but makes it clear that the word was also used in reference to the textile covers laid over such furniture. There can however be no doubt that the *banchallia duo intarsiata circa lectum* of the Italiano Invt., 1451 from Genoa was of wood, because it was decorated with *tarsie*; and it went 'round the bed'.

3 These boxes, resembling chests in every way except for their lack of a hinged lid and a lock, were called *cassoni morti* [literally, dead *cassoni*]. Two *lettiere* at Cafaggiolo (Cafaggiolo Invt., Tuscany, 1498) were described as being *col casson morto* while a simpler bed was *con casse morte dinanze* [literally with dead boxes before it]. Schiaparelli*.

Bed-hangings: the early forms pp. 120–21

1 A Tuscan painting of about 1430 shows a *lettiera* with a

small curtain attached to the frame of the head-board, down one side (Pl. 19) but such arrangements were rare, judging by the numerous pictures that survive showing beds without such a feature.

2 Seven sets of bed-hangings are mentioned by Pardi*. All comprise *cielo*, *capolletto*, and *coperta* [coverlet] and they were clearly very magnificent. Several were of tapestry, one was of velvet, and another of red cloth embroidered with silk (Este Invt. 1436, pp. 109–10).

3 See the previous note for proof that *cielo* meant the ceiling-like component, if proof be needed. In the Zambeccari Invt. of Bologna, 1412, is listed *unam littieram cum caelo*, the next item being a blue *curtina*. The Genoese residence of the Fieschi (Fieschi Invt., 1532) housed a bed with *il cello de borcato d'oro* [of gold brocade] *et de fenegieto dalta* [and with its upper valance]. Mention is subsequently made of a 'lower valance' (which went between the legs of the later forms of bed; see p. 161) but upper valances were invariably associated with the item here called *un cielo*. Several sets of bed-hangings, each comprising curtains and *uno sopra cello* with valances (in this case called *bandirolle*), are listed in the Borgia Invt., 1503. The variant, *un capocielo*, occurs in the Este inventories of 1436; see below.

4 The English had the same difficulty. In the mediaeval period the headcloth was called 'a tester' or 'dorser' [from the French *dossier*] while the *cielo* was called 'a celour'. By the 17th century, however, the horizontal *cielo* had become 'a tester' and 'headcloth' was the common term for the vertical hanging (see Eames*, Section B, and Thornton, *17th Cent. Int. Dec.*, Ch. VII).

5 *Florio** says that a *sopraletto* was 'a testerne of a bed, a canopy, or any thing over a bed', but he was writing at the time when the terminological change-over was taking place and is evidently bewildered on these points, and it is not really certain whether he is referring to the vertical or the horizontal component.

6 See n. 3 above concerning *fenogieti* and *bandirolle*.

7 In the Medici Invt., Florence, 1456 a section is headed *Fornimenti di lecti*, for example. In the Trivulzio Invt., Milan, 1465, is listed a *paramento uno da lecto* comprising *capocelo*, *testale* and *coperte*. The list of fine bed-hangings in the Este Invt., Ferrara, 1436, already mentioned (see n. 2 above) is headed *Aparamenti da lecto*.

8 *Una lettiera ... con la volta ...* (Tura Invt., Siena, 1483); *Una lettiera co la volta e cortinaggio* (Fece Invt., Siena, 1450, fn. ref. an inventory of 1492). Could the bed in Verona which was *tota revolta* not also have been 'entirely enclosed' rather than gilded as the editor of the Aleardi Invt., 1408* suggests (p. 34)?

9 The phrase *Uno fornimento da leto o Cortinazo* occurs in the Borgia Invt., 1503, which was compiled at the time when the term was not yet well understood.

The *padiglione* and the *lit a la romaine* pp. 121–9

1 The French word *pavillon* carried the same dual meaning. In England, occasionally, beds with such a feature were called 'pavilion beds' (see n. 3 below) and the fact that the mostly rather insubstantial buildings associated with the game of cricket are called 'pavilions' is a reminder that tents were commonly erected in connection with a field-sports in earlier centuries.

2 In the glossary attached to his analysis of the Fieschi Inventory (Fieschi Invt., 1532) the editor Antonio Manno (p. 64) suggests that the word *faorcheto* was a corruption of *falchetto* derived from *falcho*, a falcon, and that therefore this too was used synonymously with *sparviero* and *padiglione*.

3 See Thornton, *17th cent. Int. Dec.**, p. 159.

4 Este Invts., Ferrara, 1436, *staze di frassine da zenzaliere, dipinte in rosso*.

5 Thornton – Di Castro*, Pl. 4a.

6 e.g. A *sparviero* of *tela di Cambray*, another of *tele cambraia*, and *un moscheto di Cambrayo* (Invts.: Trivulzio 1420, Sforza 1493, Di Challant 1522). *Uno sparavero da lecto de tella de rense* and another of *tele Rheni* (Invts.: Rico, 1473 and Sforza, 1493). The Medici Invt., 1553 has one of *tela d'Olanda*, and the Requesens Invt., 1561, *Uno paviguni di tila di landa*.

7 See Thornton, *Authentic Decor*, London, 1984. Pl. 12, also Thornton, *17th cent. Int. Dec.**, Pl. 36.

8 Making pronouncements about Renaissance furniture is quite hazardous enough and I do not propose to embark on a similar exercise with regard to that of classical times, but it seems probable that they did not have beds fitted with posts with hangings attached. They are more likely to have had curtains, suspended from the architecture, as was, for instance, the practice in pre-Renaissance Italy. The very fact that the word canopy comes from a Greek word (see p. 124) suggests that the archetypal *padiglione* existed in Antiquity.

9 e.g. *Uno paviguni di lana russa vechio ... cum suo capello* (Requesens Invt., Palermo, 1561). The hangings in this case were of red cloth, and were old. In modern Italian *capello* has two p's.

10 e.g. *Uno isparvieri ... con dui ritti con suo capelleto* (Medici Invt., Florence, 1531). The *riti* were presumably the curtains; in the Requesens Invt., Palermo, 1561, a *cortinaggio* is described as being *facto a riti lavrato* [made with worked/embroidered *riti*].

11 e.g. *Un moschetto ... con uno capoletto ... con un linzolo dentro* (Trivulzio Invt., Milan, 1529). This had a sheet [*lenzuolo*] inside, this was either a makeshift curtain or the inventory-taker could not tell the difference between a linen curtain and a sheet – which was probably not great.

12 e.g. *Un padiglione ... con capuccio ...* (Vitelli Invt., Perugia, 1582); *Un scapucia da sparviero da lecto* (Della Rovere Invt., Ferrara, 1494); among the *Pavaglioni* listed separately in Lucrezia Borgia's Inventory (Borgia Invt., 1503) reference is made several times to *capuzi*.

13 e.g. The very rich *padiglione* at the Villa Medici in Rome (Medici Invt., 1598) had hangings of *taffeta a fiamme* [pres. flame-patterned] and *Un Pome di legno dipinto*[,] *da padiglione* [a painted wooden ball, for the *padiglione*]. In the Medici Invt., 1553 are listed four *pomi da sparviere di piu sorte* [i.e. of several sorts], one of them having a cord attached. In the Vitelli Invt., Perugia, 1582, similar components are called *palle da padiglione* [balls for *padiglioni*].

14 Only when the bowl (*capello, capuzzo*) was of a great diameter would there be any point in having the curtains run on rods, with rings. Otherwise the curtains were presumably fixed (nailed, if the bowl were of wood, as was usually the case; or stitched if the *capello* was of a textile material). The *girella di ferro* mentioned in the Medici Invt., 1598 may have been an iron rod running round the bowl showing that this *padiglione* was very large.

15 One of the Medici *padiglioni* had curtains made up with no less than thirty widths of materials (Medici Invt., Florence, 1553).

16 *Uno chortiginaggio ... di saia rosso per il letto grande richamato a ghironi et falconi* (Medici Invt., Florence, 1492). This was of course not a *padiglione* but it was probably suspended, as we shall show (p. 129 *et seq.*).

17 Manni*, p. 55.

The suspended *cortinaggio* pp. 129–35

1 A bed with what looks like a similar form of *cortinaggio* is to be seen in Pl. 95. One cannot see the cord which presumably holds it up but, as the bed has no posts, a cord must have been present. The picture is dated 1501.

2 The earliest reference noted is in the Este Invts., Ferrara 1436 (*Travacha ... cum li soj fornimenti de legname*, with its wooden members).

3 Manni*, p. 88

4 Bistort*, p. 249.

5 *Ibid*., p. 428.

6 Quoted by Bistort*, p. 428. It is presumably a coincidence that other references to *travacche* of walnut or with gilding that we have noted come from Sicily – Requesens Invt., 1561 from Palermo, *una trabacca di nuchi fornita* [of walnut, with its components] and *una littera di trabacca vechia dorata* [a *lettiera* of the kind with a *travacha*, old and gilded]. Daniela di Castro has suggested to me that, in view of the close link between southern Italy and Spain, one should look for a Spanish connection in the origin of the term.

The bed with posts and the camp-bed pp. 135–49

1 A posted canopy very like the posted testers of the beds just mentioned was to be seen in a painting by Cima da Conegliano that was destroyed during the last war (Pl. 148). The two principal characters were seated on confronted thrones under a tall canopy with slender posts rising from balusters and topped by small ball-finials and with a shallow scalloped valance. In proportion and style it was very like the St Ursula bed of about 1495. The picture dates from 1489 (see P. Humphrey, *Cima da Conegliano*, Cambridge, 1983).

2 Eames* believes that posted beds were occasionally made before the late 15th century. She cites a state bed made in 1242–7 for Henry III of England which had green posts powdered with gold stars and mentions other posted beds made in the 14th century in France. However, the posts of such beds *may* simply have been the ordinary corner-post that were in these instances made rather taller than usual; they need not necessarily have supported a tester. Eames at any rate states that the bed with 'four posts supporting the canopy proved to be a branch line', the main line of development being that taken by the suspended canopy (pp. 75–91).

3 See Thornton – Di Castro*, p. 2.

4 Christine de Pisan, *Le Livre des faitz et bonnes moeurs du sayge Roy Charles*, 1405, III, Ch. 71.

5 Since the distinguishing feature of a *cuccia* was its supported *cortinaggio*, some people actually came to refer to the *cortinaggio* as the *cuccia* – as here. That is the only explanation of the strange usage in these two quotations.

6 Thornton – Di Castro*, *loc. cit.*

7 Tilman Falke, Studien zur ... Geschichte der Villia Giulia in Rom, *Römisches Jahrbuch*, Vol. 13, 1971. Inventory of 1551.

8 See Heinrich Kreisel, *Die Kunst des deutschen Möbels*, I, Munich, 1968, fig. 266; but see also the diagram on p. 362 The walnut components are richly inlaid with ivory.

9 *Castra* meant a military encampment as well as a castle or fort. The phrase should be read as *una lettiera castrensis*, presumably.

10 *Fulcra* comes from *fulcio*, to support in Latin, the reference being to the *fulcrum* or head-rest which was a striking feature of Roman couches like that shown in 'The Aldrobrandini Marriage', already mentioned (see G. Richter, *The Furniture of the Greeks, Etruscans and Romans*, London, n.d., p. 107) and of the couch shown in Pl. 170. The lightweight bed shown in Pl. 365 is described as a *fulcra*.

11 Manni*, p. 103.

12 Although these beds cannot have resembled the old-fashioned *lettiera*, the term, as we have noted, was evidently sometimes used for any bed that was imposing as the Chigi camp-beds no doubt were even if they were lightweight and capable of being dismantled.

13 Havard*, 'Lit', p. 423. The bed belonged to Anne de Bretagne.

14 The title means 'On the running of a Gentleman's house, in Rome'.

15 Havard*, *loc. cit.*, quotes several descriptions of splendid French *lits de camp* of this period, including that of Anne de Bretagne already mentioned. This had hangings of cloth of gold lined with three-colour silk damask, richly fringed. Even the posts and finials were covered in cloth of gold. That was in 1498. In 1523, Marguerite d'Autriche's best camp-bed had hangings of crimson velvet decorated with gold emblems, probably embroidered. The actual curtains were of crimson taffeta. But (more important for the Italian connection) may have been that made specially, at enormous cost, by the leading Parisian upholsterer for Henri II when, in 1534, he had to go to Marseilles to meet his bride, Catherine de' Medici. This bed had crimson velvet hangings decorated with floral scrolls executed in gold, with fruit represented by pearls. He clearly wanted to impress the Italian princess. Maybe reports of this amazing piece of furniture reached the ears of Priscianese whose book was published eight years later.

16 One is for example mentioned in the Fieschi Invt., Genoa, 1532.

17 See Jervis, *Printed Designs**, especially figs 8–11, 21, 85–90, for designs by Peter Flötner (early 1530s, 1533, 1540–41), Hieronymus Rodler (1531) and Jacques Androuet du Cerceau (c.1560).

18 Jervis, *op. citt.*, fig. 15.

19 e.g. Jervis, *op. cit.*, figs. 85 and 86 (Du Cerceau, c.1560), and 153 and 154 (Hans Vredeman de Vries, 1588?).

The *lettuccio* and other forms of day-bed pp. 149–53

1 In the Gaddi Invt. 1496 from Florence, for example, each bed in the principal chambers had a *lettuccio* that was *appichato*. The latter word means 'attached' but has the same dual meaning as it does in English. These *lettucci*

may therefore all have been physically attached to their respective beds (which seems unlikely; although see below) or they were 'associated with' the beds concerned. The latter is the more probable implication. At the Capponi family's villa at Montughi, outside Florence, in 1534 (Capponi Invt.) a *lettiera* in one room had a *lettuccio* that was actually stated to be *simile alla lettiera* while in the Uzzano residence in the city (Uzzano Invt., 1424) the owner's bedchamber was furnished with a *lettiera* and a *lettuccio di brachia cinque suvvi* [five foot long, belonging to it]. A few *lettucci* do seem to have been actually built physically together with a *lettiera*, on the other hand. This must have been the case with one *apichato da pie* [attached or built-in at the foot-end] of a *lettiera* in the *camera terena* at the Medici villa at Cafaggiolo (Cafaggiolo Invt., 1498), for instance; such a combination seems to be present in Pl. 379.

2 Florio*, thought this already at the end of the 16th century. He explained that a *lettuccio* was 'a sillie poore bed or couche'.

3 As John Shearman pointed out ('The Collections of the Younger Branch of the Medici', *Burlington Magazine*, Jan. 1975, p. 18), 'Most modern handbooks on furniture call the Quattrocento *lettuccio* either *cassapanca* or *trono*' and he rightly identified a piece of furniture in the Museo Horne in Florence, very like that shown in Pl. 162 here, as being a *lettuccio*. Although John Florio, sitting in London and compiling his dictionary by reading the principal works of Italian literature and conversing with Italians, could no longer correctly envisage a *lettuccio* by 1611 (see previous note), the learned compilers of the *Vocabolario della Crusca* of 1612 got it right, telling those who consulted the fruit of their labours that this piece of furniture was *un casson grande con ispalliera e braccioli dove si dorme e si siede fra di* [a large chest with a high back and arms on which one slept or sat during the day]. Writers of dictionaries who followed *la Crusca* did not err but some 19th-century lexicographers decided that the *lettuccio* was a divan or canapé, conjuring up visions of heavy upholstery, deeply buttoned. This seems to have misled the furniture historians and it was not until 1981 that a leading Italian authority in this field, Maddalena Trionfi Honorati, developed Shearman's suggestion in an article 'A proposito de 'lettuccio'' (*Antichità Viva*, XX, 3, 1981) and firmly replaced this class of furniture in its rightful historical niche. She does, however, acknowledge that Battaglia's *Grande Dizionario della Lingua Italiana* did unearth numerous references so as to produce a correct definition in 1973.

4 King Ferrente's *lettuccio* is discussed by Eve Borsook, 'Documenti relativi alla Capelle di Lecceto e delle selve di Filippo Strozzi', *Antichità Viva*, IX, 3, 1970; his son's by Dorio Covi, 'A documented *lettuccio* for the Duke of Calabria by Guliano da Maiano', *Essays to Myron P. Gilmore*, Florence, 1978.

5 At the Medici house at Fiesole (Medici Invt., 1498) a *lettuccio* in an *anticamera* was *depinto di fiame con adornamento d'oro finno* [painted with flames and decorated with fine gold: the 'flames' were presumably some form of wavy repeating pattern like the so-called *point d'Hongrie* which became especially fashionable in the 17th century]. Kent Lydecker has very kindly drawn my attention to a description of a *lettuccio* in 1478 painted with the family arms of the Falcini and Bardi.

6 At Il Trebbio (Il Trebbio Invt., 1498), another Medici residence, near Florence, one *lettuccio* was *depinta d'una perspetiva* [painted with a perspective, which here probably means a scene with buildings rendered in highly formalized perspective although it could simply mean a view, a landscape]. At Fiesole (see previous note) there was another *lettuccio di noce intersiato e comisso di prospetiva* where the 'perspective' was executed in *commesso*, the most elaborate form of inlay involving the assembling of many small pieces of wood (p. 342). It stood in Lorenzo de' Medici's bedchamber.

7 See Shearman, *loc. cit.*; also Ronald Lightbown, *Botticelli*, 1978, p. 81; it seems the painting was executed in 1482 to go in the rooms of Lorenzo di Pierfrancesco de' Medici in the family's city residence in the Via Larga. See also Allan Braham, 'The Bed of Pierfrancesco Borgherini', *Burlington Magazine*, CXXI, 1979; this famous Florentine bed, commissioned in 1515, stood in a bedchamber in which painted panels played an important part. The panels survive and it seems that several were built into the bed itself, one forming the bed-head. There was also a *lettuccio* in the room and Vasari states that the artist (Granacci; Bacchiacca and Pontormo were also involved) provided a painting to go over [*sopra*] the *lettuccio*. If so, it would have been disposed in a similar manner to the *Primavera* but the supposed arrangement of the other panels makes this difficult to conceive; it seems more likely it fitted into the actual back of the *lettuccio*, but see note 11 below.

8 Vasari*, II, p. 148.

9 We have much information about the Tuscan form; we seem to know very little about *lettucci* made elsewhere.

10 See Shearman, *loc. cit.*, p. 18. He points out that 'A *cappellinaio* is the normal complement of a *lettuccio*' throughout the inventories he is analysing and that 'it is hard to believe that it is in all cases a hat-rack . . .'.

11 This is the view of Trionfi (see n. 3 above) but a low-backed form did exist earlier, Lorenzo de' Medici in his *camera terrena depinta* at Castello (Castello Invt., 1498) had *Uno letuzzo di br. 4 senza caplinaro*. It may have been thus constructed so that a tall back did not reach up and mask the fresco paintings on the walls which in this case may have been executed under Botticelli's supervision. A similar reason may explain why the Capponi, in their town house in 1534 (Capponi Invt.), had a *letuccio vechio sanza ispaliera* [old, without a back]. Perhaps the *Primavera* was fixed to the wall above such a backless *lettuccio*. Of course some of the low-backed *lettucci* that survive may be what is left once some art-lover has removed the painting on the *cappellinaio* and discarded the surround. Already in the 16th century Francesco Guicciardini acquired a painting that came from a *lettuccio*; he died in 1540 (see R. Ridolfi, *The Life of F. G.* 1967).

12 See Thornton, *17th Cent. Int. Dec.**, p. 172.

13 *Ibid.*, Pls. 16 and 20.

14 Honorati, *loc. cit.*, p. 43.

15 *Decameron**, Vol. II, No. 7.

16 *Un lectuchio intersiato* [with *intarsio*] (Fieschi Invt., 1532); Beatrice d'Este, the wife of Lodovico Sforza, had a splendid apartment in the castle at Milan wherein stood at least two *lettucci*, one being described in 1493 as *molto galante* while the second had a *sparviere* of gold brocade (Malaguzzi-Valeri*, pp. 330 and 331); Niccolò III had a *lettuccio* in his bedchamber in Ferrara in 1436 (Este Invt., 1436).

17 A *cappucciaio*, a rack for hoods or cowls, was of course the same as a *cappellinaio* which, strictly speaking, was for hats. What is interesting in this case is that the rack had pegs (see no. 10 above).

18 e.g. *unum magnum archo bancum cum quatuar coperchis* [i.e. large, with four lids] (Parisi Invt., Bologna, 1313).

19 e.g. a *bancale unum tarsiatum* was furnished with two mattresses, two cushions, a *bancheram* [cloth either to lay on the seat or to hang behind it] and a *boiha*; the last word is discussed on p. 53 (Riconboni Invt., Genoa, 1451). Many *banchale* were *casapanche* flanking the bed but quite a few were not evidently associated with a bed and some were in rooms that were not bedchambers.

20 See the Tura Invt., Siena, 1483, p. 116, footnote, where the term *ciscranna* is discussed by Curzio Mazzi, one of the most erudite scholars, who worked in this field in about 1900. He quotes a Florentine reference of 1493 to *Una arciscranna . . . che vi si possa sedere suso agiatamente e orrevolmente* [on which one may be seated commodiously and honourably].

21 In Lorenzo di Pierfrancesco de' Medici's *camera bella* at Fiesole (Fiesole Invt., 1498) stood a bed and a *lettuccio* but there was also *Una ciscranna di noce chon balustri e tarsia per sedere al fuocho* [of walnut with balusters and *intarsio*, for sitting by the fire]. Grand as it clearly was, it was not a *lettuccio* but it probably had a box-seat. Many *ciscranne* had locks. The *ciscranna* is further discussed on p. 171.

22 Honorati made some very plausible suggestions in her article (*loc. cit.*, pp. 45–46).

23 Malaguzzi Valeri*, p. 330.

24 Manni*, p. 102. Limewood lends itself especially well to delicate carving. The gilding was set off against a sky-blue ground.

25 Malaguzzi Valeri*, p. 332.

26 C. M. Brown, *Isabella d'Este and Lorenzo da Pavia . . .*, Geneva, 1982, p. 242 and documents 57, 62, 64, 82, 85 and 86. I am very grateful to Dora Thornton for drawing my attention to this fascinating body of material.

27 It was also very expensive. The carver was not going to charge much less than 20 ducats, Isabella was informed, and painting it blue and gilding would cost a further 15. In fact it cost 48 ducats by the time it was finished. A particularly pretty effect must have been the *historie* depicted on the blue sides in powdered gold [*oro masenado*]. We are told that the posts seem very tall in the sketch (unless the measurements are wrong, the writer adds) and that experiments in covering these slender members with stucco ornament had failed, so they would have to be carved. It took about two years to finish.

28 The writer assures her that the 'excellent beauty' [*ecelencia bela*] of this piece of furniture will particularly suit 'that small room which you want to make so beautiful' [*in quelo camerin che vole essere belisima*].

29 Fynes Moryson*, pp. 468–9.

Materials and decoration pp. 153–61

1 It is likely that only the parts of the bed that showed were made with costly materials. The hidden parts could be made of less expensive timber.

2 Schiaparelli* (p. 253–4) quotes a long description of a bed richly decorated with *tarsie*, made at Pistoia in 1468. The ornament included the arms of the owner, a band of

dancing children [*una moresca* (a kind of dance) ... *con sette spiritelli*] and a frieze of dolphins – no doubt highly stylized – amid foliage.

3 When Marco di Parente Parenti married Caterina Strozzi in 1448 he had a *lettiera* refurbished, an operation for which two new capitals were required (Lydecker, *Ceti**, p. 214). Similarly Bernardo Rinieri ordered two new capitals for the bed in his principal chamber in 1458 (Lydecker, *Thesis**, p. 264)

4 Cited also by Schiaparelli*, p. 265, who quotes many other references to painted beds and *lettucci*.

5 See Allan Braham, 'The Bed of Pierfrancesco Borgherini', *Burlington Magazine*, CXXI, 1979. The long, shallow panels (F, I and L in Braham's diagram, p. 755) must have been set into the bed-chests associated with this splendid bed. They cannot have been set into the fronts of the two *cassoni* that stood in the room as these were of walnut carved with figures (i.e. in the new fashion) which will not have offered any space for paintwork. The Borgherini bedroom of 1515 was probably one of the last major manifestations of the *quattrocento* tradition of painted chambers, with only the pair of walnut chests pointing the way forward.

6 Maddalena Trionfi Honorati, 'A proposito de 'lettuccio', *Antichità Viva*, XX, 3, 1981, p. 45.

7 Frati*, p. 22.

8 The relevant word was apparently illegible in the inventory.

9 In the *guardaroba* stood this '*letto ... dell' Indie portato a noi*' [bed from the Indies brought thence to us]; Francesco Bocchi, *Le Belleze della Città di Fiorenza*, Florence 1591, p. 86.

10 Bistort*, p. 356.

11 Florio*, explains that *retino* meant *reticella* (see p. 74).

12 Thornton – *Di Castro*, p. 3.

Bed-covers and bedclothes pp. 162–5

1 Pardi* (pp. 110–11) shows that, in Ferrara in 1436, grand beds seem invariably to have had a *coperta del letto* matching the other bed-hangings but insists, on the other hand, that *coverturi* were coverlets that did not belong to such a set. Eugene Van Overloop* (pp. 22–25) *l'inventaire Sforza, 1493*; Gemblo X, 1934 says the opposite, when analyzing a Milanese inventory of 1493. He found *copertori* that *were* en suite with bed-hangings while *coperte* seem to have been distinct items.

2 J. Shearman, 'The Collections of the Younger Branch of the Medici', *The Burlington Magazine*, Jan. 1975, p. 20.

3 See Thornton, *17th cent. Int. Dec.**, p. 112. Irish ruggs were also called "caddows" in England. Some were chequered.

4 Writing about the way Italians dressed in his day (*De gli habiti antichi et moderni*, Venice, 1590) Vecellio stated that *sopra la veste* [Genoese women] *portono una sbernia annodata con una brocca* [[over their clothes they wear a *sbernia* fixed with a brooch]. Closely related to this form of garment was the *camorra* or *gamurra*, as was also the Arab's *bernus*.

5 Shearman, *loc. cit.*, f.n. 47. For *frigio* read *fregio* = freeze, a type of woollen cloth with a nap.

6 *Schiavine* are mentioned in several 16th-century Venetian inventories (e.g. Odoni Invt., 1555; Correr Invt., 1589;

Zerlino Invt., 1589) and also in the inventory of the Castello di Narni taken in 1444 (N. Gaspari, *Archivio Storico per le Marche et per Umbria*, 1886), in all cases associated with beds.

7 A pile material of some sort, described as *savastina una piloxa*, was to be found in a Genoese bedchamber in 1456, apparently among bed-covering (Vivaldi Invt.). If this is not a mis-reading of *schiavina*, it could at any rate be a related fabric.

8 Matteo Bandello, *Novelle*, ed. G. Brogholigo, Bari, 1928. Novella III, p. 54. Published originally in 1554 and 1573.

9 The Sienese, and no doubt other Italian states, imposed an import duty on all the various sorts of *sargia francesca*. This might of course have meant lengths of serge cloth as well as the blanket-like coverlet here being discussed.

10 *essendo in piu luoghi per la piccola valle fatti letti, e tutte dal discreto siniscalco di sarge francesche e di capoletti intorniati e chiusi* (*Decameron**, VI, intro.).

11 *Decameron**, V 4.

12 *Una sargia gialla dipenta* (Fece Invt., Florence, 1450); *4 sargie rosse dipinti* (Gaddi Invt., Florence, 1496); at the Medici villa at Careggi in 1492 (Careggi Invt.) was a green *sargia dipinta a ochi di paone* (like the eyes on a peacock's feathers) and another with figures and one with roses.

13 The English name for a distinct type of woollen cloth, shalloon, derives from the same source.

14 Amato Invt., Naples, 1399–1400.

15 e.g. *unus zalonus* (Aleardi Invt., Verona, 1408 and Barzizza Invt., Padua, 1445); *claronum unum* (Vivaldi Invt., Genoa, 1456); *unum telonum de Fiandra* (Monticoli Invt., Udine, 1413).

16 For an excellent summary of our relatively scant knowledge about such materials, see Marguerite Prinet, *Le Damas de Lin. Historié ...*, Berne/Fribourg, 1982, espec. pp. 48–56. See also P. Thornton, 'Tapisseries de Bergame', *Pantheon*, VIII, pp. 85–91, March 1960. See also here, pp. 000.

17 Verga*.

18 I am indebted to Donald King for drawing my attention to this point.

19 Linen was often listed separately and, in the Capponi mansion in Florence (Capponi Invt., 1534) thirty pairs of sheets of various kinds are listed. Only one pair was *da resa* [i.e. *rensa*, from Rheims].

20 Bandello, *op. cit.*, Novella III, p. 53.

21 Bistort*, p. 356.

22 Bandello, *op. cit.*, Novella XXV, p. 276.

**Seats and Seat-Furniture
Stools pp. 168–71**

1 Manni*, p. 218. Daniela di Castro, after reading this passage in typescript, disagreed with my conclusion. However, these not uncommon stools (even if one allows for many being reproductions) *must* have had a name. No other distinguishing term presents itself.

2 This type of stool existed in France by 1539, at any rate, because in that year one was illustrated and described as *un placet* in Gilles Corrozet's *Les Blasons Domestiques*. This shows a low stool with turned baluster legs, stretchers at floor level (it seems) and a fitted textile cover to the seat. The related poem tells us that the *placet* was *Tout couvert de tapisserie* [i.e. upholstered] *Ou faeminine*

seigneurie se siet en plaisir & lyesse. Placet ou la cuisse & la fesse se reposent bien mollement. [Where fine ladies may take a seat with pleasure and comfort. *Placet* where thigh and backside rest very softly]. The full text of these verses is given in an article by Simon Jervis in *Furniture History* XXV, 1989.

3 Manni*, p. 185.

4 Manni*, p. 218. *Scani da tre piedi di raso verde con franzo d'oro* [stools with three legs, of green satin with gold fringe].

Benches and the *ciscranna* pp. 171–3

1 e.g. in a Genoese palazzo (Ponzone Invt., 1488) there was *bancheta una pro dominabus* [i.e. 'for the ladies of the household']. In a Florentine inventory (Uzzano Invt., 1424) mention is made of *I predellina da sedere da fauncilli* [a small *predella* or step for children to sit upon].

2 'Pancali, benches, formes, settles' (Florio*).

3 e.g. *bancalle unum intersiatum duarum clavatorum* [a *bancale* with *intarsio* and two locks (Negri Invt., Genoa, 1456)] and *banchale de duobus coperchiis* [with two lids; Busarini Invt., Genoa, 1461]. On the other hand there can be no doubt that the *Panchali sei a erbagi e animali di braccia 12 coll'arme* [six, with herbage and animals, 12 *braccia* wide, with coats of arms] was of verdure tapestry (Medici Invt., Florence, 1456)].

4 A rare reference to such a seat occurs in a Genoese inventory, Odoni Invt., 1555, *Quatro pezzi de banchali de spaliera bassi* [four benches with low back-rests].

5 See in Tura Invt., Siena, 1483 where Curzio Mazzi sets out all the information he could assemble on this class of furniture (p. 116–17).

6 This form was probably invented in the Netherlands about 1400 and was called a *wendelys* (turning bench). In France it was known as a *banc tourni/tourné* (see Josef De Coo, 'A Medieval Look at the Merode Annunciation', *Zeitschrift für Kunstgeschichte*, Berlin, 44, 1981

7 I discussed this problem with the distinguished furniture historian the Marchesa Maddalena Trionfi Honorati in 1987 and found we had both come to the same conclusion about the *ciscranna* – in my case, at any rate, purely on archival evidence. On that occasion I had forgotten taking a photograph of the Carmine benches in 1981 at a time when I knew nothing of this little problem. Although technically similar to northern specimens, I have no doubt these impressive seats are Italian.

Loose seat-coverings and cushions pp. 173–4

1 In one very splendid bedchamber there were no less than twenty-four cushions of gold brocade [*cosini xxiiij da sedere de broccato doro ...*] valued at the colossal sum of 204 ducats, as well as four more cushions of embroidered satin associated with the bed which may have been pillows, or may have been for display at the foot-end of the bed or on the tops of the flanking chests (Trivulzio Invt., Milan, 1465).

2 e.g. in the Sforza Invt., Milan, 1493, there is a list headed *Cusini* which includes two long, six square, and six round cushions, all covered with very costly silken materials.

3 Dante wrote of someone bringing in a *carello o cuscino* for

some people to sit upon, implying they were similar (Dante, *Fiore*, LXIII, 10) and Boccaccio has a character sit upon a *carello* [*Sopra un carello si pose a sedere* (*Decameron**, IV, 1, 17)].

4 Thornton, *17th Cent. Int. Dec.**, p. 181.

5 If this surmise is correct, we may here be dealing with one of the products of *hautelisseurs* (p. 000) who were certainly later to make special panels for seats and table-covers. If a pile-surfaced material was in question, the reference could concern a *tapis sarrasinois* or an early *moquette*.

Chairs pp. 174–91

1 For instance, in the room in which she spent much time, in the Palazzo Vecchio in Florence, Eleonora of Toledo had a *seggiola* which had a seat and back of white leather. There were three other *seggiole* in the room, presumably less imposing as they are called *da donne* which here probably meant they were used by her ladies-in-waiting (Medici Invt., 1553).

2 Pardi* (p. 153) cites a bill of 1448 *Per fare ricoprire i brazi a una scaranna* [for re-covering the arms of a *scaranna*].

3 Wanting to describe a very handsome bedchamber, Matteo Bandello (*Novella* III, publ. 1554) draws attention in some detail to the bed and then mentions the wall-hangings, a rich table-carpet, and the chests against the walls. *V'erano anco quattro catedre di velluto carmesino, e alcuni quadri di man di mastro Lionardo Vinci, il luogo mirabilmente adornavano . . .* [There were also four arm-chairs of crimson velvet, and several pictures from the hand of Master Leonardo Vinci adorned the place in a miraculous manner].

4 In a great house in Udine, in 1413 (Monticoli Invt., 1413), the only chair was *unam cathedram* in a main bedchamber. The seat-furniture was otherwise in the form of stools and benches.

5 e.g. *una chiera di covro . . . di donna* [a woman's chair of leather] and *due chiyrelli* [two small chairs] en suite with two *seggi grandi di villuto carmixino lavorato, minati* [large chairs of crimson velvet that was either figured or embroidered, with painted decoration?] (Requesens Invt., Palermo, 1561). These are late examples of an ancient usage (e.g. the *Item chiararum duarum* in the Amato Invt., Naples, 1399–1400).

6 In Tuscany the cresting or top 'rail' of the back often had an arched upper edge whereas in northern Italy an oblong rail cut away at the upper corners was popular (Pls 190, 191, 197). In all cases the top rail was partly dropped into grooves on the insides of the uprights.

7 One such reference is to *1 scranna di legname con sedere di giunchi* [an armchair of wood with a seat of rushes] Uzzano Invt., Florence, 1424. Presumably the chairs with seats *cum cordis erbarum* were likewise rush-bottomed (see Pandiani*, p. 71).

8 Havard*, 'Chaise'. In a Tuscan glassmaker's house in 1602 were *sei seggiole alla pistolesi di paglia* [six . . . of straw, i.e. 'with rush bottoms']; see Gabriella Cantini Guidotti, Accademia della Crusca, *Quaderno 2*, Florence, 1988, p. 136.

9 *Catedra desnodata* (Busarini Invt., Genoa, 1461), *una scaranna lignea desnodata* (Fiesso Invt., Ferrara, 1484).

10 e.g. *Cinque seggiole di quoio alla cardinalescha* [i.e. with leather seats and/or backs]; Medici Invt., Florence, 1492.

11 I am indebted to Dr Clive Wainwright for drawing my attention to this chair about which he intends to write an essay that will no doubt be extremely informative.

12 The actual text reads *Tomentato, o vero pulvinato, cum moderato convexo lanuginoso o vero di materia mollicula*. *Tomento* means flock.

13 See Thornton, *17th Cent. Int. Dec.**, p. 217 and f.n. 89.

14 Manni*, p. 119.

15 Pardi* (p. 98) says that animal hair was used already in the 14th century in Ferrara for stuffing saddles but he had found no references specifically to horsehair.

16 At Poggio a Caiano, during Lorenzo de' Medici's time (Poggio Invt., 1492), there were *due predelle overe seggiole di legno da malati* [two platforms or seats of wood for sick people]. No doubt they were provided with cushions and even small mattresses but they sound crude and not very comfortable.

17 e.g. *Una seggiola da dormire, di quoio rosso* [a sleeping armchair of red leather] made for the Cardinal of Ravenna (Medici Invt., Florence, 1553); *una cariega fornita di curoro rosso per dormire* [an armchair furnished with red leather, for sleeping] and another *per dormir commodo* [for sleeping comfortably] (Correr Invt., Florence, 1584).

18 Manni*, p. 37.

19 Could the *catreda de palleis* in the study in the Barzizza house in Padua (Barizza Invt., 1445) be a wickerwork armchair or was it rush-seated [*paglia* = straw]? It stood on a dais [*cum uno podio*].

20 Havard*, 'Chaise'.

21 *Scommettere*, apart from meaning to place a wager, also meant 'to disjoynt or make loose' (Florio*) but, in this context, it could simply mean that the chair folded – or was set in 'disorder', as Florio also puts it.

22 'The Gage Inventory of 1556', *Sussex Archaeological Collections*, XLV, 1892.

23 Manni*, p. 38 and p. 132.

24 Malaguzzi Valeri*, p. 83.

Chests
The large furnishing chest pp. 192–204

1 Uzzano Invt., 1424. In a main bedchamber stood a *cassone a 2 serrami* [with two locks] at the foot of the bed, so it was an important item. In the *guardaspensa* next door (a kind of store-room) was a *forziere* containing hangings associated with the aforesaid bed, a second *forziere* described as 'old', and a *forzeretto da soma* [a small *forziere* or travelling trunk suitable for loading on a mule's back].

2 Tura Invt., Siena, 1483. There were *goffani* in several rooms; some, decorated with *tarsie*, were associated with a bed and must presumably therefore have been rather low, while others were large and painted with figures [*grandi dipenti, messi a storie*]. Another pair was painted with Tura's arms and decoration *all' antica* [in the ancient (or classical) style]. In a bedroom stood two pairs of *forzieri*, iron-bound, one pair being painted with the family arms and the other being covered with hide. Another pair in another room was painted green and was iron-bound all round [*ferrati intorno*]. The single *cassone* was *grosso, di noce . . . con serratura a chiave grosse* [i.e. large, of walnut, with a lock with a large key] and was exceptional in having an inner lining of iron [*ferrato dentro da tutt' i lati*]. Other instances of *cassoni* and *forzieri* appearing together in the

one inventory are: (i) Ferrara (Della Rovere Invt., 1493); a pair of painted *forzieri* and a pair of *cassoni assepoltura* [of sarcophagus shape]. (ii) Fiesole (Medici Invt., 1498); a *cassone* of walnut with a *prospetive* [view?] executed in *intarsio*, fitted with a *spalliera* (p. 195), and two large *forseri al' anticha* painted with figures [*storiati*, i.e. with histories or stories] and gilded, also fitted with *spalliere*. (iii) Milan (Trivulzio Invt., 1529); eight *cassoni*, some of walnut and some painted with the family arms, standing alongside *Forzieri di ogni sorte No. 14* [of every kind, fourteen in all]. (iv) Genoa (Fieschi Invt., 1532); two painted *forzieri* and three *ferrati alla francese* ['iron-bound in the French manner', and perhaps therefore of oak] and several *cassoni* including one painted *alla antica*, two with inlaid ornament, and one entirely bound with iron [*ferrato tuto*]. (v) Florence (Medici Invt., 1553); the *forzieri* were by this time seemingly more utilitarian items, being covered with leather, iron-bound, with locks, and all shaped *a sepultura*, while the *cassoni* seem to have been more glamorous, one being 'large' and two painted with the family arms and stars, and one with figures.

3 e.g. *unum cassonum longum ferratum* and *unum coffanum antiquum ferratum* (Monticoli Invt., Udine, 1413); *1 cassone ferato tuto* (Uzzano Invt., Florence, 1534); *4 cassoni grandi a seppultura ferrati coperti di quoro nero . . .* (Medici Invt., Florence, 1553). Also *Quatuor cofini ferrati veteri* (Malvolti Invt., Siena, 1350); Pardi* notes references to *cofani ferrati a stagno* [with tinned iron straps] at Ferrara in 1436.

4 Randle Holme, writing in the mid 17th century, illustrates a chest with a vaulted lid and calls it 'a coffer' but goes on to say that 'If it have a flat cover, it is called a Chest' (*The Academy of Armory . . .*, 1688; reprint by the Roxburghe Club, London, 1905). See also S. Jervis, 'Furniture in the Commonwealth Inventories' in *The Late King's Goods*, ed. A. Macgregor, London and Oxford, 1989, Ch. 8, on the possessions of Charles I.

5 Paul Schubring*, whose book *Cassoni* published at Leipzig in 1915 is still by far the most thoughtful essay on this subject, came to this conclusion, saying that the term *cassone* 'is too generally used to be discarded' (pp. 13–15). See also Schiaparelli*, pp. 295–6 and 301.

6 Marcello Invt., Venice, 1534. In this same inventory mention is made of *una arcella grande* and it has been suggested that *arcella* was the Venetian name for a *cassone*. However, references to *arcelle* are too rare for this to be plausible.

7 *Decameron**, IV, 10.

8 *Unam archam parvan* [Latin: a small *arca*] (Frossasco Invt., Piedmont, 1512).

9 Vasari, speaking of Florentine 15th-century products, specifically mentions *casoni . . . a uso di sepulture, e con altre varie fogge ne' coperchi* [*cassoni* of sarcophagus shape and with other forms of lid] shows that the chief characteristic of this type lay in the lineaments of the lid which was roof-like with sloping concave sides like that shown in Pl. 222 (Vasari*, II, p. 148).

10 e.g. *duos forzerettos maioris fogie copertos corri* [two small *forzieri* of the large sort, covered with leather; Florentine inventory of 1418; see Schiaparelli*, p. 238] *Un paio di forzierj vechi, ferati, foderatj di pellj* [a pair, old, iron-bound, covered with hide; Tura Invt., Siena, 1483]; *8 fortieri a sepultura coperti di quoio nero per la compagna con lor serrami* [with black leather, for the field (i.e. for

travelling or going into the countryside), with their locks; Medici Invt., Florence, 1553].

11 e.g. *coffana duo deaurata magna* [two large gilded coffers, Vivaldi Invt., Genoa, 1456; *para doe de cofani et para doe de forzini tuti insieme* [two pairs of coffers and two of small *forzieri* all *en suite*] prepared as wedding presents for Magdalena of Brandenburg in 1487 (Borromeo-Brandenburg Invt., Milan, 1487).

12 *Unus coffinus pictus de novo a figuris magnis quatuor* [newly painted with four large figures]. The son had had this repainted after his father's death a year earlier but before the inventory was taken (Aleardi Invt., Verona, 1408*).

13 One of the major Florentine workshops, that of Apollonio di Giovanni, produced anything from two to about thirty chests a year in the middle decades of the 15th century, it taking about a month for a painter in that establishment to paint a single front-panel. A high proportion (perhaps half) of the cost lay in the gilding which surrounded the paintings – indeed, covered much of the rest of the chest. The average price was about 35 florins but even larger sums were paid for specially important commissions, for they were of course usually produced in connection with a wedding (see Schubring*, pp. 88–9, and E. Callmann, *Apollonio di Giovanni*, Oxford, 1974).

14 One should of course treat the survivors with circumspection. Those that survived the four centuries into the 19th century more or less intact must by then all have needed restoration, sometimes of a drastic nature. In some cases the decorated fronts were saved and fitted to an entirely new carcass. Feet, lids and sometimes whole framings had to be replaced, occasionally under the influence of considerable imagination. Heavy gilding, quite different in character to that of the 15th century, was too often added. As for the paintings, they too needed attention. By the time Schiaparelli* and Schubring* were studying these chests, the waters had already been considerably muddied.

15 Vasari*, II, p. 148. *In que' tempi ... i piu eccellenti pittori in così fatti lavori si esercitavano senza vergognarsi, come oggi molti farebbero, di dipingere e mettere d'oro simili cose* [in those times even the very best painters used to do this sort of work, without feeling ashamed, as many would today, of painting and gilding this sort of thing].

16 Cited by Schubring*, p. 19.

17 That of Apollonio di Giovanni; see n. 13 here. An important commission from this workshop in 1448 is discussed by J. Kent Lydecker in an article on 'Il patriziato fiorentino e la committenza artistica per la casa', Acts of a Congress on *I ceti dirigenti nella Toscana del Quattrocento*, Florence, 1983, p. 214.

18 Schubring*, p. 105.

19 *Riccordi di Baldovinetti*, ed. E. M. Londi, Florence, 1907.

20 Lydecker, *op. cit.*, p. 216.

21 G. Pardi, *Lionello d'Este*, Bologna, 1904. See also Manni*, *passim*, and p. 97, here.

22 Schubring*, p. 151.

23 *Ibid.*, p. 171.

24 Allan Braham, 'The Bed of Pierfrancesco Borgherini', *The Burlington Magazine*, CXXI, 1979.

25 *Ibid.* The walnut *cassoni* were *pieni di putti intagliati* which must mean that carved putti covered their fronts, and this clearly left no room for painting but it would anyway have been contrary to convention to paint walnut. Other *cassoni* sometimes had *spallieri* rising from their backs forming a

panel against the wall, between about 1470 and 1520 (see n. 21).

26 Schubring*, p. 166.

27 Schiaparelli* has much of great interest to say about gilded *cassoni* (see pp. 257–62) including the fact that some 'gilding' was executed with tin-leaf instead of gold-leaf: it was presumably covered with a yellow varnish to make it look like gold. This was a cheap method. Cennino Cennini, in his *Trattato della pittura*, written in the 1390s, explains how to gild chests which he said, should be treated in the same way as the gilding on paintings. He also tells one how to make moulds for appliqué relief ornament.

28 Bistort*, p. 370.

29 Schiaparelli*, p. 262. See also Vol. II, p. 74, n. 150.

30 e.g. *Una capsa grande venetiana* (Pico Invt., Modena, 1474); in the very grand Sanuti residence in Bologna, in 1505, there were such chests in the wife's room (Frati*, p. 22); Pardi*, p. 36, mentions *casse alla veneziana* in the Este inventories of 1436.

31 *Una cassone da danari* [for cash] *alla venetiana con 5 campanelli* [bells, for alarm], *di noce* (Medici Invt., Florence, 1553).

32 See Sandra Lebboroni, 'Cenni storici sulla collezione degli Ospedali Civili' in *Civiltà del Legno, Mobili dalle collezioni di Palazzo Bianco e del Museo degli Ospedali di S. Martino*, exhibition in Genoa, Palazzo Bianco, 1985.

33 Malaguzzi Valeri*, p. 81.

34 See Manni*, pls 3, 13 and 14.

35 These have sometimes been called *Nonnentruhe* [the German for nun's chests] for no very good reason.

36 Liubov Faeson, *Cassoni in Soviet Collections*, Leningrad, 1983.

37 The burdens carried on mules or asses were called *some*.

38 Trivulzio Invt., Milan, 1420 and Uzzano Invt., Florence, 1424; Fece Invt., Siena, 1450. Many instances of covers for chests slung on the backs of mules could be cited; the mule-train bringing Bianca Maria Sforza's belongings to her wedding in 1493 (Sforza Invt., Milan) must have made a fine sight with its *Coperte vigintiquinque pro mulis ad insigne Sforcianum recamate* [25 covers for mules embroidered with the arms of Sforza].

39 It is probable that the earliest chests with 'external' drawers had the drawers fitted at the bottom of the carcass, making the main compartment above less deep and easier to reach down into. This development may have taken place in some places in Italy by 1500.

40 Lydecker, Thesis*, p. 63.

41 Lydecker, *Ceti*, p. 217.

42 Domenico Gnoli, *La Roma di Leon X*, Rome, 1938.

43 Bruno Zevi, *Biagio Rossetti, architetto ferrarese*, Turin, 1960, p. 640. The cost of gilding was apparently 45 *lire*. A 'clavichord' in the dowry cost 10 and a large mirror cost 2 *lire*.

44 Vasari, in the passage mentioned in n. 9, said that *Il di dentro poi si foderava di tele e di drappi* [the insides would be lined with linen or silk (*drappi d'oro* = cloth of gold)], *secondo il grado e potere di coloro che gli facevano fare ...* [according to the rank and wealth of those who had them (the *cassoni*) made].

45 Schubring*, p. 166.

46 *Ibid.*, p. 154.

47 R. W. Lightbown, *Mantegna*, Oxford, 1986. Two of the chests are now in the cathedral at Graz in Styria and two

are in the Rudolfinum in Klagenfurt, Carinthia.

Smaller chests and cases p. 204

1 Borgia Invt., Ferrara, 1503. The fans and the shoes were in two *schatole de valentia* [from Valencia] although precisely how such boxes looked is not clear. The *caseta a modo de tomba* was empty as were the two *cassette lavorata danbri* (the amber boxes probably came from somewhere on the Baltic coast). The *Caseta lavorata da volio* [*avolio* = ivory] *venuta da Roma* was a gift to the princess but whether the *camixe* it held formed part of the present or whether she simply used it as a receptacle, we cannot say.

2 e.g. Este Invt., Ferrara, 1436; Pinelli Invt., Genoa, 1456 and Busarini Invt., Genoa, 1461, both from Genoa.

3 The Este *cassetta* mentioned in the previous note was *dipinta e dorata con figure intagliate a relievo* [painted and gilded with figures in relief] and probably belonged to one of the wives of Niccolò III of Ferrara. In the Valle Invt., Genoa, 1488 are listed *casceta una intersciata* and *Casceta una de supreso daurata* [one was decorated with *tarsie*, the other was of cypresswood, gilded (presumably only partly)]. *Cassette* of cypress are mentioned quite often (*una casetta de arcepressa lavorata tutta de releve cum 4 pome dorate de sotto*, of cypress worked overall in relief, with four gilded balls as feet; Franceschino Invt., Cesena, 1489). *Cassette* of walnut were also not uncommon but particularly striking must have been that of inlaid ivory mentioned in the Trivulzio Invt., Milan, 1420*. *Cassette* of iron [*di ferro*] must have been jewel-boxes (Valle Invt., again, this had two locks) and curious must have been the *casetta fatta di siti carmexini laurata in pagla* which was presumably covered in crimson silk and cleverly decorated with pieces of straw (Requesens Invt., Palermo, 1561). Charming caskets delightfully decorated with moresques (in Venice and perhaps elsewhere) in the late 16th century will soon be the subject of an essay by Dora Thornton.

4 Simon Jervis has been working on this problem for some years. When he publishes his findings they will undoubtedly be of the greatest interest.

Tables
Tables for meals, and the simple *credenza* pp. 205–9

1 e.g. in the *sala* of the Uzzano house in Florence in 1424 (Uzzano Invt., 1424) was *1 tavola con 2 trespoli di braccia 6 e $\frac{3}{4}$* and a smaller table of $3\frac{1}{2}$ *braccia*, while in the *saletta*, also a dining-room, stood another such table; in the De Fece mansion in Siena in 1450 (Fece Invt., 1450), there was *Una tavola da mangiare, con trepiei* in the *sala*; in store in the Correr *palazzo* in Venice in 1584 (Correr Invt., 1584) was *Un par di cavaletti con le sue tavole*. Why is *tavole* in the plural? Florio, 1611* explains that a *cavalletto* is 'any tressell or Sadlers or Armorers woodden horse'.

2 A table of cypresswood in a Bolognese house in 1335 (Belvisi Invt., 1335) had six trestles [*unam ... tabulam de*

cipresso et sex trespedes a tabula].

3 Malaguzzi Valeri*, p. 336.

4 The *Crusca* dictionary does indeed explain that *trespiedi* have three legs.

5 In the castle at Turin in 1497–8 was *une grant table de sappin a deux traicteaux a pied de grue* (Savoy Invt., 1497–8).

6 *Levate la tavola* came to mean to clear the table, i.e. remove the dishes, but the original significance was that of taking away the table itself.

7 *Decameron**, x 9 and III 10.

8 Montaigne*, p. 76.

9 See Thornton, *17th Cent. Int. Dec.**, p. 226 and Pls 212 and 213. See also Dora Thornton, Thesis*, p. 122.

10 Manni*, p. 188.

11 *Ibid*, p. 190.

12 e.g. the *dischum unum cum suis tripodibus* in the main room [*caminata*] of the Negro house in Genoa in 1456 (Negro Invt., 1456).

13 In the Medici inventory for their villa at Poggio a Caiano in 1492, a long list of objects follows this heading, and in the Gonzaga Invt., Mantua, 1582 a whole section is given to the silver reserved for two small *credenze*, comprising some fifty items in all.

14 See the Acciaiuoli Invt., 1363, p. 9, footnote. The Florentines were clearly overdoing it, with nine stages. The Queen of France at this date displayed five stages and the Duke of Burgundy six (see Eames*, p. 57). Ferrante's sons, coming from the more courtly background of Naples, may have had to hide their smiles at such ostentation.

15 Malaguzzi Valeri*, p. 337.

16 e.g. *Una tavleta per la credenza cum li trespedi*, in the Fieschi Invt., Genoa, 1532, where the next item is *El legno per le robe* [the wooden piece for the things/belongings] which must have been a staging for the better display of glamorous objects. This stood in my lady's *saletta*, a sort of private dining-room in what was one of the grandest houses in Genoa at the time.

17 e.g. at Cafaggiolo in 1498, there stood in the *sala grande* five trestle-tables (sharing seven trestles) and eight small sideboards [*deschetti*], four of them with *spalliere*. At *Trebbio* (same date) all seven *deschetti* in the *sala grande* had such back-boards.

18 See Jervis, *Printed Designs**, figs 77–84.

Tables for show pp. 209–14

1 Fynes Moryson*, p. 422. The proposed commas in squared brackets seem to make better sense of this passage.

2 Of recent books that touch upon the subject, by far the most comprehensive are those by Alvar Gonzalez-Palacios, notably his impressive series entitled *Il Tempio del Gusto*, Milan, 1984 and 1986. The bibliographical references are very full.

3 Manni*, p. 25.

4 Manni*, p. 18.

5 *Hypnerotomachia**, p. 103.

6 Capponi Invt., Florence, 1534. It stood in the main bedchamber on the ground floor. I have not seen the original manuscript but would guess that this table in fact had three legs, not two.

7 Manni*, p. 131, Pl. 64.

8 Pitti Invt., 1577

9 A former staff dining-room [*tinello*] was given over to the working of precious stones at the Palazzo Vecchio (see Medici Invt., Florence, 1553, p. 13) over which presided Maestro Raffaello di Domenico di Polo *pulitore di pietre* [polisher of stones]. In the room were tables and trestles, a *desco da sega pietre* [on which to saw stone] and one *da conciar pietre* [on which to dress stone]. Although work with *pietre dure* was akin to that of the jeweller, the scale of the work being handled here was evidently large or they would not have needed a special table for sawing the stones.

10 Manni*, p. 109.

11 It may be that the term then used was *capretto*. A table at the Villa Medici in 1598 had *capretti di legno*. See n. 13 below.

12 See Gonzalez-Palacios, *op. cit.*, I, p. 85 and fig. 175; also Olga Raggio, 'The Farnese Table; A rediscovered work by Vignola', *Metropolitan Museum of Art Bulletin*, March, 1960. The Farnese table was probably designed by Vignola. As Jervis has shown (*op. cit.*), Du Cerceau produced engraved designs for such table-supports around 1560.

13 e.g. at the Villa Medici in Rome, in 1598, a table of white marble *comessa di piu sorti di pietre fine*, measuring $10\frac{2}{3}$ *piedi* by $6\frac{1}{2}$, had *Dua capretti di legno p[er] pie di detta tavola* [two small goats (fauns?) of wood as supports . . .]. The dimensions indicate a centre-table so presumably it had two supports formed with two *pairs* of goats – unless *capretto* was a term used to describe such supports in general (like *cavelleto*, a trestle or small horse). This suggestion is strengthened by another entry in the same inventory concerning a small marble table (with engravings beneath transparent alabaster) which also has *Due capre ch[e] servano p[er] piedi . . .* [two *capre* serving as feet/supports].

14 I am greatly indebted to Daniela di Castro (Moscati) for reminding me that alabaster, lapis lazuli and basalt were sometimes decorated with painting – scenes as well as ornament – in the late 16th and 17th centuries.

Tables of other kinds pp. 214–16

1 See Thornton, 17th Cent. Int. Dec.*, p. 226. In a footnote references are cited to *une petite table à la mode d'Espaigne* in a French inventory of 1523 and to what the Dutch called a *Spaens tafelken* in one of 1619.

2 See Gonzalez-Palacios, *op. cit.*, I, Pls 434 and 438, and Pls 498–500. See also S. Jervis and R. Baarsen, 'An Ebony and Ivory Cabinet', in the *Victoria and Albert Museum Album*, IV, 1985.

3 e.g. four *Tavolle da lavar* which were probably for the laundry as they seem to be in the back areas (Ram Invt., Venice, 1592) and the *descho da chucina* mentioned in the Uzzano Invt., Florence, 1420.

Table-covers pp. 216–19

1 Pandiani* (p. 100) claimed that the *tapeta/tapeyda* lay on the floor while the *tapeto/tapeydo* lay on a table. One should hestitate before disagreeing with so distinguished a

scholar but I do not believe that the last letter could have such significance, especially as he cities in support of his case references to *una tapeyda . . . da mettere in terra* and to *uno tapeydo . . . per la tavla*; such qualification would surely have been unnecessary if the distinction had been evident from the spelling.

2 All are quoted from the Odoni Invt. Venice, 1555.

3 Bandello*, p. 53; and Medici Invt., Florence, 1492.

4 See Schiaparelli*, p. 226 for the first two, and Badoer Invt., Venice, 1521.

5 See the Pollani Invt. Venice, 1590 where *una corpetta de brocadello . . .* and another of *velludo zallo intagiada* [of brocatelle, of yellow voided velvet] are listed among items of clothing. Many of those cited by Bistort* are probably also items of costume (p. 386).

6 All four are present, in a group of table carpets, in the inventory of the sumptuous contents of the Palazzo Correr in Venice, taken in 1584.

7 Della Crusca Dictionary, *Celone. Panno tessuto a vergato, col quale ci cuopre la mensa* [cloth with stripes with which one covers a table].

8 Bistort*, p. 207.

9 See p. 73, here; also M. Prinet, *Le Damas de Lin . . .*, Berne and Fribourg, 1982, p. 46.

10 Both these terms are likely to refer to linen damask rather than plain linens. The reference to Flanders linens occurs in the Requesens Invt. of 1561 and probably concerns damasks from Courtrai where damasks were being woven by the middle of the century. The reference to Holland linen came from the Medici Invt. of 1553 by which time no damasks had apparently been produced in Holland proper, so the reference may once again be to Courtrai – unless the description concerned a plain cloth, which seems unlikely (see Prinet, *op. cit.*, pp. 67, 70, 86).

11 Eustachi Invt., Pavia, 1449.

Cupboards, Desks and Cabinets
The elaborate *credenza* pp. 220–21

1 Este Invt., Ferrara, 1436, pp. 115–16.

2 *Ibid.*, p. 58.

3 *Ibid.*, p. 53.

4 See Eames*, pp. 55–72, where much that is relevant to the present theme is surveyed, including the confusing terminology.

5 A *credenzotto di noce vecchio* [of walnut, old] stood in a bedchamber in a house at Faenza in 1567 (see E. Ciuffolotti, *Faenza nel Rinascimento. La vita privata.* Bagnacavallo, 1922, p. 20).

6 Jervis, *Printed Designs**, figs 51–72.

Desks for writing and reading pp. 222–9

1 Antonio Manno claimed that the word *scagneto* derived from *scanello* or *cancello* which meant a writing-desk. Florio.* agrees that this is what *cancello* meant but says nothing about *scagnetto*; a *scagnello*, however, was 'any little stoole . . .'. That Manno may have been right is borne out by the fact that the *scagneto* in question was *in lo scagneto* (i.e. a room). He equates this with *studiolo*, a study, although the term could also mean a cabinet in the sense of a piece of furniture (see p. 230). There is

presumably a link between *scancello* and *cancello* on the one hand, and *scancia* on the other, the latter meaning 'a shelfe or cupboard', according to Florio. Manno edited the Fieschi Invt.

Cabinets pp. 229–33

1 See Simon Jervis. 'A tortoiseshell cabinet and its precursors', *Victoria and Albert Museum Bulletin*, Oct. 1968.

2 Many of the larger examples that survive today have stands which, however, are rarely more than a century old. Whether any had stands in the 16th century is at least open to doubt. Since such cabinets were meant to be portable, it seems more likely that they stood on folding tables like those described on p. 214

3 Alvar Gonzalez-Palacios, *Il Tempio del Gusto, Roma e il Regno delle Due Sicilie*, II, figs 412–43, and text I, pp. 239–47; Simon Jervis and Reinier Baarsen, 'An Ebony and Ivory Cabinet', *Victoria and Albert Museum Bulletin*, IV, 1985.

4 As his name proclaims, he must have been Flemish and probably came from the Spanish Netherlands. *Alemanno* meant German but this should be taken no more literally than our calling the inhabitants of Holland 'Dutch', a corruption of *deutsch* which also means German.

5 See Gonzalez-Palacios, *Il Tempio del Gusto, Il Granducato di Toscana e gli State Settentrionali*, Milan 1986, II, fig. 531, and I Pl. xxxviii and pp. 351–4.

6 See Peter Thornton, *Musical Instruments as Works of Art*, London, 1968, figs 8a–c. Musical instruments, a great many of which have their date and provenance boldly inscribed on them, are a rich source of information about the dating of ornamental styles and techniques. The craftsmanship involved is closely akin to that used in the making of cabinets and other fine furniture.

7 Towards the end of the 16th century many Venetian writing-desks or cabinets (by this date, it is not clear which) seem to have been of walnut. A *scrittoretto* in 1588 might well be of the type with a sloping top; *doi scrittori* of carved walnut with compartments or perhaps small drawers [*con casselle*] in 1594 are more likely to have been of box form, as was probably also a *scrittoretto* which had *cassellette* [probably small drawers]. I am indebted to my daughter Dora Thornton for these quotations from documents in the Venetian State Archives.

8 Fynes Moryson*, p. 453 (see also p. 422). A Venetian inventory of 10 December 1597 has a reference to *Un scrittor dorato et miniado remesso drento di madreperle* [a cabinet gilt and delicated painted, inlaid with mother-of-pearl]; information kindly communicated by Dora Thornton, discovered by her in the Venetian State Archives (G. Bianchini, reg. 492, 78v.). Gonzales-Palacios (see n. 5) published two cabinets which may well be examples of this Venetian class.

9 Gonzales-Palacios (see n. 6), figs 152, 161 and 165.

10 While *scrittoio* (or variants of the term) was the commonest name for a writing-desk or writing-cabinet, the word *studiolo* became common towards the end of the 16th century. A very early use of the word, in the sense of an article of furniture made of wood, is found in the Este accounts for 1490 – *Uno studiolo de nogara posto suso quatro piede, o vero descheto* [of walnut standing on four legs, or rather a small table] (Manni*, p. 91).

11 However, Florio* tells us that a *stipo* was 'an Ambrie' which is an unusual spelling of 'aumbrie', a cupboard (in the modern sense) or press, from the French *armoire* and not far removed from the Italian *armaro*. By Florio's time most cabinets had paired doors like a cupboard but he cannot have been ignorant of the difference between a wardrobe and a cabinet. Had *stipo* been the common word for a cabinet, Florio would surely have known the fact.

Mirrors and the *Restello*
Mirrors pp. 234–9

1 Dante, *Paradiso*, XV, 113.

2 Sabba di Castiglione, *Ricordi*, Venice, 1560, p. 61. I am very grateful to Dora Thornton for drawing my attention this rich source of information.

3 A. Luzio and R. Renier, 'Il lusso di Isabella d'Este ...', *Nuova Antologia*, year XXXI, Series LXIII, Vol. XI, Rome, 1896, p. 84.

4 *Ibid*.

5 *Ibid.*, p. 60.

6 Cheap mirrors were made of tin, and very costly ones of silver and sometimes even of gold; but steel, of all the available metals, produced the sharpest and therefore most faithful reflection, its natural colour affecting the reflected colours hardly at all.

7 Information very kindly communicated by my former colleague Robert Charleston.

8 The glass-makers of Venice were forced to move out of the city itself, already in 1291, and settled instead on the nearby island of Murano where many still operate today (see R. J. Charleston and L. M. Angus-Butterworth, 'Glass', in *The History of Technology*, ed. Charles Singer and others, Oxford, Vol. III, 1957, pp. 206–44. The polishing of mirrors, on the other hand, was carried out in Venice itself. In the 16th century there were some 30,000 people living on Murano. By 1890, the figure had dropped to 4,000. No doubt it has risen somewhat since.

9 G. Marchotti (*Un Mercante Fiorentino e la sua famiglia nel secolo XIV*), published in 1881 to celebrate the Nardi–Arnaldi wedding held in Florence in that year) lists the presents exchanged at the wedding in 1466 between Bernardo Rucellai and Nannina de' Medici. One item is here recorded as being *una specciolina lavorata a Vinegia* [a small mirror worked at Venice]. Before speculating on whether this had a plate of Venetian mirror-glass, it should be noted that the same entry has more recently been interpreted as a *sechiolina lavorata a Vinegia* [i.e. a small bucket] and that the next item in the list is a bowl [*bugnolina*] which suggests the two pieces formed a hand-washing set (see p. 244) and were of metalwork, perhaps of damascened brass (see 103). This second interpretation is given in 'Giovanni Rucellai ed il suo Zibaldone', edited by Alessandro Perosa, *Studies of the Courtauld and Warburg Institutes*, London, 1960.

10 Information from R. J. Charleston (see n. 7). In this connection it is perhaps worth noting that the Duke of Burgundy in 1410 owned a circular glass mirror with a frame on the back of which was painted the figure of the Virgin Mary [*un mirouer sangle rond, d'un coste la Vierge ... et de l'autre le verre a mirer*]; E. Frémy, *Histoire de la Manufacture Royale des Glaces de France ...*, Paris, 1909, p. 3.

11 See n. 7; also G. Mariacher, *Glass from Antiquity to the Renaissance*, London, 1970 (original Italian edition, 1966).

12 Manni*, p. 68.

13 Leydecker, *Ceti**, p. 216: bill from the painters Richard and Bernardo of 1472 for *manufattura d'uno spechio di legno intagliato mi fe d'oro e d'azurro*.

14 Tura Invt., Siena, 1483; in this case the plate may have been oval rather than circular. Another ivory mirror frame is listed in the Borromeo Invt., Milan, 1497.

15 In the same inventory mention is made of a large mirror with a walnut frame, *che mostra 13 visi*. This must have been of the kind which had twelve small convex mirrors set in a ring round the main plate, so it did indeed reflect thirteen faces at once.

16 Sabba di Castiglione, *op. cit.*, pp. 90–91.

17 Letter from Ser Lapo Mazzei of 16 Jan., 1396 (G. Guasti, ed., *Lettere di un notaio*, Florence, 1890, I, p. 169).

18 Gustav Ludwig, 'Restello, Spiegel und Toiletten-utensilien in Venedig zur Zeit der Renaissance', (*Venezianischer Hausrat ... Kunsthistorisches Institut, Florenz*), Berlin, 1908, Vol. I.

19 *Ibid.*, pp. 296–300.

20 Bruno Zevi, *Biagio Rossetti, architetto ferrarese*, Turin, 1960, p. 640.

21 Giovanbattista Palatino, *Libro ... nel qual s'ingegna a Scriver ogni sorte lettere*, Rome, 1560, shows how a writer might benefit from having a mirror strategically placed in his study. *Lo specchio si tiene per conservar la vista ne lo scriver continuo* [to preserve the eyesight during constant writing].

22 Ugo Bellocchi, *Le ville di Anton Francesco Doni*, Modena, 1969, p 38.

23 Half a century later Francis Bacon recommended that a smart modern house should have two 'rich Cabinets ... Glased with Crystalline Glasse' *Essayes*, 1626, XLV 'Of Building').

24 Rabelais, *Gargantua*, I, ch. LV.

The *restello* and related forms pp. 239–41

1 *Cappellinaio* is usually spelt with only one 'p' in 15th-century inventories but the word must derive from *cappello*, a hat, not *capello*, hair. A *Capuccio* was 'a hood, cowle, a bonnet' (Florio*), and a rack for such garments was also occasionally called a *cappucciaio* (e.g. Tura Invt., Siena, 1483*).

2 David Herlihy, 'Marriage at Pistoia in the 15th century', *Cities and Society in Mediaeval Italy*, London, 1980, p. 289.

3 Bistort*, p. 369.

4 See Gustav Ludwig, 'Restello, Spiegel und Toiletten-utensilien in Venedig zur Zeit der Renaissance', *Venezianischer Hausrat ...* (Kunsthistorisiches Institut, Florenz), Berlin, 1908, which deals with this matter exhaustively but concentrates solely on the Venetian scene. In Venice, *restello*, with an 'e', was the common way of spelling the word.

5 Ludwig, *op. cit.*, chapter on 'Das Restello da Camera'.

6 Ludwig, *op. cit.*

7 *Ibid.*; also Marcello Invt., Venice, 1534.

8 *Ibid.* Many *restelli* had the family arms painted on them, which is something done mostly on items intended to catch a visitor's eye.

9 *Ibid.*

10 *Ibid.* Ludwig also cites references to *restelli* associated with paintings (one could hang a rosary on the pegs, for instance, or a kerchief for covering the head), and one *resteletto* for writings [*da scritture*] which may have been a row of spikes for bills.

11 *Ibid.*

12 Pandiani* (p. 87) does not give the date of these quotations which presumably apply to Genoese items. This particular *restello* had a picture of St Christopher painted 'in its middle'.

13 Bistort*, p. 357.

14 Philippa Glanville has kindly drawn my attention to a dressing-mirror that is mentioned in the inventory of the first Earl of Pembroke of 1561/2. It was of silver and had hooks at the bottom for toilet-accessories. Although this sumptuous object may have been made in London, it is also perfectly possible it was in fact a Venetian *restello* – just the sort of thing the use of which the Venetian sumptuary laws were seeking to suppress.

15 Ludwig, *op. cit.* The *coda* could be of white, black or red horsehair.

16 In the Tura Invt., Siena, 1483 a *strigatoio d' avorio lavorato* is listed. What was this object of carved ivory? A *stregghia* was 'a currie-combe, a horse-combe', according to Florio's dictionary of 1611* but even the rich doctor Bartolo di Tura is not likely to have used an ivory curry-comb on his horses. Presumably this was a curry-comb for human hair. Or maybe it was a *striglia* (from the Latin *strigilis*), a curved scraper used in the sauna for removing cleansing oils from the body surfaces.

17 Gilles Corrozet, *Les Blasons Dòmestiques*, 1539, (full text with illustrations published in *Furniture History*, London, 1989, Vol. XXV), under 'L'Estuy de Chambre' speaks of *pignes . . . d'ebene ou de blanc yvoire ou de bouys* [combs (*pegnes*) of ebony, white ivory or boxwood (*buys*)]. In the Venturini Invt., Venice, 1454, we find *Una pectenis de avolio et operatus et depictus auro* [a comb of carved ivory painted with gold]. In the Genoese Busarini Invt., 1461, an ivory comb is given as *Pecten unum anofancto* [of elephant], the next item being a large mirror. As for ebony combs, we have *tres pecteni eburnei ligati in una carta* [three ebony combs tied in a *carta*; the last word may mean a parchment or cardboard case] in the Ruzzini Invt., Venice, 1453.

18 Ludwig, *op. cit.*

19 See n. 17.

20 Ludwig, *op. cit.*

21 Malaguzzi Valeri* (p. 335) cites a late 15th century Milanese inventory in which is listed *uno rastello intarsiato* [decorated with *intarsio*].

22 Ludwig, *op. cit.*, tried to envisage its appearance but his drawing is not very convincing.

The Furniture of Hygiene
Wash-basins pp. 242–5

1 Fynes Moryson*, p. 419. That Italians thought themselves cleaner than foreigners is rather indicated by a letter Isabella d'Este received from a courtier visiting Vienna in 1511 whence he reports that the women have pretty faces but are rather dirty [*un poco sporche*] and have grubby and rough hands, and also by a communication from an Italian travelling in France in 1516 saying much the same [*le dame francese sono belli di molto ma . . . hanno le man sporche e pieni di rogna*] (A. Luzio and R. Renier, 'Il Lusso d'Isabella d'Este, *Nuova Antologia*, year XXI, series LXIII, Vol. XI. Rome 1896, pp. 468–9.

2 We deal with bathrooms later (p. 315). In this present section we are concerned with washing and the equipment this requires, in so far as this affects the appearance and furnishing of rooms (other than the bathroom – which was not quite such a rare feature as one might imagine).

3 Some historians today find it difficult to believe that one could keep clean without the back-up of modern plumbing but even at the beginning of this century (and perhaps much more recently, in rural districts) children were taught how to wash themselves all over, using only a basinfull of water. You do not have to lie stewing for hours in a hot bath in order to achieve this happy state; that it may be pleasanter is quite another matter.

4 Olivier de Serres (*Théâtre d'agriculture et Mesnage des Champs*, Paris, 1600) recommended rubbing the teeth with *un linge net, un peu rude* [a clean piece of linen, not too fine] and he urged his readers to do so both before and after meals using fresh water that was not too cold.

5 See E. Rodocanachi, *La Femme italienne à l'epoque de la Renaissance*, Paris, 1907, p. 104.

6 If only because Domenico Bruni, in his *Difese delle Donne* [In Defence of Women] published in 1552 assures us that 'women are by nature given to cleanliness' (see also p. 348).

7 A. Piccolomini, *La Raffaella. Dialogo nel quale si ragiona della bella creanza delle donne stordito intronato*, Venice, 1562.

8 See L. Beltrami (Polifilo), *La Guardaroba di Lucrezia Borgia*, Milan, 1903. The Duchess insisted that she and her ladies-in-waiting did not want to arrive in Ferrara *tutta sbattuta e sconquassata* [which may be translated as 'absolutely shattered and exhausted']; besides, she was of a retiring nature [*assai solitaria e remota*] and cannot have enjoyed the rigours and hurly-burly of such a journey – the noise, the discomfort, the raucous muleteers, the fussing equerries, the stolid guards, the night stops, the crossing of frontiers, and the gawping locals amazed by the passing of such a glamorous procession (Lucrezia was mounted on a white mule covered with cloth of silver; she wore cloth of gold lined with ermine). As for her hair, at one stop she complained she had not washed it for a week. At the time it was described as being 'golden'. A lock of it, sent to Cardinal Bembo, is now said to be in the Ambrosiana Library, Milan; Byron, who saw it in 1816 and stole a single hair from the lock, claimed it was 'long – and fair & beautiful' and 'the prettiest and finest imaginable – I never saw fairer' (*Byron's Letters and Journals*, Vol. 5, ed. Leslie A. Marchand, London, 1976, pp. 114–16, 118 and 123).

9 Rodocanachi, *op. cit.*

10 *Ibid.*

11 In the Pucci Invt., Florence, 1449 are listed *3 capelli di rimbiondire* [3 hats for re-enblonding].

12 F. Cognasso, *Società e Costume*, II, Turin, 1965.

13 Luzio and Renier, *op. cit.*, p. 45.

14 Filarete*, XVI, f. 129–130.

15 Giuseppe Ermini (ed.), *Ordini et Officij alla corte del Serenissimo Signor Duca d'Urbino*, Rome, 1931.

16 A. Luzio and R. Renier, *Mantova e Urbino*, Turin, 1893, pp. 230–31.

17 Pandiani* (p. 75), faced with the same entry, believed this *stangono* was a water-cistern suspended above the brass basin so that water could flow from it (presumably regulated by a tap) down over the hands into the basin below [*sotto*]. He may have been right.

18 Schiaparelli* (p. 88 *et seq.*) has an interesting section on *acquai*.

19 There has been much discussion of the meaning of the term *guardanappe* which was a cloth, usually of linen and often quite fine, which was long – anything from $3\frac{3}{4}$ to 8 *braccia* at Ferrara, according to Pardi*, and in one case 20 *braccia*, if an entry in the Guinigi Invt., Lucca, 1430 has been interpreted correctly. *Guardanappi* are not present in such large numbers as napkins. The word would seem to indicate that this cloth somehow protected the table-cloth [*nappe*]. It has been suggested that these long cloths lay across the knees of several diners sitting together on a bench, ready for them to wipe their hands on instead of using the fine tablecloth. This may have been its original purpose but what probably distinguished this cloth was its length in relation to a fairly narrow width, so when it came to be used for other purposes (like the washing of hands, the serving of wine, or holding together a stack of dishes; Pls 39, 275) it still retained its old name and, in all these roles, it served to protect other more valuable cloths – chiefly tablecloths but also sheets, if used at the bedside, or people's clothes. We can almost certainly discount the suggestion that it was a cloth somehow associated with a drinking-vessel [*nappo*].

20 A magnificent household like that of Paolo Guinigi, the powerful *signore* of Lucca, could make a brave show at meals with its small eating forks [*forchette*] already by 1430 (Guinigi Invt.). There were twelve with finials in the form of small French dogs [*cagnoletti franceschi in testa*], a dozen with lion-finials, and a further dozen with leopards, as well as three with wildmen [*homini salvatichi*] and two more, one of which had a handle of rock-crystal: all were of silver-gilt. A fork might also be called *un imbrochatoio* (see Tura Invt., 1483, p. 86).

21 By 1608, the practice was still regarded as curious to any Englishman. Thomas Coryat (*Crudities . . .*), after travelling in Italy in 1608, noted the widespread use of forks in Italy ('in all those Italian cities through which I passed'), adding that he did not believe other nations used them, 'only Italy'. Beaumont and Fletcher poked fun at 'the fork-carrying foreigner' but Ben Jonson made one of his characters speak of 'The laudable use of forks, Brought into custom here as they are in Italy, To the sparing of napkins' (*The Devil's an Ass*, 1616).

22 Filarete*, Book IX, p. 254 and 269.

23 W. Stengel, *Alte Wohnkultur*, Berlin, 1958.

24 Anton Francesco Doni, *Lettere*, Venice, 1545, No. LXXII.

Close-stools pp. 245–9

1 C. Lupi, 'La Casa pisana nel Medioevo', *Archivio Storico Italiano*, V, XXVII, 1901, p. 73. See also Schiaparelli*, p. 87. City authorities issued regulations concerning the emptying of the cesspits in which the ordure from such primitive latrines was collected.

2 Frommel*, pl. 146a; on p. 85, draws attention to a communal latrine that used to be situated in the Palazzo della Cancelleria in Rome, on a mezzanine-floor reached

by stairs leading up from the courtyard. Five seats were separated by thin walls.

3 Niccolò Machiavelli, *Le Lettere*, edited by F. Gaeta, Milan, 1961, letter of 10th Dec. 1513.

4 Gilles Corrozet, *Les Blasons Domestiques*, 1539 (reproduced recently in *Furniture History Vol.* xxv, 1989).

5 The architect Francesco di Giorgio has quite a lot to say on this question, in his treatise which dates from about 1480. One problem must have been up-draughts bringing smells back up the drainpipe. A tight-fitting stopper-like lid that sealed off the top or 'seat end' of the pipe would have gone some way to reduce this. Corrozet, *op. cit.*, speaks of the need to keep the lid shut. Lupi, *op. cit.*, claims that the cover was called a *berretta*.

6 Alberti*, v, p. 108.

7 Este Invt., Ferrara, 1436. The *guardacamera* contained a chest with clothes, a ewer and basin for washing, and the aforementioned close-stool.

8 The unsatisfactory nature of the Duchess's arrangement could perhaps go some way towards explaining a passage in Cellini's memoirs. Her husband had ordered Cellini to carry out some work that necessitated passing through the Duchess's apartment, and continuing to do so for several months. This irritated the Duchess who in consequence tried to hinder his passage by that route and had the doors locked against him. Cellini was therefore forced 'to wait a long while, because the Duchess occupied the cabinets for her personal necessities. Her habit of body was unhealthy, and so I never came without incommoding her.' Although the doors were unlocked to let him pass, nevertheless 'occasionally while walking noiselessly and unexpectedly through her private rooms, I came upon the Duchess at a highly inconvenient moment'. Not surprisingly she was furious. See *The Autobiography of Benvenuto Cellini*, ed. Charles Hope and Alessandro Nova, Oxford, 1983, p. 190.

9 Louis XIII of France, who came to the throne in 1601, remarked to a friend that he did not much enjoy being a king. There were two things he couldn't get used to – dining on his own and defecating with people present (Havard* '*Guarde-robe*'). This shows that he had not had to do these things before, and we can be fairly sure that no Italian prince, let alone his wife, would have been less fastidious with regard to the King's second point.

10 Florio*, in his dictionary of 1611, tells us that a close-stool might be called a *Moredale* but the term has not been noted in any of the inventories surveyed for the present work. In the same connection he also gives *Selletta* but our only reference to such a 'small seat' is very early (Acciaiuoli Invt., 1363) where we find one of iron with its basin (*Seletta di ferro per la camera, cho lo suo bacino*).

11 Florio, '*Cantharo* ... Also a close-stoole pan'. He says the same of a *pitale*, 'a close-stoole, or the pan for it'; however, Bianca Maria Sforza had a *pitale* of silver which makes it more likely that this served a slightly different purpose (see p. 249). *Pandiani** (p. 102) discusses these matters, suggesting that a box or vessel containing earth for scattering on the contents of the pan formed part of the equipment of a close-stool.

12 Gabriella Cantini Guidotti, 'Tre Inventari di Bicchierai Toscani ... ', Accademia della Crusca, *Quaderno 2*, Florence, 1983, p. 120.

13 Medici Invt., Paris, 1589*.

14 John Russell, in *The Book of Nurture*, a 15th-century manual on baby-care, asks the parents or nurse to 'Look

there be blankit cotyn or lynyn to wipe the nether ende.' But grown-ups too had need of what one Tudor Englishman called 'an arse wype'. Louis XI of France had some *estouppes de lin ... pour servir en ses chambres et retraict* (Gay*). In the household-regulations for the court at Urbino under Duke Guidobaldo, it was laid down that every night his close-stool should be set out and equipped with 'excrement cloths' (*spercatori de tela*) that were of a somewhat rough texture and always kept white. (G. Ermini, editor, *Ordini et Offitij alla corte del Serenissimo Signor Duca d'Urbino*, Rome, 1931).

The *orinale* p. 249

1 The actual term used in this case was *vaso urinaceo*.

2 *Uno orinario di lotono* (of latten) listed in the Di Challant Invt., Turin, 1522, where a footnote refers to the Prince of Savoy's silver *orinale* made by a Milanese goldsmith (*ung urinal dargent*).

3 *l orinale colla vesta* (Uzzano Invt., 1424*); *3 veste d'orinale di velluto co'lor cordoni* (of velvet, with their cords) (Medici Invt., 1553).

4 *2 orinali di panno rosso con lor cordoni di seta et d'oro in vesta di quoio rosso* (which implies they had an inner case of red woollen cloth and a protective case of red leather) (Medici Invt., 1553).

5 See Guidotti*, Glossary and p. 112. The same authority notes a reference of 1546 to an *orinale da stillare* which must be a flask of *orinale* shape used in the process of distilling liquids – in a still.

6 *U' seggietta coperto di panno rosso, U' horinale simile* (Medici Invt., 1598; several more sets are listed).

7 Further information about the *orinale* is to be found in Giovanni Cav, 'Urologhi, Uromanti, Uroscopi e la Matula', *Rivista di Storia delle Scienze Medicinali e Naturali*, ix, Siena, 1927.

8 Caro Invt., Rome, 1578.

9 In the Trivulzio Invt., Milan, 1529*, we find *dui bochali per andar de notte, de terra* (two bowls of earthenware, for going in the night). Florio* has '*Boccale da pisciare*, a pisse-pot'. *Pots à pisser* were not rare in France (see Havard*, 'Pot de chambre'), nor for that matter, in Germany where they were sometimes called *Nachtscherben* (night bowls; 1529) while in 1580 a document refers to *Töpfen für die betten* (bowls for the beds) in the plural, as if these were a common feature (W. Stengel, *Alte Wohnkultur*, Berlin, 1958).

10 The next item after the Trivulzio chamber-pot mentioned in the previous note is *Un pistone de bronzo* which aptly describes a clyster. In the Pucci Invt., Florence, 1449, mention is made of *un serviziale*. *Florio** gives 'Servigiale ... Also a glister'.

Perfume-burners pp. 249–51

1 M. Bandello, *Novelle*, ed. G. Brognoligo, Bari, 1928, iii, p. 53.

2 See G. Ludwig, 'Restello, Spiegel und Toilettenutensilien in Venedig zur Zeit der Renaissance', *Venzianische Hausrat ...* , (Kunsthistorisches Institut, Florenz), Berlin, 1908, pp. 268–71.

The Realm of Women
Birth-trays pp. 252–3

1 The birth of St John the Baptist is often depicted in a similar manner.

2 Men are not present in these scenes. Perhaps they called on some later occasion, after a longer interval had passed. Men, incidentally, had sometimes to be a little careful not to express their delight at seeing the new-born with too much enthusiasm. When Vittoria da Tolfa had given birth to a son in 1501, in Naples, one Roderigo of Seville rushed into the bedchamber (which was full of other well-wishers), fell on his knees and kissed the child. Next day he was found stabbed and dead in a back street (See E. Rodocanachi, *La Femme italienne à l'époque de la Renaissance*, Paris, 1907, p. 3).

3 A fine Ferrarese birth-tray is in the Museum of Fine Arts, Boston, Mass.

4 Lydecker, *Ceti**, p. 61.

5 See Tura Invt., 1483, for an erudite footnote by Curzio Mazzi on the meaning of this word which has to do with having passed through the dangers of childbirth.

6 John Pope-Hennessy and Keith Christiansen, *Secular Painting in 15th century Tuscany*, New York, (Metropolitan Museum of Art), 1980.

Cradles pp. 253–7

1 Eames*, pp. 93–107. In this important essay the author cites a reference of about 1281 to the need for two cradles on the occasion of a royal birth 'one for day and one for night', and provides much evidence for the richness of state cradles north of the Alps. When her daughter-in-law was due to bear a child, the Duchess of Burgundy ordered from Paris a cradle that was so fine it required a special travelling-case. On its arrival at Arras it was gilded and painted by the Duke's court painter. It had a red and gold coverlet lined with no less than 1200 skins of ermine.

2 The description is included in a letter written by Teodora Angelini, a lady-in-waiting at the Court of Ferrara, who was in attendance on Eleonora d'Este, princess of Aragon and the mother of Beatrice, who had come to Milan for the occasion (Malaguzzi Valeri*, pp. 329–31).

3 If the cradle really had four posts (i.e. they were not simply short posts, at the corners), and was therefore like the very newest form of bed (see p. 135), they will have supported a tester (*cielo*) with valances but at this time the form would have been so new that the writer called it a *sparviero*. As we know (see p. 124), this was a suspended form of tester that hovered 'like a sparrow-hawk', a feature rather different from the flat tester held up over a posted bed.

4 The child's grandmother, Eleonora of Aragon, Duchess of Este.

5 Malaguzzi Valeri*, p. 333.

6 Manni*, p. 42.

7 Jervis, *Design Dict**.

8 These costly objects, that embodied so much family pride, tended to be preserved. A Medici cradle was kept in a cabinet of curiosities at the Palazzo Vecchio on the *terrazzino* (*una culla di noce grande ...*); see Medici Invt., Florence, 1553.

9 Ettore Verga, 'Le Leggi suntuarie milanesi', *Archivio Storico Lombardo*, Vol. ix, year xxv, Milan, 1898, p. 63.

Flowers and Vegetation Indoors pp. 260–61

1 The vases with Madonna lilies often placed by artists between the figures of Mary and the Angel, in 15th-century scenes of the Annunciation, are there solely for symbolic reasons. Although they sometimes tell us something about costly vases, the placing of them in a vulnerable position out on the floor looks highly improbably and was probably not a practice adopted by people who valued their possessions.

2 Francesco Priscianese, *Del governo delle corte d'un signore a Roma*, Rome, 1542, explains that one of the duties of the *cameriere* [today a waiter, but in those days a servant who looked after the bedchamber (*camera*)] was to strew all sorts of flowers and greenery on the bedroom floor (*ogni cosa di fiori e di frondi*). Among the 21 best 'strewing herbs' were basil, camomile, cowslips, lavender, roses, sage, pennyroyal and hyssop, according to Thomas Tusser's *500 Points of Good Husbandry* (1610). A wider range was probably available to people living further south.

3 Cited by *Molmenti**, Ch. VIII, p. 251.

4 Battista Platina, a Cremonese humanist, also explained how you should cast flowers on the tablecloth in spring, scent the room in winter, and throw greenery on the floor in summer (*De honesta voluptate et valetudine*, Rome, 1475 (Latin edition), 1508 (first Italian edition).

5 Janet Ross, *The Early Medici*, London, 1910.

6 Priscianese, *op. cit.*, says that there were a thousand ways of composing *fiori, erbe e radici*.

7 An interesting paper in this connection is Gianni Venturi's 'Il giardino e la letteratura ...' (Acts of the Conference on giardino Storico Italiano, held at Siena and S. Quirico d'Orcia in October, 1978).

8 See Burckhardt, *Architecture**.

9 G. B. Rossetti, *Dello Scalco*, Ferrara, 1584, p. 292 *et. seq.* The key passage reads *piu cosi di verdura ... i letti nelle camere dell'istessa verdura & un tavolino per camera fatto piu di verdura.*

10 Fynes Moryson*, p. 422.

11 Ludovico Frati, 'Giuocchi ed Amori alla corte d'Isabella d'Este', *Archivio Storico Lombardo*, Vol. IX, year XXV, Milan, 1898, p. 358.

Icons and Other Wondrous Things
Detached Pictures pp. 261–8

1 There were only ten pictures in the patrician Minerbetti family's Florentine *palazzo* in 1493; four were devotional, one was a portrait, there was a hunting scene, and the remaining four were unspecified in the inventory (Schiaparelli*, p. 184; his whole Chapter III is of interest in the present connection).

2 Lydecker, Thesis*, p. 178.

3 List of objects in the trousseau of Benvenuta Marascu; see Salvatore Salomone-Marino, 'Le pompe nuziali e il corredo delle donne Siciliane ne' secoli XIV, XV e XVI', *Archivio Storico Siciliano*, new series I, 1876.

4 Lydecker, Thesis*, p. 65. f.n. 85.

5 *Ibid., loc. cit.*

6 Schiaparelli*, p. 179; see also Martin Wackernagel, *The World of the Florentine Renaissance Artist*, transl. from the German by Alison Luchs, Princeton University Press, New Jersey, 1981, pp. 103 and 173.

7 See Evelina Borea, 'Stamp figurativa e pubblico', in the Einaudi *Storia dell' Arte*, Vol. II, p. 322.

8 The Duchess asks her mother to *farme retrare al naturale la Excellentia del s. Mio padre et Vostra et tutti li miei Illustri fratelli et sorelle perche oltre adornamento delle studio a vederli me dava continua consolatione et pacere* (have made for me portrait likenesses from life of ... my father and yourself and of all my brothers and sisters (there were many as her father had married twice) as these would not only serve to adorn my *studio* but seeing them would give me continual consolation and pleasure); Dora Thornton, Thesis*; p. 14.

9 In the study of paintings listed in Parisian inventories between 1560 and 1610, three pictures with glazed frames were noted (G. Wildenstein, *Le Goût pour la peinture dans la bourgeoisie parisienne ...*, Paris, 1962, p. 19). No Italian references prior to 1600 have been noticed; Dora Thornton found two in a Venetian inventory of 1606, however (see previous note).

10 First published in Rome in 1956, ed. Adriana Marucchi. A chapter concerns the acquisition, hanging and conservation of pictures. Particularly useful in the present context is Lydecker's thesis*.

11 It was of course expected that pictures in a collection would have been chosen for their beauty – even if they were 'lascivious'. The owner should only peruse paintings of this class, Mancini insisted, when wishing 'to create offspring of equal beauty'. A century and a half earlier, Alberti had had a rather similar notion (see p. 37).

Sculptures in various media pp. 268–9

1 Schiaparelli*, p. 181.

2 *Ibid.*, p. 184.

3 In the 16th century, members of the Florentine sculptors' guild apparently had a song which they used during the Carnival. 'Who wants some elegant statuette for their delight?/You can have it above your bed or on a little stand./Our figures make every room look good.' P. Burke, *The Italian Renaissance; Culture and Society in Italy*, Cambridge, 1986.

4 Schiaparelli*, p. 187. In the Capponi Invt., Florence, 1534, we also find seven *fighure di tera colore di bronzo*. It must not be thought that this medium was only used by inferior artists. Donatello made a *Pietà 'In creta colorita a bronzo dorato'.*

5 Dora Thornton, Thesis*, p. 168.

6 Lydecker, Thesis*, p. 120.

7 Gabriella Cantini Guidotti, 'Tre Inventari di Bicchierai Toscani ... ', Accademia della Crusca, *Quaderno 2*, Florence, 1983, p. 119. On p.117 is a similar entry - a *chrosifiso quadro di gesso*.

8 Lydecker, Thesis*., pp. 72–4.

9 Much that is relevant to matters considered here is to be found in Jennifer Montagu's *Roman Baroque Sculpture*, Yale University Press, New Haven and London, 1989.

Arms and armour pp. 269

1 *Se peraventura voi mi domanderete, quali ornamenti più di tutti gli altri desiderarei in casa mia; vi risponderò senza molto pensarci Arme, & Libri ...* (Sabba di Castiglione,

I Ricordi, Venice, 1560, p. 75).

2 Montaigne noted that in Padua no one carried a sword, contrasting this with Germany where everyone did – every man, that is. The implication of his remark is that no one in Italy did so. Montaigne*, p. 1184.

3 Richard Goldthwaite, 'The Empire of Things: Consumer Demand in Renaissance Italy', *Patronage, Art and Society in Renaissance Italy*, Humanities Research Centre, Canberra, Clarendon Press, Oxford, 1987, p. 160.

Clocks and scientific instruments pp. 270–72

1 The high regard in which clockmakers were held, in the first half of the *quattrocento*, is nicely demonstrated by the way the Marquis of Ferrara, Niccolò III, arranged that the craftsman who had come to set up clocks in some Este residences (Bartolomeo da Padova) should be provided with lodging for himself and his assistant, money for whatever food he desired, as well as the fuel and iron he needed for his business. See *Manni**, p. 14.

2 Portrait by Titian in the Uffizi, Florence. The Duchess was Isabella d'Este's daughter and was used to having the best in every way. Her jewellery is superb, she carries a sable stole with a magnificent bejewelled head, she has a lap-dog that lies alongside the clock which is lantern-shaped, with a domed top surmounted by five small figures forming finials. See also n. 14 under 'Musical instruments' below.

3 Manni*, p. 126.

4 Manni*, p. 128.

5 Hour-glasses were mostly utilitarian objects but some were decorative and delicately made. We can be fairly sure that the *orologio da polvere che non sia grande* (clock with powder, which should not be large) that Isabella d'Este ordered in Venice through Lorenzo da Pavia, her discriminating agent in that city, was an exquisite object. The term *orologio da sabione* (with sand) sometimes occurs in inventories (see A. Luzio and R. Renier, 'Il lusso di Isabella d'Este', *Nuova Antologia*, year XXXL, series LXIII, Vol. XI, Rome, 1896, p. 73).

Musical instruments pp. 272–4

1 Manni*, p. 20.

2 Sabba da Castiglione, *I Ricordi*, Venice, 1560, p. 000.

3 Lorenzo da Pavia was clearly a man of discrimination. He acted as agent in the acquisition of art objects in Venice on behalf of Isabella d'Este (see p. 152).

4 Coffin*.

5 Florio* also, confusingly, gives us 'Manicord, a rigoll (regal) or claricords', 'Cembalo, a Cymball or Timbell'. 'Clavicembalo, an instrument like vigoles (virginals)' and 'Gravicembalo, an instrument of Musicke like our Claricoes'. But he seems to get nearest to the truth with his interpretation of 'Monocordo'.

6 A clavichord is clearly depicted in *tarsie* in the *studiolo* of the Duke of Urbino (1479–82). The earliest surviving Italian clavichord is dated 1543 and was made by one Domenico of Pesaro (see *The New Grove Musical Instrument Series*, ed. Edwin Ribbin, London, 1989, pp. 143–50; also Hanns Neupert, *Das Klavichord*, Kassel, 1948).

7 As the previous note makes clear, the term could be spelt in different ways. *Clavachimbrum* is a further variant (Frossasco Invt., Piedmont, 1512).

8 Boccaccio, writing in the middle of the 14th century has a character 'wrap up' or pack his harpsichord. (*rincartare il cembalo suo*); *Decameron**, VIII.

9 Illustrated in the catalogue of the *Splendours of the Gonzaga* exhibition, (Victoria and Albert Museum, 1981–2), p. 91. See also S. Bertelli and others, *Italian Renaissance Courts*, London, 1968, p. 89.

10 See the author's *Musical Instruments as Works of Art*, the Victoria and Albert Museum, London, 1968 and, in a much revised edition with some colour illustrations, in 1982. It has to be admitted that the reproduction of the photographs in the earlier edition is far clearer. The Museum's collection of 16th century Italian keyboard instruments must be second to none.

11 *Una arpa nella sua vesta di quoio nero* [a harp in its black leather case] is listed in the Medici Invt., 1553. A harp decorated with fine 'miniature' paintwork is discussed here on p. 99.

12 Medici Invt., Rome, 1598, p. 258.

13 See *Musical Instruments as Works of Art*, (n. 5, above) where this instrument is also illustrated.

14 Laurence Libin, *Keyboard Instruments*, Metropolitan Museum, New York, 1989, p. 3. The Duchess of Urbino who originally owned this instrument was also the owner of a very fine clock which was mentioned earlier (p. 270) and is depicted in her portrait by Titian.

Birds and their cages pp. 274–5

1 Manni*, p. 88.

2 Ruzzini Invt., 1543.

Lighting pp. 275–82

1 The Duke of Milan's household regulations of 1485 stipulated that all left over candle-ends should be handed in, presumably so that they could be melted down and the wax re-used for fresh candles. Those who failed to do so were to be refused candles next time. See Beltrami*.

2 L. Frati, 'Giuochi ed Amori alla corte d'Isabella d'Este', *Archivio Storico Lombardo*, Vol. IX, year XXV, 1898, Milan, p. 360.

3 Molmenti*, p. 253.

4 Snuffing is the act of trimming the wick during which process it is easy to snuff out the light by mistake. Special silver snuffing-scissors with a box on top to hold the cut off charred wick were known in England around 1550 and the form was no doubt known in Italy too (see Alistair Laing, *Lighting*, Victoria and Albert Museum, London, p 37).

5 Tura Invt., Siena, 1430, f.n. p. 72.

6 Bandello*, XXV. Priscianese* speaks of the quantity of candles required in a grand household. The proportion of tallow candles used was far higher. Especially fine wax candles were to be used on the master's dining table (only four of them, on normal occasions) which could later be carried into his bedchamber. Stout candles of 'yellow wax' (i.e. less refined) called *torce* were used when bringing food from kitchen to table or when the master went about the town.

7 (Johann Burchard), *Being an Account of the Reign of Pope Alexander VI written by his Master of Ceremonies ...* , edited and translated by Geoffrey Parker, London, 1963, p. 165.

8 Molmenti*, p. 628. Letter to her husband, Lodovico Sforza.

9 Thornton, 17th cent. Int. Dec.*, pp. 278–81.

10 *3 candelabri di legno* (Aleardi Invt., Verona, 1408*); *7 candelieri di ferro vernichati neri* (Uzzano Invt., Florence, 1424); *cinque candelieri di ferro stagnato* (tinned) (*Medici Invt., Florence, 1492*); *candelleri tri de cristallo cum li pedi e cima dargento* (three ... with feet and top of silver) (Trivulzio Invt., Milan, 1469). *Cristallo* could here possibly mean glass rather than crystal.

11 *3 candelieri a la domaschina* (Capponi Invt., Florence, 1534); *6 candelerios de damasco* (Ricobono Invt., Genoa, 1451); *candelabri damasche cum argento* (Lomellini, Genoa, 1459).

12 Frommel*, p. 72, citing G. Ermini (ed.) *Ordini et Offitij alla corte del Serenssimo Signor Duca d'Urbino*, Rome, 1931.

13 *Decameron**, VIII, X.

14 Aulo Greco, *Annibal Caro*, Rome, 1950.

15 Ermini, *op. cit.*, p. 28. It was, incidentally, also laid down that the *credenza* should be illuminated with lanterns (presumably in order to make sure the guests could see its splendour but also, no doubt, to discourage those who might think of stealing plate from the Ducal 'cup-board'. The Duke's private dining-room (*salotto*) might also be lit by lanterns in the corners of the room or by a candlestand or a page holding a candlestick standing in the middle of the room.

16 Leonardo Ginori Lisci, *I Palazzi di Firenze ...*, Florence, 1972, Vol. II, p. 714 (illus.).

Part Three: Architectural Planning
The Distribution of Rooms p. 284

1 Jean Courtonne, *Traité de la Perspective*, Paris, 1725. The key phrases are *la principale et la plus essentielle ... toutes les autres lui etant, pour ainsi dire, subordinnées*, and *à quoi serviraient vos efforts si votre plan est mal distribué*.

2 G. Fiocco, *Alvise Cornaro, il suo tempo e le sue opere*, Venice, 1965, p. 156.

3 Hoby, p. 125. He added that this was a reason why such people preferred to surround themselves with somewhat humble attendants – 'persons of no great qualitie in other things but in knowing how to attende about their [the great man's] person.' Middle-class personal staff often rose to great heights through being trusted employees of the great (see p. 13).

4 Francesco di Giorgio*, p. 72. He was writing about princely houses and those of gentlemen of consequence (*le case de' principi e gran signori*) in which it was more important to try and get these things right than in the houses of lesser mortals – although precisely where the cut-off point came must have depended on individual judgement. It also changed with the date, for what had been considered a splendid house in 1480 would seem fairly modest in 1550. But while the 'window' might have shifted, the distinction was still being made in the second half of the 16th century. Anton Francesco Doni, for instance, used the phrase *da Re, de Duca, et da potente, et*

valoroso signore (of a king, a duke, or a powerful and valiant gentleman) when speaking of a splendid building (A. F. Doni, *Le Ville*, Bologna, 1566).

The *Camera* and the *Sala* pp. 285–91

1 What follows here is about Italian Renaissance buildings but the general pattern came to be applied to the arrangements adopted in other European countries.

2 The character and function of *camere* and *sale* is amusingly set out in a conversation given in Anton Francesco Doni's *I Marmi*, Venice, 1552, p. 138. One man complains that bedchambers have become too small so that you could scarcely put a bed, a table and a couple of chests in them. The second speaker reminds him that bedchambers are for sleeping in, not for passing through or for dining, nor are they for dancing in [*le camere son fatte per dormire, & non per passegiare, o banchettarvi, ne per ballarvi*]. 'That's what *sale* are for', and he than goes on to paint a charming picture of daily life in the *sala* of what seems to be a gentleman's house of some size. The women stand near the window, both so as to benefit from the light in order to do their needlework, and also so as to be able to go to the window more easily in order to look out and see what is going on; at the high-table people are dining while to one side some are playing (cards? chess? backgammon?), several people are passing through the room and some stand by the fire – it is a place everyone can use [*Le Donne si stanno a piedi delle finestre, si per vedere a lavorare con l'Agole cose sottili & i ricami; si per potere esser commode a farsi alla finestra; alla tavola intesta si mangia, a quello lato si gioca, alcuni passeggiano, altri si stanno al fuoco et cosi v'e luogo per tutti ...*]. I am much indebted to Dora Thornton for providing me with this delightful quotation.

3 However, when there was more than one bed in a principal bedchamber, the fact was remarked upon. For example, there was a *chamera della dua letta* [the chamber of the two beds] in the Palazzo Medici in Florence at the end of the 15th century; it was on the ground floor and may have been a guest room (W. A. Bulst, Die Ursprüngliche innere Aufteilung des Palazzo Medici in Florenz, *Mitteilungen des Kunsthistorischen Institutes in Florenz*, XIV, 1970, p. 377).

4 In Caro Invt., 1578 one room described as a *stanza attigua alla sala* [next to the *sala*] contained a simple bed that was probably a servant's.

5 Alberti*, V, Ch. XVII.

6 *Decameron**, III. As Boccaccio puts it, the king would *uscire della sua camera ... ed andare alla camera della reina*.

7 Alberti*, *loc. cit.*. The 1550 translation from Latin into Italian gives this as *non bisogna che un'uomo nobile sia peggio assortito che le grue o le rondini*. The allusion is of course to the annual migration to warmer climes of these two birds.

8 R. Magnuson, *Studies in Roman Quattrocento Architecture*, Stockholm, 1958, p. 153. Nicholas V intended to have suites on *three* levels in his new apartment at the Vatican – the ground floor for spring and autumn; there is no record that the pope ever moved up and down in this way, however. Anyway, the 'winter floor' was soon to become the Borgia Apartment and the top floor Raphael's *stanze*.

9 Francesco di Giorgio*, p. 329.

10 See Ludovico Frati, 'Giuochi ed Amori alla corte

d'Isabella d'Este', *Archivio Storico Lombardo*, IX, year xxv, Milan, 1898.

11 L. B. Alberti, *Della Famiglia*, R. N. Watkins transl., Columbia Univ. of S. Carolina Press, 1969, p. 209, written in the early 1430s.

12 e.g. Boccaccio describes an abbot leaving his *camera* in order to go and eat in his *sala* (*Decameron**, I, 7). While the abbot's rooms were apparently very splendid, one gets the impression that he did not have all that many other rooms. Lydecker, Thesis*, shows that in some Florentine inventories the room is actually called a *sala de mangiare*.

13 See Frommel*, I, pp. 83–4, on the *tinello* which had been a grand dining-room in the early 14th century, for example in the Vatican, but gradually lost its status to become the dining-room of the *gentilhuomini*, the gentlemen who were not members of the owner's personal family or were not of equal standing to him. Thus when the learned Annibale Caro had to stay in the house of strangers, and he was acting as secretary to a great man who *did* dine at the owner's table, he – Caro – was expected to eat with officers of the household in the *tinello* rather than with the quality. In the Acciaiuoli Invt., 1363, we already see the distinction for there, among the long lists of silver plate, some vessels are described as being *da tinello* (for the *tinello*) and as the weight of these items seems to be less than that of similar but grander pieces, we can infer that they were more modest items for use in this secondary dining-room. Priscianese* (p. 81) explained that those who dined in the *tinello* in his day (1542) were certainly classed as gentlemen and should therefore be served politely 'even if not off plates of silver or with so many dishes in the first course' [*i gentil-'uomini del tinello anche gentil'uomini sono, e da essere come quelli servite, almeno con pulitezza, se non con piatti d'argento o con tanti antipasti*] *Tinelli* were usually situated on the ground floor whereas the principal dining-room was normally on the *piano nobile* above.

14 Alberti actually maintained that the word *sala* derives from *saltare*, to dance, but it seems more likely that it is a corruption of the Latin *aula* meaning hall which of course springs from the same root. See Frommel*, I, pp. 66–70, on this point and for a more detailed discussion of the *sala*, especially in great houses in Rome during the High Renaissance.

15 See n.2, above.

16 Pardi*, pp. 21 and 170. This was presumably the *sala* in which no less than sixty-six young women foregathered on an important occasion in 1473, in order to dance, as the Court Circular of the time records (L. A. Muratori, *Rerum Italicarum ... Scriptores*, XXIV, 'Diario Ferrarese', col. 199, 214).

17 e.g. the di Negro and Lomellini Invts.*, 1456 and 1458.

18 See J. Schulz, 'The houses of Titian, Aretino and Sansovino', in *Titian*, ed. Rosand, New York, 1982, p. 111, note 51.

19 On the plan of the château at Ancy-le-Franc, in Burgundy, which Serlio designed and insisted was 'a completely Italian building', all three terms are used (Pl. XVIII of the MS of his Book VI in Avery Library, New York, which was not published until 1978; see *Sebastiano Serlio on Domestic Architecture*, Architectural History Foundation, New York, 1978). While these three terms are inscribed on the plan, the fairly large *salotto* is described in the text as a *camera*; the same applies to a (smaller) *saletta*. Moreover, the terms *salotto* and *saletta* are not inscribed

on the Munich MS version where all are labelled as being *camere*. But Serlio quite evidently found himself confused when he tried to distinguish between the three terms, as we can see in n. 21 below.

20 However, a ground-floor *salotto* in one of the Genoese palaces described by Rubens is a mere half *braccia* larger than the *sala* on the *piano nobile* above. The distinction can also have to do with the location, a *sala* always occupying a commanding position on the main floor. (See P. P. Rubens, *Palazzi di Genova*, Vol II, 1626, fig. 30, of a house designed by G. B. Castello for two Spinola brothers in the 1580s.)

21 Serlio* VII, p. 148. The key phrases are *sala sara quella che sara di doppia lunghezza alla sua larghezza, saletta, s'ella sara tre parti in larghezza & cinque in lunghezza, ma ch'ella non sia minore in larghezza, che una delle maggior camere della casa*, and *Salotto, diro a membro che sara lungo* [he must here have meant to say *largo*] *alquanto d'una delle maggior camere, ma che non possi un quadro & mezo in lunghezza*. The passage is by no means clear and he added a further definition of *saletta* which seems to contradict his first one. I am much indebted to Caroline Elam for helping me to understand this passage. At the country palace of Belriguardo, near Ferrara, the *salotti* mentioned in a description of 1497 were of widely varying sizes and proportions – 31 × 21, 30 × 13, 83 × 21 and 27 × 9 *passi* (Gundersheimer*).

22 When describing the wonders of the palace of Belriguardo at Ferrara, Sabadino degli Argenti wrote at the end of the 15th century of its splendid *camere, sale e salotti*, making no mention of *salette* (Gundersheimer*, p. 55).

23 *da ogni capo della sala vole essere uno salotto* (Francesco di Giorgio*, p. 352).

24 Frommel*, p. 70.

25 In a large house, there could of course be more than one kitchen (see pp. 315).

26 Malaguzzi Valeri*, p. 336.

27 Manni*, pp. 37–38.

28 Francesco di Giorgio*, p. 346. He is writing about the proportions of *salotti*.

29 Scamozzi*, English trans., p. 237.

30 Serlio* VII, p. 203, shows the plan of a villa which has a covered *loggia* that forms an entrance portico at the front of the house and a second uncovered *loggia* on the garden front which, when the sun was strong, could be protected by an awning (*alle hore solari vi sarà una tenda*). The plan, Pl. 399, is based on this Serlio plate. The effect produced by such an arrangement can be seen in the Psyche Loggia at the Farnesina in Rome where Raphael and his assistants have painted the ceiling to look as if it were open to the skies with two awnings stretched on a foliage-bedecked framework.

31 This information was given in a paper by Patricia Waddy, read at the Conference on Distribution held at the Centre des Etudes supérieures de la Renaissance at Tours in June 1988, which will eventually be published. (See also her excellent book, *Seventeenth-Century Roman Palaces*, (The Architectural History Foundation, New York, and the M.I.T. Press, Cambridge (Mass.) and London, 1990) which she so kindly sent to me. As it arrived a few days before the present work had to be delivered to my publisher, I could not incorporate information from it here.) Francesco di Giorgio* (p. 350) felt that a great house should have a *salotto* for dining, next to which

should be a room for the *credenza* with a staircase leading to the kitchen [*uno salotto per desinare e cena come uno ticrino (Triclinio). Apresso del quale sia la stanza del credensiere a ripositorio al servizio di quello, con una Scala che viene de al superiore cucina*].

The *Anticamera* pp. 294–5

1 Nella Gianetto, *Vittorino da Feltre e la sua scuola*, Florence, 1983, p. 171.

2 F. W. Kent and others, *A Florentine Patrician and his Palace*, London, 1981 (Engl. edn. of *Giovanni Rucellai ed il suo Zibaldone*, 1960); essay by Brenda Preyer on 'The Rucellai Palace', p. 172.

3 See Pardi*.

4 Gundersheimer*, pp. 58–68.

5 Beltrami*, p. 35.

6 Frommel*, p. 71.

7 See J. M. Fletcher, 'Isabella d'Este. Patron and Collector'. *Splendours of the Gonzaga*, ed. D. Chambers and J. Martineau, Victoria and Albert exhib. cat., London, 1981–2, pp. 51–63. See also p. 000.

8 Francesco di Giorgio*, p. 352.

9 *Ibid.*, p. 79.

10 e.g. Serlio* VII, pp. 5, 133, 137, 149.

11 See Lydecker, Thesis*.

12 G. Ermini, *Ordini et Offitij alla corte de Serenissima Signor Duca d'Urbino*, Rome, 1931.

13 Polichetti, Urbino*, p. 217, ref. room 14h, citing a description of 1590.

14 Alberti*, Bk. V, Ch. III.

The More Private Rooms pp. 296–300

1 Bandello*, in one of his stories (*Novella* III), refers to a *camerino* (see the next paragraph) that evidently lay close to a lady's bedchamber and in which one of her personal servants slept (*una de le sue donne ... dormiva*).

2 The term is used by Cosimo Bartoli in his 1550 translation, from Latin into Italian, of Alberti's treatise on architecture; Alberti*, Bk. V, Ch. XVII.

3 Luca Pacioli speaks of a *studio overo scritoio* in his *Summa de arithmetica ...*, Venice, 1494. The term *studiolo* has come into common parlance among students of these matters because this was the title of an excellent book by Wolfgang Liebenwein (Berlin, 1977) in which he traces the early history of this room-type, chiefly from the architectural view-point. More recently, my own daughter, Dora Thornton, working at the Warburg Institute in London, submitted a doctoral thesis to London University (1990) on 'The study room in Renaissance Italy, with particular reference to Venice circa 1560–1620' which takes the matter further, reviewing in depth the character, appearance and contents of what she prefers to call the *studio*. Presumably this material will one day be published. In the meantime I am very grateful to her for allowing me to cite here a number of quotations that she has discovered, and to summarize some of the points she has made. She concluded that the meanings of the words *scrittoio* and *studiolo* varied from city to city. Florentines, for example, tended to call their studies *scrittoi* whereas the desks or cabinets in these rooms (i.e. pieces of

furniture) were known as *studioli*. In Venice, on the other hand, the room was generally called a *studio* and the piece of furniture a *scrittor*. Complete agreement on these matters did of course not exist, even within a city. One Venetian merchant called his office his *scrittor* and just occasionally Florentines referred to their studies as a *studiolo*.

4 Niccolò Macchiavelli, *Lettere familiare*, ed. Alvisi, Florence, 1955; letter of 10 Dec. 1513 to Vettori.

5 As several pictures reproduced here show, shelves set above shoulder-level and running round the whole room, was a favourite arrangement in Italian *studi* (Pls 79, 295, 257). Vasari, advising Francesco de' Medici on the design of his very handsome *studio* in the Palazzo Vecchio in Florence, recommends having such a cornice which he proposed should be supported by pilasters. This would be a good way of displaying the Duke's bronze figurines, he said (Giorgio Vasari, *Ragionamento Quarto* (c.1557) in *Ragionamenti e lettere . . .*, ed. G. Milanesi, Florence, 1882, pp. 58–59).

6 Liebenwein, *op. cit.*, p. 46.

7 For instance, there were at least three in the chief Medici residence in Florence, the *palazzo* in the Via Larga which was built in the 1440s (see Liebenwein, *op cit.*, fig.17).

8 B. Cotrugli, *Della Mercatura, et del Mercante Perfetto*, Brescia, 1602; first published in 1569. He assumes that the sort of merchant who bothered to read his manual was a habitual reader.

9 *Ibid.*

10 Erasmus, 'The Ciceronian', *The Complete Works . . .*, ed. A. H. T. Levi, Toronto, p. 350–51.

11 F. W. Kent and others, 'Rucellai's Zibaldone', *Journal of the Warburg and Courtauld Institutes* London, Vol. 11, 1981, p.172; inventory of 1582.

12 Torquato Tasso, *Dialoghi*, ed. E. Mazzali, Turin, 1959, pp. 125–6.

13 Liebenwein, *op. cit.*, p. 74. The *studietto*'s floor was laid with maiolica tiles, apparently, and there was panelling with *tarsie* on the walls, while the barrel-vaulted ceiling was faced with maiolica roundels provided by Luca della Robbia (see p. 109), painted with signs of the zodiac and activities appropriate to each month. Books, which were so evident in this *studietto*, were often decorative in the 15th century but became more so in the 16th. Claudio Tolomei recommended that a fellow scholar in Genoa should have the works of ancient authors bound in green while those by modern writers should be red. He also said that a well-chosen and displayed collection of books would form 'a complete library, which will greatly ornament first your *studio* and then your soul' (A. Hobson, 'La Biblioteca di Giovanni Battista Grimani, *Atti della Società Liguria di Storia Patria*, xx, N.S., xciv, 1980, p. 111).

14 Liebenwein, *op. cit.*, p. 106 See also D. Chambers and J. Martineau, eds. *Splendours of the Gonzaga*, Victoria and Albert Museum exhib. cat., London 1981–2, notably pp. 51–63. Isabella's sister Beatrice, Duchess of Milan, had at least two closets that were perhaps even more splendid than Isabella's in Mantua; we hear of *camerini* at Vigevano castle filled with treasures – rows of beautiful glass vessels and porcelain, works in ivory and rock-crystal, games-boards (which were often of exquisite craftsmanship), vases containing rare scents, and much else (Malaguzzi Valeri*, p. 333). Well-educated upper-

class women not infrequently had private closets, it would seem. One organized in an Italian manner was to be seen at Lyons, in France; it belonged to Marguerite du Bourg and was described by Luc Antonio Ridolfi as being "excellent and ornate", with books in Tuscan, Latin and French (note the order), when he wrote a preface to Benedetto Varchi's *Lezioni d'Amore* which was published at Lyons in 1560.

15 The term *museo*, used in the modern sense, became established in the first half of the 17th century. It appears in the title of Giovanni Pietro Bellori's *Nota delli Musei, Librerie, Gallerie . . . ne' Palazzi, nelle Case . . . di Roma*, Rome, 1644. See Liebenwein, *op. cit.*, p. 163; also Oliver Impey and Arthur Macgregor eds., *The Origin of Museums*, Oxford, 1985. However, the erudite collector, Paolo Giovio, arranged his extensive collections in a specially designed villa on Lake Como which seems to have been completed in the years 1537–43. Six years later Count Giambattista Giovio wrote a *descriptio musaei* on the building and its contents. Giovio's chief interest was in celebrated personages, past and present. (see Carl Frey, *Il Codice Magliabechiano . . .*, Berlin, 1892, p. LXVI; also Stefano della Torre, 'Le Vedute de Museo Giovano', *Quaderni Erbesi*, VII, year 1985, and the same author's 'L'inedita opera primo di Paolo Giovio ed il Museo . . .', *Atti di Convegno Paolo Giovio . . .*, Como, 1983. I am very grateful to Professor della Torre for sending me these off-prints.)

16 Liebenwein, *op. cit.*, pp. 155–160.

17 *Ibid.*, p. 143.

18 *Che non è nessun personaggio, che per la vicino passi, che a quello non voglia arrivare, come una cosa meravigliosa e singolare* (Caesare Vecellios, *Degli Habiti Antichi et Moderni*, Venice, 1590, p. 219).

19 Scamozzi*, 1615, p. 306.

20 Letter of 1566 in the Biblioteca Palatina, Parma (Farnese papers), a comment kindly communicated to me by Dora Thornton.

21 e.g. that of Bartolo di Tura (Tura Invt., Siena, 1483) whose wife had a *lettera* in her bedchamber which had *uno studio a piei* (a study at the foot-end).

22 Liebenwein, *op. cit.*, p. 144. Lydecker*, in his thesis (p. 104) cites a reference of 1473 to the purchase of a piece of verdure tapestry 'for the bed in the study' (*paramento d'arazzo a verdura per letto dello scrittoio*).

23 Francesco di Giorgio*, p. 72.

24 Frommel*, p. 78.

25 Frommel*, *loc. cit.*

26 Wolfger A. Bulst, 'Die ursprüngliche innere Aufteilung des Palazzo Medici in Florenz', *Mitteilungen des Kunsthistorischen Institutes in Florenz*, XIV, 1970, p. 381, citing the Medici Invt., 1492. In the same document reference is made to a *mezza* room above Piero de' Medici's antechamber (*stanza sopra lantichamera di piero* which follows a room called *lantichamera di piero*).

27 Dora Thornton kindly drew my attention to this incident in the play, a translation by M. V. Pfeiffer of which was published in New York in 1950.

28 Serlio*, VII, p. 102.

The Apartment pp. 300–12

1 Occasionally an apartment was shared by a husband and

his wife. A week before the typescript of my book had to be delivered I received from Patricia Waddy a copy of her important new book on *Seventeenth-Century Roman Palaces. Use and the art of the plan* (the Architectural History Foundation, New York, and the M.I.T. Press, Cambridge Mass. and London) which anyone interested in the present subject should not fail to read.

2 This matter has been entertainingly explained by Mark Girouard in his *Life in the English Country House*, New Haven and London, 1978. A seminal essay on the subject was Hugh Marray-Baillie's 'Etiquette and the Planning of the state Apartments in Baroque Palaces', *Archaeologia*, CI, 1967. See also Thornton *17th cent. Int. Dec.*, pp. 52–63. An interesting essay concerning the classical Roman background to this question is Andrew Wallace-Hadrill's 'The Social Structure of the Roman House', *Papers of the British School at Rome*, Regent's College, London, Vol. LVI, 1988. I am much indebted to Professor Michael McCarthy for drawing my attention to this essay.

3 Several 'handbooks' were published between the late 15th and early 17th century explaining how a cardinal's or great man's household should be organized, and the suggested arrangements seem to have been very complicated. See Paolo Cortese, 'De Cardinalatu', *Studies in Italian Art and Architecture*, ed. M. Millon, Cambridge, Mass., 1980, in which is set out *Qualis esse debeat domus cardinalis* (that which ought to be in a cardinal's house) It was originally published in 1510; Francesco Priscianese, *Del governo della corte d'un signore in Roma* (1542), Città di Castello, 1883; Giuseppe Ermini, ed., *Ordini et Uffity alla corte del Serenissimo Duca d'Urbino* (c.1500), Rome, 1931.

4 Alberti*, v.

5 *Ibid.*

6 *Ibid.* It must always be borne in mind that Alberti wrote in Latin but that this quotation, like those made by most other students of these matters, is taken from Bartoli's translation into Italian of 1550, a whole century after Alberti had written his treatise. Bartoli's rendering was really more of a paraphrasing of Alberti, framed in the light of mid-16th-century experience, than a precise translation.

7 Francesco di Giorgio*, p. 74.

8 Manuscript copies of the original hand-written treatise (there were at least two versions) were available to most of the people who were really interested by about 1500; none of Francesco's treatises were printed before the 20th century.

9 Francesco del Borgo was a Tuscan who died in 1468. His full name was Francesco Cereo da Borgo S. Sepolcro. He had worked for Pope Nicholas V and probably belonged to the Alberti circle. Until recently his name had been virtually fogotten; it still does not appear in general books on Italian Renaissance architecture. Professor Christoph Frommel has revealed the leading part he played in the planning of the Palazzo Venezia (and therefore in the story we are telling here); see C. L. Frommel, *Der Palazzo Venezia in Rom*, Gerda Henkel Lecture, Düsseldorf 1981, Westdeutscher Verlag, 1982, and C. L. Frommel, 'Francesco del Borgo. Architekt Pius II und Pauls II', *Römisches Jahrbuch für Kunstgeschichte*, 21, 1984, and also his paper read at the Conference on Italian Renaissance Palaces at Florence in 1986 organized by the Centro 'Andrea Palladio' in Vicenza.

10 See Sabine Eiche, 'The Villa Imperiale of Alessandro

Sforza at Pesaro', *Mitteilungen des Kunsthistorischen Institutes in Florenz*, XXIX, 1985, Vol. 2/3.

11 There is a small staircase alongside the fifth room but none after the seventh or hindermost room. Could this be because the sixth and seventh rooms were set aside for Federigo's wife? Or was it because the back part of that wing was never completed?

12 The name of Maso di Bartolomeo has been put forward as the architect responsible on site (see Polichetti*, p. 59).

13 The question of who was the supreme genius primarily responsible for conceiving the main building of the Palace at Urbino in the late 1460s and early 1470s is hotly debated (see Polichetti*, *passim*). The generally held view is that it was Luciano Laurana. It has been suggested that he had worked under Brunelleschi; he had anyway worked at the courts of Mantua, Naples and Pesaro but not much is really known about him and it has been doubted whether he possessed the intellectual scope to design the very ambitious and intricate building at Urbino. However, he was surveying the existing buildings in 1465 and, three years later, was created *Ingegnero e Capo di tutti li maestri* working on the building. This has been taken to mean that he was supreme designer and co-ordinator but it could mean that he was the senior resident architect on site, working to the designs of Francesco di Giorgio, a known genius with a wide reputation, entirely capable of conceiving the amazing structure which transformed the shape of the cliff-face on which the old castle had been built, constructing a new and extremely robust curtain wall (he was the foremost fortifications engineer of his day) to form a platform for the new building (see essay by Giancarlo De Carlo, Polichetti*, pp. 3–10). Under this platform, within the space thus encompassed, are vast stables, store-rooms, cisterns and a very complex hydraulic system. Hydraulic engineering fascinated Francesco di Giorgio, much of his treatise on architecture* (c.1480) being devoted to the subject. The strength of the curtain-wall and the fact that much of the 'plumbing' would have had to be installed while the platform was being built does rather suggest Francesco should be credited with much more of the Palace than is at present commonly supposed. The very fact that the distribution of the rooms in the main apartment of the new building is not all that convenient may perhaps also be seen as a sign of Francesco's involvement, as this does not seem to have been his *forte*, judging by the rather unimaginative ground-plans he included in his treatise.

14 Of course powerful princes had ushers and guards standing around to see that people only went through those doors they were supposed to use. Nevertheless the fully-fledged apartment system ensured this without the need for an exceptionally officious staff.

15 Vasari*, in his life of Michelozzo, the architect of the Palazzo Medici, claimed that it had been the first building *con ordine moderno* (organized in the modern manner). He was writing a century after the event, by which time the concept of apartments was well established.

16 This main suite of rooms was originally created for Piero di Cosimo de' Medici. Subsequently it was occupied by his son Lorenzo 'the Magnificent'. See Wolger A. Bulst, 'Die Ursprüngliche Innere Aufteilungen des Palazzo Medici in Florenz', *Mitteilungen des Kunsthistorischen Institutes in Florenz*, XIV, 1970.

17 In the summer apartment the 'backstairs' are in front of the bedchamber. There seem to be backstairs behind the winter apartment and some more private stairs further forward. What appears to have been the Pope's private study lies right out in front of the winter suite.

18 Alberti*, V.

19 This was claimed by J. M. Perouse de Montclos at a Conference on distribution at Tours in 1988 organized by the Centre d'Etudes Supéricures de la Renaissance, the papers of which are to be published.

20 See e.g. Serlio*, VII, pp. 50–51, pp. 118–19, pp. 148–9.

21 *Palladio**, I, Chap. XXI, 'the rooms ought to be distributed on each side of the entry and hall – those on the right correspond[ing] with those on the left ... that the walls may equally bear the burden of the roof'.

22 Scamozzi*, p. 307.

Other Rooms, other levels pp. 313–19

1 Wolfger A. Bulst, 'Die ursprüngliche innere Aufteilung des Palazzo Medici', *Mitteilungen des Kunsthistorisches Institutes in Florenz*, XIV, 1970, p. 384.

2 This *loggia* has since been enclosed. See Frommel,*, I, p. 78.

3 Although hardly touching upon Italian matters, the article by Rosalys Coope on 'The Long Gallery: Its origins, development, use and decoration', *Architectural History*, London, Vol. 29, 1986, is helpful.

4 In the same Piedmontese castle was a space called the *sopra gallaria* which seems to have been used for storage. It may not be irrelevant here to mention that Francesco di Giorgio* (c. 1480) spoke of space for recreation on the top floor of a *palazzo* [*nel terzo pavimento una sala o andata circum circa per sollazzo et esercizio de' signori ...* , p. 351]. *Sala* here implies a large space; the alternative to this was a passage or corridor (*andata*) that was *circum circa* and must somehow have followed the periphery of the ground-plan, presumably. Is it possible that the upper floor of the Strozzi Palace in Florence, which was originally empty, served a similar purpose? Angelo Poliziano (d. 1494), incidentally, stated that the upper floors of large house were always unoccupied [*le gran case sempre sone disabitate da alto*]; *Tagebuch*, Jena, 1929, p. 194. (I am extremely grateful to Professor Nicolai Rubinstein for providing this reference.)

5 Manni*, p. 143.

6 Fynes Moryson*, p. 417.

7 Scamozzi*, p. 305.

8 On this whole question, see Oliver Impey and Arthur Macgregor (eds.), *The Origins of Museums. The Cabinet of Curiosities in Sixteenth- and Seventeenth-century Europe*, Oxford, 1985, especially the first three papers and figs 1–10. On Grimani's collection, see also Francesco Sansovino, *Venetia Città Nobilissima ...*, Venice, 1663, p. 372; also M. Perry, 'A Renaissance showpiece of art: the Palazzo Grimani ...*, Apollo*, CXIII, 1981, pp. 215–21.

9 Frommel*, II, pp. 116 and 130.

10 Alberti*, V.

11 Frommel*, I, p. 54.

12 Goldthwaite, *Building**, p. 103.

13 Filarete*, p. 269, shows that the flushing of latrines was understood in mid-15th century Italy. He says that *destri ... corrispondevano ne' fondamenti, e in modo ordinati che*

l'acqua dilavava via ogni bruttura. E l'acqua che pioveva in modo ordinata era che tutta si ricoglieva per li detti luoghi, e nettava, e discoreva ne' canali sotterranei [latrines are so related to the foundations that water washes away all detritus. Rainwater is collected in such a way in these places that everything is cleaned and carried away into subterranean drains]. See also Frommel,*, i, p. 85. Where rainwater was being used, it was sensible to place the latrines close to the outside walls so that downpipes from the eaves and gutters could run vertically. Massing latrines was also practical; it meant that one downpipe could serve several 'places'.

14 The *Decameron* has a character going to a bathroom which was in a very dark part of the building, probably underground [*ove l'bagno era, una camera uscura molto*, III, 6]; in another story the bathroom is near the main entrance which must be on the ground floor [*bagno vicino all'uscio*]. Francesco di Giorgio*, p. 101, explains that bathrooms have to be downstairs. The plans of Genoese *palazzi* of the 16th century show several sumptuous bathrooms, all on the ground floor (P. P. Rubens, *Palazzi di Genova* Vol. 1, 1622, C, D and I, figs 14, 17, 21 and 54.

15 On the matter of Renaissance-period baths in general, see Gustina Scaglia,"Stanze-Stufe' e 'Stanze-Camini' nei trattati di Francesco di Giorgio Martini", *Bollettino d'Arte*, No. 39–40, Sept.-Dec. 1986. See p. 172, in the present connection; a wheel [*ruota*], presumably for a bucket-chain, already existed in a small light-well in 1514 when Antonio da Sangallo had to make some alterations there.

16 Bulst, *op.cit.*, p. 377 and fig. 3 (*stufa* = 6, kitchen = 14).

17 Scaglia, *op. cit.*

18 The *chapetium panni viridis clari et alti brachorium V balneatorum* [hood of bright green cloth five *braccia* high for the bath] must have been such a *padiglione* (Borghese Invt., Venice, 1454), and so may have been the *vellata una pro balneo cum suis frixis auri* [?screening for the bath, with its fringes of gold] mentioned in the Vivaldi Invt., Genoa, 1451. Charles V of France 1380 (Charles V Invt.), had three *Paveillons ... de toille grosse a baigner le Roy*, each with two curtains.

19 The *lensolo uno de bagno* [one sheet for the bath] and the *par unum lintianinum pro balneo* [pair of sheets] in two Genoese inventories of 1488 and 1456 (*Valle Invt.* and *Negri Invt.*) were probably for lining the bath.

20 *Decameron**, VIII, 10. There is a charming description of taking a bath in romantic circumstances.

21 Negri Invt., Genoa, 1456. In the Fieschi Invt., Genoa, 1532 similar equipment is listed; *uno caldaro da bagno con la tromba*.

22 See Thornton, *17th cent. Int. Dec.**, p. 319.

23 Scaglia, *op. cit.*, p. 164. The English word 'stews' derives from the same source as well and was used in reference to public bath-houses.

24 See n.14.

25 Scaglia, *op. cit.*, p. 182, f.n. 22.

26 D. S. Chambers, 'The Housing Problems of Cardinal Francesco Gonzaga', *Journal of the Warburg Institute*, 1976, 39.

27 Polichetti,*, *passim*, especially Plan No. 18.

28 Scaglia, *op. cit.*, p. 164. A German potter, working for the Este, seems to have been such a specialist; he produced *vaxi 134 de preda vedriadi* [vases of glazed earthenware] that were needed to *tiro suxo laqua nel bagno* of the Duke in

1485, which suggests a conduit of pipes connected with the bath (Manni*, p. 76).

29 Scaglia, *op. cit.*, fig. 12 and pp. 172–3. According to Frommel* (p. 76) the Ostia bath was designed by Baccio Pontelli.

30 Scaglia, pp. 170–2. Frommel*, p. 77, claims this bath was completed in about 1524 under Clement VII.

31 Manni*, p. 73.

32 H. Bierman, 'Lo sviluppo della villa toscana sotto l'influenza umanistica della corte di Lorenzo il Magnifico', Conference on Villas, Centro 'Andrea Palladio', XI, Vicenza, 1969.

33 Manni*, p. 102.

34 Thornton, *17th cent. Int. Dec.**, pp. 319–20.

35 See Polichetti,*, pp. 187 (f.ns. 501, 503, 634).

36 Scaglia, *op. cit.*, p. 182.

37 Manni*, pp. 88–89.

38 Bartolo di Tura was a physician who was noted for having prescribed thermal baths for the ailing Pope Pius II.

39 Tura Invt., Siena, 1483.

40 Vasari*, *Life of Antonio da Sangallo, V, p. 456*. It was perhaps just as well for the history of Western art that Pope Adrian only occupied the throne of St. Peter for a few months.

41 'The Renaissance Stufetta in Rome: The circle of Raphael and the recreation of the Antique', Ph.D. thesis, University of Minnesota, 1983, University Microfilms International, Ann Arbor, Maryland.

42 Edwards' thesis, p. 72

43 Montaigne*, p. 1265.

Symmetry pp. 319–20

1 Palladio*, I, XXI. He gives, as his reason for his insistence, the need to have 'The fabric ... in one place as in the other, and that the walls may equally bear the burden of the roof'. An experienced architect like Palladio must have known perfectly well how to support a roof even if the interior walls were not symmetrically disposed. Obviously that would make it easier but the reasons for demanding symmetry lay rather deeper.

2 Francesco di Giorgio*, p. 72.

3 Francesco di Giorgio* (p. 351) speaks of the houses of gentlemen and princes having *una ornata porta et intranta in mezzo della casa, con andito o con atrio* [an ornate doorway and entrance in the middle of the (front of the) house, with passageway or atrium (inside)].

4 See the papers of the conference on 'L'Escalier dans l' Architecture de la Renaissance', held at the Centre des Etudes Supérieures de la Renaissance, Tours, 1985. Frommel*, pp. 60–6, gives an excellent brief survey of the various types of staircase used in the 16th century in Roman *palazzi*.

5 Francesco de Giorgio*, p. 352, wanted the *sala grande e principale ... sopra a la piazza* [the great and principal *sala* facing onto the square, meaning 'at the front of the house'].

6 Another perhaps more telling reason for adhering to a symmetrical disposition sprang from the current belief that the human body, which of course is roughly symmetrical, provided a model for the organic structure of a work of art – including a piece of architecture. Symmetry was also encouraged by early perspective

theory where cityscapes with a central vanishing-point became a favourite means of demonstrating the novel system. Indeed, optical theory, at least as much as anything Vitruvius had said (or was believed to have said, because he was often difficult to interpret) must have affected the architects' thinking even more fundamentally. The human figure, incidentally, was also taken as a model for the proportions of a classical column, with a Doric column being related to a well-proportioned male body, an Ionic column being determined by female proportions, and the Corinthian (the analogy for this third variant posed a problem!) being based on those of a young woman. Goethe made fun of all this with his amusing comment, 'Give a column a dress and it will look like a girl' (*Kleid' eine Säule, sieht aus wie ein Fräule*).

7 'You cannot distribute as you would in a City so well as you can in the Country' (Alberti*, XIV).

Part Four: Creating the Interior
Costs pp. 322–3

1 Goldthwaite* has much to say on this whole question; see p. 102.

2 Peter Burke, *Tradition and Innovation in Renaissance Italy*, London, 1974, p. 291.

3 Iris Origo, *The Merchant of Prato*, London, 1957, pp. 198 and 255.

4 Delumeau*, p. 451.

5 Peter Partner, *Renaissance Rome*, Berkeley, 1976, p. 131. Pope Adrian VI, as a cardinal, had managed on 3,000 ducats a year by living outside the Roman court.

6 *Ibid.*, p. 138. See also Priscanese*.

7 *Ibid.*

8 Burckhardt*, p. 175.

9 Gage*, p. 67.

10 G. Marcotti, 'Un mercante fiorentino e la sua famiglia nel secolo XV', *Nozze Nardi-Arnaldi*, Florence, 1881, pp. 87–92. While the main costs for the banquet were for food and drink, large items were the awning and the dais which established the open-air setting. Then there was the cook's fee and that of the musicians. A considerable item (290 florins) was the many pairs of stockings that were to be given to the guests as presents. The objects making up the dowry consisted primarily of clothes and jewellery that the bride herself would be using but they were all delivered in a pair of splendid chests with backboards [*i paio di forzieri colle spaliere molto ricchi*]. Noteworthy among the presents were a small fork and a knife of silver *en suite*.

11 Delumeau*, p. 446; also Gage*, p. 28. Dowries have of course been the subject of many specialist studies as well.

12 Pio Pecchai, *Roma nel Cinquecento*, Bologna, 1948, p. 334.

13 Lydecker, Thesis*, pp. 163–4.

14 Molmenti*, p. 247.

15 Malaguzzi-Valeri*, pp. 332–3.

16 Goldthwaite*, p. 401.

17 The estimate was 18,000 ducats. The final cost came to 50,000.

18 Pius II, *Commentaries**, p. 280. 'You deserve especial honour among all the architects of our time', the Pope added, and presented Rossellino with 100 ducats and a scarlet robe. See p. 312 and Pl. 333.

Fashion and the Spread of Ideas pp. 324–8

1 Kennedy Fraser, *The Fashionable Mind*, New York, 1981, p. 9.

2 Castiglione*, p. 146.

3 Ginevra Niccolini di Camugliano, *The Chronicles of a Florentine family, 1200–1470*, London, 1933, p. 168.

4 Lydecker, *Ceti**, p. 214. Two carved capitals were supplied separately *per lettiera* (for the bed).

5 *Ibid.*, p. 215. *ripiallatura [ripigliatura] di la mia lettiera usata e rifacitura dell'architravi e fregio a lettere e chornice di noce* [the refurbishing of my used bed and remaking of the architrave and frieze with letters and a cornice of walnut].

6 Evelino Ciuffolotti, *Faenza nel Rinascimento. La vita privata*, Bagnacavallo, 1922, p. 23. There was also an *archibanco vecchio* which may have been a fine old *lettuccio*.

7 Quoted in *Giulio Romano*, exhib. cat.*, p. 225.

8 Rosita Levi Pisetzky, *Storia del Costume in Italia*, Milan, 1964, III, p. 280 provides a bibliography of Italian sumptuary regulations.

9 Giovanni della Casa (*Il Galateo*, 1550s) claimed that sumptuary regulations were introduced as an attempt to spare the feelings of the poor who could not afford costly garments and luxurious furnishings. It is most unlikely that any such altruistic motive really lay behind their introduction. Nor can many people have believed that it ran counter to the state's interests to have so much money tied up in clothes, jewellery and household furnishings and that it was better to plough that money into business 'which can produce great fruits and great utility', as the Genoese sumptuary law of 1449 put it (Gage*, p. 195). Of course luxury was condemned on moral grounds by the Church and the high-minded but such a view was hardly shared by bankers and businessmen. Jealousy was probably the prime motive, the wish among 'top people' to keep middling people down. One senses this in the Sienese sumptuary law of 1533 in which women are berated for wearing 'cloth of gold or silver, and jewels and embroidery, just as if they were princesses or queens or the like' (Clara Bonelli Gandolfo, 'Leggi suntuarie senese', *La Diana.*, *Rassegna d'arte e vita senese*, Vol. II, 4). Although these regulations were not observed too strictly, most of the time, thirty-two ladies attending a very grand Bentivoglio wedding in Bologna in 1454 were expelled from the great Church of S Petronio for wearing rich brocades that had been banned by local decree (Gage*, p. 196). Rulers and their friends, who made the laws, preferred to be the only ones who could freely enjoy great luxury. They did not like the wives of ordinary merchants treading on their heels.

10 Postal communication between Rome and the other main cities of Italy in the 16th century could be reckoned to take the following times:- Milan, 8 days; Genoa 6–7; Venice, 4–5; Bologna, Florence and Naples, 3–4. Extraordinary couriers, riding at the gallop, could reach Venice in two days and Naples in one. Travellers of course took a good deal longer than the post, and grand people, travelling with a huge train of servants, baggage and companions, took longer still. There were plenty of hazards, from atrocious roads, bandits, floods that washed away bridges, dreadful inns, and discomforts of all kinds. The *Commentaries* of Pius II* give a wonderful idea of mid-

quattrocento travel for a high papal official who later became pope. We have already said something about Lucrezia Borgia's fatiguing journey from Rome to Mantua in order to get married (for the third time) in 1503 (p. 242). She rode on a white mule, part of the time, but women of high status mostly travelled in a special carriage (*carretta da done*, i.e. for women, or *da cortexana*, for ladies of the court; Manni*, p. 43, bills of 1456 for the Este court at Ferrara). These were not coaches, which had seats, but were more probably glorified covered wagons that were well padded inside. In the Requesens Invt., Sicily, 1561, are listed two *carretti*, one of which was gilded, as well as a velvet quilted cover and two feather-filled mattresses (*piumazzi*) which presumably made the wagon rather like a day-bed on wheels.

11 Ben Jonson, *Cynthia's Revels*, Act II, Sc. IV, London, 1601.

12 When considering pictures used as room-decoration, we noted how inexpensive printed religious subjects had been produced in Italy and Germany before the middle of the century (p. 264). Until well into the 16th century, incidentally, there was no feeling that prints taken from engraved copper plates were in any way superior to those made with woodblocks. The metal plates were themselves expensive, however. See the authoritative article by Evelina Borea, 'Stampa figurativa e pubblico', in the Einaudi series on the *Storia dell'arte in Italia*, Vol. II, p. 323.

13 Peter Partner, *Renaissance Rome*, Berkeley, 1976, p. 92. The reproduction of paintings that were not absolutely modern (i.e. that had been painted some decades earlier) was not practised until after the middle of the century, by which time the books of Vasari and others had made people much more interested in the history of art (see Borea, *op. cit.*, p. 392).

14 Borea, *op. cit.*, p. 342.

15 For brief biographies of these and other key figures in this story, see Jervis, *Design Dict.**.

16 Borea, *op. cit.*, p. 389.

17 J. Addington Symonds (*Italian Literature*, 1881, p. 226) said of this allegorical romance that it was 'a treasure-house of aesthetical descriptions ... bringing before our imagination the architecture, sculpture, and painting of the fifteenth century, its gardens, palaces ... and ceremonial shows ... , its delight in costly jewels, furniture, embroidery and banquets ...'.

18 See Jervis, *Printed Designs**, *passim*.

19 Pizetsky, *op. cit.*, II, p. 218.

Patrons and Clients pp. 329–32

1 The Marquis Niccolò III of Ferrara gave instructions in 1422 that a clockmaker brought over from Padua to install clocks in the Castle should be given whatever food he needed for himself and an assistant, as well as the iron and charcoal required for the work (*Manni**, p. 14).

2 Peter Burke, *Tradition and Innovation in Renaissance Italy*, London, 1974, pp. 103–4 and 130. Ch. 4 of this book is of great interest in the present connection.

3 Mantegna, for example, had such restrictions laid upon him (*Ibid.*, p. 104), which is probably the reason that he took some months to decide whether to accept a court appointment under the Gonzaga at Mantua.

4 The artist Dosso Dossi became an artistic *factotum* at Ferrara in the 1520s, for instance. Apart from pictures, he painted and gilded window-frames and a coach, he supervised theatrical entertainment, and provided designs for maiolica (see Manni*, pp. 115–18; see also p. 109).

5 Burke, *op. cit.*, p. 103.

6 *Ibid.*, p. 97.

7 *Ibid.*, p. 93. Examples are usually taken from the lives of painters because these have been studied so much more extensively than those of architects or artisans; so much more information is therefore available about them.

8 *Ibid.*, p. 127.

9 Manni*, p. 9.

10 *Giulio Romano* exhib. cat.* p. 445.

11 Manni*, p. 25.

12 ' ... he specified the proportions and everything else', it was said (see Burckhardt, *Architecture**, p. 11.

13 See C. L. Frommel, *Die Farnesina und Peruzzis architektonisches Frühwerk*, Berlin, 1961; also Coffin*, pp. 87–110.

14 Printed books, at this early stage, were no cheaper than copies of a text produced as a manuscript.

15 Burke, *op. cit.*, p. 121f.

16 These three scholarly advisers have been mentioned elsewhere in the present work (pp. 85, 233, 315).

17 Coffin*, pp. 159–72.

18 *Ibid.*, pp. 173–4.

19 *Ibid.*, p. 320.

Architects and Other Designers pp. 333–43

1 C. E. Gilbert, *Italian Art 1400–1500. Sources and Documents*, Englewood Cliffs, N.J., 1980, p. 4.

2 Jacopo della Quercia, in the same letter of 1428, mentions a second man who could evidently manage both fortifications and palaces. His name was Fioravante; he had built 'a very beautiful palace, extremely rich, for the Pope's representative in Bologna', as well as 'the castle of Braccio in Perugia'.

3 Of the great quattrocento architects who were also fortifications engineers of repute, one may single out Francesco di Giorgio* who worked in this capacity for some of the most celebrated military leaders of the time, in various parts of Italy. Much of his treatise on architecture (see p. 338) deals with this branch of his business.

4 Many quattrocento villas and a number of city palaces have battlements and/or towers, making them look like fortresses although they were certainly not intended to withstand bombardment. These features were more symbolic, harking back to an age when the great had all lived in castles. A military architect would, anyway, have had no difficulty in introducing such features; some may even have found it rather amusing to do so.

5 Burckhardt, *Architecture**, p. 13.

6 Antonio da Sangallo (the younger) was another architect who was equally at home in the world of military engineering. The massive Fortezza da Basso (1530s), which still powerfully dominates an inner suburb of Florence, was built by him.

7 Goldthwaite, *Building**, pp. 358–9.

8 Catherine Wilkinson, 'The New Professionalism in the Renaissance', in *The Architect, Chapters in the History of the Profession*, ed. Spiro Kostof, Oxford, 1977, p. 135. The preceding chapter, by L. D. Ettlinger, is also helpful in

the present connection.

9 M. Briggs, *The Architect in History*, Oxford, 1927, p. 157.

10 R. Magnuson, *Studies in Roman Quattrocento Architecture*, Stockholm, 1958, p. 92.

11 This term was used in 1440 by officials at Montepulciano when writing to commission a design from Michelozzo (Goldthwaite, *Building** p. 371). On this general question, see Goldthwaite, pp. 371–80; also Burckhardt, *Architecture*,* Ch. VIII, 'The Architectural Model'. Both Alberti* and Filarete* are explicit about the importance of models.

12 Francesco di Giorgio*, II, p. 489.

13 Giorgio Simoncini, *Architetti e architettura nella cultura del Rinascimento*, Bologna, 1969, pp. 71–8.

14 Onians*, pp. 127–9 and Ch. XIV.

15 The builder of a great *palazzo* couched in the new style would sometimes add an inscription on its façade, in order to deflect criticism. On the Palazzo Loredan (now Vendramin-Calergi) in Venice, built in about 1500, is written, 'Not unto us, O Lord, not unto us, but unto thy name give glory ... ', while the IHS cipher appears centrally on the otherwise entirely classical Palazzo Malpiero. Such messages were undoubtedly noted; whether they did the trick is another matter.

16 The excitement that the ruins of ancient Rome could inspire, even in the breast of a sophisticated scholar-architect, is conveyed beautifully by a letter written to a friend by Claudio Tolomei in 1543 from Rome. He claims that even *un arco guasto, un tempio disfatto, un teatro caduto, un portico gettato a terra val più che tutte le case intere, i palazzi alti, le strade larghe, i tempii nuovi e i graziosi giardini* (a ruined arch, a dismembered temple, a fallen theatre, a gateway thrown to the ground, are of far greater worth than any of the undamaged modern houses, tall palaces, broad streets, new places of worship, and elegant gardens) that are to be seen there today (Claudio Tolomei, *Treatise on Architecture*, ed. Elena Bassi, Edizione Polifilo, Milan, 1985, p. 51).

17 Surveying the ruins could be a dangerous task. One had to clamber over fallen masonry, the ground might easily cave in under one, and climbing a tall ladder in order to reach and measure a capital that was still topping a standing column could be very hazardous indeed.

18 Jervis, *Design Dict** under 'Vitruvius'. Alvise Cornaro, a sober gentleman-architect (see p. 331), spoke of 'the divine Vitruvius'. Vignola (see p. 339) treated Vitruvius almost as if he were a mythological deity who was not to be criticsed in any way. Hieronymus Mercurialis, in his *Gymnastica* of about 1540, however, was outspokenly critical of him (information kindly communicated by Dr Pia Kehl) and many others had to admit that they found his text confusing.

19 Onians,* p. 40.

20 Vitruvius wrote that, while he himself had not earned widespread fame he hoped that, by bringing out his treatise, posterity would get to hear of him. His wish has been fulfilled far beyond the scope of his wildest dreams!

21 Manuscripts could be copied with considerable speed in professional *scriptoria* and manuscript copies were not all that much more expensive that those at first produced by printing. Large *scriptoria*, employing many scribes, were kept busy until late in the 15th century, so the business was clearly still profitable, at that stage. However, the rapid dissemination of a new book made possible by

printing must have stimulated discussion of its contents in a manner very different from a situation that depended on the passing from hand to hand of a comparatively rare copy laboriously produced in manuscript (see Onians*, p. 172).

22 Cesarino's *Vitruvius* was dedicated both to François I and Leo X.

23 The woodcuts were by the painter Francesco Salviati (who later wrote a book on perspective that he dedicated to Barbaro) and are said to have been based on drawings by Palladio (who designed the villa Maser for Barbaro and his brother) but this is now doubted.

24 Gustina Scaglia, 'A Vitruvianist's Thermae Plan and the Vitruvianists in Roma and Siena', *Arte Lombarda*, 84, 1988.

25 Serlio*, for instance, states in the title of the first published part of his own treatise, Volume IV, which appeared in 1537, that the things he imparts *per la magior parte concordano con la dottrina di Vitruvius* [for the most part follows the teaching of Vitruvius]; it was as well to have him on one's side!

26 The sheets of the printed edition were rushed out to Lorenzo de' Medici at his villa at Careggi, in 1468, but Lorenzo had owned a manuscript copy before that. This he lent to Duke Borso d'Este of Ferrara in 1484 as a very great favour and on condition that it was returned speedily, 'because he is very fond of it and reads it often' (L. D. Alberti, *On the Art of Building*, Cambridge, Mass., 1988, ed. J. Rykwert, his Intro., p. XVIII).

27 Alberti*, Book V, Ch. II.

28 Filarete was his nick name; his real surname was Averlino and his Christian name was either Pietro or Antonio.

29 'Mostly ridiculous', was Vasari's verdict.

30 His full name was Francesco di Giorgio Martini.

31 His origins were humble and he must have been self-taught through reading in his mature years. He no doubt took advantage of the fact that printing now made books much more readily available; indeed, he belonged to the first generation who were able to do this (Onians*, p. 172).

32 *Ibid.*

33 Fra Giocondos' and Cesarino's editions of Vitruvius did, however, appear during this interval (see p. 338).

34 Serlio's was the first original treatise on architecture (as opposed to translation or revision of an earlier work) that was intended to be published in printed form from the outset.

35 *Times Literary Supplement*, June 2–8, 1989; review of Onians' book* in which the author comments that 'Surprisingly, in view of the richness of its contents and its widespread diffusion in the 16th century, Serlio's work has never been treated seriously' (p. 264).

36 When visiting a Palladio house, it is often quite difficult to envisage where the furniture stood, or to decide what kinds of furniture were originally to be seen there. One must remember that virtually everything stood against the walls; only the occasional cicular or octagonal table stood out in the middle of the room. With so many walls covered in fresco-painting right down to the floor, there does not seem to be anywhere that furniture could stand without destroying the decoration. Howard Burns, writing of palladio's interiors, says that the architect wanted the family rooms to be 'large, middling or small, and all conveniently connected with one another' *Andrea Palladio* exhib. cat., Arts Council, London, 1975).

37 Julius von Schlosser admitted that Vignola's treatise was clear, well organized and short but felt it was 'bloodless' (*La Letteratura Aristica*, revised edition by C. Kurz, Florence and Vienna, 1964). Herman Koch spoke of Vignola's 'grey theory' (*Vom Nachleben des Vitruv, Baden-Baden, 1951*). It is beautifully illustrated.

38 An English translation in manuscript of about 1630 is bound in with a copy of the Italian printed work to be found in Sir John Soane's Museum, London.

39 Lydecker, Thesis*, p. 162. While the wooden carcass of the two chests may have been made *en suite* with the other items, the main panels were decorated by the independent painter, Lorenzo di Piero, presumably with a large scene on the front and two less important side-panels in the characteristic Florentine manner of the time (e.g. Pl. 219).

40 Giuliano da Maiano supplied another *lettuccio* in 1465 which was superbly decorated with inlay (three panels in the back, each with a *trionfo* executed in *chonmesso*, the most complicated form of *lavoro di intarsio*). Its purchase, together with that of a bed of equal elaboration provided by a different maker, is recorded in the memorandum-book of the proud owner – a sure sign of the importance to him of these acquisitions. (Lydecker, Thesis*. p. 115). At this period Giuliano was calling on talented artists like Alessio Baldovinetti to provide designs for important inlaid decoration. Earlier he had employed Tommaso Finiguerra (see p. 342); much information of this sort may be gleaned from a perusal of Jervis; *Design Dict**.

41 This phrase occurs in many Genoese inventories of around 1450. I have not come across it elsewhere. Both words mean 'of such a kind' so it is not clear precisely what is implied by the terms in these cases. The inference that an object so described had a feature similar to that of the previous item in the list can perhaps therefore be made.

42 *Giulio Romano* exhib. cat.* p. 411; letter of 1538 to the Duke of Mantua.

43 That Giulio Romano's designs possessed a uniform character is indicated by the Duke's petulent request that a clock made for him by the celebrated Maestro Cherubino of Reggio should be furnished with a plain case, 'without those ornaments designed by Giulio Romano' [*una cassa semplice, senza quell i ornamenti dessignati per G.R.*; *Giulio Romano exhib. cat.** p. 457]. The Duke evidently found that so much ornament in the same ebullient style was becoming a bit of a bore.

44 See Emmina De Negri, 'Considerazioni sull'Alessi a Genova', *Convegno Internazionale di Studi, Galeazzo Alessi*: 1974, Genoa, 1975, p. 290.

45 Manni*, pp. 20–25.

46 *Ibid.*, pp. 48–60.

47 *Ibid.*, p. 87.

48 *Ibid.*, p. 91.

49 *Ibid.*, pp. 107–18.

50 Alessandro Perosa, ed., 'Giovanni Rucellai ed il suo Zibaldone', *Studies of the Courtauld and Warburg Institutes*, London, Vol. 24, 1960, pp. 23–4.

51 Jervis, *op. cit.*, 'Schiavone'.

52 Palladio exhib. Cat. *op. cit.*, p. 52; essay by Howard Burns on 'The Interior'.

The *Maestro di Casa* and his Staff pp. 343–8

1 *Decameron**, Intro. Bk. V. Much that is relevant to the present matter is to be found in Patricia Waddy's book on *Seventeenth-Century Roman Palaces* (New York, 1990), Chapter 4, 'The Famiglia'.

2 *Decameron**, Intro. Bk. I.

3 Ryder*, p. 54.

4 Sabine Eiche, 'Towards a Study of the *Famiglia* of the Sforza Court at Pesaro', *Renaissance and Reform*, IX, 1985, p. 85.

5 Giuseppe Ermini (ed.), *Ordini et Offitij alla corte del Serenissimo Signor Duca d'Urbino*, Rome, 1931. Apparently connected with the Court of Guidebaldo da Montefeltro (d. 1508).

6 See Francesco Priscianese, *Del governo delle corte d'un signore in Roma*, Città di Castello, 1883 (written in about 1542), p. 81.

7 Giovanni Battista Rosetti, *Dello Scalco*, Ferrara, 1584.

8 When Pope Gregory XIII (1572–85) moved fom one papal residence to another, which happened frequently, his *Maestro di Casa*, a man named Bianchetti, attended to the complicated logistics of these displacements. The Pope's main base was the Vatican but he liked the Palazzo di S. Marco (the Palazzo Venezia), and also went to the Villa d'Este on Monte Cavallo where the Palazzo Barberini now stands. He also liked to visit the villa at Frascati belonging to the Cardinal of Ferrara where he spent a few days every month (Coffin*, p. 40). Even the wife of the relatively frugal Cosimo de' Medici had much to do prior to the family's annual exodus to their villa. Shortly before he died in 1464, he wrote to her complaining that 'When we go to the villa the preparations for our departure occupy thee for fifteen days' (Janet Ross, *Letters of the Ealy Medici*, London, 1910, p. 74).

9 Ryder*

10 Ermini, *op. cit.*, pp. 16–19.

11 Ryder*. These may have been the items commissioned in Flanders by the King's *comprador* (purveyor), one Andreu Pal.

12 Priscianese, Chap. XLIII.

13 *Ibid.*

14 It is worth noting that Alfonso at Naples had on his staff a *perponter*, a man who made *pourpoints* (French) which meant the article of men's clothing called a doublet – a sort of quilted tunic. In Alfonso's case, and probably also elsewhere, the *perponter* also made tents. If he could do this, there is no obvious reason why he should not also have made wall-hangings, etc. Maybe Parasina Malatesta's quilter, active at Ferrara in the 1420s, was capable of doing the same (see p. 84).

15 *Manni**, p. 185.

16 See Marco Catini and Marzio Romani, 'Le corti parallele ...', Giuseppe Papagno and Amadeo Quondam (eds.), *La Corte e lo spazio; Ferrara estense*, Rome, 1982. At a ducal court like that at Mantua, many of those on the payroll were civil servants administering the state. Duke Federigo Gonzaga had to support and feed over 800 persons: his successors cut this considerably. A courtier's immediate family had to be fed as well; this swelled the total. Duke Vincenzo had 296 courtiers; his wife had a further 36 and his children 12 more. Then there were the muleteers, stable staff and no less than 23 people whose task was to look after the ducal dogs (600 of them).

17 Ryder*.

18 Eiche, *op. cit.* This instruction with regard to making books available were *quando se mustrano a persona ignorate*

che per curiostia li volesse vedere, se non e di troppo auctoria, basta una ochiata (when you have to show an ignorant person a book which he merely wants to see out of curiosity, if he is not someone in a position of authority, allow him only a quick glance).

19 Ermini, *op. cit.* From a list of the staff, in the time of Duke Federico II of Urbino, late in the 16th century.

20 e.g. Priscianese*; Rossetti, *op. cit.*; also Paolo Cortese, *De Cardinalatu*, written before 1510 (*Studies in Italian Art . . .* , ed. Henry A. Millon, Cambridge, Mass. 1980), Cristoforo di Messisburgo, *Banchetti, Compositione di Vivande*, Ferrara, 1549; Barolomeo Scappi, *Opera*, Rome 1570; Vencenzio Cervio, *Il Trinciante*, Rome, 1593.

21 Johannes Burchardus, *Diarium romanum . . .* , edit and transl. Geoffrey Parker, London, 1963.

22 Janet Ross, *op. cit.*, pp. 129–34.

23 L. A. Gandini, *Tavola, cantina, e cucina della Corte di Ferrara nel quattrocento*, Modena, 1889, p. 55.

24 See Jennifer Montagu, *Roman Baroque Sculpture; the industry of art*, Yale University Press, New Haven and London, 1989. One Niccolò della Pigna made the sugar-paste figures for the great feast given in Venice when Henri III was welcomed there in 1574 (see Alain-Charles Gruber, 'Les Décors de Table . . . ', *Gazette des Beaux-Arts*, May-June 1974).

25 Molmenti*, p. 293.

26 Cervio, *op. cit.*

27 See n. 22 and Cervio, *op. cit.*, p. 124. At a banquet in Rome in 1593, four white peacocks suffered this fate, Their feathers were adjusted with silk thread so as to flutter when the birds were carried in on their separate chargers.

28 One of Cervio's sections is headed 'Arrangements for avoiding confusion at a major feast' (*op. cit.*, p. 108).

Women's Influence pp. 348–58

1 Domenico Bruni, *Difese della Donne*, Florence, 1552, pp. 22–3.

2 Chivalrous love has been described as 'a genuine impulse of manly hearts, inflamed by beauty, and touched with a sense of the moral superiority in woman, perfected through weakness and demanding protection' which 'served to temper the rudeness of primitive society . . . no little of its attraction [being] due to the conviction that only refined natures could experience it' (J. Addington Symonds, *Italian Literature*, London, 1881, p. 60). It arrived in Italy ready-made from Provence and France but speedily degenerated. It left its mark on Italian literature, however.

3 A long chivalric poem on the Arthurian theme, *Morgante Maggiore*, by Luigi Pulci, was written specially to be recited at Cosimo de' Medici's *palazzo* in the Via Larga (Pl. 374) at a time when it was the grandest house in Florence and the city was outwardly governed by a republic but actually governed by stolid citizens making up a mercantile oligarchy.

4 Baldassare Castiglione, in his famous *Il Cortegiano* (1529) in which he considers the formation of a courtier and the attainments he should possess, actually asks his readers at whom *tutti gli esercisi graziosi* [all those exercises in graciousness] were directed, if not at women? (Ch. III, 52).

5 Symonds, and Burckhardt, took a rosy view of Italian women's position during the Renaissance; modern scholars tend to be more sanguine (e.g. Julia O'Faolain

and Lauro Martines, *Not in God's Image*, London, 1973). Certainly not all were as learned as the daughter of Giovanni d'Andrea, a professor at Bologna University, who could take his place on the podium whenever he felt unable to give a lecture (E. Rodocanachi, *La Femme italienne à l'époque de la Renaissance*, Paris, 1907, p. 28: this work is of course of central interest to our subject, here). Castiglione, incidentally, remarked that 'the intellect of a woman could penetrate wherever a man's can'.

6 Alberti, writing in the 1430s, would have a husband commit 'the details of the housekeeping entirely into their hands', and urged wives to 'be far more eager to learn what goes on in your own house than to find out what goes on outside it.' (L. B. Alberti, *Della Famiglia*, English ed. by R. N. Watkins, Columbia University, South Carolina, p. 208). San Bernardino, the famous preacher (d. 1444), insisted that 'woman rules the house'.

7 Girls were often married at 15: husbands were usually in their thirties – in the 15th century. 'Do not penalise yourself by haste . . . , if you improve your estate in any way by delay until the age of thirty . . . you should delay' (G. Morelli, *Ricordi*, ed. V. Branca, Florence, 1956).

8 The works of David Herlihy are especially helpful in this area. See particularly *Cities and Society in Mediaeval Italy*, London 1980, which reprints some of his essays.

9 The tragedy of Shakespeare's Juliet was that she was so young and inexperienced. To lose one's head in love was considered a disaster. A mature woman was unlikely to do anything so silly.

10 Of Venetians, Fynes Moryson* (p. 410) wrote that 'theire wives and virgins are locked up at home, watched by wemen attending them abroade, have faces covered not to be seene . . . '. Thomas Coryat* also reported how Venetians would 'coope up their wives alwaies within the walls of their houses' (p. 403).

11 There are many descriptions of such formal celebrations (which must have been very tedious even if splendid). A Florentine in 1491, for instance, reported home from Naples on the *ballo solenne* [solemn dance] held in the Castel Capuano, in honour of the Duke of Calabria, at which *convenono tucte queste prime baronesse et gentil donne assai ben ornate* [were gathered all these premier baronesses and gentlewomen most finely got up] (Rodocanachi, *op. cit.*, p. 204). For descriptions of similar dazzling occasions in Venice, see Bistort*.

12 Lydecker (Thesis*, p. 120) notes an entry of 1472 in Lorenzo Morelli's memorandum-book which reads, 'My expenses when I took my wife home'. These are only minor items: we have mentioned elsewhere some of the larger items acquired for the occasion (pp. 157, 201). The two great chests he bought for his bedchamber may today be seen in the Courtauld Galleries at Somerset House, London. Lydecker's thesis contains much information on such marriage-purchases.

13 The Genoese Signoria in 1442 actually tried to forbid young men talking to the daughters of the house in the entrance hall vestibule, or elsewhere on the ground floor of the house (Roddocanachi, *op. cit.*, p. 187).

14 Marriage ceremonial varied from one region to another; the generalized picture given here is based on Lydecker, Thesis*, pp. 149–65, Pandiani*, pp. 195–9, and Rodocanachi, *op. cit.*, pp. 55–70.

15 There is a description of one such occasion, which may not have been typical. Don Joffre Borja, an illegitimate

son of Pope Alexander VI (Roderigo Borgia), in 1494 married Sancia, an illegitimate daughter of King Alfonso of Aragon in Naples. A Papal Legate attended on the Pope's behalf, to see that everything was managed properly. The young couple were undressed by women attendants in the nuptial chamber and put to bed naked, lying under linen sheets. The King and the Papal Legate entered the room to witness the ceremonial consummation. The attendants folded back the sheet so that the couple were naked to the waist whereupon Don Joffre kissed his wife 'without any embarrassment'. The King and the Legate stayed for about half an hour, talking to the couple, and then withdrew. *Autres temps, autres mœurs!* (This account was set down by Johann Burchard, Papal Master of Ceremonies, whose commentaries were edited by Geoffrey Parker in 1963).

16 Rodocanachi, *op. cit.*, p. 8.

17 Venetian procuresses were evidently able to dazzle girls in the surrounding territories with stories of the wealth and glamorous life that a *puttana* could enjoy in Venice. The city fathers of Udine in 1390 were anyway alarmed at the way they were sending *le balie e le serve dei citadini udinese a prostituirsi* [the wet-nurses and servant-girls of Udine citizens to prostitute themselves] which resulted in a serious lack of women servants in that city (Molmenti*, p. 241). On the wages of servants, see p. 322.

18 In 1491 Isabella of Aragon, Duchess of Milan, asked her agent in Venice to send her a slave who was 'more black' that those he had sent up previously (Rodocanachi, *op. cit.*, p. 255). Slaves became much less common in the 16th century but batches were still arriving in Venice at the end of that century. Fourteen slaves are listed among the goods and chattels of Don Berlinghieri Requesens (Requesens Invt., Palermo, 1561*) which suggests that the practice died out much later in Sicily. Eight were female, three of these being white; several were in their thirties and forties but the youngest were eleven, twelve and eighteen. One man, Gisuffo, was fifty-five. A rather different sense of values is revealed in the Ponzone Invt., Genoa, 1488, where the very first item is *Catarina sclava* followed by *Martinus Murus* [the Moor?], both personal slaves of the deceased master of the house.

19 Alessandra Strozzi, ever mindful of her son's well-being, wrote to him in 1465 that, 'When you marry, you will need a slave woman. I have Margherita here [in Florence] who is active. This might suggest that the duties of a slave-woman were confined to darning the son's socks and that kind of thing, but more was sometimes expected, it seems. 'What can better serve a man who enjoys his comforts than a beautiful slave girl?, asked Giovanni Maria Cecchi (1518–87). (Rodocanachi, *op. cit.*, p. 221). Slaves did not always come from far afield; pirates would sometimes snatch them from coastal villages much nearer home. A Neapolitan girl found herself carried off and sold into slavery in Genoa; a Dalmatian gentleman visiting the same city came across his sister in similar straits. Comparatively fortunate was the slave Margherita who was miraculously healed of some sickness by the Blessed Catherine of Siena in 1463, whereupon the Signoria immediately caused her to be manumitted from slavery as an example to all (Pandiani*, p. 212).

20 Ariosto advised men not to marry too beautiful a woman, for this reason. 'Many will attempt her, and even if she repulses one or two or three, do not rest in hope that no

one will win a victory'. (*The Satires of Ariosto*, translated by P. D. Wiggins, Athens, Ohio, 1976; Satire v, p. 131).

21 There are three principal sources for the study of this subject: (i) Arturo Graf, *Attraverso il Cinquecento*, Turin, 1888, in which the last section is devoted to the subject in general and the life of an important Venetian courtesan, poetess and blue-stocking, named Veronica Franco; this long section bears the title 'una Cortigiana fra mille.'; (ii) Pio Pecchiai, *Roma nel Cinquecento*, Bologna, 1948, pp. 298–317 and (iii) Georgina Masson, *Courtesans of the Italian Renaissance*, London, 1975. The present quotation comes from Graf, p. 225.

22 *Taraffa delle puttane, ... nel quale si dinota il prezzo e la qualita di tutte le cortigiane di Vinegia*, 1535. Forty *scudi* was a high fee but Tullia d'Aragona claimed to have charged a German tourist a hundred for a night's entertainment (Masson, *op. cit.*, p. 97). As for the scale of favours, Veronica Franco (see previous note) charged five or six *scudi* for a kiss but not less than fifty for what Montaigne called *la négociation entière* (Graf, *op. cit.*, p. 306).

23 Poems praising their beauty and charms are legion. Admittedly this was an age in which young men were particularly prone to claim that they were dying of love for some lady, and were apt to express their ardour in exaggerated terms, but there must have been some substance to many of these verses in praise of *cortigiane*. Aretino, for example, who could be very spiteful about such women, wrote of Angela Zaffetta (a Venetian active about 1530 who later enjoyed great success in Rome and whose portrait by Bordone hangs in the National Gallery, London) that she was *la più bella, la più dolce e la più costumata madonna che abbia Cupido in sua corte* and called her *divina giovane* ['the most beautiful, the sweetest, the most polished lady who ever had Cupid in her court' and 'a divine young woman'; Graf, *op. cit.*, p. 260]. Montaigne insisted that the women of Rome were not especially beautiful but that 'as in Paris, the most singular beauty was found among those who put it on sale'. Montaigne* was in Rome in 1580. The English traveller Thomas Coryat, on the other hand, who visited Venice in 1608 and was totally dazzled by the 'Cortezans' of that city, stated that 'few ... are so much beholden to nature, but that they adulterate their faces, and supply her defect with various cosmetics', although 'many of them which have an elegant naturall beauty, doe varnish their faces ... with these kinde of trumperies', which he thought a great pity (Coryat*, p. 266).

24 One Lucia Trevisan, a Venetian courtesan who died in 1514, apparently *cantava per eccelenzia ... e molto nominata apresso musici* [was an excellent singer, much talked of among musicians; according to her contemporary Marin Sanudo, see Graf, *op. cit.*, p. 246]. Many could play musical instruments, at least passably, just as most could dance well and cite verse from the *Decameron* or by famous authors like Petrarch and Ariosto. Not a few actually wrote verse themselves.

25 *Ella ... essendo bellissima, di corpo nettissima, sta sempre allegra con ogni persona; ... ed ha cognizione di molti e varie cose, e sanne bene ragionare* (Graf, *op. cit.*, pp. 232–3). Veronica Franco's views on the matter are given on p. 341. She, incidentally, claimed to feel happiest in the company of scholars, and wanted to be able to paint. She was a friend of Tintoretto's (p. 301). Yet even if many of her

pleasures were intellectual, this in no way prevented her from enjoying the embraces of her admirers, as some of her poems reveal (p. 305).

26 From a letter by Niccolò Martelli quoted by Masson, *op. cit.*, p. 69.

27 The twelve-year-old Marquis Federico Gonzaga, who was for a while held hostage in Rome (in a very polite and relaxed manner), dined in 1513 at the house of the Cardinal of Mantua (his uncle) where there were three other cardinals present as well as several bishops and some gentlemen – and the *cortigiana* Albina (Graf, *op. cit.*, p. 264). Many other instances could be cited.

28 'to tell a respectable lady from a courtesan' (Graf, *op. cit.*, p. 250).

29 Graf, *op. cit.*, p. 282. The poet was Ercole Bentivoglio. On Tullia's 'rapturous reception' in Ferrara, see Masson, *op. cit.*, pp. 102–8.

30 See Masson, *op. cit.*, p. 108.

31 So renowned was this courtesan that it was said that Rome had been given two supreme gifts by Mars and by Venus; the first gave Rome her Empire (*impero*); the latter gave Rome Imperia.

32 Masson, *op. cit.*, p. 37.

33 Pecchiai, *op. cit.*, p. 309. The young woman is thought to have been Lucrezia di Clarice who had the nick-name *Matrema-non-vuole* (My mother wouldn't like me to) which was apparently the rebuff she made to an unfortunate youth when she herself was still under age. Since her mother had been a prostitute before her, this spirited reaction was thought so exceptional that Roman society never forgot the incident and she appears under this nickname even in the official tax records (Masson, *op. cit.*, p. 71).

34 Graf, *op. cit.*, p. 263.

35 V. Cian, *Galanterie Italiane del Secolo XVI*, Turin, 1887, p. 15.

36 Given in full by Graf, *op. cit.*, as an appendix.

37 Coryat*, p. 000.

38 Graf, *op. cit.*, p. 244.

39 See Thornton *17th Cent. Int. Dec.*,* p. 21 and *passim*; also *Thornton, Authentic Decor.*,* London 1984, *passim*.

40 Coryat*, p. 265. In 1531 a Venetian diplomat gave a banquet at Antwerp to which he invited many local dignitaries and some Italian men of business. They fell into debating whether one could compare Antwerp with Venice, when a Frenchman who had been ambassador in Venice spoke of one form of commerce of which he had had experience there, and which in its perfection was unlike that of any other city – and then 'began to list the names of Madona Cornelia Griffo, Julia Lombarda, Bianca Saraton, le Balarine and several more' (Graf, *op. cit.*, p. 291).

41 Coryat*, p. 264. He states that 'the revenues which they pay unto the Senate for their tolleration, doe maintaine a dozen of their galleys [i.e. warships] ... and so do save them a great charge'. He also gave another reason, namely that Venetians 'thinke that the chastity of their wives would be the sooner assaulted, and so consequently they should be capricornified (which of all the indignities of the world the Venetians cannot patiently endure) were it not for these places of evacuation'.

42 Art-historians have the same problem when faced with the portrait of a beautiful young woman by Titian or Raphael, or one of the other great artists of the period.

Was she or was she not a courtesan? Once scholarship has failed to provide the answer, the poor lady's posthumous reputation usually comes to depend on the depth of her *décolletage*.

43 Although, unlike the other ladies in this list, Lucretia was the epitome of virtue and committed suicide after having failed to hold off Tarquin, her story was sufficiently sensational to become included in the erotic category.

44 See *Thornton, 17th Cent. Int. Dec.*,* Pls 20, 32, 35, 36 and 121, and *Thornton, Authentic Decor*,* London 1984 Pl. 12.

INDEX

This index lists artists and craftspeople, contemporary authors, decorative techniques and materials, and topics relevant to the planning and management of houses. At this time many people, other than nobles, did not have proper surnames, using place names (da Siena) or patronymics (di Giovanni) instead. Since there is no hard-and-fast borderline between these names and true surnames, all people have been listed under what either is, or passes for, a surname. The only exceptions are artists well known by their Christian names (Leonardo da Vinci), and some artisans known only by a Christian name and a nickname or similar label – which is indicated by printing it in italics (Zoane *Tedesco*). **The Italian terms given after English headings may not be exact equivalents. They are included to make it easier to find the reference.**